A COURSE IN MATERIALIZATION

Volume One

by

Brown Landone

Elizabeth Towne

Thomas Troward

Genevieve Behrend

Richard Ingalese

Henry Thomas Hamblin

Christian D. Larson

Julia Seton

Mary A. Dodson & Ella E. Dodson

Ralph Waldo Trine

Thomas R. Gaines

George Winslow Plummer

E. V. Ingraham

Introduction, typesetting and text editing © 2010
The Freedom Religion Press

www.thefreedomreligionpress.com

www.seeseer.com

ISBN-13: 978-0-9797267-0-5

ISBN-10: 0-9797267-0-0

This book is sold with the understanding that the editor and publisher are not engaged in rendering legal, financial, psychological or medical advice. If expert assistance or counseling is required, the services of a licensed professional should be sought. The teachings and methods described in this book are of a religious or spiritual nature.

CONTENTS

	INTRODUCTION by MIKE ALAN	4
I	BROWN LANDONE	13
II	ELIZABETH TOWNE	64
III	THOMAS TROWARD	94
IV	GENEVIEVE BEHREND	131
V	RICHARD INGALESE	167
VI	HENRY THOMAS HAMBLIN	190
VII	CHRISTIAN D. LARSON	291
VIII	JULIA SETON	493
IX	MARY A. DODSON & ELLA E. DODSON	546
X	RALPH WALDO TRINE	567
XI	THOMAS R. GAINES	601
XII	GEORGE WINSLOW PLUMMER	651
XIII	E. V. INGRAHAM	697
	AFTERWORD	737

INTRODUCTION

I began studying the art of materialization in 1977. I noticed from the beginning that the original teachings were far more powerful than the more modern teachings. Using the art of materialization I was able to retire at the young age of thirty-eight. The art of materialization brought me millions of new choices and a life that can only be described as miraculous.

The original teachings of the laws of attraction, opulence, abundance, success, supply, prosperity, power, compensation, love, affinity, harmony, imagination, ability, soul, mental control, manifestation, wholeness, increase, growth, liberty, individuality, spirit, reciprocity, the creative process, being, production, subjective mind, justice, unfolding substance, force, cause and effect, life, and related topics such as how to develop willpower, visualization, concentration, affirmations, and autosuggestion, are presented in *A Course in Materialization* with no commentary. This is very important because when someone comments on these original teachings, distortions can occur. Because there are no commentaries on these teachings, there is no barrier between you and what these original teachers wished to convey.

There are a total of five volumes in *A Course In Materialization*. You won't find any biographies in *A Course In Materialization*. Biographies tend to be fictions that reveal more about the biographer than the subject of the biography. In the case of Masters of the art of materialization, biographies reveal nothing of their true life. For every one hundred miraculous events reported, there may be ten thousand miraculous events that are not known to the biographer.

Three important keys in the art of materialization are:

1. Discerning the essential.
2. Rejecting or ignoring the non-essential.
3. Concentrating only on the essential.

Not including biographies is an example of rejecting that which is not essential and concentrating only on that which is essential.

The reason the volumes in *A Course In Materialization* are so large is because a very large number of quotes have been presented for each teacher. Presenting a small number of quotes would not have been of much use. To be able to use and apply a teaching, the entire essence of the teaching must be conveyed and to accomplish that a very large number of quotes are necessary. Beware of small books with little sound bites of information. Imagine there were two bridges across a river. Bridge number one was designed by an engineer that had eight years of education and twelve years of experience. Bridge number two was designed by someone who took a short two week seminar in engineering. Which bridge would you feel safer in crossing?

The art of materialization has allowed me to accomplish thousands of goals that are beyond anything I have ever read in testimonials. Most readers would not believe how many goals are possible that are considered to be impossible. What is important is not what I have been able to accomplish or what others have been able to accomplish. What is important is what you, the reader, are able to accomplish. That will be different for each reader.

In order to sell books and seminars many authors have claimed that these various laws will work for everyone. Some of these same modern authors admit that many readers write to them stating that they have studied and attempted to practice and yet they are not meeting their goals. The way the modern authors get around such failure is to say that the person must have some hidden or subconscious conflicting desires and that the law is giving them what they really want and not what they claim to want, therefore the law is really working.

The defect in that argument is: 1. The person was studying the teachings for the purpose of being able to achieve his or her goals. 2. That includes understanding how to remove all hidden conflicting desires. 3. If after studying and attempting to practice the teachings the person cannot remove the hidden conflicting desires, then the teaching did not work for that person.

The law may have worked, but the teachings did not work for that person. If an author really cares more about the welfare of human beings than how many books are sold, the author would point out that some people will succeed in realizing their goals with the art of materialization and some will fail. Like any aspect of life some people are better at gaining certain skills than others.

There are many different levels of skill. One person will try to hit the tennis ball one minute after it has gone past them. If, after practicing for years, that same person is still trying to hit the tennis ball one minute after the ball has passed them, they probably are never going to succeed at tennis. Fortunately the vast majority of people can acquire skill much better than that. At the other end of the scale there are those who are rated number one or number two in the world of tennis. You can fill in the current names. Most people never acquire that level of skill, but most people do not need to acquire that level of skill to enjoy tennis. So it is with the art of materialization.

I do not agree with all of the ideas that either the original or modern teachers of the art of manifestation taught. One such idea is the notion that you should *spend* money freely because if you do not *spend* money freely you are being motivated by a sense of lack, limitation or fear. This is the idea that you have to *spend* money to make money. I disagree with this idea. Some of the original teachers taught this idea and some did not. Most of the modern teachers teach this idea. Some of the so-called laws in the art of materialization are really just fantasies. This is one example of a fantasy law. This is more like a disease. I will call this disease "*spenditis.*"

There is a real law: The Law of Frugality. The Law of Frugality is: Don't *spend* even one cent that does not really need to be spent until you have met all of your financial goals. Learn the difference between wants and genuine needs and never *spend* any money on wants until you have met all of your financial goals. Save your money in a very low or *no* risk investment.

The Law of Frugality is based on real mathematical laws. The Law of Frugality is based on the formula "You have to *save* and *invest* money to make money." The *"spenditis"* formula is based on the idea "You have to *spend* money to make money." The two may sound alike, however the formulas are totally different. The results of the two formulas are totally different also.

The Law of Frugality has produced millions of millionaires. The Law of Frugality has even produced some billionaires. I read a story about one of the billionaires who is usually ranked in the top five richest people in the world. The story says that this man will not buy a luxury automobile. He calculates what the money he saves by buying the standard car instead of the luxury car would bring him if he invested it with compound returns over a period of twenty, thirty or forty years. Tens of thousands of dollars become hundreds of thousands of dollars and hundreds of thousands of dollars is too much to pay for a luxury automobile. Practicing the Law of Frugality made him a billionaire.

Suppose, as an illustration, that 2% of the people who follow the *"spenditis"* formula have met all of their financial goals after a period of twenty years and those 2% write testimonials to the value of the *"spenditis"* formula. Then people read those testimonials and believe the *"spenditis"* formula works. Unfortunately, one does not hear from the 98% who failed using the *"spenditis"* formula because that does not help to sell books and seminars. Look very carefully into the motives of those who are telling you to be loose with your money and to *spend, spend, spend*. If you are loose with your money you are more likely to buy some expensive seminar.

Another supposed law that does not hold water is the law of vibration or frequency. That notion is that the reason one's thoughts, desires, intentions and mental images materialize is because the events that materialize are on the same level of vibration or frequency as one's thoughts, desires, intentions or mental images. The defect in that explanation is that when a goal is held in mind, often the solution to the problem or the means by which the goal is obtained have never been imagined or thought of by the individual who had the goal. The solution is often very complex requiring hundreds of steps. To reduce such complexity to similar vibrations or frequencies is an error.

The true explanation is that there is a field of consciousness. That field of consciousness is omnipresent. That field of consciousness is intelligent and therefore understands the goal. That field of consciousness can arrange events to meet the goal or solve the problem with a solution that is far better than anything the individual would have imagined as a means of obtaining the goal or of solving the problem. That solution or means may be something the individual never thought of or imagined. That solution may require hundreds of steps or events that the field of consciousness can arrange.

There is another silly notion that has arisen in the manifestation teachings. That is the notion that the field of consciousness cannot understand the negative. The notion is that if you think "I don't want poverty," the field of consciousness understands that to mean "I want poverty." Oh how arrogant humans are to have such silly notions. The field of consciousness is infinite intelligence. The field of consciousness is infinitely more intelligent than a human. The notion that the field of consciousness cannot understand the negative words is absurd.

When one's desires are not fulfilled there are a number of different possible reasons. 1. The person having the desire has not fulfilled the requirements outlined in the Materialization Teachings. For example not having conflicting desires, not spending enough time holding the image in place, not having enough determination behind the intention, having too many goals or desires at once, doubting the outcome, and other reasons the teachers in this course will introduce you to. 2. If one's goal is not in harmony with the laws and goals of the field of consciousness, then the field of consciousness will not permit the materialization to occur.

This brings up another silly notion that has arisen in the manifestation teachings; the idea that there are no limits to what goals can be achieved. The field of consciousness does indeed place limits on what can be achieved and it is a very good thing that those limits are in place. Most people do not have much control over their minds and if there were no limits placed on what goals would be granted that would be a disaster.

Without limits, the first time one had a thought like "I wonder if a thought about my bursting into flames and dying might manifest" would instantly cause one to burst into flames and die. Or every time someone with great skill at materialization thought it might be nice to have another moon permanently orbiting the earth, another moon would appear and we would end up with thousands of moons. Fortunately the field of consciousness does place limits on what goals will or will not be granted.

However, that is not very limiting for one who gains great skill at the art of materialization because millions of new choices, abilities and possibilities become available that were not available before. Also, many things that most humans believe to be impossible are possible for one who gains great skill at the art of materialization. At the stage where one has millions of new choices and abilities that one did not have before, it might seem like there are no limits or feel like there are no limits.

Suppose you were going to be granted only one wish. The rule is that you could ask for anything you wanted, except for more wishes, and your wish would be granted. What would you wish for? Take a little time to think about that. *After* you decide upon what your one wish would be, *then* read further.

Suppose you wished for one billion dollars. Then for the remainder of your life anything that money could buy, you could have. Maybe your body would live for another fifty years. You would then enjoy the things that billion dollars could buy for the next fifty years. Then your body dies. Trillions of years pass.

Because you asked for something temporary, what you received only lasted fifty years. If you had asked for something eternal, you could have enjoyed it forever. Do you see how easy it would be to waste the one wish?

Most people want something from the world of the temporary. The wish might be money, or one of the thousands of things that money can buy, which are all temporary. The wish might be a new friend, husband or wife, all of which are also temporary. The wish might be a change of habits, or even a different state of consciousness, all of which is still in the realm of the temporary. The wish might be to make the earth a better place and that also is still within the realm of the temporary. For all such temporary goals *A Course In Materialization* is the best choice. If you are ever interested in how to attain the Eternal, the best book for that goal is *The Most Direct Means to Eternal Bliss* by Michael Langford. There is a link on the www.seeseer.com website to where you can purchase that book.

The whole of *A Course In Materialization* is much greater than the sum of its parts. In other words, reading these Teachings all in one place is much more powerful than reading them scattered about. *A Course In Materialization* is a transmission from the Infinite Consciousness to you.

The goal in publishing *A Course In Materialization* was to create some of the most positive and uplifting books ever written.

If you need scientific proof to help you to have faith in the Materialization Teachings there are hundreds of books you could read. Only one is being recommended here: *The Divine Matrix* by Gregg Braden. Gregg Braden has the rare ability to write in easy to understand everyday language. Only those portions of his book that refer to scientific discoveries are being recommended. The section of his book called "Three Experiments That Change Everything" is especially helpful for understanding the scientific basis of the Materialization Teachings.

There are hundreds of important safeguards in *A Course In Materialization*. Most of the more modern teachers have left out most of these safeguards. You can read more about this topic in the Afterword that begins on page 737. The question "should you use the teachings to change others" is also answered in the Afterword.

If I had a son or daughter who was about to begin the study and practice of the art of Materialization, I would give him or her the following eight suggestions:

1. Never count on the results of your practice of the art of materialization. For example, do not quit your job thinking you will be able to materialize all the money you want using the art of materialization. You may or may not be someone who will develop that level of skill. If you are not someone with that level of skill and you quit your job, you will just be someone unemployed.

2. Always obey the law of Frugality.

3. Make sure your investments are very low or *no* risk. Whenever contemplating an investment ask these questions: A. If things go terribly wrong is it possible I could lose most or all of my investment? B. Does the person recommending the investment to me have something to gain by that recommendation?

4. Never sign a contract without first having your attorney review the contract. Ask your attorney to point out all dangers.

5. Always look at the motives of the people who communicate with you. Ask: what do they have to gain by what they are communicating?

6. Always remember that what someone is communicating to you may be true or false.

7. Remember that people are often not what they appear to be or represent themselves to be. All humans are actors.

8. Use three different colors of highlighter pens while reading *A Course In Materialization*. Use a different color to circle or underline these three different categories:

    A. Those passages that emphasize morality, unselfishness, kindness, integrity, love, compassion, character building, and related topics.

    B. Those passages that describe techniques, methods, and how to make the methods and techniques more effective. For example how to visualize, concentrate, use affirmations, autosuggestion, etc.

    C. Every passage that you found to be helpful that does not fit in the above two categories.

I

BROWN LANDONE

The following quotes are from
How to Turn Your Desires and Ideals into Realities, 1922

DESIRE, IDEALS AND REALITIES

WHAT DESIRES CAN YOU MAKE COME TRUE?

Every desire is the heart of some ideal.

Your desires always come true.

Your wishes seldom do; they die by consuming themselves in forever wishing wishes.

A desire with a body or an ideal with a heart always becomes a reality!

Every desire is the heart center of some ideal which is either revealed to consciousness and understood or hidden in the ultra-consciousness and misunderstood.

The ideal is the active *body* of the desire.

Do not expect your desire to come true except you give it a body.

Construct an ideal that gives substance to each desire.

Make the ideal active – endow it with the process of attainment.

Then, it will become a reality!

It will come true!

But an *idea* is not an *ideal*!

That is where your trouble often lies!

Only a few – a very, very few – of your *ideas* ever come true. And very, very few of your thoughts and plans ever materialize if they are made up of ideas instead of ideals.

An ideal always manifests itself in action and becomes a reality. Unless it does so, it is not an ideal.

An ideal differs from an idea.

An idea is an image in the mind.

An ideal is a *perfect* image in the mind.

Every idea or ideal is composite – it is made up of parts.

Your *idea* of an orange includes, among a score of images: certain images of color, for you know it is not black; certain images of size, for you know an orange is not as small as a pinhead or as large as a watermelon; certain images of odor, it does not smell like an onion; and certain images of taste, for it does not taste like carrots or potatoes, pickles or chili-sauce.

An idea is imperfect because it lacks mind images which it should include and because it includes images which should not be included.

Your *idea* of a certain man is imperfect because your idea of him does not include all the imaged qualities a perfect man should possess and includes imaged qualities which the perfect man should not manifest.

But your perfect *ideal* of a man includes all of those qualities which such a man should possess and none of those qualities which he should not manifest.

An idea is not perfect; it is but a *partial* image, and lacking that something which is essential, seldom comes true. Usually the element an idea lacks is the very element which – if the idea possessed it – would make the idea manifest as a reality.

Differing from an idea, an *ideal* is a *perfect* image in the mind. It includes all of the component parts which it should include and it includes nothing which it should not include. Thus, in content and substance, it is perfect.

Ideas are but mental skeletons; they are without heart and body, they have no desire, no ideal.

Desire may be related to an idea or it may not. It is never a part of it. That is one of the elements an idea lacks.

An *ideal* has always a heart of desire. That is one of the reasons why ideals come true.

Mere ideas do not thrill the soul, urging and forcing man to action.

Your ideas seldom materialize. They lack desire and impulse to action.

Ideals always come true.

Change your ideas into ideals and they will become realities.

It is easy for you to do so as soon as you know what it is the idea lacks.

Which of your ideals can you make come true?

Not one of them if they exist only as desires, for desire is but the soul's *impulse* to become real!

But, give a desire a spiritual *body* – that is, embody it in an ideal – and it will always come true!

For ideals are *substance* of things that are!

CAN YOU, YOURSELF, MAKE YOUR IDEALS BECOME REALITIES?

Some of you are endowed with faith and some beset with doubt.

Of those endowed with faith based upon spiritual knowledge, there is not one whose faith is not weakened a little by trifling doubts. Of those beset with the darkest of doubts, there is not one whose doubt is not enlightened a little by a touch of faith.

When I state that ideals come true, none of you deny it or think of denying it.

But, when I assure you that every ideal always comes true and that every one of your own particular ideals can be changed to a material reality, my statement contrasts so astoundingly with your past experiences of having tried faithfully to attain that which you desire, that some of you feel it can not be true – some of you may doubt even my common sense in making such an assertion.

You who doubt that every ideal comes true, doubt sincerely, doubt because of common sense judgments based upon your *present* knowledge.

No matter what the cause, doubt interferes with your realization of your ideals: it dampens the fire of desire and lessens your effort to attain that which you wish because you think the effort is useless.

I do not wish you to accept any statement; I wish you to *know* truth! Do not change from doubt to blind belief; it will do you no permanent good – blind faith soon dies.

But what are the 'ideas' in your mind that make you doubt?

First, mistaking *ideas* for *ideals*.

Second, your 'idea' of the *density* of matter.

Third, your 'idea' of the *solidity* of matter.

Fourth, your 'idea' of matter as *motionless* and *lifeless*.

Fifth, your present incomplete knowledge of the *process* of making ideals become realities.

These are the only serious causes of doubt, five stones in the path of faith and attainment.

By and large, your doubt is based upon the seeming impossibility of etheric images of the mind being able easily to change, re-form and re-create the substance of matter which is seemingly so dense, solid and lifeless. If you could know that matter is not so dense as it seems, not so solid as it appears, not so lifeless as it is assumed to be, if you could *know* these things, then doubt would be faith and faith would be divinely certain, forever lasting, and ever impelling to action.

Most of your trouble, then, relates to your 'idea' of the nature of matter, its substance and attributes.

It is lack of knowledge of the true nature of matter that makes us think of it as dense, solid, motionless and lifeless.

If in our greater knowledge of matter we find that it is only energy in reality, that it is not restricted energy but infinite energy, and that it is of the same substance as spirit – then our concept of matter becomes so like our concept of the substance of which ideals are made, that it is possible for us to perceive some definite connection – a real relation, perhaps a similarity, perhaps even a co-existence – of the substance of every ideal and the substance of every material reality.

With such knowledge our faith that ideals come true, because they are of the same substance as matter, can be and is justified.

Such faith will fire anew our ideals and desires and impel us to cease no effort till they become realities; and with knowledge of the process of attainment, we shall know by experience that it is not so difficult as it once seemed.

And you, yourself, can make your ideals become realities.

Faith is the substance of things hoped for.

Ideals are the substance of the things that are.

THE SPIRIT OF MATTER

WHAT COMPACTNESS OF MATTER GIVES TO YOUR IDEALS

Your 'ideas' are always changing and you are ever changing your attitude regarding them. Why? They have no form, no body of spiritual substance; being without body, they are notions and very changeable notions at that.

But you are loyal to your ideals; you are steadfast in your allegiance to them. Why? Because there is something fixed and real about them; they are made of spiritual substance; they are the actual bodies of your desires.

You hold steadfastly to your ideals; but since ideals are of the spiritual and etheric substance, can you easily change them into material actualities – make them manifest in a world of matter which appears so compact and dense?

This 'idea' that matter is compact and hence dense is one of the stones in the path of faith; as an idea, it prevents you from making sufficient effort to make your ideals come true.

When you study matter as it is – as the great physical scientists now know it – and when you find that that which is called density is but the compactness of materially empty *space* – etheric substance – spiritual substance, does it not open up new visions?

Already you perceive that, if so-called density of matter is but compactness of etheric substance, that which makes density possible is similar to and co-existent with the very substance in which ideals exist and of which they are made. All of which suggests that that which appears to us as density is of aid in giving *substance* to ideals, in giving them bodies so that they can come true.

What is *density* of matter? If matter is dense, it must be compact, for idea of density depends upon the idea of compactness. Is matter a compact substance?

Read carefully and think; for this, to you, is vital. It means either that you can and will make your ideals come true or that you will slip through life forever wishing that you might have done so.

The material emptiness of the universe is a true indication of the so-called density of matter.

What is the density of the molecule?

What is a molecule?

Image the sun; image the Earth, Mars, Mercury, the other planets and their moons, all whirling and circling around the sun center to form our solar *system*. The system is a gigantic space. There is no shell to this sphere; it is just ether – conceived as a globe – within which whirl a few comparatively small specks of dust – the earth and the sun, for instance.

Look up in the air above you. Imagine the outline of a toy balloon *without* any material except a few specks of invisible dust in the space you image as a globe. That is the density of the universe; it is also as dense as the molecule which is merely an etheric globular *space* in which atoms – far, far apart – whirl around an etheric center.

Is not the density of matter already evaporating so that in it you see no hindrance to making your ideals into realities?

If not the molecule, is the *atom* dense?

The atom, like the molecule, has no shell or body. It is merely a spherical *system* of ether *space* in which electrons whirl around an etheric center.

So far nothing but infinite space and infinite energy is space! In such, what hindrance is there to your ideals and desires coming true?

There is no density of matter to hinder the manifestation of your ideals and desires.

In fact, this etheric energy-space substance, which makes matter seem to be dense, is the very substance that gives bodies to your ideals and thus makes them manifest in material actuality.

WHAT ATTRACTIVE ENERGY OF MATTER GIVES TO YOUR DESIRES

Another stone in the path of faith and the attainment of your ideals and desires is the 'idea' that matter is solid.

As density was found to be but infinite energy space – the spiritual substance in which ideals and all things exist – what will solidity turn out to be when you come to know it as it is?

Iron seems to be a solid substance and very hard.

Does its hardness reside in matter or is it due to the spirit or energy of matter? The molecules and atoms of iron are no harder or more solid than the molecules and atoms of butter. Yet, it is difficult to drive a nail into a piece of iron and easy to drive one into a chunk of butter.

That which makes it difficult to drive a nail into iron is the degree of attractive force existing between the particles. It is this force which holds molecules and their respective atoms to each other. When you drive a nail into iron, what you overcome is the attractive force which tries to prevent the molecules being pushed apart.

It is easy to force apart the molecules of butter to make space for a nail. In this case also, what you overcome is the attractive force which holds together the molecules and atoms of butter.

When the degree of attractive force is comparatively great, we say the matter is hard and solid. When it is smaller, we say the matter is not hard and not so solid. But it is not matter itself which is solid or not solid.

In truth, solidity is but the spirit of matter. It is another manifestation – the *infinite attractive energy* found throughout the universe.

Matter is not solid!

The solidity, which you feared as an evil hindrance to the manifestation of your desires and ideals, is infinite attractive spirit, the very force that gives your desires the *power* to attract all that is necessary to make them come true.

WHAT MOVEMENT IN MATTER GIVES TO THE BODY OF YOUR DESIRE

Ideals are of the substance of spirit and space; they have motion and life. Can they, then, manifest in matter if it be motionless and lifeless?

That which lives has motion of itself and within itself; that which has such motion is not dead.

All so-called matter is alive. It is alive with energy.

And, it *moves*! It moves within itself!

Matter so throbbing with energy and movement cannot hinder your ideals coming true; but your 'idea' of matter as dense, solid and motionless can hinder them by deadening your desire and lessening your effort.

Change your 'idea' of matter to a true *ideal* of matter.

For desires embodied in ideals – in bodies of etheric substance possessing infinite energy – always come true!

DESIRE-IDEALS AND THE PROCESS OF BECOMING REALITIES

THE ONLY THREE ACTIVITIES NECESSARY

First, there is the Ideal of Something Desired.

Second, the process that Leads to Attaining It; and

Third, the Act of Making the Reality yours.

These are the *three* basic activities of attaining that which you desire; they are the *only* ones which have been and can be successfully used in attaining any quality or degree of development within yourself or in obtaining any thing, condition or position in society or the world about you.

These three activities are simply stated because they are true, not because I write them. Basic truths are always simple; and, if not enveloped in a mass of superfluous words or intertwined with a web of entangled thoughts, they are always easily understood.

When simply stated and easily understood, it is easy to apply them.

If you permit your ideal to be lost in a jungle of many words and your process to be misdirected by a multitude of varying thoughts and feelings – each pointing in a different direction – why, then, of course, your ideal will not and can not become a reality.

Unless you can clearly and definitely state your *ideal*, it is not sufficiently concrete to make any process of attaining it successful.

Unless you can definitely and simply state what you are to do and how you are to do it, your plan of the *process* of attaining or obtaining that which you want will be confused and your effort will be partly wasted and probably unsuccessful.

Attaining that which you desire is easy and certain: (1) if you conceive a clear-cut ideal of what you desire; (2) if you turn the ideal to the particular process that always leads to attaining or obtaining that which you wish; and (3) if you know how to make the reality a part of you and your surroundings.

TO ATTAIN YOUR DESIRES, ALL THREE MUST BE USED

If you idealize and use *all* three of the basic activities and *only* those three, it is easy to make your ideals become realities.

You always attain when you idealize and use them; but, if you leave out any one of the three, you fail to attain your desire, and no one can be blamed except yourself.

If you idealize only that which you desire and hold faithfully to that ideal – that is if you use *only the first* of the three activities – you will succeed and justly in proportion to what you do.

Idealizing what you want and holding faithfully to the ideal for months and even years brings you the success your effort merits – even after years you will still *'be holding to'* the ideal.

And, if you idealize that which you desire and attempt to take possession of it mentally – using *the first and third* of the three basic activities – you succeed and justly in proportion to what you do.

If, when in New York, you learn of a football game to be played in Boston and desire to be present, the ideal of the *Thing Desired* is 'to be in Boston.'

If you desire to drive by automobile from New York to Boston, that is the ideal of the *Process* you intend to use to get to Boston.

If you go to your garage and sit in your car for a day, a month or a year, holding faithfully all the time to the Thing Desired and holding also a mental picture of 'being in Boston' – mentally picturing the first and third steps, *but omitting the second one* – before the year passes your friends will wish to send you to the madhouse; and only because you failed to use the second activity, that of the *process* of actually starting the machine and driving from New York to Boston.

It is not enough to hold ideals of the Thing Desired, the first step.

It is not enough even to have faith that your desire will come true, though faith is the substance of things hoped for. You must put your *ideals* into idealized *action* for ideals are the substance of things that are and idealized action is the only certain process of attainment.

HOW TO FORM AN IDEAL THAT WILL COME TRUE

First, an ideal to come true must be an *ideal*; an 'idea' will not do.

Second, an ideal to become a reality must have a *heart of desire*, and a good strong heart.

Third, an ideal to come into manifestation must be *a body of real etheric substance*.

Fourth, an ideal to become an actuality must possess *an impulse of action*.

Lacking any one or more of these, your ideals do not become realities.

First your ideal must be an ideal, not an idea.

The ideal will come true.

Since most people think and plan to ideas, their thoughts and plans seldom materialize. After repeated failures, some become discouraged, despondent or resigned and some lose faith in their capacity to attain the great goal.

Other men and women think in *ideals*; with them it is a habit. Such men and women are successful and attain to a great extent that which they desire. They attain in proportion to their ideals.

You may idealize your thoughts of ethical and spiritual advancement and attain soul consciousness; yet when it comes to other matters you may use only 'ideas' and fail.

On the other hand, although others may not idealize ethical and spiritual concepts as you do, yet they *do* idealize, that is, make perfect images of their thoughts of development, advancement, work, and business; and hence they succeed in those lines to a greater extent than you do.

You fail in that which you do not idealize; you succeed in that which you idealize.

They also fail in that which they do not idealize and succeed in that in which they use ideals.

Back of every thing in the world there is an ideal: back of the design of every chair; the decoration of every room; the cut and material of every gown and every suit of clothes; back of every thing that ever comes true.

Those who think in little ideals, succeed in little things; those who think in big ideals succeed in big things.

No advance of mankind has ever been effected except it was first formed by ideals of some kind: no painting was ever painted, no statue ever sculptured, no music ever composed – except first conceived as an ideal. No motor, no dynamo, no engine, no printing press, no linotype, no automobile, no airplane – not one was ever invented except it first existed as an ideal. Nothing in education was ever taught and no ethical or spiritual concept was ever preached that did not previously exist in ideal form in the mind.

Those who think *ideas* never attain to greatness.

Great men and women always think in *ideals*.

How? By making it a perfect image, adding *desire*, giving it *body substance*, and creating in it an irresistible impulse to manifest itself in *action*.

How can you complete an idea so as to make it an ideal?

First, by adding the factors the idea lacks.

You have an 'idea' of the color of an apple. How perfect is it? Take paints and try to paint a picture of an apple and you will discover that there are scores of tints and blends of colors which your 'idea' does not contain.

You have an 'idea' of the profile of the face of someone you love. Take a pencil and try to draw that profile!

You have an 'idea' of the shape and form of the legs of your table. Close your eyes; run your fingers over one of the legs; feel every indentation, every part that projects, the number of rings around the legs. Scores of new factors are added to your 'idea.'

How can you be certain that you have added everything the perfect image ought to contain and left out everything the image should not contain?

Although there are many millions of degrees of variation and an unlimited number of combinations, there are but a few different basic qualities that enter into our image. They are: colors, sounds, tastes, odors, movements and directions of movement, balance or lack of balance, heat or cold, lightness or heaviness.

Take any idea you wish to come true. Image it in your mind as it now is, an imperfect 'idea.' Then, take the factor of colors. Image it again, mentally seeing every color it has possessed, does possess or could possess.

In this same way go over the idea of that which you desire. Use every one of the elements of color, sound, taste, odor, heat, cold, motion, direction of motion, form, size, balance, fineness, roughness, hardness, softness, lightness, heaviness.

Do not leave out a single one.

When you have finished you will have the form of a perfect image – of an ideal – but it will still be only the *form* without a heart of desire, without an etheric body, and without impulse to impel action.

Next, add desire!

FIRING THE DESIRE OF YOUR IDEAL

Wishes are but wishes; they lead only to wishing more wishes.

Desires are heartbeats of soul; they demand and impel to action.

A wish turns ever to itself, wishing that 'something' will *come* to make itself true.

A desire goes out from self; it daringly reaches out, demanding the thing desired, and divinely creates it in reality.

Put the following truths together: Desire is the heart of your ideal; in this heart are the fires of attainment; sometimes they die down and are dim; sometimes they burn brightly and glow with hope and set fire to action; unless they thus burn with the light of hope and the fire of action your ideal will not come true.

When the fires of desire are dimmed by disappointments or discouragement, or memories of the failures of the past, what are you going to do about it?

Feed the fires with your *feelings* and *emotions*!

Your thoughts will not do; they are but damp wood and wet sand. Desires are of the heart; they cannot be made to burn brightly by adding ideas and thoughts of the mind.

Is it a *thing* – a material thing – you have desired and for which desire burns low because of past failures to attain it, or is it a new desire that dares not burn brightly for fear of disappointment should it not be attained?

Fire your desire so that it will come true.

Fire it with *your feelings* and *emotions*.

Are you a young woman and is it a dainty rose-colored gown you desire?

Image the color of it and *feel* the joy of gowning yourself in that color. *Feel* the pleasure it would give you to look at yourself in that color.

Think of its color again, the color of roses. Imagine that you have perfumed the gown with just a touch of attar of roses. *Feel* the joy of smelling the sweet odor of roses. Feel the joy of smelling the perfume with which your dress is scented.

Think of the *feel* of the material, how soft and delicate. *Feel* the joy you *feel* in *feeling* it.

Think of the lightness of the dress. *Feel* the joy you experience in handling light and dainty and fluffy things. *Feel* the joy you would *feel* in putting on that dress and in waiting for your sweetheart to call. *Feel* the joy you would feel as he admired it and complimented you upon it. *Feel* the joy you would feel dressed in that gown, when with a group of people.

Is not your desire fired and burning with impulse to act? Will not you *do* something to get that dress; and, idealizing your doing, you will do it in the right way and get it in the right way.

Are you a young man desiring a new suit of clothes? Fire your desire with your feelings.

Image the suit you wish; its color, cut, form, material, and fit to you.

Feel how happy you would feel dressed in that suit calling on the girl you love.

Feel how proud you would feel if you could wear it when going home to see mother.

Feel how satisfied you would feel walking into the office dressed in that suit.

Feel all your good *feelings* – felt under all other conditions – in relation to that suit.

Is not your desire fired to the point where you will *do* something to get it and, idealizing your doing, you will do the right thing and get it in the right way.

Is it a *position* you desire? *Feel* the joy the income of that position would give you. *Feel* the pleasures you could obtain with that income. *Feel* the joy of the opportunities that income would give. *Feel* the true pride of advancement. *Feel* the joy of knowing you have attained the position and made good. *Feel* the joy of generously helping others when in that position. *Feel* what that position would mean to you among your fellows. *Feel* what it would mean to you among business men. *Feel* all these *feelings* – feeding your desires with your *feelings* – instead of with wishes and thoughts, and you will *do* something to attain that which you desire.

Feed the desires of your ideals with your own feelings and emotions – and the higher the feelings and emotions, the stronger the fire – and your desires will turn to action that cannot be prevented. And since your desires are hearts of ideals, that which you *do* will be right.

GIVING A BODY OF ETHERIC SUBSTANCE TO YOUR IDEAL

The next step is to create a body for your ideal, a body of real etheric substance.

Image the ideal of the *thing* you want. Does the thing itself seem so compact and dense that you can not re-form and re-create it to accord with your ideal? Its form can be changed, but only if you give a body to your ideal.

First, give *form* to the substance of the ideal.

Re-idealize your image of the thing desired as made of infinite energy-space. By doing this you actually *group* the spiritual substance into *form*. This is a first step in creating the body of your ideal.

Second, give the body attractive power.

Re-image your ideal of the thing you want. Realize, that whatever the substance of the thing desired, that which makes its actuality possible is infinite attractive energy; that it is this same energy that holds all the particles of your ideal together and draws to it all the factors necessary for manifestation.

By thus imaging your ideal you give it solidity. The particles of this spiritual substance becomes fixed so that the ideal will persist; so that it will not change, as an idea changes, or evaporate in vain imagings.

By this process you also give it power to attract and draw to it all those conditions, qualities, thoughts, feelings and attitudes necessary to make it real, necessary to make its actuality possible.

Third, create the body of self-active substance.

Realize that everything you wish to change is in infinite motion, thrilling with life.

By this process you rid your soul of any idea that any so-called material thing can oppose the manifestation of your ideal.

And you give to the ideal – to its body substance – the same quality of infinite, infinitely rapid power of movement, power of action, power to make itself come true.

Image the body of your ideal composed of spirit substance, vibrating at this tremendous rate, exerting enormous power, and you give it additional power to make itself into an actuality.

To this point in the process, what is your ideal?

First, a perfect image, including only those elements it should possess and none which it should not possess.

Second, an ideal with a heart of desire, fired to action by all your feelings and soul desires: (1) increased by imaging the beauty and utility of the ideal and the pleasures it will give you and (2) augmented by every conceivable element of desire you can awaken by imaging everything composing its image, color, sound, et cetera.

Third, an ideal body, formed of the infinite spirit substance, energy-ether; a body of the same material as the essence of matter which makes it easy for the ideal to manifest as an actuality; a body held together and made permanent by infinite attractive energy; a body composed of etheric substance whose particles vibrate at a rate so rapid that imagination cannot conceive it; a body composed of etheric substance an ounce of which has gigantic power, sufficient – if freed at one time – to toss the Alps into the Atlantic Ocean.

Now give the ideal the soul impulse to act, and you can not prevent its coming true.

GIVING YOUR IDEAL THE IMPULSE OF ACTION TO MAKE IT REAL

There is one more step in the process of making your ideal complete.

It possesses infinite energy, but you must give it the *impulse of action*.

How can you do this?

In this I differ from many others. I hold that visualization is not sufficient.

Visualization, although it often accomplishes wonders, is after all but a *picturing* of an 'idea.' It does not make the idea vivid but it adds to it only one of several elements, only the images of the sight sense.

Instead of visualization I use idealization, the perfect image. This includes the factor of visualization and that of the eleven other factors. Using the other factors – especially those of motion and direction of motion – we give the ideal an impulse to move and this in turn gives it the action power that makes the ideal manifest as a reality.

Visualizing is the act of holding a mental picture; idealizing is the act of perfecting the mental image, of securing it and the act of making it real.

You often ignite the heart of your ideal by vivid mental pictures and strong feelings of desire to possess the reality; but unless connected up with your motor power of action, it remains merely an urgent unfulfilled picture of desire within you, an ideal that does not become a reality. Clutching your ideal to action cannot be effectively accomplished by a picture. Let me illustrate this clearly.

Go to an art museum; look at any painting representing a number of people. If, after going away, you close your eyes and visualize the painting, you hold in your mind a mental picture of the painting. With care and practice you can make this mental picture very vivid and increase your ability to re-see in the mind every detail of such a painting, lines, forms and colors of things and people. Yet, it is still a mere *picture*; it is flat, lacking action, and it does not impel to action.

That which I have just described is the visualizing process.

Visualizing has produced marvelous results when the person visualizing has turned such mental picture-making into the idealized process, even if they have not recognized that they have done so.

Idealizing, however, is more remarkable because it includes visualizing and adds all other elements to it. Visualization comes from using the stored-up images of but one of our senses, the sense of sight. Idealization comes from using the stored-up images not only of the sense of sight but of all other senses.

To attain that which we desire it is necessary, not only to see the visual image, but to act.

Try now another process: Idealize the painting you saw in the art museum; bring it visually to your mind; re-see it just as you did by the process previously described.

Then image action – every person in it in action; *feel* them doing the thing they are pictured as doing; feel the movement; feel the activities.

If it portrays them as speaking, hear the tones, hear what they say.

I might continue with all other elements of the picture, but I think this is sufficient to show you the difference between visualization and idealization.

Visualization produces a non-moving, non-active picture in the mind, even though it be vivid and clear. Being non-active, it does not impel to action and hence many of our pictured ideals do not become realities. But if we idealize action, if we use the mental clutch of connecting up the ideal of the thing desired with the process of obtaining that which we desire, action must result; and action is one of the essential factors in making any ideal come true.

THE PROCESS THAT MAKES IDEALS COME TRUE

Process is the *way* of doing things.

The non-idealized processes are: (1) 'mere' doing; (2) purposeful doing; (3) planned or thought-out doing.

The fourth process is the idealized process.

'Mere doing' never leads to success, for back of it there is no ideal of the process, no desire to improve it, no thought-out plan, and no ideal.

In mines and stores and factories and offices there are millions of good workers. They learn to do one thing – even learn to do it well – and then, forever afterwards, they 'merely do.' They drudge, or toil, or labor but they do not work; and they do not succeed.

You yourself may do your work perfectly, merely doing it; you may be always at it; others may be able to depend upon you doing your work exactly, with no loss of time, not missing a stroke. But all these do not lead to attainment, why, even a hay-press does those things!

'Purposeful doing' is one step in advance of 'mere doing.' It is based upon an 'idea' of progress and is stimulated by a desire. But that is not sufficient.

Why, a bank-robber has a purpose in robbing; he may succeed now and then in getting what he wants and he always succeeds in making himself a useless member of society, yet, his *life* is not successful and he is not a success.

Even well-planned, carefully thought-out doing leads to thousands of failures.

Many a young man, intelligent, enthusiastic, hard-working and earnest – starts in business for himself and fails – even after he has planned and thought out his entire problem. When he begins, he sees success – big success – within two or three years at most. But in six months the sheriff may close him up as a failure. Even planned doing, based upon ideas, desires and thought-out processes, fails unless the process is idealized.

It is only an idealized air, process and attitude that always wins.

Some time ago an additional main subway was opened in New York City. It necessitated a new routing of passengers.

For days before its opening the papers were full of the new system and how to get from one point to another.

The Result of Not Idealizing the Process: On the day of the opening, intelligent men and women crowded and jammed each other, went where they did not wish to go, even got lost, though many of them had known New York all their lives.

How I idealized the Process in this Case: I took a description of the routes from a newspaper; read it carefully. Then I quietly *visualized* the new routes. Next, I *idealized* action, idealized myself *using* the new route from my home to my office, picturing myself on the cars, changing where the description said changes must be made; idealizing every bit of the journey to my office door. Next I idealized one trip after another to other parts of the city, until I had myself mentally *used* every new and old route.

After this, it was impossible to be confused; impossible to make a mistake in using the subway.

Millions of others *thought* of the new routes, but certainly very few consciously idealized themselves traveling on them.

Yet every individual in New York could have done it in five minutes if they had only been in the habit of Idealizing the Process of Doing Things.

Others had *ideas* of the new route, of where they wanted to go, and of how to get there.

I turned my ideas into ideals.

Idealizing the process of doing the thing included more than the re-seeing of the mental picture of the new route. I did more than visualize it. I put into it an element of *action*. I kept my 'clutch' in so the picture became movement. That is always essential in attaining that which you desire.

THE ACT OF MAKING THE REALITY YOURS

This last activity – the act of making the reality yours – comprises three steps: (1) idealizing *your attitude*; (2) *unifying* the *substance* of the ideal *with* the *substance* of the *real*; and (3) making the *actual thing a part of your possessions* or *placing yourself in the actual conditions* which you have idealized and desired.

Your *attitude* relates to yourself, to others, to conditions, and to the world in general.

Begin with *yourself*. Consciously or not you do take some kind of an attitude toward yourself.

You are free to take any attitude toward yourself you desire to take; but there is only one attitude that leads to success and it is the idealized attitude!

Idealize your attitude toward *others*, "That which ye seek ye shall find."

If you think that all men are trying to crush you, you will be crushed; first, because your attitude closes your eyes to the opportunities offered you; and second, because such an attitude discovers and draws to you those who do not help you. If you idealize others as willing to help you, you draw to you men and women who will do the square thing by you and help you – in them you will find help and a just reward. This idealized attitude does not make you a trusting simpleton, for the idealized attitude also idealizes wisdom in knowing others.

The idealized attitude changes all the *conditions* of life. In business, it leads us to expect good results, and expecting good results, we plan better. When we plan better – that is, in a more idealized way – we get better results.

Idealize the *world* in general. The universe must be good. If it were not good it would go to pieces over night, for evil disrupts and destroys. Good attracts and unites and holds together.

You cannot idealize your business, your profession and your work without conducting the whole affair as an idealized service which inevitably will force your ideals to come true!

You may idealize the Thing Desired, idealize the Process of Attaining It and Carry Out the Process in Action, and, yet, by your *attitude* keep the reality from becoming yours. With a group of congenial friends, you can desire and idealize an evening's pleasure for yourself and the girl you love, you may call for her and go to the gathering together, and yet your attitude, if disagreeable, can keep the pleasure of the evening from becoming yours.

First, then, give attention to *your* attitude!

Second, *unify the substance* of your ideal *with* the *substance of the thing or condition* desired.

The substance of *your* ideal is *yours*! It is of your mind.

The substance of the reality *may not yet* be yours.

To make it *yours*, you must make the body of your ideal *coincide* with the body or actuality of that which you desire.

Recognize (1) that the material density of the thing you desire is an etheric substance coinciding in nature with the substance of your ideal; (2) that the material solidity of the thing you desire is infinite attractive energy which coincides in nature with the holding-together energy of your ideal; and (3) that the energy of the material thing desired is etheric force, exactly the same force as exists in your ideal.

Now, *image* each detail of your ideal, *project* it out of your mind to the *place* of the actuality, and *unite* it with the same detail of the material actuality you desire to be yours.

Do not miss a single detail; make the projected ideal coincide with the actual thing in *place*.

To miss no factor, *unify* step by step, as to color, sound, taste, smell, balance, heat, movement, direction of movement, form, size, fineness or roughness, hardness or softness, cold, weight, use, pleasures from use, et cetera.

Miss none of these!

Then, third, take possession of the *thing* or walk into the *condition* desired.

Idealize yourself in action: (1) the condition of yourself when in action; and (2) your use of the means to be used in performing your action.

If this afternoon you are to go to one man or a group of men to discuss or do something which it is necessary for you to present or do in order to make your ideal come true, image yourself with the man or with the men, image yourself at perfect ease, image your confidence in yourself, image your self-control when talking to them, when contradicted by them, even when ridiculed by one or more of them.

Image these conditions in your mind before you go. It builds in brain paths which makes the doing of the thing but a mere repetition of a thing already done.

I say image these things, not merely imagine them; merely thinking about them will not bring results.

Image also the impression you see yourself giving to others: Are you appearing as sincere as you are sincere? Are you appearing as reliable as you are reliable? Are you appearing active and energetic and sane and safe? Remember, it is not only what you are, but what you *communicate* to others which determines results in dealing with others.

Idealizing the action builds in brain paths. Then, when you come to the actual doing, you have already established a habit of doing it successfully.

The more times you idealize the *doing*, the stronger and more permanent these brain paths become. Hence, when you *go* into action, you are merely repeating what you have already done and what you have already succeeded in doing. Consequently there is no hesitancy, no doubt, no lack of confidence, no lack of ease, and no mistakes in your action.

And – because you center your effort rightly – the thing or condition is a reality and belongs to *you*!

Where to center your effort now follows.

WHERE TO CENTER YOUR EFFORT

It is very important that you idealize that which you desire; but, so far as the attainment of it is concerned, the process is much more important, and idealizing the process is the most important of all.

In the spring of 1919, some time after I had returned to the United States from one of my sojourns abroad, I wrote a letter to Elizabeth Towne. I had known her for many years but while I was living abroad we had been quite out of touch.

When Mrs. Towne received my letter it awakened a desire in her mind. There was to be a convention near her home town the following week. She wished me to speak at that convention. To have me speak at the convention was her ideal of the Thing Desired.

Did she stop with the Ideal of the thing desired? Not at all! She began Idealizing the Process of getting me there. She pressed the bell-button immediately; in came a stenographer; and a letter was sent telling me how I could come and return – giving information of the trains – how, by traveling at night, the trip would take the least possible time. At intervals during the day and next she went on Idealizing the Process of arranging for me while there, where I should stay, when I should speak, how many times I should speak, et cetera, et cetera.

She gave ten seconds to recognizing the Ideal of the Thing Desired and an hour or more Idealizing the Process; 10 seconds to the former; 3,600 seconds to the latter. That's about the right proportion.

Think this over; it applies to everything in life. Give about a thousand times more time and effort to idealizing and working out the process than you give to idealizing the thing you desire and your ideal will come true.

If you want to win, if you really wish that which you desire, if you truly desire to make your ideals come true, to turn them into realities, first form your ideal of the Thing Desired but give your great effort to Idealizing the Process and putting it into action.

That brings you the reality!

IDEALIZING THINGS

IDEALIZED THINGS MAKE FORTUNES

In whatever you are doing and in whatever you hope to do and attain, it is necessary to deal with three factors: things, words and people.

Consequently, idealizing the process of attaining what you want includes idealizing the *things* with which you work or the things you are to handle; and often great fortunes are made from *idealizing* little things and great failures result from *non*-idealization of things, big or little.

Here are the experiences of two men illustrating the point.

It was on the 20th Century speeding across the State of New York toward Chicago. I had left the dining car, gone to the club car and, observing that the seats about one of the card tables were empty, sat down there so that I might be alone to read.

Men were coming in from dinner and soon a man took a seat across the table. I looked up to determine whether others were with him and, if so, whether they might not wish the table for card playing. But he was alone. He had a fine face, clean, clear-cut; evidently a man of education; perhaps, a man of culture. His face, his bearing, his attitude all proclaimed him to be a 'man of ideals.' I do not mean a visionary, but a man who does and who has always done that which is right and who refuses and has refused to do that which is wrong.

In a minute we were in conversation. It started regarding the high cost of living. It went from one thing to another. He was communicative and it was not long before he mentioned that he had wished this year to send his boy to college but he had been unable to do so because he could not afford it.

"A college education costs four times as much today as it did when I went to college," he said.

The first point I wish you to remember is this: he could not afford to send his son to college.

I led him on in the conversation, learned that after graduating from college he had been a school teacher; that later he had been in Y. M. C. A. work; a welfare worker in a manufacturing plant for a year; and that in 1913, he, with a friend, had gone into a manufacturing business of his own.

"What line of manufacturing?" I asked,

"Oh, just little wicker hand satchels, such as boys use to carry books to and from school," he answered.

This is the second point I wish you to remember: "Oh, just little wicker hand satchels."

This conversation took place in the year 1920. It indicates that after having been in business seven years, manufacturing an article of use to at least ten million school children as well as hundreds of thousands of others in our country, this 'man of ideals' was unable to send his boy to college because he could not afford it.

We talked of other things; but before long he left me, going back to his Pullman.

Two other men came in and sat down. One across the table, one beside me. Later I learned that one was a coal operator of Indiana, and the other, well, the rest of the story concerns the other man.

One look at this man told me he was not a so-called 'man of ideals,' that is, not in accord with the ordinary use of the term. He looked very prosperous; he was talkative, men are always more communicative after dinner, smoking a good cigar, on a train with nothing else to do.

This man is the soap-dye king of the world. Only a few years ago he and a friend, his wife and his friend's wife, started in business making soap-dyes. Altogether they had $800. Today each of them is more than a millionaire. Their soap-dyes sell for ten cents a package, yet they do a business of many hundred thousand dollars a month. They secured the original patent and consequently, in addition to the profits they make from their own concern, they are paid royalties by all other soap-dye companies. *How did he do it?*

I have said that he is not a man of ideals. That statement is both true and not true. He is not a man of ideals of the Pharisee kind, *but he is a man who idealizes the thing with which he works.* To him the soap-dye is one of the great inventions of the age. His face glowed as he told about it; his eyes shone.

"Think what it means," he said, "for every woman in the land – in fact, all over the world, for now we're selling soap-dyes to Europe, Australia, India and Japan – to be able in two minutes to change the color of her shirtwaist, of a piece of lace, or any light trimming merely by dipping it in our dye, without any boiling, and without staining her hands."

From the very beginning he had idealized the *thing* he produced. He had idealized the soap in order to select the best for the purpose. He had idealized the dyes so as to produce the most useful dye; the most easily and quickly used dye, a dye needing no boiling, a dye that does not stain the hands of those using it.

He had idealized the chemicals used in the process of making the dye, and, as he talked of how he had built up the business, I saw that he had even idealized the kind of chemical expert he wanted and had then searched the United States until he found the man that fitted his ideal. He had idealized justice and had secured patent rights for himself and those who had worked for him.

His process of idealizing the *thing* – the soap-dye – did not stop when he had put a good product on the market and when that product had earned him millions of dollars. He told me how that very afternoon he had spent three hours with Japanese girls in New York to prove his soap-dyes would not stain the hands of the Japanese women. He had done this because reports had come from Japan that the dyes did stain the hands of Japanese girls.

He *began* his work by idealizing the *thing* he intended to manufacture; he had idealized the thing every day since he first conceived it; and he is still idealizing that same thing. Is it any wonder that his face glows, that his eyes shine, that his tone is enthusiastic and that he is making millions.

He is not a so-called 'man of ideals,' but he put idealizing into action.

He idealizes everything, even common labor; he was actually happy telling me that he and his wife made the first dyes in their own home in stew pots and dish-pans and that, while he was making the boxes in which to ship the dyes, his wife was out peddling them.

46

He has idealized the *service* the dyes render to millions of women and the just rewards to himself. Consequently, he is successful. He is worth millions, made in less than four years; he was able to send his two boys to college.

What value are your ideals unless you use them?

It is not *holding* ideals that make desires come true.

It is *using* ideals.

The first step is to idealize the *thing* with which you are working.

A BILLION DOLLARS BY IDEALIZING THE MOVEMENT OF THINGS

Can you turn a desire for money directly into money? No, certainly not! Money is the result of abundance, not abundance itself.

Let us agree upon the meaning of the term.

When one friend is thinking of a Persian cat and another is thinking of an ordinary house cat, both will disagree with what I am saying about a 'cat' if I am thinking and talking of a wild cat.

Therefore qualify at once the word 'abundance.' One meaning of the word is sufficiency – enough to meet all our true needs, present and future.

Idealizing the Process to Secure Abundance should not be limited to securing money directly. Other factors are more important. They are an abundance of ideas, recognition of the abundant opportunities that surround you, and being abundantly prepared to make use of them.

Lack of material abundance is not a lack of *ideas*; but money-lack always indicates a poverty of *ideals* regarding the right process of getting money.

Once all hairpins were made of straight wire and were always *moving*, always slipping out of the lady's hair. Millions of women were disturbed about it for scores of years and many people had *ideas* about it. Hundreds of thousands consciously desired and wished for something better and *thought* about it. Nothing, however, resulted from the *ideas* and *thoughts* of these hundreds of thousands. Not a one of them ever made a cent out of his or her ideas or thoughts. There was no abundance in them.

But, there was abundance in the *ideal* of a hairpin which of itself prevented itself from moving easily. The man who idealized and produced the crinkly wire hairpin is now a multi-millionaire.

Abundance always resides in an ideal, whether of property or management or manufacturing or position or what not; it resides in idealizing even the detailed parts of things and the *movement* of so common a substance as *oil*.

The steps in the Idealizing Process which brought success to Mr. Rockefeller were:

First, he idealized oil in *detail*. The other oil men – then wealthier than Mr. Rockefeller – *thought* of oil only as oil; as costing so much per barrel, as selling for so much, and as bringing so much profit.

Mr. Rockefeller thought of these things, but in addition he *idealized* oil in all its details. Mentally he visioned other substances in it, not at all like oil. Moreover, he idealized the process of separating these from the oil, and out of these came the by-products.

Let us be just: this wealth from the by-products was due to the fact that Mr. Rockefeller was less realistic than others; he *idealized* the oil which to others was just 'oil' and nothing more.

Second, Mr. Rockefeller idealized the *movement* of oil.

Other oil men thought of transporting oil just as barrels of flour and barrels of sugar are transported. But Mr. Rockefeller idealized it in *motion*; he saw it *flowing* and *idealized* it flowing in pipes. Hence the pipe-line system, the second great source of Standard Oil profits and supremacy.

On the other hand, Mr. Rockefeller did not idealize his relation to the rest of society. He thought of himself as a man standing alone. For forty years he was silent, unwilling that anyone within his companies should give any statement regarding their policies or methods to the public. He failed to idealize the truth that men are bound together in a social structure and consequently, separating himself from others, he failed to win the trust and good will of mankind.

Ideas, thoughts composed of ideas, and plans made up of such thoughts seldom become realities. But once the smallest or the largest thing is idealized, the soul which conceives the ideal cannot rest until the ideal has become an actuality. If you would have your desires for abundance fulfilled, idealize them and the process of obtaining them, and abundance cannot be kept from you.

IDEALIZING MEANS AND METHODS

BUILDING UP A SUCCESSFUL BUSINESS IN FACE OF THE WORST KIND OF COMPETITION

In business you fail in some things and succeed in others. You are often failing and succeeding at the same time, failing to make one part of your business successful and succeeding in making another part increase and pay. The failures are due to the ideas held; the successes, to the ideals.

If you idealize the entire process of your business you will not only avoid failures and partial failures, but will think of possibilities never thought of before, the very ones that will lead you to succeed.

To illustrate, I shall use a simple case, one of the simplest that ever came to me, yet one of the most interesting, and one, the success of which, gave me as much joy as the success of many so-called big affairs. In this instance there was a woman in the case, and it's her story I shall tell.

The Woman: A widow with four children; she then lived in a suburb of Chicago; her husband had died three months before; she was left as proprietor of a small grocery and delicatessen store.

The Conditions: As the husband had been ill three months before his death, savings had been used in doctor bills, hospital bills and funeral expenses. Though the store was a little affair, it had had a good business in this section of the wealthy suburb so long as it had been the only store there.

But, about the time of the husband's death, one of those large companies which establish branch stores all over a city built a white-tiled, plate-glass, two-story building on the corner opposite her little shop. It cut down the business of the little store so much that the woman was unable even to make a living for herself and her children.

The Problem: I confess when she first told me the entire story that it seemed impossible for her to compete with the new store with all its service, its supplies, and its million-dollar parent company back of it.

How We Went About It: We idealized (1) those to whom she could sell, (2) the business itself, and (3) the woman.

Visualizing the people of the community was a simple matter. All were mediumly well-to-do; most families had two or more maids; they entertained often at their homes, dinner parties and evening affairs.

But what could this woman sell to them which the other store could *not* supply?

Idealizing the Business: The woman told me the greatest profit was made in handling bakery goods. The big bakeries of the city delivered goods each morning and took back what was left unsold of the day before. In this line there was no waste, and no loss.

Moreover, the profit on the amount invested was made *daily*. If the woman invested ten dollars in canned goods, it might be a month before all were sold; if she made a ten percent profit she made but ten percent on ten dollars in a *month*.

But with bakery goods, if she invested ten dollars in the morning and sold the goods during the day at ten percent profit, she made ten percent on ten dollars *in one day.*

Evidently in this case bakery goods was to be the leader; but how could this little woman make her bakery goods lead over the goods of the other store, when both of them could buy from the same bakeries; and the other store had more money than she, and hence could buy better and more extensive supplies than she could?

Idealizing the Woman: All the time she talked, I had a feeling of conflicting ideas in my mind about her. These remained indefinite until it flashed upon me that, although her name was Mrs. Hansen (Scandinavian), she spoke with a *Scotch* accent.

The New Thought: Scotch – Scotland – Scotch tarts – those delicious uncovered fruit pies – two-and-a-half and three inches deep – and as big as a dinner plate – Scotch tarts, which only Scotch and English women know how to make.

"Are you Scotch?" I asked. "Yes," she replied, evidently surprised. "Can you make Scotch tarts?" "Yes; at least I used to."

"Then go down in my kitchen and make one; order anything you think necessary, but make the best one you know how to make."

That night I tasted a tart equal to any I have ever eaten; and the next morning she started the pie industry.

I sent a note out to a few acquaintances, telling them the old pagan gods on Mount Olympus would still be contentedly happy, even if nectar were taken from them, providing they could get real Scotch tarts; also that I had found a Scotch woman who could make just such tarts, and that these delicious desserts could be secured in Chicago; and I also added that they'd be wise to send their maids early in the morning with an order to Mrs. Hansen.

The Success: The first day she made a dozen pies and sold every one of them. At a good price, too – for these were no dollar pies – these pies were pies – apple tart three inches deep – with gooseberry sauce – to be served with whipped cream – they were worth much as pies, but much more as distinctive desserts not procurable elsewhere.

Of course the pie business grew and grew.

Moreover, as families bought their tarts of Mrs. Hansen, their maids also ordered other things at the same time. The idealized leader became the actual leader of group after group of other goods sold from the shelves of her store.

Common sense? Yes. Only common sense? No. It was *idealized* Common Sense.

FIVE MINUTES IDEALIZING A DAY MAKES YOU SUPER EFFICIENT

Without order in the process of your thinking and order in the act of doing things, ideals and desires do not come true.

The value of *idealizing a series of things to be done before starting to do them* is well illustrated by this experience:

The Scene: Office of a physician in a South American city. City just visited by cyclone; destruction freaky as to places; some telephone exchanges in order; houses here and there almost completely destroyed; many others not damaged; yet scores of people severely injured by falling walls.

The Work to be Done: As the cyclone passed, many telephone messages begged the physician's immediate assistance. The first asked him to hurry to a certain place to attend a woman whose scalp was torn and who evidently was suffering from internal injuries, and he was about to leave when the second message from another place begged him to come there at once and attend a man with a broken leg and an injured back. Message followed message, two score and more, each of which he listed. It was then he changed his plans; and even though he realized that each case should be attended quickly, he did not rush off.

The First Thing He Did: He took the receiver from his telephone, for there was no need of listing more calls; these and those he would find would be all he could attend to.

Then for five minutes he sat quietly at his desk, seemingly doing nothing.

The Second Thing: Quickly he wrote a list of medicines, cottons, bandages, et cetera, and calling his office girl, told her to rush to the druggist at the corner, to insist they be given her at once, and to wait for them outside the druggist's door till he came.

The Third Thing: He telephoned the department store a block from the drug store and ordered a clerk to stand ready with fifty blankets at the door of the store.

The Fourth Thing: He rapidly selected from his operating room every instrument that might be necessary in any kind of emergency case.

The Fifth Thing: Taking his bags of instruments and his medicine cases, he ran to his auto at the door; drove to the drug store corner, where – without stopping his machine – he snatched the package from the girl; and continued on to the department store, where he commanded the clerk to dump the blankets in the car.

The Sixth Thing: Then – and only then – did he begin his work of assistance, going rapidly from one injured person to another.

The Result: In no case was anything lacking that was needed; and the records show that during the afternoon he attended twice as many injured as any other physician of the city.

The result of his work shows that his efforts of the afternoon were most efficient. *But what did he do while sitting at his desk? Did he waste those first five minutes?*

This is what he did:

First, he idealized all the different kinds of injuries reported to him, and, in addition, all the possible injuries he might be called upon to treat;

Second, he visualized all of the medicines, antiseptics, accessories, et cetera, that would be required and might be required; visioned his own supply and such a surplus to be obtained at the drug store as would make any lack impossible;

Third, he idealized what should be done at once to aid the future recovery of those injured – the wisdom of wrapping each up in a warm blanket immediately after the first aid – as protections from the after-chill of the storm;

Fourth; he visualized the places where the most seriously injured were reported to be; idealized himself going from one to another by shortest routes; and repeated the process visioning the places where the less seriously injured were.

All this in five minutes!

Were the first five minutes wasted? Those five minutes more than doubled his service that afternoon and evening, and there was no failure to give aid because some necessary thing was lacking.

But we – yes, we see the value of Idealizing the Process of Doing Things in an emergency; but we forget that in our lives each hour is an emergency – a call to do the most, live the most.

CHANGING CHARACTER AND ATTAINING SPIRITUAL CONSCIOUSNESS

PREVENTING MISTAKES IN THINKING

If you know how to prevent your mind making mistakes, that knowledge and the use of it will aid you in your advancement, stop failures in business, prevent friction in social life, stop the offending and losing of friends, and help very greatly in making you happier.

Happiness is the goal of the soul. It is the end of human endeavor, the purpose of living and loving and serving.

How we have suffered because of the unintentional mistakes we have made! How we have made others suffer! And not because of our intention or their intention, but because we did not know how to idealize the process of preventing mistakes.

There are two factors in the process of thinking: (1) recognizing likenesses and (2) discriminating differences. If you idealize the process of thinking, you complete it, you use both of these. If you do not idealize the process, you use but one, or you use one almost to the exclusion of the other. And it is then that you make the mistakes which bring unhappiness.

A baby boy, reared in the tropics, was brought to New York when three years old. That winter as he looked out of the window at the first snow he had ever seen, he clapped his hands in glee and said, "oh, mamma, look at all the sugar!" He recognized the likeness in appearance of snow and sugar – its whiteness – and he made the mistake because he had had no opportunity of distinguishing the differences.

Let me repeat: *unintentional mistakes are caused by recognition of likenesses with insufficient discrimination of differences.*

Another case – the husband and wife and two young sons.

The man has worked earnestly and efficiently, and his wife has helped. They are in comfortable circumstances. One son is in high school, the other in college.

Oil is discovered in California west of the coast mountain ranges. The wells are gushing thousands of dollars worth of oil per day. The husband visits the desert lands east of the mountain range and, accidentally, in the crevices of a gulley, he finds soaked chunks of earth that are oily. He feels of it; it feels oily. He looks at it; it looks oily. It feels and looks *like* the oil-soaked chunks of earth found in the oil region west of the mountains.

In his mind, he sees oil gushers in this region *like* those west of the mountains. In his imagination he sees himself many times a millionaire *like* the men who discovered oil west of the mountains. As many know he is on this trip he does not confide his discovery to others. So he says nothing, but invests all his savings in this desert land. At the bank he borrows all he can borrow, to secure additional options. To this point, all his thought and action is based upon recognition of *likenesses*.

Then the expert finds a *difference*. It looks like oil, but it is not oil. It feels greasy, just as petroleum feels greasy, but it is not petroleum. It is of no value.

It is so easy to see likenesses. It is the lowest type of mind action. It is incomplete. It leads to mistakes. It brings unhappiness – so much unhappiness!

To prevent mistakes in individual life, in home life, in business, in industrial and in national affairs, idealize the process of recognizing differences.

Idealize your thoughts, and your plans of action; whatever you *are* to do, idealize the process. Sit quietly, vision the likenesses, do *not* omit them; but idealize the differences also. Idealize the differences again and again, to be certain you include all of them.

CHANGING WEAK WILLS TO STRONG WILLS

What a tragedy it is to live with the will so weak that one cannot carry out that which one sincerely intends to do or live as one has conscientiously resolved to live.

And, it is easy, so very easy, to change what is called a weak will to a strong will if you idealize the process which was used in the beginning to form the original intention or resolution.

If you do this, the original intention – with all its desires – is ever present and no effort is necessary to sustain the will. All success depends, however, upon the process being *idealized*, being made perfect in the mind. In the case of will, the idealizing applies most of all to idealizing vivid images in the mind.

Will is the power that makes us persist in our efforts to carry out a decision long after the decision is made. A man with a weak will often makes a decision with the same good intention as a man with a strong will, but the power to carry out his decision does not persist after a lapse of time because he ceases to visualize the images that led him to make the decision in the first place.

Why does a man of good intentions, having made a promise in all sincerity, fail to keep it? Because of lack of will. Because he allows the images that led him to make the promise to become less vivid day by day. And as these images fade, as they become weaker and weaker, he leaves undone many things that should be done to enable him to keep the promise. A strong will keeps the images in mind day after day; a weak will permits them to fade.

The decision at the time a promise is made is strong because the images, ideas and ideals that lead one to make the decision are vivid at the time. If the images are kept vivid, the decision remains, and the will grows stronger instead of weaker.

The case of a Boy and His Mother: The boy is lovable, dutiful, obliging, sociable and idealistic; not a single bad habit. His mother is partly dependent upon him. He left the little Connecticut town to accept a position in New York City because the increased pay would make it possible for him to give more to his mother. Before leaving he vowed to himself and promised her that every Saturday night he would send her at least six dollars; that when his salary was increased he'd send her more.

Failure Due to Weak Will: The six dollars were sent the first, second, third, and fourth Saturday nights, but only five dollars were sent the fifth; and then the amount varied. Finally one Saturday night he had nothing to send; he did not even have enough to pay his room rent for the next week.

He was just as lovable, obliging, and idealistic as when he left home; but when he went out with the other office men to lunch, he did not wish to seem miserly, so ordered what they ordered. When they invited him to join, them – dutch treat – at a good theatre, he went because he liked good entertainments. And so his money was spent.

His habits were still good, but his will was not strong enough to resist the temptation to spend money for the things of the city.

His Struggle: The night he was unable to send anything to his mother was a night of agony. He was not selfish, and, consequently, he suffered the more. He prayed, and he resolved, and he vowed that he'd never fail again. But – he did. Though he sent six dollars a week regularly for four succeeding weeks, the seventh week he sent but four and two of these he had borrowed.

How He Developed a Strong Will: He chummed with a fellow-worker in the office. One night the boy, in desperation, opened his heart to his friend, and the chum, who knew me, brought him to me.

The boy felt his whole life would be a failure: "If I have not strength of will to resist these temptations, what will become of me when big ones come?"

The Process of Idealizing: I asked him to close his eyes, to think of his home, to picture in his mind the house and the rooms in the house, to visualize his mother there, to visualize her love for him and his love for her; to visualize her needs, and how much the six dollars a week added to her comfort.

That was all there was to it.

"You now feel strong enough to keep your promise, do you not?"

"Certainly," he replied, "I am strong enough *now*."

"Then always keep this condition of the *now* with you; make it permanent in your mind; visualize, for fifteen minutes every morning and every night these same images of your mother's home, her needs, and the extra comforts your six dollars a week will provide. So long as these images are strong in your mind your will to keep your promise is strong. But when these images fade and the images of expensive lunches and theatres become stronger, your will to keep your promises becomes weak. To keep your will strong to keep the promise you made, idealize the images which led you to make the promise."

Twenty-four hours later he said over the telephone: "It's easy, desire to help mother is so strong I've not even a desire to waste money." And a year later he said the same thing, and he had lived up to it, too!

NORMAL MEANS OF ATTAINING SPIRITUAL CONSCIOUSNESS

Spiritual Consciousness completes life; it gives life the true balance, the balance of *knowing* both its actuality and its spirituality.

Spiritual Consciousness is a condition, a condition of being consciously in touch not only with all other souls but with Cosmic Consciousness, Divine Mind, The Infinite, Principle – anything you wish to name it. It is not recognition, nor acceptance, nor faith.

Certainly, I'd not write a word on how to attain Spiritual Consciousness if I thought you were looking for a means of attaining a sort of non-active state of etherealized super-holiness.

The aim of all religion and idealistic thought is to extend the scope of life, to get in closer touch with and be more *responsive* to The Infinite.

This gives the *keynote* of the process by which we attain spiritual consciousness, *making ourselves more responsive*.

Responsiveness necessitates likeness, for only like qualities or conditions respond one to another. The vibration of one string of a violin produces a responsive vibration only in a string or wire or vibrating body capable of vibrating to a like note. Even seemingly contrasting people are drawn to each other by those qualities of soul which are common, although perhaps unconsciously common.

Intelligences of men differ much more than their love-natures. The ignorant peasant knows love as deep and pure and noble as the best schooled man of the world.

Consciousness of universal love is the first step in attainment of spiritual consciousness.

But love's spiritual nature is not personal, hence the method must idealize it – eliminate personality.

No matter what the bickerings of the day, the annoyances and disturbances, the disagreements, and perhaps even the quarrels, they all disappear when the family gathers about the open hearth-fire. Little by little conversation ceases – which means that thought ceases – and the vague consciousness of universal love permeates each, taking each in his reveries to the very borderland of spiritual consciousness.

So also around the campfire of the army. No matter what the friction of the day between officers and men, or the discontent, or the horrors of the struggle, they disappear, and the same vague consciousness of universal love quiets the men, and takes them also to the borderland.

And the same is true – perhaps to a greater extent – before the altar-fire.

One cannot attain spiritual consciousness by thinking.

Thinking is mind activity; the mind reaches out into all the world in search of new impressions and new ideas to be taken within itself and treasured up for its own use.

Love is emotion, it is a *moving out*, its nature is to give.

Unselfishness is not attained by selfishness, therefore thinking, thought, or thought affirmations will not awaken a consciousness of universal love. Moreover, thinking, thought and thought affirmations prevent the attainment of spiritual knowing and establish instead thought *about* spiritual consciousness.

The first step, then, is to quiet thought; the second, to awaken universal love by the most idealized process of all the ages – and that is idealization before the fire.

You know the effects, whether before the open-fire in the home or the campfire in the woods.

First, you cease to think – conversation lags, then stops – and the body relaxes;

Second, daily troubles vanish, and a kindly attitude and an indefinite contentment come to you;

Third, there comes not a conscious but a super-conscious condition, beginning with reverie; and then all thought ceases, and since all thought has ceased you are not even conscious that it has ceased; until

Fourth, with a start, you come back to yourself, that is, back to normal consciousness. But you have been on the borderland of spiritual consciousness.

Continued, before the open fire – impersonally the most idealized process of all times – the super-conscious state soon becomes illuminated and spiritual consciousness is attained.

Awakened in this way, it does not unfit one for the daily work of life; it becomes the balance, the proper balance of Cosmic Realization and Practical Life.

II

ELIZABETH TOWNE

The following quotes are from
How to Grow Success, 1904

SUCCESS – WHAT IT IS

Success is not money, nor is it fame. The King in the ancient fable turned to gold all that he touched and starved to death.

Success is *liberty to command, coupled with a clear conscience and loving heart.*

Liberty to command must not be overworked, lest it cease to be liberty and become the drudgery of *taking care* of things.

A successful man is not necessarily a rich man, but he is a man who can command *all he desires.* Among money kings it is said J. Pierpont Morgan is not rated a very rich man. But he commands more money than any other man in the world. It is said men confide in him because of his fine business sense, gained by *using his own* judgment; and because "*he does exactly what he agrees to.*" He never asks advice and he keeps his mouth shut unless he has something special to say. Then he says it, in the simplest and fewest words possible. This is concentration, the mode of success.

Money is not success, but success *includes the power to command money.*

Success includes the liberty to command money enough to gratify all one's aspirations to better his own condition, and the condition of those dependent upon him. This does not mean that success includes money enough to enable one to outshine his neighbor. *No man with that aim in life was ever successful, or ever will be.*

Not to *out*-shine, but to *shine upon* his neighbors, is the successful man's mission.

SUCCESS IS ALIVE

It germinates, sprouts and grows. It grows first underground. In due time it appears and keeps on unfolding.

It is just as easy to grow success as to grow potatoes. Yes, it is easier; for success will grow out of potatoes, and *it will grow where potatoes won't.*

Success may outgrow a place and need transplanting; but it will *sprout anywhere.*

And at any time. Potatoes must be started at a certain time. The time to plant and tend success is *now.*

You plant potatoes and you *know* they will grow. You go off and do something else whilst they germinate and sprout. You can't *see* them grow but you *know* they are growing, and whilst you are working away at other things you have a nice little warm glow in your heart, over the fine crop that is coming on out there in the tater patch. You *love* that patch. You planted it just as well as you could, with the best seed potatoes, and you are proud of it, even before there is the first peep of green. When that comes your love increases. You hoe every hill carefully and you take good care of the bugs. In due time you exhibit some of those spuds at the State Fair and you get a prize. And at last you *command more money* for your potatoes than others get for theirs.

Now do you imagine you had no success until you got the gold for those potatoes? Then you are greatly mistaken. You *planted success* with every blessed tater hill. You loved it and beamed on it, hoed the weeds away, picked the bugs off, and reveled in success all summer long. You *lived on success all summer.*

Perhaps you say, "Oh, that is a very pretty picture but *my* potato patch was a failure." Then you planted failure with your potatoes. When you were plowing and planting and hoeing you were telling yourself all the time that "there is no use – *nothing* ever did well for you – it seemed to be your lot to drudge and pinch and worry along and never have anything – there is John Smith over the way – *he can* take it easy and have fine stock and hire men to do the drudgery whilst he rides around and bosses – and here *you* are – everything is against you – damn the stones on this land anyhow – your spuds never do well – ground is no good – why can't you take it easy like other folks?" And so on, ad infinitum, *ad nauseum*, your mind meanders, whilst you, with less than half a heart get through the "drudgery" any old way, just so you get through.

Potatoes are not the only thing you planted. You planted *thoughts* in every hill. You *cursed* every hill you planted – cursed it with mean thinking. You planted *failure* and you will reap ditto. Every idle thought will bring its meed of *failure* and subtract from the money that might have been yours.

It takes the finest seed potatoes, good land *and thinking to match*, to insure a good crop and good prices.

The successful man puts his thought *into* his work. The unsuccessful one turns his thought *away* from it; as if when he was supposed to be watering his garden he should turn the stream over the fence into the road, leaving his garden dry and gasping.

YOU MUST LOVE

And *think* about your work if you are to make a success of it and make it pay.

If you are doing work you dislike you will not succeed, and all the treatments in creation can't make you succeed.

Get into line with a work you do love – something in which you can express yourself.

If you think you must remain where you are then put your interest, your love, *yourself*, into that business. One touch of *yourself* will make business go. A young man laid in coal, opened shop, placed his card in the local paper and sat down to wait for custom that did not come. When he went home to dinner one day his wife remarked that she had a headache which had been aggravated by the noise of putting in coal at the next house. That young man went to the newspaper office and added a line to his ad – "Coal delivered without noise!" He delivered his coal in sacks. Yes, delivered it. One touch of *himself* did the business and he was custom-less no longer.

A man's success is measured on the unseen side by the amount of *love* he feeds his work with; and on the seen side it is measured by money.

I do not mean that the amount of money a man manages to corner by fair means or foul, his own or his father's is the measure of his success. Not at all. But the amount of *real love* a man puts *into* his work determines exactly the amount of money he or some other man can get *out* of it. If he respects himself *and the rest of mankind*, if he *knows that justice rules now* – really *knows* it – he will himself get the money. If he "knows just what mean and grasping liars men are," he attracts men who will rob him of the money due his work. But in either event *he* is at the bottom of the whole business.

The individual himself is Lord of his own circumstances; circumstances and other men are puppets in his hands. As a man realizes this he moves circumstances and people at will, *by pulling the right strings in himself.*

YOU MUST LOVE

People in order to be able to move them. You must be able to see them *as they see themselves*, and you must meet them *heart*-ily. Love is not sentimental gush; love is not a self announcer. Love is divine emotion, that which *moves outward* from the point where the Universal meets the personal. Love manifests in the person as pure *Good Will*. It shines in his face, beams from his eyes and impels his every action. The successful man is a man of pure *Good Will*.

Remember, Success is the liberty to command, *coupled with a clear conscience and loving heart*. In proportion as a man is possessed of *Good Will* his conscience is clear. Good Will is the outward-moving power of a loving heart.

Only such a heart ever has liberty to command.

In proportion as a man succeeds in *letting* Good Will flow outward to each person, thing or circumstance with which he comes in touch, in that proportion will he be able to *influence* persons, things and circumstances according to his will – his *Good Will* – which is just to all.

The art of succeeding is the art of *concentrating Good Will*, and *using* it for definite purposes.

GOOD WILL

Must go out to all mankind, collectively and individually.

It is *your* grudge that has the power to destroy your success – *your* grudge against person, place, work, or "fate."

THE ESSENTIALS

Of success are these:

1. Good Will toward all. This includes justice, honesty, a clear conscience and loving heart.

2. An Aim; a stake to be reached.

3. Eternal stick-to-it-iveness.

4. Concentration of thought and effort upon the *details* of reaching the stake set.

A man's aim in life is the *reflection* of his opinion of himself. A man with a pretty low opinion of himself has no aim at all. He feels himself merely a fallen twig borne helplessly on the bosom of life. Wake up dearie, exalt yourself, and set your stake *just as high as you dare*. Then, as you find you can face your stake with a feeling that you are really going to make it after all, congratulate yourself upon your soul stature, *and move your stake higher*.

Ella Wheeler Wilcox says: "There is no chance, no destiny, no fate, can circumvent or hinder or control the firm resolve of a determined soul."

Concentration of thought upon the details of getting there: You *can't afford* to waste thought upon grumblings and resentments, against individuals, circumstances or "fate." You may imagine you have brains enough to divide between your work and these petty fault findings and resentments; but you have not. Every idle thought subtracts a *definite* amount from your success *and your cash*. Put your thought into business.

This does not mean you are never to think of anything but business; but it *does* mean that you are never to separate thought *from Good Will*.

Whatever you can think of with Good Will, will aid you to self-expression; will increase your power.

Concentrate; on the *details* of getting there. I was once lost above the snow line on a great mountain and had to retrace my steps upward to the point where I had taken the wrong trail. I was so anxious to get to that point that my whole soul seemed to leap upward and away toward that place leaving me so utterly paralyzed that I was actually unable to take a step. In a few moments I collected myself and put my thought into the climbing, when I made the distance easily and quickly. Where the thought runs ahead like that the will, the real motive power of the body, actually goes out of the body, leaving it unable to accomplish what is expected of it. When you are *doing* something *put* your *thought* into it. Will follows thought and thus you work easily and effectively. When you are relaxed and resting you may without injury let thought take any flight.

Work done in this way actually *rejuvenates* the body; whilst a scattered mind scatters or disintegrates the body. You are a *unit*, a One. *Work* as a One.

NEVER FEAR FEAR

Fear is a great bugaboo and like most bogies he is merely a shadow. No amount of fear will hinder your success if you will *keep your eye on the stake you have set*, and keep *sticking to it mentally*, fears or no fears. When I ride the wheel I see stones to be avoided. If I look at one and say to myself, "I am afraid I'll probably run over it," then I go over it every time. But I may have *more* fear, it may be a larger stone, but if I *say to myself* "I shall go *around* that," I invariably *go* around it.

It is *the Word*, the mental statement, that determines whether I miss or hit those stones. I have proven by hundreds of careful observations that *fear* has absolutely *nothing* to do with it.

I may be scared over something; I may not be able to keep my eyes off the obstacle; but if I *affirm* resolutely, "I shall miss that" – I miss it *every time*.

Our bodies are just bundles of mental statements, which are being hourly augmented and *revised* by more statements. It is these mental statements that *incite* motion. *Every thought* sends vibrations clear to the tips of the nerves and on out through the personal and universal auras. *Every thought incites corresponding muscular activity.*

Fear literally has *no* power over your body except as you *state to yourself* that it has. Deny it – *deny* that fear has power. Make persistent mental statements of what you desire; make them in the face of fear, until fear tucks his tail betwixt his legs and gets off the earth.

Kate Boehme gives this sentence to her students to "concentrate" upon:

"I am open on my inner side to the inexhaustible ocean of Divine Love and Power. I flow forth from it and am one with it. All success is mine through the working of this power. I shall succeed in all my undertakings." *Be still and know.*

MONEY MAKING

"Please treat me that I may be useful to the world. I will trust the money to follow."

All right; you will find the money following; but it will follow such a long way off that you will never see it except in some-other-body's possession.

"Make me useful to the world" is the cry of *self-depreciation*; it presupposes that you are *now* a weak, useless piece of furniture.

As you think of yourself so the world thinks. Just so long as you carry that prayer in your heart, just so long will you remain weak and useless *in your own esteem*, which the world will continue to reflect.

The world has an eye to the Main Chance. If you think you are worth little to the world, the world will not fall over itself to lay its coin at your feet. It will take all you can give and when you've nothing more to give it will dump the remains in the potter's field. Possibly it may beautify its parks and sooth its conscience with a monument inscribed to you when you are well out of the way. And it may hold memorial services where it will congratulate itself on the bargain it got out of you.

But pay you? – never! Not a cent will you get beyond what you *really think in your heart* you are worth to the world.

Ungrateful? Hard? Wrong? Not at all. The world is governed by the immutable *Law* that "as a man thinketh so he *is;*" and the world is too wise to give gold for nothing.

Every man gets just as much gold out of the world as he *puts into it*. All things are thought made. Every man must *think his own gold into being*. Or, to turn it around that we may get a clearer view, there is money enough in existence but each individual must *stake his claim and then work it*.

In our country it is not the "big I" corporations, trusts or individuals who are the cause of squalor and wretchedness. *It is the "little I" in the working man*. The only cure for poverty of mind or body is to *educate* the individual "little I" until he grows up. These pinched conditions are necessary to wake up the individual to his own I AM – his "big I."

Every man gets the mental claim he stakes, works and *sticks* to.

NOW AND THEN

Discouragement is due to just one cause – letting the mind run on one thing whilst you are doing another. At such times you are a house divided against itself and you are falling. You are a stream of energy running in two channels instead of one, and you are therefore too weakened to accomplish anything in either channel. And you *feel* weak and discouraged. You are practicing mental scatteration, which is the way not to live.

You are allowing yourself to be pulled to pieces by conflicting centers of attraction outside you. You are becoming the puppet of environment for the time being.

Of course it don't feel good. It is an unnatural state, a painful state, to be in.

And you don't have to be there a single minute. Only your own ignorance can keep you there.

You are a center of attraction, with greater force than is in all your environment beside. You can literally *pull yourself together* and become master instead of puppet.

And it is the easiest thing in the world to do it, and the most natural. So natural that the tiniest infant can do it, and does it habitually.

Living is the art of adjusting one's self to the *now*. Whatever one is really adjusted to one enjoys. Whenever one is *not* enjoying it is because he is hanging with one hand to the *now* and with the other to the fleeting past, or is straining out toward the future.

The *now* is the only point one can become thoroughly adjusted to, the only place one can really enjoy. And the only way one can enjoy the *now* is to put *all* of himself into it, so that there is no straining out in different directions.

One no sooner becomes comfortably adjusted to the *now* than the *now* changes.

Well, *let* it change and do thou likewise. Readjust as *now* readjusts. *Let go* what is fleeting away, accept what is arriving, and *get interested* in cuddling comfortably down into it.

Dearie, this is something that is all in your mind. Keep adjusting your mind to things as they come.

Of course you will have a lot of Desires that certain particular things come.

Desire is the Index to the Book of Life. Just read the index and smack your lips over the good things that are coming in that big book, and then settle down to *enjoy* every one of the chapters as it comes.

I know lots of folks think they must dip into the last chapter first and then they lose interest in what comes before and skip slightingly over it all. They don't get half the pleasure of the book. But the Book of Life is a serial story and you can't get at the last chapter first, fortunately for you. So don't try. Just glance over the index, your desires, and then cuddle comfortably down with each chapter as it comes. *Enjoy it*. And then enjoy the next and the next.

What is the use anyway in eternally hashing over the table of contents of our lives? Lots of us look backward continually and dwell upon the hard places. Why? Just because we want to be pitied and made much over – because we want somebody to get down with us and wail over the terrible things we have been through. Or if we have been through some nice things we want folks to weep with us because the particular chapter we are now giving the small part of our attention to isn't quite so nice.

It is astonishing how determined we are to weep and make other folks weep over our Book of Life.

We are so set on "sympathy" that we don't even see one-tenth of the good cheer and fun and frolic and real wit that is so plentifully bespringling every Book of Life. We pass over the good things because we don't half read the *now* chapter.

Then if we have perchance grown tired of looking over the table of contents of our past lives we go stumbling over the future. We study our Desires assiduously but we *don't believe them*.

So we fail to make the best of what goes before and we postpone the day of getting to the thing Desire promises, or when we get there we don't half enjoy it because we have failed to pay *attention* to what went before.

Now, dearie, this is no joke and no meaningless figure of speech. It is a literal *fact*, as solid as any rock that ever grew. You never strive and strain over the table of contents of any printed book – you *never doubt* that it will all be in the book. So you set comfortably to work at the beginning and read one chapter at a time until you get to the Supreme Climax. Your desires are just as accurate and trustworthy an index to what is coming. Then *Let* it come and *enjoy the vicissitudes by which it comes*. Cuddle comfortably down with the *now* chapter and *pay attention* to each thing as it turns up. That is the way to get there.

UNITED WE ACHIEVE

Do I believe in turning *all* the attention upon each detail of every day work? Yes. Pour *all* your thought into *this* piece of work until you can do it to perfection and *with joy*. As long as you have irksome tasks or "drudgery" you may rest assured it is because you have not yet put in interested thought enough.

This is the finest "concentration" practice in the world – just to put your whole soul into the one thing you are doing. When you have used this practice long enough you will do the thing beautifully and with joy.

About this time you will find your thought force has flowed into this work and filled it *full* of energy *and is overflowing*. You will take happy little mental flights away from your work; little inspirations will come to you, and always your thought will come back to your work with joy.

Do you see now what "concentration" upon daily tasks is for? To *fill* your members, the different parts of your body, *with loving intelligence in expressing thought*.

There is a vast difference between putting *all* your thought into an action until you can do it sub-consciously, and your thought is freed on a higher plane, and the common way of putting half – or less – of your thought energy into "drudgery," done in a slipshod, ungraceful fashion, whilst the main body of your thought goes gallivanting around *where it has no business to be*.

Thought is *vitalizing*, energizing. When you try to work with half your thought switched *off* and *out* of your activities you rob and devitalize your body. To a fully vitalized body every act is *joy*. Whenever your work is "drudgery" stop short, call your thought home, take three or four very slow, full breaths of *fresh* air – straighten up to do it! – and then *quietly turn all* your thought into your actions. Every time you catch it wandering again bring it quietly but firmly, back to business. This is the sort of "concentration" that gives self-command and fits you to think higher thoughts and *fill higher places*. And the moment you are *ready* the omnipresent Law of Attraction will whisk you into place.

You are not a separate and distinct creation rolling around loose in the world. You are part of The Whole – a part that has its own peculiar position and uses in the economy of The Whole, and in all creation there is, never has been, and never will be, a duplicate of you. If you get misplaced in the world, or if you are not properly polished and beautified it is not you alone who suffer. The Whole travails in pain until you are satisfied and satisfying; *until you fit* in and glory in your fitness and beauty.

All the universe bestirs itself to help you fit in and be happy. All the beauty of the universe is pressing *out* through you into expression.

Eye hath not seen or ear heard, nor hath it yet entered into the heart of you to conceive the glories that are aching to flow through you and be free. There is more beauty, and art, and brilliance, wit and wisdom, fine raiment and *money* trying, trying to come upward and outward through *you*, dearie, than this blessed world has yet seen.

Whether you believe it or not, *it is true*.

What is more, all these beautiful and desired things *are coming* through you. They are pressing out *now*, with fast increasing impetus.

It is true, dearie, it is true.

Do you *want* to believe it? Do you want to help the universe into expression? Oh, you do.

But there are so many things, and you don't know where to begin. You don't have time for "these other things outside."

Well, *begin right where you are with the thing you are doing now*. You don't have to go outside to let the beautiful things of the universe come through you. You don't have to have special times for beauty culture, or wisdom or money growing. Did you ever see a rose tree that had special hours for growing, or a rose that needed special times for improving its complexion or its perfume? No more do you need special times and places for such things. All desirable things well up within you and are radiated, just as the rose's beauty is radiated.

One of the reasons why some people and corners of earth are not beautiful now is because they continually shut themselves up and try to get along any old way whilst they do up the so-called business of life. They promise themselves the ease and leisure to be beautiful and enjoy it away off some time in the future. Or, maybe, they just put it off until six o'clock, when the store closes. They try to live all day on business with a promise of what little beauty and leisure they can manage to crowd in after hours. The result is that when six o'clock comes they are literally starved – "too tired to move" – and must take that precious time that they meant to make beautiful, for resting. That is, they must needs lie down and *let the unseen beauties* rest them.

Beauty is harmony. Harmony may be seen, felt, tasted, smelt or heard. It may affect us through one or all the senses, either consciously or unconsciously. At night we sleep and the fine harmonies of the universe play through us and bring us into tune again. All unconsciously to us. Or, we may listen to exquisite music and so come consciously into harmony again. Or we see a beautiful, quiet place and *let* ourselves "catch" the harmony there expressed.

In either of these cases, or any other that we might think of, we simply *quit straining* – we quit *promising* ourselves beauty, harmony, at some other time. We *let go* and *enjoy* the harmony that *is now*. We "vibrate with" the things that are and forget that tired feeling.

That tired feeling comes from *living on promises*. You see, promises point to something just out of reach and to save your life you can't help straining out after those promised good things. Your *energy* flows right out in the direction of the promised good things.

There *are* good things ahead – better things than any yet beheld. But, dearie, if you keep watching them they will ever *keep ahead. Your thought fixes them in the future* and keeps them moving, just as every "tomorrow" is kept moving.

There is really no future, *only as you think it*. Some people are literally almost *made up* of the future – they live so eternally on promises. Then there are so many poor, down-hearted back-number folks who are in the same way nearly wholly composed of *the past*. Rarely do we meet one who is built of *the present*. When we do meet such an one we see a radiant individual.

The knowledge that saves is the certainty that all that is, was, or ever will be, is now.

When one knows *that, he lets go* and vibrates with the All-Love-Life *now*. He is an epitome of the universal harmonies. His life is not only a song but an exquisite blending of accompaniment beside.

So it is not "time for these other things outside" that you need, dearie, but *time now* to *be* what you have been promising yourself. What you need is to haul taut on the life line and get those beautiful things right down into the *now*. Your visible self is a "statement of beliefs." Quit stating *anything* in the future tense. Say "I AM beauty, joy, everything I want – I AM! I AM!" Stick to it until you have made yourself *accept* the statement. That statement alone, *lived on* morning, noon and night, not to mention between-times, will work in you the mightiest revolution your world has ever seen. That statement lived on will make a new creature of you – will move you to new ideas and activities – will open up the way for *all* those unseen beauties you so ardently desire to *literally come into the now*. This is no frill on the garment of Truth – it *is* Truth itself. You prove Truth as you do the pudding. *Live on* beauty *now* and you will prove that all beauty *is* now – that you *are* what you desire to be. You will find all you desire unfolding to your gaze, to *all* your senses.

Remember that what you desire is *not coming to you* now or ever. It comes *through* you, from the unseen into the seen world. Whilst you are in the shop waiting upon a customer, the things you desire are *forming within you*.

You cannot *see* the beauty you desire but you can *feel* it if you are mindful of it, if you look for it – you can feel it as a still, warm calmness at the center of you. *And your customer can see it shining in your face and feel its thrill in your quiet, whole-hearted attention.* It will mayhap quiet the turbulent waters of her soul. And it will surely help your soul into expression of the beauties you crave. Be still, dearie, and let the unseen harmonies be seen through you.

Every action that ever was made is really a vehicle for the *letting* of harmony from the unseen into the visible. The true art of living is only the art of letting – the art of being still.

Be still and *let* what you are into *this* act *now*.

Rejoice in what you *are*, as well as in what you have.

Dearie, this is an accurate description of each and every step of the way from behind that counter to *any place you may determine upon*.

Go in to *win*. Keep cool and sweet and *be now* what you desire.

HOW TO BE WEALTHY

At last I "caught on" to the knack of spending like an opulent queen what I *did* have to spend, and from that day things began to get better. I do not mean that all at once I went to spending recklessly for all sorts of things I happened to fancy at the moment – a glass of ice-cream soda, or a new ribbon I saw in the window, a new shirtwaist I thought pretty – I still denied myself all "luxuries."

And right here I want to tell you that it is these little *wishes of the moment* which are the real leakages that keep our pocketbooks flat. Not only that, but the gratifying of every momentary whim *depletes your stock of Desire* just so much.

The cutting off of these little leaks permits the tide of desire to rise higher within you, *for the accomplishment of things worthwhile.* In the same way it permits the rising of the money tide in your purse. Cogitate this well.

I not only did not fly into all sorts of momentary indulgences, but I began to put *more* thought than ever into *each* expenditure I made. I bought nothing that was not necessary, and I always "slept on it" before I decided that it *was* necessary. Then I consulted my cash and decided what was "the limit" I could use for this purpose. Then I went over in my mind all the things I *couldn't* have if I bought this. I let go *definitely* of *each one* of these. I said, "Get thee behind me – I *choose* this *one* thing and you may go away into forgetfulness – *I do not want you.*" Then I went down town and "looked around" until I found just the right thing to suit me. Sometimes it was on the bargain counter, sometimes among the new goods at highest price; but when I found it I was *pleased* with it, and I paid *gladly* for it, and took it home and *enjoyed it forever after.*

I used to be a great hand to be "sorry I hadn't got something else," but I never made a purchase in this new way which I did not enjoy fully until it was worn to shreds.

This was the beginning of opulence for me. After a time I found my desires growing *stronger and more definite and less numerous.* And at the same time I began to discover *more money in my purse, and fewer drains upon it.* I know by right of discovery and experience, that *this* is the road to wealth. And I know that what I have done in this line every one of you can do if you will. It will take you a longer or shorter time to accomplish just in proportion as you work faithfully at it *all* the time, or just spasmodically once in a while.

It is all a matter of establishing a right *habit* of thought. A few thoughts once in a while will not do it, but persistent effort *will.*

DESIRE FOR THIS, THAT AND THE OTHER

You will never reach the place where you have all you want to spend except by commanding yourself to spend, and to *want* to spend, less than your income, whatever that may happen to be; for having all you want to spend is a *state of mind*, not a matter of hundreds, thousands or millions of dollars income. With all Anna Gould's millions, her French husband, de Castellane, has never had all he wanted to spend.

You will never have "enough for your needs" except by *ruling your needs*; for this too is a state of mind, not a matter of the size of your income. You "need" what you *think* you need; and in order to have "enough for your needs," you must *change your mind* as to your needs.

This is the only sure way to do it. To enlarge your income will never do it, because *your "needs" will grow with your income, as long as your state of mind remains unchanged, always outstripping your income*. Your "needs" will continue to suck the life out of your income and howl for more. Try it if you will, but you will only prove that what I tell you about is true. And I know from a full experience.

To seek to increase your income to cover your needs is to follow a will-o'-the-wisp which will lead you into quagmires of dissatisfaction if not debt. That way lies defeat.

Every human being is a little garden patch of desires, where one desire or set of desires must thrive at the expense of another desire or set of desires; just as your strawberry plants must thrive at the expense of the weeds which try so hard to grow along with your berry plants. As you nip those weeds in the bud in order to give the strawberry plants a chance to grow and bear fruit, so in the garden of your heart you must continually nip in the bud the undesirable desires in order to allow the desirable desires to gain in stature and bear fruit.

We cut off the tops of some of our weeds – we run in debt as far *as we dare*, for This, That and The Other, *and promise* to pay, when we know perfectly well that unless a miracle occurs we can't do it; when we know that unless our *wildest* hopes are realized we shall not be able to pay when the time comes; *when we know that emergencies are continually arising to prevent us from keeping promises.* We cut off the tops of our *tallest* weeds of Desire for This, That and The Other, but we *leave the roots* and the "most necessary" sprouts – we "only Have It Charged when it's absolutely necessary;" which is in 999 cases out of 1,000 a mere sophistry.

There *might* be in any life an occasional time when it is "absolutely necessary" to Have It Charged or to borrow – which is the same thing – just as there might come up a weed over night; *but there is never a continued necessity for buying what one has not the money to pay for.*

Of course this does not refer to Having It Charged as a matter of convenience, when one *already has in bank* the money to pay for it. I refer to the habit of buying today that which one hopes to pay for out of tomorrow's work; the living this week on money one hopes to earn next week; the spending of money which is still On The Books; or *even living this week off money we expect to receive on Saturday night*. All living ahead of *the money in hand*, no matter when that money may be "due," is done at the expense of that homely plant, the Desire to Live Within Your Income, the essence of which is *Honesty*. And that plant, dearie, is the *only* one from which we can distill the essence of Honesty. That is why I so strongly desire us to cultivate it.

The *habit* of Having It Charged is an ugly, gnarled and distorted weed whose root is the Desire for This, That and The Other; Desire which has been permitted to burrow and spread itself until it is in a fair way to completely starve that homely plant from which we distill honesty.

Don't you know how, when you get the new chair you desired, the one like Mrs. Smith's, immediately your room looks shabby and you find yourself desiring a new cushion or two to match – and new curtains – and then a new carpet to take the place of the old one which looks old fashioned now beside the new chair – and a dozen other things? And then when the door is open into the next room *that* looks shabby and you desire new things for that. And so your Desire for This, That and The Other goes running like a noxious weed in an untended garden, all over your house and premises, and yourself and children and husband, until it sucks the life all out of your income and the *peace out of your heart* and the hearts of those around you.

All these things are lovely in themselves, but *when purchased at the price of your conscience and the peace of mind of yourself and husband they are not expedient*; that is, *they do not speed your soul's expression*; they do not help you to express the *best* of yourself. In other words *they retard your development*.

FACTORS OF SUCCESS

There are a lot of things in this world that simply will not "go in" success. Disobedience to the letter *or spirit* of an employer's regulations is one of them. And every employer has a lot of *mental* regulations, besides the expressed ones, by which you must cheerfully abide if you are to *succeed* with him. He is not wholly conscious of all these little mental regulations himself, so how can he put them down in black and white? But if your *attentive desire* is turned toward pleasing him you will *feel* his desires as opportunity offers. You will please him and be successful.

Of course laziness, lack of promptitude, inattention to details, lack of order, slovenly dress, a glum or wooden expression, a slouchy shuffling gait, a mind not on your work, an eye on the clock, a nose or tongue in other people's business, inaccuracy of statement, or "sticky fingers," – all these are *not* factors which will go in success.

Neither will the sort of ridicule and criticism some employees indulge in when the employer's back is turned.

And it makes no difference who your employer is. You may be *your own* employer, but still it remains true that none of these things will "go in" success. When we get down to the foundations of things we find we are *all* employees of the One Spirit which is running this universe. There is no use trying to fool ourselves with the idea that we have nobody to please but our own small, personal selves.

In order to please ourselves, in order to realize the success we want we have got to *please the Spirit that's over us all*.

Consecration is the first requisite of success – consecration to the Spirit of Truth *as it speaks to the individual*.

When in doubt *don't do it*.

Wait until you are *sure you will not regret*; then go ahead to victory. *Be still* and the Spirit of Truth will teach you.

Do not drive ahead on some doubtful line and try to *make* it come out right by "affirming" that it will.

Here is a wail from a woman. She says she went into the canvassing business expecting to succeed, and she has been treated to succeed, and she has continually affirmed that she would. But she failed. She "just hates" to ring door bells and she despises to meet strangers and she would never have gone into such work except for the money there was in it. Is it any wonder there was no money in it for her? Hating one's work is another factor which simply will not "go in" success.

There *must* be a degree of love for the work, outside the money there is in it.

And this love for your business must be cherished and coaxed to *grow*, or your business success will not grow.

Dearie, when you get right down to the foundation of things there is but *one* Law of Success, and that is the same Law which governs all creation – *the Law* of *Love*. The man who *loves* every bit of his work will coin his very highest *soul* into it. He will make it such a beautiful and glorified thing that the world will run to see, and will pay for his work almost any price he can ask.

Success is a certainty to him who *keeps in line* with his own ideals and aptitudes.

TO BE SQUARE

What does it mean to be "square?" It means a different thing to every man on earth, and yet it means always *one thing* – to do what *your own* spirit says is right, and to *keep your word*, actual or implied.

To be square one must control his feelings instead of letting them run away with him. The boy who plays hookey when he feels like it is not square with himself nor the world. *There is an "ought" in his heart which he is not square with.*

Life is full of mournful fizzles who habitually play hookey when they *feel* like it. They *feel* like slighting this thing and that, and – they play hookey. They *feel* like lying in bed late in the morning, though that little "ought" inside, and mayhap an employer outside, admonishes them to get up even if they don't happen to *feel* like it. Something is *expected* of them and they shirk. Tacitly their *word* is given to be on time, and they are not on time. They are not square.

The little "ought" inside is the well laid track upon which the individual's life may *safely* run.

When he jumps that track and runs on *feeling alone* he is *not square* with the world and there is danger ahead. And he ploughs along in the wrong direction, injuring himself *and others*.

He follows feeling and lies in bed. He is late at his work and dumpy when he gets there. His employer *feels* that he is not fairly treated. If he acts upon *his* feeling the sleepy-head will get his salary reduced.

Then he will tell folks what a stingy old curmudgeon his employer is. For he will never see that his own lack of square dealing has anything to do with his lack of funds or success. If there is anything the feeling-follower is really proficient in – anything where he shows himself a glorious genius – it is in *finding excuses* for himself and to himself.

You must mind *your* conscience if *you* would win.

And you must mind your conscience *as it is* – not as you'd like to have it be. If your conscience tells you to hop out of bed *now* it will not do to lie still and philosophize about it, and explain away the "ought" and conjure up an excuse for flying its track.

Until you can educate your conscience up to the point of letting you do what you want to do you would better do what it bids you even if you don't happen to *feel* like it.

It is easy for a man to do as he "ought" in little things. And if he takes pains to do it in little things he will find he has grown power to do as he "ought" when big things turn up. It is this doing as he ought – as *his own* soul says he ought, which enables a man to learn the lessons set for him in his particular class in life.

And it is the learning of the lessons in one class which fits him for those of a higher class.

JOY WORDS

"All my life I have been searching for happiness in many different ways, but have never found the real thing."

You have been hunting happiness outside of you. You have expected happiness to flow from *things* into you. You have expected happiness as a result of making your environment fit you. All your efforts have been put forth in this direction, and you have constantly met with disappointment – and unhappiness. As everybody will whose happiness is pinned to his conditions.

Conditions, like people, are *growing* things; never two minutes in exactly the same state. If you pin your happiness to a thing, or a friend, you will probably have to unpin it before night.

Happiness, real happiness of the abiding, *growing* kind, *never* comes as a result of fitting circumstances to your notions. *It comes from fitting yourself to circumstances.*

After all this is much easier to do. There is but *One* of *you* to be adjusted; while all the rest of creation goes to make up your environment.

What power has a convict over his prison walls and keepers? But he has *all* power over his *mind*; and he has all power over his body *within the limits* set by his prison walls and his keeper's rules.

A convict can be a fool and fret away his life within those walls; he can sulk mentally, and refuse to use his physical powers as far as permitted.

Or, the prisoner may use as he pleases that part of himself which cannot be walled in by any number of bolts and bars. He may think as high and as bravely and well as he *chooses*; and he may use his physical energies as bravely and well as he *may*.

He may make the best of his opportunity to learn a trade, and to cheer and help others as he may, even in a prison. If he does this he will be in those grim environs a happier man than are three-quarters of the men who are outside prison walls. Not only this, but he will *win* from his keepers kindness and consideration not accorded the indifferent or defiant prisoner; and he will *shorten his term of sentence.*

Now, every human being is in a prison of circumstances. He is there because he deserves to be. He has "attracted" it to himself.

It is stocked with just the sort of things he needs to exercise mind, will and muscles upon, to fit him for the next higher class *in the line of his desires.*

Will he *adjust himself* to it all and work happily, faithfully, willingly; and thus *shorten his sentence*? Or will he kick the walls and curse his work – and *lengthen his sentence*? Will he *accept* things and work happily? Or will he grumble and kick, and be unhappy?

It all depends upon *himself*. His environment is his friend if he works *with* it; his foe if *he turns against it*. One is happy with his friends, no matter in what garb they come; one is unhappy with those he is *turned against*, no matter how richly they are dressed or how fair they may appear.

Do you really *want* to be happy? Do you want happiness enough to pay the price for it?

Happiness and Good Will are Siamese twins. You simply must have 'em both, or live without either. Growls and dislikes always send Good Will into the dark closet and then happiness flies away. You must *choose* Good Will, and keep on choosing, until it fills you and radiates such positive energy that growls and dislikes simply shrivel and cannot get into your mind or heart at all.

If you *choose* a grumble as it presents its frowzy, bristly head, it hops over the sill and comes in. And the very first thing it does is to touch the button and shut off your *Good Will* radiations. Next it throws open the doors and windows of your mind and invites in all its relations.

To keep out growls just paste up a big notice:

NO GROWLS ADMITTED! NOT EVEN ON BUSINESS!

Now growls are quite as intelligent as other folks. If they get an unvarying and decidedly warm brogan they give it up and go hunt for somebody who is in the *habit* of letting 'em in. All you have to do is to cultivate the habit of firing them. Then your Solar Center will shine brighter and brighter and Good Will and Happiness will hold open house to every little thought-body that's nice.

And your sentence will be commuted and you will go into a bigger, better place.

And happiness will keep right on growing.

Smile. Smile alike upon just or unjust.

Get interested in seeing how happy you *can* be.

Take a few minutes the first thing every morning to cultivate *real* happiness, which is joy. Sit down with a pencil and paper, in a good comfortable, *straight-backed* chair. Place the paper on the table and hold the pencil ready for business. Now say to yourself "*Joy*"; and as you say it make a firm, bold dot with your pencil. Repeat. Make the next dot firmly *right over* the first one – right in it, I mean – simply make the one mark blacker and firmer. And mentally *put* that single word "*Joy*" right *into* that firm pencil dot. Put the real *Joy* into it. See how perfectly *One* you can make the pencil mark and the mental word. Bring *Joy down to a fine point.*

Do this twenty-five or thirty times at a sitting, saying *Joy* very positively with each dot of the pencil. Do it very *deliberately*, calmly, positively, resolutely.

Then go quietly about your work. You will be surprised to see how smoothly and pleasantly your work goes.

Whenever things seem to get into a snarl, or you feel discouraged or burdened, drop everything like a hot potato, go into another room and use this little Joy-exercise a few minutes. It's magic. Just *do* it and see.

And you will be surprised to see how little time it takes: and you will be amazed at how *much* time it *saves*; time saved from wrangles and jangles, to be used in *Joy*.

SUCCESS LETTERS

Think "*Power, power, power*" and think it emphatically and *slowly*. It is not necessary to face the visible sun always, but face the I AM SUN *in you*.

It takes *thought* to keep ourselves from being ruled by our work. And ruined, too. But we *can* keep from it! Oh, yes! There is just nothing we can't do when once we see the point and go in to *win*.

And we not only can rule these things, but we *glory in doing it*. We *glory* in our power and in showing it! When once we get the notion of using our power on *ourselves* we are on the high road to greater achievements than the world has ever before dreamed of! And we are on that road *now*. And we are making rapid progress. We rejoice in our growth, and our appetite is whetted for more Self-command and more growth. Oh, we are The People and we are inheriting the earth! And the sun, too! Glory to the I AM in us!

Success is the natural result of intelligent effort. Failure is the natural result of unintelligent effort. The *degree* of success in any man's life is determined by the exact amount of intelligence *he puts into* his efforts.

Take a careful inventory of *today's* efforts, dearie. How much of it is done perfunctorily, grumblingly, from *habit*, or "compulsion"; and *not* because you have *waked up*, surveyed conditions and *ideals*, and decided that under these circumstances, and *just now, this* is the highest, best thing you can do? Unless you have thus *decided*, this particular effort you are engaged in is *not* an intelligent effort and therefore is *not* adding to your success. It is a thought*less* effort, a drudgery, and *is wasting your energy and your success.*

Now quit, *short*. If you cannot *put* intelligence, *will, interest,* into *this* effort and make it serve a purpose, then stop short and sit or lie perfectly relaxed until you *can* make your efforts tell. Far better do *nothing at all* than to waste energy in such wasteful effort. At least *be still* and let energy accumulate.

After a bit you will find yourself again able to put *intelligence* into your motions. When you do not know just what to do and how to do it, *be still*. Be still all over – see how still you *can* be. Intelligence and power will well up inside and *fill* you again, to overflowing. *Then* you will know what to do and how, and it will be joy to do it. In the meantime, whether you are putting intelligence into effort *or into being still, success grows.* I AM with you.

Relax your body definitely and all over and rise into the realm of imagination. See what wild and happy flights you can take. Picture yourself as you *desire* to be – stretch your imagination in this direction! Then *affirm* all those happy things for yourself, in the present tense – say "I AM all those things! – and by thunder I'll prove it!!"

Then go in to win some more – to prove some more – to *work out* some more of the delightful things that are *within you*. Don't you know your imagination is within you? And whatever you see in imagination is within you. *And anything that is within you can be worked out.*

An imagination filled with desirable things is inspiration – the real thing that enables you to do anything. And an imagination filled with undesirable things is a paralyzer. Think about it now and see if it is not so.

And imagination is the one place where you can do *anything*. You can imagine good things or bad things at will. So be sensible, dearie, and imagine good things and then *work them out*. It is fun to work out good things! If you find working is not fun, just stop short and see how far you can stretch your imagination again, in desirable directions. That's where the power comes from. Go often into your power house.

Be still and know. *Be still and know.* Be *still* and *know*.

Be still and *will* success. Be still. Relax. *Let go* definitely of everything you don't want. Wave your hand and banish each one. Then *let go* each thing you *do* want. *Let go.* You were tired and strained from hanging on. You were so strained that the life force could not flow through and fill you and *forward your work*. Now you are resting, all limp and loose, and life is pouring through your body and *re-charging* it with the magnetism that *attracts to you what you desire*. Now you are rested and filled with quiet, good feeling and *will*.

Rise now and see how well you can *use* your fresh energy. *Success is yours* and I AM with you.

Attention is to you what the lens is to a camera – it *focuses power* for you. *Keep your attention upon success*, upon opulence; until *success* is imprinted upon every brain cell – I AM Success.

III

THOMAS TROWARD

The following quotes are from
The Dore Lectures on Mental Science, 1909

ENTERING INTO THE SPIRIT OF IT

We all know the meaning of this phrase in our everyday life. The Spirit is that which gives life and movement to anything, in fact it is that which causes it to exist at all. The thought of the author, the impression of the painter, the feeling of the musician, is that without which their works could never have come into being, and so it is only as we enter into the *idea* which gives rise to the work, that we can derive all the enjoyment and benefit from it which it is able to bestow. If we cannot enter into the Spirit of it, the book, the picture, the music, are meaningless to us: to appreciate them we must share the mental attitude of their creator. This is a universal principle; if we do not enter into the Spirit of a thing, it is dead so far as we are concerned; but if we do enter into it we reproduce in ourselves the same quality of life which called that thing into existence.

Now if this is a general principle, why can we not carry it to a higher range of things? Why not to the highest point of all? May we not enter into the originating Spirit of Life itself, and so reproduce it in ourselves as a perennial spring of livingness? This, surely, is a question worthy of our careful consideration.

The spirit of a thing is that which is the source of its inherent movement, and therefore the question before us is, what is the nature of the primal moving power, which is at the back of the endless array of life which we see around us, our own life included? Science gives us ample ground for saying that it is not material, for science has now, at least theoretically, reduced all material things to a primary ether, universally distributed, whose innumerable particles are in absolute equilibrium; whence it follows on mathematical grounds alone that the initial movement which began to concentrate the world and all material substances out of the particles of the dispersed ether, could not have originated in the particles themselves. Thus by a necessary deduction from the conclusions of physical science, we are compelled to realize the presence of some immaterial power capable of separating off certain specific areas for the display of cosmic activity, and then building up a material universe with all its inhabitants by an orderly sequence of evolution, in which each stage lays the foundation for the development of the stage which is to follow – in a word we find ourselves brought face to face with a power which exhibits on a stupendous scale, the faculties of selection and adaptation of means to ends, and thus distributes energy and life in accordance with a recognizable scheme of cosmic progression. It is therefore not only Life, but also Intelligence, and Life guided by Intelligence becomes Volition. It is this primary originating power which we mean when we speak of "The Spirit," and it is into this Spirit of the whole universe that we must enter if we would reproduce it as a spring of Original Life in ourselves.

Now in the case of the productions of artistic genius we know that we must enter into the movement of the creative mind of the artist, before we can realize the principle which gives rise to his work. We must learn to partake of the feeling, to find expression for which is the motive of this creative activity. May we not apply the same principle to the Greater Creative Mind with which we are seeking to deal? There is something in the work of the artist which is akin to that of original creation. His work, literary, musical, or graphic is original creation on a miniature scale, and in this it differs from that of the engineer, which is constructive, or that of the scientist which is analytical; for the artist in a sense creates something out of nothing, and therefore starts from the standpoint of simple feeling, and not from that of a preexisting necessity. This, by the hypothesis of the case, is true also of the Parent Mind, for at the stage where the initial movement of creation takes place, there are no existing conditions to compel action in one direction more than another. Consequently the direction taken by the creative impulse is not dictated by outward circumstances, and the primary movement must therefore be entirely due to the action of the Original Mind upon itself; it is the reaching out of this Mind for realization of all that it feels itself to be.

The creative process thus in the first instance is purely a matter of feeling – exactly what we speak of as "motif" in a work of art.

What then can this original feeling of the Spirit be? Since the Spirit is Life-in-itself, its feeling can only be for the fuller expression of Life – any other sort of feeling would be self-destructive and therefore inconceivable. Then the full expression of Life implies Happiness, and Happiness implies Harmony, and Harmony implies Order, and Order implies Proportion, and Proportion implies Beauty; so that in recognizing the inherent tendency of the Spirit towards the production of Life, we can recognize a similar inherent tendency to the production of these other qualities also; and since the desire to bestow the greater fullness of joyous life can only be described as Love, we can sum up the whole of the feeling which is the original moving impulse in the Spirit as Love and Beauty – the Spirit finding expression through forms of beauty in the centers of life, in harmonious reciprocal relation to itself. This is a generalized statement of the broad principle by which Spirit expands from the innermost to the outermost, in accordance with a Law of tendency inherent in itself.

It sees itself, as it were, reflected in various centers of life and energy, each with its appropriate form; but in the first instance these reflections can have no existence except within the originating Mind. They have their first beginning as mental images, so that in addition to the powers of Intelligence and Selection, we must also realize that of Imagination as belonging to the Divine Mind; and we must picture these powers as working from the initial motive of Love and Beauty.

Now this is the Spirit that we need to enter into, and the method of doing so is a perfectly logical one. It is the same method by which all scientific advance is made. It consists in first observing how a certain law works under the conditions spontaneously provided by nature, next in carefully considering what principle this spontaneous working indicates, and lastly deducing from this how the same principle would act under specially selected conditions, not spontaneously provided by nature.

The progress of shipbuilding affords a good example of what I mean. Formerly wood was employed instead of iron, because wood floats in water and iron sinks; yet now the navies of the world are built of iron; careful thought showed the law of floatation to be that anything could float which, bulk for bulk, is lighter than the mass of liquid displaced by it; and so we now make iron float by the very same law by which it sinks, because by the introduction of the *personal* factor, we provide conditions which do not occur spontaneously – according to the esoteric maxim that "Nature unaided fails." Now we want to apply the same process of specializing a generic Law to the first of all Laws, that of the generic life-giving tendency of Spirit itself. Without the element of *individual personality* the Spirit can only work cosmically by a *generic* Law; but this law admits of far higher specialization, and this specialization can only be attained through the introduction of the personal factor. But to introduce this factor the individual must be fully aware of the *principle* which underlies the spontaneous or cosmic action of the law. Where, then, will he find this principle of Life? Certainly not by contemplating Death. In order to get a principle to work in the way we require it to, we must observe its action when it is working spontaneously in this particular direction. We must ask why it goes in the right direction as far as it does – and having learnt this we shall then be able to make it go further. The law of floatation was not discovered by contemplating the sinking of things, but by contemplating the floating of things which floated naturally, and then intelligently asking why they did so.

The knowledge of a principle is to be gained by the study of its affirmative action; when we understand *that* we are in a position to correct the negative conditions which tend to prevent that action.

Now Death is the absence of Life, and disease is the absence of health, so to enter into the Spirit of Life we require to contemplate it, where it is to be found, and not where it is not – we are met with the old question, "Why seek ye the living among the dead?" This is why we start our studies by considering the cosmic creation; for it is there that we find the Life Spirit working through untold ages, not merely as deathless energy, but with a perpetual advance into higher degrees of Life.

We have seen that the action of the Originating Mind must needs be *generic*, that is according to types which include multitudes of individuals. This type is the reflection of the Creative Mind at the level of that particular *genius*; and at the human level it is Man, not as associated with particular circumstances, but as existing in the absolute ideal.

In proportion then as we learn to dissociate our conception of ourselves from particular circumstances, and to rest upon our *absolute* nature, as reflections of the Divine ideal, we, in our turn, reflect back into the Divine Imagination its original conception of itself as expressed in generic or typical Man, and so by a natural law of cause and effect, the individual who realizes this mental attitude enters permanently into the Spirit of Life, and it becomes a perennial fountain of Life springing up spontaneously within him.

INDIVIDUALITY

Hence by the requirements of the case man should be capable of placing himself either in a positive or a negative relation to the Parent Mind, from which he originates; otherwise he would be nothing more than a clockwork figure.

In this necessity of the case, then, we find the reason why the life, love, and beauty of the Spirit are not visibly reproduced in every human being. They are reproduced in the world of nature, so far as a mechanical and automatic action can represent them, but their perfect reproduction can only take place on the basis of a liberty akin to that of the Originating Spirit itself, which therefore implies the liberty of negation as well as of affirmation.

Why, then, does the individual make a negative choice? Because he does not understand the law of his own individuality, and believes it to be a law of limitation, instead of a Law of Liberty. He does not expect to find the starting point of the Creative Process reproduced within himself, and so he looks to the mechanical side of things for the basis of his reasoning about life. Consequently his reasoning lands him in the conclusion that life is limited, because he has assumed limitation in his premises, and so logically cannot escape from it in his conclusion. Then he thinks that this is the law and so ridicules the idea of transcending it. He points to the sequence of cause and effect, by which death, disease, and disaster, hold their sway over the individual, and says that sequence is law. And he is perfectly right so far as he goes – it is *a* law; but not *the* Law. When we have only reached this stage of comprehension, we have yet to learn that a higher law can include a lower one so completely as entirely to swallow it up.

The fallacy involved in this negative argument, is the assumption that the law of limitation is essential in all grades of being. It is the fallacy of the old shipbuilders as to the impossibility of building iron ships.

The recognition of this is the discovery of our own relation to the whole world of the relative.

As our minds become open to the full meaning of this position, the immense possibilities and also the responsibility contained in it will become apparent.

It means that the individual is the creative center of his own world. Our past experience affords no evidence against this, but on the contrary, is evidence for it. Our true nature is always present, only we have hitherto taken the lower and mechanical side of things for our starting point, and so have created limitation instead of expansion. And even with the knowledge of the Creative Law which we have now attained, we shall continue to do this, if we seek our starting point in the things which are below us and not in the only thing which is above us, namely the Divine Mind, because it is only there that we can find illimitable Creative Power. Life is being, it is the experience of states of consciousness, and there is an unfailing correspondence between these inner states and our outward conditions. Now we see from the Original Creation that the state of consciousness must be the cause, and the corresponding conditions the effect, because at the starting of the creation no conditions existed, and the working of the Creative Mind upon itself can only have been a state of consciousness. This, then, is clearly the Creative Order – from states to conditions. But we invert this order, and seek to create from conditions to states. We say, "If I had such and such conditions they would produce the state of feeling which I desire;" and in so saying we run the risk of making a mistake as to the correspondence, for it may turn out that the particular conditions which we fixed on are not such as would produce the desired state. Or, again, though they might produce it in a certain degree, other conditions might produce it in a still greater degree, while at the same time opening the way to the attainment of still higher states and still better conditions. Therefore our wisest plan is to follow the pattern of the Parent Mind and make mental self-recognition our starting point, knowing that by the inherent Law of Spirit the correlated conditions will come by a natural process of growth. Then the great self-recognition is that of our relation to the Supreme Mind.

It is thus, not a compelling power, but an expanding and illuminating one; so that the more the individual recognizes the reciprocal action between it and himself, the more full of life he must become.

Then also we need not be troubled about future conditions because we know that the All-originating Power is working through us and for us, and that according to the Law proved by the whole existing creation, it produces all the conditions required for the expression of the Life, Love and Beauty which it is, so that we can fully trust it to open the way as we go along.

This does not, of course, mean that we are not to exert ourselves.

We are to use our common sense and natural faculties in working upon the conditions now present. We must make use of them, *as far as they go*, but we must not try and go further than the present things require; we must not try to force things, but allow them to grow naturally, knowing that they are doing so under the guidance of the All-Creating Wisdom.

Following this method we shall grow more and more into the habit of looking to mental attitude as the Key to our progress in Life, knowing that everything else must come out of that; and we shall further discover that our mental attitude is eventually determined by the way in which we regard the Divine Mind.

And as we advance in this knowledge we shall find that we transcend one law of limitation after another by finding the higher law, of which the lower is but a partial expression, until we shall see clearly before us, as our ultimate goal, nothing less than the Perfect Law of Liberty – not liberty without Law which is anarchy, but Liberty according to Law.

THE NEW THOUGHT AND THE NEW ORDER

So far as we can form any conception of these things at all we see that they are universal principles applicable to all nature, and, at the human level, applicable to all men: they are general laws the recognition of which is an essential preliminary to any further advance, because progress is made, not by setting aside the inherent law of things, which is impossible, but by specializing it through presenting conditions which will enable the same principle to act in a less limited manner.

In what does the specialization of a natural law consist? It consists in making that law or principle produce an effect which it could not produce under the simply generic conditions spontaneously provided by nature.

This selection of suitable conditions is the work of Intelligence; it is a process of consciously arranging things in a new order, so as to produce a new result. The principle is never new, for principles are eternal and universal; but the knowledge that the same principle will produce new results when working under new conditions is the key to the unfoldment of infinite possibilities. What we have therefore to consider is the working of Intelligence in providing specific conditions for the operation of universal principles, so as to bring about new results which will transcend our past experiences. The process does not consist in the introduction of new elements, but in making new combinations of elements which are always present; just as our ancestors had no conception of carriages that could go without horses, and yet by a suitable combination of elements which were always in existence, such vehicles are common objects in our streets today.

All the practical attainments of science, which place the civilized world of today in advance of the times of King Alfred or Charlemagne, have been gained by a uniform method, and that a very simple one. It is by always inquiring what is the affirmative factor in any existing combination, and asking ourselves why, in that particular combination, it does not act beyond certain limits. What makes the thing a success, so far as it goes, and what prevents it going further? Then, by carefully considering the nature of the affirmative factor, we see what sort of conditions to provide to enable it to express itself more fully. This is the scientific method; it has proved itself true in respect of material things, and there is no reason why it should not be equally reliable in respect of spiritual things also.

Taking this as our method, we ask, what is the affirmative factor in the whole creation, and in ourselves as included in the creation, and this factor is Spirit – that invisible power which concentrates the primordial ether into forms, and endows those forms with various modes of motion, from the simply mechanical motion of the planet up to the volitional motion in man. And, since this is so, the primary affirmative factor can only be the Feeling and the Thought of the Universal Spirit.

The scientific method of inquiry therefore brings us to the conclusion that the required conditions for translating the racial or generic operation of the Spirit into a specialized individual operation is a new way of *thinking* – a mode of thought concurring with, and not in opposition to, the essential forward movement of the Creative Spirit itself. This implies an entire reversal of our old conceptions. Hitherto we have taken forms and conditions as the starting point of our thought and inferred that *they* are the causes of mental states; now we have learnt that the true order of the creative process is exactly the reverse, and that thought and feeling are the causes, and forms and conditions the effects. When we have learnt this lesson we have grasped the foundation principle on which individual specialization of the generic law of the creative process becomes a practical possibility.

Then, still employing the scientific method of following up the affirmative factor, he realizes that this universal causative power, by whatever name he may call it, manifests as Supreme Intelligence in the adaptation of means to ends. It does so in the mechanism of the planet, in the production of supply for the support of physical life, and in the maintenance of the race as a whole.

Now, one of these conditions is to recognize it as Intelligence, and to remember that when working through our own mentality it in no way changes its essential nature, just as electricity loses none of its essential qualities in passing through the special apparatus which enables it to manifest as light.

When we see this, our line of thought will run something as follows: "My mind is a center of Divine operation. The Divine operation is always for expansion and fuller expression, and this means the production of something beyond what has gone before, something entirely new, not included in past experience, though proceeding out of it by an orderly sequence of growth. Therefore, since the Divine cannot change its inherent nature, it must operate in the same manner in me; consequently in my own special world, of which I am the center, it will move forward to produce new conditions, always in advance of any that have gone before."

In this way we throw out certain aspirations with the result that we intensify our attraction of the Divine forces in a certain specific manner, and they then begin to act both through us and around us in accordance with our aspirations.

Then, when these external facts appear in the circle of our objective life, we must work upon them from the objective standpoint. This is where many fall short of the completed work. They realize the subjective or creative process, but do not see that it must be followed by an objective or constructive process, and consequently they are unpractical dreamers and never reach the stage of completed work. The creative process brings the materials and conditions for the work to our hands; then we must make use of them with diligence and commonsense.

He receives guidance because he seeks guidance; and he both seeks and receives according to a Law which he is able to recognize; so that he no more sacrifices his liberty or dwarfs his powers, than does an engineer who submits to the generic laws of electricity, in order to apply them to some specific purpose. The more intimate his knowledge of this Law of Reciprocity becomes, the more he finds that it leads on to Liberty, on the same principle by which we find in physical science that nature obeys us precisely in the same degree to which we first obey nature. As the esoteric maxim has it "What is a truth on one plane is a truth on all." But the key to this enfranchisement of body, mind, and circumstances is in that new thought which becomes creative of new conditions, because it realizes the true order of the creative process. Therefore it is that, if we would bring a new order of Life, Light, and Liberty into our lives we must commence by bringing a new order into our thought, and find in ourselves the starting point of a new creative series, not by the force of personal will, but by union with the Divine Spirit, which in the expression of its inherent Love and Beauty, makes all things new.

THE LIFE OF THE SPIRIT

The three preceding lectures have touched upon certain fundamental truths in a definite order – first the nature of the Originating Spirit itself, next the generic relation of the individual to this All-embracing Spirit, and lastly the way to specialize this relation so as to obtain greater results from it than spontaneously arise by its merely generic action, and we have found that this can only be done through a new order of thought. This sequence is logical because it implies a Power, an Individual who understands the Power, and a Method of applying the power deduced from understanding its nature. These are general principles without realizing which it is impossible to proceed further, but assuming that the reader has grasped their significance, we may now go on to consider their application in greater detail.

What, then, is the Power which we are to distribute? It is the Originating Spirit itself. We are sure that it is this because the new order of thought always begins at the beginning of any series which it contemplates bringing into manifestation, and it is based upon the fact that the origin of everything is Spirit. It is in this that its creative power resides; hence the person who is in the true new order of thought assumes as an axiomatic fact that what he has to distribute, or differentiate into manifestation is nothing else than the Originating Spirit. This being the case, it is evident that the *purpose* of the distribution must be the more perfect expression of the Originating Spirit as that which it is in itself, and what it is in itself is emphatically Life. What is seeking for expression, then, is the perfect Livingness of the Spirit; and this expression is to be found, through ourselves, by means of our renewed mode of thought. Let us see, then, how our new order of thought, with regard to the Principle of Life, is likely to operate.

When we realize the truth about the Creative Process, we see that the originating life is not physical: its livingness consists in thought and feeling. By this inner movement it throws out vehicles through which to function, and these become living forms because of the inner principle which is sustaining them; so that the Life with which we are primarily concerned in the new order is the life of thought and feeling in ourselves as the vehicle, or distributing medium, of the Life of the Spirit.

Then, if we have grasped the idea of the Spirit as the great *forming* Power, as stated in the last lecture, we shall seek in it the fountainhead of Form as well as of Power: and as a logical deduction from this we shall look to it to give form to our thoughts and feelings. If the principle is once recognized the sequence is obvious. The form taken by our outward conditions, whether of body or circumstance, depends on the form taken by our thoughts and feelings, and our thoughts and feelings will take form from that source from which we allow them to receive suggestion. Accordingly if we allow them to accept their fundamental suggestions from the relative and limited, they will assume a corresponding form and transmit them to our external environment, thus repeating the old order of limitation in a ceaselessly recurring round. Now our object is to get out of this circle of limitation, and the only way to do so is to get our thoughts and feelings molded into new forms continually advancing to greater and greater perfection. To meet this requirement, therefore, there must be a forming power greater than that of our own unaided conceptions, and this is to be found in our realization of the Spirit as the Supreme Beauty, or Wisdom, molding our thoughts and feelings into shapes harmoniously adjusted to the fullest expression, in and through us, of the Livingness which Spirit is in itself.

Now this is nothing more than transferring to the innermost plane of origination, a principle with which all readers who are "in the thought" may be presumed to be quite familiar – the principle of Receptiveness. We all know what is meant by a receptive mental attitude when applied to healing or telepathy; and does it not logically follow that the same principle may be applied to the receiving of life itself from the Supreme Source? What is wanted, therefore, is to place ourselves in a receptive mental attitude towards the Universal Spirit with the intention of receiving its forming influence into our mental substance. It is always the presence of a definite intention that distinguishes the intelligent receptive attitude of mind from a merely sponge-like absorbency, which sucks in any and every influence that may happen to be floating round: for we must not shut our eyes to the fact that there are various influences in the mental atmosphere by which we are surrounded, and some of them of the most undesirable kind. Clear and definite intention is therefore as necessary in our receptive attitude as in our active and creative one; and if our intention is to have our own thoughts and feelings molded into such forms as to express those of the Spirit, then we establish that relation to the Spirit which, by the conditions of the case, must necessarily lead us to the conception of new ideals vitalized by a power which will enable us to bring them into concrete manifestation.

It is just here that subconscious mind performs the function of a "bridge" between the finite and the infinite as noted in my "Edinburgh Lectures on Mental Science," and it is for this reason that a recognition of its susceptibility to impression is so important.

Knowing, then, that by its inherent nature this Intelligence can only work to the expansion of the individual life, we can rest upon it with the utmost confidence and trust it to take an initiative which will lead to far greater results than any we could forecast from the standpoint of our own knowledge. So long as we insist on dictating the particular form which the action of the Spirit is to take, we limit it, and so close against ourselves avenues of expansion which might otherwise have been open to us; and if we ask ourselves why we do this we shall find that in the last resort it is because we do not believe in the Spirit as a *forming* power. We have, indeed, advanced to the conception of it as executive power, which will work to a prescribed pattern, but we have yet to grasp the conception of it as versed in the art of design, and capable of elaborating schemes of construction, which will not only be complete in themselves, but also in perfect harmony with one another. When we advance to the conception of the Spirit as containing in itself the ideal of Form as well as of Power, we shall cease from the effort of trying to force things into a particular shape, whether on the inner or the outer plane, and shall be content to trust the inherent harmoniousness or Beauty of the Spirit to produce combinations far in advance of anything that we could have conceived ourselves. This does not mean that we shall reduce ourselves to a condition of apathy, in which all desire, expectation and enthusiasm have been quenched, for these are the mainspring of our mental machinery; but on the contrary their action will be quickened by the knowledge that there is working at the back of them a Formative Principle so infallible that it cannot miss its mark; so that however good and beautiful the existing forms may be, we may always rest in the happy expectation of something still better to come. And it will come by a natural law of growth, because the Spirit is in itself the Principle of Increase. They will grow out of present conditions for the simple reason that if you are to reach some further point it can only be by starting from where you are now. Therefore it is written, "Despise not the day of small things." There is only one proviso attached to this forward movement of the Spirit in the world of our own surroundings, and that is that we shall cooperate with it; and this cooperation consists in making the best use of existing conditions in cheerful reliance on the Spirit of Increase to express itself through us, and for us, because we are in harmony with it. This mental attitude will be found of immense value in setting us free from worry and anxiety, and as a consequence our work will be done in a much more efficient manner. We shall do the present work *for its own sake*, knowing that herein is the principle of unfoldment; and doing it simply for its own sake we shall bring to bear upon it a power of concentration which cannot fail of good results – and this quite naturally and without any toilsome effort.

It is simply the assurance of a man who knows that he is working in accordance with a law of nature. He does not claim as a personal achievement what the Law does *for* him: but on the other hand he does not trouble himself about outcries against his presumptuous audacity raised by persons who are ignorant of the Law which he is employing. He is therefore neither boastful nor timorous, but simply works on in cheerful expectancy because he knows that his reliance is upon a Law which cannot be broken.

In this way, then, we must realize the Life of the Spirit as being also the Law of the Spirit. The two are identical, and cannot deny themselves. Our recognition of them gives them a new starting point through our own mentality, but they still continue to be the same in their nature, and unless limited or inverted by our mental affirmation of limited or inverted conditions, they are bound to work out into fuller and continually fuller expression of the Life, Love, and Beauty which the Spirit is in itself. Our path, therefore, is plain; it is simply to contemplate the Life, Love, and Beauty of the Originating Spirit and affirm that we are already giving expression to it in our thoughts and in our actions however insignificant they may at present appear. This path may be very narrow and humble in its beginning, but it ever grows wider and mounts higher, for it is the continually expanding expression of the Life of the Spirit which is infinite and knows no limits.

ALPHA AND OMEGA

Alpha and Omega, the First and the Last. What does this mean? It means the entire series of causation from the first originating movement to the final and completed result. We may take this on any scale from the creation of a cosmos to the creation of a lady's robe. Everything has its origin in an idea, a thought; and it has its completion in the manifestation of that thought in form. Many intermediate stages are necessary, but the Alpha and Omega of the series are the thought and the thing. This shows us that in essence the thing already existed in thought. Omega is already potential in Alpha, just as in the Pythagorean system all numbers are said to proceed from unity and to be resolvable back again into it. Now it is this general principle of the already existence of the thing in the thought that we have to lay hold of, and as we find it true in an architect's design of the house that is to be, so we find it true in the great work of the Architect of the Universe. When we see this we have realized a general principle, which we find at work everywhere. That is the meaning of a *general* principle: it can be applied to any sort of subject; and the use of studying general principles is to give them particular application to anything we may have to deal with. Now what we have to deal with most of all is ourselves, and so we come to the consideration of Alpha and Omega in the human being.

But if we grasp the truth that the thing is already existent in the thought, do we not see that this transcendent Omega must be already existent in the Divine ideal of every one of us? If on the plane of the absolute time is not, then does it not follow that this glorified humanity is a present fact in the Divine Mind? And if this is so, then this fact is eternally true regarding every human being. But if it is true that the thing exists in the thought, it is equally true that the thought finds form in the thing; and since things exist under the relative conditions of time and space, they are necessarily subject to a law of Growth. The expression of the thought in the thing is a matter of gradual development. This is a point which we must never lose sight of in our studies; and we must never lose sight of the perfection of the thing in the thought because we do not yet see the perfection of the thought in the thing. Therefore we must remember that man, as we know him now, has by no means reached the ultimate of his evolution. We are only yet in the making, but we have now reached a point where we can facilitate the evolutionary process by conscious cooperation with the Creative Spirit. Our share in this work commences with the recognition of the Divine ideal of man, and thus finding the pattern by which we are to be guided. For since the person to be created after this pattern is our self, it follows that, by whatever processes the Divine ideal transforms itself into concrete reality, the place where those processes are to work must be within ourselves; in other words, the creative action of the Spirit takes place through the laws of our own mentality. If it is a true maxim that the thing must take form in the thought before the thought can take form in the thing, then it is plain that the Divine Ideal can only be externalized in our objective life in proportion as it is first formed in our thought; and it takes form in our thought only to the extent to which we apprehend its existence in the Divine Mind. By the nature of the relation between the individual mind and the Universal Mind it is strictly a case of reflection; and in proportion as the mirror of our own mind blurs or clearly reflects the image of the Divine ideal, so will it give rise to a correspondingly feeble or vigorous reproduction of it in our external life.

This being the rationale of the matter, why should we limit our conception of the Divine ideal of ourselves? Why should we say, "I am too mean a creature ever to reflect so glorious an image."

In saying such things we expose our ignorance of the whole Law of the Creative Process. We shut our eyes to the fact that the Omega of completion already subsists in the Alpha of conception, and that the Alpha of conception would be nothing but a lying illusion if it was not capable of expression in the Omega of completion.

Now the fact which, in our past experience, we have not grasped is that the human mind forms a new point of departure for the work of the Creative Spirit; and in proportion as we see this more and more clearly, the more we shall find ourselves entering into a new order of life in which we become less and less subject to the old limitations. This is not a reward arbitrarily bestowed upon us for holding dogmatically to certain mere verbal statements, but it is the natural result of understanding the supreme law of our own being. On its own plane it is as purely scientific as the law of chemical reaction; only here we are not dealing with the interaction of secondary cause but with the Self-originating action of Spirit. Hence a new force has to be taken into account which does not occur in physical science, the power of Feeling. Thought creates form, but it is feeling that gives vitality to thought. Thought without feeling may be constructive as in some great engineering work, but it can never be creative as in the work of the artist or musician. It is this indissoluble union of Thought and Feeling that distinguishes creative thought from merely analytical thought and places it in a different category; and therefore if we are to afford a new starting point for carrying on the work of creation it must be by assimilating the feeling of the Originating Spirit as part and parcel of this thought – it is that entering into the Mind of the Spirit of which I spoke in the first address.

Now the images in the Mind of the Spirit must necessarily be *generic*. The reason for this is that by its very nature the Principle of Life must be prolific, that is, tending to Multiplicity, and therefore the original Thought-image must be fundamental to whole races, and not exclusive to particular individuals. Consequently the images in the Mind of the Spirit must be absolute types of the true essentials of the perfect development of the race, just what Plato meant by archetypal ideas. This is the perfect subsistence of the thing in the thought.

Then it is that his recognition of the originating creative movement, as arising from combined Thought and Feeling, becomes a practical working asset. He realizes that there is a Heart and Mind of the Spirit reciprocal to his own heart and mind, that he is not dealing with a filmy abstraction, nor yet with a mere mathematical sequence, but with something that is pulsating with a Life as warm and vivid and full of interest as his own – nay, more so, for it is the Infinite of all the he himself is.

But this self-recognition through the individual cannot in any way change the inherent nature of the Creative Spirit, and therefore to the extent to which the individual perceives its identification with himself, he places himself under its guidance, and so becomes one of those who are "led by the Spirit." Thus he begins to find the Alpha and Omega of the Divine ideal reproduced in himself – in a very small degree at present, but containing the principle of perpetual growth into an infinite expansion of which we can as yet form no conception.

THE CREATIVE POWER OF THOUGHT

One of the great axioms in the new order of ideas, of which I have spoken, is that our Thought possesses creative power, and since the whole superstructure depends on this foundation, it is well to examine it carefully. Now the starting point is to see that Thought, or purely mental action, is the only possible source from which the existing creation could ever have come into manifestation at all, and it is on this account that in the preceding addresses I have laid stress on the origin of the cosmos.

But if our thought possesses this creative power, why are we hampered by adverse conditions? The answer is, because hitherto we have used our power invertedly. We have taken the starting point of our thought from external facts and consequently created a repetition of facts of a similar nature, and so long as we do this we must needs go on perpetuating the old circle of limitation. And, owing to the sensitiveness of the subconscious mind to suggestion, (See Edinburgh Lectures, chapter V) we are subject to a very powerful negative influence from those who are unacquainted with affirmative principles, and thus race-beliefs and the thought currents of our more immediate environment tend to consolidate our own inverted thinking. It is therefore not surprising that the creative power of our thought, thus used in a wrong direction, has produced the limitations of which we complain. The remedy, then, is by reversing our method of thinking, and instead of taking external facts as our starting point, taking the inherent nature of mental power as our starting point. We have already gained two great steps in this direction, first by seeing that the whole manifested cosmos could have had its origin nowhere but in mental power, and secondly by realizing that our own mental power must be the same in kind with that of the Originating Mind.

When we realize this on the one hand, and on the other that all external conditions, including the body, are produced by thought, we find ourselves standing between two infinities, the infinite of Mind and the infinite of Substance – from both of which we can draw what we will, and mold specific conditions out of the Universal Substance by the Creative Power which we draw in from the Universal Mind. But we must recollect that this is not by the force of personal will upon the substance, which is an error that will land us in all sorts of inversion, but by realizing our mind as a channel through which the Universal Mind operates upon substances in a particular way, according to the mode of thought which we are seeking to embody.

These are not mere fancies but the expression of strictly scientific principles in their application to the deepest problems of the individual life; and their basis is that each one's world, whether in or out of the flesh, must necessarily be created by his own consciousness, and, in its turn, his mode of consciousness will necessarily take its color from his conception of his relation to the Divine Mind – to the exclusion of light and color, if he realizes no Divine Mind, and to their building up into forms of beauty in proportion as he realizes his identity of being with that All-Originating Spirit which is Light, Love, and Beauty in itself.

THE GREAT AFFIRMATIVE

The Great Affirmative appears in two modes, the cosmic and the individual. In its essence it is the same in both, but in each it works from a different standpoint. It is always the principle of Being – that which *is*, as distinguished from that which is not; but to grasp the true significance of this saying we must understand what is meant by "that which is not." It is something more than mere nonexistence, for obviously we should not trouble ourselves about what is nonexistent. It is that which both is and is not at the same time, and the thing that answers to this description is "Conditions." The little affirmative is that which affirms particular conditions as all that it can grasp, while the great affirmative grasps a wider conception, the conception of that which gives rise to conditions.

It is the direct contradiction of the maxim "nothing can be made out of nothing"; and it is the recognition of the presence in ourselves of this power, which can make something out of nothing, that is the key to our further progress.

We shall realize in ourselves the working of a new principle whose distinguishing feature is its simplicity. It is *one*-ness and is not troubled about any second. Hence what it contemplates is not how its action will be modified by that of some second principle, something which will compel it to work in a particular manner and so limit it; but what it contemplates is its own Unity.

Realizing this he deliberately places his thoughts under the guidance of the Divine Spirit, knowing that his outward acts and conditions must thereby be brought into harmony with the great forward movement of the Spirit, not only at the stage he has now reached, but at all future stages. He does not at all deny the power of his own personal world, on the contrary it is precisely on the knowledge of this fact that his perception of the true adjustment between the principles of Life is based; but for this very reason he is the more solicitous to be led by that Wisdom which can see what he cannot see, so that his personal control over the conditions of his own life may be employed to its continual increase and development.

In this way our affirmation of the "I am" ceases to be the petulant assertion of our limited personality and becomes the affirmation that the Great I AM affirms its own I AM-ness both in us and through us, and thus our use of the words becomes in very truth the Great Affirmative, or that which is the root of all being as distinguished from that which has no being in itself but is merely externalized by being as the vehicle for its expression.

Thus in our measure and station each one of us will receive the mission of the I AM.

The fulfilling of anything is the bringing into complete realization of all that it potentially contains, and so the filling of any law to its fullness means bringing out all the possibilities which are hidden in it. This is precisely the method which has brought forth all the advances of material civilization.

Why should we not, then, apply the same method to ourselves and see whether there are no potentialities hidden away in the law of our own being which we have not as yet by any means brought to their fulfillment? We talk of a good time coming and of the ameliorating of the race; but do we reflect that the race is composed of individuals and that therefore real advance is to be made only by individual improvement, and not by an Act of Parliament? And if so, then the individual with whom to begin is our self.

The mistake is in supposing that Life can be generated in ourselves by an intellectual process; but, as we have seen in the preceding lectures, Life is the primary movement of the Spirit, whether in the cosmos or in the individual. In its proper order intellectual knowledge is exceedingly important and useful, but its place in the order of the whole is not that of the Originator. It is not Life in itself, but is a function of life; it is an effect and not the cause.

The reason why this is so is because intellectual study is always the study of the various laws which arise from the different *relations* of things to one another; and it therefore presupposes that these things together with their laws are already in existence. Consequently it does not start from the truly creative standpoint, that of creating something entirely new.

Now the only thing that can release us from the inextricable confusion of an infinite multiplicity is the realization of an underlying unity, and at the back of all things we find the presence of one Great Affirmative principle without which nothing could have existence. This, then, is the Root of Life; and if we credit it with being able, not only to supply the power, but also the form for its manifestation we shall see that we need not go beyond this *single* Power for the production of anything. It is Spirit producing Substance out of its own essence, and the Substance taking Form in accordance with the movement of the Spirit.

Now the ultimate Law is that of production. All subordinate laws are merely the measurements of the relations which spontaneously arise between different things when they are brought into manifestation, and therefore, if an entirely new thing is created it must necessarily establish entirely new relations and so produce entirely new laws. This is the reason why, if we take the action of pure unmanifested Spirit as our starting-point, we may confidently trust it to produce manifestations of law which, though perfectly new from the standpoint of our past experience, are quite as natural in their own way as any that have gone before. It is on this account that in these addresses I lay so much stress on the fact that Spirit creates out of no preexisting forms, but simply by its own movement within itself.

The Spirit can never change its essential nature as the essence of Life, Love, and Beauty; and if we adopt these characteristics, which constitute the Law of the Spirit, as the basis of our own thinking and reject all that is contrary to them, then we afford the broad generic conditions for the specialized thinking of the Spirit through our own minds: and the thinking of the Spirit is that *involution*, or passing of spirit into form, which is the whole being of the creative process.

That is what makes the difference between our old thought and our new thought. Our old thought was based upon a comparison of limited facts: our new thought is based upon a comprehension of principles. The difference is like that between the mathematics of the infant, who cannot count beyond the number of apples or marbles put before him, and that of the senior wrangler who is not dependent upon visible objects for his calculations, but plunges boldly into the unknown because he knows that he is working by indubitable principles.

Our thought will not be objectless or unintelligible to ourselves. It will be quite clear as far as it goes. We shall know exactly what we want to do and why we want to do it, and so will act in a reasonable and intelligent manner. But what we do not know is the greater thought that is all the time giving rise to our smaller thought, and which will open out from it as our lesser thought progresses into form. Then we gradually see the greater thought which prompted our smaller one and we find ourselves working along its lines, guided by the invisible hand of the Creative Spirit into continually increasing degrees of livingness to which we need assign no limits, for it is the expansion of the Infinite within ourselves.

It is the distinction between a knowledge which is merely that of comparisons between different sorts of conditions, and a knowledge which is that of the Life which gives rise to and therefore controls conditions. Only we must remember that the control of conditions is not to be attained by violent self-assertion which is only recognizing them as substantive entities to be battled with, but by conscious unity with that All-creating Spirit which works silently, but surely, on its own lines of Life, Love, and Beauty.

The creative level is where new laws begin to manifest themselves in a new order of conditions, something transcending our past experiences and thus bringing about a real advance; for it is no advance only to go on in the same old round even if we kept at it for centuries: it is the steady go-ahead nature of the Spirit that has made the world of today an improvement upon the world of the pterodactyl and the ichthyosaurus, and we must look for the same forward movement of the Spirit from its new starting-point in ourselves.

The remedy is to go back to the original starting point of the Cosmic Creation and ask: where were the preexisting forms that dictated to the Spirit then? Then because the Spirit never changes it is *still the same*, and is just as independent of existing conditions now as it was in the beginning; and so we must pass over all existing conditions, however apparently adverse, and go straight to the Spirit as the originator of new forms and new conditions. This is real New Thought, for it does not trouble about the old things, but is going straight ahead from where we are now. When we do this, just trusting the Spirit, and not laying down the particular details of its action – just telling it what we want without dictating *how* we are to get it – we shall find that things will open out more and more clearly day by day both on the inner and the outer plane. Remember that the Spirit is alive and working here and now, for if ever the Spirit is to get from the past into the future it must be by passing through the present; therefore what you have to do is to acquire the habit of living direct from the Spirit here and now.

The material form stands in the same relation to Spirit that the image projected on the screen stands to the slide in the lantern. If we wish to change the exhibited subject we do not manipulate the reflection on the screen, but we alter the slide; and in like manner, when we come to realize the true nature of the creative process, we learn that the exterior things are to be changed by a change of the interior spiritual attitude.

We have found that the originating movement of Spirit from which all creation proceeds can only be Self-contemplation. Then, since the Original Spirit cannot change its nature its self-contemplation through our own minds must be as creative in, for, and through us as it ever was in the beginning; and consequently we find the original creative process repeated in ourselves and directed by the conscious thought of our own minds.

In all this there is no place for the consideration of outward conditions, whether of body or circumstances; for they are only effects and not the cause; and therefore when we reach this standpoint we cease to take them into our calculations. Instead we employ the method of self-contemplation, knowing that this is the creative method, and so we contemplate ourselves as allied to the infinite Love and Wisdom of the Divine Spirit which will take form through our conscious thought, and so act creatively as a Special Providence entirely devoted to guarding, guiding, providing for, and illuminating us.

The following Thomas Troward quotes are from
The Edinburgh Lectures on Mental Science, 1909

FURTHER CONSIDERATIONS REGARDING SUBJECTIVE AND OBJECTIVE MIND

An intelligent consideration of the phenomena of hypnotism will show us that what we call the hypnotic state is the *normal* state of the subjective mind. It *always* conceives of itself in accordance with some suggestion conveyed to it, either consciously or unconsciously to the mode of objective mind which governs it, and it gives rise to corresponding external results. The abnormal nature of the conditions induced by experimental hypnotism is in the removal of the normal control held by the individual's own objective mind over his subjective mind and the substitution of some other control for it, and thus we may say that the normal characteristic of the subjective mind is its perpetual action in accordance with some sort of suggestion. It becomes therefore a question of the highest importance to determine in every case what the nature of the suggestion shall be and from what source it shall proceed; but before considering the sources of suggestion we must realize more fully the place taken by subjective mind in the order of Nature.

If the student has followed what has been said regarding the presence of intelligent spirit pervading all space and permeating all matter, he will now have little difficulty in recognizing this all-pervading spirit as universal subjective mind. That it cannot *as universal mind* have the qualities of objective mind is very obvious. The universal mind is the creative power throughout Nature; and as the originating power it must first give rise to the various *forms* in which objective mind recognizes its own individuality, before these individual minds can react upon it; and hence, as pure spirit or *first cause*, it cannot possibly be anything else than subjective mind; and the fact which has been abundantly proved by experiment that the subjective mind is the builder of the body shows us that the power of creating by growth from within is the essential characteristic of the subjective mind. We may say that wherever we find creative power at work there we are in the presence of subjective mind, whether it be working on the grand scale of the cosmos, or on the miniature scale of the individual. We may therefore lay it down as a principle that the universal all-permeating intelligence is purely subjective mind, and therefore follows the law of subjective mind, namely that it is amenable to any suggestion, and will carry out any suggestion that is impressed upon it to its most rigorously logical consequences. The incalculable importance of this truth may not perhaps strike the student at first sight, but a little consideration will show him the enormous possibilities that are stored up in it. For the present it will be sufficient to realize that the subjective mind in ourselves is *the same* subjective mind which is at work throughout the universe giving rise to the infinitude of natural forms with which we are surrounded, and in like manner giving rise to *ourselves also*.

It may be called the supporter of our individuality; and we may loosely speak of our individual subjective mind as our personal share in the universal mind. This, of course, does not imply the splitting up of the universal mind into fractions, and it is to avoid this error that I have discussed the essential unity of spirit in the third section, but in order to avoid too highly abstract conceptions in the present stage of the student's progress we may conveniently employ the idea of a personal share in the universal subjective mind.

To realize our individual subjective mind in this manner will help us to get over the great metaphysical difficulty which meets us in our endeavor to make conscious use of first cause, in other words to create external results by the power of our own thought. Ultimately there can be only one first cause which is the universal mind, but because it is universal it cannot, *as universal*, act on the plane of the individual and particular. For it to do so would be for it to cease to be universal and therefore cease to be the creative power which we wish to employ. On the other hand, the fact that we are working for a specific definite object implies our intention to use this universal power in application to a particular purpose, and thus we find ourselves involved in the paradox of seeking to make the universal act on the plane of the particular. We want to effect a junction between the two extremes of the scale of Nature, the innermost creative spirit and a particular external form. Between these two is a great gulf, and the question is how is it to be bridged over. It is here, then, that the conception of our individual subjective mind as our personal share in the universal subjective mind affords the means of meeting the difficulty, for on the one hand it is in immediate connection with the universal mind, and on the other it is in immediate connection with the individual objective, or intellectual mind; and this in its turn is in immediate connection with the world of externalization, which is conditioned in time and space; and thus the relation between the subjective and objective minds in the individual forms the bridge which is needed to connect the two extremities of the scale.

The individual subjective mind may therefore be regarded as the organ of the Absolute in precisely the same way that the objective mind is the organ of the Relative, and it is in order to regulate our use of these two organs that it is necessary to understand what the terms "absolute" and "relative" actually mean. The absolute is that idea of a thing which contemplates it as existing *in itself* and not in relation to something else, that is to say, which contemplates the essence of it; and the relative is that idea of a thing which contemplates it as related to other things, that is to say as circumscribed by a certain environment. The absolute is the region of causes, and the relative the region of conditions; and hence, if we wish to control conditions, this can only be done by our thought-power operating on the plane of the absolute, which it can do only through the medium of the subjective mind.

For this purpose the student cannot too strongly impress upon himself that subjective mind, on whatever scale, is intensely sensitive to suggestion, and as creative power works accurately to the externalization of that suggestion which is most deeply impressed upon it.

The object of our desire is necessarily first conceived by us as bearing some relation to existing circumstances, which may, or may not, appear favorable to it; and what we want to do is to eliminate the element of contingency and attain something which is certain in itself.

This separation from the elements of condition implies the elimination of the idea of *time*, and consequently we must think of the thing as already in actual existence.

The simplest practical method of gaining the habit of thinking in this manner is to conceive the existence in the spiritual world of a spiritual prototype of every existing thing, which becomes the root of the corresponding external existence. If we thus habituate ourselves to look on the spiritual prototype as the essential being of the thing, and the material form as the growth of this prototype into outward expression, then we shall see that the initial step to the production of any external fact must be the creation of its spiritual prototype. This prototype, being purely spiritual, can only be formed by the operation of *thought*, and in order to have substance on the spiritual plane it *must* be thought of as actually existing there.

By thus making intelligent use of our subjective mind, we, so to speak, create a *nucleus*, which is no sooner created than it begins to exercise an attractive force, drawing to itself material of a like character with its own, and if this process is allowed to go on undisturbed, it will continue until an external form corresponding to the nature of the nucleus comes into manifestation on the plane of the objective and relative. This is the universal method of Nature on every plane.

All branches of physical science demonstrate the fact that every completed manifestation, of whatever kind and on whatever scale, is started by the establishment of a nucleus, infinitely small but endowed with an unquenchable energy of attraction, causing it to steadily increase in power and definiteness of purpose, until the process of growth is completed and the matured form stands out as an accomplished fact. Now if this be the universal method of Nature, there is nothing unnatural in supposing that it must begin its operation at a stage further back than the formation of the material nucleus. As soon as that is called into being it begins to operate by the law of attraction on the material plane; but what is the force which originates the material nucleus? Let a recent work on physical science give us the answer; "In its ultimate essence, energy may be incomprehensible by us except as an exhibition of the direct operation of that which we call Mind or Will." The quotation is from a course of lectures on "Waves in Water, Air and Ether," delivered in 1902, at the Royal Institution, by J. A. Fleming. Here, then, is the testimony of physical science that the originating energy is Mind or Will; and we are, therefore, not only making a logical deduction from certain unavoidable intuitions of the human mind, but are also following on the lines of the most advanced physical science, when we say that the action of Mind plants that nucleus which, if allowed to grow undisturbed, will eventually attract to itself all the conditions necessary for its manifestation in outward visible form. Now the only action of Mind is Thought; and it is for this reason that by our thoughts we create corresponding external conditions, because we thereby create the nucleus which attracts to itself its own correspondences in due order until the finished work is manifested on the external plane. This is according to the strictly scientific conception of the universal law of growth; and we may therefore briefly sum up the whole argument by saying that our thought of anything forms a spiritual prototype of it, thus constituting a nucleus or center of attraction for all conditions necessary to its eventual externalization by a law of growth inherent in the prototype itself.

CAUSES AND CONDITIONS

The expression *"relative* first cause" has been used in the last section to distinguish the action of the creative principle in the individual mind from Universal First Cause on the one hand and from secondary causes on the other. As it exists in *us*, primary causation is the power to initiate a train of causation directed to an individual purpose. As the power of initiating a fresh sequence of cause and effect it is first cause, and as referring to an individual purpose it is relative, and it may therefore be spoken of as relative first cause, or the power of primary causation manifested by the individual. The understanding and use of this power is the whole object of Mental Science, and it is therefore necessary that the student should clearly see the relation between causes and conditions. A simple illustration will go further for this purpose than any elaborate explanation. If a lighted candle is brought into a room the room becomes illuminated, and if the candle is taken away it becomes dark again. Now the illumination and the darkness are both conditions, the one positive resulting from the presence of the light, and the other negative resulting from its absence: from this simple example we therefore see that every positive condition has an exactly opposite negative condition corresponding to it, and that this correspondence results from their being related to the *same cause*, the one positively and the other negatively; and hence we may lay down the rule that all positive conditions result from the active presence of a certain cause, and all negative conditions from the absence of such a cause. A condition, whether positive or negative, is never *primary* cause, and the *primary* cause of any series can never be negative, for negation is the condition which arises from the absence of active causation. This should be thoroughly understood as it is the philosophic basis of all those "denials" which play so important a part in Mental Science, and which may be summed up in the statement that evil being negative, or privation of good, has no substantive existence in itself. Conditions, however, whether positive or negative, are no sooner called into existence than they become causes in their turn and produce further conditions, thus giving rise to the whole train of secondary causes. So long as we judge only from the information conveyed to us by the outward senses, we are working on the plane of secondary causation and see nothing but a succession of conditions, forming part of an endless train of antecedent conditions coming out of the past and stretching away into the future, and from this point of view we are under the rule of an iron destiny from which there seems no possibility of escape. This is because the outward senses are only capable of dealing with the relations which one mode of limitation bears to another, for they are the instruments by which we take cognizance of the relative and the conditioned. Now the only way of escape is by rising out of the region of secondary causes into that of primary causation, where the originating energy is to be found before it has yet passed into manifestation as a condition. This region is to be found *within ourselves*; it is the region of pure ideas; and it is for this reason that I have laid stress on the two aspects of spirit as pure thought and manifested form. The thought-image or ideal pattern of a thing is the *first cause* relatively to that thing; it is the substance of that thing untrammeled by any antecedent conditions.

If we realize that all visible things must have their origin in spirit, then the whole creation around us is the standing evidence that the starting-point of all things is in thought-images or ideas, for no other action than the formation of such images can be conceived of spirit prior to its manifestation in matter. If, then, this is spirit's modus operandi for self-expression, we have only to transfer this conception from the scale of cosmic spirit working on the plane of the universal to that of individualized spirit working on the plane of the particular, to see that the formation of an ideal image by means of our thought is setting first cause in motion with regard to this specific object. There is no difference in kind between the operation of first cause in the universal and in the particular, the difference is only a difference of scale, but the power itself is identical. We must therefore always be very clear as to whether we are *consciously* using first cause or not. Note the word "consciously" because, whether consciously or unconsciously, we are always using first cause; and it was for this reason I emphasized the fact that the Universal Mind is purely subjective and therefore bound by the laws which apply to subjective mind on whatever scale. Hence we are *always* impressing some sort of ideas upon it, whether we are aware of the fact or not, and all our existing limitations result from our having habitually impressed upon it that idea of limitation which we have imbibed by restricting all possibility to the region of secondary causes. But now when investigation has shown us that conditions are never causes in *themselves*, but only the subsequent links of a chain started on the plane of pure ideal, what we have to do is to reverse our method of thinking and regard the ideal as the real, and the outward manifestation as a mere reflection which must change with every change of the object which casts it. For these reasons it is essential to know whether we are consciously making use of first cause with a definite purpose or not, and the criterion is this. If we regard the fulfillment of our purpose as contingent upon any *circumstances*, past, present, or future, we are not making use of first cause; we have descended to the level of secondary causation, which is the region of doubts, fears, and limitations, all of which we are impressing upon the universal subjective mind with the inevitable result that it will build up corresponding external conditions. But if we realize that the region of secondary causes is the region of mere reflections we shall not think of our purpose as contingent on any conditions whatever, but shall know that by forming the idea of it in the absolute, and maintaining that idea, we have shaped the first cause into the desired form and can await the result with cheerful expectancy.

It is here that we find the importance of realizing spirit's independence of time and space. An ideal, as such, cannot be formed in the future. It must either be formed here and now or not be formed at all; and it is for this reason that every teacher, who has ever spoken with due knowledge of the subject, has impressed upon his followers the necessity of picturing to themselves the fulfillment of their desires as *already accomplished* on the spiritual plane, as the indispensable condition of fulfillment in the visible and concrete.

When this is properly understood, any anxious thought as to the *means* to be employed in the accomplishment of our purposes is seen to be quite unnecessary. If the end is already secured, then it follows that all the steps leading to it are secured also. The means will pass into the smaller circle of our conscious activities day by day in due order, and then we have to work upon them, not with fear, doubt, or feverish excitement, but calmly and joyously, because we *know* that the end is already secured, and that our reasonable use of such means as present themselves in the desired direction is only one portion of a much larger coordinated movement, the final result of which admits of no doubt. Mental Science does not offer a premium to idleness, but it takes all work out of the region of anxiety and toil by assuring the worker of the success of his labor, if not in the precise form he anticipated, then in some other still better suited to his requirements. But suppose, when we reach a point where some momentous decision has to be made, we happen to decide wrongly? On the hypothesis that the end is already secured you cannot decide wrongly. Your right decision is as much one of the necessary steps in the accomplishment of the end as any of the other conditions leading up to it, and therefore, while being careful to avoid rash action, we may make sure that the same Law which is controlling the rest of the circumstances in the right direction will influence our judgment in that direction also. To get good results we must properly understand our relation to the great impersonal power we are using. It is intelligent and we are intelligent, and the two intelligences must cooperate. We must not fly in the face of the Law by expecting it to do *for* us what it can only do *through* us; and we must therefore use our intelligence with the knowledge that it is acting *as the instrument of a greater intelligence*; and because we have this knowledge we may, and should, cease from all anxiety as to the final result. In actual practice we must first form the ideal conception of our object with the definite intention of impressing it upon the universal mind – it is this intention which takes such thought out of the region of mere casual fancies – and then affirm that our knowledge of the Law is sufficient reason for a calm expectation of a corresponding result, and that therefore all necessary conditions will come to us in due order. We can then turn to the affairs of our daily life with the calm assurance that the initial conditions are either there already or will soon come into view. If we do not at once see them, let us rest content with the knowledge that the spiritual prototype is already in existence and wait till some circumstance pointing in the desired direction begins to show itself. It may be a very small circumstance, but it is the direction and not the magnitude which is to be taken into consideration. As soon as we see it we should regard it as the first sprouting of the seed we have sown in the Absolute, and do calmly, and without excitement, whatever the circumstances may seem to require, and then later on we shall see that this doing will in turn lead to further circumstances in the same direction until we find ourselves conducted step by step to the accomplishment of our object. In this way the understanding of the great principle of the Law of Supply will, by repeated experiences, deliver us more and more completely out of the region of anxious thought and toilsome labor and bring us into a new world where the useful employment of all our powers, whether mental or physical, will only be an unfolding of our individuality upon the lines of its own nature, and therefore a perpetual source of happiness; a sufficient inducement, surely, to the careful study of the laws governing the relation between the individual and the Universal Mind.

THE WILL

The business of the will is to retain the various faculties of our mind in that position where they are really doing the work we wish, and this position may be generalized into the three following attitudes: either we wish to act upon something, or be acted on by it, or to maintain a neutral position; in other words we either intend to project a force, or receive a force, or keep a position of inactivity relatively to some particular object. Now the judgment determines which of these three positions we shall take up, the consciously active, the consciously receptive, or the consciously neutral; and then the function of the will is simply to maintain the position we have determined upon; and if we maintain any given mental attitude we may reckon with all certainty on the law of attraction drawing us to those correspondences which exteriorly symbolize the attitude in question. The willpower when transferred from the region of the lower mentality to the spiritual plane, becomes simply a calm and peaceful determination to retain a certain mental attitude in spite of all temptations to the contrary, knowing that by doing so the desired result will certainly appear.

The training of the will and its transference from the lower to the higher plane of our nature are among the first objects of Mental Science. The man is summed up by his will. Whatever he does by his own will is his own act; whatever he does without the consent of his will is not his own act but that of the power by which his will was coerced; but we must recognize that, on the mental plane, no other individuality can obtain control over our will unless we first allow it to do so; and it is for this reason that all legitimate use of Mental Science is towards the strengthening of the will, whether in ourselves or others, and bringing it under the control of an enlightened reason.

IV

GENEVIEVE BEHREND

The following quotes are from
Your Invisible Power, 1927

ORDER OF VISUALIZATION

The exercise of the visualizing faculty keeps your mind in order, and attracts to you the things you need to make life more enjoyable in an orderly way. If you train yourself in the practice of deliberately picturing your desire and carefully examining your picture, you will soon find that your thoughts and desires proceed in a more orderly procession than ever before. Having reached a state of ordered mentality you are no longer in a constant state of mental hurry. Hurry is Fear and consequently destructive.

In other words, when your understanding grasps the power to visualize your heart's desire and hold it with your will, it attracts to you all things requisite to the fulfillment of that picture by the harmonious vibrations of the law of attraction.

Everyone visualizes, whether he knows it or not. Visualizing is the great secret of Success. The conscious use of this great power attracts to you multiplied resources, intensifies your wisdom, and enables you to make use of advantages which you formerly failed to recognize.

For example: A lady once came to me for help in selling a piece of property. After I explained to her just how to make a mental picture of the sale, going through the details mentally exactly as she would do if the property was sold, she came a week later and told me how, one day she was walking along the street when the thought suddenly occurred to her, to go and see a certain real estate dealer, to whom she had not yet been.

She hesitated for a moment when she first got the idea as it seemed to her that that man could not sell her property. However upon the strength of what I had told her, she followed the lead and went to the real estate man, who sold the property for her in just three days after she had first approached him. This was simply following along with the natural law of demand and supply.

We now fly through the air, not because anyone has been able to change the laws of Nature, but because the inventor of the flying machine learned how to apply Nature's laws and, by making orderly use of them, produced the desired result. So far as the natural forces are concerned, nothing has changed since the beginning. There were no airplanes in "the Year One," because those of that generation could not conceive the idea as a practical working possibility. "It has not yet been done" was the argument, "and it cannot be done." Yet the laws and materials for practical flying machines existed then as now.

Troward tells us that the great lesson he learned from the airplane and wireless telegraphy is the triumph of principle over precedent, the working out of an idea to its logical conclusion in spite of accumulated contrary testimony of all past experience.

With such an example before you, you must realize that there are still greater secrets to be disclosed. Also "That you hold the key within yourself, with which to unlock the secret chamber that contains your heart's desire. All that is necessary in order that you may use this key and make your life exactly what you wish it to be, is a careful inquiry into the unseen causes which stand back of every external and visible condition. Then bring these unseen causes into harmony with your conception, and you will find that you can make practical working realities of possibilities which at present seem but fantastic dreams."

For example: A woman came to me in New York City asking for help as she was out of work. I spoke the word of ever present supply to her and intensified it by mentally seeing the woman in the position she dreamed of but which she had been unable to make a practical reality. That same afternoon she called up and told me she could hardly believe her senses as she had just taken exactly the kind of a position she wanted. The employer told her she had been wanting a woman like her for months.

We all know that the balloon was the forefather of the airplane. In 1766 Henry Cavendish, an English nobleman, proved that hydrogen gas was seven times lighter than air. From that discovery the balloon came into existence, and from the ordinary balloon the dirigible, a cigar-shaped air ship, was evolved. Study of aeronautics and the laws of aerial locomotion of birds and projectiles led to the belief that mechanism could be evolved by which heavier-than-air machines could be made to travel from place to place and remain in the air by the maintenance of great speed which would overcome by propulsive force the ordinary law of gravitation. Professor Langley of Washington who developed much of the theory which others afterward improved upon was subjected to much derision when he sent a model airplane up only to have it bury its nose in the muddy water of the Potomac. But the Wright Brothers, who experimented in the latter part of the Nineteenth Century, realized the possibility of traveling through the air in a machine that had no gas bag. They *saw* themselves enjoying this mode of transportation with great facility. It is said that one of the brothers would tell the other (when their varied experiences did not turn out as they expected): "It's all right, brother, I can *see* myself riding in that machine, and it travels easily and steadily."

Those Wright Brothers knew what they wanted, and kept their pictures constantly before them. And though transportation through the air is in its infancy, we all feel sure that it will become as ordinary a method of travel as is the automobile.

In visualizing, or making a mental picture, you are not endeavoring to change the laws of Nature. You are fulfilling them. Your object in visualizing is to bring things into regular order both mentally and physically. When you realize that this method of employing the Creative Power brings your desires, one after another, into practical, material accomplishment, your confidence in the mysterious but unfailing law of attraction, which has its central power station in the very heart of your word-picture, becomes supreme. Nothing can shake it. You never feel that it is necessary to take anything from anybody else. You have learned that asking and seeking have as their correlatives, receiving and finding. You know that all you have to do is to start the plastic substance of the Universe flowing into the thought-molds your picture-desire provides.

HOW TO ATTRACT TO YOURSELF THE THINGS YOU DESIRE

The power within you which enables you to form a thought picture is the starting point of all there is. In its original state it is the undifferentiated formless substance of life. Your thought picture makes the mold (so to say) into which this formless substance takes shape. Visualizing, or mentally seeing things and conditions as you wish them to be, is the condensing, the specializing power in you which might be illustrated by the lens of a magic lantern. The magic lantern is one of the best symbols of the imaging faculty. It illustrates the working of the Creative Spirit on the plane of initiative and selection (or in its concentrated specializing form) in a remarkably clear manner.

The picture slide illustrates your own mental picture – invisible in the lantern of your mind until you turn on the light of your will. That is to say, you light up your desire with absolute faith that the Creative Spirit of Life, in you, is doing the work. By the steady flow of the light of the will on the Spirit, your desired picture is projected upon the screen of the physical world, an exact reproduction of the pictured slide in your mind.

For example: A woman came to me for help to cause her husband to return to her. She said she was very unhappy and lonely without him and longed to be reunited. I told her she could not lose love and protection because both belonged to her. She asked what she should do to get her husband back again. I told her to follow the great power of intuition and think of her husband as perfectly free and the embodiment of all that a husband should be. She went away quite happy but returned in a few days telling me that her husband desired a divorce in order to marry again. She was quite agitated and had evidently relaxed her will in following the instructions given at the former interview. Again I told her to hold constantly in her mind that the loving protection of the Spirit of Life would guide her in perfect happiness. A month later she came again telling me her husband had married the other woman. This time she had completely lost her mental grip. I repeated the words to her as before and she regained her poise. Two months later she came back to me, full of joy. Her husband had come to her begging her forgiveness, telling her what a terrible mistake he had made as he could not be happy without her. They are now living happily together and she, at least, learned the necessity of holding her pictured desire steadily in place by the use of her will.

Visualizing without a will sufficiently steady to inhibit every thought and feeling contrary to your picture would be as useless as a magic lantern without the light. On the other hand, if your will is sufficiently developed to hold your picture in thought and feeling, without any "ifs"; simply realizing that your thought is the great attracting power, then your mental picture is as certain to be projected upon the screen of your physical world as any picture slide put into the best magic lantern ever made.

Try projecting the picture in a magic lantern with a light that is constantly shifting from one side to the other, and you will have the effect of an uncertain will. It is as necessary that you should always stand back of your picture with a strong, steady will, as it is to have a strong steady light back of a picture slide.

The joyous assurance with which you make your picture is the very powerful magnet of Faith, and nothing can obliterate it. You are happier than you ever were, because you have learned to know where your source of supply is, and you rely upon its never failing response to the direction you give it.

All said and done, happiness is the one thing which every human being wants, and the study of visualization enables you to get more out of life than you ever enjoyed before. Increasing possibilities keep opening out, more and more, before you.

A business man once told me that since practicing visualization and forming the habit of devoting a few minutes each day to thinking about his business as he desired it to be in a large, broad way, his business had more than doubled in six months. His method was to go into a room every morning before breakfast and take a mental inventory of his business as he had left it in the evening before, and then enlarge upon it. He said he expanded and expanded in this way until his affairs were in a remarkable successful condition. He would see himself in his office doing everything that he wanted done. His occupation required him to meet many strangers every day. In his mental picture he saw himself meeting these people, understanding their needs and supplying them in just the way they wished. This habit, he said, had strengthened and steadied his will in an almost inconceivable manner. Furthermore, by thus mentally seeing things as he wished them to be, he had acquired the confident feeling that a certain Creative Power was exercising itself, for him and through him, for the purpose of improving his little world.

When you first begin to visualize seriously, you may feel, as many others do, that someone else may be forming the same picture you are, and that, naturally, would not suit your purpose. Do not give yourself any unnecessary concern about this. Simply try to realize that your picture is an orderly exercise of the Universal Creative Power specifically applied. Then you may be sure that no one can work in opposition to you. The universal law of harmony prevents this. Endeavor to bear in mind that your mental picture is Universal Mind specifically exercising its inherent powers of initiative and selection.

Many people ask, "But why should we have a physical world at all?" The answer is: Because it is in the nature of Originating Substance to solidify, under directivity rather than activity, just as it is the nature of wax to harden when it becomes cold, or plaster of paris to become firm and solid when exposed to the air. Your picture is this same Divine Substance in its original state taking form through the individualized center of Divine operation, in your mind; and there is no power to prevent this combination of Spiritual Substance from becoming physical form. It is the nature of Spirit to complete its work and an idea is not complete until it has made for itself a vehicle. Nothing can prevent your picture from coming into concrete form except the same power which gave it birth – yourself. Suppose you wish to have a more orderly room. You look about your room and the idea of order suggests boxes, closets, shelves, hooks and so forth. The box, the closet and the hooks, are all concrete ideas of order because they are the vehicles through which order and harmony suggest themselves.

RELATION BETWEEN MENTAL AND PHYSICAL FORM

We all possess more power and greater possibilities than we realize, and visualizing is one of the greatest of these powers. It brings other possibilities to our observation.

This same power that brought universal substance into existence will bring your individual thought or mental picture into physical form. There is no difference in the power. The only difference is a difference of degree. The power and the substance themselves are the same. Only in working out your mental picture it has transferred its creative energy from the Universal to the particular, and is working in the same unfailing manner from its specific center, your mind.

OPERATION OF YOUR MENTAL PICTURE

The operation of a large telephone system may be used as a simile. The main, or head, central subdivides itself into many branch centrals, every branch being in direct connection with the main central and each individual branch, recognizing the source of its existence, reports all things to its central head. Therefore, when assistance of any nature is required; new supplies, difficult repairs to be done, or what not, the branch in need goes at once to its central head. It would not think of referring its difficulties (or its successes) to the main central of a telegraph system (though they might belong to the same organization). These different branch centrals know that the only remedy for any difficulty must come from the central out of which they were projected and to which they are always attached.

For example: A man came to me in great distress saying he was about to lose his home in the South. In his own words, it was mortgaged to the hilt and his creditors were going to foreclose. It was the house he was born in and grown to young manhood in, and the thought of losing it filled his heart and mind with sorrow, not only from a money standpoint, but from the standpoint of sentimental association. I explained to him that the Power that brought him into existence did so for the purpose of expressing its limitless supply through him; that there was no power on earth which could cut him off from his source except his own consciousness and in reality he would not be cut off then. I explained to him that he had it but was unable to recognize that it was there, and said: "Infinite substance is manifesting in you right now." The next week, on Sunday, just before leaving my dressing room in the Selwyn Theatre to give my afternoon message, I received the following note: "Dear Mrs. Behrend: I want you to know that I am the happiest man in the whole city of New York. My home in the South is saved. The money came in the most miraculous way, and I have telegraphed enough to pay off the mortgage. Please tell the people this afternoon about this wonderful power."

You may be sure I did, explaining to them everything animate or inanimate is called into existence or outstandingness by a Power which itself does not stand out. The Power which creates the mental picture, (the Originating Spirit Substance of your pictured desire) does not stand out. It projects the substance of itself which is a solidified counterpart of itself, while it remains invisible to the physical eye.

There is nothing unusual or mysterious in the idea of your pictured desire coming into material evidence. It is the working of a universal natural Law. The world was projected by the self contemplation of the Universal Mind, and this same action is taking place in its individualized branch which is the Mind of Man. Everything in the whole world has its beginning in mind and comes into existence in exactly the same manner; from the hat on your head to the boots on your feet. All are projected thoughts, solidified. Your personal advance in evolution depends upon your right use of the power of visualizing, and your use of it depends on whether you recognize that you, yourself, are a particular center through and in which the Originating Spirit is finding ever new expression for potentialities already existing within Itself. This is evolution; this continues the unfolding of existing through outwardly invisible things.

Your mental picture is the force of attraction which evolves and combines the Originating Substance into specific shape. Your picture is the combining and evolving power house, so to say, through which the Originating Creative Spirit expresses itself. "It proceeds stage by stage, each stage being a necessary preparation for the one to follow."

Now let us see if we can get an idea of the different stages by which the things in the world have come to be. Troward says, "If we can get at the working principle which is producing these results, we can very quickly and easily give it personal application. First, we find that the thought of Originating Life, or Spirit, about Itself is its simple awareness of its own being and this produces a primary ether, a universal substance out of which everything in the world must grow."

Troward also tells us that "though this awareness of being is a necessary foundation for any further possibilities, it is not much to talk about." It is the same with individualized Spirit, which is yourself. Before you can entertain the idea of making a mental picture of your desire as being at all practical, you must have some idea of your being; of your "I am"; and just as soon as you are conscious of your "I-am-ness" you begin to wish to enjoy the freedom which this consciousness suggests. You want to do more and be more, and as you fulfill this desire within yourself, localized spirit begins conscious activities in you. The thing you are more concerned with is the specific action of the Creative Spirit of Life, Universal Mind specialized.

You want to enjoy life and liberty. You want freedom in your affairs as well as in your consciousness, and it is natural that you should. With this progressive wish there is always a faint thought-picture. As your wish and your recognition grow into intense desire, this desire becomes a clear mental picture. For example, a young lady studying music wishes she had a piano in order to practice at home. She wants the piano so much that she can mentally see it in one of the rooms. She holds the picture of the piano and indulges in the mental reflection of the pleasure and advantage it will be to have the piano in the corner of the living room. One day she finds it there just as she had pictured it.

As you grow in understanding as to who you are, where you came from, what the purpose of your being is, and how you are to fulfill the purpose for which you are intended, you will become a more and more perfect center through which the Creative Spirit of Life can enjoy itself. And you will realize that there can be but one creative process filling all space, which is the same in its potentality whether universal or individual. Furthermore, all that there is, whether on the plane of the visible or invisible, had its origin in the localized action of thought, or a mental picture, and this includes yourself, because you are Universal Spirit localized, and the same creative action is taking place through you.

Now you are no doubt asking yourself why there is so much misery in the world. If the same power and intelligence which brought the world into existence is in operation in the mind of man, why does it not manifest itself as strength, joy and plenty? If one can have one's desires fulfilled by simply making a mental picture of that desire, holding on to it with the will, and without anxiety, doing on the outward plane whatever seems necessary to bring the desire into fulfillment, then there seems no reason for the existence of poverty. The first reason is that few persons will take the trouble to inquire into the working principle of the Laws of Life. If they did they would soon convince themselves that there is no necessity for the poverty which we see about us. They would realize that visualizing is a principle and not a fallacy. There are a few who have found it worthwhile to study this simple, though absolutely unfailing law which will deliver them from bondage. However, the race as a whole is not willing to give the time required for the study. They may make a picture of their desire with some little understanding of visualizing for a day or two, but more frequently it is for an hour or so.

If you will insist upon mentally seeing yourself surrounded by things and conditions as you wish them to be, you will understand that the Creative Energy sends its substance in the direction indicated by the *tendency* of your thoughts. Herein lies the advantage of holding your thought in the form of a mental picture.

For example: A man in the hardware business in New Jersey came to me in great distress. He would have to go into bankruptcy unless something happened in a fortnight. He said he had never heard of visualizing. I explained to him how to make a mental picture of his business increasing instead of a picture of losing it. In about a month's time he returned very happy and told me how he had succeeded. He said "I have my debts all paid and my shop is full of new supplies." His business was then on a solid basis. It was beautiful to see his Faith.

The more enthusiasm and faith you are able to put into your picture, the more quickly it will come into visible form, and your enthusiasm is increased by keeping your desire secret. The moment you speak it to any living soul, that moment your power is weakened. Your power, your magnet of attraction is not so strong, and consequently cannot reach so far. The more perfectly a secret between your mind and your outer self is guarded, the more vitality you give your power of attraction. One tells one's troubles to weaken them, to get them off one's mind, and when a thought is given out, its power is dissipated. Talk it over with yourself, and even write it down, then destroy the paper.

However, this does not mean that you should strenuously endeavor to compel the Power to work out your picture on the *special* lines that you think it should. That method would soon exhaust you and hinder the fulfillment of your purpose. One of the doormen in the building in which I lived heard much of the mental picturing of desires from visitors passing out of my rooms. The average desire was for $500. He considered that five dollars was more in his line and began to visualize it, without the slightest idea of where or how he was to get it. My parrot flew out of the window, and I telephoned to the men in the courtyard to get it for me. One caught it and it bit him on the finger. The doorman, who had gloves on, and did not fear a similar hurt, took hold of it and brought it up to me. I gave him five one-dollar bills for his service. This sudden reward surprised him. He enthusiastically told me that he had been visualizing for just $5, merely from hearing that others visualized. He was delighted at the unexpected realization of his mental picture.

All you have to do is to make such a mental picture of your heart's desire, hold it cheerfully in place with your will, always conscious that the same Infinite Power which brought the universe into existence brought you into form for the purpose of enjoying

Itself in and through you. And since it is all Life, Love, Light, Power, Peace, Beauty and Joy, and is the only Creative Power there is, the form it takes in and through you depends upon the direction given it by your thought indicator. In you it is undifferentiated, waiting to take any direction given it as it passes through the instrument which it has made for the purpose of self-distribution.

It is this Power which enables you to transfer your thoughts from one form to another. The power to change your mind is the individualized Universal Power taking the initiative, giving direction to the unformed substance contained in every thought.

It is the simplest thing in the world to give this highly sensitive Substance any form you will through visualizing. Anyone can do it with a small expenditure of effort. Once you really believe that your mind is a center through which the unformed substance of all there is in your world, takes involuntary form, the only reason why your picture does not always materialize is because you have introduced something antagonistic to the fundamental principle. Very often this destructive element is caused by the frequency with which you change your pictures. After many such changes you decide that your original desire is what you want after all. Upon this conclusion you begin to wonder why, (being your first picture), it hasn't materialized. The Substance with which you are mentally dealing is more sensitive than the most sensitive photographer's film. If, in taking a picture, you suddenly remembered you had already taken a picture on that same plate, you would not expect a perfect result of either picture. On the other hand, you may have taken two pictures on the same plate unconsciously. When the plate has been developed, and the picture comes into physical view, you do not condemn the principle of photography, nor are you puzzled to understand why your picture has turned out so unsatisfactorily. You do not feel that it is impossible for you to obtain a good, clear picture of the subject in question. You know that you can do so, by simply starting at the beginning, putting in a new plate, and determining to be more careful while taking your picture next time. These lines followed out, you are sure of a satisfactory result. If you will proceed in the same manner with your mental picture, doing your part in a correspondingly confident frame of mind, the result will be just as perfect. The laws of visualizing are as infallible as the laws governing photography. In fact, photography is the outcome of visualizing.

Again, your results in visualizing the fulfillment of your desires may be imperfect and your desires delayed through the misuse of this power, owing to the thought that the fulfillment of your desire is contingent upon certain persons or conditions. The Originating Principle is not in any way dependent upon any person, place or thing. It has no past and knows no future. The law is that the Originating Creative Principle of Life is "the universal here and everlasting now." It creates its own vehicles through which to operate. Therefore, past experience has no bearing upon your present picture. So do not try to obtain your desire through a channel which may not be natural for it, even though it may seem reasonable to you. Your feeling should be that the thing, or the consciousness which you so much desire, is normal and natural, a part of yourself, a form of your evolution. If you can do this, there is no power to prevent your enjoying the fulfillment of the picture you have in mind, or any other you may create.

EXPRESSIONS FROM BEGINNERS

Hundreds of persons have realized that "visualizing is an Aladdin's lamp to him with a mighty will." General Foch says that his feelings were so outraged during the Franco-Prussian war in 1870 that he visualized himself leading a French army against the Germans to victory. He said he made his picture, smoked his pipe and waited. This is one result of visualizing with which we are all familiar.

A famous actress wrote a long article in one of the leading Sunday papers last winter, describing how she rid herself of excessive avoirdupois by seeing her figure constantly as she wished it to be.

A very interesting letter came to me from a doctor's wife while I was lecturing in New York. She began with the hope that I would never discontinue my lectures on visualization, making humanity realize the wonderful fact that they possess the means of liberation within themselves. Relating her own experience, she said that she was born on the East Side of New York in the poorest quarter. From earliest girlhood she had cherished a dream of marrying a physician some day. This dream gradually formed a stationary mental picture. The first position she obtained was in the capacity of a nursemaid in a physician's family. Leaving this place she entered the family of another doctor. The wife of her employer died, and in time the doctor married her, the result of her long pictured yearning. After that both she and her husband conceived the idea of owning a fruit farm in the South. They formed a mental picture of the idea and put their faith in its eventual fulfillment. The letter she sent me came from her fruit farm in the South. Her second mental picture had seen the light of materialization.

Many letters of a similar nature come to me every day. The following is a case that was printed in the New York Herald last May: "Atlantic City, May 5 – She was an old woman, and when she was arraigned before Judge Clarence Goldenberg in the police court today she was so weak and tired she could hardly stand. The Judge asked the court attendant what she was charged with. 'Stealing a bottle of milk, Your Honor,' repeated the officer. 'She took it from the doorstep of a downtown cottage before daybreak this morning.' 'Why did you do that?' Judge Goldenberg asked her. 'I was hungry,' the old woman said. 'I didn't have a cent in the world and no way to get anything to eat except to steal it. I didn't think anybody would mind if I took a bottle of milk.' 'What's your name?' asked the Judge. 'Weinberg,' said the old woman, 'Elizabeth Weinberg.' Judge Goldenberg asked her a few questions about herself. Then he said: 'Well, you're not very wealthy now, but you're no longer poor. I've been searching for you for months. I've got $500 belonging to you from the estate of a relative. I am the executor of the estate.'

Judge Goldenberg paid the woman's fine out of his own pocket, and then escorted her into his office, where he turned her legacy over to her and sent a policeman out to find her a lodging place."

I learned later that this little woman had been desiring and mentally picturing $500, while all the time ignorant of how it could possibly come to her. But she kept her vision and strengthened it with her faith.

In a recent issue of Good Housekeeping there was an article by Addington Bruce entitled "Stiffening Your Mental Backbone." It is very instructive, and would benefit anyone to read it. He says, in part: "Form the habit of devoting a few moments every day to thinking about your work in a large, broad imaginative way, as a vital necessity to yourself and a useful service to society."

Huntington, the great railway magnet, before he started building his road from coast to coast, said that he took hundreds of trips all along the line before there was a rail laid. It is said that he would sit for hours with a map of the United States before him and mentally travel from coast to coast just as we do now over his fulfilled mental picture. It would be possible to call your attention to hundreds of similar cases.

The method of picturing to yourself what you desire is both simple and enjoyable, if you once understand the principle back of it well enough to believe it. Over and above everything else, be sure of what you really want.

SUGGESTIONS FOR MAKING YOUR MENTAL PICTURE

Perhaps you want to feel that you've lived to some purpose. You want to be contented and happy; you feel that a successful business would give you contentment. After you have decided once and for all that this is what you want, you proceed to picture your business just as great a success as you can naturally conceive it growing into. The best time for making your definite picture is just before breakfast and before retiring at night. As it is necessary to give yourself plenty of time, it may be necessary to rise earlier than you usually do. Go into a room where you will not be disturbed, meditate for a few moments upon the practical working of the law of visualizing, and ask yourself, "How did the things about me first come into existence? How can I get more quickly in touch with my invisible supply?"

Someone felt that comfort would be better expressed and experienced by sitting on a chair than on the floor. So the very beginning of a chair was the desire to be at ease. With this came the picture of some sort of chair. The same principle applies to the hat and the clothes you wear. Go carefully into the thought of the principle back of the thing. Establish it as a personal experience; make it a fact to your consciousness. Then open a window, take about ten deep breaths, and during the time draw a large imaginary circle of light around you. As you inhale (keeping yourself in the center of this circle of light) see great rays of light coming from the circle and entering your body at all points, centralizing itself at your solar plexus. Hold the breath a few moments at this central point of your body (the solar plexus) then slowly exhale. As you do this, mentally see imaginary rays, or sprays, of light going up through the body and down and out through the feet. Mentally spray your entire body with this imaginary light. When you have finished the breathing exercise, sit in a comfortable upright chair and mentally know there is but one Life, one Substance, and this Life Substance of the Universe is finding pleasure in self-recognition in you. Repeat some affirmation of this kind, until you feel the truth and stimulating reality of the words which you are affirming. Then begin your picture. If you are thorough in this, you will find yourself in the deep consciousness beneath the surface of your own thought-power.

Whether your desire is for a state of consciousness or a possession, large or small, begin at the beginning. If you want a house, begin by seeing yourself in the kind of house you desire. Go all through it, taking careful note of the rooms, where the windows are situated, and such other details as help you to feel the reality of your picture. You might change some of the furniture about and look into some of the mirrors just to see how wealthy and happy you look. Go over your picture again and again until you feel the reality of it, then write it all down just as you have seen it, with the feeling that:

"The best there is, is mine. There is no limit to me, because my mind is a center of divine operation" and your picture is as certain to come true, in your physical world, as the sun is to shine.

THINGS TO REMEMBER

In Using Your Thought Power for the Production of New Conditions

1. Be sure to know exactly what conditions you wish to produce. Then weigh carefully what further results the accomplishment of your desire will lead to.

2. By letting your thought dwell upon a mental picture, you are concentrating the Creative Action of Spirit in this center, where all its forces are equally balanced.

3. *Visualizing* brings your objective mind into a state of equilibrium which enables you to *consciously* direct the flow of Spirit to a definitely recognized purpose and to carefully guard your thoughts from including a flow in the opposite direction.

4. You must always bear in mind that you are dealing with a wonderful potential energy which is not yet differentiated into any particular form, and that by the action of your mind you can differentiate it into any specific form that you will. Your picture assists you to keep your mind fixed on the fact that the inflow of this Creative Energy is taking place. Also by your mental picture you are determining the direction you wish the sensitive

Creative Power to take, and by doing this the externalization of your picture is a certainty.

5. Remember when you are visualizing properly that there is no strenuous effort to hold your thought-forms in place. Strenuous effort defeats your purpose, and suggests the consciousness of an adverse force to be fought against, and this creates conditions adverse to your picture.

6. By holding your picture in a cheerful frame of mind, you shut out all thoughts that would disperse or dissipate the spiritual nucleus of your picture. Because the law is Creative in its action, your pictured desire is certain of accomplishment.

7. The seventh and great thing to remember in visualizing is that you are making a mental picture for the purpose of determining the quality you are giving to the previously undifferentiated substance and energy rather than to arrange the specific circumstances for its manifestation. That is the work of Creative Power itself. It will build its own forms of expression quite naturally, if you will allow it, and save you a great deal of needless anxiety. What you really want is expansion in a certain direction, whether of wealth or what not, and so long as you get it (as you surely will, if you confidently hold to your picture) what does it matter whether it reaches you by some channel which you thought you could not count upon, or through some other of whose existence you had no idea. You are concentrating energy of a particular kind for a particular purpose. Bear this in mind and let specific details take care of themselves, and never mention what you are doing to anyone.

Your conscious Oneness with the great Whole is the secret of success and when once you have fathomed this you can enjoy your possession of the whole, or a part of it, at will, because by your recognition you have made it, and can increasingly make it yours.

Never forget that every physical thing, whether for you or against you, was a sustained thought before it was a thing.

Thought as thought, is neither good nor bad; it is Creative Action and always takes physical form. Therefore, the thoughts you dwell upon become the things you possess or do not possess.

For example: A man came to me telling me how he longed to marry a certain young woman but felt he could not afford to as his salary was small and work uncertain. I spoke the word of ever present *Certain, Unlimited Supply* and explained that *Love* knows no failure. "It is yours to enjoy. See yourself in the kind of a home you *both* want. Do your part; keep on loving the girl, and believe absolutely in that which Lives and Loves in you." A few months later they both came to my study looking radiantly happy. I knew they were married. The wife said to me, "Dear Mrs. Behrend, we are very happy because we now know how to use our thought power and hold our consciousness as one, with all we want."

So be yourself and enjoy Life in your own Divine way. Do not fear to be your true self for, *everything you want, wants you.*

WHY I TOOK UP THE STUDY OF MENTAL SCIENCE

I have frequently been questioned about my reasons for taking up the study of Mental Science, and as to the results of my search, not only in the knowledge of principles, but also in the application of that knowledge for the development of my own life.

When about to abandon the search for contentment and resign myself to resume a life of apparent amusement, a friend invited me to visit the great Seer and Teacher, Abdul Baha. After my interview with this most wonderful of men, my search for contentment began to take a change. He had told me that I would travel the world over seeking the truth, and when I had found it, would speak it out. The fulfillment of the statement of this Great Seer then seemed to be impossible. But it carried a measure of encouragement, and at least indicated that my former seeking had been in the wrong direction. I began in a feeble, groping way to find contentment within myself, for had he not intimated that I should find the truth? That was the big thing, and about the only thing I remember of our interview.

A few days later, upon visiting the office of a New Thought practitioner, my attention was attracted to a book on his table entitled "The Edinburgh Lectures on Mental Science," by T. Troward. It interested me to see that Troward was a retired Divisional Judge from the Punjab, India. I purchased the book, thinking I would read it through that evening. Many have endeavored to do the same thing, only to find, as I did, that the book must be studied in order to be understood, and hundreds have decided, just as I did, to give it their undivided attention. After finding this treasure book I went to the country for a few days, and while there studied the volume as thoroughly as I could.

It seemed extremely difficult and I decided to purchase another book of Troward's in the hope that its study might not require so much of an effort. Upon inquiry I was told that a subsequent volume, "The Dore Lectures," was much the simpler and better of the two books. When I procured it, I found that it must also be studied. It took me weeks and months to get even a vague conception of the meaning of the first chapter of Dore, which is entitled "Entering Into the Spirit of It." I mean by this that it took me months to enter into the spirit of what I was reading.

But in the meantime a paragraph from page 26 arrested my attention, as seeming the greatest thing I had ever read. I memorized it and endeavored with all my soul to enter into the spirit of Troward's words. The paragraph reads:

"My mind is a center of Divine operation. The Divine operation is always for expansion and fuller expression, and this means the production of something beyond what has gone before, something entirely new, not included in the past experience, though proceeding out of it by an orderly sequence of growth. Therefore, since the Divine cannot change its inherent nature, it must operate in the same manner with me; consequently, in my own special world, of which I am the center, it will move forward to produce new conditions, always in advance of any that have gone before."

It took an effort on my part to memorize this paragraph, but in the endeavor toward this end the words seemed to carry with them a certain stimulus. Each repetition of the paragraph made it easier for me to enter into the spirit of it. The words expressed exactly what I had been seeking for. My one desire was for peace of mind. I found it comforting to believe that the Divine operation in me could expand to fuller expression and produce more and more contentment – in fact, a peace of mind and a degree of contentment greater than I had ever known. The paragraph further inspired me with deep interest to feel that the life-spark in me could bring into my life something entirely new. I did not wish to obliterate my past experience, but that was exactly what Troward said it would not do. The Divine operation would not exclude my past experience, but proceeding out of it would bring some new thing that would transcend anything that I had ever experienced before.

Meditation on these statements brought with it a certain joyous feeling. What a wonderful thing it would be if I could accept and sincerely believe, beyond all doubt, that this one statement of Troward's was true. Surely the Divine could not change its inherent nature, and since Divine life is operating in me, I must be Divinely inhabited, and the Divine in me must operate just as it operates on the Universal plane. This meant that my whole world of circumstances, friends and conditions would ultimately become a world of contentment and enjoyment of which "I am the center." This would all happen just as soon as I was able to control my mind and thereby provide a concrete center around which the Divine energies could play.

Surely it was worth trying for. If Troward had found this truth, why not I? The idea held me to my task. Later I determined to study with the man who had realized and given to the world so great a statement. It had lifted me from my state of despondency. The immediate difficulty was the need for increased finances.

HOW I ATTRACTED TO MYSELF TWENTY THOUSAND DOLLARS

In the laboratory of experience in which my newly revealed relation to the Divine operation was to be tested, the first problem was a financial one. My income was a stipulated one, quite enough for my everyday needs. But it did not seem sufficient to enable me to go comfortably to England where Troward lived, and remain for an indefinite period to study with so great a teacher as he must be. So before inquiring whether Troward took pupils or whether I would be eligible in case he did, I began to use the paragraph I had memorized. Daily, in fact, almost hourly, the words were in my mind: "My mind is a center of Divine operation, and Divine operation means expansion into something better than has gone before."

From the Edinburgh Lectures I had read something about the Law of Attraction, and from the Chapter on "Causes and Conditions" I had gleaned a vague idea of visualizing. So every night, before going to sleep, I made a mental picture of the desired $20,000 which seemed necessary to go and study with Troward. Twenty $1,000 bills were counted over each night in my bedroom, and then, with the idea of more emphatically impressing my mind with the fact that this twenty thousand dollars was for the purpose of going to England and studying with Troward, I wrote out my picture, saw myself buying my steamer ticket, walking up and down the ship's deck from New York to London, and, finally, saw myself accepted as Troward's pupil. This process was repeated every morning and every evening, always impressing more and more fully upon my mind Troward's memorized statement: "My mind is a center of Divine operations." I endeavored to keep this statement in the back part of my consciousness all the time with no thought in mind of how the money might be obtained. Probably the reason why there was no thought of the avenues through which the money might reach me was because I could not possibly imagine where the $20,000 would come from. So I simply held my thought steady and let the power of attraction find its own ways and means.

While these reflections were going on in my mind, there seemed to come up from within me the thought: "I Am all the substance there is." Then, from another channel in my brain the answer seemed to come, "Of course, that's it; everything must have its beginning in mind. The 'I' the Idea, must be the only one and primary substance there is, and this means money as well as everything else." My mind accepted this idea, and immediately all the tension of mind and body was relaxed. There was a feeling of absolute certainty of being in touch with all the power Life has to give. All thought of money, teacher, or even my own personality, vanished in the great wave of joy which swept over my entire being. I walked on and on with this feeling of joy steadily increasing and expanding until everything about me seemed aglow with resplendent light. Every person I passed was illuminated as I was. All consciousness of personality had disappeared, and in its place there came that great and almost overwhelming sense of joy and contentment.

That night when I made my picture of the twenty thousand dollars it was with an entirely changed aspect. On previous occasions, when making my mental picture, I had felt that I was waking up something within myself. This time there was no sensation of effort. I simply counted over the twenty thousand dollars. Then, in a most unexpected manner, from a source of which I had no consciousness at the time, there seemed to open a possible avenue through which the money might reach me.

At first it took great effort not to be excited. It all seemed so wonderful, so glorious, to be in touch with supply. But had not

Troward cautioned his readers to keep all excitement out of their minds in the first flush of realization of union with Infinite supply, and to treat this fact as a perfectly natural result which had been reached through our demand? This was even more difficult for me than it was to hold the thought that "all the substance there is, I Am; I (idea) Am the beginning of all form, visible or invisible."

Just as soon as there appeared a circumstance which indicated the direction through which the twenty thousand dollars might come, I not only made a supreme effort to regard the indicated direction calmly as the first sprout of the seed I had sown in the absolute, but left no stone unturned to follow up that direction, thereby fulfilling my part. By so doing one circumstance seemed naturally to lead to another, until, step by step, my desired twenty thousand dollars was secured. To keep my mind poised and free from excitement was my greatest effort.

This first concrete fruition of my study of Mental Science as expounded by Troward's book had come by a careful following of the methods he had outlined. In this connection, therefore, I can offer the reader no better gift than to quote Troward's book, "The Edinburgh Lectures," from which may be derived a complete idea of the line of action I was endeavoring to follow. In the chapter on Causes and Conditions he says:

"To get good results we must properly understand our relation to the great impersonal power we are using. It is intelligent, and we are intelligent, and the two intelligences must cooperate. We must not fly in the face of the Law expecting it to do *for* us what it can only do *through* us; and we must therefore use our intelligence with the knowledge that it is acting as *the instrument of a greater intelligence*; and because we have this knowledge we may and should cease from all anxiety as to the final result."

"In actual practice we must first form the ideal conception of our object with the definite intention of impressing it upon the Universal Mind – it is this thought that takes such thought out of

155

the region of mere casual fancies – and then affirm that our knowledge of the Law is sufficient reason for a calm expectation of a corresponding result, and that therefore all necessary conditions will come to us in due order. We can then turn to the affairs of our daily life with the calm assurance that the initial conditions are either there already or will soon come into view. If we do not at once see them, let us rest content with the knowledge that the spiritual prototype is already in existence and wait till some circumstance pointing in the desired direction begins to show itself. It may be a very small circumstance, but it is the direction and not the magnitude which is to be taken into consideration. As soon as we see it we should regard it as the first sprouting of the seed sown in the Absolute, and do calmly, and without excitement, whatever the circumstances seem to require, and then later on we shall see that this doing will in turn lead to a further circumstance in the same direction, until we find ourselves conducted, step by step, to the accomplishment of our object. In this way the understanding of the great principle of the Law of Supply will, by repeated experiences, deliver us more and more completely out of the region of anxious thought and toilsome labor and bring us into a new world where the useful employment of all our powers, whether mental or physical, will only be an unfolding of our individuality upon the lines of its own nature, and therefore a perpetual source of happiness; a sufficient inducement, surely, to the careful study of the laws governing the relation between the individual and the Universal Mind."

To my mind, then as now, this quotation outlines the core and center of the method and manner of approach necessary for coming in touch with Infinite Supply. At least it, together with the previously quoted statement, "My mind is a center of Divine operation," etc., constituted the only apparent means of attracting to myself the twenty thousand dollars. My constant endeavor to get into the spirit of these statements, and to attract to myself this needed sum, was about six weeks, at the end of which time I had in my bank the required twenty thousand dollars. This could be made into a long story, giving all the details, but the facts, as already narrated, will give you a definite idea of the magnetic condition of my mind while the twenty thousand dollars was finding its way to me.

HOW TO BRING THE POWER IN YOUR WORD INTO ACTION

In every word you use there is a power germ which expands and projects itself in the direction your word indicates, and ultimately develops into physical expression. For example, you wish the consciousness of joy. Repeat the word "joy" secretly, persistently and emphatically. The repetition of the word sets up a quality of vibration which causes the joy germ to begin to expand and project itself until your whole being is filled with joy. This is not a mere fancy, but a truth. Once you experience this power, you will daily prove to yourself that these facts have not been fabricated to fit a theory, but the theory has been built up by careful observation of facts. Everyone knows that joy comes from within. No one can give it to you. Another may give you cause for joy, but no one can be joyous for you. Joy is a state of consciousness, and consciousness is purely mental.

Troward says the "Mental faculties always work under something which stimulates them, and this stimulus may come either from without, through the external senses, or from within by the consciousness of something not perceptible on the physical plane. The recognition of this interior source of stimulus enables you to bring into your consciousness any state you desire." Once a thing seems normal to you, it is as surely yours, through the law of growth and attraction, as it is yours to know addition after you have learned the use of figures.

This method of repeating the word makes the word in all of its limitless meaning yours, because words are the embodiment of thoughts, and thought is creative; neither good nor bad, simply creative. This is the reason why Faith builds up and Fear destroys. "Only believe, and all things are possible to you." It is Faith that gives you dominion over every adverse circumstance or condition.

It is your word of Faith that sets you free, not faith in any specific thing or act, but simple Faith in your best self in all ways. It is because of this ever-present Creative Power within the heart of the word that makes your peace of mind and your financial condition a reproduction of your most habitual thought. Try to believe and understand this, and you will find yourself Master of every adverse circumstance or condition for you will become a Prince of Power.

HOW TO INCREASE YOUR FAITH

But, you ask "How can I speak the word of Faith when I have little or no faith?" Every living thing has faith in something or somebody. Faith is that quality of Power which gives the Creative Energy a corresponding vitality and the vitality in the word of Faith you use causes it to take corresponding physical form. Even intense fear is alive with faith.

You fear poverty and loneliness because you *believe* them possible for you. It is the Faith which understands that every creation had its birth in the womb of thought-words that gives you dominion over all things, your lesser self included, and this feeling of faith is increased and intensified through observing what it *does*.

Your constant observation should be of your state of consciousness when you *did; not* when you hoped you might, but feared it was too good to be true. How did you feel that time when you simply had to bring yourself into a better frame of mind and did, or you had to have a certain thing and got it? Live these experiences over again and again (mentally) until you really feel in touch with the self which knows and does, and then the best there is, is yours.

THE REWARD OF INCREASED FAITH

Your desire to be your best has expanded your faith into the faith of the Universe which knows no failure, and has brought you into conscious realization that you are not a victim of the universe, but a part of it. Consequently you are able to recognize that there is that within yourself which is able to make conscious contact with the Universal Law, and enables you to press all the particular laws of Nature, whether visible or invisible, into serving your particular demand or desire. Thereby you find yourself Master, not a slave of any situation. Troward tells us that this Mastering is to be "accomplished by knowledge, and the only knowledge which will afford this purpose in all its measureless immensity is the knowledge of the personal element in universal spirit" and its reciprocity to our own personality.

The words you use are the instruments – channels – through which the creative energy takes form. Naturally, this sensitive Creative Power can only reproduce in accordance with the instrument through which it passes. All disappointments and failures are the result of endeavoring to think one thing and produce another. This is just as impossible as it would be for an electric fan to be used for lighting purposes, or for water to flow through a crooked pipe in a straight line. The water must take the shape of the pipe through which it flows. Even more truly this sensitive, invisible, Substance must reproduce outwardly the shape of the thought-word through which it passes. Hence, when your thought or word-form is in correspondence with the Eternal constructive and forward movement of the Universal Law, then your mind is the mirror in which the Infinite Power and Intelligence of the Universe sees itself reproduced, and your individual life becomes one of harmony.

HOW TO MAKE NATURE RESPOND TO YOU

It should be steadily borne in mind that there is an Intelligence and Power in all Nature and all space which is always creative and infinitely sensitive and responsive. The responsiveness of its nature is twofold: it is creative and amenable to suggestion. Once the human understanding grasps this all important fact, it realizes the simplicity with which the law of life supplies your every demand. All that is necessary is to realize that your mind is a center of Divine operation, and consequently contains that within itself which accepts suggestions, and expect all life to respond to your call. Then you will find suggestions which tend to the fulfillment of your desire coming to you, not only from your fellowmen, but also from the flowers, the grass, the trees and the rocks which will enable you to fulfill your heart's desire, if you act upon them in confidence on this physical plane.

FAITH WITH WORKS – WHAT IT HAS ACCOMPLISHED

It is said of Tyson, the great Australian millionaire, that the suggestion to "make the desert land of Australia blossom as the rose" came to him from a modest little Australian violet while he was working as a bushman for something like three shilling a day. He used to find these friendly little violets growing in certain places in the woods, and something in the flower touched something akin to itself in the mind of Tyson. He would sit on the side of his bunk at night and wonder how flowers and vegetable life could be given an opportunity to express themselves in the desert land of Australia. No doubt he realized that it would take a long time to save enough money to put irrigating ditches in the desert lands, but his thought and feeling assured him it could be accomplished, and if it could be done, he could do it. If there was a power within himself which was able to capture the idea, then there must be a responsive power within the idea itself which could bring itself into a practical physical manifestation. He resolutely put aside all questions as to the specific ways and means which would be employed in bringing his desire into physical manifestation, and simply kept his thought centered upon the idea of making fences and seeing flowers and grass where none existed at that time. Since the responsiveness of Reproductive Creative Power is not limited to any local condition of mind, his habitual meditation and mental picture set his ideas free to roam in an infinitude, and attract to themselves other ideas of a kindred nature. Therefore, it was not necessary for Tyson to wait until he had saved from his three shilling a day enough money to irrigate the land, to see his ideas fulfilled, for his ideas found other ideas in the financial world which were attuned in sympathy with themselves, and doors of finance were quickly opened.

All charitable institutions are maintained upon the principle of the responsiveness of life. If this were not true, no one would care to give, simply because another needed. The law of demand and supply, cause and effect, can never be broken. Ideas attract to themselves kindred ideas. *Sometimes* they come from a flower, a book or out of the invisible. You are intent upon an idea not quite complete as to the ways and means of fulfillment, and behold along comes *another* idea, from no one can tell where, and finds friendly lodging with your idea; one idea attracting another, and so on until your desires are physical facts.

You may feel the necessity for an improvement in your finances, and wonder how this increase is to be brought about, when there seems suddenly to come from within the idea itself that everything had its birth in thought, even money, and your thoughts turn their course. You simply hold to the statement or affirmation that the best, and all there is, is yours. Since you are able to capture ideas from the Infinite through the instrument of your intuition, you let your mind rest upon that thought *knowing* full well that this very thought will respond to itself. Your inhibition of all doubt and anxiety enables the reassuring ideas to establish themselves and attract to themselves "I can" and "I will" ideas, which gradually grow into the physical form of the desire in your mind.

In the conscious uses of the Universal Power to reproduce your desires in physical form, three facts should be borne in mind:

First – All space is filled with a Creative Power.

Second – This Creative Power is amenable to suggestion.

Third – It can only work by deductive methods.

As Troward tells us, this last is an exceedingly important point, for it implies that the action of the ever-present Creative Power is in no way limited by precedent. It works according to the essence of the spirit of the principle. In other words, this Universal Power takes its creative direction from the word you give it.

Troward says, "If you think your thought is Powerful, your Thought *is* Powerful."

Only the reproductive Creative Spirit of Life knows what you think until your thoughts become physical facts and manifest themselves in your body, your brain or your affairs.

Suggestions as to How to Pray or Ask,
believing you have already received:

SCIENTIFIC THINKING – POSITIVE THOUGHT

Suggestions for Practical Application

Try, through careful, positive, enthusiastic (though not strenuous) thought, to realize that the indescribable, Invisible Substance of Life fills all space; that its nature is Intelligent, Undifferentiated Substance.

Rise every morning at five o'clock, sit in a quiet room in a straight-backed chair, and think out the affirmation of the previous evening, and you will realize and be able to put into practice your Princely Power with the realization to some extent, at least, that your mind *really* is a center through which all the Creative Energy and Power there is, is taking form.

THE PRINCIPLE UNDERLYING SCIENTIFIC PRAYER

In prayer for a change in condition; physical, mental or financial for yourself or another, bear in mind that the fundamental necessity for the answer to prayer is the understanding of the scientific statement:

"Ask, believing you have already received, and you shall receive."

This is not as difficult as it appears on the surface, once you realize that:

Everything has its origin in the mind, and that which you seek outwardly, you already possess. No one can think a thought in the future. Your thought of a thing constitutes its origin.

Therefore:

The Thought Form of the Thing is Already Yours As soon as you think it.

Your steady recognition of this Thought Possession causes the thought to concentrate, to condense, to project itself and to assume physical form.

Items to be remembered about Prayer for Yourself or Another

Remember that that which you call treatment or prayer is not, in any sense, hypnotism. It should never be your endeavor to take possession of the mind of another.

Remember that it should never be your intention to make yourself believe that which you know to be untrue.

First Cause has endowed every man with the Power and Ability to bring into his personal environment whatever he chooses.

Cause and Effect in reference to Getting

If you plant an Acorn, you get an Oak. If you sow a grain of Corn, you reap a stalk and many kernels of Corn.

You always get the manifestation of that which you consciously or unconsciously *affirm* and *claim*, habitually declare and expect, or in other words *"As you sow."*

Therefore, sow the seeds of *I am...I ought to do...I can do...I will do.*

Realize that because you *are* you *ought* to do; that because you *ought* to, you *can* do; that because you *can* do, you *do* do.

The manifestation of this Truth, even in a small degree, gives you the undisputable understanding that *dominion is your charter right.*

All is yours, and you know that all you have to do is to *reach out your mental hand* and take it.

Intensify your thought by meditating upon the fact that there is that in you which finds the way, which is the Truth and is the Life.

Prayer as a method of thought is a deliberate use of the Law which gives you the Power of Dominion over everything which tends in any way to hamper your perfect liberty.

You have been given life that you may enjoy it more and more fully.

The steady recognition of this Truth makes you declare yourself a *Prince of Power.*

The work must be perfectly done. Your mind is a center of divine operation.

Hints for application and Practice

For every five minutes given to reading and study of the theories of Mental Science, spend fifteen minutes in the use and application of the knowledge acquired.

1. Spend one minute in every twenty-four hours to conscientiously thinking over the specification that must be observed in order to have your prayers answered.

2. Practice the steady recognition of desirable thought possession for two periods of fifteen minutes each, every day. Not only time yourself each period to see how long you can keep a given conception before your mental vision, but also keep a written record of the vividness with which you experience your mental image. Remember that your mental senses are just as varied and trainable as your physical ones.

3. Spend five minutes every day between 12 noon and 1 o'clock with a mental research for new sources of wealth.

THINGS TO REMEMBER

All that is really worthwhile is contentment. Self-command alone can produce it.

Absolute dominion is yours when you have sufficient self mastery to conquer the negative tendency of thoughts and actions.

Ask yourself daily:

"What is the purpose of the Power which put me here?"

"How can I work with the purpose for life and liberty in me?"

After having decided these questions, endeavor hourly to fulfill them. You are a law unto yourself.

If you have a tendency to overdo *anything*; eat, drink, or blame circumstances for your misfortunes, conquer that tendency with the inward conviction that *all power* is yours. Eat less, drink less, blame circumstances less, and the best there is will gradually grow in the place where the worst seemed to be.

Always remember that *all* is yours to use as you will.

You can if you *will*: if you *will* you do.

The reason for greater success when you first began your studies and demonstrations in Mental Science was your joy and enthusiasm at the simple discovery of Power within which was greater than you were able to put into your understanding later. With increased understanding, comes increasing joy and enthusiasm, and the results will correspond.

V

RICHARD INGALESE

The following quotes are from
The History and Power of Mind, 1923

MEDITATION, CREATION AND CONCENTRATION

Thought is the product of mind; it is a rate of vibration sent forth from mind, and therefore is force. This thought force is continually being used or misused, because to live is to think, either rightly or wrongly, with the objective or subjective mind. Thought, per se, is neither good nor bad, but, like any other force, the use of it determines its character.

Thought has one chief characteristic, I might almost say but one characteristic, and that is vibration. From this standpoint we may divide thought into two general classes, that of the positive and negative. Positive thought is a high rate of vibration sent forth from the mind, and negative thought is a low rate of vibration.

The will is the positive side of the subjective mind, and corresponds to the desire or the positive side of the objective mind. The will plays a very important part in human affairs, whether it becomes active in the subjective mind as will power, or whether it operates in the objective mind as desire. In connection with thought the will has three functions:

First, it determines the nature of the thought sent forth from the mind, whether it be constructive or destructive.

Second, will determines the intensity of the thought, whether it shall vibrate at a high rate and travel with great rapidity, or whether it shall proceed at a low rate, and reach but a short distance. In other words, the will determines whether the thought shall be positive or negative.

Third, will determines the direction of thought; that is, the person, place or thing to which it shall be sent and how long it shall remain in each place.

Knowing the functions of this tremendous force, which in its higher aspects is latent in most persons, you can see how essential it is that it should be awakened; for, like the muscles of the body, will grows stronger with use. It is left with each of us to determine whether we shall remain infirm of purpose and weak in will, or awaken, and arouse this force and use it for our upbuilding.

The first mental mode to cultivate in order that the mind may draw to itself whatever it desires is Philosophical Meditation. (I use the word philosophical as qualifying this state of mind, because there are various other modes of so-called meditation.)

In order to understand more fully the elements which compose this kind of meditation, we will analyze them. The first condition of mind is a receptive one. In using the word "receptive" I do not mean negative. Never, under any circumstances, permit yourself to be in a negative condition, because the moment you become negative you become subject to malevolent subjective entities and influences which may control or obsess you and perhaps dominate your mind throughout this life.

If there is one idea that will be emphasized more than another during this course of lectures it will be the necessity of being mentally positive.

A receptive condition of mind is the same mental condition that you are now in. A quiet, listening, expectant attitude; not intense but waiting, giving positive attention to what I am saying while your bodies are in a relaxed but comfortable position. No one could control any mind in this room at this moment because each one is positive and is in an active instead of a passive condition.

Having placed yourself in this receptive condition you desire to receive knowledge. Knowledge is the second element in our definition, and is all that you can receive through meditation; since qualities or things are brought through other modes of mind.

Now direct your demand or prayer to the Universal Consciousness – not to an individual, for there must be no intermediary.

You go into meditation for the purpose of receiving knowledge from the highest source of knowledge, and this is the third element in our definition.

It may seem that your demand or prayer has gone into space somewhere to diffuse itself throughout the great Consciousness. It may be of help to you to consider the Universal Consciousness as another individual mind near you that you may speak to as you would to another person. Or better still, you may picture it as a golden sun or center of vibrating light within your own heart – for the heart center is one of the chief points of contact between the individual and the Universal Mind.

I wish to impress upon your mind the thought of your nearness to this Universal Consciousness.

You should take the great Consciousness into every thought and act of life; whisper to It in the darkness of the night and It will hear and answer you. See It in a mental picture of golden yellow light and It will fill your body with Its uplifting vibrations. Depend upon It, instead of persons and things, to bring you what you need and your demands will never fail to be met.

There are two reasons why your demands should be made of the Universal Consciousness. First, because if you do not address your demands to the Highest your objective mind will immediately assert itself and assume the responsibility of answering you.

Nothing but perfect self-control will ever fully prevent the attempted intervention by the objective mind.

The second reason for addressing your demand to the Supreme Consciousness, as if it were another mind, is that you thereby have a tendency to cut off communication with all other individual minds who are thinking along the same general line with yourself; otherwise you may get into a current of thought and be as likely to get wrong thoughts as right ones.

Many persons "go into the silence," or try to meditate by sitting and waiting for any thought to come to them. In this way they receive any impressions that may sweep into their minds, believing such impressions are Divine Inspiration. But all this is not Philosophical Meditation and cannot possibly bring the good you desire. The proper way to meditate is to get your subject before going into meditation and then ask for knowledge concerning it and wait patiently for your impression. It is absolutely necessary that you should have a concrete subject because concreteness is the secret of success along mental as well as along all other lines. The subject for meditation may be anything concerning which you desire knowledge. It may be knowledge pertaining to any plane of being, the Spiritual, Mental, or Physical; but it must be concrete.

The majority of persons do not think, they merely dream. You often hear the remark, "A penny for your thoughts," and the reply usually comes, "Why, really I don't know what I was thinking about." People think they think, but in point of fact they jump from subject to subject as a bird flits from one limb of a tree to another. There is no logical sequence to their thought, there is no continuity. Many persons think of words, not of concepts or of concrete mental things; and this is sometimes true even with persons who are called scientific. What concept do most persons have of Love, Force, Mind, Thought? If these words mean anything then these are things.

It is possible to have thoughts without words and this kind of thinking is mental picture making, or concrete thought, which is the real, creative thought. Your careless thinking has very little or no results, while your concrete thoughts have absolute, mathematical results.

Returning to the subject of meditation we should first consider the best time for this practice, for in the beginning it is better to have a definite time set apart for it – after a while you will be able to meditate at any time or place. The early morning hours are the best for meditation because at that time great forces of nature are sweeping through you and through that part of the world where the sun is beginning to shine. At that time all your own magnetic forces have been drawn back to you during the previous sleep and you have not as yet been drawn into the world's thought.

When you demand knowledge from the Universal Consciousness there go forth from you, according to the intensity of your thought, many little magnetic lines into the ether. These lines look like blue rays of light and connect you with the person or thing which will be the best instrument to answer your demand. Sometimes this instrument is another ego who consciously through telepathy sends you an answer to your question.

It is true the answer does not always come immediately after the demand is made, and you may continue to demand for a day, a week or a month before it comes. The concreteness and intensity of your thought determine the promptness of the response. And if there should be a delay it will be through no fault of the Universal Consciousness or of the law of supply and demand, any more than an error in your calculations would prove wrong a rule in mathematics. The fault will be in yourself; because you do not think clearly enough or hold your thought picture sufficiently long. If you will persistently follow the rules given in this lecture, your impressions will always come in time for you to use them.

Here are some rules which may help you in your work:

First, mistrust all *immediate* answers; because the chances are that when your reply comes at once, your objective mind is speaking to you.

Second, examine the answer closely when it comes in the form of words, and consider it well because the objective mind invariably expresses itself in words and sometimes in a long dissertation. The Universal Consciousness usually conveys the answer to your mind in an impression or conviction.

Third, test the answer by your reason until your intuition has become fully awakened and can tell you where the answer came from. For example, suppose you ask if it is best for you to do a certain thing and the answer comes back "yes," and shocks your sense of justice or of truth, of expediency or of probability. Sit in judgment upon it with your reason until your intuition is awakened and do not act hastily.

The second mode of mind is Creation. Thought creation is the imaging or putting into concrete form a selected subject. By concrete form is meant a mental picture of the selected subject invested with all the qualities of that subject in its natural state. Mental creation will bring you any quality or any thing you want, except knowledge, which comes through meditation. Imagination is not fancy; it is the image-making faculty which is used for the purpose of making a concrete picture of the thing we desire. Do you want love? What is love? If you are going to create a thing you must have a concrete picture of it. Love is a force. Being a force it must have a rate of vibration, and having a rate of vibration it must have a color. Therefore when you picture love you must picture it according to your highest conception of what that force would be, and the color of the highest force upon this planet is yellow.

If it is Divine love you want, see yourself standing in a flood of this golden vibrating force; see It bathing you in Its rays, penetrating every part and particle of your being till your body and you vibrate in response to It, and until the atmosphere around you pulsates and throbs with Its golden glow. If you desire to send love to another, picture the Universal Love flowing into yourself and then see it passing from your heart's center as a golden stream flowing outward till it reaches the heart to which it is sent. Some of your own being will enter and warm the heart of the one to whom you send that love force, and you will have the joy that comes through loving and being loved. If you wish to demonstrate love from another, see that golden current of force flowing from that other person to you.

If you wish to work upon the mental plane, if you wish to demand a greater mentality, picture the blue Cosmic Force flowing into you. Picture yourself as suffused with this blue force until your whole being vibrates with it. Let it magnetize your brain and thrill you through and through with its uplifting force. After a demonstration of this kind you will feel capable of accomplishing any mental undertaking. Do not deceive yourself into the belief that one treatment with this blue Cosmic Force will make of you a genius, because it will not. But constant treatments of this kind will gradually increase your mental power, which you can direct into any channel you desire, and the picture you make creates the center or matrix into which the Universal Consciousness can bring that which you demand.

On the material plane the same picture-making faculty is used. Do you want to build up a fine law practice? Then picture your clients coming in large numbers to your office, engaging your services and paying you liberally – this last part of the picture is an essential portion of the whole. Do you wish to develop a business? Then see crowds of people coming and waiting for you to serve them. But good, bad and indifferent business will come unless you limit your creation to a certain class; then that kind or class of business which you have created will come.

But while you are waiting for your creations to materialize, for your demands to be met, you should do cheerfully and faithfully such duties as are presented to you to do. In this way you will cooperate with the Supreme because you will never know till a duty is done what good may come to you from doing that duty well.

Do you want money? Then make a concrete picture of the amount you want – say a one hundred dollar bill; or if you do not want your money all of one denomination picture a sufficient number of bills, of the denomination you want, to make the amount you desire. But in any event make a picture of a definite amount and after making it, hold to it till it stands out as distinct as though it had materialized and you could see it before you. Then say to the Universal Consciousness, "Give me this creation," and repeat this demand day after day and many times a day if you want to. You can do this instead of dreaming or reading the signs in the street cars, etc. The concreteness of your picture makes your creation a mental reality and the more tenaciously you hold to the mental creation the sooner will the material reality come. Creative thought is always in pictures.

Everything that is, existed first on the mental plane, even to the clothes you wear and the chair you sit on.

Let us further examine the working of the law, and we'll take for example the concrete picture of a bundle of money – one hundred dollars. You have made a mental picture or image of this creation and now you are sending your force, which is simply thought vibrations, into that picture until it becomes clearly defined in the ether which surrounds your own aura. The clearness of your thought and the intensity of your picture make a photograph, as it were, in the Universal Mind, and this is your matrix or plan. If the matrix of your thumb nail should be destroyed you could never have another thumb nail in this life, but so long as the matrix is there, although the nail may be for the time being destroyed, another will grow.

And so it is with your mental matrix, so long as it is not destroyed it will sometime draw to you the material thing pictured. The constant or frequent vibration which your thought causes, sets the Universal Consciousness surrounding you and your picture into action. Then out from you goes the small magnetic cord which the Universal Consciousness directs to the sum of money you have demanded. This money is somewhere upon the material plane when you make your demand for it, and the Universal Consciousness directs your demand, with its tiny magnetic cord attached, to this amount of money. It is no affair of yours where this one hundred dollars shall come from. The avenue through which it may come is for the Universal Consciousness to select, and, being Justice, It will bring it from the source whence it should come, and no one will be unjustly treated by the transference of it to your possession.

At this point of our evolution we create mental pictures of things already in existence and draw them to us according to the operation of the law I have just explained. But the time will come in our development when we can imagine a thing and have the power to draw together the particles necessary to its composition, and create the thing itself. This power is called precipitation, and is really the highest form of creation.

Mental Concentration is the third mode of mind. It is not in its nature creative, but it is the direction of force which hastens the materialization of creations. Concentration is holding the mind on one subject to the exclusion of every other subject. Here, again, you must have a specific subject to concentrate upon, and it may be any quality, thought or thing. This mode of mind is perhaps the most forceful of the three modes mentioned in this lecture. It is therefore always an active, positive condition of mind. The habit of concentration is not acquired in a short time, but is a matter of growth, a matter of practice. You will be surprised to know that the average person cannot – or does not, perhaps I should say – hold his mind for ten consecutive seconds on one subject.

For example, take this creation we last selected, the bundle of money. Try to hold your mind on that one hundred dollar creation for a moment. After a few seconds you begin to wonder whether that creation is really coming, and then you bring your mind back to your subject, and look at that mental picture for another couple of seconds. Then you suddenly remember that there is a magnetic cord attached to each demand that goes forth from you, and you wonder if that magnetic cord is all right; then you try to see the cord and the first thing you know you have lost sight of the money, and are creating a magnetic cord attachment to your demand. Suddenly you become conscious that your mind is wandering and you wonder if you are concentrating right; and thus your thoughts skip from one thing to another and you learn by experience that concentration is gained only by patient and constant practice.

Some suggestions may be helpful to you in acquiring this art of concentration and making it a habit of thought. Select an hour in the morning, or take a part of the same hour that you give to meditation; give the first ten or twenty minutes to meditation and the remainder of the time to concentration. If this practice is persisted in for several days in succession you will find your concentration becoming easier, because the law of periodicity will be operating with you; and the impetus thus given to concentration soon makes the practice a habit of mind.

Look at your mental creation quietly, but intensely. Think of the picture – say the money – for about twenty minutes. Concentration means looking at your picture. It is not very hard work to sit and look at one hundred dollars; indeed, it can be made a very pleasant thing to do, if you realize that it is yours. Concentration should always be a pleasant exercise of will, a quiet but positive condition of mind. Let the mind rest entirely upon your mental picture and claim it by saying or thinking "that is mine, because I have created it."

Many persons make hard work of trying to concentrate. This is a mistaken waste of physical force. When you see a pretty flower and look at it admiringly, you are thinking of that flower and are concentrating upon it, because for the moment you are thinking of it to the exclusion of everything else. When you go to the theater, and become absorbed by the acting, you are concentrating upon the acting. With most persons, in trying to concentrate, the tendency is to imagine that they are placing themselves in a false or unnatural condition of mind; they feel that they are going to do something they have never done before, or something they are not accustomed to do. Perhaps they will shut their teeth together, and whisper tragically, "Now I am going to concentrate," and then, with clenched fists and corrugated brows, they knot their muscles till the perspiration starts, and the breath comes hard and fast. Dismiss the mistaken idea, for that is an artificial condition of mind. Concentration is not a fiery ordeal; it is a natural and a pleasant recreation, or should be.

Put your body in an easy position, and whenever your attention is attracted to your body you may know it is getting tense; then relax and forget about it, because all your force is needed in looking at your picture.

You may believe these principles, but you will never know them until you demonstrate them for yourself. If you persist in practicing the rules given, you can draw to yourselves anything you care to picture. If you desire success, social position, any spiritual, mental or physical thing, it can be gained by simply creating and holding the picture in your mind.

If you misuse your powers or direct your forces to the detriment of another, you must take the consequences and these are very direful, because the law of Justice acts much more quickly upon persons who consciously misuse mental forces than upon those who do wrong in a half conscious manner.

It is always well to meditate before you create a thing. So many persons are continually creating and demanding things they do not really want. Ask the Supreme Consciousness, whatever you choose to call the Great Source, if there is any reason why you should not have the thing you desire.

THE LAW OF OPULENCE

A great mistake most people make is in limiting the meaning of the word "work" to purely physical labor. Work does not necessarily mean physical effort. Man is mind, and mental strength and growth can come only through the exercise of his mental powers.

Last year when these lectures were first delivered several persons said, "It is very wrong to teach that you can draw material things to yourself by the use of mental forces; you should teach that people must work for what they get."

It is obvious that these cautious souls have not developed beyond the physical plane and are unable to appreciate the fact that there may be mental as well as physical labor. Then there are other persons who do not desire to use Spiritual forces to draw to themselves material things and therefore protest against teaching this knowledge. It is quite reasonable to suppose that such persons find it difficult to manipulate spiritual forces and because they do not understand how to use them, they object to others using them. To such persons I have nothing to offer except good wishes for their progress along the lines of development they have chosen.

Man's evolution has enlarged the meaning of the word "work," and we now say, "In the sweat of thy face or through mental effort shalt thou earn bread." Employers, capitalists, and thinkers plan day after day and work very hard mentally, yet many of them never raise a hand to do physical labor, but leave that part of the work to be done by those persons who still believe they must earn bread in the sweat of their faces.

There are three classes of workers; first, the physical workers; second, the physico-mental workers; and the third, or purely mental workers, and each of these classes marks a period of human evolution. By purely physical workers I mean the hewers of wood and the drawers of water – the mass of humanity. The physico-mental workers are those who, while recognizing that the laws of mind have a wonderful power to aid a man in his development and resources, use their minds for planning and enlarging their work and drawing Opulence to themselves and yet use physical means also for the purpose of manifesting it. The third class embraces all who are purely mental workers, those who have learned to use their minds along all lines and who use mental forces so fully and so completely that they receive whatever they desire without manual labor of any kind. These are conscious users of what is commonly called the Law of Opulence or the law which brings opulence. Some students call this the law of Demand and Supply. It really does not matter what it is called, it operates as unfailingly on the plane of mind as it does in the realm of economics.

Each person places himself in one of these three classes of workers, according to his evolutionary development. In the first mentioned class the law of opulence never manifests. Those who only work physically and individually can never acquire opulence. They earn a living, plus a little more than an actual living and that is all. The law of opulence commences to manifest in the second class, the physico-mental workers, and passes by slow gradation up through it to the third class where it manifests in its fullness. Every person in the course of his evolutionary career must pass through each of these three classes, and most persons who have reached our point of development are in the second class. This class is working with the laws of nature consciously while having a center through which to draw opulence. By a "center" I mean a certain definite vocation or avocation through which money comes. For example, suppose you have a small business – a news-stand perhaps. You have learned that there is such a thing as the law of mental demand and supply and you desire to use this law for your financial betterment.

The small business is your center, and having a center you wish to enlarge it. You make a mental picture of a larger business and see yourself with a cigar and news-stand combined. You continue to look at that picture day after day and mentally demand that it shall be yours. If you never destroy your picture, in the course of time your demand will be met and the ways and means will be provided for you to get what you want.

Or perhaps you do not wish to have a news-stand. You may be engaged in another kind of business and are working for a salary. Perhaps you would like an advancement in your salary and a better position. Then you should make a mental picture of yourself occupying the position you want and drawing the salary you require, and by using this position for your center you will work upward and onward to any height you desire.

If we do not like our occupation, there is no reason why we should continue to work at it forever; but we should hold the thought that we shall use it only for the present until we can draw to ourselves a better and higher one. Faith in the law and the power of mind enables us to demonstrate over adverse financial conditions and make them what we desire.

A master of this art, whom I knew, was once a newsboy. Born of poor parents in one of the poorest quarters of Paris, he lived like all other children of his class in great destitution. His father and mother were rag-pickers and lived in a cellar. One day when he had reached the age of eighteen or twenty years a great Soul came into his life, and after engaging the boy to do some work for him became interested in his welfare, and commenced to teach him something about the power of mind. He also gave him a manuscript and told him to study and practice the teachings he would find therein.

The boy took the manuscript home and spent his last penny for a candle to give him light while he read about the Law of Demand and Supply; and as he read he began to believe that he could use this law to help himself out of his wretched condition. Looking around the tiny place which he called his bedroom, with its bare walls and stone floor, he said: "I shall commence now to create opulence for myself and the first thing I need to make me comfortable is a piece of carpet three feet long, that I can stand on while dressing when I get out of bed on cold mornings." He made the mental picture of the carpet and held steadily to his creation. After a while a piece of new carpet was given him by a woman whom he had served and from the moment his first demonstration was made, his faith in the law never wavered. He became a master at making demonstrations and when I first met him was possessed of a great many hundred thousand dollars.

Faith in something we cannot understand is hard to acquire and rarely amounts to anything more than a hope; but faith based upon immutable law grows to be knowledge. The small demonstrations made in the beginning of our work with the law are often the most important, because they prove to us that we have the power to put the law into operation.

In the class of the physico-mental workers we find the progressive student increasing his center and also attempting to make demonstrations independently of it. Such persons have made a marked advance in their evolutionary progress. For example, let us take the attorney who knows how to use the law of demand. He says, "I want a good law practice," and pictures clients coming in large numbers into his office. After a time the clients come as he has pictured, and then he begins to make a distinction between them. He says: "I want to represent only those whose cases I can win," and in this way he works for the mutual benefit of all who are interested. Then he begins to create things separate and distinct from his law practice.

He wishes to go to Congress, perhaps, and makes a picture of himself representing his district at the Capitol, and after holding the picture for a while and earnestly making his demands that it shall come to him, an opportunity will be given and his pictures will materialize, because the law has been put into operation by his power of mind.

In the third class are those individuals who are able to draw to themselves whatever they desire irrespective of any center. Constant practice has made these persons skilled operators of the law and with them faith has grown into absolute knowledge. When a person has reached this point in his development he may go out of business and go wherever he desires because he can draw to himself anything he wants at any time or in any place he may happen to be. Many students pass through the second stage, that of the physico-mental workers, very slowly. A few pass rapidly since some have more faith than others.

To put this law of opulence into operation it is necessary to realize three things:

First: That everything you want exists now in Divine Mind. Do you want jewels, gold, silver? They are all in the market; besides, there are in the mines as yet undiscovered all these things in great abundance. All these things exist and you can put into operation the law which will bring them to you. The history of the world shows that every mental demand of man has been met. Man grew tired of walking and carrying things and the cumbersome ox cart was evolved to supply his needs. But he was not satisfied with this crude vehicle and demanded something better. Then came the horse and a lighter wagon, and after that came steam cars, bicycles, and automobiles; and still man is not satisfied; he wishes to fly and flying machines are in the process of evolution. By degrees, from the boat made by burning out the center of an old log, has the modern steam yacht been evolved, and from the slow, tedious process of sending verbal messages by footman from place to place has been evolved the wireless telegraph.

There is no lack of anything in the world; and there should be no envy or jealousy between men, because there is enough of everything for everyone who lives.

Second: Realize that all things belong to Deity and that you can only have a temporary use of them. We should not be so vainglorious as to think we own anything. We came into the world destitute of everything and go out of it with nothing except character – and some even go without that. While we remain here we may borrow of Deity something or nothing according to our manner of thinking.

Third: We should realize that all things are distributed by the Universal Consciousness according to law. One man is not poverty-stricken and another man a millionaire by chance, fatalism or caprice; but everything is distributed according to the law of mental demand, or of asking and receiving.

Everyone who stops to think knows that the successful man of business has always been, is, and always will be, the man who can demand – i.e. make a positive picture of what he desires. If you want anything, create it mentally, demand it and according to your faith be it unto you.

There are certain rules whereby you may hasten your creations whether you work with or without a center, and your experiences will demonstrate the accuracy of the rules:

Rule First: Meditate and ask Deity if there is any reason why you should not have the thing you desire to create.

This removes all uncertainty from your mind about the advisability of creating it. Uncertainty produces a negative condition, disturbs your aura and therefore delays the materialization of your creations.

When you have received the answer from the Universal Consciousness that it is right and proper for you to have the thing that you desire, you are then in a positive condition of mind and can forcefully put the law into operation.

Rule Second: Having decided to create something make your mental picture of it and demand it unfalteringly until it comes.

Rule Three: A positive demand accomplishes more and better results than a request or a petition.

The mental attitude while making a demand should always be reverential but very positive.

Rule Four: Demand specifically what you want.

Every word of this rule is important. First you must make a demand. Then that demand must be specific. Make your mental picture clear-cut. The clearer your picture the sooner will it materialize. Demand specifically what you want – not what someone else wants you to have, not what you think you ought to have, not what you believe it your duty to want – but what you, yourself, wish to have.

The converse of this rule is equally important. Never demand what you do not want. If you want money do not demand work, but always be ready and willing to work for it – if necessary. Almost everyone in the beginning makes the mistake of demanding what he does not want, because it is difficult to break the customs of many years. Unpleasant environment is the result of demands we have made in the past for things we do not want now.

This rule is very likely to be misunderstood even by some metaphysicians. A local teacher of metaphysics who heard this rule given in last year's lectures said it was misleading; that if a person had a drug store, for instance, and wanted money, he should demand patrons because they would bring money.

To an Occultist this is strange logic. The druggist might have a thousand patrons and sell his entire stock. If all his customers bought goods on credit and neglected to pay for them afterwards, his desire for money would not be fulfilled although his demand for patrons had been fully met. It is best to demand the specific thing you want and then you will make no mistakes.

A member of last year's class who thought she understood this rule, said to me several weeks after the lecture course ended that she had created a trip to Europe. When I asked her to describe her mental picture she said, "Oh, I just created a one thousand dollar bill which I shall use for my trip." She had not created a trip to Europe, but had created the money to pay for one. This was not surety of her getting the trip, because when the money came an infinite number of things might occur to prevent her going. She should have created the picture of herself on board ship crossing the ocean; and should have seen herself landing safe and well on the other side.

Rule Fifth: Demand only when your desire is strong.

When you feel the need of a thing your desire for it is strongest. Many students begin enthusiastically to make their demands, but soon grow lukewarm. A good way to intensify your desires is to think of the pleasure the possession of the thing would give you, and when the desire for it comes sweeping over you then make your demand for it. Do not demand because the hour set apart for demanding has come, or because you regard it as a duty you have assumed. Demands made under such conditions amount to nothing, and the time put to work of that kind is wasted.

Rule Sixth: Mind works best when the body is still.

If you are drumming with your fingers or swinging your feet while making demands, a part of your mental force goes into the physical motions you are making; and your forces being divided the mental work is robbed of much of its power.

You should conserve your force. At intervals during the day you may think of your demands and you can hold them subconsciously in mind much of the time; and while this kind of picture making does not accomplish as much as when the body is at rest, yet it does have an effect.

Rule Seventh: Never demand when excited.

You may have a strong desire but no excitement. A demand made during intense excitement is always met forcefully. This is an important rule, the observance of which may save you much inconvenience. We are quite likely to become impatient at times and are often tempted to make violent demands. It is a dangerous thing to do, as I shall show you in an illustration.

There was a student of Occultism in this city who had met with several misfortunes. Disasters followed each other till everything he had on the material plane was swept away. But he was possessed of a great deal of force, and knowing how to make demands for what he wanted, he commenced making new creations. He demanded ten thousand dollars, which to him was financial opulence. The demand was not met immediately, and the young man became impatient and finally angry. And when he wakened one morning to find himself without money enough to pay for his breakfast, he walked to the park, threw himself upon the ground and lay there for several hours with his teeth set, hands clenched and with the perspiration standing out all over his body, so intense was his excitement while making his demand for the money he had pictured. The next day he boarded a freight train and, after the usual delays and inconveniences attending upon transportation of that kind, the student of Occultism managed to reach a Western town. But he had no sooner entered that place than a cyclone came along and swept it off the face of the earth. When the young man of violent demands came to consciousness he was lying on the ground some distance from the place where he was at the last moment of his recollection.

His body was a mass of bruises, and when he tried to rise to his feet he found one leg broken. Bodies of dead animals and men lay all around him, and wagonloads of debris were strewn in all directions; but just within reach of his arm lay a plethoric leather wallet. The young man reached his best arm out and got the wallet and immediately examined its contents. There were just ten one thousand dollar bills in it and not a scrap of paper or a card to tell to whom it belonged. He placed his prize in the pocket of his ragged coat and crept on his hands and knees for some distance till someone came to his relief. He was cared for and finally got well. The owner of the money could not be found, and the young man kept it as an answer to his violent demand, which so nearly cost him his life.

Please do not misunderstand me to say that the young Occult student's violent demand created the cyclone, because it had nothing to do with its creation. But the student was drawn into the cyclone, and suffered the horrors of it, because of his own tempestuous mental condition when making a demand, which had to be met after the manner that it was made.

Rule Eighth: Always be deliberate and quiet but positive when demanding.

Never demand in a hurry. Mental perturbation engendered by hurry, delays the materialization of your creation.

Rule Ninth: Avoid speculating on the time when, or on the way in which, your demonstrations will be made.

When you begin speculating about the ways and means by which your demonstrations will come, immediately your force becomes scattered or divided and a repellent expectancy arises. There is an expectancy that draws and also one that repels. The quiet expectancy, such as is used in meditation, is helpful in drawing to you whatever you have demanded.

But the impatient expectancy of the objective mind is repellent, because it causes your aura to become disturbed and then nothing you want can reach you.

For example: You have made a demand and have commenced to wonder through whom that demand will be met. Your objective mind suggests Mr. Blank as the most probable person, and if you accept the suggestion when you meet Mr. Blank you are not mentally poised because of your impatient expectancy. Mr. Blank feels your mental condition and if he were inclined to form a business connection with you he would hesitate and become uncertain because of your perturbed condition; thus the ways and means that you expected to bring your demonstration would not be used because of your repellent expectancy.

Rule Tenth: Anger, discontent, envy and lack of self-control repel and delay a demonstration.

If you make a mental picture of a thing and hold it for a time it will materialize, but it will be delayed if you indulge in any of the mental attitudes just mentioned; because any of these puts your aura into a perturbed condition, which is repellent. Divine Mind may be likened to the ocean which is bearing a boat laden with your creations to you who are standing upon the shore. If you are perturbed your mind acts upon Divine Mind as the wind off shore acts upon the ocean. It is forever driving back the craft in which are the things you desire.

This rule is one of the hardest to observe, but like anything else it can be followed. It is the disregard of this rule which leads investigators and beginners to disbelieve in the law or power of mind, and which makes so many students finally abandon in despair their efforts to use the forces of nature. But if we do not use nature's forces then we shall be used by them.

Rule Eleventh: The earnestness with which a demand is made, the frequency with which it is made and the persistency with which the mental image is consciously held in mind hasten the demonstration.

Rule Twelve: The realization that you are using an immutable law hastens your demonstrations.

Claim it. You know your demand has been met on the mental plane, and since it is law that you are using, it is yours as much before it has materialized as it will be afterward.
This declaration gives you a positive realization of possession which has a tendency to bring more quickly your creations and removes anxiety and perturbation from your mind. If this lecture on opulence has been made clear, you will understand that I am not teaching a *mental-get-rich-quick* affair, nor the getting of something for nothing; but that you must work mentally in order to accomplish whatever you desire. The particular advantage of this system of mental work over physical work is this: you can select your own time to do it, and arrange your own compensation. Your experiences with prosperous businessmen and all successful persons in the world show that unconsciously they work along these lines. I say unconsciously because the majority of them as yet only unconsciously put the law into operation. If you will but persist in your faith there can be no limit to your possibilities. If you can demonstrate a piece of carpet three feet long you can demonstrate a million dollars. If you can be happy a week you can be happy for a lifetime, because what can be done in a small degree can, with persistency, be done in a large degree. It rests with you whether you will or will not use this law consciously. There are some of you who will. There is always a percentage of persons who succeed and a percentage who do not. Each of you can do with your knowledge what you choose. This much is true, if you persist for two years to consciously use these laws in your daily affairs of life, by the end of that time your environment will have changed sufficiently, and demonstrations enough will have been made, to prove to you that you are dealing with *Law*.

VI

HENRY THOMAS HAMBLIN

The following quotes are from
Dynamic Thought, 1923

THINGS TO OBSERVE

Do not worry because you cannot follow the course exactly to the letter. Do what you can of it, adapt it to your life, and do the best you can in present circumstances.

The principal thing is to get twice daily into what is called the Silence, to quiet the senses, and get in touch with the Unseen.

Another vital thing is to use affirmations and denials; these will be explained more fully later. Yet another is meditation, for you gradually grow into the likeness of that upon which you meditate. Still another is visualizing. Always visualize the good, the beautiful, and true, and your life will reflect these things. Incidentally, the practice of visualization greatly increases one's powers of concentration.

Also while you are receiving this course and for some time after, refrain from all hazardous speculation. Do not launch out in business without sufficient capital and then expect everything to turn out all right. Instead wait until the way is made clear. Guidance and help will come *in time*, therefore do not try to force things.

Remember that although as soon as you start right thinking, you begin to build up your life, yet it takes time to manifest. At first things may seem to be worse, if so keep on and they will soon settle down. You cannot fail in the long run if you will persist and persevere.

I want you to realize:

That within you are infinite power and possibilities.

That the inward Power can be aroused and brought into expression by holding high ideals in the mind and by affirmations and meditation.

That it is necessary to spend a short time in the Unseen both night and morning.

That by doing so you can enter a super-conscious realm where your word is creative.

That what you speak comes to pass, that what you mentally picture must come true.

That it is only by following high ideals that true success can be achieved.

Therefore, picture a higher life – the highest you can conceive, and affirm that it is yours.

LESSON ONE

The objects of this course are: 1. To alter your mental attitude. 2. To direct your thoughts into those channels which lead to success, achievement, happiness and perfect good. 3. The arousing of the inward *power*. 4. The overcoming of bad habits. 5. The building up of character. 6. The discovery and development of the creative faculty.

How these are accomplished will be explained to you in their proper place and at the proper time, but first of all I want you to consider, thoughtfully, what is before you. It is not exactly an easy road which you have chosen. No path that leads upward ever is. The path of victory is always thorny; but when the thorns hurt the feet most, we can console ourselves with the thought that the path really does lead *somewhere*, and we know definitely that it leads to *Success, Achievement, Happiness and Satisfaction*. Difficulties there will be, disappointments, failures and setbacks, but to him who sets his face towards the light, and will keep steadily onward, there *must come* success and accomplishment and victory, above all expectation.

It is the *doing* of it that will change your character and your life.

Therefore, stop now and think carefully over the path that lies before you; estimate its difficulties, do not think lightly of them, be prepared for difficulty, and make up your mind, here and now, to conquer.

You may have failed in the past, but this time *you must, you will, and you shall overcome* every difficulty and weakness, and achieve dominion over yourself, victory over your circumstances and complete control over your life.

There must and shall be no failure this time. This time you are going to succeed through the power that is within you.

Now close your eyes, and mentally picture yourself, radiant, strong, successful, happy, full of the joy and zest of life. *See* yourself treading a path that leads ever upwards. Behind you the air is murky and gloomy, but in front is increasing brightness and loveliness. *See* yourself progressing, climbing, winning. *See* yourself trampling old habits and weaknesses under your feet. *See* yourself meeting difficulties in your path, and *see* yourself, sustained by a mighty inward power, brushing all obstructions aside, and never faltering in your upward climb.

Concentrate with all your powers upon this mental imagery. Persevere until you can see yourself radiant, sublime, shorn of all weaknesses and imperfections, the perfect image of your perfect self.

See yourself successful, attracting both people and affluence to you. Make a concrete, sharply defined image in your mind of yourself as you desire to be; see yourself master of circumstances, attracting all good things by the power of your mental forces.

Whatever you create, in this manner, in your mental world, will later be manifested in your outward life.

You will gradually grow into the likeness of the image you are now creating. Therefore create the right image. Let your ambition be a high one; do not picture yourself as a common man, satisfied with vulgar pleasures, instead, create a perfect man, the most perfect of which you can conceive.

In the same way when you throw your mind forward and foresee the task before you and "will" that all difficulties shall be overcome, and that if you get weary of well doing, you will not give up but will persevere, and arouse fresh interest in the task of self culture and achievement, then you are already winning the battle in advance, you are making your ultimate success doubly sure.

I want you to realize that this journey of yours is not a walk over, I want you to understand that it is a fight all the way, but at the same time to realize that it is a *winning* fight all the time; for although difficulties are real, yet you have within you the Powers which make difficulties and obstacles melt away. Great and omnipotent is the Power within you. Nothing can stay your upward climb, there is nobody who can prevent you succeeding except *yourself*; there is nothing that can stop your progress but your own doubt and fear. All things are possible if you believe that they are possible.

Unbounded confidence, the keynote of Success. You cannot fail, you, yourself, are Success.

Another word for "unbounded confidence" is "faith." Every successful man is a confident man. He believes wholeheartedly in his own power to succeed. This is not vanity or being too "cocksure," instead it is either conscious, or unconscious, or subconscious realization of the *Inward Power*. This is why so few men are really successful, so few men ever arouse the mighty powers that are within them, so few men think the kind of thoughts that bring these powers into life and action.

Every successful man is a man of "faith," every successful man is a man who cultivates "hope."

Therefore I want you first of all to cultivate Hope and Faith.

That you have these two qualities is proved by the fact that you are reading this course. You have had the hope of winning your way to a life of Success, and Power, and you have had the Faith to believe that within you are the powers and forces which make this possible. Without Hope a man is as good as dead, without Faith he is like a rudderless ship drifting hither and thither with every wind and current. On the other hand *all things are possible* to the man who has both these qualities.

Hope reaches forward and claims success, faith holds on until success is attained. Therefore seek to develop these qualities to their fullest extent.

It is a well known fact that when a man turns his face round and determines to fight his way to success, or to overcome evil habits, or to raise himself in any way either mentally, morally, physically or spiritually, then everything seems to happen to thwart his new intention and to throttle his new desires. So long as he goes on in his old way, drifting with the tide, floating about helplessly, the sport of fate and the prey of outside circumstances, so long as this goes on, nothing unusual happens. But directly as a start is made in an upward direction, then all kinds of psychic powers seem to be let loose, whose object appears to be to prevent the student from making any progress in his new life.

When a man realizes his own interior powers and understands the vastness and wonder of his subliminal forces, and determines to make use of them, and thus become a king among men instead of a slave, then such disturbance takes place that unless he possesses Hope and Faith he will be tempted to turn his back on the new life and to sink back again into the old sluggish drifting existence, which leads to disappointment and despair.

When the entities that cause the disturbance realize that you mean to keep on, and that you cannot be bullied into going back to the old life, they will quickly leave you. In any case there is nothing to be afraid of, because these entities are *helpless* if one does not *fear* them. In other words, if you have Hope and Faith you can win through. Hope for better times although the present may be discouraging. Faith in the sure belief that soon all the disagreeable symptoms will disappear.

Hope on; by Faith, hang on, and keep hanging on and you will win through. Do not be discouraged by seeming failure, nothing was ever won without effort. What can be had without effort is not worth having.

Take encouragement from the fact that this disturbance in your life proves that vital changes are taking place within, that the vast powers of your subliminal mind are beginning to awaken, and that the entities of your old erroneous beliefs and habits are taking their departure.

Believe now that you can conquer and win through, and you *will* conquer and win through. What you believe you can do, you *can* do, because all power is within you. There is nothing in all the world that can stop you, except your own doubt and fear.

I want you to trust me to the extent of doing something, the underlying principle of which cannot be explained in this first lesson. I want you to make what is known as an "affirmation," I want you to affirm the following:

"The old life is dead and buried. I have severed myself from it once and for all. Henceforth I live the new life of success and power, of self-mastery and all accomplishment."

First of all memorize these words. Keep repeating them over until they sink deeply into your memory, and their meaning finds a place in your consciousness. If you can get a few moments to yourself during the day, practice making the affirmations. The right way is as follows: Go into a quiet place, whether you sit, stand, or lie down is immaterial. Now close your eyes and say the words over very earnestly.

Strive to realize all that they mean and address the words to your *inner mind*. It is your submerged mind that you are influencing, so address the affirmation very earnestly to it. Do this for several minutes, and finish by making the affirmation into space. Hurl it out as a message to the Universe and by so doing you will come into harmony with innumerable invisible forces, who will help and strengthen you.

Do not make the affirmation while in a state of strain and nervous tension. Relax yourself, take a deep breath, and as you exhale let your muscles go limp; smooth out your nerves until your whole body is in a peaceful easy state. Concentrate your thoughts on what you are doing. If they wander bring them back and begin again. The more you concentrate the better will be the result.

The most important, in fact *the* time above all times for making the affirmation is just as you are falling to sleep. There is a great psychological reason for this. If you can fall asleep while making the affirmation, or while visualizing it, so much the better. Therefore take no food or stimulants (it is better to avoid the latter altogether) just before retiring. The reason cannot be given here because it would take too long, but it is an important one.

In the early morning immediately on waking is the next best time, both times should be made use of, and on no account be missed, but of the two the one just before sleep is by far the more important.

The influence of these affirmations will be felt during the day, they will have an effect upon your mental outlook, and upon the way in which you will deal with the problems of your day's work; but this influence can be intensified and buttressed up, as it were, by "retiring into yourself" at intervals, during the day, and mentally repeating the affirmation. This will give you a sense of power and confidence and hope, such as you have never experienced before. This is not "imagination," it is your hitherto unsuspected interior powers being aroused into activity.

When you have finished making the affirmation, again close your eyes and make a mental picture of yourself in the manner already taught. Endeavor to see yourself as a radiant being, with the old life and its murkiness and imperfections left far behind you. Picture yourself pressing forward to higher and better things, meeting difficulties, it is true, but overcoming them, trampling old habits, weaknesses and imperfections under your feet. Try and realize that you have the power to raise yourself above the ordinary things of life, that you can breathe a rarer and purer atmosphere. Picture yourself as a new being, happier, brighter and more radiant than ever you have been even at your most sublime moments.

This will not be easy. It requires concentration and perseverance. You will find it difficult to see yourself as you wish to see yourself, or you will find it not easy to see yourself clearly at all, also you will find it difficult to keep your mind concentrated upon the making of the image. There is only one thing to do and that is to keep on trying. Thus in the first lesson do you come face to face with a battle royal. With most students this visualizing is a great difficulty, but no matter how difficult it may be, it has to be overcome. If you fail to overcome this difficulty then you fail in this course of lessons; if you fail to overcome now, you will fail in the larger things of life.

The best way to overcome a difficulty is by getting interested in it. When you have developed interest, enthusiasm is aroused, and after that concentration becomes comparatively easy, and this commands success. Therefore get interested in this problem of visualizing.

Everything is first created in the unseen before it is manifested in the seen. When you, by dint of practice, can visualize clearly and distinctly, you will have developed creative power, not figuratively, but literally so.

Whatever you create in your mental world by means of visualizing will in time be manifested in the outer physical world. *The outer world of matter is subservient to the inner world of mind.*

I hope enough has been said to arouse your interest in, and enthusiasm for, visualizing. The more clearly you can visualize, the more clean cut will be the results in your daily life.

By visualizing, and by denials and affirmations (which will be explained later), by meditation and by the exercise of Hope and Faith, the life, character and circumstances can be transformed. The results are so extraordinary that it is very difficult to get people to believe them, but they are none the less real. Therefore practice your affirmations and persevere with your visualizing, they will lead to results of which you can at present form but a faint conception.

To obtain the best results from this course it is necessary to set apart a *special time every day* for meditation and concentration. The reason man is so weak and unhappy is because he lives the whole of his time in the objective life, the shallow material life of the senses, and neglects the deeper, grander transcendental life of the inner mind. It is the *inner* life that gives power and peace and satisfaction. The *outer* material life of the infinite mind of the senses brings worry and care. The *inner* life of the deeper mind brings strength, wisdom, understanding and the ability to accomplish.

It is a proved scientific fact that you grow into the likeness of that upon which you meditate. If you meditate upon evil then evil will come into your life; if you meditate upon revenge, your life will be turned into an inferno of trouble; on the other hand, if you meditate upon happiness and other higher mental states, then happiness will be yours, and if you let your thoughts dwell upon "peace" then peace of mind will result. All these states and many others are within you; they can be called forth by meditation. You can call forth either good or evil, success or failure, strength or weakness, happiness or woe, everything is in your own hands.

MEDITATION

To be used every day and twice a day if possible, between the hours of 6 and 9 A.M. and 9 and 11:30 P.M. Other times are suitable, but those mentioned will be found especially valuable to students, as between these hours their teacher is meditating upon the same thoughts, and the vibrations from his mind will be helpful to all who are "tuned to receive them."

Try and arrange to spend half an hour in meditation before retiring for the night. Sit in a quiet place, relax your body and concentrate upon these words:

Within me are infinite powers seeking expression. In the past, because I did not know of their existence, they have been stifled and suppressed. Now I "will" that they shall be called into activity, and find perfect and full expression in my life in the form of success and achievement in my heart in the form of a mighty upwelling of joy and happiness. Now that I have discovered this hidden and inexhaustible store of power and energy, my life is transformed; weakness gives place to strength, sorrow to happiness, morbidity to radiant joy, pessimism to divine optimism, despair to hope, failure to success, poverty to prosperity. Henceforth only the highest good can come into my life. Now by the power of my thought-forces I am allied with and joined to the Infinite Principle of Good, and we have become *one*. Henceforth for me there is, and can be, no evil, only Infinite Good. All evil is now cast out of my life, because I am one with the Infinite Good. "No evil can come nigh my dwelling;" "nothing can harm or destroy." Henceforth by scientific thinking I control my life, for my life is the result of the effect of my thoughts. When evil thoughts, or weak thoughts, or impure thoughts, or failure thoughts, or fear thoughts, or poverty thoughts, or hate thoughts assail me, I will cast them out and think only of thoughts of love and strength, of prosperity and success, and of the Infinite Perfection with which I am now allied, and of which I form a part.

When meditating upon the above, take each thought separately in turn and concentrate all your thoughts upon it. Not only grasp its meaning, but try and picture what it means. For instance: "My life is transformed." When you think upon these words, try and *see* your life being transformed, *see* your weaknesses falling away from you like an old garment, and instead, strength, success and noble qualities being born in their place. Practice and concentrate and *feel* the power of this meditation.

This ends the metaphysical part of this week's lesson; the following are some brief hints of great value to the student beginning the study of Scientific Thought: 1. Everything works according to Law, we each of us have what we deserve. 2. Covet no man's goods, possessions or happiness; he deserves them, let him alone. Realize that the Universe holds all that you can possibly desire – for you. 3. Hate no man. Hatred will come back like a boomerang and hurt you far more than it can the object of your hatred. Ignore what you cannot like, and concentrate your mind on pleasant things. 4. Be true, be honest, be faithful. All these create vibrations which will bring back blessings and happiness to you.

You have entered a life, the power and possibilities of which you at present have no conception. If I described it now you would not understand. But, believe me, it is a life of Power to accomplish and Victory over all weaknesses. It is a life of Prosperity and true Success. It is a life of transcendent Joy. It is a life of peace.

Keep on affirming. Keep on visualizing. Keep on meditating. Keep on believing. Keep on hoping. What you hope for, and believe, and affirm, and visualize, is *yours*. Remember also that you grow into the likeness of that which you meditate on.

The brain is a very delicate instrument; it is the vehicle through which the mind finds expression. The mind cannot manifest its power if the brain is clouded by the grossness of the body. The one who would improve his or her mind, who would awaken the mighty powers within, must give up hurtful physical habits. It is useless to attempt to eradicate bad mental habits while the body is suffering from indulgence of any kind. For instance, it would be a waste of time to affirm all or any of the higher qualities of the mind and then to go to bed intoxicated or full of pork chops and fried onions. Let your diet be on the light side, always rise from the table slightly hungry rather than replete, and never eat later than three hours before retiring to bed. For instance, if you go to bed at 11 P.M. do not eat at a later hour than 8 P.M. This is a most important point, *the affirmations have more power if made when fasting*, therefore the last thing at night and the time of waking in the early morning are the best times at which to perform them.

Let only thoughts of good, purity, strength, success, love, self-control, courage and determination enter this greater mind of vast intelligence and power. Do this, and your Subliminal Mind will take these thoughts as orders, and will shape your life accordingly. Thus in a general way your Subliminal Mind will be led to develop your life on successful, noble, and harmonious lines.

The main object of this lesson is to make a dent or impression on the Subliminal Mind and to make it realize that the old life is dead and that you have now entered a new life of success and power. Your Subliminal Mind will accept this if you persevere with the visualizing and affirmations, and will thus be prepared for the more advanced training which is to follow.

LESSON TWO

Gaze up into the sky at night and sense the infinite majesty of the Universe. Get mentally into touch with those patient stars that flash and twinkle like gems of purest water. Realize that they are suns, situated millions of miles away. Then think of our own little spot in the Universe – the Solar System. Think of the majestic Magnetic Sun; the planets all following certain paths guided by a wonderful system of Universal Law. Observe the precision of the rising and setting of the Sun, the lunar periods, the rhythmic ebb and flow of the tidal sea. Let your mind grasp what all this means, let it sweep right from the grandest aspect of Nature down to the atom itself and what does it see? A Power expressing itself in an infinite variety of ways, in everything, and through everything. There is nothing, not a grain, not an atom, not an electron, that does not contain this wondrous Power. Man has been described as an epitome of the Universe; an atom clairvoyantly observed has been described as a replica of the Solar System; therefore we have universe within universe, solar system within solar system, and all animated, controlled and directed by the Universal or Infinite Mind.

Therefore the Power that animates man is an Infinite Power. In man the Infinite Mind finds its highest expression on the visible plane.

The cause of all man's weakness, mistakes and failures, has been that he has not realized the Power within; instead, he has thought himself to be separate and friendless, weak and helpless, adrift, without chart or compass upon the sea of life. He has thought himself to be the victim of circumstance, the sport of fate, and the puppet of forces outside himself. He has called himself a worm instead of looking upon himself as a king. He has thought himself to be worthless and insignificant instead of realizing his wonderful interior *Powers* and the grandeur of his being.

Instead of being a worm, man is a king. Potentially all the powers of the Infinite Mind are his. Instead of being the victim of circumstances he can control them. Instead of being the puppet of forces outside himself, he has within him the Power to be what he will; to do what he will; to accomplish all that he desires.

Now at last the darkness is being pierced and man realizes that he is a mental creature, and that he is *Mind* as well as matter, that is, as Mind, is one with the Universal or Infinite *Mind*. That the difference between him and the Infinite or Universal *Mind* is not one of kind, but of degree.

Like a traveler lost in the bush, who, almost dying, at last finds his way to a permanent spring of water, and drinks and drinks again, knowing that he can never exhaust the everlasting supply; so does man after long wanderings, at last realize, that within him is a fountain of never failing Power and Wisdom, and that his subliminal mind is linked up with, and forms a part of, the Infinite Mind of the Universe.

This is the greatest discovery in the history of the World; this is the crowning revelation of all the ages; this is the blinding knowledge that dwarfs every other knowledge: *that within man dwells the infinite mind of the universe.*

Call how he may on these hidden forces; they can never fail to respond, for they are infinite and inexhaustible. Man stands alone and apart from all other creatures, in this visible world around him, in that he has the power to govern his own actions, choose right and wrong, to mold his own fate, and create his own life and circumstances.

To other creatures, life and the visible world are fixed quantities. To man, life and the world are reflexes of inward mental states. Thus, can he make life what he will; thus can he live in a world of his own creating.

Man alone has the power to realize and recognize the inward Power of the Infinite, and to consciously bring It into objectivity.

The inward powers of the mind are potentially illimitable, but they lie dormant and unexpressed, until they are recognized, and aroused into action, by the individual.

This is why the majority of people are so worried and distressed. Why they either fail to make life worth living or achieve only partial success, and that with great difficulty. They try to achieve without the power to achieve. They marvel at their own weakness, not realizing that within them lie immeasurable powers which are patiently waiting to find expression.

Until man calls these powers into activity they can never act. Within him is that which is connected with the Power-House of the Universe, yet he never feels its power. Within him is Infinite Wisdom, Knowledge, Inspiration, Creative Power and driving Force, yet he slumbers on, unconscious of their existence. But to those who realize their own interior Powers, what a mine of inexhaustible treasure do they find, what force and energy for all accomplishment.

When you, dear reader, enter into the realization of the mighty Power within you, you enter into possession of all good and perfect things. You cease to strive, and squabble, and snatch, with selfish anxious hand, the bread from another's mouth. You leave off striving, with palpitating heart and careworn face, to push your way in front of the one next to you. Instead, you set your ambitions high, and sustained and carried forward by invisible forces, enter into possession of all that you desire.

Work? Yes, you will work, for right thinking, and this realization of the Power within you is the result of right thinking and is the inspiration of all right action. You will work hard enough but the difference will be that your work will be the greatest joy in your life. Joy! There is no joy like the joy of work well loved and well done, and which leads to accomplishment and victory. Work! Yes, you will work, but not with the feverish haste or with the fear of failure and bankruptcy ever before you. Instead, you will work with confidence and power, sure in the knowledge that your efforts lead definitely to Success.

When you have realized the inward Power, you will feel it pushing you in the back and impelling you forward, you will feel yourself borne along to the goal of your endeavor.

Whereas formerly you were chasing Success, and waiting on it cap in hand; in the future you will realize that you are master; that you command and Success obeys.

You realize that instead of as in the past, running after fame and fortune, which, like a will o' the wisp, constantly eluded you, you have now the power to attract all desirable things to you.

Instead of feverish anxiety and joyless quest, you possess calm confidence and the power to accomplish everything that you desire.

There will be no anxiety, no care for the morrow; instead – the confidence of exact knowledge – the knowledge that the results will be exactly as arranged. Just as today is the result of past thinking, so the future will be the result of what is built today. Therefore you do certain things today and you *know* with mathematical certainty what the future results will be.

That is the basis of all success, the confidence, the exact knowledge that what you are sowing now will be reaped a hundredfold; that in the future you will enter into occupation of that which you are building now, that what you claim as your own *now*, out of all the riches of the Universal Store House, will be yours in the future. It is yours *now*; you enter into possession in the days to come.

You will now begin to see why I ask you to use affirmations. In succeeding lessons will be explained what affirmations are, their object and the manner in which they work.

In the meantime make use of the same affirmation that you have been using in the past week, but with something added. It will now read:

The old life is dead and buried. I have severed myself from it once and for all. Henceforth I live the new life of Success and Power, Self-Mastery and all Accomplishment. This I do, not in the strength of my ordinary consciousness, but by the Infinite Power of my deeper inner *Mind* which is one with, and forms a part of, the Infinite Universal Mind.

Make the affirmations earnestly. Think of what you are saying. Enter into all that the words mean. Try and feel their power. Do not, however, bring yourself up to a nervous tension, instead let yourself relax. First your body with its muscles and nerves – let them all go limp, then your mind – let that unbend also. Now affirm calmly and confidently as instructed, and then visualize a picture of yourself, radiant, calm, and possessed of a new power. See yourself master of all weaknesses and passions, directing yourself, guiding your life with unerring wisdom, shaping your course to a glorious destiny. Practice and keep on practicing the art of visualizing. Remember that you are dealing with finer matter than that which is discerned by the senses, but it is none the less real; in fact, it is far more real.

If, therefore, you create in your mental realm a picture of yourself, radiant, successful, self disciplined, master of your life and destiny, then you are creating a new *you*, which in the process of time, will become objectified in your outward life. In other words, the new *you*, the radiant being of your mental imagery, will later manifest itself in a new outside physical *you*. Whatever is created in the Unseen, later becomes manifested in the Seen. This is an immutable Law. By mental imagery you create in the Unseen.

Be careful what you create, whatever it is, good or bad, will find its way into your life and be read and known of all men.

Whenever you meet with temptation or difficulty or if you let yourself get flustered at business, just "retire into yourself" for a moment and make the affirmation mentally, and *"realize"* that you are a new creature. You will then become conscious of *The Inward Power*.

MEDITATION

Sit very quietly and relax nerves and muscles, and concentrate your thoughts upon a conception of an ideal world. Picture a world of indescribable beauty, without pain or care; without hate, unkindness or selfishness; without poverty, want or any lack. Picture mentally a world in which love and good will reign supreme, where beauty, joy, happiness, plenty and profusion of all good things are unstinted and for all. Picture a world where there is no limitation, where you can know everything, possess all the wisdom, and where you can be everywhere at the same time.

In this world the colors of the flowers and of the sky are more beautiful than anything you have seen before, the singing of the birds more ravishing than anything yet heard. The inhabitants are all comely and strong; they are all animated by goodwill and indescribably happy. This is the perfect World of *Mind*.

Now concentrate upon this image. You will most probably find worry thoughts intruding. Thoughts of the rent, of the mistake one of your clerks has made in your business, of threatened competition, or of some slander or unkind imputation that may have been made against you. Whenever a thought tries to enter your mind dismiss it at once and concentrate your mind upon your ideal world. This will not be easy, but continue to persevere. It is *most important* that you should master this, as by so doing you are cultivating one of the most wonderful faculties of your mind. Therefore keep on dismissing the unwelcome thought by *denying it*.

For instance, you are disturbed by the thought that something grossly unfair has been done to you, it makes your blood boil when you think of it. Immediately when this thought comes to you, say at once, "in this perfect world of Mind there is no unfairness, injustice or unkindness, all is truth and honor and goodwill," and raise your thoughts above this imperfect material life, and concentrate your mental gaze upon your ideal world. Again, a thought may come suggesting that the new competition in your business will ruin you. Immediately deny it by saying, "in this perfect world there is no competition, there is no failure; I am a perfect mental creature gifted with Infinite Powers, and I am above competition, I am success." Keep your mental vision on your ideal world the whole time and keep denying all your troubles one by one, and affirming their opposites.

By your denials you "kill" the worry thought and by affirming its opposite you build up a character and mental outlook that are superior to worry and incapable of failure.

It was seen in last weeks lesson that in a general way the Subliminal Mind could be influenced for good by allowing only thoughts of good, courage, success, etc., to pass the citadel of the mind. This is the foundation of all happiness and harmony in one's life, but if it is desired to arouse your latent powers, and to train your Subliminal Mind to solve all your problems, to give you true inspiration and supply you with original ideas, other methods must be employed. Your great Subliminal Mind is not going to yield up its wonderful store of knowledge, neither is it going to act as the solver of all your problems, in response to a mere pious wish. What is necessary is that very strong, concentrated, forceful directed thoughts should be sent down into this greater mind, continuously and persistently. Whatever message you keep sending down into your Subliminal Mind, provided it is not changed or altered, and that it is sufficiently *strong* and *concentrated*, will be obeyed *in time*.

For some students it will take a longer amount of time than others, but everyone, sooner or later, who follows these instructions, will develop the power of *directed* Subliminal thinking.

The first step is to impress very powerfully upon the Subliminal Mind that it is capable of solving all your problems. At present unless you are a very rare exception, your Subliminal Mind is hypnotized into the belief that it cannot solve your problems. So long as it believes that it cannot solve your problems it never will attempt the task, but once you can convince your Subliminal Mind that it has the power, the wisdom and the knowledge to do so, then you will at once pass from weakness to power. You will have at your disposal a mind so vast and wonderful that the finite mind of the senses will be unable to grasp its full significance.

In order to convince your Subliminal Mind that it can solve all your problems you must: 1. Believe in yourself that it can do so. 2. Have a strong desire to use your hidden powers. 3. Make strong affirmations that your Subliminal Mind can think constructively and, drawing upon the All-knowledge, solve every perplexity and problem. 4. Visualize yourself meeting with problems and having them solved immediately by referring them to your greater mind within.

Within you are limitless powers, but they only become available when you consciously call upon them and make use of them. Therefore carry this thought strongly in your mind, "My Subliminal Mind can draw upon the Universal Intelligence and solve all my problems."

When seeking to impress the Subliminal Mind it is necessary to be alone and to still the objective mind and the senses. When all thoughts of worry, business and material life, have been dismissed from the mind and perfect calm obtained, then you will be in a state favorable to: 1. The sending of directions to the Subliminal Mind. 2. Receiving inspiration from it.

The Unseen is greater than the Seen; therefore to work in the Unseen is to deal with the "cause" of which the outward life is the "effect." By working in the Unseen by means of meditation, affirmation, visualizing and by holding in our mind the highest ideals we arouse the Power that lies hidden within us.

The Power that is within us is the power of the Universal Mind or Spirit, therefore it is infinite and illimitable; the only limit there can be is the limitation we place upon it by our lack of faith.

Therefore in all your difficulties and battles remember that the Power within you is infinite. You are one with the Infinite if you will only believe it, if you can only realize it.

Rise up and go forward with confidence, your highest ideals can be attained too, if you will believe and have faith and reach upward to higher and better things.

I affirm for you the inward knowledge of these things.

LESSON THREE

While the existence of the subliminal mind is a modern discovery to Western minds, it is ancient knowledge in the East. For centuries this knowledge has been treasured by certain orders of mystics. Dating right back to the earliest times we find evidence of signs and wonders being worked through the power of the subliminal mind.

In the West, however, there has always been a tendency toward materialism. A materialist believes in matter. He wants to see, touch and handle before he will believe.

Literally he will only believe what he sees through the senses.

Modern science has, however, knocked the ground from under the materialist's feet, because it is constantly proving that there is far more in the unseen than there is in the seen. Science, in spite of all its achievements, realizes that, up to the present, it has only been paddling on the edge of a mighty ocean of mystery.

Science has, slowly and with huge and clumsy effort, now proved the existence of many things which scientists would not believe before, but which were known in the East for centuries. One of these is the existence of the subliminal mind. Mesmerism and Hypnotism have proved that man is composed of more than one *mind*. There is the surface or outside mind of the senses. This mind reasons, learns from books and other outside sources, and functions generally, on the physical plane. It is only a minute fraction of the total mind of man. Like the iceberg, which only shows one-twelfth of itself above the surface of the sea, the other eleven-twelfths being submerged, the objective mind of man is only an infinitesimal portion of the whole.

The surface or objective mind is the finite mind, the Subliminal is joined up with the Universal Mind of the Universe, therefore it can never be measured and it is beyond comprehension. Sufficient for us to know that its power is limitless, and that we can use this power in creating our lives anew, and for the realization of all our desires.

The Subliminal Mind is:
1. Inspiratory.
2. Intuitive.
3. Creative.

It is a storehouse of knowledge and the powerhouse of energy. It is much more than all this. In this lesson we will consider the first three descriptions in the order named.

1. Inspiration. It is through the subliminal mind that all inspiration has come to men. It was through this channel that Wordsworth, Shakespeare, Milton, Emerson and all great teachers and leaders have drawn their inspiration.

That some are giants in their accomplishments and others pigmies is simply due to differing degrees of expression. Some express more of the Power within them, some express less. The Power is there, it is for us to express it. We cannot all be Shakespeares and Miltons, neither is it possible for all men to be Gladstones or Lincolns, but there is a niche somewhere in the world where we can each find a useful field of congenial work. We can, if we will, be guided by inspiration, find somewhere a field of labor where we can pour out our pent up passion for achievement, where we can command success beyond our wildest dreams.

You, dear reader, have not been sent into this world for a joke, you have been sent to achieve a certain purpose, to accomplish something which no one can do but you. There is no one in all the world just like you, and all that you do is colored by your individuality. No one in all the world could do your work just as you do it; there are fields of conquest in front of you which no one but you can conquer. Therefore, *listen to the voice of inspiration*.

2. Intuitive. Those who learn to recognize the voice of intuition are brought into touch with infinite wisdom. They do by intuition that which other people can only do by cumbersome effort, if indeed they can do it at all. One who has developed this power has no perplexities, because all his problems are solved for him by his subliminal mind. He listens to the inner voice of wisdom, acts accordingly, and the result always justifies his faith in this inward power.

President Lincoln, when confronted by a perplexing problem, used to make a habit of dismissing it to his inner mind, and then going for a short walk. During his walk he would interest himself in the birds and trees and other things around him and then give no thought to the perplexity which was demanding an answer. When he got back from his walk the answer would be ready because his subliminal mind had solved the problem. Others, puzzled by an intricate matter, may go to bed with the problem still unsolved, and awake in the morning with the solution of their difficulty already formed in their conscious mind; or it may come to them, like a flash, while they are dressing; the subliminal mind has solved their problem.

In the subliminal mind is all wisdom and understanding. You, too, can use this wisdom and understanding if you develop the faculty of inward hearing.

3. Creative. The subliminal mind is creative. Being one with the Universal Mind, which is the Creative Power of the Universe, it partakes of the same nature. The difference is not one of kind but of degree.

As in the macrocosm, so in the microcosm. Just as Infinite Mind is absolute through the whole Universe, so is man king of his life, master of his fate, captain of his soul, creator of his life and circumstances.

The difference between men is a difference of vision. The difference between their vision is the difference between their accomplishment. Some men create more than others – it is because theirs is a greater vision.

People who pride themselves on being "practical" look askance at imagination, thinking it to be something impractical and shadowy; something belonging to the realm of dreams. They confuse constructive imagery with daydreaming. Daydreaming is the aimless frittering away of the mental powers; creative imagination, on the other hand, gathers together the mental forces, and by focusing the powers of the hidden mind bring into being a definite image.

The reason that here and there in the world's history there have been great characters who have achieved the noblest ends is because theirs have been the noblest visions. As the image is, so your life will be. Therefore if you hold in your mind the vision, or mental picture, of great success or noble endeavor, then in your life these things will become manifested.

A person of poor powers of concentration cannot hold a definite image in his mind, but must be always changing and modifying it, with the result that he gets nothing but confusion and lack of achievement manifested in his life.

What you are inwardly, what you think inwardly, what you visualize inwardly, is what your future life will be. Your outward life is modeled on your inward life – it is an exact replica of the life within.

Therefore your subliminal mind is not only the source of inspiration and intuition, it is creative also. Your life is in your own hands, you can make it what you will. Your future is yours entirely; you can build it up with mathematical precision into any form you please. You are free to make or to mar, to build up or destroy. You can climb to the highest heights or descend to the lowest depths. You can be weak or strong, filthy or pure, miserable or happy, unsuccessful or successful, poverty stricken or prosperous, hated or loved: It is all a matter of Thought-control and Scientific Thinking.

It is now time that you begin to apply some of the things you have learned. Add to your affirmation at night the following:

Mine is a life of overcoming and power.

Henceforth I will cease doing _____
and will instead do _____.

I do this by the Infinite Power within me which can never fail.

Where I have left blanks I want you to fill in with 1. Whatever bad habit you most wish to eradicate. 2. The virtue you wish to put in its place.

For instance, suppose you have been in the habit of getting up late, swallowing your breakfast hurriedly and rushing to business, getting all behind with appointments and correspondence. Supposing this is the case (of course I only use this as an illustration), you will fill in the words to suit, so that the sentence will read something like this, supposing your proper time for rising is 7 A.M.:

"Henceforward I will cease getting up late and will instead get up punctually at 7 A.M."

Or better still, you can command yourself to wake at 6:30 and spend half an hour in meditations and the saying of affirmations. You will then be quite ready to rise at 7 o'clock.

Immediately following the affirmation, visualize a picture of yourself waking in the morning. "See" yourself open your eyes and look at the clock. "See" that the time is 6:30. "See" yourself engaged in concentration, meditation and making affirmations. "See" yourself look at the clock again, and at 7 o'clock "see" yourself get up and go to the bathroom. The more clearly you can picture this scene, the easier you will find the task of getting up.

You may not be successful the first morning or two, but if you *persevere* you will find that you have, by the use of affirmations, complete control over yourself. The more successful you become, the stronger your Willpower grows.

If you are in the habit of going to bed too late, you can add to your morning affirmation the following:

"Henceforward I will cease going to bed late. I will instead go to bed at 10. At 10 o'clock tonight I shall feel sleepy and tired. I will then go to bed."

After making this affirmation, visualize yourself as you will appear at 10 P.M. You are, we will say, sitting reading or working. You "see" yourself look at the clock. You "see" yourself put your book or work away and go to bed. Persevere with the visualizing until you can see every detail with great vividness and distinctness.

Make this affirmation and create this mental picture and you will find that what you have affirmed and visualized will come to pass exactly as desired. Before you is unfolding a life of perfect self-control and overcoming. When you have become master of yourself, first in small things and then in the greater, you will have become master over your life, your circumstances and your destiny.

Not only is it necessary that you should overcome habits in this way by reversing them, but it is also necessary that you should reverse all your wrong ideas of life and the Universe, replacing wrong and harmful ideas by Truth. One of the objects of this course is to dispel old erroneous beliefs, and thus to change your mental outlook.

In addition it is necessary that you should reverse every thought and suggestion of a harmful character directly as it comes to you. A thought may come to you such as: "You will fail, you can never succeed." Now if you allow that thought to enter your mind it will weaken you, paralyze your efforts and bring failure into your life, just as surely as day follows night. Therefore, as soon as it comes to you, you must kill it by denial. In this case you would raise yourself in thought to your perfect mental world and say, "There is no failure. I am a perfect Mental creature living in a perfect Mental World and all of the potentialities of the Infinite Mind are mine. I cannot fail." Say this over several times and then affirm: "I am success in all that I undertake."

Every time that you do this you drive failure further and further away and establish success more firmly in your life. The more often you do this, provided that you get a clear concept of your perfect Mental World, and, as it were, breathe in its atmosphere, the more rapidly you will progress. Do not, however, strain and worry after results, instead seek to adopt and maintain a calm, serene, confident attitude, above the worries and cares of life.

Remember to always retire into yourself and to rise to your Perfect World of Mind before making a denial or affirmation.

MEDITATION

To be pondered over between the hours of 6 A.M. and 9 A.M. and 9 P.M. and 11 P.M. Especially just before retiring is recommended.

In the past I have listened to the distracting voices of this imperfect unsatisfying life of the senses. I have been pulled this way and that, by desire, by impulse, by uncontrolled emotions, and have been influenced by the advice of those who have had no inward knowledge. Henceforth I turn a deaf ear to all these voices and listen only to the inward voice which always speaks with perfect wisdom. No more shall I be perplexed and worried not knowing which way to turn or what to do, instead I shall be guided perfectly by the inward voice of inspiration. I raise my mind above this life of the senses and dwell in the perfect World of Mind. All thoughts and suggestions and states that are not in harmony with the highest good, I reverse into their opposites. Thus do I cleanse my mind, my thought, my life, my circumstances, my world, and build up my life anew.

When perplexed or faced with difficult problems, I retire into my inner self, and by thought control, I keep out, or "reverse," the unwanted thought, until my inner mind is stilled and calmed, and I can hear the inner voice of wisdom. This voice of wisdom never errs, *never* leads astray, but always guides me toward the highest good. Therefore, I have no worry or care or perplexity, because I always know how to act even in the most perplexing circumstances, being guided perfectly by the inner voice of wisdom.

Henceforth there is for me no care, anxiety or worry, because I am guided into all good. Every good and perfect thing is mine *now*. Prosperity, happiness, peace of mind, all are mine here and now.

Having for this past week impressed on your Subliminal Mind that it *can* think constructively and drawing upon the All-Knowledge, solve your every problem, it is now necessary for you to tell your Subliminal Mind that it *does* solve all your problems. This week's meditation indicates the way – to retire into yourself – this is the secret. To most students it is a difficult task to still the senses and inhibit unwanted thought, but it is comparatively easy, if, instead of trying to inhibit all thought, you keep on concentrating upon it and dismiss every thought of care, worry, business, or anything to do with the senses, which comes to you. It must be a thought which will draw you away from the life of the senses to the greater life of the mind and spirit.

Continue to dismiss all other thought until all worry is killed and the mind and Spirit are at rest. Then say in your own words, something like this: My Subliminal Mind draws upon the All-Wisdom and solves my every problem and difficulty.

The life that lies before the student of Truth is one of great glory – of infinite expansion and unfoldment. It does not, however, always appear thus to him. In order to test his mettle, it often appears drab and hopeless. Everything seems to go wrong, and voices whisper "Go back, why trouble any longer, the pursuit is hopeless." The one who will keep on in spite of all discouragements and opposition, and who proves his worth, passes on to a life of indescribable joy, victory, achievement and peace of mind.

I affirm for you the life of true freedom.

LESSON FOUR

We now have to deal with that part of your Mind which is the center of all action and the seat of all memory. Not only the memory of this life, but the race memory of all mankind.

This division of the mind we will call the subconscious mind, we will do so in order to distinguish it from the mind of creation, intuition, and inspiration, which we have already considered, and also from the objective or conscious mind which will be described later.

This subdivision is not orthodox according to the ordinary teachings of psychology. The usual practice is to term the whole of the submerged mind subconscious. That this is not correct must, if we think for a moment, be apparent. The subconscious mind acts only according to instruction and instinct. Thoughts and commands flow from the seat of the Will through the conscious mind down into the subconscious mind and are immediately acted upon. The subconscious mind is a blind intelligence. It cannot reason – it can remember, it can act – but it cannot think, plan or reason.

Yet we have a mind within us that can inspire, create, and bring forth the most wonderful thoughts. A mind which can solve our most complicated problems; that can guide us through the most difficult situations if we will but trust it. This cannot be the subconscious mind because we have already seen that this is a blind intelligence acting only upon instruction, suggestion and animal instinct. Therefore, there must be a mind or minds other than the subconscious, and this I have termed, for the want of a better word, the subliminal.

The subconscious mind is a kind of sleepy giant, or a slumbering volcano. It only requires arousing to cause it to manifest extraordinary power.

This subconscious mind of ours is subject to our will and guidance. Within us is this wondrous power – the almost infinite intelligence; yet its use and control are in our own hands.

Unto us is given the ability to govern a power whose extent we cannot gauge, to direct an intelligence so great that it is impossible for us to grasp its full significance.

The subconscious mind is the center of all action. It is by this mind that everything that we do is accomplished.

It is the personification of tireless energy. It works constantly; it never sleeps; for while *we* sleep the subconscious mind is busily engaged in repairing and rebuilding the body.

Whatever thought we allow to pass into the subconscious mind is translated into action. This is why a thought has been described as "an action in the process of being born."

The great lesson for you, dear reader, to learn is this, that if the subconscious mind translates each thought into action, then thought control is the one great transcendental fact of life. If you possess the power to control your thoughts, you have at once the power to control your actions. If you can control your actions, what a life of possibility opens before you!

One of the principal causes of failure in life is due to the inability to control thoughts. Wrong thoughts reach the subconscious mind, these are translated into wrong actions and these bring failure and disaster in their train.

When the thoughts are uncontrolled, then the subconscious mind will act upon any thought or suggestion that may "float" in.

Now thoughts and suggestions are born not only within the consciousness, they are also received from without.

Like a wireless apparatus which receives messages through vibrations in the ether, so does the human mind receive impressions from without.

Thoughts impinge upon your consciousness and unless you are able to reject them they will enter the subconscious mind and bring forth action in your life and conduct.

If, therefore, the thought be evil, then evil will result, if of weakness, then failure will follow.

In the same way, if you entertain a noble thought, a noble action will result. If thoughts of success and power are dwelt upon, then success and the power to accomplish will be manifested in your life and circumstances. It is thought that rules your life, therefore, if you govern your thoughts, you control your life.

"How then," you ask, "can I escape all this harmful suggestion? I am conscious of evil in my life. I do not know what to expect next. How then can I cast out evil and avoid all these harmful suggestions that impinge upon my consciousness from a thousand different sources?"

The answer is: *By Denials.*

First of all I want you to understand that your life consists only of that which is in your mind. Your world also is really nothing more than a reflection of your own mind and what is in your own mind. It is because of this that two people in precisely the same circumstances will each find life and the world very different. One will see in life great joy and much cause for thankfulness, and the other may experience only unhappiness and disappointment. The difference is not in the circumstances but in the mind. The mind is the real thing, the world is transient and fleeting, and has, philosophically speaking, no *real* existence, but *mind* endures.

The natural or "mortal mind" view of life and the world is almost always the exact opposite of what is the real spiritual truth and fact. Metaphysics tells us that the visible world is an inverted reflection of the real. If then it is inverted, it is natural, until our spiritual or inner eyes are opened to the truth, for us to see things as the exact opposite of what they really are. Therefore, it is not surprising to find that, whereas the mortal or animal mind of the senses thinks the world is the real thing and the mind only a shadow, the real *truth* is, that mind and spirit are real and eternal, and the visible world but a transient and impermanent thing which has no actual reality.

Such being the case, the only thing that really matters is what is in the mind or what is not in the mind. If we have a belief in evil, and thoughts of evil, in our mind, then we have evil in our life. If, however, we can cast the thought of, and belief in evil, out of our mind, then it will cease to appear in our life.

By raising ourselves above the sensuous life, and realizing our permanent world of Mind, and there denying evil, poverty, failure, unhappiness, or whatever our trouble may be, we kill the thought which is the cause of all our troubles. Then whatever we affirm will take their place. If we deny "evil," then we follow by affirming "good."

By denials, we can take all the care, fear and worry out of our lives, and build up in their place, by means of affirmations, perfect good, success, affluence, happiness, love, peace and courage.

Everything being in the mind, everything that is taken out of the mind is taken out of the life, and everything that is put into the mind comes into the life.

Affirmations are concentrated thoughts. Back of each affirmation is a strong emotion, and this gives it tremendous driving force.

By the use of affirmations, all the finer forces are aroused to action, and the life is transformed from weakness or ineffectiveness to strength or purposefulness.

By the use of affirmations, the Will is strengthened, until it becomes so strong, all else has to bend to it.

By the use of affirmations, difficult tasks and unpleasant duties become easy of accomplishment.

By the use of affirmations, it is possible to break bad habits of lifelong standing, and replace them with good ones.

By the use of affirmations, we can build up character, mold our circumstances, shape our destiny, captain our soul, be what we will, do whatever we desire, attain all our ideals.

Therefore, it is of the utmost importance that you should be most diligent in practicing the affirmations – always. Never let a single night or morning pass without spending several minutes in quiet concentration on the affirmation given you in this course.

Mental and Physical lethargy must be overcome. It is by sustained action that you can accomplish, you cannot dream yourself to success, *you have to win it*.

Therefore, you must concentrate, concentrate, concentrate, upon the affirmations and visualizing exercises. The latter are a form of affirmation and are of equal importance.

A word of warning: Do not keep changing your affirmations. Do not affirm one thing one day and another the next; it causes confusion in your mental World, and makes "confusion worse confounded" in your life. Of course, as you overcome weaknesses and bad habits, you will alter your affirmations accordingly. You will always find some defect that wants eradicating. Otherwise, keep to the affirmations given in these lessons.

By this I do not mean, that you are not to make denials, reversions and affirmations, at all times adapted to all the varying circumstances and difficulties of life, because these are, for your own protection, necessary.

You will doubtless have some plan towards which you are moving. You have some ambition to be realized, some creative purpose in your mind, which you wish to accomplish. To attain to this end, you deny failure, you affirm success, you visualize a picture of that which you wish to achieve. That being so, and having made up your mind, now *stick to it*. Do not change your affirmation; do not alter your mental image. *Keep it unchanged* until it is accomplished. If you vary it and change it, you will bring the utmost confusion into your life. See to it that the image remains unimpaired, getting clearer and more sharply defined, from day to day. If you do this, you will see it working out with mathematical precision in your life.

This course has been prepared so as to guide students by a sure and safe path to the goal of their ambitions.

Concentrate on this teaching, persevere with the "doing" of this teaching, and you will be able, like the writer, to prove and demonstrate its truth in your life and circumstances.

I want you to start seriously to develop your visualizing powers. By this you will improve your memory of all knowledge, but that is quite a minor matter. What is of importance is that what you create in the form of a mental vision, if persistently held in mind, will assuredly manifest itself in your life. Thus you have two methods by which you can alter your life, create better circumstances, and achieve success. First, by Denials and Affirmations, and, second, by Meditation, Concentration and Visualizing. The two should work together. For instance, you make an affirmation, preceded by a denial; next, you conjure up a mental picture of what you have affirmed yourself to be.

You wish to be successful, therefore first of all, you must deny evil and affirm Good, because evil is the general cause of all your troubles and lack of success; next you will affirm Success and follow this by visualizing, either yourself in your perfect mental world, radiant and successful, or else dwell only on the perfect world of *Mind* where there is no failure or limitation of any description.

Having killed failure and poverty by denial, then affirm "I am Success, I am a perfect mental creature, one with the Source of all Good, part of the Universal Mind." "I am Success, like a magnet I attract to me all that I need." "A thousand invisible forces hasten to do my bidding." I am carried along by an irresistible power; I am Success, Success, Success.

Make this affirmation, preceded by the denials, night and morning, always making the affirmation in "Your perfect mental world," buttress it up by repeating it during the day, each time raising yourself to your higher world; do this, and *you will revolutionize your life*.

In order to increase your powers of mental imagery, do the following exercise:

Take a simple flower, or picture, and gaze at it very attentively for several minutes. Examine it in every possible way. Impress every detail upon your mind, then close your eyes and call up an exact mental image of the thing you have been looking at. If the image is crisp, and sharply defined, with no details missing, you will have done well, if not, keep on trying until you succeed.

When you go into a strange room or office, examine carefully every detail; where each piece of furniture is, what pictures are on the walls, what is on the floor, the kind of fireplace, and everything else that forms part of the furnishing. After you get home or when on the train, close your eyes and recall, by making a mental image, as much as you can, of what you saw. Practice this visualizing as much as possible during the coming week, and make affirmations to suit your growing developments. Whatever your need may be, you can make a denial and affirmation to supply that need. Whatever difficulty you have to face, you can overcome it by denial and affirmation, made in your perfect World of Mind.

This course seeks first to build a firm foundation of character, upon which you can later erect the superstructure of success. Seek first to eradicate all weaknesses of character, and in their place install their opposites. For instance, if you have been a procrastinator, become instead noted for your instant action. If you have been pessimistic, become cheerful and optimistic instead. If unpunctual, become the most punctual person who ever lived. If you have been sullen and morose, seek to be bright and cheerful. All this is possible, and really quite easy of accomplishment, by the use of denials, affirmations and mental imagery.

When you have built up your character, the road of success will become comparatively easy, because success is principally a matter of character.

For meditation this week,
think upon these words of James Allen:

"The soul that is impure, sordid and selfish, is gravitating with unerring precision toward misfortune and catastrophe; the soul that is pure, unselfish, and noble, is gravitating with equal precision toward happiness and prosperity. Every soul attracts its own, and nothing can come to it, that does not belong to it. To realize this is to recognize the Universality of Divine Law."

And again, these further words of James Allen: "Your own thoughts, desires and aspirations comprise your world, and, to you, all that there is in the Universe, of beauty and joy and bliss, or of ugliness and sorrow and pain, is contained within yourself. By your own thoughts, you make or mar your life, your world, your Universe."

Quicker results will be obtained, if in addition to visualizing yourself radiantly successful, you will create a sharply defined picture of the exact success that you wish to achieve. If it is money that you want, then "see" the money falling in showers upon your desk.

Whatever you picture in this way persistently, will, in time, be brought to pass in your life. Nothing ever "happens," it is always "brought to pass." You cannot get what you want merely by a pious wish, you have to work for it by mental imagery, then, in time, the way will open for you in a most marvelous manner.

Continue to practice concentration, on one thought or mental image, inhibiting all other thoughts, until the senses are entirely stilled. Then say as before: "My Subliminal Mind draws upon the All-Wisdom, and solves my every problem."

LESSON FIVE

The Objective or Conscious Mind is the outer or surface mind of mind. It is the finite mind of very close limitations. It receives impressions through the organs of sight, hearing, taste, touch and smell. It learns from books, speech, experience and experiment.

We have seen that the subliminal mind is one with the Infinite Mind of the Universe, differing only in degree and not in kind, yet this is useless if the objective mind does not make use of the potential powers lying dormant within.

We have also seen that the so-called subconscious mind is pregnant with tremendous power, and that it is a wonderful intelligence far exceeding anything that the objective consciousness can grasp or understand. Further, that this is regulated and controlled by thoughts, impressions and suggestions, coming through the conscious mind. Therefore, this great intelligence is ruled and governed, or ought to be, by the objective mind. Yet of what use is all this if the mind of the senses does not govern wisely or does not govern at all, but lets the subconscious mind run amuck, as it were, and acting upon instincts and false impressions, untruths and harmful suggestions, turn the whole life into an inferno of trouble and difficulty?

Suppose you wish to succeed in an undertaking. We will imagine that "this undertaking" is a course of study which requires a great deal of application and perseverance, and a certain amount of sacrifice of pleasure for its accomplishment. It necessitates working while others are playing, the resisting of entreaties on the part of friends to join them in their pleasures.

After receiving its instruction, the Will passes on the order through the conscious to the subconscious mind, but unless your Will is naturally very strong, it does this in a halfhearted manner. Although this supposed course of study is of the utmost importance, for without it you cannot succeed in your profession or calling, yet the Will is so weak it cannot impress this sufficiently upon the subconscious mind, with the result that there is very little driving force behind your efforts.

For a time, the studies go along successfully. For one thing the first lessons are always easy, and for another, there is the novelty and freshness of the new work, and the glow of self satisfaction at having entered upon a self-appointed task.

But after a time, the tasks get more difficult, and require more application and concentration, the calls of friends to join them in their pleasures become more insistent, and the Will, not being strong, can no longer deal with the situation. The Will, through weakness, allows suggestions such as "the task is too difficult," "others are enjoying life why should not you?", "others can get on in life without working themselves to death, so why not you?" to pass down into the subconscious mind. The latter, knowing no better, and acting entirely upon suggestion, responds accordingly, with the result that the lessons are flung aside, games are indulged in, and another failure is written large on the scroll of your life.

Suppose, on the other hand, that your Will has been reinforced by affirmations. First, the subconscious mind is deeply impressed. It realizes that this self imposed task *has* to be accomplished somehow, no matter what the cost may be in hard work, perseverance, discomfort and self-sacrifice. Therefore, from the very first, there is great driving power put behind your efforts. A concrete, well-defined image, of the object of your endeavor, the successful ending of your studies, the pride of achievement, the pleasure it will give your friends, the great assistance it will be to you in your profession, the increased status, the enlarged income, the better house, the improved condition of living for those dependent upon you, all these combined in one sharply defined image, are impressed upon the subconscious mind so deeply, that they form a pattern upon which the mind will concentrate all its intense energies, activities and powers. The energies and powers of the mind, working on definite lines laid down by the Will, create in the life a complete replica of the image which has been held in the mind.

When studies become difficult, instead of faltering, the mind puts forth greater effort, generates more power, and overcomes the subject of difficulty. When friends try to entice you to leave your task and join them in their pleasure, then entreaties fall upon deaf ears. You reply, "I must complete this course of study," or "I must pass this examination," or "when I have succeeded and won the position I seek, then, and not until then, I will unbend a little."

This is why very few men succeed, and many fail. Most men have not the staying power to succeed. They have the desire to succeed, but they lack the force of character, and the necessary willpower, to carry their plans to fruition. Some men are full of splendid ideas, but they never carry them out. They see their opportunities, but lack the strength to take advantage of them.

Such a man always has plenty of excuses for his nonsuccess, any reason but the right one. He will never admit that it was his Will that failed. Circumstances, he tells you, were against him.

Nobody would help him at the critical moment. Something or other "happened," which accounted for his failure.

The number of men endowed with the necessary strength of will to succeed by willpower alone, is comparatively small. For one who can succeed in this way, there are thousands who must fail. These thousands of failures might be turned into successes, if they only realized the Power within them, and understood the wonders that can be wrought from affirmations and mental imagery. Men and women endowed with but the ordinary amount of willpower can achieve success beyond their wildest dreams, when they have learnt to use their true Inward Powers, and to reinforce their Wills by the use of affirmations and mental imagery.

But it must not be thought that because you are being taught valuable metaphysical knowledge that you can neglect your Will. On the contrary the training of the Will is of the utmost importance.

In order to succeed you need imagination and vision – faith in yourself and the power within you – but more than all else, staying power is required, and this is largely dependent upon the strength of the Will.

Desire to succeed, energy, ambition, ability, intellect, imagination, capacity, large ideas, all are good, all vitally necessary for the achievement of success, but they are all useless if "staying power" is lacking.

Therefore, one of the primary objects of this Course is the building up within you of that staying power, that strength of purpose, that stability of character, that inflexibility of Will, that are necessary for the achievement of the highest success.

While it teaches valuable metaphysical knowledge, which gives you a tremendous advantage in life, because it reveals to you your inward powers, and shows you how to use them, yet these powers and forces have to be controlled by your Will, otherwise they may work harm instead of good.

Do not misunderstand me, I do not teach that, except in a very few cases, success can be won by willpower alone. It is not willpower that creates, inspires and attracts success. It is the subliminal mind that is the fountain of perpetual power and the storehouse of wisdom. It is the subconscious mind that provides the driving power, but it is the Will that provides the staying power.

The Ego decides what is to be done. It is the Will that compels the subconscious mind to carry out the wishes of the Ego. It is not the will that executes; it is the power of the subconscious mind.

All other systems of instruction, with which I am acquainted, teach a series of gymnastics for the objective mind, and a kind of Will training by brute force. It is a joyless quest seeking success along these lines. It is equivalent to trying to start an automobile engine with the petrol turned off, or without first switching on the electric current.

"Scientific Thought" arouses the latent powers within, puts the student in touch with all the Cosmic Forces, and trains the Will in order to direct them towards the accomplishment of his ambitions.

The ordinary and time-honored way, of trying to develop the Will by brute force, is almost always unsuccessful, and, even when it succeeds, is an extremely slow, and painful method.

In this course of lessons, the strength of the Will grows almost imperceptibly. All the affirmations and exercises, if done systematically and thoroughly, will strengthen your willpower. If you will pay great attention to the affirmations, and persevere with the visualizing, you will find that your willpower will increase to such an extent that you will become a new creature. Therefore, pay the greatest attention to these things, so that your willpower may increase, and its development keep pace, with your increase of knowledge.

Affirmations rob the training of the Will of half its terrors. If you affirm calmly, and steadily, and confidently, that you will perform some difficult or unpleasant duty, at a certain time, you will find, when the time comes, that there will be an impulse urging you to perform that duty. And when you increase your courage, and go and do the thing you dread or dislike, you find to your surprise that it is not half as difficult or unpleasant as you thought it would be.

This is the power of the subconscious mind. It not only urges you to act at the proper time, it also supplies you with the power to act.

If you affirm that you are going to do a certain act, and then not do it, even when your faithful subconscious mind gives you the helpful impulse, then you are destroying your mental powers root and branch. You are deliberately slamming the door of progress and achievement in your own face.

So it is with the subconscious mind. When it prompts, obey it, for if you do not, it will soon cease its promptings, and this wonderful power will be lost to you.

So you see, by the use of affirmations, you can so influence the powers within you, that things impossible to you before, become comparatively easy of accomplishment. The only condition being that you act with decision – that you go fearlessly forward, and do exactly what you have planned to do.

Now I want you, from this time forward, to do each day something that is unpleasant or difficult, but which you really ought to do.

It may be that you really ought to go to your dentist, you are aware that your teeth are getting rapidly worse and that the dentist could stop the mischief if he were given the opportunity, thus saving you much pain, loss and ultimate expense. You know that your digestion, and consequently your general health, are suffering through this neglect and yet you keep putting the matter off. It means the trouble of arranging appointments, the sacrifice of a certain amount of time, and the expenditure of money; also, it is unpleasant to say the least, so you have been letting the matter drift.

Or it may be that there is a certain man you ought to go and interview. You know that if you could get him interested, a lot of profitable business would follow. You have, however, put off visiting him from time to time because he is a great man and has an antipathy to people such as yourself. You know that if you do see him, you will most probably be snubbed most unmercifully, and that no business will result. For these two reasons you have avoided what promises to be an unpleasant interview.

Whatever the unpleasant duty may be that you decide to perform, you should prepare the way by denials and affirmations.

For your visit to your dentist you can deny and affirm as follows: "There is nothing to fear at the dentist; there is nothing he can do to me that I cannot take smiling." Therefore, tomorrow at 11 A.M. I will write (or phone) for an appointment with Mr. _____. He will put my mouth in splendid order and this will benefit my health.

After saying the affirmation over several times, visualize a picture of yourself in your office. You see yourself look at the clock on your desk. It is 11 o'clock. You see yourself take up the telephone and ring up Mr. _____ and hear yourself arrange an appointment. Or you see yourself dash off a note to your dentist asking for an appointment.

Next, you picture yourself in perfect health and your mouth in splendid order.

The next day you will have no difficulty in carrying out what you have affirmed.

If it is a difficult interview, that you decide to undertake, make the affirmation for three, or even seven days, if possible, before the interview takes place. Proceed as follows: Raise yourself up mentally into your perfect World of Mind and deny fear. Say: "I am a perfect radiant mental creature, I am one with the Infinite Universal Mind, therefore, I am full of courage. No one can make me afraid." On _____ day at noon (or any other time you can arrange) I will interview Mr. _____. He will hear what I have to say and the result of the interview will be satisfactory to me. I do this not by mind domination, but by the Law of Attraction."

After affirming in the usual way, visualize your interview. Imagine yourself engaged in conversation with Mr. _____, who seems interested in what you are saying. See yourself entirely at ease and quite natural in your manner. See yourself making a satisfactory end to your interview. Do this very earnestly every night and morning until the interview takes place. When it does take place you will find it will be more satisfactory than ever you dared hope.

When you have learned this way to act with courage and decision, you can leave off using affirmations for such small matters and use them for more important things.

As you progress in Scientific Thinking, you will find wonderful possibilities opening up before you, so that you will always find a use for all the time that you can devote to denials and affirmations. Your character is constantly growing in strength, and things that were impossible at one time, become easy of accomplishment, but always in front of you lie fresh fields to conquer; there is no limit to the life of the Mind.

Continue to practice concentration upon one thought or image, to the exclusion of all other thoughts and images, until the mind is perfectly calm. When you have thoroughly mastered this, and *not* before, you may begin to make use of this wonderful intelligence which you have harnessed to your service. This is explained fully in Lesson eleven, but in order that you may start getting results at once, the following instruction is given: Just as you are falling asleep, calm and still the mind, and when you have succeeded, bring your problem before your mind, and affirm that while you sleep your Subliminal Mind will solve your problem, and give you the answer in the morning. Next, dismiss the matter from your mind, and go to sleep. In the morning, when you are awake, refuse to worry about your problem, or engage in nerve-racking thought about it; instead, still the mind as before, and the answer will come.

Read this lesson over as often as you can find time to do so; it cannot be absorbed all at once.

Hold in your mind a sharp definite picture of the success you have planned. If it is money that you desire, then see money in abundance pouring in streams on to your desk.

If it is a wealthy practice, then mentally "see" yourself in a perfectly appointed office, receiving wealthy clients in large numbers, and "see" them waiting patiently in queues for their turn to see you. Whatever it is that you desire, no matter whether it be invention, genius, love, friends, house, lands or service to others, picture it very definitely and distinctly and hold this image before your mind, keep constantly calling it up, and every time that you do so let the sight thrill you with pleasure. As you call up the picture affirm "I am Success," and believe that it is already yours. Keep on affirming success, and visualizing success, and it will surely come, and in much larger volume than ever you imagined possible.

I wish you the highest possible success.

LESSON SIX

The Objective or conscious mind is the mind of the senses. It learns from books, persons, experience and experiments. It reasons on things learnt, and on thoughts received from a variety of sources, and having passed judgment, rejects some things as error, and accepts others as truth. Things considered to be truth are passed down into the subconscious mind to add to its existing store of memory and experiences.

Whatever is passed to the subconscious mind becomes translated into action. Thus, if immoral or impure thoughts are entertained, then immediately physical changes take place in the body, which are simply these thoughts being translated into action by the subconscious mind. Thus, if one repeatedly imbibes this class of thought, a time arrives when one is compelled by the subconscious mind to indulge in immoral practices. This is why many people who have been all their lives apparently quite moral, and well behaved, suddenly break out into flagrant immorality. It is a great surprise and causes great distress to relations and friends. They think that it is a sudden transformation, or that it is due to a certain temptation, or to the evil influence of a certain wicked person. It is instead none of these things. It is simply the result of evil thinking. Evil thoughts produce evil actions. Evil thoughts also attract other thoughts just as evil as themselves. In the same way a person who indulges in evil thinking, attracts other people of similar character.

There is a law running through the Universe which is that "like attracts like." Think evil thoughts, and you will assuredly attract others just as evil, which will help to drag you down. Let him think evil thoughts, and he will attract other people even worse than himself. In the same way, if you entertain thoughts of failure, if you doubt your ability to succeed, if you feel that circumstances will arise which will "swamp" your business, then you will attract streams of "failure" thoughts which will help to keep success away.

The reverse is of course equally true. If you entertain "pure" thoughts you will attract thoughts of a similar kind from the ether, and be strengthened and blessed thereby. By the same law you will attract other people of lofty minds who will aid you in your upward climb.

If you entertain beautiful thoughts, you will draw to yourself a constant stream of thoughts of a like nature, and you will attract to yourself friends of a noble and inspiring character.

In the same way, if you allow thoughts of success only to be held in the mind, and chase away all thoughts of failure, you will attract to yourself a full measure of successful thoughts. These will strengthen your determination and inspire you to greater effort. By the same law you will also attract to yourself men and women of a successful type of mind. You will find yourself sought after by successful people and they will bring with them opportunities for your more abundant success.

Therefore, you will readily see how important it is that only the right type of thoughts should be allowed to enter the subconscious mind.

The Will and the Conscious Mind stand as sentinels at the door of the subconscious mind. To them is given the important task of deciding what shall, or what shall not, enter. Every kind of thought and suggestion, inimical to our welfare, meet us and strike us on every hand. Harmful thoughts seek to enter our minds at every turn. Books, magazines, race thought, the mental outlook of friends and acquaintances are all against our mental development. The attitude of mind of the average person, of the common ruck, is not inspiring. It does not suggest "success," it expresses at best, only a passive acceptance of life. It takes life as it is; things as they come. It is not often that you meet a man who is conscious that he is "Master of his fate, the Captain of his soul."

How then can you escape all this deadening, destroying mental atmosphere?

First: You must, in habit of thought, separate yourself from "the crowd." You must shut out their pessimistic-belief-in-circumstances – weak-failure-low-lewd type of thoughts altogether, and live in an entirely different world – the inner world of your own creative thought.

I do not mean that you are to look down upon your fellows. You must mix with your fellows, and while holding yourself proof against low and weak types of thought, seek to raise their minds by your own hopeful suggestions. When a friend talks as though failure were a possibility in his life, suggest instead that success is hastening his way. When people are sad, try to cheer them by hopeful suggestions. When they look on the dark side of life, show them the bright side. When they rail and rave, pour oil on the troubled waters. Seek to cheer people up and resolutely refuse to accept the suggestions of their minds.

Second: You must remember that books, papers, magazines, letters, unless you consciously prevent them, will convey suggestions to your subconscious mind and in course of time become translated into action. Therefore, if you read books of passion, your life will be unbalanced and perhaps wrecked by gusts of violent desire, which call loudly to be satisfied. On the other hand, if you will read books written by lofty minds, you will receive thoughts which inspire and strengthen you.

You should therefore choose your reading wisely. Read the best literature, and do not then accept as Truth all that you read. Refuse resolutely to accept any idea that is not in agreement with your new conception of life. All ideas of man being the puppet of powers outside himself, of being the sport of fate and the victim of circumstances must be rigorously rejected. All that tends to strengthen your new conception of life, which is, that all things are delivered into your hands, and that you have the power to conquer both yourself and all difficulty and thus make your life sublime – all that tends to strengthen this mental attitude should be accepted.

The Will and the Conscious Mind stand at the gate; by them you must examine every thought, every suggestion. Hold everything up and examine it in the light of your newly found knowledge, and if it cannot stand this searching test, cast it from you.

You can never be successful if you allow thoughts of weakness or failure or fear to enter your subconscious mind. The one great outstanding characteristic that distinguishes successful men from the unsuccessful, is their absolute belief and faith in their own ability to succeed. Thoughts of failure, or fear, never enter the mind of the truly successful man. If you examine the character of any great and truly successful man, you will find this dominating characteristic – absolute faith in his own success, and with it an entire absence of fear or weakness.

Therefore, it is certain that you can never be successful if you allow doubt or fear to enter your mind; it is only when by mind control you have cast out fear and doubt that you can enter the path that leads to success.

Some men are successful and are not conscious of the laws which govern success. They unconsciously work according to law – by instinct rather than knowledge. It is because they are naturally men of *large faith* and *unfailing courage* that they have become successful.

Therefore you, too, in order to succeed must have a large faith and unfailing courage. Faith in the power within you and a courage that is born of knowledge. Thus can you be placed on the same footing as that of any other successful man, in fact you will be better equipped than the naturally successful man, for possessing knowledge will enable you to avoid many errors, into which he, through ignorance of the law, might fall.

Therefore, in your reading you must close your eyes to all suggestions which are antagonistic to your newly found knowledge.

Third: By denial and affirmation you create a new mental outlook.

By denial we obtain immediate relief from our troubles.

Denial kills the evil thought which is the cause of all the trouble, and cleanses and purifies the mind, making it ready for the affirmation.

Always precede an affirmation by the necessary denial.

If you are going to affirm success, first deny failure, if you wish for prosperity and plenty, then first deny poverty and want, so as to get the mind ready for the affirmation "I am success; prosperity and plenty are already mine."

But, you exclaim, how can I truthfully affirm that I am that which I know myself not to be? The answer is: There are two of *you*. There is the finite, outside, surface, material *you*, and there is the great and glorious inner spiritual being which is the real *you*. The former is a weak and coarse reflection of the latter. This glorious and real *you* is perfect.

When you affirm in your perfect Mental World, that you are perfect, you mean the real and sublime *you*, and you are telling the truth. Whatever good quality you affirm is quite true, because you (yourself, the real *you*) are perfect. By denial of evil and imperfection and by the affirming of infinite perfection, you destroy evil in your material life, and bring it more into harmony with the perfect life. Therefore, what you affirm in your perfect mental world, is later, and sometimes instantaneously, manifested in your material world.

An affirmation has been described by one writer as "a statement of Truth consciously used so as to become the directing power of Life's expression." This is a good and true definition. Scientists will tell you that the submerged mind of man acts only upon suggestion. So powerful is the hidden mind and so subject is it to suggestion that we have in affirmations a weapon of extraordinary power for good, and in negative suggestion a terrible power for evil.

When we use an affirmation we make a statement of Truth which, if repeated often enough, will sink down into the recesses of our mind and become part of our very life. It will galvanize the hidden forces of our mind into activity and guide them into the path of achievement.

If in the past you have been a failure, then by constantly affirming "I am Success," you will gradually eradicate the weak-fearing-give-up-too-soon attitude of your material mind, and build up in its place the mental outlook of courage, cheerfulness, optimism and belief in your ability to succeed.

Failure or lack of success in life is not, as I have already pointed out, due to outward circumstances, but is simply a weakness of character. By affirmations you can build up your character and make its former weak points strongest in your armor.

It is by affirmations, then, that man can control himself, build up his character and shape his own destiny.

You will look upon life in a different way, you will act in a different manner, you will attract a different kind of people. Soon you begin to see evidences of the truth of these teachings manifested in your life and circumstances.

Therefore, you can by affirmations make yourself proof against the harmful suggestions that meet you on every hand. By affirmations you build up the courageous, confident, hopeful, cheerful, absolutely certain attitude of mind, which is the only type of mind that can readily succeed.

As you begin to see evidences of the working of your newly found power, you feel lifted up in a strange and wonderful way. You feel as if you are being carried forward, by invisible powers, to success; it is as though some impelling force were pushing you in the back and urging you forward to the goal of your endeavor.

Therefore, persist and persevere with your affirmations. Continue to look for difficult tasks, and unpleasant, but very necessary duties, and aided by the power of affirmations, *do them*.

Make affirmations to suit your own peculiar needs. If you are too energetic and inclined to run yourself to pieces, and rush and tear about and get your own nerves and everybody else's, on edge, affirm as follows: "I am perfectly calm, cool and collected. I refuse to get excited or flustered. I work quietly and methodically." Then mentally picture yourself at work in a very calm, cool and collected way, without hurry, fluster or excitement. You will find your work goes much better in consequence, and certainly not less quickly.

If, on the other hand, you are inclined to be lazy or lethargic, affirm as follows: "I am the personification of industry and energy. I am busy from morning until night." Then picture yourself hard at work, doing good work and plenty of it. This you will find will help you vastly in enabling you to "stick" to your task, and to keep sticking to it day after day.

Thus you have within your grasp the power by which you can overcome every weakness of character; a key which will unlock every door; an art which is the open sesame to the unlimited treasure house of the Universal Mind.

By the use of this wonderful power you can turn failure into success, sorrow into joy, mediocrity into genius.

To you all things are possible – strength of purpose, the joy of achievement, all the glories of a life of self-mastery.

Unto him who attains to the dazzling height of self-mastery, unto him who can stand erect, and unafraid, and untroubled by the things that vex and rend the hearts of men; unto him who is master of his passions, his emotions, his circumstances and his life; unto such a one has come that for which the world has longed and strived in vain, about which philosophers, poets and seers have, for centuries, spoken and written, and yet never have been able to grasp or hold.

He who overcomes himself, overcomes the world.

For visualizing exercises, picture the window frame of your bedroom, trace the wood of which it is made, step by step, process by process, right back to its original form, the tree in the forest. See clearly and distinctly every stage, leave out no detail.

LESSON SEVEN

An American writer speaking of Universal Mind says:

"It thinks, and Suns spring into shape;
It wills, and Worlds disintegrate;
It loves and Souls are born."

It will thus be seen that thought is the origin of the visible Universe. All that we see around us is the result of thought. We may even go further, and say that all the invisible forces, which keep the wonderful machinery of the Universe working perfectly and smoothly, are but the thought-energies of the same Universal Mind.

As in the macrocosm so is it in the microcosm; the subliminal mind of man is the same in essence as the Universal Mind of the Universe; the difference is not one of kind but of degree.

Thought is so subtle, so elusive, that it has by the majority of men, been considered impossible to control, but the greatest philosophers, seers and leaders in the World's history have known differently. All that they achieved, they accomplished through the power of thought; and this was possible because they had learned the art of thought control.

"What man has done, man can do." This was never so true as it is today, because the science of Mind is now being spread abroad, and that it is possible for quite ordinary people to learn how to control their thoughts, is now known to be a scientific possibility.

The Law which keeps the Universe running so smoothly is the law of Attraction. It is this law that brought it together; it is this law that keeps it from falling apart.

All the Universe, in all its planes, is ruled by this law; in the Spiritual World it is called the Law of Love; in the Mental World the Law of Attraction; in the Material World it is known as the Law of Affinity. They all mean the same – in essence they are the same.

Just as the electrons are called together in the invisible ether, thus to form an atom, so in turn, are atoms brought together, and by vibrating at different rates of speed, create what we call form. Thus is matter (so-called) built up into all the beautiful forms we see, simply by the Law of Attraction.

It is this law that holds all matter together. If it failed, rocks would fly asunder and all things would disintegrate, because the power that attracted one atom to another would have ceased to operate.

It is the same in the Mental World; everything works according to this same law. It is because "like creates like" and "like attracts like" that it is possible to revolutionize our lives by the power of thought.

"Thoughts," said Prentice Mulford, "are things." "Thoughts," says T. Sharper Knowlson, "so far from being mere brain flashes, are, judging solely from their effects, real entities, apparently composed of spiritual substance, the nature of which is outside the range of discovery of our present faculties." "Thought," says Levy, "is not an event which dies in a world ethereal, supersensible, imperceptible; it has continually its likeness and repercussion in our organism."

In our laboratory experiments we are demonstrating the great fact that thoughts are forces. They have form, and quality, and substance, and power, and we are beginning to find that there is what we may term a science of thought.

We are beginning to find also that through the instrumentality of our thought forces we have creative power in reality. Many more authorities could be quoted, but these will suffice to show that thoughts are just as much "things" as town halls or mountains are "things." It is a great mistake to imagine that because you can see a thing with your physical eyes, feel it with your hands, or hit it with a hammer, that it is for that reason more real than something you can neither see nor feel. On the contrary, the "Unseen" is vastly more powerful, lasting and forceful than anything you can see with your physical eyes. What you see with your eyes is only the effect of greater causes which are invisible.

"Everything exists in the unseen before it is manifested in the seen, and in this sense it is true that the unseen things are real, while the things that are seen are the unreal. The unseen things are *cause;* the seen things are *effect*."

Thoughts then are "entities," are "things," are "forces," are vital subtle "powers." They, like everything else, and every other force in the universe, are subject to law. This law is the Law of Attraction.

Whatever thoughts you think will attract to you thoughts of a similar nature. According as you create good or bad thoughts, so do you determine whether your life shall be blessed or cursed.

Thus, if you think "Success" thoughts, and affirm them, and cling to them in the face of apparent defeat and failure, you will attract to yourself such a wave of powerful, upbuilding and inspiring thoughts, that you will be lifted right over your difficulty and carried, as by invisible forces, along the path of accomplishment.

On the other hand, it is equally true that if you think a weak thought, a low thought, a vile thought, or a thought of failure, there will be attracted to you a host of thoughts of like character, which by their nature will curse you and drag you down.

Think "Success" and thousands of invisible forces will fly to your aid. Think "failure" and innumerable forces will help to make your failure even more complete.

By choosing your thoughts you choose either success or failure, happiness or misery, hope or despair.

Says one of deep insight into the nature of things: "The things that we see, are but a very small fraction of the things that are. The real, vital forces at work in our own lives, and in the world we see about us, are not seen by the ordinary physical eye. Yet they are the causes of which all things we see are merely the effects. Thoughts are forces; like builds like, and like attracts like. For one to govern his thinking then is to determine his life."

By the right use of your thought-forces you can make yourself a magnet and attract to yourself all that you *deserve*. We each get what he or she deserves. As we improve the quality of our thoughts, so do we become deserving of better results; as we become deserving of better results, so do better things flow to us by the operation of Universal Law.

By the use of carefully graded denials and affirmations, we break the power of evil thought-habit, and in its place create a new mental attitude, hopeful, strong, cheerful, successful, confident, an attitude of mind that knows not failure, can never be discouraged; that stands firm and unafraid amid the changing scenes of life; an attitude of mind that overcomes, conquers and achieves. An attitude of mind that lives in a sea of positive, helpful, stimulating thoughts, that are the products of the best minds of all ages.

Thus it all comes down to this. It is by the use of denials and affirmations, and by persevering in their use, that the life can be changed, circumstances altered, and ambitions realized.

By denials and affirmations we can direct our thought-stream into the right channel; by denials and affirmations we can impress upon our subconscious mind thoughts which, becoming translated into actions, lead to success and all accomplishment. By denials and affirmations we can break down the force of evil habit, and in its place install habits that ennoble and enrich our lives. By denials and affirmations we can build up our characters, changing what was weak and vacillating into that which is powerful and stable. By denials and affirmations we can concentrate our consciousness upon thoughts of Power, Success and Courage and these, in turn, will attract to us multitudes of other thoughts of a similar nature. Do you realize, dear Reader, the extent of the wonderful power that you hold in your hands?

Make denials and affirmations to suit your particular needs. Whatever you desire to do, affirm beforehand that you can do it, and that you *will* do it when the time for doing comes.

Whatever disagreeable or difficult duty lies before you, deny failure, and affirm beforehand that you can and will do it, that already in your Mental World it is accomplished; then visualize yourself doing the thing calmly and without effort. Mentally see yourself dealing with a difficult or unpleasant matter, with calm dignity and ease. When the time for action arrives you will succeed.

MEDITATION

Concentrate your whole attention upon the meditations. If you find your thoughts wandering through lack of concentrative power, make use of the following denial and affirmation. First of all, cleanse the mind by the denial of evil, and calm and strengthen it by the affirmation of good. You have by so doing raised yourself into your perfect Mental World, breathing the pure air of perfect mental freedom. Now say, "Mind wandering cannot affect me. I am a perfect *mind*, part of the great Universal Mind that is everywhere and works in and through everything. Therefore, my mental powers are perfect. It was a mistake that made me think I could not concentrate; it was simply a delusion of the physical senses.

Now affirm as follows: "Now I know that I can concentrate on any subject I please. My potential powers are infinite, I have only to develop them, I have only to 'try' and I must succeed." Working in this way you will develop tremendous powers of Concentration.

MEDITATION

I send out my thoughts to all mankind and say: "Dear everybody, I love you." Like the beams of a searchlight, my mental vision sweeps over all the continents and islands of the world, and visualizes all peoples, sending out to them a great beam of Love. It embraces all animals again affirming, "I love you, I love you." Then into my heart flows a great wave of divinest peace.

For this week's visualizing exercise, take six small articles and examine them very carefully, one at a time. For instance, if one article is a pencil, look at it and see in what respects it differs from other pencils. You notice its color; its shape, either round, hexagon or oval; its point, well sharpened or otherwise; the maker's name and trademark; the name of the pencil itself; its condition, scratches on the surface of the polish; all these and many other points should be minutely noticed. Examine each article in turn and just as minutely. When you have examined them all, shut your eyes and visualize each article, and see every point and peculiarity in your mind's eye, just as you did with your physical sight. Change the articles for new ones from day to day.

If you lack knowledge of a certain subject and desire to gain this knowledge, then tell your subliminal mind what it is that you require; it will then either supply direct the knowledge that you need or bring to your notice the very book or course of lessons that you require. Also, in solving your problems, your subliminal mind may bring a sentence to your notice, which, directly as you read it, tells you that it is the answer to your riddle. The more you can quieten the senses and the objective mind, and rely upon your subliminal mind, the greater will be your wisdom and understanding.

LESSON EIGHT

There has been a lot of nonsense written and spoken about the Law of Attraction. People have been solemnly taught that all they need to do is to adopt a certain mental attitude, think thoughts of success and abundance, and then to sit and wait for abundance of all good things to drop from the skies at their feet. The folly of it is seen when we find that these teachers of "abundance" and "opulence" have themselves to work for a living, by teaching the very thing which, if true, would save them from all necessity of working.

There is no such thing as getting something for nothing. The principle of the "square deal" runs right through life and the Universe. A businessman who tries to get something for nothing, who, in other words, fails to give value for money, finally finds himself without a customer. Those who try to evade this law by creating trusts and combines will find that their ill gotten gains will be confiscated by a power greater than themselves. The "square deal," reasonable profits, fair wages, honest straightforward business integrity, all these will succeed and continue to succeed, as long as their remain people to do business with; but the "ring" or "combine" or "trust," squeezing its swollen, dishonest profits out of the life and blood of the common people, can only do business so long as the community allows them to.

Even if, however, a man can filch a fortune by unfair means, i.e. by not giving good value for money, by extortion or profiteering, he will lose in one direction exactly in proportion to that which he gains in another. Let him make a fortune by sharp practice; let him snap his fingers and sneer at integrity and honor and universal law; let him rejoice at what he has done; let him think himself a fine, clever fellow; nevertheless nemesis awaits him. He will lose in love, peace of mind and happiness in exact proportion to his dishonest gain. He makes money, granted, but he loses that which money cannot buy.

There is a Law of Compensation running through life and the Universe and you cannot avoid it. If you are to succeed you must work and accomplish; if you are to receive the riches of the world you must give of your best in exchange.

"Then give to the world the best you have, and the best will come back to you."

This is where the Law of Attraction operates, not by your sitting still and expecting the impossible to happen, but by the giving in faith and confidence of your best efforts to the World. By calling upon your hidden powers, and by creating powerful thoughts, you attract to yourself armies of thoughts of a similar kind, which passing into your subconscious mind are translated into actions of the highest type, the type that glories in achievement, and that wins Success. Thus if you give your best to the world, then in the form of a rich and abundant success "the best will come back to you."

These people who expect to be successful without working for it, take, many of them, great comfort from John Burrough's famous poem, the first verse of which is as follows:

"Serene, I fold my hands and wait,
Nor care for wind, or tide, or sea;
I rave no more 'gainst Time or Fate,
For lo! my own shall come to me."

Its meaning is the exact opposite to that which the "no work" people attach to it. It does not mean that we can literally sit and "think," without effort, good things into our lap. Instead, it describes the mental attitude of the man of faith – the man who believes he can succeed. Having adjusted his mind to the correct attitude, he is serene and calm, knowing that his efforts in the objective world of effort will be successful, owing to his mental world being in tune with all the higher cosmic forces. These words therefore represent the mental attitude of a well poised, confident man, and have no connection with his physical life. Such a man owing to his mind being at peace, is always capable of the best and highest effort. It is those whose minds are at rest who work the best. Therefore, those who think that they can become successful without translating their thoughts into actions are deluding themselves.

The principle of "the square deal" runs through all life and the universe. Should an artist conceive a picture, and be content that it remains in his mind; can he rightly expect payment for his creation? Would it be right if payment were made to him for a picture that existed only in his imaginative mind? No, because he has not rendered any service to his fellows, he has not given value for money. Let him therefore put his picture on canvas and thus bring joy and refreshment to many, and for his service payment will be made, and the greater his conception, the greater will be the reward.

Again, an engineer conceives a bridge. Shall he be deserving of payment if he keeps it in his mind? No, let him transfer his mental image to paper and translate his drawings into actual steel and stone construction, and he will become a blessing to thousands. Then will he be worthy of the greatest rewards. Life demands of us a square deal, a fair exchange. If we are to receive, we must give. If we give, we shall receive. Do not believe for one moment that chicanery, or sharp practice, or underhand dealing, or hiding up faults, or taking advantage of other people's ignorance or weaknesses is going to lead to success, because it will not, and cannot. I have known plenty of men splendidly equipped for the battle of life, "brainy," resourceful, capable, and not lacking in courage, yet they have not succeeded, simply because they were not "straight." They were clever and plausible and could always do well at first interviews, but they could never keep their clients or customers because they failed to give honest service in exchange for honest money.

This world is crying aloud for honest, straightforward and sincere lawyers, doctors, businessmen, politicians and teachers. It calls for men of integrity, men who live their lives according to a principle instead of being mere opportunists; for men who love honor and truth, for men who believe in the principle of the square deal. The world wants men who will give of their very best, and upon such is willing to pour out its treasures in rich profusion. Principle and sincerity are more than ever needed today. Men who can be trusted, men on whom a nation, a world, can rely.

No great success is, or ever can be, possible without the quality of sincerity; no great achievement was ever won except by those to whom honor and principle were as the very breath of life.

Look at the lives of all the truly great and successful ones that have ever lived, and we can only find sincerity of purpose – a giving of their very best service to the world. The extent of their sincerity was the measure of their greatness.

To win success of any kind you must be sincere, you must give of your very best, you must somehow find expression for that which is within you.

As you come into conscious realization of the powers within you, you will have more to express. Therefore, "your best" will be constantly getting better, with the consequence that your reward will be greater. In other words, as you develop "within," as you build up in the "unseen," so in like manner will your power to achieve be manifested in your life, and success and prosperity be attracted to you. All this is dependent upon your giving freely. If you give grudgingly, you will receive but a scanty reward; if you give fully and freely of the best that is within you, you will reap a rich and abundant harvest.

Give the best that is within you. How can I find words with which to express all that I mean? Give your best thoughts, hold nothing back; give your most faithful service, do not spare yourself, for all the cosmic forces are yours; give to the utmost of all the powers, the forces, the emotions, the inspirations that are within you; do this, and you will never lack. The universe is not run by caprice or chance, everything is according to Law. The Law of Compensation is immutable, it can never be evaded.

Thus do we hold our lives and destinies in our own hands. We can give our best to the world – our best in service, in love, in devotion, in honesty, in faithfulness, in inspiration, in beauty – our best in all that we do or attempt to do; and back to us will come unerringly the highest good, the greatest joy, the best that life can offer. Or, on the other hand, we may give poor service, try to get what we do not deserve, endeavor by slimness, trickiness and sharp practice to snatch an advantage at the expense of others, and in return we shall reap a harvest of trouble, disappointment, unhappiness and failure.

"Then give to the world the best you have, and the best will come back to you."

No longer can you offer the world the more or less imperfect service which has hitherto been the best that you could offer. Now are you entering into the fullness and glory of the vast powers of your subliminal mind, now are you controlling an ever-growing stream of creative thoughts; now are all these inward forces being translated into action, and that action can only be better service, better work, higher accomplishment, more abundant success than ever you have known before.

Let imperfect work belong only to the past; the badly scrubbed doorstep, the mediocre poem, the commonplace picture, the halfhearted service in parliament; time-serving, men pleasing, instead of working for a grand ideal; let it all go, it belongs to yesterday and yesterday is dead. It belongs to the imperfect past. Now you live in a more perfect present, and press on to a still more perfect future.

Mistakes and shortcomings of the past shall have no more dominion over you; in your hands is the key which opens up the way to all freedom and accomplishment.

From now onward the new and wonderful life within you will well up with ever-increasing power and find expression in better work, in tasks more perfectly performed, in service more generously given, in more complete self-control.

Leave the past and its failures; you have nothing to do either with it or them; today is yours and the future shall be according as you build today.

This week's affirmation is:

*I give to the world the best I have,
and the best comes back to me.*

Then visualize yourself giving the very highest and best service of which you are capable, and then picture the highest good coming back to you in return. Make this mental picture very real; it will have a great effect for good in your life.

As a visualizing exercise, take a flower and picture its "growth" backwards from the full bloom right back to the planted seed. Actually "see" the whole process.

MEDITATION

There is no need for me to anxiously snatch and grab, to hoard and scrape, to cheat and squeeze my fellow men. I do not have to run after success and fortune; instead, they kneel down at my feet and pay me homage. I need stoop to no subterfuges, no low cunning, no doubtful methods, for everything I need is mine, all that I desire comes to me, by the operation of Natural Law. I realize now that I am one with, and form a part of, the Infinite Mind. I realize that the Infinite Mind is "everything there is," and that everything there is, is Infinite Mind. Therefore, as I am a part of the Infinite Mind, I too am all things and all things are in me.

Therefore, everything that I can possibly require, peace of mind, achievement of friends, love, prosperity, success, these are all mine.

I am a magnet; I attract to myself only the highest good.

I am attuned only to the highest vibration of success, accomplishment, happiness; the lower vibrations of failure, want and unhappiness can find no echo in my mind, no manifestation in my life.

I pour out unstintedly upon my fellows my best work and efforts, my richest thoughts and emotions; I give to the World the very best that is in me. Yet the more unselfishly I give, the more abundantly are life's choicest gifts showered upon me.

Give to the world the best you have, not merely your labor, your work, your earnest endeavor, but your inspiration, the very best that is in you. Not only work in the usual sense of the word, not only labor by accomplishing your daily task better than ever before, but in addition work mentally, work creatively, work along original lines. Strive to do something fresh, create something new, add something to the world's total sum of joy and happiness. This can only be done by spending your spare time, not in frivolous pleasures, but in concentration in the Silence. Still the outer mind and the senses, and then in the Silence listen to the still small voice of inspiration.

LESSON NINE

Mankind is divided into two types, positive and negative. Let me try and describe each to you.

Positive man is magnetic, attractive, courageous, happy, cheerful, energetic, is full of vitality, power and ability to succeed. He never doubts his ability to win; he never worries when things go wrong; he does not complain when things are not smooth. If he meets with a temporary set-back he becomes the more determined to succeed. He does not lay upon other people the blame of his own mistakes, but instead learns a lesson from his temporary failure which shall be a guide and beacon in all future undertakings. The positive man can always find people to believe in him and to finance his operations. He never lacks friends, for just the type of people he wants are always anxious to be his friends. Consequently men, and with them, opportunities, are always coming his way. He is an optimist, but is not foolish or blind in his optimism. He is above being petty or mean, or selfish or cruel; neither does he let hate or anger sway him or influence his life or business. He inspires confidence, compels attention, is a leader rather than a follower, and literally exudes an atmosphere of success.

A negative man is, of course, the antithesis of this type. He is fearful, given to worry, apt to look on the dark side of things. Is afraid to act too much on his own responsibility and seeks the help and advice of other people. Has difficulty in making up his mind, and when he has made it up, he often changes it. He lets others pass him in the race of life and then worries because he fails to get on. He is never much of a success in life; no matter what he achieves he might have done very much better. He seldom realizes that his failures are due to his own failings, but instead lays the blame upon other people's shoulders or ascribes his troubles to chance or ill fortune. His company is not cheerful and is not sought by other people, except one or two as miserable as himself.

All his thought and conversation are tinged with pessimism and his face, in course of time, becomes lugubrious and miserable, an accurate index of the state of mind within. He has no belief in himself. He believes in fate and the influence of outside circumstances. He is, so he says, as environment has shaped him. If he is a failure, it is, he thinks, not his fault, and if his character is not all that it might be, it is due to heredity and environment.

There are, of course, infinite degrees of positiveness and also of negativeness. Therefore, one may be said to be more positive or less positive according to one's stage of development, or one can be more negative or less negative according to the degree of helplessness and misery in which one may be steeped; but the essential difference is this, that whereas the positive man looks *within* for his power to achieve, and looks forward with confidence to the future, the negative person, on the contrary, having no confidence in himself, looks to others and outside sources for help and assistance and fears what fate may bring him. The positive man believes in himself completely and absolutely, the negative person does not; that is the great difference.

We are what we are as a result of past thinking. Our mental attitude is built up by the thoughts we habitually harbor or cultivate. Thus, if we entertain positive thoughts only, and deny negative thoughts, replacing them by their opposites whenever they intrude, we gradually build up a positive attitude of mind, which means that we become positive men or women, and as such cannot fail to be successful in life. Therefore, it all comes back to the old question of thought control. "For one to govern his thinking, then, is to determine his life."

Thoughts are positive if they dwell upon the following: Success, achievement, accomplishment, overcoming, conquering, mastering, prosperity, power, courage, calmness, dignity, perseverance, purposefulness, patience, wisdom, faithfulness, confidence, faith, hope, cheerfulness, love, joy, peace and happiness.

Thoughts are negative if they dwell upon the following: Failure, difficulty, bad luck, hard lines, I can't, fear, dread, grief, worry, care, anxiety, loss, fate, unfaithfulness, grievances, criticizing others, imputing bad motives to others, hate, envy, covetousness, brooding, lust, impurity, immorality, selfishness, sensuality, misery and unhappiness.

If you concentrate your thoughts upon the former for a few minutes and let the imagination play round each word, and call up in the mind just what it means, a sense of power, unlimited and all comprehensive will pervades one's being. This is the infinite powers of the subliminal mind being aroused. All these positive qualities which these words represent are within you; otherwise you could not arouse this sense of power. If, by concentrating your thoughts for a few minutes upon Success, a sense of unlimited powers of accomplishment stirs within you, then you have actually within you unlimited powers of accomplishment. If, by thinking only of Joy for a few minutes, a sense of intense Joy pervades the mind, then you have simply called into activity an inexhaustible reservoir of Joy that already existed within you. You cannot call into activity that which does not exist. In the same way, if you concentrate your thoughts upon a negative quality, such as misery, you will after a few minutes become gloomy and depressed, or if your mind dwells on fear, you will soon become full of dread and apprehension.

Therefore, your success and happiness all depend upon the type of thought that you entertain. If your mind dwells upon positive thoughts only, then you become positive and by sustained action, successful. If, however, you think negative thoughts, you become negative and consequently a failure.

How then shall you so control your thinking that only positive thoughts are allowed? The answer is, by eternal vigilance, constant watch and guard, and by incessant denials and affirmations. Whenever a weak or vile or unworthy thought attempts to enter your mind, deny its existence in your perfect Mental World, and affirm in its place a thought the exact opposite of the one which you have denied. For instance, the thought may come to you that you will fail at the examination for which you have shortly to sit or that a certain important interview will end disastrously for you. Whatever the thought may be, if it is negative, deny it from the mind. Raise yourself into your perfect World of Mind and say "There is and can be no failure, man is a perfect mental creature, potentially all the powers of the Infinite are his, therefore he can never fail." And then affirm:

I am success.
Everything that I attempt I completely accomplish.
I am success.

Then visualize yourself successful in that which you have attempted, the examination passed, the interview successfully ended. See yourself radiant with success, feel yourself lifted up by the power within. Let the thought, "I am success," sink deeply into your subconscious mind; let this be projected into the space to gather unto itself thoughts of similar quality and power, and you will find the negative fearing thought will flee away. Thus will you become master in your own house and captain of your soul. Thus will you be built up in character and strengthened with determination and ability to accomplish. Thus will you be enabled to go forward with joy and confidence to possess your glorious heritage.

The following affirmation used at night just as you are falling asleep will be helpful; after a few weeks it will have become unnecessary and should be discarded:

When negative thoughts assail me
I will deny them
and replace them
by thoughts of power.

Then visualize yourself pursuing the path of achievement which you have so often before seen in your mind's eye. Imagine that you see people trying to drag you from the path and seeking to persuade you to travel down a side turning. See yourself shake them off easily and firmly, continuing your journey to that bright vision which to you is Success.

I have said that there are varying degrees of Positiveness, just as there are varying degrees of Negativeness. For instance, the lowest form of "success" thought is "I can succeed." A student may have all his life thought that he could not succeed. He may have thought that others might succeed because they were "clever" or had better opportunities, or were blest with "luck"; but he, poor fellow, being neither clever, lucky nor presented with opportunities, cannot succeed; he must forever be content to remain a mere hewer of wood and drawer of water. But one day, we will imagine, he reads a "Pass me on" pamphlet and reads for the first time that he has within him the power to succeed and accomplish, and like a flash he realizes his true inward powers, and cries "I can succeed."

That, of course, is the first step. Very soon he says to himself, "I will succeed," and thus finds himself on the second step, and, for some time, progresses on these lines. This is a rugged and stony path because progress depends almost entirely upon Willpower and progress by Willpower alone is exhausting and trying to a degree, but soon the student realizes that he has acquired a new or wider consciousness and says with joy and wonder, "I am success." He has now reached a higher region of the mind; he is now exercising a larger and deeper faith. He realizes for the first time that success is not something that is outside himself, or that has to be searched for or chased. He realizes that not only is success within him, but that he himself is Success. I cannot explain it further. I am dealing with a state of mind which cannot be described, but which can be experienced. When the student has attained to this stage of consciousness he can no longer fail in life. His life henceforth becomes a constant progression, a passing onwards to higher heights and more glorious achievements.

This is the reason why I have made the affirmation to read "I am Success" instead of "I will be successful." To say that you will be successful is good, but it puts off your success to a future time. To affirm that you are success or successful *now* is to make your success to begin here and now.

Conscientious readers will say at once: "How can I say truthfully that I am success when all the time failure enters so much into my life? I have just failed to pass an examination, and through lack of energy and perseverance have let the opportunity of a lifetime slip by; how then can I affirm myself success?" The answer is that you are success in reality. In your inward inner self you are success and have all the elements of unbounded success inherent within you.

If you affirm that you are Success, and will persist and persevere with that affirmation, then in your inner self you are success, and later this will be translated into your outward life. What is created in the Unseen is later manifested in the Seen. By the affirmation "I am Success," you create Success "within"; later this finds expression in your outward life, in the form of achievement, accomplishment and material prosperity.

Therefore, when a thought or suggestion of failure attempts to gain admission to the citadel of your mind, kill it by denial, and affirm in its place the "Success" formula that I have given you. Thus will the attitude of your mind be built up into a definite form. By affirming "I am Success" and by visualizing yourself as the embodiment of success. By seeing, with your mental eyes, yourself with your ambitions realized, and with all things at your feet, you will construct a concrete image in your mind, which will form a matrix, out of which will proceed the material success and accomplishment which are its visible expression.

It cannot be emphasized too much that success is not a something to be won; instead it is rather a mental state, an attitude of the mind. The mind itself has unlimited power, and mental power or thought is the power or force to accomplish all things and is within us. This potent power however, cannot find expression in the life if the attitude of the mind is wrong. When the mind is naturally of the success type or is made so by training, then its intense powers become focused into one powerful beam, which shapes and molds the outward life, on the form of the inward pattern. There is nothing of "magic" about this; it is capable of the simplest explanation. When your mind is of this type, the impulses sent to the subconscious mind can only result in successful actions. As we have already seen, the subconscious mind is the seat of all action and contains unlimited power and energy. This power and energy only needs directing into the right channel to accomplish anything that we may desire to accomplish. When therefore, the mind is cast in the "Success" mold, then only "success" thoughts and suggestions can go to the subconscious mind, and these in turn must of necessity be translated into successful actions.

The only difference between a successful type of man and an unsuccessful type, provided they are of equal energy, is one of mind – of thought. The successful man's attitude of mind is such that he generates the right kind of thought, which passing to his subconscious mind, is transmuted into the right type of action. The unsuccessful man, on the other hand, through his mind being of a negative type, generates the wrong kind of thought and this in turn results in the wrong type of action. This is why it is impossible to keep the "success" type of man down for any length of time. It is impossible to keep such a man down for long, simply because his mind will not allow it. This also is why it is impossible to help a man of a negative type. The more one helps such a man the weaker and more hopeless he becomes, and the more helplessly he clings round one's neck for sustenance and support. Place him in affluent circumstances, find him work, prospects, influence, friends, place in his hands everything possible with which to aid him, and he will let it all slip through his fingers and come right down to want and penury. Therefore, success in life is the result of "success" actions, which are the result of "success" thoughts, which are the result of a "success" attitude of mind, and this is the result of the affirmation "I am success."

As the attitude of the mind alters from negative to positive there is developed what is called personal magnetism; one radiates an influence which attracts people. It is impossible to estimate the difference which this alone makes to one's prospects of success. If a man is in business for himself, what an enormous difference the drawing influence of a well-ordered mind will make to that business. Success and prosperity crowd in upon the man or woman who cultivates the right type of mind. Once the right attitude of mind has been built up, the trouble is not how to get business, but how to execute it. It comes crowding in so rapidly, it is difficult to cope with.

Again, in all businesses difficulties appear from time to time, and although these may and do extinguish men of the negative type, they cause only temporary trouble to one whose mind has been trained on "success" lines.

As explained in other parts of this course there are ways by which all difficulties can be overcome by the power of the mind, but it is only those whose minds are controlled aright who can make use of them.

Again, as the mind becomes more positive, the Will is greatly strengthened, the staying power is increased, and the powers of concentration vastly strengthened. Anyone acquainted with the difficulties and trials of establishing a business or professional practice will appreciate the value of this. Success generally comes to those with the greatest staying power. The power to "stick to it" is often the deciding factor in the struggle. Most men give up the struggle when they are just at the turning of the corner, and only a little more push and staying power would ensure success. Instead they give up through lack of "stick-ability" just when success is ready to crown their efforts.

Many other illustrations could be given to show how it is that success is really more an attitude or quality of the mind than something outside of us, but these will suffice. The great thing to aim at is to build up within you this "success" attitude of mind. When this is established and the habit of action well developed, there is nothing that can stay your success. Affirm that you are success now, steep yourself in the success idea, visualize yourself successful and all conquering, breathe the success atmosphere, live, dream and be success, and nothing can prevent you from being successful, because you, yourself, are success.

Do not, however, strain after success; rather realize that you yourself are "Success" and that you therefore attract to you all that you desire. Go about your duties calmly and with confidence, *knowing* that you are "success" and therefore must succeed. A hundred times a day, if necessary, affirm "I am success." The last thing at night, just as you fall to sleep; the first minute of your waking day, affirm it and affirm it again, always picturing yourself happy, successful and all-conquering.

The special visualizing exercise for this week is as follows: Sit upright in a quiet place and, closing your eyes, send out to all mankind the best and noblest thoughts of which you are capable, thoughts of goodwill and love to everybody in all the wide world. Now feel these thoughts being projected from you in all directions, and mentally see them being sent forth like the beams of light from the lighthouse. See them penetrating further and further, all over your own country and then through every other country. Do this for some time and then reverse the process. Feel the thoughts coming back laden with other thoughts of a like nature. See innumerable beams of light pouring into you from all over the world. Feel yourself filled up and overflowing with the riches of all the most glorious thoughts which the world has ever known. The first part of the exercise may exhaust you, but the latter part will fill you with courage, confidence, calm, serenity and peace.

Persevere and endeavor to make this exercise as real as possible. By this exercise you enrich the world by your own noble thoughts; you lessen its pain and sorrow, and help to assuage its grief. In return you are blessed and strengthened in a way which could never otherwise be possible. The more freely you give of your best thoughts the more bountifully you will receive.

MEDITATION

Meditate daily upon the following words of James Allen: "You say you are chained by circumstances; you cry out for better opportunities, for a wider scope, for improved physical conditions, and perhaps you inwardly curse the fate that binds you hand and foot. It is for you that I write. It is to you that I speak. Listen, and let my words burn themselves into your heart, for that which I say to you is the truth: You may bring about that improved condition in your outward life which you desire, if you will unswervingly resolve to improve your inner life. I know that pathway looks barren at its commencement (truth always does, it is only error and delusion which are at first inviting and fascinating), but if you undertake to walk it; if you perseveringly discipline your mind, eradicating your weaknesses, and allowing your soul-forces and spiritual powers to unfold themselves, you will be astonished at the magical changes which will be brought about in your inward life. As you proceed, golden opportunities will be strewn across your path, and the power and judgment to properly utilize them will spring up within you. Genial friends will come unbidden to you; sympathetic souls will be drawn to you as the needle is to the magnet, and books and all outward aids that you require will come to you unsought."

Spend as much time as possible in the Silence, for in quietness and confidence shall be your strength. Also, whenever during the day you have to make a decision, mentally retire into the Silence and gain wisdom and inspiration from the Infinite. Thus shall you be kept from all mistakes and blunders, and your life become rich with blessing, because it is lived in obedience to Universal Law.

LESSON TEN

There are two great obstacles in the path to success: They are fear and hate. Not only do they bar the path to success, they also destroy all happiness and peace of mind. They are the most negative of all negative qualities and give rise to the most negative of thoughts and the most destructive emotions. They break down the fabric of the character, and create disharmonies and disturbances which effectually keep success, peace of mind and happiness at a distance.

Great characters, accomplishers of great achievements, the truly successful, know full well that they can only do great deeds, or accomplish mighty purposes, to the extent that they are able to banish fear and hate from their minds and lives.

Fear is the deadly enemy of accomplishment; it paralyzes effort, destroys initiative and corrodes the mental machinery. Fear and worry go hand in hand, the one produces the other. Worry never yet succeeded in overcoming a difficulty, neither has it ever succeeded in elucidating a problem; all it can do is to wreck happiness and peace of mind, and make the difficulties more difficult to overcome and the problems less easy of solution.

Fear, worry, care, what a terrible trinity! How destructive they are, what numberless lives they have marred and ruined. Mental gifts, high attainments, university education, opportunities due to birth, breeding and influence, help of friends and relatives, even genius or ability almost approaching genius, all in vain, all are rendered futile, if the mind is allowed to entertain fear.

Unless fear is cast out of the life *utterly* there can be no success. Entertain fear in your mind and you slam and bolt the door on all achievement, you sound the death knell of your hopes and ambitions:

"Fear is everywhere: fear of want, fear of starvation, fear of public opinion, fear of private opinion, fear that what we own today may not be ours tomorrow. Fear has become with millions a fixed habit. The thought is everywhere. The thought is thrown upon us from every direction… To live in continual dread, continual cringing, continual fear of anything, be it loss of love, loss of money, loss of position or station, is to take the readiest means to lose what we fear we shall."

Fear, worry, anxiety, dread, this dreadful negative family, are rendering miserable lives of millions of people, and they are all the offspring of lack of faith and courage. Have faith in the omnipotence of the Power within you, and all fear will cease, and worry, care and anxiety flee away. Get right hold of the Truth that your life, your circumstances, everything that comes into your life, is the result of your thinking; that your future will be modeled exactly on how you think today. Realize that everything is in your own hands and that as you are building well today, the future must and will be well. You cannot build well today and have a bad future, neither can you build badly today and reap a good future.

Think right thoughts *now* and the future can take care of itself. There is *nothing* to fear, henceforth there is nothing capricious or uncertain in your life, all is according to Eternal Law. All that you have to do is to think aright and to act aright, and all things will be added unto you.

As you bring your life, by the control of your thoughts, into harmony with the unseen higher forces, you enter into a life of peace and power. There is nothing whatever about which you need fear or worry, because you are in harmony with all the Universe. The power that maintains the stars in their places and guides the planets in their courses, is the same power that animates you. Nothing can come by chance into your life, only that which is the result of your thinking.

Now is given into your hands the power and the knowledge whereby you can control your thinking; the power and the knowledge by which you can choose those thoughts which will build up your life in beauty and strength, and ensure a harmonious future. Nothing can go wrong in your life if your thoughts are right. Right cannot produce wrong, neither can wrong produce right. Get your thoughts under control and all evil must flee away.

Therefore, there can be nothing to fear, your life is in your own hands. He who is established in truth and courage need fear no evil, for evil has no power over one whose soul has cast out fear. When thoughts of fear assail you, and at all available times, make use of the following denial:

There is nothing in all the universe that can make me afraid.

The only power that evil and fear, and the things feared, have, is the power that we invest them with, by our thoughts. Nothing exists apart from our minds. Everything is mind or thought, and its phenomena or manifestation.

This is proved up to the hilt by the fact that when you have, by the power of the denial, "There is no evil," and the affirmation, "There is only Infinite Good," cast the thought of, and belief in, Evil out of your mind, then you discover that there is no evil outside of human thought and that there is, and always has been, only Infinite Good. In the same way, when you by denial and affirmation have cast out fear, you discover, to your joy, that there is nothing to fear, and never has been, and never can be, anything to fear.

Having raised yourself mentally above the world of petty strife, limitations, and time and sense, into the Perfect World of Mind, realize that you are in harmony with and form a part of, the great Power behind the Universe, that Infinite Mind or Principle of Perfect Good, which is the guiding spirit behind all life's mysteries. Get into touch with, and realize your oneness with, this Infinite Mind of Perfect Good, and you will realize that there can be nothing to fear.

Stand firm then, looking up, realize your one-ship with the Highest Powers, your harmony with all the Divine Forces, and use the denial unceasingly:

"There is nothing in all the Universe
that can make me afraid."

Having purged your mind of fear, next build it up and strengthen it by this affirmation:

"I am in harmony with the Infinite Principle of Good
that permeates the Universe,
and against which evil has not the slightest power.
Therefore I am unafraid,
nothing can harm or destroy,
nothing can ruffle me,
or disturb my peace of mind.
I am carried forward by the invisible forces of Good.
All is well."

Then realize this stupendous truth, and visualize yourself standing dauntless and unafraid, serene and calm, borne up by Higher Powers.

There are, of course, testing times in all lives, but, to the well-trained mind, these should give no cause for fear.

"It is how we bear ourselves at such time that determines our real worth and use, whether we have stamina, backbone, courage – real character – and if at such times we can stand unfaltering, uncomplaining, desirous of neither sympathy nor pity, patient but resolute, and doing today what today reveals to be done and so ready for the morrow when it comes, there can be but one outcome. The Higher Powers of all the universe stand back of such a life, they uphold it, they sustain it, they stamp it with success, they crown it with adoration and with honor." - R. W. Trine in "The Wayfarer on the Open Road"

Therefore, you have nothing to fear, so cast out fear and meet the future with joy and gladness.

The other great obstacle to success is hate. He who hates emits a force which rebounds back upon himself. Hate is negative and destructive, love is positive and upbuilding. Hate affects adversely all the vital processes. It wrecks happiness and turns the life into an inferno of trouble. Have you ever noticed the lives of those who indulge in hate? They are a continual round of trouble. Before they finish one brawl they find themselves engaged in another. They are at loggerheads with nearly everybody, and misfortunes seem to dog their footsteps. Misfortunes and troubles are attracted to them as a direct result of their hate. Through indulging in negative thoughts and emotions, negative conditions are produced and attracted. That is why people who hate are not always in trouble through other people's hatred, but they attract to themselves troubles and disasters which seem to have no connection with hate, but which are in reality a direct result of that condition of mind. Therefore, dear reader, if you have hatred, malice or resentment in your mind or life, pluck it out and cast it away.

The best way to cast out hate is to hold your mind continually in the attitude of good will to all men. If, just as you are falling asleep you use the following combined denial and affirmation, you will find it much easier to conquer your negative feeling during the next day. First of all, raise yourself into your Perfect World of Mind, deny evil and affirm Infinite Good, then say:

I forgive and forget all my enmity and anger,
I send out thoughts of love and good will to all mankind.

Get your mind into this attitude and all will be well.

It may seem strange to insist upon forgiveness and love in lessons on mind training and success development, but believe me there can be no true all-round success, no happiness or harmony in life, so long as hatred, malice and uncharitableness are cherished. These are negative qualities, and success, real, lasting and true, can come only to those who overcome and cast out, root and branch, all negative thoughts, beliefs and habits. Great minds are above all such petty, mean feelings as hatred, spite and malice. It is the truly great who can best afford to be magnanimous. By regulating and controlling your thinking, by casting out fear and hate and all other negative states, you, too, can become great in mind, and noble in action.

Therefore, when you make the above affirmation, visualize yourself raised above the petty cares and strifes of men, looking with a broader outlook above those who hate and squabble and disagree. There is a mental realm of peace and quietude which is far above earth's troubles. But before you can enter into it, you must first put yourself right with your fellow men. We cannot dwell there if we are not dealing fairly with the world, and giving our very best service to the cause of humanity. We cannot dwell there if we fear; we must first of all banish fear and possess our hearts with courage. We cannot dwell there if we are selfish, nor if we desire or demand for ourselves anything or state which we are not anxious that all should partake of or enjoy. But when we have put ourselves in harmony with all the higher forces, then we can rise above the things which vex and grieve the hearts of men. We can rise to a plane where absolute calm and peace continually abide.

I can hear some of my readers saying, "What has this got to do with success in life?" My answer is, "everything." It is because the majority of people are so full of worry and care that they are perplexed and anxious. It is because they are so perplexed and anxious and so wrapped up in little, petty, nonessential things, that they are never able to take the broad view and consequently can never be successful. A man or woman with a small, petty mind can never be successful; it is only those with imagination and breadth of view who can plan a successful campaign, and successfully carry it through. It is impossible for anyone to put forth his best effort if he is worried and careworn, or fearful, or full of hate. The nervous system is so weakened, the life force is so corroded, there is none of that vital, living, overpowering energy which is so necessary to success. Neither can the mind be concentrated upon the business in hand nor the problem to be solved, nor the difficulty to be overcome, if it is engaged in worry, anxiety, hate, or fear.

Therefore I say, learn to rise to that higher state of the mind where peace and calm and confidence continually abide.

The special visualizing exercise this week is as follows:

Sit yourself in a quiet place, upright in a chair, close your eyes. Now mentally send out to all the World your best service. If you are a great writer of books, see them being sent by the thousand, by rail and steamship, all over the globe. If you are a merchant or manufacturer, see your goods being dealt with in the same way. If you are an artist, see your pictures going to many lands. If you are a poet, see your poems bringing joy and peace to thousands of hearts everywhere. No matter what your occupation may be, or may be in the near future, see the effects of your service going out to all mankind. Do this for a few minutes, and then reverse the process. See money coming back to you from all over the world. Call up a clear and perfect image of money arriving by every post, in the form of drafts, checks, money orders, or cash. See it after the envelopes are opened. See yourself counting it and piling it up. Do this for a few minutes and then dismiss that matter from your mind.

MEDITATION

There is infinite plenty and profusion in Nature for all man's wants and needs. Nature is prodigal in her provision, and would willingly clothe every son of man in plenty and abundance, if he did not create his own poverty by wrong thinking. Prosperity and abundance, in wealth, beauty, and happiness, in every perfect good, these are all waiting for man, did he but know it, could he but believe it. There is for every man all that the heart can wish for, but he fails to enter, because of wrong thinking, into his glorious heritage. When I have got rid of hate and fear and selfishness and weakness, and have built up my mind in love and courage, unselfishness and strength, then shall I find that there is nothing in life that is too good for me, nothing in all the Universe that can be denied me. Nature withholds nothing from the man who is unafraid, and whose thoughts are in harmony with the Universal Mind, whose heart is free from hate and malice. Therefore, Nature shall withhold nothing from me.

And what I affirm for myself, I desire also for all my fellow creatures, that they too may experience all the joy that I experience, and learn how to bring their lives into harmony with the Infinite Principle of Good.

Continue to develop subliminal thinking. Take all your difficulties and perplexities into the Silence and let your great inner mind, drawing upon the Eternal Wisdom of all the Ages, give you the true answer that you need. Whenever you desire inspiration or original ideas, seek them in your Subliminal Mind because there alone can they be found.

LESSON ELEVEN

What is success? To one it means one thing and to another it may mean something quite different. Some desire happiness and love above all things, and could they but gain these, would count themselves successful in the highest degree, even though their circumstances remained humble and comparatively poor. Some desire fame and distinction in science, their ambition is to invent, to discover or investigate, to do something that has never been done before, the only reward that they seek being the joy of accomplishment. Some desire to be great in music, painting or sculpture; others seek to be leaders in their chosen profession of medicine, law or politics. Others have ambitions to serve their day and generation, to give and be spent in the service of humanity. Some seek mental, and others, spiritual attainments. Success in its lowest form is the acquisition of wealth, the building up of large businesses, or the earning of a large income. Although this aim is not so lofty as its predecessors, yet it is not an unworthy ambition, and if kept within bounds, will result in benefit to the community, and not too great a burden to the individual.

It is useless to try and be successful if you are a round peg in a square hole. Before you can make your life a full and abundant success, you must find your "niche" and fill it. There is, somewhere in the world, work for you to do; work, which no one else can do as well, and which no one else can do in quite the same way. Many are the illustrations one could bring forward in support of this. Men who were anything and everything and unsuccessful in all, until at last they hit upon something which they could do a little better than anybody else and which brought them amazing success.

Seek, and keep on seeking, and interior illumination will show you the path, and open up the way. While searching for your niche, do not neglect your business or profession or work. Some have been foolish enough to throw up their present calling before looking for a fresh one. Needless to say this is not the course that these lessons recommend.

Mix caution with your ambition, do not be headstrong, be a blend of tremendous energy, burning ambition and wholesome caution and restraint.

The way out of undesirable conditions, the path by which you will find your niche in life where your work will be an everlasting and surpassing joy, is by doing your duty in your present sphere and listening to, and obeying, *the inward voice of wisdom.*

If you shirk your duty and responsibility in order to "get on" you defeat yourself and curse your life. On the other hand, if you do your duty, however unpleasant, and shoulder, with cheerfulness, your responsibilities, no matter how heavy, affirming success, visualizing better conditions, listening to the inward voice of wisdom, you will find that sooner or later the way will be opened up before you in a wonderful manner, and you will enter into a life of great joy and usefulness. The outward life will and must conform to the inward life, sooner or later the change must come, but only if you are calm, untroubled and serene.

No matter how anxious you are to change your conditions, do not be persuaded to do anything that will not bear the strictest examination in the light of your highest concept of Truth.

Therefore, take these "Nevers" as signposts and beacons to warn you from shortcuts, so-called, which lead only to disaster and failure.

Never wrong anyone. Never betray a trust. Never go back on your word. Never do anything selfish. Never repudiate an agreement. Never shirk your responsibilities. Never do anything that looks mean in the light of your Perfect World of Mind.

Finally, live your life to a principle, the principle of Truth, Justice and Love.

In choosing your ambition, but more often, of course, it is that ambition chooses you, but whichever it is, examine it carefully and see just where it is going to lead you. Even if ambition chooses you, you still have the power to exercise restraint and to modify it according to reason. Ask yourself the question, "Am I prepared to pay the price of success?" If it is money and business success that you are going to seek, are you prepared to pay the price? Remember that men of this type live laborious days. They can never get away from their business. Many have telephones by their bedside, some have a bedroom and bathroom at their office, so that in times of stress they need not go home, but can work twenty and sometimes even twenty-two hours a day. Unless gifted with constitutions of iron, such men become nervous wrecks, and most of them have no enjoyment in life outside of their business. Their wealth is of no use to them. Their only joy is the joy of accomplishment, the glow of satisfaction at having achieved. Are you prepared to pay the price that such a success demands? If you are, go forward, and if you really believe you can succeed, and have built up your mental powers and character on the lines laid down in these lessons, you *must* succeed. Do not blame me, however, if you find wealth and success of this type rather a burden. The only satisfaction to be got out of it is the satisfaction of having built up a big business. I speak from experience. I went in for this type of success and in three years created, out of nothing, one of the largest businesses of its kind in the United States. When I had lived in a very small house and had to economize on a very tiny income, I had been very happy. When I became passing rich, the owner of a big business, and could keep one or two motor cars and other things to match, I certainly was not as happy. I would have been happier if I had modified my ambition, and had been satisfied with a smaller business, a less generous income, and had in consequence more leisure and opportunity for self improvement.

If you will sacrifice part of your ambition and thus live a more normal and well-balanced life, your life will, in its broad sense, be more successful than if you sacrifice everything to the accomplishment of your desires. One can become a millionaire and be but a poor shriveled soul in other respects. Far better is it, and I speak from experience, to aim for a broader ideal, to aspire to prosperity rather than great wealth; to desire happiness and peace of mind rather than to sacrifice these things at the altar of ambition.

Far better is it to build up character than a great business, to develop an insight into Nature's beauties than to own a million dollars; it is far better to enjoy refreshing sleep, and a splendid appetite, than to own a kingdom.

Your mind actually has creative power, not in a figurative sense but in reality. All that you see with your bodily eyes is matter vibrating at different rates. The matter that you can see in this way is coarse matter. With your mind's eye you can see other matter of a finer nature. With your mind you can mold this finer matter into any pattern you please. What you create in your mind in this way, in other words, that which you visualize, if persistently held to, will form the matrix out of which will grow your outer life. The coarser particles of the outer life are shaped on the model of the pattern formed in the finer matter of the mind. This is why these lessons have persistently taught you to cast your mind in a certain attitude of thought and to visualize all that you wished to accomplish.

Visualization is a form of concentrated thought. It is only possible as a result of intense concentration. It is thought materialized in the fine matter of mind-stuff. Therefore, the more real and clear and sharply defined your mental image is, the greater your powers of concentration. The power to concentrate can be developed, and it is developed, as your power of visualizing grows.

The value of concentration in business, in study, in fact, in any effort to accomplish and achieve is too well-known to need any comment. It enables you when confronted with a difficult task to get your teeth right into it and to go right to the very heart of the subject without fatigue or brain weariness. The greatest lawyers and counsel, the ablest scientists and investigators, the most successful men of affairs and business, are those with the greatest powers of concentration. Some possess this power naturally, others can acquire it. By the methods taught in this course you can, by the constant use of affirmations, and by persevering in the visualizing lessons, develop a degree of concentration power almost unknown in the West, approximating somewhat to the power of certain Eastern adepts who have made concentration and mind control the study of centuries.

The writer can concentrate his whole mind and thought upon the point of a pencil for minutes at a time. Try it, and see how soon your attention wavers, how your mind wanders about the point of the pencil, but never on it. You think of other things such as concentration, of being determined to think of nothing but the point; the mind wanders off into a hundred and one things and has to be brought back again and again by an effort of the will, finally you give it up and acknowledge that it is a very difficult thing to do.

When you can concentrate your whole mind and thought on the point of a needle for one minute, you will be able to accomplish anything to which you give your attention. You will have the power to take up a subject, examine it, decide upon it and then to dismiss the matter entirely from your mind. Can you estimate this power at its proper value? Instead of lying awake all night worrying over a business problem, you dismiss it from your mind and have a good night's rest, and arise in the morning with fresh energy and strength *and with your problem solved*.

All your powers of concentration must be focused on the achievement of your ambition. A clear and well defined image of what you intend to accomplish must be constantly held in the mind, *and never changed until the object aimed at is achieved.*

Visualize and affirm success, denying evil and failure, constantly and perseveringly, this is the path to success.

Remember that success is not only a matter of concentration – it is also a question of staying power. How many a promising career has been ruined by lack of perseverance and "stickability." In business and in other competitive walks of life, it is frequently the one with the longest wind who wins. The brilliant, the clever, the ones with every advantage, drop out by the way, and leave the field clear for the plodder and sticker. Therefore, hold the thought "I am Success" constantly in your mind, let it color all your actions and inspire all your deeds. Hold the perfect image of your success as a clear picture in your mind, persevere and hang on, and grow not weary in well doing; then whatever it is that you are aiming for will be accomplished. Be assured of this, and, again, I speak from experience, not only will your vision of success be accomplished, but it will be exceeded beyond your wildest dreams. March on; your ultimate success is as certain as the rising and setting of the sun.

Make your own denials and affirmations now and henceforth, and use them as difficulties arise. Do not try to do anything without consulting your inner self and thus bringing your inward powers to action. If you feel gloomy, affirm that you are bright and cheerful; then will your gloom be chased away like mist before the morning sun. If you feel tired, affirm that you are fresh and vigorous and free from fatigue; then act accordingly, and you will find that your lethargy has flown away. If you feel care-worn, raise yourself mentally above the petty things of life, and you will find yourself dwelling on a plane, where worry and care cannot exist.

If you need guidance in the face of difficulty, when the finite mind of the senses is perplexed and at the limit of its resources, then retire into yourself and receive wisdom and guidance from the

Great Within. Put the matter that is perplexing you out of your mind and dismiss every thought as it comes, until at last the mind is entirely free from thought – until it is a complete blank. When you have done this you have separated yourself entirely from the world and the life of the senses and you are in touch with the Infinite Mind of the Universe. Then will the answer come, in the still, small voice which is in every man, if he would but know it and listen for it.

Another method is to raise oneself mentally above the fret and fever of life, and deny evil and affirm the Infinite Good until you get a clear concept of your Perfect World of Mind. The worry or perplexity will follow you even there, but when it does, deny its existence and affirm perfect peace, perfect wisdom, perfect knowledge, perfect understanding. Affirm that man is a perfect mental creature, one with the Infinite Mind, and, therefore, in his higher self, can never be perplexed or troubled by the trivial things of the material life. Again and again the worry will come, but if you will each time deny it and affirm your perfect higher self, the possessor of all wisdom and knowledge and understanding, the thought will get weaker and weaker until it is killed altogether. Now contemplate the wonders and delights of the perfect World of Mind for a time, and after that turn immediately to, and occupy the mind with, some other matter. The answer will come, the problem will be solved, and the way will be opened before you in a wonderful manner.

Another way is as follows: Just as you are going to sleep, after conquering the worry thought and rising superior to it, in your Perfect World of Mind, simply hold the problem in your mind in an expectant way, believing and affirming that in the morning the problem will be solved. When the morning arrives you will find on awaking, the solution of your perplexity, or it will come to you as you are getting up.

For a visualizing exercise, imagine that you have received a momentous letter from overseas. Trace its journey back to the beginning. First the postman, the local sorting office, the mail-train, the general post office of the large city, the mail-train from the coast, the mail-carrying steamship, the journey across the seas, the journey from the foreign port, by rail to your friend's home. Then see your friend sealing the letter, then see him writing it. Now look into your friend's mind and see the thought that inspired the letter.

MEDITATION

I am Success. By constant and eternal vigilance, I kill by means of denials, every thought of fear, of failure, of poverty and lack, and replace them by affirmations of Success, Prosperity and Achievement. I think only of *positive* things, states, and emotions, and never of Negative. My mind is being constantly lifted up into a higher realm where I receive inspiration and strength. My inner Mind is one with the Universal Mind; therefore I draw upon the inexhaustible strength, energy and wisdom of the Infinite. Through thinking *positive* thoughts and meditating upon *positive* states, I attract to myself streams of thoughts and emotions of a like character, which strengthen and help me.

I grow into the likeness of that upon which I meditate, I become more Positive, I become a magnet, I draw and attract to myself all that I need. Difficulties are smoothed out, people and opportunities come to me unbidden, the way is made clear before me, and all things work together for my good. My services to the world become increasingly valuable, I get greater and deeper insight into my work, I am inspired in such a way that I can do better work, and more work, and greater work, than ever before. Therefore I can see in my mind's eye all desirable things coming to me. All are seeking me, instead of my seeking them. Friends, wealth, position, power, all are coming to me. I am a magnet. I am Success.

The reason some people cannot remember is because they do not pay sufficient attention. If you were making phonograph records you would have to arrange things so that a deep, sharp impression was made in the wax. If only a faint impression was made, then only a faint jumble of sounds could be reproduced. It is the same with the mind, if you fail to observe and to pay attention, then facts, happenings, orders, etc., which should be remembered are only faintly impressed upon the mind with the unfortunate consequence that many important points and details are forgotten. The great thing to do is to observe and pay attention, to mentally impress upon your mind those things which you ought to remember. A table-knife lying on the table to one person would be a knife and nothing more. If pressed for a description he might be able to say that it was either a dinner knife or a cheese knife but that would be all. A more observant person would be able to tell us that the knife was made in Sheffield and give us the name of the maker, that the blade was Firth's stainless steel, that the handle was real ivory and the tag of the knife went right through to the other end of the handle. A primrose to one may be a mere yellow flower, to another it is a universe of beauty and delight. A telegraph post to one is a telegraph post only, to another it is old or new, it carries so many wires, has a crack down one side, has a certain number burned into it and shows signs of having been recently climbed by a workman with steel spikes.

Two persons may be so alike that they frequently get mistaken, the one for the other, yet if you examine them carefully, you will see so many points of difference, you wonder why you ever thought they were alike. Their teeth are different, their ears are very dissimilar, the eyes of one are much wider apart. The hands too will show differences, the nails being of a different shape and in many other points one can find marked differences.

In order to improve one's memory, one must learn to observe, to pay more attention, to examine more minutely, and to consciously impress matters that one wishes to remember upon one's mind.

Not only should you learn to take more notice, to pay more attention, to observe more closely, but you should also memorize something during the day, and just as you are falling asleep at night recall what you have learned, and after repeating it over, tell your subliminal mind that you will never forget it, and you never will. This is the direct natural way of remembering, and is far better than any method which employs the Law of Association. If you follow these instructions, increasing the amount memorized each day, you will develop a memory above the average.

Look within for Power. Man has, in his subliminal mind, transcendental faculties, but to the multitude, these are unsuspected and undiscovered. To you has been given the knowledge that has put you in touch with the Great Within. This is the key to all wisdom, knowledge, truth, understanding, achievement and power. It unlocks for you the Treasure House of the Universe, opens up to you the Wisdom of the Ages; it links you up to the Power House of the Infinite. If you are perplexed, look within, and light and leading will come, for you are one with, and form a part of, the Great Universal Mind. Have you a great task to perform? Look within, and you will find all the strength, energy, perseverance and ability that you require. No matter what your need, you will find within you every quality necessary for your success.

LESSON TWELVE

Said Charles Godfrey Leyland, when over seventy years of age, "Man has within him, if he would but know it, tremendous powers or transcendental faculties of which he has never had any conception." These powers are within *you*, and by the use of affirmations and the power of mental imagery, you can arouse these vast potencies, and harness them to your service, for the enrichment of your life and the accomplishment of your ambitions.

Every act of life can be influenced by affirmations, but do not confuse yourself by employing too many at once. Seek to progress by steps, not by huge bounds which may land you anywhere but in the right place. Day by day, and step by step, is the sure road to success. Do not attempt too much, a little at a time well done is far better than a huge and ambitious scheme that may have to be abandoned. If you have a little shop, do not attempt to turn it, all at once, into a huge department store. Seek first to make it by far the best small shop in the district. Make yourself very efficient in your small shop, and it will not be very long before the opportunity comes for you to take a large one, or to buy a bigger business. As you outgrow that, other opportunities for expansion will come your way, and thus will you grow from small beginnings to great things. Suppose you have a small law practice, do not try to blossom out all at once into a high class, lucrative, exclusive practice. Seek first to make yourself so exceedingly efficient in your small practice that you will be prepared for the high class practice when it comes. Affirm success and keep visualized in your mind the exact kind of success that you desire, and ways and means will in time be provided. But remember to travel step by step, to grow gradually, to develop, like a plant, on natural lines. Remember nature is never in a hurry; all her vast works are accomplished slowly, methodically, step by step, cell by cell, but whatever she seeks to do is ultimately accomplished. So will it be with you. You have the knowledge by which you can develop your success with mathematical exactitude. All you have to do is to put the Law into action and to advance step by step. Begin with small things; when you have conquered in small things, you can pass to greater, and from greater things to boundless power.

Do not expect the maximum of success at once. If you get only partial success at first, be satisfied, knowing that you will keep on improving. Even if you fail utterly, you will be stronger and better for having tried. "It is the law of the reflex nerve system that whenever one does, or endeavors to do, any given thing in a certain way, a modicum of power is added whereby it is a trifle easier at the next effort, an added trifle at the next and the next, until that which is difficult and is done only with great effort in the beginning becomes easy of accomplishment – that which we do haltingly and stumblingly at first, by-and-by, so to speak, does itself, with scarcely or even without any conscious effort on our part. This is the law; it is the great secret of habit forming, character building, of all attainment."

Above all, live your life according to a principle. This will steady the most vacillating character. It is possible for a simple person to estimate with mathematical exactness the result of right action, but the wisest and cleverest cannot foretell the result of an unprincipled one. The first is according to Law and produces certain results; the second, i.e. an unprincipled action, is against the Law and no one can tell where the evil will end.

Live your life to a principle and you will always know how to act in all cases of uncertainty. Set up as your standard the highest aspect of Truth of which you know and bring everything into line with it. When confronted with two or three courses of action and you do not know which to follow, compare each line of action with your principle, and adopt that one which is in harmony with it.

When once you have learned to live your life according to a principle, you will feel a great load lifted from your mind. For the first time there will be certainty and precision in your life and absolute peace of mind. You will have nothing to worry about because you know that your line of action will always be right, and can only bring the highest good into your life.

Never wrong any man, never take advantage of one with less knowledge than yourself, never sacrifice your principles, never give up your ideals. See that you are known for your integrity and absolute honesty, as well as for your cleverness and capacity. It may look, on the face of things, that this course of action is not going to lead to success. You see so many of your competitors making money by sharp practice, and you feel that by adopting an honest line of action you are simply putting yourself up as a target for people of less principle to shoot at. That is what it looks like, but I can assure you, speaking from experience, that the reverse is the case. It is the man of probity and honor who scores in the long run.

When in business I was more successful than anyone in my line had ever been before, and I never found it necessary to be "sharp" or "over-reaching." I never practiced "salesmanship" yet I had more business than I wanted; I never went out of my way to get customers, yet they swarmed into my place from morning till night.

I once knew a theatre manager who suddenly began to live his life to a principle. Instead of covering up occasional defects in his shows as he had formerly done, he made it a principle to point them out to his customers. Many of his friends said he was a fool and prophesied his ruin and failure, but instead his business grew and flourished. His friends were very surprised at his success, but they need not have been. The theatre manager was simply coming into line with eternal law; he was putting into action forces which could not fail to bring him success and prosperity. Do not misunderstand me; it is not enough to be honest or to live one's life to a high principle, but all other things being equal, it will be the man of integrity who will win in the end.

Therefore, live your life to a principle, and persevere with the course which you have laid out for yourself. Be constant, be true, be faithful, be strong, be persevering, be fair to yourself, be fair to the wondrous inward powers which are seeking to find expression in your life.

Remember the law of compensation; if you are to receive the highest good in your life, you must give the world your best service.

If people are to prefer your business or your professional services to those of others there must be a sufficient reason. They are not going to do this simply because you affirm that they will. The only way to get them is by supplying better goods, more perfect service, higher skill, greater probity and trustworthiness.

Another great factor in winning success is the mental attitude of cheerfulness and brightness. People are attracted to the cheerful, optimistic person, and repelled by one who is gloomy and pessimistic. Be cheerful and bright under all circumstances and this alone will be worth a king's ransom to you. These qualities alone will bring you in more money every year than most people get by hard work, to say nothing of the joy and cheeriness which this attitude of mind will attract to you. By your brightness, cheerfulness, and optimism, by your appearance and personality, you will create a good impression wherever you go. I mention appearance advisedly, because the face becomes in time an index of the soul. Just as vice becomes deeply marked on the faces of its devotees, so does the face of one whose mind and thoughts are directed into right channels, reflect the calm and peace and courage of the mind within. As time goes on, the face as well as the attitude and carriage of the body alter considerably, and this makes one more attractive; thus do you attract success, because if you attract to yourself people of the right kind they bring potential success with them.

One word of warning and it is this: exercise a wise business prudence. Do not, just because you feel within you the fluttering of a new and wondrous power, rush thoughtlessly into business speculation, which may either ruin you or seriously jeopardize your business. Be prudent, be wise, be not carried away by your enthusiasm; instead, go slowly and feel your way, as it were, step by step. Be sure and steady; do not risk failure for the sake of getting on more quickly.

Keep your expenditure within your income. He is a happy man who spends less than he earns. The troubles of many families are due to their expenditure being in excess of their income. This leads them into endless difficulties and cares.

Success is no success that does not extend to the home. By scientific right thinking, happiness, peace and harmony can be made to reign supreme where formerly there was bickering.

Cleanse your own heart and mind by denials; build up your own character by affirmations, calm your own spirit by dwelling in the perfect purity of the transcendental World of Mind, and you will find, strange though it may seem, that everybody else in your household will get more lovable, and helpful, and restful, in their attitude toward you.

Remember to "reverse" every undesirable thought, suggestion, sight, or impression that comes to you. Deny them each and all in your perfect World of Mind, and affirm their opposite.

Remember the three great Laws: 1. The Law of Love and Attraction. "Give love, and love to *your* heart will flow, a strength in your utmost need." 2. The Law of Compensation. "Then give to the World the best you have, and the best will come back to you." 3. The Law of Absolute Justice.

Therefore, the ability to win the highest and truest success, to draw to yourself the greatest happiness, to create in your life the highest good, all depend upon giving. The mistaken idea of the animal mind that, to be happy and successful, one must seize and grab, is entirely false, and leads to bitter disappointment. The voice of Wisdom that is heard in the "Silence" tells us that only as we give do we receive. That if we give of our best – our best thoughts, emotions, service, love – then the best will come back to us in the exact proportion, no more, no less.

Again let me emphasize the necessity for "stickability" and perseverance. Keep at it, never know failure, let this word be purged from your vocabulary. It is the man with the greatest staying power who wins through hard times.

Possess your soul in courage. Remember that if you use your inward mental powers aright, and bring your business and your life and your conduct into harmony with the Law, you can never fail. Great are the possibilities of your life, because great, beyond all human ken, is the Infinite Power within you. You have nothing to be afraid of. Big corporations cannot smash you. You can always beat them by personal service, by individuality and originality. By straight dealing, by integrity, by honesty combined with efficiency, and businesslike procedure, you can make for yourself an enduring reputation. When faced by problems, difficulties and perplexities, you can at once raise yourself into your perfect World of Mind, and realize that you, your real self, can never be perplexed, because, being one with the Universal Mind, all wisdom is yours. You know that in the "Silence," having hushed the loud voices of the surface, material mind, you can hear the still small voice of intuition, of infinite wisdom. For you, having learnt how to raise yourself above the life of the senses, to the perfect World of Mind, there is wisdom, understanding and illumination; there can be no perplexity or worry, only infinite calm and peace.

Study the lessons and practice their teachings for the rest of your life. Do not expect immediate results. The effects of thought are slow in manifesting. It is my experience that what we think today becomes manifest in about two years time. By that I do not mean that by affirming certain qualities, I do not immediately begin to develop these qualities, because I do right from the first affirmation. What I do mean is this: suppose I want to demonstrate a big business, a large practice, or say a house in the country all bought and paid for, or a greater advancement in spiritual unfoldment, then if I hold in my mind a sharply defined picture of what I want, and vitalize it by joyful emotion, and confident affirmations, and spend at least a quarter of an hour every night and morning holding this picture in my mind, besides calling it up at intervals during the day, then in about two years time what has been held in the mind will become an actual accomplished fact in my life. I may have many setbacks and disappointments, but if I persevere and persist and concentrate, then whatever I desire *must* objectify in my life. Actually, of course, I have been progressing all the time towards the realization of my desire, but it is in about two years time that tangible results usually are seen.

After that one can never look back, because success attracts success, and once one has "demonstrated," one becomes so full of success vibrations that success becomes the habit of one's life.

Therefore, keep on persevering, persisting. Never cease mentally to picture and affirm confidently. It is by this mental activity that you win success; it is not done by striving so much as "thinking" and visualizing. Of course one must work, but it is the mental activity that crowns the work with lasting success.

By bringing into play, as taught in these lessons, the illimitable powers of your subliminal mind, by the use of denials and affirmations, by harmonizing with Immutable Law, and by the art of visualizing, you can accomplish all that you desire. There is no height to which you cannot climb, no success that you cannot achieve, no happiness that you cannot attract into your life. All things are yours. Everything has been delivered into your hands. You can achieve what you will, you can be all that you desire. Act according to the teachings of this course, making in future your own denials and affirmations as are required, extemporizing your own meditations, and you will have set your feet in a path that leads ever upward.

I affirm for you Success in its richest and fullest sense, and all the joys of overcoming.

VII

CHRISTIAN D. LARSON

The following quotes are from
The Ideal Made Real, 1912

To have ideals is not only simple but natural. It is just as natural for the mind to enter the ideal as it is to live. In fact, the ideal is an inseparable part of life; but to make the ideal real in every part of life is a problem, the solution of which appears to be anything but simple. To dream of the fair, the high, the beautiful, the perfect, the sublime, that everyone can do; but everyone has not learned how to make his dreams come true, nor realize in the practical world what he has discerned in the transcendental world. The greatest philosophers and thinkers in history, with but few exceptions, have failed to apply their lofty ideas in practical living, not because they did not wish to but because they had not discovered the scientific relationship existing between the ideal world and the real world.

To understand the scientific relationship that exists between the real and the ideal, the mind must have both the power of interior insight and the power of scientific analysis, as well as the power of practical application; but we do not find, as a rule, the prophet and the scientist in the same mind. The man who has visions and the man who can do things do not usually dwell in the same personality; nevertheless, this is necessary. And every person can develop both the prophet and the scientist in himself. He can develop the power to see the ideal and also the power to make the ideal real. The large mind, the broad mind, the deep mind, the lofty mind, the properly developed mind can see both the outer and inner side of things. Such a mind can see the ideal on high, and at the same time understand how to make real, tangible and practical what he has seen. The seeming gulf between the ideal and the real, between the soul's vision and the power of practical action is being bridged in thousands of minds today, and it is these minds who are gaining the power to make themselves and their own world as beautiful as the visions of the prophet; but the ideal life and the world beautiful are not for the few only. Everybody should learn how to find that path that leads from the imperfections of present conditions to the world of ideal conditions – the world of which we have all so frequently dreamed.

The problem is what beginners are to do with the beautiful thoughts and the tempting promises that are being scattered so widely at the present time. The average mind feels that the idealism of modern metaphysics has a substantial basis. He feels intuitively that it is true, and he discerns through the perceptions of his own soul that all these things that are claimed for applied metaphysics are possible. He inwardly knows that whatever the idealist declares can be done will be done, but the problem is how. The demand for simple methods is one of the greatest demands at the present time – methods that everyone can learn and that will enable any aspiring soul to begin at once to realize his ideals. Such methods, however, are easily formulated, and will be found in abundance on the following pages. These methods are based upon eternal laws; they are as simple as the multiplication table and will produce results with the same unerring precision. Any person with a reasonable amount of intelligence can apply them, and those who have an abundance of perseverance can, through these methods, make real practically all the ideals that they may have at the present time. Those who are more highly developed will find in these methods the secret through which their attainments and achievements will constantly verge on the borderland of the marvelous. In fact, when the simple law that unites the ideal and the real is understood and applied, it matters not how lofty our minds and our visions may be we can make them all come true.

To proceed, the principal obstacle must first be removed, and this obstacle is the tendency to lose faith whenever we fail to make real the ideal the very moment we expect to do so. This tendency is present to some degree in nearly every mind that is working for greater things, and it postpones the day of realization whenever it is permitted to exercise its power of retrogression. Many a person has fallen into chronic despondency after having had a glimpse of the ideal, because it was so very beautiful, so very desirable, in fact, the only one thing that could satisfy, and yet seemingly so far away and so impossible to reach. But here is a place where we must exercise extraordinary faith. We must never recognize the gulf that seems to exist between our present state and the state we desire to reach. On the other hand, we must continue in the conviction that the gulf is only seeming and that we positively shall reach the ideal that appears in the splendors of what seems to be a distant future, although what actually is very near at hand.

Those who have more faith and more determination do not, as a rule, fall down when they meet this seeming gulf; they inwardly know that every ideal will some time be realized. But even to these the ideal does at times appear to be very far away, and the time of waiting seems very long. They are frequently on the verge of giving up and fears arise at intervals that many unpleasant experiences may, after all, be met before the great day of realization is gained; however, we cannot afford to entertain such fears for a moment nor to think that anything unpleasant can transpire during the period of transition; that is, the passing from the imperfections of present conditions to the joys and delights of an ideal life. We must remember that fear and despondency invariably retard our progress, no matter what our object in view may be, and that discouragement is very liable to cause a break in the engine that is to take our train to the fair city we so long have desired to reach.

The time of waiting may seem long during such moments as come when the mind is down, but so long as the mind is on the heights the waiting time disappears, and the pleasure of pursuit comes to take its place. In this connection we should remember that the more frequently we permit the mind to fall down into fears and doubts the longer we shall have to wait for the realization of the ideal; and the more we live in the upper story of life the sooner we shall reach the goal in view. There are many who give up temporarily all efforts toward reaching their ideals, thinking it is impossible and that nothing is gained by trying, but such minds should realize that they are simply making their future progress more difficult by retarding their present progress. Such minds should realize the great fact that every ideal can be made real, because nothing is impossible.

To reach any desired goal the doing of certain things is necessary, but if those things are not done now they will have to be done later; besides, when we give up in the present we always make the obstacles in our way much greater than they were before. Those things that are necessary to promote our progress become more difficult to do the longer we remain in what may be termed the "giving up" attitude, and the reason why is found in the fact that the mind that gives up becomes smaller and smaller; it loses ability, capacity and power and becomes less and less competent to cope with the problems at hand. Whenever we give up we invariably fall down into a smaller mental state. When we cease to move forwards we begin to move backwards. We retard progression only when we cease to promote progression. On the other hand, so long as we continue to pursue the ideal we ascend into larger and larger mental states, and thus increase our power to make real the ideals that are before us. The belief that it is impossible to make real the ideal has no foundation whatever in truth. It is simply an illusion produced by fear and has no place in the exact science of life. When you discern an ideal you discover something that lies in your own onward path. Move forward and you simply cannot fail to reach it; but when you are to reach the coveted goal depends upon how rapidly you are moving now.

Knowing this, and knowing that fear, doubt, discouragement and indifference invariably retard this forward movement, we shall find it most profitable to remove those mental states absolutely.

The true attitude is the attitude of positive conviction; that is, to live in the strong conviction that whatever we see before us in the ideal will positively be realized, sooner or later, if we only move forward, and we can make it sooner if we will move forward steadily, surely and rapidly during every moment of the great eternal now. To move forward steadily during the great eternal now is to realize now as much of the ideal as we care to appropriate now; no waiting therefore is necessary. To begin to move forward is to begin to make real the ideal, and we will realize in the now as much of the ideal as is necessary to make the now full and complete. To move forward steadily during the great eternal now is to eternally become more than you are; and to become more than you are is to make yourself more and more like your ideal; and here is the great secret, because the principle is that you will realize your ideal when you become exactly like your ideal, and that you will realize as much of your ideal now as you develop in yourself now. The majority, however, feel that they can never become as perfect as their ideal; others, however, think that they can, and that they will sometime, but that it will require ages, and they dwell constantly upon the unpleasant belief that they may in the meantime have to pass through years and years of ordinary and undesirable experience; but they are mistaken, and besides, are retarding their own progress every moment by entertaining such thoughts.

If all the time and all the energy that is wasted in longing and longing, yearning and yearning were employed in scientific, practical self-development, the average person would in a short time become as perfect as his ideal. He would thus realize his ideal, because we attract from without what corresponds exactly to what is active in our own within. When we attain the ideal and the beautiful in our own natures, we shall meet the ideal and the beautiful wherever we may go in the world, and we will find the same things in the real that we dreamed of in the ideal. When we see an ideal we usually begin to long for it and hope that something remarkable may happen so as to bring it into our possession, and we thus continue to long and yearn and wait with periods of despondency intervening. We simply use up time and energy to no avail. When we see an ideal the proper course to pursue is to begin at once to develop that ideal in our own nature. We should never stop to wait and see whether it is coming true or not, and we should never stop to figure how much time it may require to reach our goal. The secret is, begin now to be like your ideals, and at the proper time that ideal will be made real.

The very moment you begin to rebuild yourself in the exact likeness of your ideal you will begin to realize your ideal, because we invariably gain possession of that of which we become conscious; and to begin to develop the ideal in ourselves is to begin to become conscious of the ideal. To give thought to time is to stop and measure time in consciousness, and every stop in consciousness means retarded progress.

The only time that seems long is the time that is not well employed in continuous attainment, and the only waiting time, that seems the hardest time of all, is the time that is not fully consecrated to the highest purpose you have in view. When we understand that we all may have different ideals we will find that we have an undeveloped correspondent in ourselves to every ideal that we may discern, and if we proceed to develop these corresponding parts there will be some ideals realized every day. Today we may succeed in making real an ideal that we first discovered a year ago. Tomorrow we may reach a goal towards which we have been moving for years, and in a few days we may realize ideals that we have had in view during periods of time varying from a few weeks to several years; and if we are applying the principles that underlie the process of making real the ideal, we may at any time realize ideals of which we have dreamed for a life time. Consequently, when we approach this subject properly we shall daily come into the possession of something that is our own.

All the beautiful things of which we have dreamed will be coming into our world and there will be new arrivals every day.

This is the life of the real idealist, and we cannot picture a life that is more complete and more satisfying; but it is not only complete in the present. It is constantly growing larger and more desirable, thus giving us daily a higher degree of satisfaction and joy. When we discern an ideal, that ideal has come within the circle of our own capacity for development, and the power to develop that ideal in ourselves is therefore at hand. The mind never discerns those ideals that are beyond the possibility of present development. Thus we realize that when an ideal is discerned it is proof positive that we have the power to make it real now.

Those who have not found their ideals in any shape or form whatever have simply neglected to make their own ideal nature strong, positive and pronounced. To live in negative idealism is to continue to dream on without seeing a single dream come true; but when the ideals we discern in our own natures become strong, positive working-forces our dreams will soon come true; our ideals will be realized one after the other until life becomes what it is intended to be, a perpetual ascension into all that is rich, beautiful and sublime.

Whether we speak of environments, attainments, achievements, possessions, circumstances, opportunities, friends, companions or the scores of things that belong in our world, the law is the same. We receive an ideal only when we become just like that ideal. If we seek better friends, we shall surely find them and retain them, if we develop higher and higher degrees of friendship. If we wish to associate with refined people, we must become more refined in action, thought and speech. If we wish to reach our ideals in the world of achievement, we must develop greater ability, capacity and power. If we desire better environments, we must not only learn to appreciate the beautiful, but must also develop the power to produce those things that have true quality, high worth and real superiority.

The great secret is to become more useful in the world; that is, useful in the largest and highest sense of that term. He who gives his best to the world will receive the best in return.

The world needs able men and women; people who can do things that are thoroughly worthwhile; people who can think great thoughts and transform such thoughts into great deeds; and to secure such men and women the world will give anything that it may hold in its possession. To make real the ideal, proceed to develop greatness, superiority and high worth in yourself. Train the mind to dwell constantly upon the borderland of the highest ideals that you can possibly picture; but do not simply yearn for what you can see, and do not covet what has not yet become your own. Proceed to remake yourself into the likeness of that ideal and it will become your own. To proceed with this great development, the whole of life must be changed to conform with the exact science of life; that is, that science that is based upon the physical and the metaphysical united as the one expression of all that is great and sublime in the soul. The new way of thinking about things, viewing things and doing things must be adopted in full, and this new way is based upon the principle that the ideal actually is real, and therefore should be approached not as a future possibility, but as a present actuality. Think of the ideal as if it were real and you will find it to be real. Meet all things as if they contained the ideal, and you will find that all things will present their ideals to you, not simply as mere pictures, but as realities. View the whole of life from the heights of existence; then you will see things as they are and deal with things accordingly; you will see that side of the whole of existence that may be termed the better side, and in consequence, you will grow into the likeness of that better side. When you grow into the likeness of the better side of all things, you will attract the better side of all things, and the ideal in everything in the world will be made real in your world.

HOW TO BEGIN: THE PRIME ESSENTIALS

To formulate rules in detail that will apply to each individual case is neither possible nor necessary. All have neither the same present needs nor the same previous training; but there are certain general principles that apply to all, and these, if followed according to the individual viewpoint, will produce the results desired. If the proper beginning is made, the subsequent results will not only be greater and be realized in less time, but much useless experience and delay will be avoided. These principles, or prime essentials, are as follows:

1. *Learn to be still.* When you undertake to live an ideal life and seek to promote your advancement in every direction, you will find that much cannot be gained until your entire being is placed in a proper condition for growth; the reason being that the ideal is ever advancing toward higher ideals, and you must improve yourself before you can better your life. It has been found that all laws of growth require order, harmony and stillness for proper action; therefore, to live peacefully, think peacefully, act peacefully and speak peacefully are important essentials. This will not only put the entire being into proper condition for growth, but will also conserve energy, and when you begin to live the larger life you will want to use properly all your forces; neither misusing or wasting anything. To acquire stillness never "try hard," but simply exercise general self-control in everything you do. Never be anxious about results, and they will come with less effort, and in less time. Whenever you have a moment to spare, relax the whole person, mind and body; just let everything fall into the easiest position possible. Make no effort to relax, simply let go.

While in this relaxed condition be quiet; do not move a muscle; breathe deeply but gently, and think only of peace and stillness. Before you go to sleep at night relax your entire system, and fall asleep with peace in your mind; bathe your mind and body, so to speak, in the crystal sea of the beautiful calm. These methods alone will work wonders in a few weeks. While you are at work hold yourself from anxious hurry or disturbed action; work in the attitude of poise and you will accomplish much more in the same given time and you will be a far better workman. Train yourself to come into the realization of perfect peace by gently holding a deep strong desire for peace and by ordering all your actions to harmonize with the peaceful goal in view. The result will be "the peace that passeth understanding," and for this alone your gratitude will be both boundless and endless.

2. *Rejoice and be glad.* Cheerfulness is not only a good medicine, but it is food for mind and body. The cheerful life will fill every atom with new life, and it is to the faculties of the mind what sunshine is to the flowers and trees. To be happy always is one of the greatest things that man can do, and there are few things that are more profitable in every sense of that term. No matter what comes, be glad; and live in the conviction that all things are working together for good to you. As your conviction is so is your faith; and as your faith is so it shall be unto you. When you live in the conviction that all things are working together for good you will *cause* all things to work together for good, and you will understand the reason why when you begin to apply the real science of ideal living. No matter how dark the cloud, look for the silver lining; it is there, and when you always look at the bright side of things you develop brightness in yourself. This brightness will strengthen all your faculties so that you can easily overcome what obstacles may be in your way, and thus gain the victory desired. However, do not try hard; gently direct your attention to the bright side and know that you can. Ere long it will be second nature for you to live on the sunny side. The value of this attainment is very great; first, because joyousness will increase life, power, energy and force; this we all know from personal experience, and we wish to have all the life and power that we can possibly secure; second, because the happiest soul never worries, which is great gain. Worry has crippled thousands of fine minds and brought millions to an early grave. We simply cannot afford to worry and must never do so under any condition whatever. If we have that habit we can remove it at once by the proper antidote, which is joyousness. After

you have trained yourself to look only for the bright and the best, the bright and the best will come to you, because you will be using your powers to bring those very things to pass; therefore, rejoice and be glad every moment. Let your heart and your soul sing at all times. When you do not feel the joyous music within, produce it with your own imagination, and ere long it will come of itself with greater and greater abundance; your soul will *want* to sing because it *feels* music, and there are few joys that equal the joy that comes when music is felt in the soul. There are so many things that are sweet and beautiful in life that when we once find the key to harmony we shall always rejoice. In the meantime, be happy for the good you have found, and through that very attitude you will develop the power to attract better things than you ever had before.

3. *Love everybody and be kind*. If you wish your path to be strewn with roses, just be kind. Give your best to the world, and the best will come to you without fail; if it does not come today, never mind; just go on being kind and refuse to consider disappointments. Never hold in mind those things that you do not wish to retain; you thus cause those things to pass away. This "shall also pass away" is true of everything that is not pleasant; but unpleasant things will not pass away so long as we hold them in thought. That which you let go from your mind will pass away from you entirely. Train yourself to be kindness in a permanent state of mind, because you cannot afford to criticize, condemn or be angry at any time. Be good and kind to everybody; it is one of the royal paths to happiness and peace. When anyone does wrong, do not condemn; help him out; help him find the better way. "Cast your bread upon the waters;" it will surely return; sometimes more quickly than you expect it. Therefore, give abundantly of all that is best in your life, and nothing is better than kindness and love. When you begin to live an ideal life you will desire more and more to live the largest life possible, and to accomplish this you must learn to be much to everybody. Your purpose must be to be useful in the largest and truest sense of that term; and nothing can promote this purpose so thoroughly and so extensively as universal kindness. This does not imply, however, that you are to permit

yourself to be imposed upon or unjustly used by the unscrupulous. It is our duty, as well as our privilege to demand the right at all times, and to demand justice for everybody and from everybody, but this should be done in kindness, with the antagonistic attitude eliminated. The love that loves everybody is not the love that seeks to gain personal possession of some object of affection. We refer to that larger kindness that excludes no one from our whole souled good wishes. This form of love is the greatest power in the world, and the one who loves the most in this larger, truer sense will accomplish the most. The reason why is found in the fact that a great love invariably brings out all that is large, great and extraordinary in human nature. To state that the one who takes the greatest interest in the welfare of the world does the most to promote his own interests may seem to be a contradiction of terms; but it is true, and it proves conclusively that the one who gives his best to the world will invariably receive the best in return. Never permit yourself to say that you cannot love every creature that lives; say that you do love everything that lives, and mean it. What you say you are doing, that you will find yourself doing. This greater love illumines the mind, gives new life to every fiber in your being, removes almost every burden and eases the whole path of existence. Love removes entirely all anger, hatred, revenge, ill-will, and similar states, a matter of great importance, for no one can live an ideal life while such states of mind remain. To have a sweet temper and loving disposition and a kind heart is worth more than tons of gold. We are all finding this to be true, and we realize fully that the person who loves everybody with that larger loving kindness has taken a long step upward into that life that is real life. This is not mere sentiment, but the expression of an exact scientific fact. A strong, continuous love will bring good to anyone who lives and acts as he inwardly feels.

4. *Have faith in abundance.* We all know the value of self-confidence, but faith is infinitely deeper, larger and higher. Self-confidence helps us to believe in ourselves, as we are at present, and thus helps us to make a better use of the talents we now possess; but faith elevates the mind into the consciousness of our

larger and superior possibilities, and thus increases perpetually the power, the capacity and the efficiency of the talents we now possess. Faith brings out the best that is within us and puts that best to work now. He who follows faith may frequently go out upon the seeming void, but he always finds the solid rock. The reason is that faith has superior vision and goes instinctively to the very thing we desire to find. Faith does not expect things to come of themselves. Faith never stands and waits; it does things; but while at work *believes* that the goal will be reached and the undertaking accomplished. The person who works in the attitude of faith can never fail; because through faith he draws upon the inexhaustible. The person who works in the attitude of doubt can never be at his best. Through the feeling of doubt he lowers his own ability; he holds back his best power and employs but a portion of his capacity; but the one who works in faith will press on to the very limit of his present capacity and then go on further still, because the more faith he has the more fully he realizes that there is no limit to his capacity, that the seeming void that lies before is positively solid rock all the way and he may safely proceed. Whatever you do *believe* that you can succeed in; do not for a moment permit yourself to doubt; know that the Infinite is your source, that you live in the universal and have the boundless upon which to draw for supply. If people or things do not come up to your ideal, never mind; give them time; continue to have faith in their better selves; they will also scale the heights. Expect them all to do their best, and most of them will do so now; the others will soon follow, if you live in the faith that they will. The unbounded faith of one soul can elevate the lives of thousands. This is a statement that is just as true as it is great, and we should constantly give it the highest place in mind. Many a person has risen rapidly in the scale because someone had faith in him. Faith is the greatest elevating power that we know in the world. Faith can convert any failure into success and can promote the advancement of everybody, no matter what the circumstances may be. Have faith in yourself and you will advance as you never advanced before. Have faith in others and they will inevitably follow. Have faith in the Infinite and the Supreme Power will always be with you. This power will see you through, whatever your goal may be. Therefore, if you would enter the new life, the better life, the ideal life, and inspire others to do the same, have faith in abundance.

5. *Pray without ceasing.* The true prayer is the whole-souled desire for the larger, the higher and the better while the mind is stayed upon the Most High; and to pray without ceasing is to constantly live that lofty desire. The forces of mind and body always follow our desires; therefore, if we would use our powers in building up a larger life we must have high desires and true desires. Turn your desires upward and keep them there; desire the greater things only; never desire anything less. Those powers within you will cause you to become as true, as great and as perfect as your heart has prayed that you might become. To cause our desires, thoughts and states of consciousness to rise to the very highest states of being, we should employ the silence daily; that is, we should enter into the absolute stillness of the secret life of the soul. Through the silence we shall find the secret of secrets, the path to that inner world from which everything proceeds. To begin, be alone and comfortably seated. Or, you may enter the silence in association with someone that is in perfect harmony with yourself. Relax mind and body; close your eyes and be perfectly quiet; turn your attention upon the inner life of the soul and gently hold your mind upon the thoughts of stillness and peace. Affirm with deep, quiet feeling, "Peace is mine." "I am resting in the stillness of the spirit." "I have entered the beautiful calm." "I am one with the Infinite." "I am in the secret places of the Most High," and similar states. While you make these statements *feel* that you are peaceful and still and that you are now in that inner world where all is quiet and serene. When you feel this deep, sublime stillness you can use other affirmations according to your present needs. You may affirm that you are well and strong and happy and harmonious, and that you have full possession of all those qualities that you know have existence in real life. To feel the perfect peace of the soul, however, is the first essential. After that is attained, your consciousness will deepen and you will enter the great within to a greater and greater degree. While the mind is in this interior

state of being, every thought you think will be a power, and every desire you express will modify or change everything in your life according to the nature of that desire and in proportion to its depth and unity with the Supreme. For this reason you should train yourself to think only right thoughts and create only the truest desires while you are in the silent state. That which you think or do while in the silence will have a greater effect upon your life than that which you may attempt while on the surface of outer consciousness. Therefore, everything that is important should be taken into the silence and through the silence to the Infinite. The real purpose of the silence is to enable the mind to enter the inner life and not only re-create all thought according to the higher truth, but to enter into a more perfect touch with the divine source of things. The silence should be entered every day for ten, twenty or thirty minutes. This is a daily practice of extreme value. Though you may not have any real results at first, simply continue; you will reach your goal. When you begin to become conscious of your interior life and begin to live more or less in touch with the world beautiful that is within you, you will find that you can live in this high, peaceful state the greater part of the time and thus be in the silence almost constantly. This is not only a most desirable attainment, but it is *the one great* attainment toward which every soul should work. When a person can live in these higher realms always and constantly, and desire the realization of the highest and the best that he knows, the prayer without ceasing, the true spiritual prayer is being fulfilled. Every day will bring us something that we truly wished for, and every moment will be supplied with all that is necessary to make the present full and complete.

6. *Think the truth.* When we learn to think the truth we have actually come to the "parting of the ways." Here we find where the old leaves off and the new begins. In this state the wrong disappears and the right is discerned and realized in an ever increasing manner. Each individual is now in possession of infinite wisdom, infinite power, infinite love, eternal life, perfect peace, everlasting joy, universal truth, universal freedom, universal good,

divine wholeness, spotless virtue, boundless supply. True, these attributes exist principally in the potential state, that is, they are possibilities waiting in the within for unfoldment, development and expression; nevertheless, they do exist in every soul and to a degree that is limitless. Therefore, every soul does actually possess those attributes, and to speak the truth we must recognize their existence and even now claim their possession. To think the truth you must think that you are divine in your true being, and that you possess these attributes, because this is the truth. To think contrary to this would be wrong thought, and from wrong thought comes all the wrong in the world. The average person does think contrary to this thought; therefore, he is almost constantly in bondage to sin or trouble of some kind. You are not the body; you possess a body, and that body may be indisposed, if you create wrong thought, but that body is not you. When the light reigns supremely, darkness cannot enter. Wrong thought comes from a false conception of yourself, and false conceptions will continue to form in mind so long as you are ignorant of the truth. When we think the truth about ourselves we shall always think the truth about others; we shall, therefore, not think of them as they appear on the surface but as they are in the perfection of real spiritual being. We shall overlook, forgive and forget the wrong appearance, knowing that it is but a temporary effect of wrong thought, and we shall proceed to inspire everyone to change that appearance by thinking right thought, the thought of truth.

7. *Live in the spirit*. To express this statement in its simplest terms, we would say that to live in the spirit is to live in the upper story of mind and thought, or to live on the good side, the bright side and the true side of everything. To the beginner this is sufficient, because this simple change in living must come before the higher spiritual consciousness can be realized; but the change though simple at first will completely revolutionize life. Ere long, however, the consciousness of the true side and the better side will become so clear that to live in the spirit will mean infinitely more than to simply dwell in the upper story of mind, and when this larger experience comes we shall know from our own illumined

understanding what it means to live in the spirit. When we begin to think the truth all kinds of illusions and false beliefs will gradually vanish, and we shall not only understand that we are spiritual beings, but we shall feel that we are all that divine life can be. We shall positively know that we are eternal souls living in a spiritual world now, expressing ourselves in a physical world, and we shall realize that we are actually created in the image and likeness of the Infinite, united with the Infinite and living in the life of Infinite being. Through the fuller realization of truth we will learn that the spiritual is not some vague, far away something that saints alone can know, but that spirit is the essence of all things, the very life of all things visible and invisible, and that spirit is in itself absolutely good and perfect. We will realize that there is but one substance from which all things proceed and that substance is the expression of spirit; we will see that there is but one life, the spiritual life. We will find through the spirit that evil is but a temporary condition produced by man's misunderstanding of the goodness and the completeness of real being and that to so live that we realize the absolute goodness and the perfect harmony of the whole universe is to live in the spirit. When we realize this we are on the true side of all things and we feel that we are. When we are in harmony with all things we are in harmony with the Infinite; and we also find that to "dwell in the secret places of the Most High" is to realize that we are in that great sea of life, the great spiritual sea, the universal state of being, the world of divine existence. While we are in this upper state, that is, in the spirit, we are away from the false, and actually in the true. We are in the spirit, and from the light of the spirit we can see clearly the truth concerning everything. From this place we may ascend to other and greater heights and enter into the ever increasing realms of life where existence becomes fairer and higher, too beautiful for tongue to ever describe. What is held in store for the soul that lives in the spirit, eternity alone can reveal, but that the life that is lived in the spirit is the only true life thousands have learned, both in this age and in ages gone by. To the beginner, however, the first essential is to get away from material life, that is, the common, the gross, the superficial, the ordinary, the perverted and the wrong; then to go up higher, to enter the world of light and live in the more beautiful realms of sublime existence. To live in the spirit, live in the highest and most perfected state now, and do not for a moment come down. At first this state will simply be a life that is finer, larger and more harmonious, where things move more smoothly and where the value of life seems to constantly increase; but ere long living in the spirit will mean far more than merely a pleasing state of existence, and the further we advance the more this wonderful life will be. However, before we begin we must be convinced of the great truth that the spiritual life is not mere sentiment nor a mere feeling of mind and soul. The spiritual life is the real life, the foundation of all life, the essence of all life, the soul of all life, and every true statement concerning the spiritual life is an exact scientific fact readily demonstrated by anyone who will apply the principle. And happy is the soul that does apply this principle, for such a soul will find life in the spirit, not only to be real, but to be infinitely more perfect, more wonderful and more beautiful than anyone has ever dreamed.

THE FIRST STEPS IN IDEAL LIVING

Give your best to the world no matter how insignificant that best may be, and the world will invariably give its best to you. When we give our best we not only receive the best in return from the outer world, but we also receive the best from the inner world. When you give your best, you bring forth your best, and it is the bringing forth of your best that causes you to become better and better. When you become better you will meet better people and enter into better environments, and everything in your life will change for the better, because like does attract like. To give much is to become much, provided we give our best and give with the heart. The giving that comes simply from the hand does not count, no matter how large it may be. It brings nothing back to us nor does it bring permanent good to anybody else. When you give your best you do not give from your over-supply or from that which you cannot use. If you have something that you cannot use, it does not belong to you, and you cannot give, in the true sense of the term, what is not your own. To give does not mean simply to give money, unless that is the best you have; but rather to give your own service, your own talents, your ability, your own true worth and your own real self. The man who lives a real life at all times and under all circumstances is giving his best and the very best possible that can be given. A real life truly lived in the world is a power, and the person who lives such a life is a power for good wherever he may be. The presence of such a person is an inspiration and a light, as we all know. The man who loves the whole world with heart and soul, and loves without ceasing is doing far more for the race than he who endows universities, and will receive a far greater reward. We must remember, however, that such a love is not mere sentiment. Real love is a power and will cause the person who has it to do his very best for everybody under every possible circumstance. That person whose heart is with the race will never be satisfied with inferior work. He will never shirk nor leave the problems of life to somebody else; he will go in and push wherever something good is being done, and he will constantly endeavor to render better and better service wherever his field of action may be. Such a person will give his best to the world, whether he gives through the channels of art or mechanics, music or literature, physical labor or intellectual labor, ideas or real living. What he does will be the best, and what he receives in return will be the best that the world is able to give. Give the best that you are through every thought, word and deed; that is the principle; and your life will be constantly enriched both from without and from within. Through the daily application of this principle you will develop superiority in mind, soul, character and life, and the world will be better off because you are here.

Expect the best from everybody and everybody will do their best for you. There may be occasional exceptions to this rule, but through close examination we shall find that these exceptions are due solely to our own negligence in applying the law to every occasion. The man who expects the best from everybody and has faith in everybody will certainly receive more love, more kindness, better friendship, better service and more agreeable associates by far than the one who has little or no faith in anyone. But our faith in people must be alive, and our expectations must have *soul*. To live constantly in the fear that people will do this or that, and that such and such mistakes may be made, is to live in a confused mental world, and where there is much confusion there will be many mistakes. Mental states are contagious; how that can be is not a matter for present discussion, but the fact that they are is extremely important, and we all know that they are; therefore, if we live in fear and confusion we will be a disturbing element among all those with whom we associate, and if our associates are not mentally strong and positive, they will be more or less confused by our presence, and they are very liable to produce the very mistakes we feared. On the other hand, when we have faith in people we help them to have faith in themselves, and the more faith a person has in himself, the fewer his mistakes and the better his work.

Look for the best everywhere and you will find the best wherever you go. Why this is so is a matter upon which many delight to speculate, but the why does not concern us just now. It is the fact that this law works that concerns us, and concerns us very much. Not everybody can fully understand why the best is always found by him who never looks for anything but the best, but everybody *can* look for the best everywhere and thereby find the best; and it is the finding of the best that attracts our attention. It is real results that we are looking for, and the simpler the method the better. The man who will constantly apply this law will not remain in undesirable environments very long, nor will he occupy an inferior position very long; better things will positively come his way and he will not have to wait an age for the change. The man who looks for the best is constantly thinking about the best and constantly impressing his mind with the best thought about everything; and since man is as he thinks, we can readily understand why such a man will become better and better; therefore, by looking for the best everywhere he will not only find the best in the external world, but he will create the best in his mental world; this will give him a greater mind, which in turn will produce higher attainments and greater achievements. That man, however, who is always looking for the worst, will constantly think about the worst and will fill his mind with inferior thoughts; that he, himself, will become inferior by such a process is a foregone conclusion. We shall positively find, sooner or later, what we constantly look for; it is, therefore, profitable to look for the best everywhere and at all times; we become like those things that we constantly and deeply think about; it is, therefore, profitable to think only of the best whatever may come or not. The average person may not find the best the very first day this principle is applied. Most of us have strayed so far away from this mode of thinking and living that it may take some time to get back to the path that leads to the best; but one thing is certain, whoever will look for the best everywhere, and continue to do so for a reasonable length of time, will find that path; besides, he will have more delightful experiences while he is training himself to apply this principle than he has had for any similar period before. This, however, will be only the beginning; the future has far greater things in store, if he will continue to look for the best.

When things are not to your liking, like them as they are. In other words, while you are working for greater things, make friends with the lesser things, and they will help you to reach your goal. The person who is dissatisfied with things as they are and discontented because things are not to his liking is standing in his own way. We cannot get away from present conditions so long as we antagonize those conditions, because we are held in bondage to that which we resist. If you want present conditions to become steppingstones to better things, you must get on the better side of present conditions, and you do that by liking things as they are while they remain with you. We must be in harmony with the present if we wish to advance, because in order to advance we must use the present, but we cannot use that with which we are not in harmony. This is a fact that deserves the most thorough attention, and will, when understood, explain fully why the average person seems powerless to rise above his surroundings. We must be on friendly terms with everything that exists in our present world if we wish to gain possession of all the building material that our present world can give, and we cannot secure too much material if we desire to build a larger life and a greater future. That which we dislike becomes detrimental to us, no matter how good it may be; nevertheless, it will always be with us because it is impossible to eliminate permanently that which we antagonize; when we run away from it in one place we shall meet it elsewhere in some other form; but that which we love will constantly serve us and help us on to greater things; when it can serve us no longer it will disappear. To like those things, however, that are not to our liking may seem difficult, but the question is why they are not to our liking; when we know that everything in our present world is a steppingstone to something still better it will be natural for us to like everything. Those things may not come up to our ideals, but that is not their real purpose; it is not the mission of present things to serve as ideals, their mission is to help us to reach our ideals, and they positively can do this if we will take them into friendly cooperation. When you take a drive to an ideal country place you do not dislike the horse because he is not that country place; if you are humane, you will love that horse because he is willing and able to take you where you wish to go. If you should dislike and mistreat that horse or should fail to hitch him to the vehicle, you would not reach your destination. This, however, is the very thing that the average person does with the things of his present world; these things are the horses and the vehicles that can take us to the ideal places we desire to reach; but we must hitch them up; we must treat them right and use them. To cause all things that are about us now to work together with us, we must be in perfect harmony with them; we must like them as they are, and that becomes comparatively easy when we know that it is necessary for them to be what they are in order that they may serve as our steppingstones; if they were different there would be no steppingstones, and we would have to remain where we are. When we realize that everything that exists in our present world has the power to promote our advancement, if we properly use that power, and when we realize that it is necessary to be in harmony with all things to use the power that is within those things, we shall no longer dislike anything; we shall even make friends with adversity, because the power that is in adversity can be tamed by kindness and love; and when that power is tamed it becomes our own. These are great facts and easily demonstrated by anyone, and whoever will apply these principles will find that, by liking everything that he finds, he will secure the cooperation of everything, and anyone can move forward rapidly when all things are working with him; consequently, by liking what he finds, he will find what he likes.

When you do not get what you want, take what you can get and call it good. It is better to have something than nothing; besides, we must use what we can get before we can become so strong and so able that we can get whatever we may want. When a person fails to realize his ideals, there is a reason; usually the cause is this: He simply longs for the ideal but does not work himself up to the ideal. And to work himself up to the ideal he needs everything that he can get and use now; by taking what he can get he secures something to work with in promoting his present progress, and by looking upon this something as good, he will turn it to good account. It is a well-known fact that we get the best out of everything when we meet everything in the conviction that it is *good for something,* because this attitude invariably brings the mind into conscious touch with the real value of that which is met. What we constantly look for we are sure to find, therefore, by calling everything good that we get and by constantly looking for the real worth of that which we get, the good in everything that we get will be found; the result is that everything we receive or come in contact with will be good for something to us and will have something of value to give us. Gradually, the good will so accumulate that we shall have all that we want; life will be filled with that which has quality and worth, which means that the development towards greater worth will constantly take place, and development towards greater worth means the constant ascension into the realization of our ideals. By accepting and using the good that we can now secure we add so much to the worth of our own life that we become worthy of the greater good we may desire; in consequence, we shall positively receive it. This process may not satisfy those who expect to reach the top at once or expect to receive the better without making themselves better, but it will satisfy those who would rather move forward gradually and surely than stand empty handed waiting and waiting for ages hoping that some miraculous secret may be found through which everything can be accomplished at once. The idea, however, is not that we should meekly submit to things as they are and be satisfied with what little fate may seem willing to give us; that is the other extreme and is just as detrimental to human welfare. Take everything that legitimately comes your way; do not refuse it because it seems too small; take it and call it good, because it is good for something; then make the best possible use of it with a view of getting greater good through that use; expect everything to multiply in your hands; have that faith; accept little things, as well as large things in that conviction, and every good that you do accept will be instrumental in bringing greater good to you. To live in the attitude of turning everything to good account has a most wholesome effect upon mind and character, because that mental attitude will tend to turn everything within yourself to good account; the result will be the constant development of a finer character and a more capable mind. By combining all the results from this mode of living and by noting the greater results that will invariably come from these combined results, we must conclude that the total gain will be great, and that he who turns to good account everything that comes into his life, will positively receive everything that he may require to live an ideal life.

Live in the cheerful world, even if you have to create such a world in your own imagination. Resolve to be happy regardless of what comes; you cannot afford to be otherwise. Count everything joy; meet everything in the spirit of joy, and expect everything to give you joy. By creating a cheerful world in your own imagination you develop the tendency to a sunny disposition, and by meeting everything in the attitude of joy you will soon meet only those things that naturally produce joy. Like does attract like. Much sunshine will gather more sunshine, and the happiest mind meets the most delightful experiences. When exceptions occur pass them by as of no consequence, because they are of no consequence to you; you are interested only in happy events; it is only such events that you desire to meet. It is a fact that the less attention we pay to unpleasant conditions the less unpleasantness we meet in life. That person who looks for the disagreeable everywhere, and expects to find it everywhere, will certainly find what he is looking for in most places if not in all places. On the other hand, the person who expects only the pleasant will seldom find anything else. We attract what we think of the most. The greatest value of cheerfulness is found in its effect upon the mind; that is, in its power to make faculties and talents grow, just as sunshine makes flowers grow. It is a well-known fact that the most cheerful mind is the most brilliant mind, other things being equal, and that the brightest ideas always come when you are in the brightest frame of mind. This makes cheerfulness indispensable to those who wish to improve themselves and develop superior mental power. The depressed mind is always dull and never sees anything clearly; while the cheerful mind learns more readily, remembers more easily and understands more perfectly; but we must not conclude that cheerfulness is all that is necessary to the development of a fine intelligence; there must be mental power and mental quality as well; but the power and the quality of the mind, however great, cannot be fully expressed without an abundance of mental sunshine. There are thousands of fertile minds in the world that are almost wholly unproductive, because they lack mental sunshine. If these would cultivate real genuine mental brightness, every part of the world would sparkle with brilliant ideas. What the acorn is to the oak, bright ideas are to a great and successful life, and we all can produce bright ideas through the development of mental ability and the cultivation of mental sunshine. To attain the cheerful state we must remember that it is a product of the inner life and does not come from circumstances or conditions; therefore, the first essential is to create a cheerful world in the imagination; picture in mind the brightest states of existence that you can think of and impress joy upon mind at all times; feel joy, think joy, and make every action of mind and body thrill with joy; ere long you will have created within yourself the subconscious cause of joy, and when this is done cheerfulness and brightness will become permanent elements in yourself.

Live in the present only. It is what we do for the present that counts; the past is gone, and the future is not ready to be acted upon. Give your time, your talent and your power to that which is now at hand and you will do things worthwhile; you will not waste thought upon what you expect to do, but you will turn all your energies upon that which you now can do; results will positively follow. The man who does things worthwhile in the present will not have to worry about the future; for such a man the future has rich rewards in abundance. The greater the present cause, the greater the future effect. Nine-tenths of the worries in the average life are simply about the future; all of these will be eliminated when we learn to live in the present only. Instead of giving anxious thought to the bridge we may have to cross, we should give scientific thought to the increase of present ability and power; thus we make ourselves fully competent to master every occasion that may be met. To judge the present by the past is not sound doctrine, because if we are advancing, the present is not only larger than the past, but quite different in many if not all respects. To follow the past is to limit one's self to the lesser accomplishments of the past and thus prevent the very best from being attained in the present. The present moment should be dealt with according to the needs of the present moment regardless of what was done under similar conditions in the past. There is sufficient wisdom at hand now to solve all the problems of the present moment, if we will make full, practical application of that wisdom. He who lives for the present only will live a larger life, a happier life, a far more useful life; this is perfectly natural, because he will not scatter his forces over past ages and future ages, but will concentrate his whole life, all his power and all his ability upon that which he is trying to do now; he will be his best today, because he will give all of his best to the life of today, and he who is his best today will be still better tomorrow.

Never complain, criticize or condemn, but meet all things in a constructive attitude of mind. The critical mind is destructive to itself, and will in time become wholly incompetent to even produce logical criticism. To complain about everything is to constantly think about the inferior side of everything, thus impressing inferiority upon the mind; this will cause the entire process of thinking to become inferior; in consequence, the retrogression of the man himself will inevitably follow. Refuse to complain about anything; complaints never righted a wrong and never will. When you seek to gain justice through complaint, you temporarily gain something in one place and permanently lose something in another; besides, you have harmed your own mind. The fact is that the more you complain the worse things will become; and the more you criticize what you meet today, the more adverse and inferior will be the things you are to meet tomorrow. The reason why is simple; the complaining mind attracts the cheap and the common, and the critical spirit goes directly down into weakness and inferiority. However, we must remember in this connection that there is a marked difference between the critical attitude and the discriminating attitude. When things are not right we should say so, but while saying so we should not enter into a "rip and tear" frame of mind; the facts should be stated firmly but gently and without the slightest trace of ill feeling or condemnation; simply discriminate between the white and the black and state the facts, but let no hurt whatever appear in your voice. What we say is important, but the way things are said is far more important; even truth itself can be expressed in such a way that it hurts, harms and destroys; this, however, is not true expression. It is truth misdirected and always produces undesirable effects. To state your wants in a friendly manner is not complaint, but when there are hurts and whines in your voice, you are making complaints, and you are harming yourself; besides, you are producing unfavorable impressions upon those with whom you come in contact. It is far better to have faith in people than to criticize and complain, even though everything seems to go wrong, because when we have faith in people we shall finally attract those who are after our own hearts, and who are competent to do things the way we wish to have them done. The very day we establish faith in the place of complaints, criticisms and distrust, the tide will turn; things will change for the better in our world, and continue to improve perpetually.

Make the best use of every occasion, and nothing but opportunities will come your way. He who makes the best of everything will attract the best of everything, and it is always an opportunity to meet the best. There are occasions that seem worthless, and the average person thinks he is wasting time while he is passing through such states, but no matter how worthless the occasion may seem to be, the one who makes the best use of it, while he is in it, will get something of real value out of it; in addition, the experience will have exceptional worth, because whenever we try to turn an occasion to good account, we turn everything in ourselves to good account. The person who makes the best use of every occasion is developing his mind and strengthening his own character everyday; to such a person every occasion will become an opportunity and will consequently place him in touch with the greater world of opportunities. Much gathers more and many small opportunities will soon attract a number of larger ones; then comes promotion, advancement and perpetual increase. "To him that hath shall be given." Every event has the power to add to your life, and will add to your life, if you make the best use of what it has to give; this will constantly increase the power of your life, which will bring you into greater occasions and better opportunities than you ever knew before. Make the best use of everything that comes your way; greater things will positively follow; that is the law, and he who daily applies this law has a brilliant future before him.

Never antagonize anything, neither in thought word or deed. The antagonistic mind develops bitterness in itself and thereby becomes just as disagreeable as the thing disliked; frequently more so, and we cannot expect to be drawn into the more delightful elements of the ideal while we ourselves are becoming less and less ideal. To live in the antagonistic attitude is to perpetuate a destructive process throughout mind and body, and at the same time suffer a constant loss of energy. We therefore cannot afford to be antagonistic at any time, nor even righteously indignant, no matter how perfectly in the right we may be; though in this connection it is well to remember that indignation never can be righteous. There are a number of minds that have the habit of feeling an inner bitterness towards those beliefs or systems of thought which they cannot accept. Frequently there can be no logical grounds for such a feeling. In many instances it is simply hereditary, or the result of foundationless prejudice; nevertheless, it is there and is actually sapping life and power out of the mind that has it. Be on friendly terms with the entire universe and feel kindly towards every creature in existence.

THE FIRST THOUGHT IN IDEAL THINKING

Every part of the outer world is filled and permeated with an inner world, and everything that appears in the outer world is a partial manifestation or expression of what exists in a perfect and complete state in the inner world.

In the life of man we have the outer and the inner worlds; the personal life in the without and the great spiritual life in the within. What appears in the outer world of man, that is, in his personal existence, is the result of what he has sought and brought forth from his inner world. According to one of the greatest of metaphysical laws, we express whatever we become conscious of. We, therefore, understand clearly why the personal man, or his outer world, is the direct result of what he has become conscious of in his interior world. Man is what he is in the without, because he has sought the corresponding elements in the within, and he may change the without in any manner desired by seeking first in the within those qualities and attributes that he may desire.

To seek and find the within is to become conscious of the within.

The power of the spiritual must be made the soul of all power, and the law of spiritual action must be made the rule and the guide in all action. When the spiritual is lived in all life, the richness and the quality and the worth of the spiritual will be expressed in all life, and spiritual worth means the sum-total of all worth. There are any number of minds in the world who now realize this greater worth and who have found the spiritual riches within to an extraordinary degree, but they have not in every instance sought righteousness; therefore, these spiritual riches have been of no use; frequently they have become obstacles in the living of a life of personal welfare and growth.

Real righteousness means right living and exact scientific thinking; that is, the correct expression of everything of which we are now conscious. To be righteous does not simply mean to be moral and truthful and just, but to live in harmony with all laws, physical, mental, moral and spiritual. To be in harmony with physical law, is to adapt one's self orderly to everything in the external world; to resist no exterior force, but to constructively use every exterior force in such a manner that perpetual physical development may take place. To be in harmony with mental laws is to promote scientific thinking; that is, to think the truth about everything and to see everything from the universal viewpoint. Scientific thinking is that mode of thinking that causes all the forces of mind and thought to constantly work for greater things. To be in harmony with moral laws is to live a life of complete purity; and purity in the true sense of the term is the doing of all things at the right time, in the right place and with the right motive; in other words, every action is a pure action that leads to higher and better things. All other actions are not pure, therefore not moral. To be in harmony with spiritual laws is to live in constant conscious touch with the inner or higher side of everything. To apply the spiritual law is to seek the spiritual first, no matter what the goal in view may be; to seek first the spiritual counterpart that is within everything, to make the spiritual thought the predominating thought and to dwell constantly in the spiritual attitude. We enter the spiritual attitude when we enter the upper story of the mind and mentally face that supreme side of life that is created in the likeness of the Supreme. Briefly stated, to be righteous is to be in harmony with the outer side of life, to think the truth, to live in real purity, to dwell on the spiritual heights and to give full and complete expression to the highest and the best of which we are now conscious. The righteous man is right and perfect as far as he has ascended in the scale of life at present, though not simply in a moral sense, but in every sense, including body, mind and soul.

The righteous man is never weak and is never in a state of discord or disorder. This is a great truth that we should not fail to remember. Weakness, discord and all other adverse conditions come from the violation of law somewhere in human life, but the righteous man violates no law. He is true to life as far as he has ascended in the scale of life.

Righteous action is that action that is always harmonious and that always works for better things, greater things, higher things. The great majority of those minds that are awakened to the reality of the spiritual side of things have already found an abundance of good things in the vast interior life that is ready for manifestation in personal life, but as most of these have neglected the law of real righteousness, this abundance remains inactive in the potential state and all other things as promised are not added.

When we desire more wisdom and a greater understanding it is evident that we can obtain these things only by entering real mental light, and that light is within us in the spirit. By entering into the consciousness of the illumined world within we naturally receive more light. We, ourselves, become illumined to a degree, frequently to a great degree, and we thus gain the power to understand perfectly what we could neither desire nor comprehend before. When we seek more life and power we can find the greater life only in the eternal life.

Whenever we enter into the presence of the Infinite, we enter into the life of the Infinite, and we are thus filled through and through with the supreme power of that life.

There is no limit to the power of the spirit, and the more power we enter into or become conscious of, the more power we shall give to mind and body; in consequence, the more spiritual we become, the stronger we become, the more able we become, the more competent we become and the more we can accomplish whatever our work may be; and he who can do good work in the world invariably receives the good things of the world.

There is no bondage in the spirit, and as we grow in the spirit we grow out of every form of bondage. One adverse condition after another disappears until absolute freedom is gained.

Perfect freedom in all things and at all times will positively be added.

As the only way to permanently increase anything is to increase the expressions of its source, we understand perfectly why greatness can come only when we begin to live in the great within. We must always bear in mind that what we become conscious of we bring forth into personal expression, but we cannot become conscious of the larger source of any quality or talent unless we enter into the spirit of that quality and talent.

The truth is that adverse conditions will positively disappear after one begins to actually live the full spiritual life. Poverty has two causes; lack of ability and the misplacing of ability. To improve ability to any degree the within must be awakened. We must learn to draw upon the inexhaustible sources of the inner life and become conscious of the greater capacity that lies latent within us.

By giving your first thought, your predominating thought, to the great and mighty world within, your mind will gradually enter more deeply into the life of this inner world. You thus become conscious of the larger powers within, because consciousness always follows the predominating thought. What you think of the most develops in yourself. When you think the most of the spiritual, consciousness will follow your spiritual thought and thus enter more deeply into the spirit. The result is you become conscious of a larger spiritual domain every day, you become conscious of a greater capacity within yourself every day, and since you always express what you become conscious of, you will cause greater ability and capacity to be developed and expressed in yourself every day; you thereby remove the first cause of poverty and place yourself in a position where you will be in greater demand, and the greater the demand for your service, the greater will be your recompense.

There are a number of people who have misplaced their talents that may have considerable ability, but they are not in the work for which they are adapted, and therefore do not succeed. They may have been forced into their present positions by necessity, or they may have chosen their present places through inferior judgment, but both of these causes may be changed. When we enter the spiritual everything clears up. We not only see our mistakes, but also how to correct them.

If you do not know whether you are in the proper sphere or not, enter the spirit. Constantly live in the spirit and you will soon know; you will also know when and how to change. By entering this state where the outlook is infinitely greater, you will see opportunities, open doors, possibilities, and pastures green that you never saw before, and you will also see clearly which one you have the power and the capacity to take advantage of now.

Instead of adversity and constant need, you will have peace, harmony and abundance. You will pass from the world of poverty and limitations to a world that can offer a future as brilliant as the sun.

The man who fights adversity and complains of his lot will continue in poverty and need. He will remain in mental darkness; he will be daily misled, and will always be doing the wrong thing at the wrong time. Such a life breeds ill luck and misfortune and perpetuates the poverty that already exists. However, let this person enter into harmony with his present fate, count everything joy, and realize that he can make his present misfortune a steppingstone to better things; then let him give his first thought to the greater life and power and capacity within, to the superior creative powers of his own mind, those powers that are able even now to create for him a better fate if he will but place before them a better pattern; the results will be peace of mind first, then hope of the better, then the vision of great changes near at hand, then the faith that the new life, the new time and the better days are now being created for his world. And when a person begins to inwardly feel that things are taking a turn, that better days are coming, and that the good is beginning to accumulate in his life, the victory is nearly won. A little more faith and perseverance and the crowning day is at hand. From that moment all things will begin to work together for good things and for still greater things, providing all the laws of life are employed according to the highest ideal of righteousness.

Many a person, however, has failed while on the very verge of his victory. By giving his first thought to the material benefits that he expected to secure, his consciousness is taken away from the spirit and becomes confused in those things that had not as yet been placed in the true order of perpetual increase. The result is a scattering of forces and his loss upon the hold of the good things that were beginning to gravitate towards his world. While ascending this upward path we must at every step keep the eye single upon the spiritual, upon the larger and the higher life within.

We shall enjoy these other things so much the more, if we continue to give the first thought to the spirit. This is evident, because while giving the first thought to the spirit everything that comes into our world will be spiritualized, refined and perfected, and will thus be given added power and worth.

We are always at our best when we are on the heights, and we gain the power to create, produce and attract those things from every part of life that correspond to the life on the heights.

Giving our first thought to the spiritual and seeking to live righteously according to this larger view of righteousness, all problems of life will be made straight; obstacles will disappear; our circumstances will change to correspond with our ideas, and we will daily enter into a better life and a greater state of existence than we ever knew before. The problems of the world can be solved in the same way.

The human race is the product of human thought.

To make the ideal real upon earth, all thinking must be ideal; and to cause all things to become ideal the foundation of all things must be based upon pure spiritual thought.

We receive only in proportion to what we give, and it is only as we work well that we produce great results; but by entering the spiritual life we receive everything that we may require in order to give as much as we may desire, to do as much as we may desire. We gain the power and the talent to do everything that is necessary to give worth and superiority to our entire state of existence. When we enter the spiritual life we gain every quality that is necessary in making life full and complete now, and we gain the power to produce and create in the external world whatever we may need or desire. In other words, we receive everything we want from within and we gain the power to produce everything we want in the without. We, therefore, need never take anxious thought about these other things.

The way will be open to all that is rich, beautiful and superior in life, and we shall be abundantly supplied with the best that life can give.

THE IDEAL AND THE REAL MADE ONE

When the elements of the ideal are blended harmoniously with the elements of the real, the two become one; the ideal becomes real and the real gives expression to the qualities of the ideal. To be in harmony with everything, at all times and under all circumstances, is therefore one of the great essentials in the living of that life that is constantly making real a larger and larger measure of the ideal; and so extremely important is continuous harmony that nothing should be permitted to produce confusion or discord for the slightest moment. Discord wastes energy, while harmony accumulates energy. If we wish to be strong in mind and body and do the best possible work, harmony is absolutely necessary and we must be in the best possible condition to make real the ideal. The person who lives in perpetual harmony with everything will accomplish from ten to one hundred per cent more than the average during any given period of time; a fact that gives the elements of harmony a most important place in life. When harmony is absent there is always a great deal of mental confusion, and a confused mind can never think clearly, therefore it makes mistakes constantly. To establish complete and continuous mental harmony will reduce mistakes to a minimum in any mind; another fact that makes the attainment of harmony one of the great attainments.

To live in harmony is to gain the joy everlasting, the contentment that is based upon the real value of life, and that satisfaction that grows larger and better for every day that passes by. On the other hand, to live in discord is to live in perpetual torment, even though our personal attainments may be great and our personal possessions as large as any mind could wish.

To live the good life, the ideal life, the beautiful life, we must be at peace with all things, including ourselves, and every thought, word and deed must be harmonious. Whatever we wish to do or be it is wisdom to make any sacrifice necessary for the sake of harmony, although that which we sacrifice for the sake of harmony is not a sacrifice. When we enter into harmony we will regain everything that we were willing to lose in order that we might possess harmony. When we establish ourselves in perfect harmony we shall be reunited with everything that we hold near and dear and the new unity will be far sweeter, far more beautiful than the one we had before. "My own shall come to me" is a favorite expression among all those who believe that every ideal can be made real, and many of these are waiting and watching for their own to come, wondering in the meantime what can be done to hasten that coming. There are many things to be done, but one of the most important is the attainment of harmony. No person who lives in perpetual harmony will be deprived very long of his own, whatever that own may be. Whatever you deserve, whatever you are entitled to, whatever belongs to you will soon appear in your world, if you are living in perfect harmony.

To enter harmony is to enter a new world where everything is better, where opportunities are greater and more numerous, and where persons, conditions and things are more agreeable. You will not only enter a better world, but the attitude of harmony will relate your life so perfectly to the good things in all worlds that may exist about you, that the best from every source will naturally gravitate towards your sphere of existence. But harmony will not only cause the good things of life to gravitate towards you; it will also cause you to radiate the good qualities in your own being and thus become a perpetual benediction to everybody. To be in the presence of a person who dwells serenely in the beautiful calm is, indeed, a privilege, especially to those who can appreciate the finer elements of a truly harmonious life. Whenever we are in touch with real harmony, whether it comes from the music of human life, the music of nature or the music of the spheres, we are one step nearer the Beautiful. We can therefore realize the great value of being able to actually live in perfect harmony at all times. The life of harmony is the foundation of happiness and is one of the greatest essentials to achievement and real success. When we look into the past we can always find that our failures originated in the confusion; likewise our troubles. On the other hand, all the good things that have happened to us in the past, or that are happening in the present, had their origin and their growth in the elements of continuous harmony; the ideal and the real were made one, and we consequently reached the goals in view.

The mind that works in perpetual harmony does more work and far better work than is possible in any other condition; besides, harmonious work is invariably conducive to higher development and growth. To work in harmony is to promote increase and development in all the qualities and powers of the personality; while to work in confusion is to weaken the entire system and thus originate causes that will terminate in failure. The majority state that they have no time for self-development, but to live in harmony and work in harmony is to promote self-development every moment, and this development will not be confined simply to those muscles or faculties that we use directly, but will express itself throughout the entire system; and the mind especially will, under such conditions, steadily gain both in power and in worth. In the presence of these facts we can realize readily that no person can afford to permit discord, disturbance or confusion at any time. The many declare, however, that they cannot help it, but we must help it and we can. There is no reason why our minds should be excited or our nerves upset at any time. We can prevent this just as easily as we can refuse to eat what we do not want.

To proceed, we must apply exact reason to this great subject. We should learn to understand that no wrong will be righted because we permit ourselves to "fly to pieces;" also that the act of becoming nervous over a trouble will never drive that trouble away. To live in a constant strain will not promote our purpose nor arrange matters the way we want them. This is a fact that we should impress deeply upon our minds, and then impress our minds to take another and a better course. The average person feels that it is a religious duty to be as excited as possible, and to string up all his nerves as high as possible, whenever he is passing through some exceptional event; in consequence, he spoils all or practically all of that which might have been gained.

There are many reasons why such a large number of undertakings fail, but one of the principal reasons is found in the fact that few people have learned to retain perfect harmony under all kinds of circumstances. Discord and confusion are usually present to a great degree, and in consequence, something almost invariably goes wrong. But when a person is in perfect harmony and does his very best, he will succeed at least in a measure every time, and he will thus prepare himself for the greater opportunities that are sure to follow. To believe that intelligent, well educated people almost daily break down over mere trifles is not mere simplicity, but the fact that it is the truth leads us to question why. Intelligence and education should give those who possess it the power to know better. Modern education, however, does not teach us how to use ourselves. We have learned how to mix material substances so as to satisfy every imaginable taste, and we have learned how to use the tangible forces of nature so as to construct almost anything we like in the physical world, but we have not learned how to combine the elements of mind so as to produce happiness, strength, brilliancy and harmony whenever we may so desire. A few, however, have made the attempt, but the elements of the mind will not combine for greater efficiency and higher states of expression unless the mind is in perfect harmony.

We have all learned to remember, but few have learned to think. To repeat verbatim what others have thought and said is counted knowledge and with such borrowed knowledge the majority imagine they are satisfied, the reason being they have not discovered the art of thinking thoughts of their own. This is an art that every person must learn; the sooner the better, if the ideal is to be made real. Original thinking is the secret of all greatness, all high attainments, all extraordinary achievements and all superior states of being; but no mind can create original thought until a high state of mental harmony is attained. To produce mental harmony we must first bear in mind the great fact that it is not what happens that disturbs us, but the way we think about that which happens; and our thought about anything depends upon our point of view. The way we look at things will determine whether the experience will produce discord or harmony, and it is in our power to look at things in any way that we may desire. When we are face to face with those things that usually upset the mind, we should immediately turn our attention upon the life and the power that is back of the disturbing element, having the desire to find the better side of that life and power constantly in view. Everything has its better side, its ideal side, its calm and undisturbed side, and a mere desire to gain a glimpse of that better side will turn the mind away from confusion and cause attention to be centered upon that calm state that is being sought. This will decrease discord at once, and if applied the very moment we are aware of confusion, we will entirely prevent any mental disturbance whatever. To meet all circumstances and events in this way is to develop in ourselves a harmonious attitude towards all things, and when we are established in this harmonious attitude nothing whatever disturbs us; no matter what may happen we will continue to remain in harmony, and will consequently be able to deal properly with whatever may happen.

The mind that is upset by confused circumstances will lose ground and fail, but the mind that continues calmly in harmony with everything, no matter what the circumstances may be, will master every occasion and steadily rise in the scale. He will continue to make real the ideal, because he is living in that harmonious state of being where the ideal and the real are harmoniously blended into one. To promote the highest and most perfect state of continuous harmony we must learn to meet those persons, things and events, with which we come in daily contact, in the right mental attitude. The result of such an attitude is determined directly by the nature of our own attitude of mind, and as we can express ourselves through any attitude we desire, it is in our power either to spoil the most promising prospects, or convert the most unpromising conditions into the greatest success. We should train ourselves to meet everything in that attitude of mind that expects all things to work out right. When we deeply and continually expect all things to work out right we relate ourselves more perfectly with that with which we come in contact; we take things, so to speak, the way they ought to be taken, and we thereby promote harmony and cooperation among all things concerned.

Though this be extremely important, it is insignificant, however, in comparison with another great fact in this connection; that is, the way things respond to the leading desires of the ruling mind; whether it is the exercise of the mysteries of mental force or the application of a mental law not generally understood, does not concern us just now; but it is a fact that things will do, as a rule, what we persistently expect them to do. To understand why this is so may require some study of the great laws of mind and body, and everybody should seek to understand these laws perfectly; but in the meantime anyone can demonstrate the fact that things will work out right if we constantly expect them to do so. No matter what may happen we should continue in the faith that all things will come right, and as our faith is, so it shall be. To place ourselves in perfect harmony with all things, the domineering attitude of mind must be eliminated completely. The mind that tries to domineer over things will not only lose control of things, but will lose control of its own faculties and forces. At first it may seem that the domineering mind gains ground, but the gain is only temporary. When the reaction comes, as it will, the loss will be far greater than the temporary gain. When you try to domineer over persons and things you gain possession and control of those things only that are too weak to control themselves. That is, you gain a temporary control over negatives, and negatives have no permanent value in your life; in fact they soon prove themselves to be wholly detrimental. Occasionally a domineering mind may attract the attention of better things, but as soon as his domineering qualities are discovered those better things will part company with him at once. The law of attraction is at the foundation of all natural constructive processes; therefore, to promote construction, growth, advancement and real success we must work in harmony with that law. If we wish to attain the superior, we must become superior, because it is only like that attracts like. If we wish to make real the ideal, we must live the ideal in the real.

When you want good things, make yourself better, and better things will naturally be attracted to you; but good things do not submit to force. Therefore, to try to secure better things through forceful methods, or through the domineering attitude, can only result in failure; such methods gain only the inferior, those things that can add neither to the welfare nor the happiness of any one. This fact holds good, not only among individuals, but also among nations and institutions. The more domineering an institution is the more inferior are its members, and the more autocratic the nation, the weaker its subjects. On the other hand, we find the best minds where the individual is left free to govern himself and where he is expected to act wisely, to be true to the best that is within him. In order that the individual may advance, he must steadily grow in the mastery of himself, and must so relate himself to the best things in life that he will naturally attract the best things; but these two essentials are wholly interfered with by the domineering attitude. Such an attitude repels everything and everybody that has any worth. It spoils the forces of mind, thus weakening all the mental faculties, and it steadily undermines whatever self-control a person might possess. Never try to control anything or domineer over anything, but aim to live in perpetual harmony with the highest, the truest and the best that is in everything.

Whatever happens we should approach that event in that attitude that believes it is all right. We should never permit the attitude that condemns, not even when the things concerned have proved themselves to be wrong. The attitude that condemns is detrimental to our own minds, because it invariably produces discord. When you meet all things in the expectation of finding them right, you always find something about them that is right. This something you may appropriate, and thus gain good from everything that happens. That person, however, who expects to find most things wrong, will fail to see the good that may exist among the things that come his way; therefore, he gains far less from life than his wiser neighbor. But what is equally important, the man who expects to find everything right wherever he may go will gradually gravitate towards those people and circumstances that are right. The man who expects to find everything wrong usually finds what he expects. The effect of these two attitudes upon mind and character is even more important, because the man is as his mind and character, and as the man is, so is his destiny. The man who expects to find most things wrong, and meets the world in that attitude, is constantly impressing the wrong upon his mind, and as we gradually grow into the likeness of that which we think of the most, he is building upon sinking sand. The mind that is constantly looking for the wrong cannot be wholesome. Such a mind is not in harmony with the law of growth, power, and ability; and therefore can never do its best. Unwholesome thoughts will steadily undermine the finest character and mind, and the world is full of illustrations. There is always something wrong in the life of that person who constantly expects to find things wrong, and the reason why is simple. His own expectations are reacting upon himself; by thinking about the wrong, he is creating the wrong, and thus bringing forth the wrong in every part of his life.

The man, however, who expects to find everything right, and meets the world in that attitude, is daily nourishing his mind with right thoughts, wholesome thoughts, and constructive thoughts; he thinks the most of that which is right, and is therefore steadily growing more and more into the likeness of that which is right, perfect, worthy and good; he is daily changing for the better, and through this constant change he steadily rises in the scale and thereby meets the better and the better at every turn. By expecting to find everything right he finds more and more of that which is right, and as he is becoming stronger in mind, character and soul, he is affected less and less by those few things that may not be as they should be. When you meet a disappointment, meet it in the conviction that it is all right, because through this attitude you enter into harmony with the power that is back of the event at hand, and you thus convert the disappointment into a channel through which greater good may be secured. Those who doubt this should try it; they will find that it is based upon exact scientific fact. Transcend disappointment, and all the powers of adversity will begin to rise with you and will begin to work with you and help you reach the goal you have in view. You will thus find that it is all for the best, because through the right mental attitude you made everything work out in such a way that the best transpired as a final result.

To live in what may be termed the "all right" attitude, that is, in that attitude that expects to find everything all right and that constantly affirms that everything is all right, is to press on to the realization and the possession of those things that are as you wish them to be. Disappointments and failures, when met in this attitude, simply become open doors to new worlds where you find better opportunities and greater possibilities than you ever knew before. When the average person meets disappointment he usually declares, "Just my luck;" in other words, he enters that mental attitude that faces ill luck; he thus fails to see anything else but misfortune in that which has happened; and so long as that person, consciously or unconsciously expects misfortune, into more misfortune he will go. He who believes that he is fated to have bad luck will have bad luck in abundance. The reason is, he lives in that mental attitude that places his mind in constant contact with those confused elements in the world that never create anything else but bad luck. That person, however, who thoroughly believes that everything that happens is simply a step to greater good, higher attainments and greater achievements, will steadily rise into those greater things that he expects to realize; the reason being that he is living in that mental attitude that places his mind in contact with the building power of life. Those powers will always build greater things for those with whom they are in harmony, and we all can place ourselves in harmony with those powers.

What we expect comes if our expectation is filled with all the power of life and soul, and what we believe our fate to be, that is the kind of fate we will create for ourselves. To meet ill luck in the belief that it is your luck, your particular kind of luck, and that it is natural for you to have that kind of luck is to stamp your own mind as an unlucky mind. This will produce chaotic thinking, which will cause you to do everything at the wrong time, and all your energies will be more or less misdirected; in consequence, bad luck comes from doing the wrong thing, or from being your worst; while good luck comes from being your best and from doing the right thing at the right time. It is therefore mere simplicity to create good luck at any time and in the measure that we may desire. The person that fears misfortune or expects misfortune and faces life in that attitude is concentrating attention upon misfortune; he thereby creates a world of misfortune in his own mind; and he who lives in mental misfortune will produce misfortune in his external life. Like causes produce like effects; and this explains why the things we fear always come upon us. We create mental causes for those things, and corresponding tangible effects always follow. Train the mind to expect the right and the best, regardless of present circumstances, conditions or events. Call everything good that is met. Declare that everything that happens, happens for the best. Meet everything in that frame of mind, and no matter how wrong or adverse conditions seem to be, you cause them all to work out right.

When the mind expects the best, has the faith that the right will prevail, and constantly faces the superior, the true mental attitude has been gained. Through that attitude all the forces of mind and all the powers of will become constructive, and will build for man the very thing that he expects or desires while his mind is fixed upon the ideal. He relates himself harmoniously to the best that is in all things and thus unites the ideal with the real in all things; and when the ideal becomes one with the real, the ideal desired becomes an actual fact in the real; and this is the goal every true idealist has in view. He takes those elements that have been revealed to him through the vision of the soul and blends them harmoniously with the actions of daily life. He thus brings the ideal down to earth and causes the real of every day life to express the ideal in everything that he may undertake to do. His life, his thought, his action, his attainments, his achievements, all contain that happy state where the ideal and the real are made one. His dreams have become true.

THE FIRST STEP TOWARDS COMPLETE EMANCIPATION

To forgive everybody for everything at all times, regardless of circumstances, is the first step towards complete emancipation. Heretofore, we have looked upon forgiveness as a virtue; now we know it to be a necessity. To those who possessed the spirit of forgiveness we have given our highest praise, and have thought of such people as being self-sacrificing in the truest sense of that term. We did not know that the act of forgiving is the simplest way to lighten one's own burdens. According to our former conception of this subject, the man who forgives denies himself a privilege, the privilege of indignation and revenge; for this reason we have looked upon him as a hero or as a saint, thinking that it could not be otherwise than heroic and saintly to give up the supposed pleasure of meting out revenge to those who seemed to deserve it. According to the new view, however, the man who forgives is no more saintly than the one who insists on keeping clean, because in reality the act of forgiving simply constitutes a complete mental bath.

It is profitable, most highly profitable, to forgive everybody, no matter what they have done, and this includes also ourselves. It is just as necessary to forgive ourselves as to forgive others, and the principal reason why forgiveness has seemed to be so difficult is because we have neglected to forgive ourselves.

We cannot let go of that which is not desired until we have acquired the mental art of letting go, and to acquire this art we must practice upon our own minds. That is, we must learn to let go from our own minds all those things that we do not wish to retain.

Whatever you held against yourself or others, you now drop entirely out of your mind; in consequence, you are freed from your mental burdens, and when mental burdens disappear, all other burdens will disappear also. The ills that we hold in mind are the only things that can actually burden our lives.

Many persons will state that they hold no ill against anyone yet suffer just the same. So they may think, nevertheless they are mistaken and will see their mistakes when they learn the truth about mental laws. You may not hold direct ill against any person just now, but your mind has not always been absolutely pure and absolutely free from every wrong thought.

To have wrong desires is to hold ills against yourself, as well as others. To blame yourself, criticize yourself, feel provoked at yourself, or condemn yourself for your shortcomings, is to hold ills against yourself, and there are very few who are not doing this every day to some degree.

When you have trouble, forgive those who have caused the trouble; forgive yourself for permitting yourself to be troubled, and your troubles will pass away. When you have made a mistake, do not condemn yourself or feel upset; simply forgive yourself, and resolve that you will never make the mistake again. As you make that resolution, desire more wisdom, and have the faith that you will secure the wisdom you require. "According to your faith, so shall it be." There are many who will think that the practice of forgiving everybody for everything will produce mental indifference and thus weaken character, but it is the very opposite that will take place. To forgive is to eliminate the useless, everything that is not good; and to free the mind from obstacles and adverse conditions is to enable that mind to be its best, to express itself fully and completely. This will not only strengthen the character and enlarge the mind, but will cause the greatness of the soul to come forth. There is many a character that appears to be strong on account of its open hostility to wrongs, but such a character is not always strong. Too often it is composed of a few borrowed ideas about morality backed up by mere animal force. The true character does not express hostility and does not resist or antagonize, but overcomes evil by giving all its power to the building of the good. A strong character meets evil with a silent indifference; that is, indifference in appearance only. The true character does not pass evil by because he does not care, but because he does care. He cares so much that he will not waste one single moment in prolonging the life of the wrong; he therefore gives his whole time and attention to the making of good so strong that evil becomes absolutely powerless in the presence of that good. No intelligent person would antagonize darkness. By giving his time to the production of light he causes the darkness to disappear of itself.

When we apply the same principle to the elimination of evil, a marvelous change for the better will come over the world. No person can forgive everybody for everything until he desires the best from every person and from every source. In other words, we cannot forgive the wrong until we desire the right. Therefore, the letting go of the inferior, and the appropriation of the superior, constitutes one and the same single mental process. We cannot eliminate darkness until we proceed to produce light, and it requires only the one act for removing the one and bringing forth the other. From these facts it is evident that when we let go of the wrong we gain more of that power that is right, and we thus increase the strength of character.

To eliminate all ill feelings, all hatred, all wrong thoughts and all false beliefs from the mind will increase the power of the mind, and place every mental faculty in proper condition for higher development.

The man who finds it easier to forgive than to condemn is on the verge of superior wisdom and higher spiritual power. He has entered the path to real greatness and may rapidly rise in the scale by applying the laws of true human development. Instead of producing weakness and indifference, the act of absolute forgiveness will produce a more powerful character, a more brilliant mind and a greater soul. Try this method for a year. Forgive everybody for everything, no matter what happens, and do not forget to forgive yourself.

Forgive the imperfect, and with heart and soul desire constantly the realization of the perfect; the imperfect will thus pass away and the more perfect will be realized in a greater and greater abundance.

Whatever our place in life may be, we must eliminate every burden of mind or body, if we wish to rise in the scale, and the first step in this direction is to forgive everybody for everything. When you begin to practice forgiveness on this extensive scale you will find obstacles disappearing one after the other. Those things that held you down will vanish and that which was constantly in your way will trouble you no more; your pathway will be cleared. You will have nothing more to contend with, and everything in your life will move smoothly and harmoniously towards greater and greater things.

To absolutely remove hatred for the wrongdoers in the world, we must cultivate a higher order of love, that love that loves every living creature with the true love of the soul, and such a love is readily attained when we train ourselves to look for the ideal soul of life that exists in everything, everywhere in the world. This idea may cause many to come to the conclusion that the act of forgiving the wrongdoer will have an undesirable effect upon society, because we may be liable to let people in general do as they please; but in this they are wholly mistaken. Reason declares that you cannot justly blame anyone, and love does not wish to blame anyone; forgiveness must therefore inevitably follow when reason and love are truly combined; but reason and love will never permit man in general to do as he pleases. When we love people we are not indifferent about their future. We do not wish them to go down grade. We want them to improve, to do the right and the best and we will do everything in our power to emancipate and elevate the entire race. Reason understands how the laws of life can be applied in producing those results we may have in view; therefore, the desires of love can be carried out through the understanding of reason, and thus every high purpose may be promoted by the right spirit and the proper methods.

If we can forgive everybody for everything now, we should do so, whether the world in general can do so or not. The man who wishes to move forward must not wait for the race. It is his privilege to go in advance of the race; thus he prepares the way for millions.

Be what you can be now. Do what you can do now, no matter how far in advance of this age such actions may be.

PATHS TO PERPETUAL INCREASE

The universe is overflowing with all manner of good things and there is enough to supply every wish.

The bitterness that sometimes appears in life is not a real part of life. The greatness of existence alone is intended for man. To know the bitter from the sweet, and to appropriate the latter, and always reject the former, is a matter, however, that is not clearly understood. There may be thousands who know the bitter when they see it, but they do not always know how to reject it. To throw off the ills of life is an art that few have mastered. But those who can eliminate the wrong are not always able to distinguish the right from the wrong, the reason being that we have not looked at things from the viewpoint of that power that produces things. The philosophers, the theologians and the scientists, as a rule, make life very complex and difficult to live. Their profound expressions confuse the multitudes, while ills and troubles continue as before; but to live is simple.

All things are possible, and the most difficult things become comparatively easy when we know how; therefore, the way of wisdom is not to look for those difficulties that ignorance has connected with things, but look for that simplicity that is the soul of all knowledge. When we learn to do things as they should be done, all difficulties disappear, and even the largest life becomes simple.

The doing of things is the universal theme in this age. Those who simply tell us what to do are no longer acceptable. We want practical instructions that tell us how. The greatest man of this age and of the future will not be the one who can move as he wishes the emotions of multitudes by the magic art of eloquence and bring whole nations to his feet by the artistic juggling of eloquent phrases. The great man will henceforth be the man who can tell us how, and who can express himself so clearly that anyone can understand. This, however, we are now beginning to do, and ere long the many will come back to the truth itself and understand the real truth in all its original simplicity. The path of truth and life is perfectly straight and is illumined all the way. It is therefore simplicity itself to follow this path when we find it, but the many have strayed into the jungles of illusions and misconceptions. These must all come back to the simple path, and when they do, the difficulty of living will wholly disappear.

To teach the race how to find the simple things, the true things, and the real things, is now the purpose of every original thinker, and whoever can add to the world's wisdom in this respect becomes a light to the race, indeed. One of the first principles in this new understanding of things is that which deals with man's power to place himself in perfect touch with the source of limitless supply; in other words, to enter the path of perpetual increase.

We do not have to take from another to have abundance, because there is more than sufficient for all. The fact that some one has abundance does not prove that he has taken some or all of his wealth from others, although this is what a great many believe to be the truth. Whenever we see some one in luxury, we wonder where and how he got it, and we usually add that many are in poverty because this one is in wealth. Such doctrine, however, is not true. It is thoroughly false from beginning to end. The world is not so poverty stricken that the few cannot have plenty without stealing from the many. The universe is not so bare and so limited that multitudes are reduced to want whenever a few persons undertake to surround themselves with those things that have beauty and worth. True, there is injustice in the world. There are people who have secured their wealth, not upon merit, but through the art of reducing others to want; but the remedy is not to be found in the doctrine that thousands must necessarily become poor when one becomes very rich. This doctrine is an illusion, and illusions cannot serve as foundations for a better order. There is enough in life to give every living person all the wealth and all the luxury that he can possibly appropriate.

The universe is overflowing with abundance. If we have not everything that we want, there is a reason; there is some definite cause somewhere, either in ourselves or in our relations to the world, but this cause can be found and corrected; then we may proceed to take possession of our own. Among the many causes of poverty, and the lack of a full supply, there is one that has been entirely overlooked. To overcome this cause is to find one of the most important paths to perpetual increase, and the remedy lies within easy reach of everyone who has awakened to a degree to the finer elements in his life.

There may be exceptions to the rule, but there are thousands who are living on the husks of existence because they were not grateful when the kernels were received. Multitudes continue in poverty from no other cause than a lack of gratitude.

We are now beginning to realize more and more that the greatest thing in the world is to live closely to the Infinite.

In fact, this mode of living is the very secret of secrets revealing everything that the mind may wish to know or understand in order to make life what it is intended to be. We also realize that the more closely we live to the Infinite, the more we shall receive of all good things, because all good things have their source in the Supreme; but how to enter into this life, of supreme oneness with the Most High, is a problem.

The mind that dwells constantly in the presence of true worth is daily adding to his own worth. He is gradually and steadily appropriating that worth with which he is in constant contact; but we cannot enter into the real presence of true worth unless we fully appreciate the real worth of true worth; and all appreciation is based upon gratitude.

The more grateful we are for the good things that come to us now, the more good things we shall receive in the future. This is a great metaphysical law, and we shall find it most profitable to comply exactly with this law, no matter what the circumstances may be. Be grateful for everything and you will constantly receive more of everything; thus the simple act of being grateful becomes a path to perpetual increase. The reason why is found in the fact that whenever you enter into the mental attitude of real gratitude your mind is drawn into much closer contact with that power that produces the good things received. In other words, to be grateful for what we have received is to draw more closely to the source of that which we receive. The good things that come to us come because we have properly employed certain laws, and when we are grateful for the results gained, we enter into more perfect harmony with those laws and thus become able to employ those laws to still greater advantage in the immediate future. This anyone can understand, and those who do not know that gratitude produces this effect should try it and watch the results.

The attitude of gratitude brings the whole mind into more perfect and more harmonious relations with all the laws and powers of life. The grateful mind gains a firmer hold, so to speak, upon those things in life that can produce increase. This is simply illustrated in personal experience where we find that we always feel nearer to that person to whom we express real gratitude. When you thank a person, and truly mean it with heart and soul, you feel nearer to that person than you ever did before. Likewise, when we express whole-souled thanksgiving to everything and everybody for everything that comes into life, we draw closer and closer to all the elements and powers of life. In other words, we draw closer to the real source from which all good things in life proceed.

When we consider this principle from another point of view we find that the act of being grateful is an absolute necessity, if we wish to accomplish as much as we have the power to accomplish. To be grateful in this large, universal sense is to enter into harmony and contact with the greatest, the highest and the best in life. We thus gain possession of the superior elements of mind and soul and, in consequence, gain the power to become more and achieve more, no matter what our object or work may be. Everything that will place us in a more perfect relation with life, and thus enable us to appropriate the greater richness of life, should be employed with the greatest of earnestness, and deep whole-souled gratitude does possess a marvelous power in this respect. Its great value, however, is not confined to the laws just mentioned. Its power is exceptional in another and equally important field.

To be grateful is to think of the best, therefore the grateful mind keeps the eye constantly upon the best; and, according to another metaphysical law, we grow into the likeness of that which we think of the most. The mind that is always dissatisfied fixes attention upon the common, the ordinary and the inferior, and thus grows into the likeness of those things. The creative forces within us are constantly making us just like those things upon which we habitually concentrate attention. Therefore, to mentally dwell upon the inferior is to become inferior, while to keep the eye single upon the best is to daily become better. The grateful mind is constantly looking for the best, thus holding attention upon the best and daily growing into the likeness of the best. The grateful mind expects only good things, and will always secure good things out of everything that comes. What we constantly expect we receive, and when we constantly expect to get good out of everything, we cause everything to produce good. Therefore, to the grateful mind all things will at all times work together for good, and this means perpetual increase in everything that can add to the happiness and the welfare of man. This being true, and anyone can prove it to be true, the proper course to pursue is to cultivate the habit of being grateful for everything that comes.

All things are so situated that they can be of some service to us, and all things have somewhere at sometime been instrumental in adding to our welfare. We must therefore, to be just and true, express perpetual gratitude to everything that has existence. Be thankful to yourself.

If you wish to live an ideal life, then aim to make real the most beautiful life that you can think of today. If you are longing for greater accomplishments and a larger sphere of usefulness, then be your very best in the place that you occupy now.

The great mistake of the age is to strive, to go about our work as if it were extremely difficult. The man who works the hardest usually accomplishes the least; while the truly great man is the man who has trained his life and his power to work through him.

The human race today resembles in too many instances the useless weed. Millions in every generation come and go without accomplishing anything whatever. They do not even live a life that gives contentment.

We have worked hard for results, not knowing that the only cause of results was within us, ready to produce the very results we desired, just for the asking. We have in many instances destroyed our brains trying to invent methods for producing happiness, power and success, not knowing that these things already existed within us in abundant supply, and that by wholesome thinking they would appear in full external expression.

The secret of secrets is to let the best within us have full right of way; this, however, most of us have failed to do. In consequence, the majority are undeveloped weaklings of little use to themselves or to the world. The lily permits that which *is* to have right of way. It does not interfere, but man does interfere. He usually refuses to accept the gifts which nature wishes to bestow upon him, and he hardly ever accepts assistance from a higher power. He sets out for himself and works himself into old age and death trying to gain what was actually given to him in the beginning. He leaves the real riches of life and enters the world of personal ambition expecting to find something better and create something superior through his own efforts, but he fails because man alone can do nothing. The average person does not realize that to create something from nothing is impossible, nor has he learned that the necessary something can come only from the life that is within. He may try to accomplish much and become much through personal ambition and hard work, but no one can build without material, and the material that is needed in building greatness can be secured only by giving right of way to the life and the power of the inner world. The man who expects to build greatness upon personal limitations will pass away in the effort, leaving his unfinished work to be taken up by some one else who will possibly build upon the same useless foundation. Thus one generation after another comes and goes, each expecting to succeed where predecessors failed; in the meantime very little is accomplished by man, and he fails to receive what infinite life is ever waiting to give.

This is the truth about man in general. The multitudes have come and gone during countless ages and have accomplished but little. There have been a few great exceptions in every age, but these were exceptions because they refused to follow the ways of the world. They learned the lesson that the lilies have taught, and they chose to let life live, to let the greatness from within come forth, to let power work, and to let that which *is* in the real of man have full right of way. When a person discovers what he is and permits that which he is to have full expression, his days of weariness, trouble and failure are gone. Henceforth he will live as the flower. His life will be full.

When a flower, which has so little of soul within itself, can become so much by permitting itself to be itself, how much more might man become if he would permit himself to be himself.

Since every step in advance comes when we refuse to go the way of the world, we should now understand that the way of the world is a mistake. We should therefore free ourselves from that mode of life, thought and action, absolutely.

The true way to attain greater things is to permit the greatness that is within to have full expression; likewise, when we seek happiness and harmony or a beautiful life, the true course is to permit those things to come forth and act through us; they are ready to appear.

They are now at hand and will express themselves through us the very moment we grant them permission. We have all discovered that whenever we become perfectly still, and permit supreme life to live in us, we can feel power accumulating in our system until we feel as if we could move mountains. We have also felt that while turning attention to the everlasting joy within, and opening the mind fully to this joy, that there came into being a state of happiness, comfort and contentment that seemed infinitely more perfect than the imagination has ever pictured.

In this age personal ambition is one of the ruling factors, and nearly everybody is trying to outdo some one else. The result is we build up and tear down in the outer world, but as a race we improve but little. The great within is ignored, held back or prevented from free expression, while there are few things in the great without that are really worthwhile.

The human race is breaking itself down striving to gain hold upon phantoms, while the great prize that has already been given is lost sight of in the dust and confusion.

It is the living of life that will change the life of the world. The world at large does not listen to reason, nor can those who are in the mad rush stop to think; besides, such minds are not sufficiently clear to understand the principles upon which the living of life is based.

Give the life within permission to really live in us. The life within will live our life and give us a beautiful life. The power within will do our work and do that work extremely well.

What we are required to do, that such things may come to pass, is to live, think and act in the likeness of the Infinite.

The soul becomes great and beautiful by permitting its own greatness and loveliness to come forth unhindered and undisturbed.

Thousands of people are at present trying to develop higher powers. Many of these actually try to work hard in their efforts to gain the various gifts of mind and soul, and because they do not succeed to any great extent they frequently become discouraged and give up, wondering whether or not the real truth has been found. Others being ambitious to become great in the world try to employ spiritual laws in the furthering of their personal aims, but they find the reactions so disagreeable that the prize is not worth the labor. To fly to the top at once is the ruling passion among many, and when they fail with whatever methods they may employ, they conclude that what passes for truth is nothing but manmade doctrines. The fact is, however, that the truth always appears to be the untruth when misdirected. To apply the principles of real truth in the furthering of any lofty aim we may have in mind, the first essential is to establish life in perfect touch with eternal life; the second essential is to positively determine what we expect to attain and become in actual personal living; and the third essential is to proceed in the attainment of happiness and harmony. Without happiness our talents will be as the flowers without sunshine, and without harmony most of the power we might receive would be thrown away.

To obtain happiness and harmony we need simply let life live. Real life already has these things, and when we let life live in us, those things will be expressed through us.

If you are miserable, it will profit nothing if everybody may know your name. It is not the praise of man that we should seek, but the life of the Infinite. The praise of the world can give us nothing, but life from within can give us everything.

Those who are accustomed to the worldly methods of thinking and working may feel that it is hardly possible to apply these new ideas while associated with worldly minds, but we must remember that it is not where we work or at what we work, but how we work that determines what results are to be. To so work that you permit the boundless power within to work through you is the secret, and this will not only cause your work to be pleasant, but will also cause you to do better and better work every day. It is therefore the royal path to pleasantness today and greater things tomorrow. In the old way you are compelled to almost wear yourself out today in order that you might provide for tomorrow; but not so in the new. While you are providing for tomorrow, you are not only enjoying life today, but you are, through the expression of greater and greater power from within, making yourself larger, stronger and greater today. In the development of talents you employ the same principle. You do not strive for greatness; you know that you are potentially great already, and by permitting this greatness to become alive in you, you will accomplish great things.

When you apply this principle in everything that you do, you will find your advancement to be steady and even rapid; you will move forward in all things, making the ideal real as you ascend in the scale.

When we begin to live, think and act according to these principles, we feel that we are carried on and on by some mysterious presence that seems to be doing everything for us while giving us the pleasure and the glory.

To engage in some extraordinary work becomes one of our greatest pleasures, because nothing is hard or difficult any more; obstacles disappear the very moment we enter their presence, and we realize inwardly that whatever we undertake to do will be accomplished. We no longer tremble when in the midst of events that require exceptional wisdom and power; we know that wisdom is ready to speak whatever may be necessary now, and that power is at hand to do whatever may be necessary to be done now. We are in touch with the greatness of the great within and may draw upon that great, inexhaustible source whatever we may need at any time. Fear takes flight, while faith becomes stronger, higher and more perfect; sorrow and despair are no more, because all things are working for the best. Even in the presence of death and loss we see more life and greater gain.

We know that what passes away merely ascends that it may live more and be itself in a larger, higher measure than it ever was before. We know that whatever comes will bring the new and the more beautiful. It could not be otherwise, because having chosen to be all that we are, the all can never cease to come, and the more the all continues to come, the more the all will continue to bring. We have laid aside the illusions of the world and adopted the ways of truth. We have beheld the beauties of nature and have opened our minds to the visions of the soul. These have given us the secret, and like the lilies of the field, we have learned to be still and live.

COUNT IT ALL JOY

We meet something at almost every turn that we think ought to be different. If we have high ideals, we may not feel satisfied to permit those conditions to remain as they are; we may even complain or antagonize. On the other hand, if our ideals be low, we may feel wholly indifferent, but then we find that those things go from bad to worse. What we seek, however, is our present comfort on the one hand and the betterment of everything about us on the other hand, and we wish to know how this may be brought about in the midst of the confusion, the ignorance and the ills that we find in the world. When we are indifferent to the wrong it becomes worse; therefore, even for our own good we must do something with those adverse conditions that exist in the home, in society, or in the state. We must meet all those things and meet them properly, but the problem is, how?

To antagonize, criticize or condemn never helps matters in the least; besides, such states of mind are a detriment to one's own peace. The critical mind wears itself out while thinking about the wrong, but the wrong in the meantime goes on becoming worse. To feel disappointment because the universe does not move according to our fancy will not change the universe, but it will produce weakness in our own mind.

The usual way of dealing with the problems of life solves nothing. The ordinary way of meeting temptation gives the tempter greater power, while the person who tries to resist is usually entrapped in adversity and trouble.

Count it all joy. That is the secret. Count it all joy no matter what may come, agreeing with all adversity at once, antagonizing nothing, condemning no one, leaving criticism alone. Never be disappointed or discouraged, and have nothing whatever to do with worry. Whatever comes, count it all joy. He who meets adversity in the attitude of peace, harmony and joy will turn enemies into friends and failures into greater good.

When things do not come your way, never mind. Continue to count everything joy, and everything will change in such a manner as to give you joy.

That which is good is always good; it is always welcome whenever it comes. In the meantime you are living in harmony and joy, and that in itself is surely a great good. That person who lives constantly in gloom drives even the sunshine out of his own mind; the clouds of gloom are so heavy that he fails to see the brightness that is all about him. That person, however, who counts everything joy will change everything to brightness and thus receive joy from everything. When you fail to receive what you sought, never for a moment be disappointed. Count it all joy. In fact, be supremely happy; you have a reason so to be. When you fail to get what you seek it simply means that there is something still better in store for you; then why should you not count such an event great joy. This is always the case when your whole desire is to receive the best; and when you train yourself to count everything joy, your mind develops that desire that always desires the best.

When you seek only the best, the best only will come, and you must not feel disappointed when you are taken away from a hovel in order that you may enter a palace.

The Infinite is your supply. When one door closes another opens, and if you depend upon the Supreme to open that other door, it will be a door opening into far greater and far better things than what you seemingly lost; besides, by being kind to your adversary you lifted yourself up. You are now a higher and a greater being. That means that you will now draw to yourself higher and better things; consequently, it was not the enemy that got the best terms; it was you.

Whatever you are called upon to do, do it and be happy. Count it all joy that you are given the opportunity to bring sunshine into dark places and develop your own latent power by doing what seemed difficult. You are equal to the occasion, if you think so; therefore you should consider it a privilege to prove it. The world is waiting for great souls – souls that are ready to do what others failed to accomplish. You can become one of these great souls by proving to yourself that you are equal to every occasion; and you will be equal to every occasion, if you count everything joy. When you are in the midst of temptations, rejoice with your whole heart.

Millions of people have died unhonored and unsung who might have arisen to greatness and become leaders and saviors in the world, if they would have demonstrated their superiority in the midst of temptation, tribulation and wrong.

Count it all joy; besides, the result will not only produce joy to yourself, but possibly to millions.

He who remains below must be counted with the small and the ordinary.

Whatever comes, or whatever you meet, or whatever you are called upon to do, proceed with peace and joy. Be glad that you have the opportunity to prove your own power, and thus elevate yourself thereby. Be supremely happy to know that you may change many things for the better through this attitude, and thus bless the lives of multitudes.

Train yourself to look at things according to this principle, and you will find that everything can produce joy. Everything can give cause for rejoicing; that is, providing everything is met in that attitude that counts everything joy. The same principle may be employed to great advantage in overcoming difficulties.

Every person desires to make the most of himself, but to accomplish this all latent power must be awakened, and there is nothing that will bring forth our latent powers more thoroughly than the doing of what seems difficult. When you find yourself shrinking from certain tasks, you have discovered a weak faculty within yourself. Refuse to let that faculty remain in such a condition. Go and do what you feared to do and let nothing hold you back. In this way the weak faculty will be made strong and your entire nature will pass through most valuable discipline and training. Nothing is really disagreeable unless we think so. That is, we may approach the disagreeable in such a way that it ceases to be disagreeable; and the secret is, count everything joy. You may enter darkness and gloom, but if you are living in a world of brightness and cheer, that darkness will not be darkness to you, nor will gloom enter your mind for a moment. You can remain in your own happy world, no matter what may happen, no matter what may take place in your immediate environment.

When you resolve to do certain things and proceed with a conviction that you will enjoy the work thoroughly, you will find real pleasure in that work; besides, you will do the work very well. Pleasure comes from within, and when the fountain of joy within is overflowing, it will give joy to everything that exists about us. To cause this fountain within to overflow at all times, count everything joy at all times. We should never look for weakness, but when we find it we should proceed at once to change it into strength. Whenever we meet difficulties, or whenever we are called upon to do what we dislike, we have found a weakness. We may remove that weakness by doing with a will what the moment demands, and resolve to enjoy it. Never permit such occasions to pass by without being changed. The opportunity is too valuable.

When you fail to gain or realize in the present what you expected, do not feel disappointed. Make up your mind to be just as happy in those conditions that are, as you expect to be in those conditions that you are looking for. The feeling of disappointment is not produced by events. It is produced by your own attitude toward events. You can meet all events in such a frame of mind that you never feel disappointed in the least, and that frame of mind is the result of counting everything joy.

We do not gain joy from things, but from the way we think about things, and we can think as we choose at any time, no matter what the circumstances may be. When the present demands happiness from something, different than what you were looking for in the present, grasp the opportunity to prove that you are equal to this occasion. You thus develop latent ability. When you count everything joy, you know that you can always produce joy. You know that whatever happens is best, because you have the power to cause it to become the best. The best always happens to those who seek only the best; therefore, whatever comes should be received as the best, and we must give it the opportunity to prove that it is better than anything that could have happened. You are not dependent upon events for happiness. Happiness does not come from what we do or where we go. Happiness comes from what we are now or what we create out of what is present now. Whether we be alone in a garret or in a gorgeous ballroom, the amount of happiness we are to receive in either place will depend entirely upon our own frame of mind. The frame of mind that you desire for the present moment you may have; if it does not come of itself, you can create it; you are the master.

When things do not come the way we like, we can like them the way they are coming. This is how we agree quickly with our adversaries; we thus *receive* the enemy, instead of fighting the enemy; and that which we receive in the true attitude of mind becomes our own. Count everything joy and every adversity will give up its power to you.

We always attract the best from everything when we meet everything in the conviction that all things work together for good. When nothing comes to give us happiness in the external, we can open the fount of everlasting joy in the great within.

We shall fail to see the fountain of joy within, however, so long as our whole attention is fixed upon those worldly pleasures that failed to come into our world; but if we count everything joy we no longer feel disappointed about what did not happen; on the other hand we enter into that joyous state of mind that will place us in direct contact with the source of limitless joy within the mind. When people speak unkindly of you, you will become offended if you thought they spoke unkindly, but if your eyes are too pure to behold iniquity, you will go on your way as if nothing had been said; you count everything joy and thus you will receive joy from your own lofty position in the matter.

When you are asked to do certain things, do not proceed with a feeling that you are compelled to. Go and do it because you want to; say that you want to, and count it all joy. We should never say "I have a duty to perform," but rather, "Here is an opportunity which I have the privilege to embrace." Train yourself to want to do whatever your present sphere of life may demand. He who loves and thoroughly enjoys what he is doing today will be asked to do greater things tomorrow. The large soul never asks if things are unpleasant or difficult; such thoughts never enter his mind. Whatever he finds to do, he proceeds to do, with his mind full of will and his heart full of joy. If you dislike anybody, you have found a weakness in yourself. You have found a difficulty that must be overcome at once. Do not permit such obstacles to remain in your way.

When we hate anything, we recognize the existence and the power of those things that have neither real existence nor real power; we therefore enter into a confused state of mind.

When you dislike anybody, overcome that weakness by giving that person all the love of your heart. Love that person and *mean* it, no matter what he has said or done. There is nothing in the world that lifts the soul so high above darkness and illusion as strong, pure, spiritual love.

THE TRUE USE OF KINDNESS AND SYMPATHY

The ordinary use of sympathy is responsible for a very large portion of the ills and the troubles we find in the world; the reason being that nearly all suffering is mental before it is physical, and that mental suffering is almost invariably produced when we enter into sympathetic touch with the ills that we meet among relations, friends or associates. The average person would suffer but little if he suffered only from the troubles that arise in his own system. It is the pain that is felt through sympathy for others that gives him most of the burdens he finds it necessary to bear. It is considered a sign of kindness, goodness and high regard, however, to sympathize with others in this manner, or rather to suffer with others, but this is not the true use of kindness.

We do not help others by entering into the same weakness that is keeping them in a world of distress. We do not help the weak by becoming weak. We do not right the wrong by entering into the wrong, or doing wrong. We do not free man from failures by permitting ourselves to become failures. We do not emancipate those who are in bondage to sin by going and committing the same sin. This is very simple; but ordinary sympathy is based upon the idea that we sympathize with a person only when we suffer with that person. We expect to relieve pain by proceeding to produce the same pain in our own systems; but we cannot remove darkness by entering into the dark. We can remove wrong only by removing the cause of that wrong, and to remove the cause of wrong we must produce the cause of right. Darkness disappears when we produce light; likewise, trouble will vanish when we produce harmony, but we cannot produce harmony by entering into trouble.

This, however, is what ordinary sympathy does; it has, therefore, failed to relieve the world. The ordinary use of sympathy multiplies suffering by making suffering contagious. It causes the suffering of the one to give pain to the many, and then in turn causes the pain of the many to give additional pain to each individual person whose sympathy is aroused in the same connection. Therefore, one of the first essentials in producing emancipation or in making real the ideal is to find the true use of sympathy.

Sympathy itself must not be removed, because it is one of the highest virtues of the soul. The average person, however, misapplies this virtue continuously, and in consequence brings pains both to himself and others, that could easily have been prevented. There is a better use for sympathy, and through this better use we cause all the good things in life to become contagious. Instead of entering into sympathetic touch with the weakness that may temporarily exist in the personality of man, we enter into sympathetic touch with the strength that permanently exists in the soul of man. Instead of morbidly dwelling upon the wrongs which we find, we proceed to gain the highest possible realization of the good, the right, the superior and the beautiful that we know has existence back of and above the superficial life of human nature. According to a metaphysical law, when we enter into mental contact with the good in man, we awaken the power of that which is good in man, and the most perfect mental contact is produced by sympathy.

To sympathize with the soul is to increase the active power of the soul, because we always arouse into greater action that with which we sympathize. To sympathize with the power of harmony in man will increase the power of harmony throughout his entire system and the elimination of trouble must inevitably follow. To sympathize with the pain a person may feel is to do nothing to relieve that person. You take the pain to yourself, but you do not take the pain away from the person with whom you sympathize.

You thus double the suffering instead of removing it entirely, as you should. On the other hand, when we proceed to awaken in that person that something that can remove the suffering, we protect ourselves from pain, while we actually do something to relieve that person from pain. We do not suffer with the person that suffers, but we do something to remove suffering absolutely from everybody concerned; instead of entering into the pain we take that person out of pain. That is sympathy that *is* sympathy. That is kindness that really results in a kind act. It does not weep, but does better. It removes both the cause and the effect of the weeping. It awakens that superior power in man that positively does produce emancipation. It does not cause suffering to be transmitted to a score of other persons who have done nothing to merit that suffering, but it stops the pain where it is and puts it out of existence absolutely.

Every form of suffering comes from the violation of some law in life. It is therefore wrong, but it cannot be righted by making a special effort to spread the results of that wrong among as many others as possible. This, however, ordinary sympathy does; it makes a special effort to make everybody feel bad because some one is not feeling as he should; but the pains of the many cannot give ease and comfort to the one, nor can many minds in bondage set one mind free. When any one is feeling bad it will not help him to have a group of morbid minds suffer with him. When any one is sorry it will not remove the cause of his grief to have others decide to be sorry also. Do something so that person will not feel bad any more. Take him out of his trouble. That is real sympathy; and while you are helping him out make him feel that your heart is as tender as tenderness itself. Do something so that the grief may be removed through the realization of that greater truth that knows that all is well. That is kindness worthy of the name.

Those, however, who are in the habit of sympathizing in the ordinary way, may think the new way cold, and devoid of feeling or love, but the fact is that it is the ordinary form of sympathy that is devoid of love.

When you love a person who is in pain you will not stand around and weep pretending that you are also feeling bad. You will put on the countenance of light and cheerfulness and actually do something tangible to remove his pain. That's love; and if you have real sympathy, you will minister to him with so much depth of feeling and tender kindness that you will touch the very innermost life of his soul. All love, all tenderness, all kindness and all real feeling come from the soul. Therefore, he whose sympathy is of the soul will receive his love and his kindness directly from the true source; in consequence, he will have more love and more kindness by far than the one whose sympathy is a form of morbid feeling.

The real purpose of true sympathy is twofold; first, to arouse in a greater measure that finer something in life that is not only tender and sweet and beautiful, but is also immensely strong – strong with the strength of the Infinite; and second, to awaken everything in man that has quality, superiority and worth; that is, to make man feel the supreme power of his own inherent divinity. There is something in man that is greater than all weakness and all wrongs, and when this something is awakened, developed and expressed, all weakness and all wrongs must disappear. To sympathize with this greater something in everybody with whom one may come in contact will arouse this greater something, not only in others, but also in him who lives in this form of sympathy. In other words, to sympathize with the superior in man is to banish the wrong and the inferior by causing the expression of that divine something within that has the power to make all things well. Such a sympathy will tend to build a stronger life, a better life, a superior life, a more beautiful life; and to give such a sympathy to everybody is kindness indeed.

There may seem to be kindness in weeping with those who weep, but it is a far greater kindness to give those people the power to banish their sorrows completely, and he who does this is not cold; he is the very essence of the highest and most beautiful love. There is no joy in having sorrow. There is no pleasure in having pain.

Therefore, what greater good can man do for man than to help him gain complete emancipation from all those things, and this is the purpose of this higher use of sympathy. True sympathy is neither cold nor purely intellectual. It is real soul-feeling, while ordinary sympathy is simply a morbid mental feeling. True sympathy is the very fire of real spiritual love, because it springs from the very soul of love and is in constant touch with the unbounded power of that love. That such a sympathy should have extraordinary emancipating power is therefore most evident. The ordinary use of sympathy may appear to be kind. It may mean well, but it is usually misdirected kindness, and is nearly always weak. The higher use of sympathy, that is, the expression of divine sympathy, is not only kindness itself, but it has the spiritual understanding and the spiritual power to do what kindness wants to do. Ordinary kindness is usually crippled. It lacks both the power to do and the understanding to know what to do. The true sympathy, however, not only has the power to feel kindly, but has the power to act kindly. It not only gives love and makes everybody feel that they are in the presence of real love, but it also gives that something that can cause the purpose of love to come true. Real love invariably aims to produce comfort, peace, and emancipation. That is its purpose, and real sympathy can fulfill that purpose. Therefore, this higher sympathy is the sympathy that *is* sympathy.

The same principle should be employed in the use of every form of emotion, because every emotion is a movement of the mind conveying mental elements and powers with certain definite objects in view. Therefore, the way the emotion acts will determine to a very great extent whether these mental powers will build for better things, or produce undesirable conditions. Those movements of the mind or emotions that express themselves in love, heartfelt joy and spiritual feeling have a beneficial effect; while that mental feeling that is usually termed emotionalism is never wholesome. True spiritual feeling is calm, but extremely beautiful and awakens orderly and harmoniously all the finer elements of human life.

The mind that permits itself to be aroused by intense, emotional feeling will gradually lose its power of clear thought. The understanding will become so weakened that the principles of real truth cannot be fully comprehended, while the judgment will follow more and more the illusions of an overwrought imagination. The fact that religious feeling among millions is so closely associated with this overwrought state of emotionalism proves the importance of a better understanding of the use of these finer mental elements. Emotionalism compels the mind to follow mere feeling, and mere feeling, when not properly blended with clear understanding, will be misdirected at every turn. Emotionalism also stupefies the finer perceptions by intoxicating the mind and by burning up the finer mental energies; and since these finer perceptions are required to discern real truth, we understand readily why highly emotional people cannot comprehend the principles of pure, spiritual metaphysics.

There is something in man that is called religious feeling. It is present to a greater or lesser degree in everybody and cannot be removed, because it is a part of life itself. When in action, and it is never inactive very long, it expresses itself in some power of emotion. When this emotion or delicate mental movement is permitted to act without any definite purpose it becomes emotionalism; that is, mental energy running rampant, and becoming more and more intense until it destroys itself, as well as all the energy it originally contained. On the other hand, when this feeling is directed towards the highest and the most perfect conception of truth, life and being that the mind can possibly picture, all that is lofty, ideal and beautiful will be developed in the mind and soul of that individual. This is natural, because there is nothing that has greater developing power than deep, spiritual feeling; a fact that those who desire to develop remarkable ability, extraordinary talent and rare genius will do well to remember.

Emotionalism invariably excites the imagination, and an excited imagination will imagine all sorts of things that are not true.

The mind will thus be filled with illusions, and in consequence, false beliefs, wrong thoughts, perverted states and misdirected mental energy will follow. The result will be trouble, mistakes and failures in one or more of their many forms. It is now a well demonstrated truth that every thought has a definite power of its own, and that that power will produce its natural effect in some part of the human system. If the thought is not good the effect will naturally be undesirable, and conditions will be produced in mind that we do not want. But whatever we imagine, that we think; therefore, when we excite the imagination we imagine all manner of things that are untrue, unreal or abnormal; we produce false or perverted thought action in the mind; we think the wrong, and wrong thoughts invariably produce wrong conditions in the mind.

What we imagine we reproduce in ourselves to some degree, frequently to a marked degree; but an excited imagination simply cannot imagine what is good and wholesome. In every form of development, whether in the body, the mind or the soul, the imagining faculty is employed extensively. All growth is promoted by combining and recombining the elements of life in higher and higher forms, and since it is one of the functions of the imagination to produce these higher, more complex and more perfect combinations, development cannot take place unless the imagination works orderly, constructively and progressively. An excited imagination will produce false mental combinations or may waste energy by attempting to combine mental elements that will not combine. An orderly imagination may be likened to a skilled workman who builds a beautiful mansion out of his bricks, while an excited imagination might be likened to some one who can do nothing more than pile those bricks into a heap. The fact that emotionalism always excites the imagination proves therefore how impossible it is for minds with uncontrolled emotions to develop the greatness that is latent within them.

Another fact of great importance in this connection is that emotionalism will intensify every mental tendency that may be active in mind at the time.

If there is a tendency towards abnormal desires, emotionalism will intensify those desires so that it will be very difficult to resist temptation should it appear. On the other hand, pure spiritual feeling would transmute those desires, and produce instead, an ascending tendency, thus leading all the forces of mind towards higher ground. To overcome emotionalism, intense mental feeling, anger, excitability and all overwrought or abnormal mental states, turn attention upon the spiritual heights of the soul whenever such mental feelings are felt.

To cause all the emotions to follow ascending tendencies will increase remarkably the power, the fineness, the life and the rapture of every phase of feeling, not only in the soul, but in the mind and the body as well. Every trace of coldness, indifference or lack of feeling will entirely disappear, and we shall develop instead that higher form of kindness, sympathy and spiritual emotion that is created in the likeness of divine emotion. Whoever employs this method will not permit his feelings to run wild at any time, but will cause the life and the power of every feeling to accumulate in his system. He will hold them all in poise and use their energies intelligently in the building up of his whole life and in adding to the joy, the rapture and the delight of the living of a full, strong, ever-ascending state of existence. That person who controls his feelings and turns all the energies of those feelings upon the spiritual heights of the soul will actually become a living flame of love, sympathy and sublime emotion. Such a person will enjoy everything intensely, but his joy will be in such a high state of harmony that he will waste nothing in his life; instead, all the elements and powers of his life will continue to accumulate, thus giving added strength, worth and superiority to everything that he may physically, mentally or spiritually possess.

TALK HAPPINESS AND PROSPERITY

Talk happiness. When things look dark, talk happiness. When things look bright, talk more happiness. When others are sad, insist on being glad. Talk happiness, and they will soon feel better. Talk happiness; it pays in every shape and form and manner. Give sunshine to others, and others will be more than pleased to give sunshine to you. Talk happiness and your mind will be brighter and your personality far more attractive; but the qualities that happiness will give to you will also be given to those who have the pleasure to listen to you when you talk happiness.

Talk happiness, and you will always remain in a happy frame of mind. You will encourage thousands of others to do the same. You will become a fountain of joy in the midst of the garden of human life, and who can tell how many flowers of kindness and joy unfolded their rare and tender beauty because you were there. When others have lost courage, talk happiness. The future is bright for everybody. Talk happiness, and you turn on the light in their pathway, and they will see the better things that are before them. When the mind is depressed it is blinded; it sees only darkness; but when the light of joy is admitted everything is changed. Therefore, talk happiness to all persons and on all occasions.

We cannot have too much light in the world, and the more we talk happiness the more light we produce wherever we may be. What greater pleasure could anyone desire than to realize that he has eased the way of life for thousands and sent the sunbeams and joy into the mental world of tens of thousands? You can do this by talking happiness. Thus by constantly talking happiness you produce perpetual increase in your own happiness. What we give in abundance always returns in abundance; that is, when we give in the right spirit. When in the midst of discord, trouble or confusion, talk happiness. Harmony will soon be restored. The majority can easily change their minds for the better when some one takes the lead. You can take the lead by talking happiness.

Talk prosperity. When times are not good, man himself must make them better, and he can make them better by doing his best and having faith in that power that produces prosperity. When men have faith in prosperity they will think prosperity, live prosperity and thus do that which produces prosperity; and you can give men faith in prosperity by constantly talking prosperity. They may not listen at first, but perseverance always wins. Prosperity is extremely attractive, and the more you impress it upon the minds of others, the more attractive it becomes until no one can resist it; and when we admit the idea of prosperity into our own minds we will from that moment begin to produce prosperity. Think prosperity, talk prosperity, and live prosperity; and you will rise in the scale no matter what the circumstances may be. Hold to the power that produces abundance by having unbounded faith in that power and you will overcome all adversity and reach the highest goal you have in view. The fear of failure produces more failure than all other causes combined. You can remove that fear by talking prosperity.

When the sins of the world are in evidence, talk virtue. When the power of virtue is in evidence, talk more virtue. Eternally emphasize the good; give it more and more power, and it will soon become sufficiently strong to produce that ideal of power that you wish to make real. Talk virtue, and people will think of virtue; they will dwell more and more upon the beauty of virtue. Ere long they will desire virtue, and that desire will become stronger and stronger until it thrills every atom in human life. To desire virtue is to become virtuous. To live for the attainment of purity is to place in action all the purifying elements in your being, and you will soon realize that perfectly clean condition that every awakened mind has learned to worship. You can purify the minds of thousands by constantly talking virtue, and these thousands will in turn convey the power of virtue to as many thousand times thousands more. On the surface many things may seem to be what they ought not to be, but the surface is not all there is. It is an insignificant part of the whole. There is a hidden richness in life that the many do not see, because their attention has never been turned in that direction.

You can lead mankind into the gold mines of the mind and into the diamond fields of the soul, and the secret lies in the words you speak. You can guide the mind of man by the way you talk. Talking therefore should not be empty, but should ever have a sublime goal in view. Your words point the way and they who hear what you have to say will, to some degree, be influenced to go whatever way your words may point. Your power, therefore, in directing other minds towards greater and better things is hidden in every word you speak, and how important that that power be wisely employed.

We are responsible for every word we express. It will affect somebody either for good or otherwise. Talk sin and trouble and you will cause many to go directly into more sin and trouble. Talk happiness and prosperity and you will cause many to find happiness and prosperity in greater and greater abundance. When the world complains, do not forget to emphasize the great fact that universal good is even now at hand. The complaining mind wears colored glasses. He cannot see things as they are. You can help him to remove those glasses by calling his attention to the fact that things are not what they seem to him. Everything lies in the point of view. Look at things from the right point of view and you will be happy, cheerful and optimistic under all sorts of circumstances. But look at things from the wrong point of view, and you will see nothing clearly; everything will appear to be what it is not. You will thus live in confusion and your mistakes will be many. Remove this confusion by placing yourself in harmony with the eternal good, and you can do this by talking about the good, thinking about the good and emphasizing most positively every expression of good with which you may come in contact. That which we think of and talk of constantly will multiply and grow in our own world.

Talk peace. You will thus not only prevent confusion, but you will remove those confused conditions that may already exist. You can still the storms of life everywhere by talking peace.

When man thinks the most of peace he will be in peace, and he cannot fail to think of peace so long as he is faithfully talking peace. Talk success, and you will inspire everybody with the spirit of success. You will help to turn the energies of life upon the goal of success, and thus you will help all minds to move towards success. Never say that anything is impossible. Talk success, and you help to make everything possible. Everybody should succeed. It is not only the privilege of everybody to succeed, but every person, to be just to himself, must succeed. The fear of failure, however, is the greatest obstacle. You can remove that fear by talking success. Hold the idea of success before every mind with which you come in contact; you will thus become one of the greatest philanthropists in the world.

New and greater opportunities may be found everywhere. Talk of these things and forget the missteps of the past. We can leave the lesser that is behind only by pressing on towards the greater that is before. Talk success to everybody, and everybody will press on towards the greater goal of success. Be an inspiration among all minds; and you can be by holding up the light of success, prosperity and attainment at all times. Use your words in promoting advancement, in awakening new interest in the better side, the brighter side, the sunny side, and turn the mind of man upon those things that *can* be done. He can who thinks he can, and you help every person to think that he can by talking prosperity and success. Impress the greater upon every mind, and every mind will think the greater; and he who thinks the greater is constantly building for greater things. Emphasize the sunny side in all your speech and you provide a never failing antidote for complaints; and since the complaining mind soon becomes the retrogressing mind, this antidote has extreme value. It may change for the better the destiny of anyone when brought squarely before his attention, and this your words can do.

When one door closes another opens; sometimes several. This is the law of life. The man who talks happiness, prosperity, power and progress is working in harmony with the universe, and is helping to promote the great purpose of the universe; and who would not occupy a position of such value and importance? Whenever you talk trouble, failure or sin you arraign your own mind against the law of life and the purpose of the universe. You will thereby be against everything, and everything will, in consequence, be against you. You must, therefore, necessarily fail in everything you undertake to do. But how different everything will be when you turn and move in the other direction. Go with the universe, and all the power of the universe will go with you, and will help you to reach whatever object you may have in view.

Harmonize yourself with the laws of life and you will steadily rise in the scale of life. Nothing can hold you down. Everything you undertake to do you will accomplish, because everything will be with you. You will reach every ideal, and at the best time and under the best circumstances cause that ideal to become real. When you cease to talk failure and begin to talk success you invariably meet the turn in the lane. You find that a new world and a better future is in store. Things will take a turn when you take a turn, and you will take a turn when you begin to talk about those things that you desire to realize. The way you talk you go. The way you talk others will go. Therefore, talk happiness and prosperity, and help everybody, yourself included, to move towards happiness and prosperity. The power of words is immense, both in the person that speaks and in the person that is spoken to. The simplest way to use this power is to train yourself to talk the things you want; talk the things that you expect or desire to realize; talk the things you wish to attain and accomplish. You thus cause the power of words to work for you and with you in gaining the goal you have in mind. Whatever comes, talk happiness and prosperity. Say that you are happy; say that you are prosperous. Emphasize everything that is good in life, and the power of the Supreme will cause your words to come true.

WHAT DETERMINES THE DESTINY OF MAN

The destiny of every individual is being hourly created by himself, and what he is to create at any particular time is determined by those ideals that he entertains at that time. The future of a person is not preordained by some external power, nor is fate controlled by some strange, mysterious force that masterminds alone can comprehend and employ. It is ideals that control fate, and all minds have their ideals wherever in the scale of life they may be. To have ideals is not simply to have dreams or visions of that which lies beyond the attainments of the present; nor is idealism a system of ideas that the practical mind may not have the privilege to entertain. To have ideals is to have definite objects in view, be those objects very high or very low, or anywhere between those extremes.

The ideals of any mind are the real wants, the real desires or the real aims of that mind, and as every normal mind invariably lives, thinks and works for that which is wanted by his present state of existence, it is evident that every mind must necessarily, either consciously or unconsciously, follow his ideals. When those ideals are low, ordinary or inferior the individual will work for the ordinary and the inferior, and the products of his mind will correspond in quality with that for which he is working. Inferior causes will originate in his life and similar effects will follow; but when those ideals are high and superior, he will work for the superior; he will develop superiority in himself, and he will give superiority to everything that he may produce. Every action that he originates in his life will become a superior cause and will be followed by a similar effect.

The destiny of every individual is determined by what he is and by what he does; and what any individual is to be or do is determined by what he is living for, thinking for or working for. Man is not being made by some outside force.

Man is making himself with the power of those forces and elements that he employs in his thought and his work; and in all his efforts, physical or mental, he invariably follows his ideals. He who lives, thinks and works for the superior, becomes superior; he who works for less, becomes less. It is therefore evident that any individual may become more, achieve more, secure more and create for himself a greater and greater destiny by simply beginning to live, think and work for a superior group of ideals. To have low ideals is to give the creative forces of the system something ordinary to work for. To have high ideals is to give those forces something extraordinary to work for, and the fate of man is the result of what his creative forces hourly produce. Every force in the human system is producing something, and that something will become a part of the individual.

These forces, however, are not directed or controlled by the will. It is the nature of the creative forces in man to produce what the mind desires, wants, needs or aspires to attain, and the desires and the aspirations of any mind are determined by the ideals that are entertained in that mind. The forces of the system will begin to work for the superior when the mind begins to attain superior ideals, and since it is the product of these forces that determines both the nature and the destiny of man, a superior nature and a greater destiny may be secured by any individual who will adopt the highest and the most perfect system of idealism that he can possibly comprehend. To entertain superior ideals is to picture in mind and to hold constantly before mind the highest conception that can be formed of everything of which we may be conscious. To mentally dwell in those higher conceptions at all times is to cause the predominating ideas to become superior ideas, and it is the predominating ideas for which we live, think and work. When the ruling ideas of any mind are superior, the creative force of that mind will produce the superior in every element, faculty, talent or power in that mind; greatness will thus be developed in that mind, and the great mind invariably creates a great destiny.

To entertain superior ideals is not to dream of the impossible, but to enter into mental contact with those greater possibilities that we are now able to discern; and to have the power to discern an ideal indicates that we have the power to realize that ideal. We do not become conscious of greater possibilities until we have developed sufficient capacity to work out those possibilities into practical, tangible results. Therefore, when we discern the greater we are ready to attain and achieve the greater; but before we can proceed to do what we are ready to do we must adopt superior ideals, and superior ideals only. When our ideals are superior we shall constantly think of the superior, because as our ideals are so is our thinking, and to constantly think of the superior is to steadily grow into the likeness of the superior.

When the ideals are very high all the forces of the system will move towards superior attainments; all things in the life of the individual will work together with greater and greater greatness in view, and continued advancement on a larger and larger scale must inevitably follow. To entertain superior ideals is not simply to desire some larger personal attainment or to mentally dwell in some belief that is different from the usual beliefs of the world. To entertain superior ideals is to think the very best thoughts and the very greatest thoughts about everything with which we come in contact. Superior idealism is not mere dreaming of the great and the beautiful, but is actual living in mental harmony with the very best we can find in all things, in all persons, in all circumstances and in all expressions of life. To live in mental harmony with the best we can find everywhere is to create the best in our own mentality and personality; and as we steadily grow into the likeness of that which we think of the most, we will, through ideal thinking, perpetually increase our power, capacity and worth. In consequence, we will naturally create a greater and a more worthy destiny.

The reason why the majority fail to secure any tangible results from higher ideals is because they entertain too many of the lower ideals at the same time.

They may aim high; they may adore the beautiful; they may desire the perfect; they may live for the better and work for the greater, but they do not think their best thoughts about everything, and this is the reason why they do not reach the goal they have in view. Some of their forces are building for greater things, while other forces are building for lesser things, and a house divided against itself cannot stand.

Superior idealism contains no thought that is less than the very greatest and the very best that the most lofty states of mind can possibly produce, and it entertains no desire that has not the very greatest worth, the greatest power, and the highest attainment in view.

To apply the principles of superior idealism in all things means advancement in all things. To follow the superior ideal is to move towards the higher, the greater and the superior, and no one can continue very long in that movement without creating for himself a new world, a better environment and a greater destiny. To create a better future begin now to select a better group of ideals. Select the best and the greatest ideals that you can possibly find, and live those ideals absolutely. You will thus cause everything in your being to work for the higher, the better and the greater, and the things that you work for now will determine what the future is to be. Work for the greatest and the best that you know in the present, and you will create the very greatest and the very best for the future.

TO HIM THAT HATH SHALL BE GIVEN

The statement that much gathers more is true on every plane of life and in every sphere of existence; and the converse that every loss leads to a greater loss is equally true; though we must remember that man can stop either process at any time or place. The further down you go the more rapidly you will move towards the depths, and the higher up you go the easier it becomes to go higher still.

When you begin to gain you will gain more, because "To him that hath shall be given." When you begin to lose you will lose more, because from "Him that hath not, even that which he hath shall be taken away." This is a great metaphysical law, and being metaphysical, man has the power to use it in any way that he may desire. As man is in the within, so everything will be in his external world. Therefore, whether man is to lose or gain in the without depends upon whether he is losing or gaining in the within.

The basis of all possession is found in the consciousness of man, and not in exterior circumstances, laws or conditions. If a man's consciousness is accumulative, he will positively accumulate, no matter where he may live; but whether his riches are to be physical, intellectual or spiritual will depend upon the construction of his mind. When the mind has the greatest development on the physical plane an accumulative consciousness will gather tangible possessions. When the mind has the greatest development on the intellectual or metaphysical plane, an accumulative consciousness will gather abundance of knowledge and wisdom. When the mind has the greatest development on the spiritual plane an accumulative consciousness will gather spiritual riches. However competent you may be on the physical plane, if your consciousness is not accumulative, you will not gain possession of a great deal of this world's goods.

To have is not simply to possess in the external sense. Those who are conscious of nothing have nothing. Those who are conscious of much have much, regardless of external possession. Before we can gain anything we must have something, and to have something is to be conscious of something.

We must be conscious of possession in the within before we can increase possession in any sphere of existence. All possession is based upon consciousness and is held by consciousness or lost by consciousness. All gain is the result of an accumulative consciousness.

All loss is due to what may be termed the scattering of consciousness; that is, that state of consciousness that lets go of everything that may come within its sphere. When you are conscious of something you are among those that hath and to you shall be given more. As soon as you gain conscious hold of things you will begin to gain possession of more and more things.

When you inwardly feel that you are gaining more and more, or that things are beginning to gravitate towards your sphere of existence, more and more will be given to you until you have everything that you may desire. How we feel in the within is the secret, and it is this interior feeling that determines whether we are to be among those that have or among those that have not. When you feel in the within that you are gaining more you are among those that have, and to you shall be given more.

When we learn that mind is cause and that everything we gain may come from the action of mind as cause, we discover that all possession is dependent upon the attitude of mind, and since we have the power to hold the mind in any attitude desired, all the laws of gain and possession are in our own hands. When this discovery is made we begin to gain conscious possession of ourselves, and to him that hath himself all other things shall be given. To feel that you, yourself, are the power behind other powers, and that you may determine what is to come and what is to go, is to become conscious of the fact that you are something. You thus become conscious of something in yourself that is real, that is substantial and that is actually supreme in your world. To become conscious of something in yourself is to have something, and to have something is to gain more; consequently, by gaining consciousness of that something that is real in yourself you become one of those that hath, and to you shall be given.

To gain consciousness of the real in yourself is to gain consciousness of the real in life, and the more you feel the reality of life the more real life becomes. The result is that your consciousness of the reality of life becomes larger and larger.

Whatever you become conscious of in yourself, that you gain possession of in yourself. Whatever you gain possession of in yourself, that you can constructively employ in your sphere of existence, and whatever is constructively employed is productive; it produces something. Therefore, by becoming conscious of something you gain the power to produce something, and products on any plane constitute riches on that plane.

The more you become conscious of in yourself and in your life the greater your power to create and produce in your sphere of action, and the more wealth you produce the greater your possession, providing you have learned how to retain the products of your own talent. When we analyze these laws from another point of view we find the consciousness of the real in ourselves produces an ascending tendency in the mind, and whenever the mind begins to go up, the law of action and reaction will continue to press the mind up further and further indefinitely. Every upward action of mind produces a reaction that pushes the mind upward still farther. As the mind is pushed upward a second upward action is expressed that is stronger than the first; this in turn produces a second reaction stronger than the first reaction, and the mind is pushed upward the second time much farther than it was the first time. The fact is, when the mind enters the ascending scale the law of action and reaction will perpetuate the ascension so long as the mind takes a conscious interest in the progress made; but the moment the mind loses interest in the movement the law will reverse itself and the mind enters the descending scale.

When the mind is in the ascending scale it is steadily becoming larger, more powerful and more competent, and will consequently be in demand where recompense is large and the opportunities more numerous. Such a mind will naturally gain step by step in rapid succession. To such a mind will be given more and more continually, because it has placed itself in the world of those who have. The great secret of gaining more, regardless of circumstances, is to continue perpetually to go up in mind. No matter how things are going about you, continue to go up in mind.

Every upward step that is taken in mind adds power to mind, and this added power will produce added results in the tangible world. When these added results are observed mind gains more faith in itself, and more faith always brings more power. On the other hand, when we permit ourselves to go down in mind, because things seem to go down, we lose power. This loss of power will prevent us from doing our work properly or from using those things and conditions about us to the best advantage. In consequence, things will actually go down more and more; and if we permit this losing of ground to make us still more discouraged, we lose still more power, to be followed by still more adversity and loss. It is therefore evident, that the way we go in mind, everything in our world will go also, and that if we change our minds and stay changed, everything else will change and stay changed. If we continue to go up in mind, never permitting retrogression for a moment, everything in our world will continue to go up, and there will not even be signs of reverse, much less the loss of anything which we wish to retain.

When things seem to go wrong we should stay right and continue to stay right, and things will soon decide to come and be right also. This is a law that works and never fails to work. When we permit ourselves to go wrong because things seem to go wrong, we produce what may be termed the letting go attitude of mind, and when we cease to hold on to things, things will begin to slip away. We must hold on to things ourselves, if we wish to retain them for ourselves; and the secret of holding on to things is to continue positively in that attitude of mind that is perpetually going up into the larger and the greater. The laws of life will continue perpetually to give to those who have placed themselves in the receiving attitude, and those same laws will take away from those who have placed themselves in the losing attitude. When you create a turn in yourself you will feel that things are also taking a turn to a degree; and if you continue persistently in this feeling, everything in your life will positively take the turn that you have taken. As you go everything in your world will go, providing you continue to go; the law of action and reaction explains why.

THE LIFE THAT IS WORTH LIVING

To the average person life means but little, because he has not discovered the greater possibilities or his real existence. He has been taught to think that to make a fortune or to make a name for himself are the only things worth while, and if he does not happen to have the necessary talent for these accomplishments there is nothing much else for him to do but to merely exist. However, if he has been touched with the force of ambition, or if he has had a glimpse of the ideal, mere existence does not satisfy, and the result is a life of unhappiness and dissatisfaction. But such a person must learn that there are other openings and opportunities in life besides mere existence, regardless of what the mental capacity of the individual may be. These other opportunities, when taken advantage of, will give just as much happiness, if not more, than what is secured by those who have won the admiration of the world; besides, when one learns to live for these other things real living becomes a fine art, and he begins to live a life that is really worth while.

There is many a person whose present position in life depends almost wholly upon his financial returns, and if these are small, with no indications of immediate increase, his life seems to be almost, if not wholly, a barren waste; not because it is a barren waste, but because he has not found the real riches of existence. The trouble with this person is the point of view; he is depending upon things instead of depending upon himself. He must learn that there is something more to live for besides his salary and what his salary can buy. The value of the individual life is not measured by the quantity of possessions, but by the quality of existence. The value of life comes not from having much, but from being much; and happiness is invariably a state of mind coming, not from what a person has, but from what he is. We must remember, however, that he who is much will finally gain much, providing the powers in his possession are practically applied; and his gains will have high quality whether they be gains in the world of things or in the world of mind, consciousness and soul.

The problem for the average person to solve is what he actually can do with himself in his present position. He may not be earning much now, and his opportunities for earning more may not be clearly in evidence, but he is nevertheless living in a great sea of opportunities, many of which may be taken advantage of at once. The first of these is the opportunity to make of himself a great personality, and in taking advantage of this opportunity he should remember that to do great things in the world is not the only thing worth while. To be great in the world is of equal if not greater worth, and he who is now becoming great in his own life will, without fail, do great things in years to come. The majority of those who have practical capacity are making strenuous efforts to do something great, something startling, that will arrest the attention of the world; while those who do not possess this practical capacity are not satisfied because they are not similarly favored. In the meantime neither class gains happiness, and the best forces of life are employed in the making of things, most of which are valueless, while the making of great personalities is postponed to some future time.

The capacity to make great things is not the only capacity of value in the possession of man; but all minds do not possess this capacity; all minds, however, do possess the power to remake themselves in the exact likeness of all that is great and beautiful and ideal.

The average person usually asks himself how much money he can make during the next ten years, but why should he not ask himself how much happiness he can enjoy during those same years, or how much brilliancy he can develop in his mind, or how much more beautiful he may become in body, character and soul? He would find that by living for these latter things he would not only perpetually enrich his life and live a life that is thoroughly worth living, but he would find that the earning of money would become much easier than if he simply lived for material gain alone.

There are a number of ambitions outside of the usual ones that could engage our attention with the greatest of profit, because they not only have worth in themselves, but they lead to so many other things that have worth. The desire to secure as much out of life as life can possibly give will not only make living intensely interesting, but the more life a person can live the more power he will get. Live a great life and you gain great power. The increase of your power will enable you to carry out a number of other ambitions, thus adding to the richness of your life from almost every imaginable source.

If your present life does not hold as much as you would wish, do not think of it as an empty state of existence. Do not depend upon those few things that you are receiving from the external world; but begin to draw upon the limitless life and power that exists in the vastness of your interior world. Then you will find something to live for.

When the world of things does not seem to hold any new opportunities for you, resolve to grow more and more beautiful in body, character and soul with the passing of the years. Make this your ambition, and if you do your utmost to carry out this ambition, you will gain far more satisfaction from its realization than if you had amassed an immense fortune. Live to express in body, mind and soul all that is high and beautiful and ideal in your sublime nature, and you will not only give yourself unbounded joy, but you will become a great inspiration to the entire world. The life that is not expressed through the beautiful nor surrounded by the beautiful is not worth a great deal to the mind of man; but there is practically no end to the joy and richness that man may gain through that which is actually beautiful. The beautiful not only gives happiness, but it opens the mind of man to those higher realms from which proceed all that is worthy or great or ideal. To look upon the beautiful is to gain glimpses of that vast transcendent world where supreme life is working out the marvelous destiny of man.

Remember that no matter how insignificant your position in life may be today, or how small your income, or how limited your opportunities, you can begin this moment to give expression to the vast riches of your interior life; and before you take your departure from this sphere you may become such a great light in the world of higher illumined attainment that your accomplishments in this unique sphere of action will continue to inspire the world for ages yet to come.

To live for the purpose of unfolding the latent powers of your being is a work that will not only prove interesting to an exceptional degree, but will prove exceedingly rich in future possibilities. That there is practically no end to the possibilities that are latent in man is now the firm conviction of all real psychologists.

The problem to solve is to know the greatest thing we can do now; and the solution may be found by resolving to live for that which is nearest at hand, whatever that may be. Accept the greatest opportunity that you can take advantage of now, and then begin to live for the working out of everything that that opportunity may contain. Do not long for opportunities that are out of reach. The majority do this and thus waste their time. Do not wait for opportunities to do great things. The opportunity to make of yourself a great soul, a marvelous mind and a higher developed personality is at hand, and by taking advantage of this opportunity you will awaken within yourself those powers that can do great things. You will thus cause your present to become all that you may wish it to be; you will build for a future that which will be nothing less than extraordinary; and you will be living a life that is thoroughly worth living. You will be making the ideal real at every step of the way, but every moment will lead you into worlds that are richer and realms that are fairer than you ever dreamed of before.

WHEN ALL THINGS BECOME POSSIBLE

When the mind is placed in conscious contact with the limitless powers of universal life, all things become possible, and faith is the secret. To have faith is to possess that interior insight through which we can discern the marvelous possibilities that are latent in the great within, and to possess the power to enter into the very life of the great within. To most minds there seems to be a veil in consciousness between the spheres of present understanding and the spheres of the higher wisdom, and though there are many who feel distinctly that there is something greater within them, yet it seems hidden, and they cannot discern it. Faith, however, has the power to perceive those greater things within that previously seemed hidden, and this is the reason why faith is the evidence of things not seen. Faith does not simply believe. It knows; it knows through higher insight, because faith is this higher insight. Faith is not blind, objective belief, but a higher development of consciousness through which the mind transcends the circumscribed and enters into the life of the boundless.

When faith is active, consciousness is expanded so much that it breaks all bonds and penetrates even those realms that objective man has never heard of before. In this way new truth and discoveries are brought to light, and this is how man gains the understanding of what previously seemed to be beyond his comprehension. When we define faith as that power in mind through which consciousness can penetrate into the larger sphere of life, we perceive readily why almost anything can be accomplished through faith, and we also understand why no one can afford to work without faith. When consciousness enters a larger sphere of action its capacity is naturally increased, and the greater power that can be drawn upon in performing any kind of work increases in proportion; likewise, the knowing how to work will be promoted in the same manner. To do anything successfully one must know how to do it and have the power to do what one knows should be done, and both these essentials are increased in proportion to the enlargement of consciousness.

The art of extending consciousness into the realms of unlimited life and power and wisdom is the secret through which all great attainments and great achievements become possible; but without faith this enlargement of consciousness cannot take place, because faith is that power that perceives and enters into the greater things that are still before us. Faith looks into the beyond of every faculty, talent or power and perceives that there is much more of these same talents and powers further on. In fact, there is no visible limit to anything when viewed through the eyes of faith.

No matter how much wisdom or power we may require to reach the goal we have in view, we can finally secure the required amount through the perpetual enlargement of consciousness. This is evident, and since faith is that something in mind that leads consciousness on and on into larger fields of action it becomes indispensable to all growth, to all great achievements, to all high attainments and to the realization of all true ideals. The man who has no faith in himself can neither improve himself nor his work. When nothing is added to his ability, capacity or skill there can be nothing added to the quality or the quantity of what he is doing. The effect will not improve until we have improved the cause; and man himself is the cause of everything that appears in his life.

Modern psychology, however, has discovered and conclusively demonstrated that no faculty can be improved until the conscious sphere of action of that faculty is enlarged and thoroughly developed. Therefore, to promote the efficiency of any faculty the conscious action of that faculty must become larger and imbued with more life. This is the fundamental principle in all advancement, but consciousness will not enlarge its sphere of action until it perceives that there is reality beyond its present sphere, and it is only through the interior insight of faith that the greater reality existing beyond present limitations is discovered to be real. The lack of this interior insight among the great majority is the principle obstacle that prevents them from becoming more than they are. Their minds have not the power to see the potential side of their larger nature.

They are aware of the objective only and can do only as much as the limited power of the objective will permit. But they are not aware of the fact that there is limitless power within, nor do they realize that they can draw upon this great interior power and thus accomplish not only more and more, but everything that they may now have in view. Not having the power to look beyond present attainment, the little world in which they live is all that is real to them. Occasionally there is a dream or a vision of greatness, but it soon fades away, and in those rare instances when the high vision continues for some time the knowledge of how to make real the ideal is usually not at hand.

The human race is divided into three classes; first, those who live in the limited world and never see anything beyond the limited; second, those who live in the limited world but have occasional glimpses of greater things, though having neither the knowledge nor the power to make their dreams come true; and third, those who are constantly passing from the lesser to the greater, making real every ideal as soon as it comes within the world of their conscious comprehension. The last group is small, but there are millions today who are on the verge of a larger sphere of existence, and for this reason we should usher into the world at once a greater movement for the promotion of faith than has ever been known before. It is more faith that these millions need in order to enter into the beautiful life they can see before them. It is more faith they must have before they can become as much as they desire to be. To make real the ideal in any life faith must be combined with work, and no work should be undertaken unless it can be animated thoroughly with the power of faith. The reason why is found in the fact that all practical action is weak or strong, depending upon the capacity of that part of the mind which directly controls that action; and the capacity of the mind increases in proportion to the attainment of faith. To accomplish what we have in view, it is not only necessary to know how to go about our work, but it is necessary to have sufficient power, and faith is the open door to more and more power.

The very moment you obtain more faith you feel stronger; you are then certain of results and the very best results; and the reason why is found in the fact that faith always connects the mind with the larger, the greater and the inexhaustible. On the other hand, you may have an abundance of energy, but do not see clearly how to apply that energy in such a way that results will be as desired; again the remedy is more faith. Faith elevates the mind and lifts consciousness up above doubt, uncertainty and confusion. When you go up into faith you enter the light and can see clearly how to proceed; but in this connection we must avoid a very common mistake. When we discover the remarkable power of faith there is a tendency to depend upon faith exclusively and ignore other faculties. We sometimes come to the conclusion that it matters little how we work or think or act so long as we have an abundance of faith, because faith will cause everything to come right. The fact, however, that we sometimes come to this conclusion proves that we have not found real faith, because when we have an abundance of real faith we can see clearly the great truth that all thought and action must be right to secure results, and that all faculties and power must be employed in their highest states of efficiency if we wish to make real the ideal. Though it is absolutely necessary to have the vision, still the vision is not sufficient in itself. After the vision has been discovered in the ideal it must be made real; the principle must be applied; the new discovery must be worked out in practical action; but these things require both fine intelligence and practical skill.

When work and faith are combined then everything becomes possible. The power of faith is placed in action; work becomes greater and greater, and whatever our purpose may be we shall positively scale the heights. The great principle is to combine unlimited faith with skillful work. Work with all the skill that you can possibly cultivate, but inspire all your efforts with the mighty soul of a limitless faith.

Faith comes to fill all physical and mental action with renewed life and power.

It comes to open that door through which all our efforts may pass to higher and greater things. Faith is not simply for the moral and spiritual life; it is not simply for what is sometimes called higher endeavor. It is for all endeavor, and it has the power to push all endeavor with such energy and force that we simply must succeed, no matter what our work may be.

When you have real faith you never undertake anything without first placing your entire being in the very highest attitude of faith. Even the most trivial things you do are done invariably in the spirit of faith. This is very important, because by training yourself to be at your best in little things, it soon becomes second nature for you to be your best in all things, and when you are called upon to do something of exceptional importance, something that may seem very difficult, you do not fall down; you are fully equal to the occasion. The more we exercise faith the more it develops; it is therefore profitable to use faith at all times and in everything that we do.

When we know that faith is that something that takes mind into the superior side of life and thus places in action superior powers, it is not difficult to understand how to proceed when we place ourselves in faith. As we think more and more of this higher side of our nature, this better side, this wonderful side, we gradually become conscious of its remarkable possibilities and soon we can feel the power of superiority becoming stronger and stronger in everything that we do in mind or body. To develop the power of faith the first thing to do is to train the mind to hold attention constantly upon the limitless side of life; that is, to live in the upper story of being and to think as much as possible about the true idea of faith, as well as the interior essence of faith itself. When you begin to see clearly that faith is this higher development of mind, this insight that leads to higher wisdom, greater power and more abundant life, you actually find yourself entering into the realization of those greater things whenever you think of faith.

By concentrating your attention upon the inner meaning of faith your mind becomes clearer, your faculties become stronger and your entire being feels the presence of more life; and that you can do much better work while in this condition is too evident to require any more elucidation. While in the attitude of faith you cannot only do your present work better, but you will steadily develop the ability and the capacity to do more difficult work – work that will prove more useful to the community and more remunerative to yourself. The world wants everything well done and is more than willing to pay for good work. We are all seeking the best and the majority aim consciously or unconsciously to give their best, but without faith it is not possible for anyone to be his best, give his best, or do his best.

Do your best and the best will come to you in return. The universe is founded upon justice, and justice will positively be done to you if you have faith in justice. Everything in life is moving towards greater worth, and since justice is universal, the greater the worth of a man, the greater the value of those things that he will receive in life. The worthy soul is always rich in those things that have real worth; and when we learn to harmonize ourselves more fully with all the laws of existence, we shall place ourselves in that condition where we not only can give more that has worth but will also receive everything of worth that actually is our own. Whether you are working in the commercial world, the professional world, the artistic world, the intellectual world; in brief, whatever your work may be, to have the best results you must have faith, and it is practical results in practical everyday life that determines how rapidly and how perfectly the ideal shall be made real in your own world. Whoever will do his present work as well as he possibly can, and continue to work in the highest attitude of faith, will positively advance and perpetually continue to advance. He may not have accomplished much thus far; but if he takes this course, combining efficient work with supreme faith, he certainly has a splendid future before him.

If your present work is not to your liking, do not plan to change at once. First proceed with your present work in this higher attitude of faith. You may thus find your present work to be the very work you want; or your present work, if it is not what is intended for you, will become the open door through which you will reach that field of action that will be to your liking, providing you animate your present work with all the faith that you can possibly realize. Make yourself the best of your kind, whatever your sphere of action may be, because by so doing you are not only increasing the number of great minds in the world, but you are adding immeasurably to the world's welfare and joy; and he who combines his work with limitless faith will become the greatest and the best in his sphere. In the application of faith, however, the whole of attention must not be directed upon the improvement of yourself. The more you improve, the better you can do, but while you are improving yourself, your improvement will be incomplete and insufficient unless you each day practically employ in your work what you have developed in yourself. Give the power of every moment to greater attainment in yourself and to greater achievement in your present occupation, and you will fulfill that dual purpose in life that invariably leads to the heights. Develop more power, more ability and more faith and combine these in everything that you do. Through the power of faith you will not only discern higher and higher ideals, but you will also give greater capacity to your practical ability. In other words, you will not only gain the power to see the ideal, but you will gain the power to practically apply what you have seen; you will make tangible in real life what the visions of the soul have revealed in the ideal life; and as you grow in faith, so great will this power become that there is no ideal you cannot make real. You will have placed yourself in touch with limitless power – the power of the Supreme, and therefore to you, all things become possible.

THE ART OF GETTING WHAT IS WANTED

Mere personal desires are usually out of harmony with the present process of soul-growth, and therefore there is no supply in our immediate mental vicinity for what those desires naturally need. This is the reason why more time is required for the fulfilling of these desires, and frequently the time required is so long that when the desire is fulfilled we do not need it any more. When we desire only those things that are best for us now, that is, those things that are necessary to a full and complete life in the present, we shall receive what we desire at the very time when those things are needed. What is best for us now is ready in the mental world to be expressed through us. Every demand has its own supply in the immediate vicinity, and every demand will find or attract its own supply without any delay whatever, but the demand must be natural, not artificial.

The average person is full of artificial desires – desires that have been suggested by what other people possess or require. But the question is not what we need now to compete with other people so as to make more extravagant external appearances than other people. The question is, what do we need now to make our present life as full, as complete and as perfect as it possibly can be made now. Ask yourself this question and your artificial desires will disappear. In the first place, you will try to ascertain what you are living for, and what may be required to promote that purpose of life that may seem true to your deeper thought on the subject. In the second place, you will realize that since it is the present and the present only for which you are living, you will concentrate your attention upon the living of life now. This will bring the whole power of desire down upon the present moment and engage all the forces of life to work for the perfection of the present moment. The result will be the elimination of nearly everything that is foreign to your present state of existence.

To know what to desire and what to ignore in the present may seem to be a problem, but it is easily solved by depending upon the demands of the soul instead of the demands of the person. The desires of the average person are almost constantly colored or modified by suggestions from the artificial life of the world; they are therefore not normal and not true to real life.

We live to live a larger and a greater life perpetually; therefore every desire must desire only those things that are conducive to growth, advancement, attainment and superior states of existence. The expression of desire, however, must not confound cause with effect, but must so place every desire that the power of cause invariably precedes the appearance of effect. To promote advancement in life we must advance in our own conscious beings before true advancement in the external world can follow.

What life may require now, that life *can* receive now. This is the law. But every artificial desire that we may hold in mind interferes with the workings of this law, and since the average person is full of artificial desires, he usually fails to receive what is needed to promote the welfare of real life. Every desire that is held in mind uses up energy; therefore, if the desire is artificial, all that energy is thrown away, or it may be employed in creating something that we have no use for when it does come.

The majority are entirely too reckless about their desires; they desire things because they want them at the time, but do not stop to think whether the things desired will prove satisfactory or not when they are received; and since we usually get, sooner or later, what we persistently desire, knowing what to desire is an art, the development of which becomes extremely important.

We must remember that it is not best for anyone to pass through trouble and misfortune. When people have misfortune they sometimes console themselves with the belief that it is all for the best, but this is not the truth; though we can and should turn every adverse circumstance to good account.

When you come into trouble you have not been living for the best. You have made mistakes or entertained artificial desires, and that is why trouble came. Had you lived in the faith that all things are working together for good, nothing but good would have come; and had you lived in the strong desire for the best and the best only, you would have received the very best that you could appreciate and enjoy now. The belief that we have to pass through trouble to reach peace and comfort is an illusion that we have inherited from the dark ages, and the belief that we are purified through the fires of adversity is another illusion coming from the same source. We are purified by passing through a perpetual refining process, and this process is the result of consciousness gaining a deeper, a higher, a truer and a more beautiful conception of that divinity in man that is created in the image and likeness of the Supreme; and it is well to remember that this refining process can live and act only where there is peace of mind, harmony of life and the joy of the spirit.

Higher states of life do not come by passing through adversity but by living the soul-life so completely that you are never affected by adversity. The peace that passeth understanding does not come from the act of overcoming trouble, but is the product of that state of mind that is so high and so strong that it is never moved by trouble. The greatest victory does not come through successful warfare, but through a life that is so high and in such perfect harmony with all things that it wars against nothing, resists nothing, antagonizes nothing, pursues nothing, overcomes nothing. The life that is above things does not have to overcome things, and it is such a life that brings real peace, true joy and sublime harmony.

When we fail to get what is wanted, our wants are either artificial or so full of false and perverted wants that the law of supply is prevented from doing its proper work for us. Under such conditions it is necessary to ask the great question:

"What am I living for?"

Then eliminate those desires that are suggested by the world, and retain only those that desire the highest state of perfection for the whole man.

He who desires more life will receive more life, and with the greater life comes the greater power – that power with which man may create his own destiny and make everything in his life as he wishes it to be. In order to get what is wanted or what is needed the usual process of desire must be reversed. Instead of desiring things, desire that greater life and that greater power that can produce things. First, desire life, power, ability, greatness, superiority, high personal worth, and exceptional spiritual attainments. Never desire definite environments, special things or certain fixed conditions. Leave those things to Higher Power, because when Higher Power begins to act you will receive the very best environments, the richest things and the most perfect conditions that you can possibly enjoy.

PATHS TO HAPPINESS

Happiness does not come from having much, but from being much; therefore, anything that will tend to bring forth into tangible expression more and more of the real being of man will add to his joy. To promote the larger and larger expression of the real being of man; in other words, to promote the living in the real of more and more of the ideal, a number of methods may be presented; but as happiness is based upon simplicity, methods for producing the cause of happiness must also be based upon simplicity, therefore only those principles that are purely fundamental need be employed. These principles however must not be applied singly. It is necessary to combine them all in practical everyday living, and when this is done, more and more happiness will invariably follow. The principles necessary to the perpetual increase of happiness are as follows:

1. *Live the simple life.* The complex life is not only a burden to existence, but is invariably an obstacle to the highest attainments and welfare of man; and the majority, even among those whose tangible possessions are very insignificant, are living a complex life; but when the average person is told to remove complexity from his world and adopt simplicity, he almost invariably destroys the beauty of life. The art of living a life that is both simple and beautiful is an art that few have mastered, though it is by no means difficult. Most of the life that is called simple is positively devoid of beauty and has nothing whatever that is attractive about it. In fact, it is positively a detriment both to happiness and advancement. To live the simple life is not to return to primitive conditions nor to decide to be satisfied with nothing, or next to nothing. It is possible to live the simple life in the midst of all the luxuries that wealth can buy, because simplicity does not spring from the quantity of possession but from the arrangement of possession. The central idea in the living of a simple life is to eliminate non-essentials. The question should be, "Which of the things that are about me do I need to promote the greatest welfare of my life?" To answer this question will not be difficult, because almost anyone can determine at first thought what is needed and what is not needed to a complete life. When the decision is made, non-essentials should be removed as quickly as possible. True, we must avoid extremes, and whatever we do we must do nothing to decrease the beauty or harmony of life.

There are a great many things in the world of the average person that he simply thinks he needs, though he knows that those things never did anything but retard his progress. It is therefore necessary to remove non-essentials from the mind before we attempt to simplify our immediate surroundings. The simple life is a beautiful life, with all burdens removed, and it is only the unnecessary that is burdensome. To live the simple life, surround yourself only with those things that are directly conducive to your welfare, but do not consider it necessary to limit the quantity of those things.

Surround yourself with *everything* that is necessary to promote your welfare, no matter how much it may be, although do not place in your world a single thing that is not a direct power for good in your world. You thus establish the harmony of simplicity without placing any limitations whatever upon your possessions, your welfare or your highest need. You thus eliminate everything that may act as a burden; and we can readily understand that when all burdens are removed from life the happiness of life will be increased to a very great degree.

2. *Live the serene life.* Be calm; be peaceful, quiet and undisturbed in all things and at all times. Confusion and hurry waste energy. The serene life, if lived in poise, will keep the system brimful of energy at all times, and so long as you are filled through and through with life and energy you will be full of spirit and joy. Our saddest moments are usually the direct results of reactions from turbulent thinking and living; therefore, such moments will be eliminated completely when thinking and living are made peaceful and serene. It is not necessary to live the strenuous life in order to accomplish a great deal, although on the other hand it is not quantity but quality that we seek. Our object should not be to do many things, but to do good things. If we can do many things that are good, very well, but we must have quality first in the mind; the quantity will increase as we grow in capacity, and there is nothing that promotes the increase of mental and physical capacity more than calm, serene living. The sweetest joys that the mind can feel usually come from those deep peaceful realizations of the soul when all is quiet and serene. Therefore, to cultivate the habit of living always in this beautiful calm will invariably add happiness to happiness every day of continued existence.

3. *Be in love with the world.* He who loves much will be loved much in return, and there is nothing in the world that can give more joy and higher joy than an abundance of real love. The selfish love, that is only personal, and that *must* be gratified to be enjoyed, gives but a passing pleasure, the reaction of which is always pain.

When we love with such a love we are always unhappy when not directly loved in return, and the purely selfish love never brings real love in return. When we love everybody with the pure love of the soul, that love that does not ask to be loved in return but loves because it *is* loved, we shall positively be loved in return; and not simply by a few here and there, but by great numbers. To feel that you are loved unselfishly, that you are loved not because anything is expected in return, but because the love is there and *must* come – to feel this love is a source of joy which cannot be measured, and this joy everybody can receive in abundance now. The simple secret is to love the whole world at all times and under every circumstance; love everybody with heart and soul and *mean* it, and everything that happens to you will add both to the pleasure of the mind and to the more lofty joys of the soul.

4. *Be useful.* "Give to the world the best that you have and the best will come to you." Hold nothing back. If you have something that you can share with the world, let everybody have it today. Do all that you can for everybody, not because you expect reward, but because it is a part of your nature. Be all that you can be and do all that you can do. Never say, "I will do only as much as I am paid for." Such an attitude has kept many a person in poverty for life. Reward is an effect, not a cause. Do not place the reward first, and the service second. Increase your service and the reward will increase in proportion; you will thus not only place yourself in a position where you can secure more and more of the good things of life, but you will live in that position where you are bringing into expression more and more of the good things that exist in your own life. And we must remember that the greatest joy does not come from gaining good things from the without, but from the expression of good things from the within; and when both of these are combined harmoniously we shall secure all the joys of life – the joys that come from the outer world and the joys that come from the beauty and the splendor of the inner world. To combine these in your life, be useful; express your best; be your best; do your best. You thus bring forth riches from within and attract riches from without.

Give richly of the best you have and good things in an ever increasing number will constantly flow into your life. That deep soul-satisfaction that comes to mind when we have rendered valuable service to man is entirely too good to be ignored; it is one of the deepest and highest joys that man can know. Those people who are the most valuable wherever they go are always the happiest; and we all can be of service in a thousand ways; therefore, we may add to our happiness in just as many ways, if we will always remember to be and do the best we can wherever we may go in the world.

5. *Think and speak the beautiful only.* Every word or thought that you express will return to you. Never say anything to make others discouraged or unhappy; it will come back to yourself. He who gives unhappiness to others is giving unhappiness to himself. He who adds to the joys of others is perpetually adding to his own joy. You can say something good about everybody. Then say it. It will give joy to everybody concerned, yourself included.

When every word is animated with the spirit of kindness and joy, you will not only increase the power of joy in your own life, but you will be sowing the seeds of joy in the garden of the universal life; and one of these days you will reap abundantly from what you have sown.

6. *Forgive and forget everything that seems wrong.* We have spent many a weary day simply because we persisted in remembering something that was unpleasant. Forget the wrong and it will disturb you no more. Forgive others for what they have done and you will have no unpleasant memories to cloud the sky of your mental world. When people speak unkindly of you, never mind. Let them say what they like, if they must. Nothing can harm you but your own wrong thinking and living. If people do not treat you right remember they would act differently if they knew better, and you know better than to become offended. So therefore forgive it all and resolve to be happy. Forgive everybody for what is not right and forget everything that is not conducive to the right.

You have no time to brood over troubles that exist only in your memory. Your memory is created for a better purpose. Remember the good, the true and the beautiful; this is one of the greatest secrets of perpetual happiness. When you forgive those who have wronged you, you usually come to a place where you think more of those very persons than you ever did before, and when you come to that place you will realize a joy that is far too sweet and beautiful for pen to ever describe.

He who can forget and forgive the wrongs of the lowlands of undeveloped life, invariably ascends to the heights, and it is upon the heights that we find real happiness. Such is the reward of forgiveness. It will therefore not be difficult to forgive when we know that the results are so rich and so beautiful; indeed, to forgive and forget everything that seems wrong will thus become a coveted pleasure.

7. *Be perfectly contented with the present.* We have heard a great deal about the value of divine discontent, but discontent is never divine any more than indignation is ever righteous. Perfect contentment is one of the highest states of the soul and is one of those attainments that invariably follows ideal living. Discontent, however, in any of its shapes or forms, always indicates that we are not on the true path. So long as there is discontent there is something wrong in our living, but the moment this wrong is righted, perpetual contentment will be realized. If your present lot is not what you wish it to be, discontent will not make it better. Be perfectly content with the present and create more lofty mansions for the future; thus you will not only improve your condition every year, but you will be supremely happy every day. The more perfect your present contentment, the more power you will have to create for yourself a greater future, and the more mental light you will have to build wisely for days to come. The more contentment you realize in your mind, the more brightness and strength there will be in your mind.

Find the good that you already possess, then enjoy it. Better things are even now on the way and through the harmony of contentment you will be prepared to receive them. You will also be in that higher state of mental discernment where you can know good things when you see them.

Contentment does not mean to be so satisfied with present conditions that we do not care to change them. True contentment not only appreciates the full value of the present, but also appreciates those greater powers in life that can perpetually add to the value of the present.

Those things that are not quite right can be made better. Proceed to make them better, and one of the greatest joys in life comes directly from that action of life that is causing things to become better.

When we aim to improve everything that we meet, we bring out all the good that is latent in our world, and to increase the expression of the good in our world is to increase our own measure of joy.

8. *Seek the ideal.* Look for the ideal everywhere; live in ideal environments when possible; but if not possible in an external sense create for yourself an ideal environment in the internal sense. Live in ideal mental worlds no matter what external worlds may be.

We have no time to give to the common and the ordinary. We want the best. We deserve the best, and we can secure the best by seeking the best and the best only. Live your own ideal life. Seek the ideal both in the within and in the without, and aim to make the ideal real in every thought, word and deed; you will thus cause every moment to add to your joy.

9. *Develop the whole man.* The more perfectly you are balanced, the greater will be your joy, because a balanced nature is conducive to harmony, and harmony is conducive to happiness.

10. *Open the mind to beautiful thoughts only.* The world is full of thoughts, all kinds of thoughts, but only those that are invited will come to you. There is nothing that affects life more than the thoughts we think; and the thoughts we are to think will depend almost entirely upon our mental attitude towards that which we meet in life. When we resolve to receive only the beautiful thoughts from everything with which we come in contact, the change for the better in life will be simply remarkable.

11. *Be in touch with the harmony of life.*

12. *Consecrate every moment to the higher life.*

CREATING IDEAL SURROUNDINGS

We all believed, not so very long ago, that the circumstances in which each individual was placed were produced by inevitable fate, and that the individual himself could not change them, but would have to remain where he was until something in his favor happened from external sources. What was to cause that something to happen we did not know, nor did we give the matter much thought. We believed more or less in chance and luck, and had no definite conception of the underlying laws of things. But now many of us have changed our minds, as we have received a great deal of new light on this most important subject. The many, however, are still in the old belief; they are ignorant of the fact that man can create his own destiny, and that fate, circumstances and environments are but the products of man himself, acting alone, or in association with others. But this is the fact, and it can be scientifically demonstrated by anyone under any circumstance.

This new idea that man can change his surroundings or transport himself to more agreeable environments through the use of psychological and metaphysical laws may seem unthinkable and far-fetched to a great degree; but when we study the subject with care we find that the principles, laws and methods involved are not only natural but thoroughly substantial and can be applied in tangible everyday affairs. If the surroundings in which you live are not what you wish them to be, know that you can change them. You can make those surroundings ideal. You can make those surroundings better and better at every step in your advancement, thus making real higher and higher ideals in your life. This is a positive truth and should be impressed so deeply upon every mind that no former belief on the subject can cause us to doubt our possession of this power for a moment. The importance of thus impressing this fact upon the mind becomes very evident when we understand that no matter how much we may know, we will have no results so long as we are in doubt as to whether what we have undertaken is really possible or not. There are thousands of people who believe, in a measure, that they can better their own conditions and they understand fully all the principles involved, but they have no satisfactory results because one moment they believe that the change is possible while at the next moment they entertain doubts. To have real results in any undertaking, especially in the changing of one's surroundings, one must believe with his whole heart that he can, and he must constantly employ all the necessary principles in that conviction.

You must think that you can so as to fully annihilate the belief that you cannot. Know that you can, and in that attitude continue to apply the necessary methods. Let nothing disturb your faith in the possibility of what you have undertaken to do in this respect, and you will positively succeed.

To create ideal surroundings, the first essential is to gain a clear understanding of what actually constitutes your surroundings. The world in which you live is a state of many elements, factors, forces and activities. The physical environment with all its various phases and conditions has been considered the most important, but this is not necessarily true, because the mental environment is just as much a part of the world in which you live as the physical.

The term "world" is not confined simply to visible things; it also includes states of mind, mental tendencies, thoughts, desires, motives and all the different phases of consciousness. The place in which you live physically, the place in which you live mentally, the place in which you live morally and spiritually, these places combined constitute the world in which you live. All of these states and conditions are necessary parts of our surroundings, and it is our purpose to make these necessary parts as beautiful, as perfect and as ideal as possible.

The place where you work with your hands and with your brain is a part of your world, but the same is true of the place where you work in your dreams, in your aspirations and in your ideals. The circumstances and events of your life, physically and mentally; the opportunities that are constantly passing your way; the people you meet in your work; the people you think of in your thoughts; the people you associate with and friends that are near; the various elements of nature, both visible and invisible; the many groups of things in all their various phases that you come in contact with in your daily living; all of these belong to your world. To enter into details it would be possible to mention many hundreds of different elements or factors that compose the world in which the average person lives; but to be brief we can say that your world is composed of everything that enters your life, your home, your experience, your thought and your dreams of the ideal. All of these play their part in bringing to you the good that you may desire or the ills that you may receive. Consequently, since the world in which you live is so very complex and since so much of it belongs to the mental side of life, the process of change must necessarily involve mental laws, as well as physical laws; but here the majority have made their mistake.

Many great reformers and human benefactors have tried to emancipate the race through the change of exterior laws and external conditions alone, forgetting that most of the troubles of man and nearly all of his failures have their origin in the misuse of the mind.

We all know that the mind is the most prominent factor in the life of man, and yet this factor has been almost entirely overlooked in our former efforts to change the conditions of the race. Everything that man does begins in his mind; therefore, every change that is to take place in the life of man must begin in his mind. This being true, we understand readily why modern metaphysics and the new psychology can provide the long looked for essentials to human emancipation and advancement. When we examine all the various things that go to make up the world in which we live, we may find it difficult to discover the real source of them all. How they were produced; who produced them; why they happened to come to us, or why we went to them; these are problems that we are called upon to solve before we can begin to create ideal surroundings.

To solve these problems the first great fact to realize is that we are the creators of our own environments; but at first sight this fact may not be readily accepted, because there are so many things that seem to be the creation of others. There are two kinds of creation, however, the direct and the indirect. In direct creation you create with the forces of your own life, your own thought and your own actions, and your own creations are patterned after the ideas in your own mind; but in what is termed indirect creation some one else creates what you desire. It is your creation, however, in a certain sense, because it was your desire that called it forth. To state the fact in another manner, the world in which you live may be your own direct creation or it may be the creation of another, but you went into that other one's world to live. In the majority of cases, the world in which the individual lives is produced partly by his own efforts and partly by the efforts of others, though there is nothing in his world that he has not desired or called forth in some manner and at some time during his existence. There are a number of people who are living in worlds created almost entirely by others; in fact, the world of the average person is three-fourths the creation of the race mind; but the question is, why does a person enter into a world that is created by others; why does he not live exclusively in a world created by himself?

There are many fine minds who are living in the world of the submerged tenth, but they did not create that world. That inferior state existed long before the birth of its present inhabitants; but why have those gone to live there who were not born there, and why have those who were born there not gone away to some better world of their own superior creation? Why do the people who live in that inferior world continue to perpetuate all its conditions? No world can continue to exist unless the people who live in that world continue to create those conditions that make up that world. Then why do not those people who live in the world of the submerged tenth cease the creating of that inferior world and begin the creation of the superior world when we know they have the power to do so? These are great questions, but they all have very simple answers. To answer these questions the first great fact to be realized is that the mind of man is the most important factor in everything that he does, and since no person can change his environments until he changes his actions, we realize that the first step to be taken is the change of mind. Learn to change your mind for the better, and you will soon learn how to change your surroundings for the better. Before you proceed, however, there is another important condition to be considered; it is the fact that a portion of what is found in our world is created by ourselves, while the rest is the product of those minds with which we work or live. In the home each individual contributes to the qualities of the world which all the members of that home have in common, but each individual lives in a mental world distinctly his own, unless he is so negative that he has not a single individual purpose or thought. When the mental world of each individual is developed to a high degree it will become so strong that the fate of that individual will not be affected by the adverse conditions that may exist in the home.

The same is true of the environments that we meet in our places of work. No man need be affected very long by adverse surroundings or obstacles that he may meet in his work. He will finally become so strong that he can overcome every adversity that may exist in his physical world and thus gain entrance to better surroundings.

However, we can readily see how a great deal of discord can be produced in a home or in our place of work where the different members are not in harmony with each other, and we can also understand how the events, circumstances and conditions of all those members, as well as each individual member, will be affected more or less by that inharmony; providing however, that each individual is not developing that power of his mental world that can finally overcome all adversity. We can also understand how harmony and cooperation in a home or in a place of work would become a powerful force for good in the life of each individual concerned. Where a few are gathered in the right attitude, there immense power will be developed; in fact, sufficient power to do almost anything that those few may wish to have done. This has been fully demonstrated a number of times; therefore, where many minds are associated in the creation of a world in which all will live, more or less, these higher mental laws should be fully understood and most thoroughly applied.

    To enter a world that does not correspond with yourself and to go in and live where you do not naturally belong is to go astray, and such an action will not only cause all the forces and elements of your life to be misdirected, but you will place yourself in that position where nothing that is your own can come to you. There are vast multitudes, however, who have gone astray in this manner, and that is the reason why we find so many people who are misplaced, who do not realize their ideals, and who have not the privilege to enjoy their own. But we may ask, why do people go astray in this manner; why do we associate with people that do not belong in our world; why do we enter environments that do not correspond to our nature; why do we enter vocations for which we are not adapted, and why do we pursue plans, ideas and ambitions that lead us directly away from the very thing that our state of development requires? These are questions that we must answer, because no one can get the greatest good out of life or make the most of himself unless he lives in a world where he truly belongs.

There are two reasons why we stray from our own true world and enter worlds where we do not belong; first, because we frequently permit the inferior side of our nature to predominate; and second, because we permit the senses to guide us in almost everything that we do. No person who has qualifications for the living of life in a superior world will ever enter an inferior world if he does not permit inferior desires to lead him into destructive paths; and no person, no matter what his work may be, will go down the scale so long as he follows the highest mental and spiritual light that he can possibly see during his most lofty moments. Follow the highest and the best that is in you, and you will constantly ascend into higher and better worlds; all your creative forces will thus build for you better and better surroundings, because so long as you are rising in the scale, everything in your life in the external as well as in the internal must necessarily improve continuously. There is no need whatever of any person ever entering an inferior world. No one need pass into environments and surroundings that are less desirable than the ones in which he is living now. In fact, a person may take the opposite course. Endeavor constantly to attain superiority and you will steadily work yourself up into superiority, and as you become superior you will find an entrance into those worlds, those environments and those surroundings that are superior. There is a higher light, a better understanding within yourself that will guide you correctly in all your associations with people and environments. Do not follow physical desires or physical senses; let these be servants in the hands of higher wisdom. Follow this higher wisdom and you will make few mistakes, if any. You will constantly pass into better and better surroundings, because you will constantly pass into a higher, a better and a superior life. To follow the highest and the best that is within you under all circumstances does not constitute supernaturalism. It is simply good sense enlarged, and those who take this course will continue to make real the ideal in everything that may exist in the world in which they live.

CHANGING YOUR OWN FATE

When you discover that you are living in a world that you did not create and that does not correspond with your ideals, there is a tendency to break loose from external conditions at the earliest possible moment; but this tendency must be checked. Nothing is gained through an attempt to change from one world of effect to another world of effect without first changing the cause. The majority believe that when things are wrong in the outer world, the only remedy is to change external conditions; but the fact is that external conditions are simply effects from internal causes, and so long as those internal causes remain the same, no attempt to change external conditions will prove of permanent value. So long as there are adverse causes in your inner life, there will be adverse effects in your outer life, no matter how many times you may change from one condition to another or from one place to another.

When you begin to seek emancipation from the false world in which you are living now; in other words, when you begin to take positive measures to change your own fate, the first thing to do is to resolve not to make any forceful effort to change external conditions without first changing the inner cause of those conditions. Let outer things be as they are for the time being and continue to remain where you are until you can open a door to better things; but while you are waiting for this door to open do not be idle in any manner whatever. Although you are letting things be as they are in the external sense, and although you are not forcing yourself into different places or circumstances, still your purpose must be to entirely remake yourself. You came to this false state of life because you were misled by your own judgment, and if you should break loose, this same judgment will mislead you again; you will thus pass from one world that is not your own into some other world that is not your own, and there will be no improvement in the change. If you have not improved yourself in any manner whatever, your judgment will be just as inferior and unreliable as it was before, and no attempt to follow this judgment into different conditions will help matters in the least.

Your object is not to set yourself free from the false world in which you are living now and then enter some other world that is not your own. You are not ready to move, neither physically nor mentally, until you have created a world of your own just as you would have it in your present state of development. Therefore, all thought of change will but divert your attention from the real purpose in view. So long as you are constantly thinking about external changes, your mind cannot concentrate upon internal changes. So long as you are trying to change external conditions you cannot change yourself, and as you, yourself, are the cause of the new world which you are trying to create, you must recreate yourself before you can create the external world as desired.

To change your fate begin with yourself. If the environments in which you live are beneath your ideal, nothing can be gained by leaving those environments until the way is opened naturally to better things. If you simply get up and leave, you will gravitate into something elsewhere that will be just as uncongenial as those conditions you left behind. First, find the reason why you are living in your present environments, then proceed to remove that cause. There may be many reasons, but in most cases the principal reason is a lack of ability or the lack of power to apply the ability you possess. In such a case you must remove inability by becoming more proficient, and as soon as you are competent to render better service you will readily find a better place. This means larger remuneration, and you will thus be able to secure more desirable surroundings. The many, however, will think that to promote sufficient improvement so as to command greater recompense, and do so in a short time, is practically impossible under the average conditions; but all difficulties that may be met in this connection may be readily removed through the principles of modern metaphysics.

Continuous improvement in everything pertaining to the life, the power, the capacity or the mentality of the individual can be readily promoted by anyone and decided results secured in a very short time.

Therefore, no person need remain in adverse or limited conditions. He can, through the awakening and the expression of the best that is in himself, become competent to take advantage of greater opportunities and thus change his fate, his future and his destiny. If you wish to improve your physical environments, remain content where you are while you develop the power to earn and create better environments. Contentment with things as they are and harmony with everything about you are indispensable essentials if you wish to increase your ability, your capacity and your worth.

Whatever comes, meet all things in the attitude of perfect harmony and you will find that all things, even the most adverse, can be readily handled and turned to good account. We all know the marvelous power of the man who can harmonize contending factions, be they in his own life or in his circumstances. He not only gains good from everything that he meets, but he becomes a most highly respected personage, and is sought wherever opportunities are great and where great things are to be accomplished. Learn to harmonize the contending factions in your own life and experience, and you will find yourself entering new worlds where circumstances are more congenial and opportunities far greater. You will thus meet more desirable events, more desirable people, and superior advantages of every description will appear in your pathway.

Make yourself over, so to speak, in your own friendship; increase your personal worth; polish your own character; refine your mind, and make real more and more of the ideal; double and treble your love and your kindness and constantly increase your admiration for everything that has real quality and high worth. Continue this until you have results, whether those results begin to come at once or not; they will positively come ere long, and the things that you develop in your self you will meet in your external world. Change yourself for the better in every shape and manner, and you change your fate for the better, but the change that you produce in yourself must not simply be negative in its action.

It is the positive character, the positive mind, the positive personality that meets in the external world what has been developed in the internal world. The fact that a change in yourself can produce a similar change in your fate, your environments, your circumstances, in brief, everything in your outer world, may not seem clear at first; but it is easily demonstrated to be the truth when we analyze the relationship that exists between man and the world in which he lives. Everything that exists in your outer world has a correspondent in your inner world. This inner correspondent is the cause that has either created or attracted its external counterpart, and the process is easily understood.

To state it briefly, environment corresponds with ability. Circumstances are the aggregation of events brought about by your own actions and associations and friends, which follow the law of like attracting like. That environment is the direct effect of ability may not seem true when we observe that there are many people living in luxury that have practically no ability, but we must first demonstrate that these people have no ability. We shall find that those who have actually accumulated their own wealth have ability, in fact, exceptional ability, though they may not always have employed it according to the exact principles of justice. On the other hand, when we understand the process of creation we shall find that ability employed according to principle will produce far greater results than when it is employed unjustly. Therefore, the law underlying the power of ability to create its own environment acts wholly in the favor of him who lives according to the highest ideals of life.

This fact becomes more evident when we discern that success is not measured simply by the accumulation of things, but also by the accumulation of those elements in life that pertain to quality and worth in man's interior nature. It is wealth in the mental and the spiritual worlds that has the greatest value or the greatest power in promoting the welfare and the happiness of man, and this higher wealth can be accumulated only by those who are living according to their ideals.

However, the accumulation of mental and spiritual wealth will have a direct tendency to increase the power and the capacity of practical ability, and practical ability when scientifically applied will tend to increase tangible wealth; that is, to improve the value and the worth of external environments.

We shall also find that when a person increases the power of his own life he will bring about, through his own actions, new events, and these new events will produce new circumstances.

To change circumstances is to change fate; and whatever the change may be in fate, circumstances or events, it will be a change for the better, if the increase of power is applied according to the principles of ideals. Again, when a person develops quality and superiority in himself, he will, through the law of attraction, meet friends and associations that are after his own heart. In other words, he will enter a world where his ideals, both as to persons and as to things, are constantly being made real in every sphere of his present state of existence. He is thus creating for himself a better fate in every sense of the term and opening doors and pathways to a larger and a more beautiful future than he has ever realized before; but the beginning is in himself; in fact, every change for the better must begin within the life of man himself, and whoever will begin to change for the better in the within will positively realize greater and greater changes for the better in the without.

BUILDING YOUR OWN IDEAL WORLD

To build your own ideal world, the first essential is to begin to build in the real everything that you can discern in the ideal; and the second essential is to continue to rebuild your ideal world according to higher and higher ideals. However congenial or desirable or perfect our world may be, we should continue to improve upon it constantly. When we cease to promote progression we return to the ways of retrogression.

One of the principal causes of undesirable environments or unexpected reverses among the more capable is found in the tendency to "stop, rest and enjoy" what we have gained whenever conditions are fairly satisfactory.

To begin, your entire mentality must be changed and constantly changed so as to correspond perfectly with your newest thoughts on every subject and your highest ideals of everything that you can discern in your life. The mind is the cause and is the source of every force that can act as a cause of whatever may be developed, expressed or worked out through yourself into your external world. Therefore, begin with the mind and with all the elements of the mind. All desires, motives and ambitions must be concentrated upon the larger and the perfect in their various spheres of action. All the mental states must be in harmony with each other, and with the outer as well as the inner conditions of life. All mental qualities must be expanded and enlarged constantly, and consciousness must be trained to act perpetually upon the verge of the limitless. The entire world of thought must be perpetually renewed, enlarged and perfected, and every step taken in the mental world must be practically expressed and applied in the outer world. In order to bring all the creative forces of mind into harmony with the goal in view the ideal wished to be realized must be thoroughly established in consciousness, and the goal in view must be constantly held before the mental vision.

In the rebuilding of your own world one of the principal causes of failure will be found in a tendency to change in your plans, motives or desires; therefore, do not permit yourself to entertain one group of desires today and a different group tomorrow, and do not permit your faith to fall into periodical states of doubt.

The powers within you follow the predominating states of mind, and when these states are constantly changing, the creative forces will be employed simply in taking initial steps, but never in completing anything.

On the other hand, when your mental states, desires, motives, plans, etc., continue to concentrate upon the one supreme goal in view, your creative forces will perpetually build towards that goal, and you will be daily rebuilding your entire world according to the higher, the better and the greater that you have in view. There are thousands of fine minds that are down in the scale today and cannot get up, because they are constantly changing their plans, motives and desires. To create a new world you must fix in your mind what you wish to create, and then continue to build until the complete structure is finished. Recreate your present world, then constantly make it better, larger and more beautiful. All the elements of your mind, both conscious and subconscious, must be constantly inspired with your highest thought of the larger, the better and the more beautiful.

The mind must be clean, strong and high. It is the mind that does things. It is the mind that originates things. Therefore, if you wish to build for yourself an ideal world, the mind must be ideal in every sense of the term, and every element of the mind must always be its best and act at its best. To promote the right use of mind the imagination must be guided with the greatest of care. The imagination is one of the most important powers in the mind. The imagination when misdirected can produce more ills than any other faculty, and when properly directed can produce greater good than any other faculty. In fact, the imagination when scientifically applied becomes a marvelous power in the great creative process of the vast mental domain. Train the imagination to picture, not only the goal you have in view but all the highest ideals that you can possibly imagine as might exist within the realms of that goal. Train the imaging faculty to impress upon the mind only those superior qualities that you wish to incorporate in your new world, and whatever you impress upon the mind will be created in your mental world. To create superior qualities in the mental world means that you will create, as well as attract, the superior in your outer world, and you thus promote the building of an ideal world.

To build your own ideal world, the more opportunities that you can take advantage of the better, but opportunities come only to those who have demonstrated their worth. Prove to the world that you have worth, and you can have your choice of almost any opportunity that the world can offer. There is nothing that is in greater demand than great men and women – minds of ability and power, people who can do things. The great mind is constantly in the presence of opportunities to change his environment and his field of action; therefore, he may enter into a new world almost any time. Those opportunities, however, do not come of themselves; they come because he has made himself equal to those opportunities. Make yourself equal to the best and you will meet the best.

Make yourself a great power in your present sphere of action. Learn to do things better than they have ever been done before. Produce something for the world that the world wants and the gates to new and greater opportunities will open for you. Henceforth, you may secure almost anything that you may wish, and all the elements that may be necessary for you to employ in order to build the ideal world you have in mind may be readily obtained because you have placed yourself in touch with the limitless supply of the best that life can give.

Those who are in search for new and greater opportunities should eliminate the belief that the best things have been said, that all great things have been done and that all remarkable discoveries have been made. The fact is we are just in the A B C of literature, invention, art, music, industrial achievements and extraordinary human attainments. The human race is now on the verge of hundreds of undeveloped fields that have just been discovered, and they have more possibilities in store than we have ever dreamed. Many of these possibilities when developed will supply the world with the very things that the present development of the race is demanding in every expression of thought and desire. It is therefore easier to attain greatness, and do something of exceptional value at the present time than it ever was before.

The opportunities of this age are very numerous, and some of them hold possibilities that are actually marvelous. Those who will prepare themselves to meet the requirements of this age will therefore find a number of rich fields already at hand, and all minds can prepare themselves as required.

Train all the elements of your being to work towards a higher goal and you will bring forth into expression those greater powers that will make for you a mentality that the world will demand for its highest places of action and achievement. When you proceed to build in yourself an ideal mental world – a mental world of power, ability, capacity and high worth you will find it necessary to adapt this mental world to the external world in such a way as to promote harmony of action. The added power of your new mental world must work in harmony with your external world if practical results are to be secured. Circumstances come from personal actions; therefore, to change circumstances, personal actions must be changed, and to change personal actions your ideal mental life must be expressed in your personal life, and to this end the development of a high degree of harmony becomes necessary. Harmony, however, will not only promote the united action of the inner world with the outer world, but will also tend to eliminate mistakes from personal actions, and when we eliminate mistakes from personal actions we will cease to produce adverse circumstances. When you are in perfect harmony with yourself and everything you eliminate mental confusion. You thus place your mind in that position where you can think clearly, reason logically and judge wisely. The result is, you will do the right thing at the right time. The elements of your life will be properly blended, and this is necessary in order to create an ideal world.

Another essential in the practical application of your ideals to real life is the development of what may be termed interior insight. This faculty will guide you through the tangible things of life; in other words, you will see clearly how to combine the ideal with those actions that are promoted for the purpose of rebuilding the real.

To combine the ideal with the real and make the two one, we must come into the closest possible relationship with the finer things in life and learn to use that phase of mind that is always in a cleared-up condition. The lower story of the mind is often darkened with false conclusions about things, and is frequently more or less filled with ideas that have been impressed through the senses; but the upper story of the mind, the cleared-up side of consciousness where the sun is always shining and where there are no clouds, is called interior insight. This interior insight not only discerns the ideal, but can discern the practical possibilities that every ideal may contain, and we make the ideal real when we proceed to develop and apply in actual life those practical possibilities that our ideals may contain. Interior insight will also elevate all our mental faculties and cause those faculties to function with far greater efficiency. In fact, the entire mind will be lifted up into a state of greater power, greater brilliancy and greater ability for high and efficient mental expression.

To develop interior insight aim to use consciousness in the discernment of what may be termed the spirit of all things. Do not simply think of things as they appear on the surface, but try to think of things as they are in the spirit of their interior existence. The mere effort to do this will develop the power to look through things or to look into things; and the growth of this power promotes interior insight. You may thus discern clearly the real worth and the real possibilities that exist in the lofty goal that you have in view, and by keeping the eye single upon that lofty goal, never wavering for a moment, all the powers of your being will work together and build for those greater things that you can see upon the heights of that goal. Thus your entire world in the within as well as the without will constantly be recreated and rebuilt according to the likeness of your supreme ideals; in consequence, you will not only build for yourself an ideal world, but you will be building for yourself a world that is ever becoming more and more ideal, and to live in such a world is ideal living indeed. The world that is ever becoming more and more ideal is *the* world in which to live, and the power to create such a world is now at hand.

The following Christian D. Larson quotes are from
Concentration, 1920

Whatever your work or purpose may be, a good concentration is indispensable. It is necessary to apply, upon the object or subject at hand, the full power of thought and talent if you are to secure, with a certainty, the results you desire, or win the one thing you have in view. But the art of concentration is not only a leading factor in the fields of achievement and realization; it is also a leading factor in another field – a field of untold possibility.

Concentration in general may be defined as an active state of mind wherein the whole of attention, with all available energy and talent, is being applied upon the one thing that we are doing now. We concentrate in the full meaning of the term when we give ourselves completely to the thought or the action of the present moment; and this is true whether we work with muscle, brain or mind, or express ourselves through thoughts, words or emotion.

The principle of concentration is to do one thing at a time, and to do that one thing with all the talent and power we possess. We literally turn on the full current of mental and personal energy – not only the full current of what we may feel on the surface of thought – but all that we can arouse in deeper consciousness, and bring forth from the greater self within. It is a leading purpose in concentration to lay hold upon deeper and greater possibility; for we are not giving our whole best self to the work in hand unless we apply all the life, energy and talent that we can through super-effort to awaken and develop now.

There are many things that we may expect to accomplish through concentration; and in order that we may become familiar with this art from every aspect – which is necessary to its highest development – we will consider briefly the most important of these accomplishments.

First of all we gain the power to hold attention upon any object or subject for a sufficient length of time to complete the work in hand, and the power to do this at any time and under any circumstances. This is vitally important as we all meet distractions at every turn, and must learn to give our work undivided attention whatever our surroundings may be.

When we concentrate well we may, at will, cause all the available energies of mind and personality to work together, with full capacity, upon the work in hand. This will increase remarkably the working capacity and the dependable endurance of both mind and body, and will mean a high degree of mental mastery. To be able to master the elements and energies of the mind sufficiently to bring them all together to work together anywhere any time – this is an advantage for which we would pay almost any price; but it comes as a natural emolument with the development of concentration.

You are equal to any occasion when the whole of your mind is called into action; and this very thing concentration has the power to do. More than that, the whole of the mind will be called to higher ground, thereby working itself out of mediocrity and restricted channels, and gradually developing itself into that wonder state where everything seems possible. Real concentration can lead the way; the whole mind will follow; and concentration invariably leads into worlds of greater results. When we concentrate well we exercise a peculiar influence over the whole mind; we create, in every part of the mind, an irresistible desire to go to work; and we inspire every element of the mind with a definite ambition to excel.

The act of concentration tends not only to apply effectively all available energy of mind and personality; but tends also to draw forth latent energies. The fact is that real concentration becomes in the mind a remarkable force of attraction – attracting to itself unused and latent energies from all sources in the mental world.

That is one reason why the mind that concentrates well becomes so powerful, and why such a mind will invariably forge ahead, regardless of what the obstacles or difficulties may be.

Concentrate the mind upon any problem, and if you concentrate wonderfully well, you will find the solution. The solution of any problem is locked up in that problem; and concentration is the key. The psychology of this involves a most fascinating study; but sufficient in this stage of our study to know that these things can be done. The same is true of any subject, situation or circumstance. You can, through concentration, find the main points or the inside facts of any subject or situation that you may consider. Real concentration has the power to break through the shell; to get beneath the surface; to get in behind the scenes; to enter into the very life of the thing, and thus get hold of bedrock information.

These things we may accomplish through concentration; and there is good reason therefore why it has always been looked upon as the master art; but there is one thing more, the greatest of them all. Mental action, when perfectly concentrated, tends to go farther and farther into the life, substance or principle that is acted upon at the time. Concentration develops a penetrating tendency – a tendency to lead the mind out of the usual and on into the unknown. Concentration forges ahead. It goes straight on. It does not tarry with known facts. It goes farther. It sets out upon a journey; and such a journey will invariably prove a journey of discovery. The mind will find and enter new fields of thought. New laws and principles will be discovered. A new region of possibility will open before the mind, and long sought secrets may come to light. Positively, we can, through a highly developed concentration, cause Nature to give up her secrets, and cause the mysteries of Life to be revealed.

When we realize what may be accomplished through concentration, we shall make every conceivable effort to develop this master art; and our persistence, determination and enthusiasm will know neither pause nor measure; we will purpose positively to learn how to concentrate, and therefore will want to know how to proceed – what principles to adopt and what methods to apply.

When we examine the psychology of concentration, we find that it is based upon mental actions that are deeply interested in a certain subject or object; that is, we concentrate naturally and without effort whenever or wherever we are vitally interested. This then is the first principle. Be really interested in that to which you are to address yourself, and you will give it your undivided attention.

The problem, however, is how to become really interested in subjects or objects that do not, on their own account, attract our attention; or that do not, on the surface, appeal to us in the least. This is the first and possibly the greatest obstacle we have to meet in the development of concentration; but the solution is very simple; and we proceed upon the fact that *everything is interesting from a certain point of view* – that everything can attract our attention if permitted to reveal its chief attraction.

We concentrate naturally and perfectly when we are vitally interested. Everything is, in its chief attraction, extremely interesting. Therefore, we may, by seeking the chief attraction in everything, concentrate naturally and perfectly anywhere any time.

It is only necessary at first to proceed upon the conviction that everything is interesting from certain points of view; and to drill that fact into the mind with positive action and depth of thought.

When you convince the mind that everything is interesting from a certain point of view, you establish, in the subconscious, a natural tendency to be on the alert for this interesting viewpoint.

When the mind is on the alert, and keenly looking for the interesting element, the mind is really interested in that subject or object.

In practical life this is how the plan will work. You are called upon to give attention to something you do not understand, or something that does not appeal to you in the least. You are not interested, and therefore you cannot, at the moment, concentrate properly, or give the matter undivided attention. But you remember the great fact noted in this study, that everything is interesting from a certain point of view. Instantly you become curious to know what the interesting element in the matter in hand might be. You have made your own mind curious; and a curious mind is on the verge of becoming an interested mind.

If this be your first attempt in the application of this method, nothing more than a mild interest may arise; and even that might aid you decidedly at the time; but suppose you make use of this method many times every day for weeks and months. Suppose you make it a part of your daily work to impress upon your mind, again and again, the fact that everything is interesting from a certain point of view. The subconscious will soon receive these impressions and make that fact its very own. Then suppose you are called upon to consider a subject towards which you have been wholly indifferent. But the subconscious has been advised that there are elements of interest everywhere, and the subconscious never forgets what it has once really learned. Accordingly, the mind will be prompted, by powerful impulses from within, to seek the interesting elements in the subject before you; and, before you are hardly aware of the fact, this subject has become interesting and attractive. Suddenly, a keen desire has come over you to look into this subject thoroughly. You want to know. You are vitally interested. You are giving the matter undivided attention. You are concentrating perfectly in that direction.

Wherever we meet what does not seem interesting, we should proceed at once to examine that particular thing with a view of finding something of interest; and we will find it. And when we have work that does not seem interesting – work upon which we must concentrate in order to do it well – we should take up such work in the same attitude; that is, we should inquire deeply and scientifically as to what there is about such work that is in reality interesting. This question coming up will cause the mind to become interested; and at once concentration will begin.

The rule is simple: Look for the interesting, and the mind becomes interested; and wherever the mind is interested, there you concentrate naturally and effectively; provided, of course, that you subconsciously *feel* that there are interesting elements in everything; and, provided further, that your mind is keenly alive with the desire to know, to achieve, to excel.

To develop the tendency to enter the deeper states of the mind, we should work in harmony with a leading law in the mental world; that is, the peculiar proneness of the mind to produce within itself any state, condition or tendency that we continue to desire with persistence and sincerity. It is the truth that *your mind will do anything for you if you really want it done*.

The purpose must be to live beneath the surface; to make the great within our chief realm of life and concern.

The secret is to want what you want with all the life and power there is in you. We can reach any goal, or realize any ideal when we concentrate perfectly, and with the full force of a perfect concentration; and persistent desire proceeds to give concentration more and more of the two chief essentials; that is, deeper mental interest and greater mental power.

In this connection inquiry may arise as to the best methods for creating this deeper and more persistent desire, especially where we may not be personally interested in the final results; but here we should remember that we always gain personally from anything that is done right. If we develop greater mental power through the use of any psychological law, we gain to that extent, even though the greater portion of the tangible results may, in this instance, go elsewhere.

The future is long; every form of gain will come to each one of us in due time – in very short time if we take advantage of every opportunity to increase our own capacity and power. We should therefore be interested, personally, in the best and most thorough use of every psychological law we may have the privilege to employ.

Realizing this fact, we will want to desire success, the greatest possible success, for every enterprise with which we may be connected. Such a desire will improve remarkably, not only our own concentration, but also all other powers and talents we may possess. Our own gain therefore will be strictly personal, and most direct; and although tangible gain may not come at once, it positively will come in the near future. The future is both larger and richer for those who improve themselves in the present; and greater opportunities are waiting everywhere for greater minds; but improvements must be genuine, not merely superficial.

To increase the power of desire we should deepen and intensify all such desire in every form and manner, realizing the fact that the more the mind acts in a certain direction the greater becomes its power to act still more in the same direction. The force of desire therefore may through this simple rule become immense. And the more we increase the force of desire the more we increase results in every field of thought or action. Furthermore, we may cause the forces of concentration and desire to act and react upon each other to great advantage; that is, the more we concentrate for the increase of desire – worthwhile desire – the more powerful and persistent will such desire become; and the more deeply we desire the power to concentrate well – wonderfully well – the more life, energy and action we express in the building of real concentration.

As a practical suggestion we should, whenever we begin to concentrate, proceed to imagine all the forces of the mind coming to a focus at the point of concentration. This simple rule will not only produce some startling results in the process of concentration itself, but will also train imagination for definite and practical work.

Herewith, let us note that imagination does have the power to take the lead in the mental world; and therefore whenever we imagine that a certain thing is being done in the mind, we lead a majority of the energies of the mind to go and do that very thing; provided of course that imagination be vivid and highly positive in its actions. Here then we have within easy reach a most remarkable possibility.

An excellent practice is to turn attention frequently upon the great within, concentrating the deeper forces of the mind upon the vast and marvelous possibilities that exist in the fathomless depths of the mental world. This practice will not only aid the mind remarkably in gaining this interior hold upon the finer energies, but will also awaken latent forces and new talents; and will invariably arouse increased capacity and power in every faculty and talent we may be using now.

The possibilities of concentration are many; but here is one possibility in particular that we all should seek to understand most thoroughly, and develop to the highest degree conceivable. The results will be amazing; and every step in advance will open new worlds to conquer.

The principle is this, that we can through concentration clear the way for almost any achievement, attainment or discovery within the range of human life and power; and this range is a thousand times greater than we have supposed; in fact, no limits or restrictions can be found.

This principle can be applied to almost anything that we may wish to find or accomplish; and for practical illustration we will consider first the problems we meet in daily life. It is the usual custom, when we have difficult problems to solve, to waste a vast amount of time and energy worrying about how we are to find the solution; and as we know this is an easy way to failure and defeat.

The new way is to concentrate; to concentrate upon the problem with all the energy and intellect we possess; and this is what will happen: The full light of the mind will be focused upon that problem; that problem will be placed under the penetrating gaze of a powerful mental search light; and, accordingly, the mind will be able to look into and look through the entire situation. Thus the solution will be found; for the fact is that situations or problems seem difficult or perplexing only when viewed in the dark or in subdued light. When we can look through the thing, then we know what to do.

Turn on sufficient light and all mystery disappears. Problems cease to be problems when viewed in the clear light; and we can, through a highly developed concentration, turn the full light of the mind upon any subject, circumstance or situation. Therefore, we should concentrate upon those things; concentrate with all the energy and intellect we possess; concentrate for days or weeks, if necessary, and with unflinching faith and determination. We will soon penetrate the mystery and find what is wanted. We will see through it all, and see clearly what to do.

The same principle will apply if you are working on some invention. Do not give up at any stage; concentrate upon the thing you wish to develop or perfect; and concentrate with more and more persistence until the thing is done. Nothing is impossible. Nature will give up her secrets to those who really want them, or to those who will come into her greater realms and get them; and concentration has the penetrating power to go anywhere.

The majority among those who entertain high ideals do not give sufficient thought to concentration. They dream and dream, hoping the dream will come true; or, when they do try to concentrate, they journey off into abstractions and transcendental speculations – a process that does not call into action the power that is able to make those dreams come true.

The same is true of young minds who are ambitious. Most of them merely hope and hope that their ambitions will be realized somehow; but they do not concentrate persistently and continually upon the great goal they have in view. They do not call into concerted and organized action the sum total of their forces and faculties; and, in consequence, their ambitions never materialize. The fact is that where one ambitious mind scales the heights of achievement, fifty give up their early ambitions after a few years and decide to resume an average existence; and the chief reason is, that these fifty do not concentrate; or, if they do concentrate, it is only for a time and in a weak, uncertain fashion. The successful one, however, turns on the full current of concentration, and persists, with undaunted faith and determination, until the goal in view is realized.

This should be the rule: Whatever you want, concentrate; concentrate upon the purpose you have in mind; concentrate upon those greater forces and possibilities within you that can get you what you want – that can see you through successfully. For it is positively true that your own mind can get you anything within reason; provided of course that your whole mind is working for you; and your whole mind will work for you – will work for you with the highest degree of effectiveness – if you concentrate wonderfully well.

The possibilities of concentration are not confined, however, to the usual fields of achievement, or to those mental domains with which most of us are familiar. There are other and greater worlds that we may discover and take possession of through the use of this master art. To illustrate, if we wish to evolve or develop something that is entirely new, or decidedly different, the principle is to concentrate in that direction. Thus we shall make a super-effort in that direction; that is, if we concentrate with full capacity and marvelous skill; and we will, with absolute certainty, develop something that is beyond all previous effort – something that is distinctive, that stands out in a class by itself, that reveals clearly the master touch of genius.

The elements of genius are latent in every mind; and any mind may, through the super-efforts of a marvelous concentration, call those elements together into positive, creative action. Thus something new or startling may be developed. It may be a new and most brilliant idea; or, a new and superior plan for the realization of certain highly desired changes in life; or, an entirely new way of doing things – ways and methods, which when applied, might revolutionize everything in that sphere of human thought or endeavor.

The most wonderful possibility of all is this, that concentration can lead the mind on and on, out of present restrictions and beyond present states of knowledge and consciousness, into new realms, richer kingdoms and greater worlds. We know that concentration does have the tendency to go farther; and that it has real penetrating power, so that it may delve into anything in the vast domains of Life, Mind or Nature. It is possible therefore to cause the power of concentration to go so far into any state of reality that new and marvelous domains will open before the mind. Thus we might find long sought secrets in the natural world, or make discoveries in any field or region that would prove amazing to the mind and invaluable to human progress.

It is the positive truth that a highly developed concentration can carry the mind farther and deeper in any direction. This is something that the great minds of every age have demonstrated repeatedly. And if we go deeper or farther into Life, into Mind, into Nature, we are going to make discoveries. We are going to find secrets that no mind has known before. We are going to meet forces, laws and principles, the knowledge of which may reduce to simplicity a thousand so-called impossibilities. We are going to discern the inner workings of things in many fields and regions, and thus secure information that wise men have sought all through the ages.

These things are not exaggerations nor the mere picturing of a highly stimulated imagination; for when we accept the fact that concentration can lead the mind farther and deeper in any direction we realize that we may, through this use of concentration, discover or accomplish almost anything; that is, if we carry on the process far enough. It is a matter therefore of deciding to concentrate until we find or secure what we want. The outcome will be as expected; for in due time we shall meet the great and the wonderful; we shall learn how this remarkable power can open to the mind regions beyond regions of untold possibility.

When we realize that the mind holds marvels and possibilities far beyond what we ever dreamed; and when we know that these mental marvels can be gathered and trained for super-effort – for creative work on any scale – or for going out upon expeditions of discovery, even entering into the secrets of life and the heart of things – when we note these things we stand amazed at what might be done. But the mind of faith and courage will stand amazed only for a moment. Such a mind will resolve to master this wonder art at once – for in it there is a power that never knew failure nor defeat – a power that is fully able to cast the mountains of impossibility into the sea of oblivion.

The following Christian D. Larson quotes are from
Your Forces And How To Use Them, 1912

THE RULING PRINCIPLE IN MAN

Whenever you act, realize that it is the *"I Am"* that gives initiative to that action, and whenever you think of yourself or try to be conscious of yourself, realize that the *"I Am"* occupies the throne of your entire field of consciousness.

Another important essential is to affirm silently in your own mind that you are the *"I Am,"* and as you affirm this statement, or as you simply declare positively, *"I Am,"* think of the *"I Am"* as being the ruling principle in your whole world, as being distinct and above and superior to all else in your being, and as being you, yourself, in the highest, largest, and most comprehensive sense. You thus lift yourself up, so to speak, to the mountain top of masterful individuality; you enthrone yourself; you become true to yourself; you place yourself where you belong.

Through this practice you not only discover yourself to be the master of your whole life, but you elevate all your conscious actions to that lofty state in your consciousness that we may describe as the throne of your being, or as that center of action within in which the ruling *"I Am"* lives and moves and has its being. If you wish to control and direct the forces you possess, you must act from the throne of your being, so to speak; or in other words, from that conscious point in your mental world wherein all power of control, direction and initiative proceeds; and this point of action is the center of the *"I Am."* You must act, not as a body, not as a personality, not as a mind, but as the *"I Am,"* and the more fully you recognize the lofty position of the *"I Am,"* the greater becomes your power to control and direct all other things that you may possess.

In brief, whenever you think or act, you should feel that you stand with the *"I Am,"* at the apex of mentality on the very heights of your existence, and you should at the same time, realize that this *"I Am"* is *you* – the *supreme you*. The more you practice these methods, the more you lift yourself up above the limitations of mind and body, into the realization of your own true position as a masterful individuality; in fact, you place yourself where you belong, over and above everything in your organized existence.

When we examine the mind of the average person, we find that he usually identifies himself with mind or body. He either thinks that he is body or that he is mind, and therefore he can control neither mind nor body. The *"I Am"* in his nature is submerged in a bundle of ideas, some of which are true and some of which are not, and his thought is usually controlled by those ideas without receiving any direction whatever from that principle within him that alone was intended to give direction. Such a man lives in the lower story of human existence, but as we can control life only when we give directions from the upper story, we discover just why the average person neither understands his forces nor has the power to use them. He must first elevate himself to the upper story of the human structure, and the first and most important step to be taken in this direction is to recognize the *"I Am"* as the ruling principle, and that the *"I Am"* is *you*.

Another method that will be found highly important in this connection is to take a few moments every day and try to feel that you – the *"I Am"* – are not only above mind and body, but in a certain sense, distinct from mind and body; in fact, try to isolate the *"I Am"* for a few moments every day from the rest of your organized being. This practice will give you what may be termed a perfect consciousness of your own individual *"I Am,"* and as you gain that consciousness you will always think of the supreme *"I Am"* whenever you think of yourself. Accordingly, all your mental actions will, from that time on, come directly from the *"I Am;"* and if you will continue to stand above all such actions at all times, you will be able to control them and direct them completely.

In the exercise of consciousness, we find that the *"I Am"* employs three fundamental actions. When the *"I Am"* looks out upon life we have simple consciousness. When the *"I Am"* looks upon its own position in life we have self consciousness, and when the *"I Am"* looks up into the vastness of real life we have cosmic consciousness.

In simple consciousness, you are only aware of those things that exist externally to yourself, but when you begin to become conscious of yourself as a distinct entity, you begin to develop self consciousness. When you begin to turn your attention to the great within and begin to look up into the real source of all things, you become conscious of that world that seemingly exists within all worlds, and when you enter upon this experience, you are on the border land of cosmic consciousness, the most fascinating subject that has ever been known.

When we come to define body, mind and soul, we must reverse the usual definition. In the past, we have constantly used the expression, "I have a soul," which naturally implies the belief that "I am a body;" and so deeply has this idea become fixed in the average mind that nearly everybody thinks of the body whenever the term "me" or "myself" is employed. But in this attitude of mind the individual is not above the physical states of thought and feeling; in fact, he is more or less submerged in what may be called a bundle of physical facts and ideas, of which he has very little control. You cannot control anything in your life, however, until you are above it. You cannot control what is in your body until you realize that you are above your body. You cannot control what is in your mind until you realize that you are above your mind, and therefore no one can use the forces within him to any extent so long as he thinks of himself as being the body, or as being localized exclusively in the body.

Proceed this very moment to the mountain tops of the strength you now possess, and whatever may happen do not come down. Do not weaken under adversity. Resolve to remain as strong, as determined and as highly enthused during the darkest night of adversity as you are during the sunniest day of prosperity. Do not feel disappointed when things seem disappointing. Keep the eye single upon the same brilliant future regardless of circumstances, conditions or events. Do not lose heart when things go wrong. Continue undisturbed in your original resolve to make all things go right. To be overcome by adversity and threatening failure is to lose strength; to always remain in the same lofty, determined mood is to constantly grow in strength.

HOW WE GOVERN THE FORCES WE POSSESS

Whenever you think or whenever you feel, whenever you speak, whenever you act, or whatever may be taking place in your life, your supreme idea should be that you are above it all, superior to it all, and have control of it all. You simply must take this higher ground in all action, thought and consciousness before you can control yourself and direct, for practical purposes, the forces you possess.

THE USE OF MIND IN PRACTICAL ACTION

We sometimes wonder why there are so many capable men and admirable women who do not reach those places in life that they seem to deserve, but the answer is simple. They do not apply the power of mind as they should. Their abilities and qualities are either misdirected or applied only in part. These people, however, should not permit themselves to become dissatisfied with fate, but should remember that every individuality who learns to make full use of the power of his mind will reach his goal; he will realize his desire and will positively win.

Generally speaking, we may say that the power of mind is the sum total of all the forces of the mental world, including those forces that are employed in the process of thinking. The power of mind includes the power of the will, the power of desire, the power of feeling, and the power of thought. It includes conscious action in all its phases and subconscious action in all its phases; in fact, it includes anything and everything that is placed in action through the mind, by the mind or in the mind.

To use the power of the mind, the first essential is to direct every mental action toward the goal in view, and this direction must not be occasional, but constant. Most minds, however, do not apply this law. They think about a certain thing one moment and about something else the next moment. At a certain hour their mental actions work along a certain line, and at the next hour those actions work along a different line. Sometimes the goal in view is one thing, and sometimes another, so the actions of the mind do not move constantly toward a certain definite goal, but are mostly scattered. We know, however, that every individual who is actually working himself steadily and surely toward the goal he has in view, invariably directs all the power of his thought upon that goal. In his mind not a single mental action is thrown away, not a single mental force wasted. All the power that is in him is being directed to work for what he wishes to accomplish, and the reason that every power responds in this way is because he is not thinking of one thing now and something else the next moment. He is thinking all the time of what he wishes to attain and achieve. The full power of mind is turned upon that object, and as mind is the ruling power, the full power of all his other forces will tend to work for the same object.

In using the power of mind as well as all the other forces we possess, the first question to answer is what we really want, or what we really want to accomplish; and when this question is answered, the one thing that is wanted should be fixed so clearly in thought that it can be seen by the mind's eye every minute. But the majority do not know what they really want.

They may have some vague desire, but they have not determined clearly, definitely and positively what they really want, and this is one of the principle causes of failure. So long as we do not know definitely what we want, our forces will be scattered, and so long as our forces are scattered, we will accomplish but little, or fail entirely. When we know what we want, however, and proceed to work for it with all the power and ability that is in us, we may rest assured that we will get it. When we direct the power of thinking, the power of will, the power of mental action, the power of desire, the power of ambition, in fact, all the power we possess on the one thing we want, on the one goal we desire to reach, it is not difficult to understand why success in a greater and greater measure must be realized.

To illustrate this subject further, we will suppose that you have a certain ambition and continue to concentrate your thought and the power of your mind upon that ambition every minute for an indefinite period, with no cessation whatever. The result will be that you will gradually and surely train all the forces within you to work for the realization of that ambition, and in the course of time, the full capacity of your entire mental system will be applied in working for that particular thing.

On the other hand, suppose you do as most people do under average circumstances. Suppose, after you have given your ambition a certain amount of thought, you come to the conclusion that possibly you might succeed better along another line. Then you begin to direct the power of your mind along that other line. Later on, you come to the conclusion that there is still another channel through which you might succeed, and you proceed accordingly to direct your mind upon this third ambition. Then what will happen? Simply this: You will make three good beginnings, but in every case you will stop before you have accomplished anything. There are thousands of capable men and women, however, who make this mistake every year of their lives. The full force of their mental system is directed upon a certain ambition for a short time; then it is directed elsewhere.

They never continue long enough along any particular line to secure results from their efforts, and therefore results are never secured.

Then there are other minds who give most of their attention to a certain ambition and succeed fairly well, but give the rest of their attention to a number of minor ambitions that have no particular importance. Thus they are using only a fraction of their power in a way that will tell. The rest of it is thrown away along a number of lines through which nothing is gained. But in this age high efficiency is demanded everywhere in the world's work, and anyone who wants to occupy a place that will satisfy his ambition and desire, cannot afford to waste even a small part of the power he may possess. He needs it all along the line of his leading ambition, and therefore should not permit counter attractions to occupy his mind for a moment.

If you have a certain ambition or a certain desire, think about that ambition at all times. Keep that ambition before your mind constantly, and do not hesitate to make your ambition as high as possible. The higher you aim, the greater will be your achievements, though that does not necessarily mean that you will realize your highest aims as fully as you have pictured them in your mind; but the fact is that those who have low aims, usually realize what is even below their aims, while those who have high aims usually realize very nearly, if not fully, what their original ambition calls for. The principle is to direct the power of mind upon the very highest, the very largest and the very greatest mental conception of that which we intend to achieve. The first essential therefore, is to direct the full power of mind and thought upon the goal in view, and to continue to direct the mind in that manner every minute, regardless of circumstances or conditions.

The second essential is to make every mental action positive. When we desire certain things or when we think of certain things we wish to attain or achieve, the question should be if our mental attitudes at the time are positive or negative.

To answer this we only have to remember that every positive action always goes toward that which receives its attention, while a negative action always retreats. A positive action is an action that you feel when you realize that every force in your entire system is pushed forward, so to speak, and that it is passing through what may be termed an expanding and enlarging state of feeling or consciousness. The positive attitude of mind is also indicated by the feeling of a firm, determined fullness throughout the nervous system. When every nerve feels full, strong and determined, you are in the positive attitude, and whatever you may do at the time will produce results along the line of your desire or your ambition. When you are in a positive state of mind you are never nervous or disturbed, you are never agitated or strenuous; in fact, the more positive you are the deeper your calmness and the better your control over your entire system.

The positive man is not one who rushes helter-skelter here and there regardless of judgment or constructive action, but one who is absolutely calm and controlled under every circumstance, and yet so thoroughly full of energy that every atom in his being is ready, under every circumstance, to accomplish and achieve. This energy is not permitted to act, however, until the proper time arrives, and then its action goes directly to the goal in view.

The positive mind is always in harmony with itself, while the negative mind is always out of harmony, and thereby loses the greater part of its power. Positiveness always means strength stored up, power held in the system under perfect control, until the time of action; and during the time of action directed constructively under the same perfect control. In the positive mind, all the actions of the mental system are working in harmony and are being fully directed toward the object in view, while in the negative mind, those same actions are scattered, restless, nervous, disturbed, moving here and there, sometimes under direction, but most of the time not. That the one should invariably succeed is therefore just as evident as that the other should invariably fail.

Scattered energy cannot do otherwise but fail, while positively directed energy simply must succeed. A positive mind is like a powerful stream of water that is gathering volume and force from hundreds of tributaries all along its course. The further on it goes the greater its power, until when it reaches its goal, that power is simply immense. A negative mind, however, would be something like a stream that the further it flows the more divisions it makes, until, when it reaches its goal, instead of being one powerful stream, it has become a hundred, small, weak, shallow streams.

To develop positiveness it is necessary to cultivate those qualities that constitute positiveness. Make it a point to give your whole attention to what you want to accomplish, and give that attention firmness, calmness and determination. Try to give depth to every desire until you feel as if all the powers of your system were acting, not on the surface, but from the greater world within.

The third essential in the right use of the mind is to make every mental action constructive, and a constructive mental action is one that is based upon a deep seated desire to develop, to increase, to achieve, to attain – in brief, to become larger and greater, and to do something of far greater worth than has been done before. If you will cause every mental action you entertain to have that feeling, constructiveness will soon become second nature to your entire mental system; that is, all the forces of your mind will begin to become building forces, and will continue to build you up along any line through which you may desire to act.

Inspire your mind constantly with a building desire, and make this desire so strong that every part of your system will constantly feel that it wants to become greater, more capable and more efficient.

Do not turn the power of your mind upon others, but turn it upon yourself in such a way that it will make you stronger, more positive, more capable, and more efficient, and as you develop in this manner, success must come of itself.

The way to control circumstances is to control the forces within yourself to make a greater man of yourself, and as you become greater and more competent, you will naturally gravitate into better circumstances. In this connection, we should remember that like attracts like. If you want that which is better, make yourself better. If you want to realize the ideal, make yourself more ideal. If you want better friends, make yourself a better friend. If you want to associate with people of worth, make yourself more worthy. If you want to meet that which is agreeable, make yourself more agreeable. If you want to enter conditions and circumstances that are more pleasing, make yourself more pleasing. In brief, whatever you want, produce that something in yourself, and you will positively gravitate towards the corresponding conditions in the external world. But to improve yourself along those lines, it is necessary to apply for that purpose all the power you possess. You cannot afford to waste any of it, and every misuse of the mind will waste power.

Avoid all destructive attitudes of the mind, such as anger, hatred, malice, envy, jealousy, revenge, depression, discouragement, disappointment, worry, fear, and so on.

Make the best use of your own talent and the best that is in store for you will positively come your way. When others seem to take advantage of you, do not retaliate by trying to take advantage of them. Use your power in improving yourself, so that you can do better and better work. That is how you are going to win in the race. Later on, those who tried to take advantage of you will be left in the rear. Remember, those who are dealing unjustly with you or with anybody are misusing their mind. They are therefore losing their power, and will, in the course of time, begin to lose ground; but if you, in the meantime, are turning the full power of your mind to good account, you will not only gain more power, but you will soon begin to gain ground. You will gain and continue to gain in the long run, while others who have been misusing their minds will lose mostly everything in the long run. That is how you are going to win, and win splendidly regardless of ill treatment or opposition.

A great many people imagine that they can promote their own success by trying to prevent the success of others, but it is one of the greatest delusions in the world. If you want to promote your own success as thoroughly as your capacity will permit, take an active interest in the success of everybody, because this will not only keep your mind in the success attitude and cause you to think success all along the line, but it will enlarge your mind so as to give you a greater and better grasp upon the fields of success.

Those people who fail, and who continue to fail all along the line, fail because the power of their minds is either in a habitual negative state, or is always misdirected. If the power of mind is not working positively and constructively for a certain goal, you are not going to succeed. If your mind is not positive, it is negative, and negative minds float with the stream. We must remember that we are in the midst of all kinds of circumstances, some which are for us and some which are against us, and we will either have to make our own way or drift, and if we drift we go wherever the stream goes. But most of the streams of human life are found to float in the world of the ordinary and the inferior. Therefore, if you drift, you will drift with the inferior, and your goal will be failure.

When we analyze the minds of people who have failed, we invariably find that they are either negative, non-constructive or aimless. Their forces are scattered, and what is in them is seldom applied constructively.

There is nothing of a positive, determined nature going on in their mental world. They have not taken definite action along any line. They are dependent upon fate and circumstances. They are drifting with some stream, and that they should accomplish little if anything is inevitable. This does not mean, however, that their mental world is necessarily unproductive; in fact, those very minds are in many instances immensely rich with possibilities. The trouble is, those possibilities continue to be dormant, and what is in them is not being brought forth and trained for definite action or actual results.

What those people should do, is to proceed at once to comply with the three essentials mentioned above, and before many months there will be a turn in the lane. They will soon cease to drift, and will then begin to make their own life, their own circumstances and their own future.

In this connection, it is well to remember that negative people and non-constructive minds never attract that which is helpful in their circumstances. The more you drift, the more people you meet who also drift, while on the other hand, when you begin to make your own life and become positive, you begin to meet more positive people and more constructive circumstances.

As you begin to grow and become more capable, you will find that you will meet better and better opportunities, not only opportunities for promoting external success, but opportunities for further building yourself up along the lines of ability, capacity and talent. You thus demonstrate the law that "Nothing succeeds like success," and "To him that hath shall be given." And here it is well to remember that it is not necessary to possess external things in the beginning to be counted among them "that hath." It is only necessary in the beginning to possess the interior riches; that is, to take control of what is in you, and proceed to use it positively with a definite goal in view. He who has control of his own mind has already great riches. He has sufficient wealth to be placed among those who have. He is already successful, and if he continues as he has begun, his success will soon appear in the external world. Thus the wealth that existed at first in the internal only will take shape and form in the external. This is a law that is unfailing, and there is not a man or woman on the face of the earth that cannot apply it with the most satisfying results.

The reason why so many fail is thus found in the fact that they do not fully and constructively apply the forces and powers they possess, and the reason why so many succeed only to a slight degree is found in the fact that only a small fraction of their power is applied properly.

But anyone can learn the full and proper use of all that is in him by applying faithfully the three essentials mentioned above. The reason why those succeed who do succeed is found in the fact that a large measure of their forces and powers is applied according to those three essentials, and as those essentials can be applied by anyone, even to the most perfect degree, there is no reason why all should not succeed.

When you think of yourself do not think of that part of yourself that appears on the surface. That part is the smaller part and the lesser should not be pictured in mind. Think of your larger self, the immense subconscious self that is limitless both in power and in possibility.

Believe in yourself but not simply in a part of yourself. Give constant recognition to all that is in you and in that have full faith and confidence.

Give the bigger man on the inside full right of way. Believe thoroughly in your greater interior self. Know that you have something within you that is greater than any obstacle, circumstance or difficulty that you can possibly meet. Then in the full faith in this greater something proceed with your work.

THE FORCES OF THE SUBCONSCIOUS

If you continue to desire greater ability along a certain line and expect the subconscious to produce greater mental power along that line, your ability will increase as expected, but it is necessary in this connection to be persistent and persevering. To become enthusiastic about these things for a few days is not sufficient. It is when we apply these laws persistently for weeks months and years that we find the results to be, not only what we expected, but frequently far greater.

TRAINING THE SUBCONSCIOUS FOR SPECIAL RESULTS

If we want power, we should direct the subconscious not simply to give us a great deal or a certain amount of power, but to give us more and more power. In this manner, we shall secure results from the very beginning. If we try to train the subconscious to produce a certain amount, it might be some time before that amount can be developed. In the meantime, we should meet disappointment and delay, but if our desire is for steady increase along all lines from where we stand now, we shall be able to secure, first, a slight improvement and then added improvement to be followed with still greater improvement, until we finally reach the highest goal we have in view.

We all know of instances where great things were accomplished simply through the fact that the individual was carried on and on by an immense power within him that seemed to be distinct from himself and greater than himself; but it was simply the greater powers of the subconscious that were aroused and placed in positive, determined action. These instances, however, need not be exceptions. Any man, under any circumstances, can so increase the power of his mind, his thought and his will as to be actually carried away with this same tremendous force; that is, the power within him becomes so strong that he is actually pushed through to the goal he has in view regardless of circumstances, conditions or obstacles.

When demands are urgent, the subconscious responds more readily, especially when feelings at the time are also very deep. When you need certain results, say that you *must* have them, and put your whole energy into the "must." Whatever you make up your mind that you must do, you will in some manner get the power to do.

There are a number of instances on record where people were carried through certain events by what seemed to be a miraculous power, but the case of it was simply this – that they had to do it, and whatever you have to do, the subconscious mind will invariably give you the power to do. The reason for this is found in the fact that when you feel that you must do a thing and that you have to do it, your desires are so strong and so deep that they go into the very depths of the subconscious and thus call to action the full power of that vast interior realm.

If you have some great ambition that you wish to realize, direct the subconscious several times each day and each night before you go to sleep, to work out the necessary ways and means; and if you are determined, those ways and means will be forthcoming. But here it is necessary to remember that we must concentrate on the one thing wanted. If your mind scatters, sometimes giving attention to one ambition and sometimes to another, you will confuse the subconscious and the ways and means desired will not be secured. Make your ambition a vital part of your life, and try to feel the force of that ambition every single moment of your existence. If you do this, your ambition will certainly be realized. It may take a year, it may take five years, it may take ten years or more, but your ambition will be realized. This being true, no one need feel disturbed about the future, because if he actually knows what he wants to accomplish, and trains the subconscious to produce the idea, the methods, the necessary ability and the required capacity, all these things will be secured.

When you are about to undertake anything new, do not proceed until you have submitted the proposition to the subconscious, and here we find the real value of "sleeping over" new plans before we finally decide. When we go to sleep, we go more completely into the subconscious, and those ideas that we take with us when we go to sleep, especially those that engage our serious attention at the time, are completely turned over, so to speak, during the period of sleep, and examined from all points of view.

Sometimes it is necessary to take those ideas into the subconscious a number of times when we go to sleep, as well as to submit the matter to the subconscious many times in the day during the waking state, but if we persevere, the right answer will finally be secured. The whole mind, conscious and subconscious, does possess the power to solve any problem that may come up, or provide the necessary ways and means through which we can carry out or finish anything we have undertaken.

When there are no results, do not lose faith. You know that the cause of the failure was the failure of the conscious to properly touch the subconscious at the time the directions were given, so therefore try again, giving your thought a deeper life and a more persistent desire.

Always be prepared to give these methods sufficient time. Some have remarkable results at once, while others secure no results for months; but whether you secure results as soon as you wish or not, continue to give your directions every day, fully expecting results. Be determined in every effort you may make in this direction, but do not be overanxious.

Every effort you may make to direct or train the subconscious, will bring its natural results in due time, provided you are always calm, well balanced, deeply poised and harmonious in all your thoughts and actions.

When you have made up your mind what you want to do, say to yourself a thousand times a day that you will do it. The best way will soon open. You will have the opportunity you desire.

If you would be greater in the future than you are now, be all that you can be now. He who is his best develops the power to be better. He who lives his ideals is creating a life that actually is ideal.

There is nothing in your life that you cannot modify, change or improve when you learn to regulate your thought.

Our destiny is not mapped out for us by some exterior power; we map it out for ourselves. What we think and do in the present determines what shall happen to us in the future.

THE POWER OF SUBJECTIVE THOUGHT

Make it a point to have definite results in mind at all times. Permit no thinking to be aimless. Every aimless thought is time and energy wasted, while every thought that is inspired with a definite aim will help to realize that aim, and if all your thoughts are inspired with a definite aim, the whole power of your mind will be for you and will work with you in realizing what you have in view. That you should succeed is therefore assured, because there is enough power in your mind to realize your ambitions, provided all of that power is used in working for your ambitions.

We frequently hear the expression, "I can never do anything right," and it is quite simple to understand that such a mode of thought would train the mind to act below its true ability and capacity. If you are fully convinced that you can never do anything right, it will become practically impossible for you to do anything right at any time, but on the other hand, if you continue to think, "I am going to do everything better and better," it is quite natural that your entire mental system should be inspired and trained to do things better and better.

The more you think of what is right, the more you tend to make every action in your mind right. The more you think of the goal you have in view, the more life and power you will call into action in working for that goal. The more you think of your ambition, the more power you will give to those faculties that can make your ambitions come true.

It is when the individual goes all to pieces, so to speak, that adversity gets the best of him; but no individual will go to pieces unless his thinking is chaotic, destructive, scattered, confused and detrimental.

Continue to possess your whole mind and you will master the situation, no matter what it may be, and it is scientific thinking that will enable you to perform this great feat.

To make thinking scientific, there are three leading essentials to be observed. The first is to cultivate constructive mental attitudes, and all mental attitudes are constructive when mind, thought, feeling, desire and will constantly face the greater and the better. A positive and determined optimism has the same effect, and the same is true of the practice of keeping the mental eye single on the highest goal in view. To make every mental attitude constructive, the mind must never look down, and mental depression must be avoided completely. Every thought and every feeling must have an upward look, and every desire must desire to inspire the same rising tendency in every action of mind.

The second essential is constructive mental imagery. Use the imagination to picture only what is good, what is beautiful, what is beneficial, what is ideal, and what you wish to realize. Mentally see yourself receiving what you deeply desire to receive. What you imagine, you will think, and what you think, you will become. Therefore, if you imagine only those things that are in harmony with what you wish to obtain or achieve, all your thinking will soon tend to produce what you want to attain or achieve.

The third essential is constructive mental action. Every action of the mind should have something desirable in view and should have a definite, positive aim. Train yourself to face the sunshine of life regardless of circumstances. When you face the sunshine, everything looks right, and when everything looks right, you will think right. It matters not whether there is any sunshine in life just now or not. We must think of sunshine just the same. If we do not see any silver lining, we must create one in our own mental vision.

Be optimistic, not in the usual sense of that term, but in the real sense of that term. The true optimist not only expects the best to happen, but goes to work to make the best happen.

The true optimist not only looks upon the bright side, but trains every force that is in him to produce more and more brightness in his life, and therefore complies with the three essentials just mentioned. His mental attitudes are constructive because they are always facing greater things. His imagination is constructive because it is always picturing the better and the ideal, and his mental actions are constructive because he is training the whole of his life to produce those greater and better things that his optimism has inspired him to desire and expect.

In training the mind in scientific thinking, the larger part of attention should be given to that of controlling our feelings. It is not difficult to think scientifically along intellectual lines, but to make our feelings move along wholesome, constructive, optimistic lines requires persistent training. Intellectual thought can be changed almost at any time with little effort, but feeling usually becomes stronger and stronger the longer it moves along a certain line, and thus becomes more difficult to change. When we feel discouraged, it is so easy to feel more discouraged; when we feel dissatisfied, it is only a step to that condition that is practically intolerable. It is therefore necessary to stop all detrimental feeling in the beginning. Do not permit a single adverse feeling to continue for a second. Change the mind at once by turning your attention upon something that will make you feel better. Resolve to feel the way you want to feel under all circumstances, and you will gradually develop the power to do so. Depressed mental feelings are burdens, and we waste a great deal of energy by carrying them around on our mental shoulders. Besides, such feelings tend to direct the power of thought towards the lower and the inferior. Whenever you permit yourself to feel bad, you will cause the power of mind and thought to go wrong. Therefore, persist in feeling right and good. Persist in feeling joyous. Persist in feeling cheerful, hopeful, optimistic and strong. Place yourself on the bright side and the strong side of everything that transpires in your life, and you will constantly gain power – power that will invariably be in your favor.

HOW MAN BECOMES WHAT HE THINKS

So long as you think that you are thus or so in the personal sense, your thought will be on the surface.

To change yourself you must go to that depth of mind where the causes of your personal condition exist. But your mind will not enter the depth of the within so long as your thought is on the surface, and your thought will be on the surface so long as you are thinking exclusively about your personal self.

THE ART OF CHANGING FOR THE BETTER

The tendency of all life is onward and upward. Therefore, to ask anything to come down is to violate the very purpose of existence. If we wish to be with the higher, the greater and the superior, we must change ourselves and become higher, greater and superior; and this we all can do.

When we have formulated in our minds what changes we wish to make, the course to pursue is to love the ideal that corresponds to those changes. This love must be deep and strong, and must be continued until the desired change has actually taken place. Know what better qualities you want; then love those qualities with all your mind and heart and soul.

To love the higher and the greater qualities of life is to cause the creative qualities of mind to produce those same qualities in our own nature; and in consequence, we steadily grow into the likeness of that which we constantly love. This is the great law – the law that governs all change for the better.

In the average person, love is directed almost exclusively upon the personal side of life. In consequence, the love nature becomes so personal, so limited and so superficial, that materialism follows.

In many other minds, it is mere appearances that attract the power of admiration, and the finer things in mind, soul and character are wholly ignored. The result is that the finer qualities of such people gradually disappear, and grossness, both in thought and in appearance naturally follow. But we must not conclude in this connection that it is wrong to admire the beautiful wherever it may be seen in the external world. We should love the beautiful everywhere, no matter where it may be found; we should admire the richness of life, both in the external and in the internal; and by living a complete life, we shall enjoy more and more of the richness and the beautiful in life, in the within as well as in the without. But the power of love must direct the greater part of its attention upon that which is rich and beautiful in mind and soul. It is that which is finer than the finest of external things that must be loved if man is to grow into the likeness of the great, the superior and the ideal, because man is as he thinks, and he thinks most of what he loves the best.

When any individual begins to love the finer qualities in life, and gives all the power of mind and soul to that love, he has taken the first step in the changing of his destiny. He is laying the foundation for a great and a better future, and if he continues as he has begun, he will positively reach the loftiest goal that he may have in view. There are many laws to apply in the beginning of a great life, but the law that lies at the foundation of them all is the law of love. It is love that determines what we are to think, what we are to work for, where we are to go, and what we are to accomplish. Therefore, among all great essentials, the principal one is to know how to love.

To apply this essential for all practical purposes, the secret is to love the great, the beautiful and the ideal in everybody and in everything; and to love with such a strong, passionate love that its ascending power becomes irresistible.

The whole of life will thus change and go up with the power of love into the great, the superior and the ideal; everything, both in the being of man and his environment will advance accordingly, and the dreams of the soul will come true. The ideal will become real, the desires of the heart will be granted, and what man has hoped to make his own will be absent no more.

When failure comes be more determined than ever to succeed.

The more feeling there is in your thought the greater its power.

You steadily and surely become in the real what you constantly and clearly think that you are in the ideal.

The more you believe in yourself the more of your latent powers and possibilities you place in action. And the more you believe in your purpose the more of your power you apply in promoting that purpose.

To him who thinks he can everything is an opportunity.

Depend only upon yourself, but work in harmony with all things. Thus you call forth the best that is in yourself and secure the best that external sources have to give.

HE CAN WHO THINKS HE CAN

When we think that we can, we must enter into the very soul of that thought and be thoroughly in earnest. It is in this manner that we awaken the finer creative energies of mind, those forces that build talent, ability and genius – those forces that make man great. We must be determined to do what we think we can do. This determination must be invincible, and must be animated with that depth of feeling that arouses all the powers of being into positive and united action. The power that can do what we think we can do will thus be placed at our command, and accordingly we may proceed successfully to do what we thought we could do.

The fact that you have failed to get the lesser proves conclusively that you deserve the greater. So therefore, dry those tears and go in search of the worthier prize.

Count nothing lost; even the day that sees "no worthy action done" may be a day of preparation and accumulation that will add greatly to the achievements of tomorrow. Many a day was made famous because nothing was done the day before.

Know what you want and continue to want it. You will get it if you combine desire with faith. The power of desire when combined with faith becomes invincible.

Some of the principal reasons why so many fail to get what they want is because they do not definitely know what they want, or because they change their wants almost every day.

HOW WE SECURE WHAT WE PERSISTENTLY DESIRE

The purpose of desire is to inform man what he needs at every particular moment to supply the demands of change and growth in his life; and in promoting this purpose, desire gives expression to its two leading functions. The first of these is to give the forces of the human system something definite to do, and the second is to arouse those forces or faculties that have the natural power to do what is to be done.

In exercising its first function, desire not only promotes concentration of action among the forces in man, but also causes those forces to work for the thing that is wanted. Therefore, it is readily understood why the wish, if strong, positive, determined and continuous, will tend to produce the thing wished for. If you can cause all the elements and powers in your being to work for the one thing that you want you are almost certain to get it.

What you can appreciate, enjoy and use in your present sphere of existence, you have the power, in your present state of development, to produce; that is, you can produce it if all your power is applied in your effort to produce it; and when you desire any particular thing with the full force and capacity of your desire you cause all your power to be applied in producing that particular thing.

In exercising its second function, desire proceeds directly into that faculty or group of forces that can, if fully applied, produce the very thing that is desired. In its first function it tends to bring all the forces of the system together, and inspires them with the desire to work for what is wanted. It acts upon the system in general and gives everything in the system something definite to do, that something definite in each case being the one thing desired. In its second function it acts upon certain parts of the system in particular; always upon those parts that can do what is wanted done; and it tends to arouse all the life and power that those particular parts may contain.

No matter how sluggish a faculty may be, if it is thoroughly charged, so to speak, with highly active energy, it simply must become more active. And no matter how small it may be, if it continues to receive a steady stream of added life, energy and power, day after day, month after month, year after year, it simply must increase in size and capacity. And whenever any faculty becomes greater in capacity and more alive in action it will do better work; that is, it will gradually gain in ability and power until it has sufficient ability and power to produce what you wished for.

It is not occasional desire, or half-hearted desire that gets the thing desired. It is persistent desire; and persistent desire, not only desires continually, but with all the power of life and mind and soul. The force of a half alive desire, when acting upon a certain faculty, cannot cause that faculty to become fully alive. Nor can such a desire marshall all the unused forces of the system and concentrate them all upon the attainment of the one thing wanted.

And it is true that the desires of most people are neither continuous nor very deep. They are shallow, occasional wishes without enough power to stir to action a single atom.

Then we must also remember that results do not necessarily follow the use of a single force. Sometimes the force of persistent desire alone may do wonders, but usually it is necessary to apply in combined action all the forces of the human system. The force of desire, however, is one of the greatest of these, and when fully expressed in connection with the best talents we may possess, the thing desired will certainly be secured.

Before you begin to apply the power of desire, know with a certainty what you want because when you get what you have desired, you may have to take it. If you do not know definitely what you really do want, desire a better judgment, a clearer understanding and a more balanced life. Desire to know what is best for you, and the force of that desire will tend to produce normal action in every part of your system. Then you will feel distinctly what the highest welfare of your nature actually demands.

In deciding upon what you want, however, do not be timid, and do not measure the possible with the yardstick of general appearances. Let your aspirations be high, only be sure that you are acting within the sphere of your own inherent capacity; though in this connection it is well to remember that your inherent capacity is many times as great as it has been supposed to be; and also that it can be continuously enlarged.

The power of desire not only tends to arouse added life and power in these faculties upon which it may act, but it also tends to make the mind as a whole more alert and wide-awake along those lines. This is well illustrated by the fact that when we have a strong, continuous desire for information on a certain subject, we always find someone or something that can give us that information.

And the reason is that all the faculties of the mind are prompted by the force of this desire to be constantly on the lookout for that information.

That the same law will apply in the desire or search for wisdom, new ideas, better plans, better opportunities, more agreeable environments and more ideal companions, is clearly understood. And when we couple this fact with the fact that the power of desire tends to increase the life, the ability, the working capacity and the efficiency of these faculties or forces that can produce what we desire, we must certainly admit that those who have found the secret of using desire have made a great find indeed. But, as stated before, and it cannot be repeated too often, the desire must be persistent and strong, as strong as all the life and soul we possess.

In other words, we must wish hard enough, and we wish hard enough when our desires are sufficiently full and deep and strong to thoroughly arouse those faculties that have the natural ability to fulfill those desires. Many desires are only strong enough to arouse their corresponding faculties to a slight degree – not enough to increase the activity or working capacity of these faculties, while most desires are too weak to arouse any force or faculty in the least.

The act of wishing hard enough, however, does not imply hard mental work. If you make hard work of your wishing, you will use up your energy instead of turning it into those channels where it can be applied to good account. It is depth of desire and fullness of desire combined in an action that is directed continuously upon the one thing desired that constitutes true desire. To wish hard enough is simply to wish for all that you want with all that is in you. But we cannot wish with all that is in us unless our wish is subconscious as well as conscious because the subconscious is a part of us – the larger part of us.

To make every desire subconscious, the subconscious mind should always be included in the process of desire; that is, whenever we express a desire we should think of the subconscious, and combine the thought of that desire with our thought of the subconscious mind. Every desire should be deeply felt as all deeply felt mental actions become subconscious actions.

It is an excellent practice to let every desire sink into the deeper mental life, so to speak; and also to act in and through that deeper mental life whenever we give expression to desire; or, in other words, when we turn on the full force and power of that desire. To become proficient in these methods requires some practice, though all that is necessary to become proficient is to continue to try.

CONCENTRATION AND THE POWER BACK OF SUGGESTION

The purpose of concentration is to apply all the active forces of mind and personality upon that one thing which is being done now, and it may therefore be called the master key to all attainments and achievement. In its last analysis, the cause of all failure can be traced to the scattering of forces, and the cause of all achievement to the concentration of forces. This does not imply however, that concentration is the only essential, but it does imply that concentration must be perfect, or failure is inevitable no matter how many good methods one may employ. The ruling thought of concentration is, "This one thing I do," and it can be stated as an absolute truth that whenever the mind works completely in the attitude of that thought, concentration is perfect.

The value of concentration is very easily illustrated by taking, for example, a wheel of twenty spokes with every spoke a pipe, and all those pipes connected with another conveying steam. The steam will thereby pass out through twenty channels. Then connect an engine with one of the pipes. That engine will accordingly receive only one-twentieth of the steam conveyed through the wheel, while nineteen-twentieths will pass out in waste.

But suppose the other nineteen pipes were plugged so that all the steam would pass out through the one pipe connected with the engine. The engine would then have twenty times as much power as before.

The average mind is quite similar to such a wheel. An enormous amount of energy is generated at the hub, so to speak, or at the vital center of mental life; but as a rule, that power passes out through a score of channels, so that the channel of action receives only a fraction of the power generated in the human system. But here we must remember that you can apply your power effectively only in one direction at a time; therefore, if all your power is to be applied in that one direction, all other channels must be closed up for the time being; or in other words, all the power of mind and thought must be concentrated where you are acting at the time.

There is no use trying to concentrate unless the action of the mind is deep. That is the first essential. In other words, the mind must go into the psychological field; the mind must act, not on the surface of things, but through the deeper life of its thought process.

The first method is to train the mind to act in the subjective or psychological field; in other words, cause all thinking, all feeling and all actions of thought, will and desire to become deeper and finer; in fact, deepen as far as possible all mental action. Whenever you concentrate or turn your attention upon any subject or object, try to feel deeply, try to think deeply and try to turn thought into deeper realms of feeling. The moment your mental action begins to deepen, you will find your attention directed upon the object in mind with perfect ease and with full force. Whenever you are thinking about anything, try to feel your thought getting into the vital life of that something, and wherever you turn your attention, try to feel that the force of that attention acts through your whole mind instead of simply on the surface of your mind. To state it briefly, whenever you concentrate, deepen your thought, and the deeper your thought becomes, the more perfectly will the full force of your mind and thought focus upon the point of concentration.

Whatever you have to do, deepen your thought while giving that work your attention. You will find that you will thereby give all your energy to that work and this is your purpose.

The second method is to become interested in that upon which you desire to concentrate. If you are not interested in that subject or object, begin at once to look for the most interesting point of view. You will be surprised to find that no matter how uninteresting a subject may seem, the very moment you begin to look for the most interesting viewpoints of that subject, you will almost immediately become interested in that subject itself. And it is a well known fact that whenever we are thoroughly interested in a subject, we concentrate thoroughly and naturally upon that subject.

Another important essential in the use of the forces of mind and thought is that of understanding suggestion and the power back of suggestion; and this becomes especially true when we realize that there is no factor or condition that we may come in contact with anywhere or under any circumstances that does not suggest something.

To define suggestion, it may be stated that anything is a suggestion that brings into mind some thought, idea or feeling that tends to undermine some similar idea, thought or feeling that happens to be in the mind at the time. When you have certain ideas or feelings, and you meet circumstances that tend to remove those ideas or feelings, the power of suggestion is working in your mind.

The great majority are receiving all sorts of suggestions every hour, and they respond to a very large number of them; in fact, we can truthfully say that most people are controlled, most of the time, by suggestions that come to them from their environment. Those minds, however, who understand the power of thought, and who know the difference between detrimental and beneficial suggestions, can close their minds to the former and open them fully to the latter.

And the method to apply is this, that whenever you are in the presence of an adverse suggestion, concentrate your attention upon some idea or mental state which you know will act as a counter suggestion; in other words, when adverse suggestion is trying to produce in your mind what you do not want, persist in suggesting to yourself what you do want. This practice, if employed frequently, will soon make you so strong in this direction that you will unconsciously, so to speak, be on your guard; in fact, the very moment that an adverse suggestion is given, your mind will spring up of its own accord with a wholesome suggestion to meet the requirements. To avoid becoming a victim to adverse suggestions – and we have such suggestions about us almost constantly – fill your mind so full of good, wholesome thoughts and suggestions that there is no room for anything else. Feel right at all times, and nothing from without can tempt you to think wrong.

A great many suggestions do not produce results, a fact which should be perfectly understood, because every thought that we think does contain some suggestion. When we are trying to impress good thoughts upon our minds, we want the good suggestions conveyed by those thoughts to take effect, but frequently they do not, and the reason is that a suggestion takes effect only when we exercise the power that is back of suggestion.

To explain further, we might say that you use the power back of suggestion whenever you mentally feel that vital idea which the suggestion aims to convey. When you feel that idea, you respond to the suggestion, but when you do not feel it, you do not respond.

THE DEVELOPMENT OF THE WILL

Among the many functions of the will, the principal ones are as follows: The will to initiate; the will to direct; the will to control; the will to think; the will to imagine; the will to desire; the will to act; the will to originate ideas; the will to give expression to those ideas; the will to will into action any purpose; the will to carry through that purpose; the will to employ the highest and most perfect action of any force or faculty in mind; and the will to push up, so to speak, any talent in the mind to its highest point of efficiency. This last mentioned function has been ignored, but it is by far the most important in the practical life of attainment and achievement.

In brief, when a faculty is backed up, so to speak, with a powerful will, it easily doubles its capacity and efficiency; in other words, it is pushed to a higher state of action.

A powerful will, however, is never domineering or forceful. In fact, a domineering will is weak. It may be seemingly strong on the spur of the moment, but it cannot be applied steadily for any length of time. A strong will, however, is deep, continuous and persistent. It calls into action your entire individuality, and as you exercise such a will you feel as if a tremendous power from within yourself had been calmly, though persistently aroused.

When we analyze the human mind, in the majority we find the will to be weak, and in fact, almost absent in a great many. Such people do not have the power to take a single original step. They have no initiative, and accordingly drift with the stream. Among others, who are a little higher in the mental scale, we find a will somewhat stronger, but not sufficiently strong to exercise with any degree of efficiency a single one of its functions.

A great many people have good intentions, and they have sufficient will power to originate those intentions, but they have not sufficient will power to carry them out; in other words, they have the will to think, but not the will to act.

Thousands of people start out right, but they have not the power of will to continue, so that where ten thousand make a good beginning, less than a score finish the race.

Realizing the importance of a strong will, and knowing that the will is weak in the minds of the great majority, we may well ask what might be the cause of this weakness; and the answer is that there are several marked causes, all of which we shall proceed to consider.

The first among these causes is alcohol. The use of alcohol weakens the will, not only in the individual who partakes of it, but in his children and grandchildren, and many generations following. It has been estimated by those who have studied this subject carefully, that the use of alcohol from generation to generation through the centuries is one of the principal causes for this weakness in the human will that we find to be almost universal. And when we study the psychology of the subject we soon discover the reason why.

Nearly every nation, as far back in history as we can go, has been using alcohol in some form or other, and as its weakening effect upon the will is transmissible from one generation to another, we realize that practically every member of the race has been burdened, more or less, with this adverse inheritance. But in this connection, we must remember that it is not necessary to be disturbed by this dark picture, because no matter what we have inherited, we can overcome it absolutely.

The fact that the human race has transmitted a weak will from generation to generation explains why the human family does not have enough power to produce more than an occasional mental giant. Here and there we find in history, men and women who tower above the rest. Their minds are strong, their wills are powerful, and their souls invincible; but how different is the condition among the majority. Most of them constitute mere driftwood, and follow blindly the leadership of these mental giants the race has produced.

When you permit an outside agency to control your feelings and emotions at frequent intervals for a prolonged period, your system will soon get into the habit of submitting to the control of this outside agency, and will not respond any longer to any effort that the will may make to regain its original power of control. This being true, we find an explanation for a number of perplexing questions. We learn why great men and women are not more numerous. We learn why the majority are so easily influenced by temptations. We learn why powerful characters are found only here and there, and we also learn why every great nation of past history has fallen.

If man wants to live his own life as it should be lived; if he wants to master circumstances and determine his own destiny, he must have the power to say under all sorts of conditions what he is going to think and what he is going to do; but he cannot exercise this power unless his own will is permitted to have absolute control over every thought, effort and desire in his life.

Emotional excess is another cause that weakens the will, and by emotional excess we mean the act of giving way to uncontrolled feelings of any kind. To give way to anger, hatred, passion, excitability, intensity, sensitiveness, grief, discouragement, despair, or any other uncontrolled feeling, is to weaken the will. The reason is that you cannot control yourself through your will when you permit yourself to be controlled by your feelings; and any act that rules out the will, weakens the will.

Whenever you permit yourself to become angry, you weaken the will. Whenever you permit yourself to become offended or hurt you weaken your will. Whenever you permit yourself to become despondent or discouraged, you weaken your will. Whenever you give way to grief, mental intensity or excitability, you weaken your will. You permit some artificial mental state to take possession of your mind, and your will at the time is put aside. We therefore should avoid absolutely all emotional excess.

We must not permit any feeling whatever to take possession of us, or permit ourselves to be influenced in any form or manner by anything that may enter the mind uncontrolled through the emotions; but this does not mean that we should ignore emotion. Emotion is one of the most valuable factors in human life, and should be used and enjoyed under every normal circumstance, but should never become a ruling factor in mind, thought or feeling.

Another cause of weakness in the will is what might be called mental dependence. To depend upon anybody or anything outside of yourself, is to weaken the will, for the simple reason that you let the will of someone else rule your actions, while your own will remains dormant. Nothing, however, that remains dormant can grow or develop. On the other hand, it will continue to become weaker and weaker, like an unused muscle, until it has no strength whatever. We therefore understand why those multitudes of people, who have followed blindly the will and leadership of others, not only in religion but in all other things, have practically no will power at all. And here we wish to state that it is positively wrong for any individual or any group of individuals to follow any one man or any one woman or any group of men or women under any circumstances whatever.

Another cause which is too large and diversified to outline in detail, is that of intemperance; that is, immoderation in anything in life. To indulge excessively any desire or appetite, be it physical or mental, is to weaken the will. Partake only of that which is necessary and good, and observe moderation.

Whenever you will to do anything, will it with all there is in you. If no other practice than this were taken, the power of the will would be doubled in a month. Depend upon the power that is in you for everything, and determine to secure the results you desire through the larger expression of that power. Never give in to anything that you do not want.

When a certain desire comes up that you do not care to entertain, turn your attention at once upon some favorable desire, and give all the power of your will to that new desire. This is very important, as the average person wastes more than half of his energy entertaining desires that are of no value, and that he does not intend to carry out. Whenever any feeling comes up in the system ask yourself if you want it. If you do not, turn your attention in another direction; but if you do want it, take hold of it with your will and direct it towards the highest states of mind that you can form at the time. In brief, every action that enters the system, whether it comes through thought, feeling, desire or imagination, should be redirected by the power of the will and turned into higher and greater actions.

The more easily you are disturbed, the weaker your will, while the stronger the will, the more difficult it is for anything to disturb your mind. When the will is strong, you live and exercise self-control in a deeper or interior mental world, and you look out upon the confusions of the outer world without being affected in the least by what takes place in the external.

He who would become great must live a great life.

Happiness adds life, power and worth to all your talents and powers. It is most important, therefore, that every moment should be full of joy.

However much you may do, always remember you have the ability to do more. No one has as yet applied all the ability in his possession. But all of us should learn to apply a greater measure every year.

While you are waiting for an opportunity to improve your time, improve yourself.

The man who never weakens when things are against him, will grow stronger and stronger until he will have the power to cause all things to be for him.

THE BUILDING OF A GREAT MIND

A great mind does not come from ancestors, but from the life, the thought and the actions of the individual himself; and such a mind can be constructed by anyone who understands the art of mind building, and who faithfully applies his art.

You may have a small mind today, and your ancestors for many generations back may have been insignificant in mental power; nevertheless, you may become even exceptional in mental capacity and brilliancy if you proceed to build your mind according to the principles of exact science; and those principles anyone can apply.

There are two obstacles, however, that must be removed before this building process can begin, and the first one of these is the current belief in heredity. That we inherit things is true, but the belief that we cannot become any larger or any better than our inheritance is not true. As long as man believes that greatness is not possible to him because there were no great minds among his ancestors, he is holding himself down, and cannot become any more than he subconsciously thinks he can; while on the other hand, the man who expects to become much because he had remarkable grandfathers is liable to be disappointed because he depends too much upon his illustrious forefathers and not enough upon himself.

When we live only with that love that centers attention upon a limited number of persons, one of the greatest actions of mind will work in a limited world. When our sympathies go only to a chosen few, the same thing occurs, and when our purpose in life has a personified goal, we keep the mind within the limitations of that personification.

To give universality to our feelings and actions may require considerable training of the mental tendencies, but it is absolutely necessary if we will develop a great mind.

It is only those mental forces that move towards the verge of the limitless in every direction that can cause the mind to transcend limitations; therefore, all the forces of the mind should be given this transcending tendency.

In the mental actions of love, we find many forces, all of which are true in their own places, but all of these forces must be exercised universally; that is, they must act upon a scale that is without bounds in the field of your own consciousness.

The idea is not only to love the tangible, but also that other something that transcends the tangible – that something that appears to the soul in visions, and predicts wonders yet to be. That such a love will expand and enlarge the mind anyone can understand, because practically all the elements of the mind will tend to follow the actions of the love nature, when that nature is exceptionally strong.

In the fields of motives, objects, aims and purposes, we find that nearly every mental action is occupying a limited scope, and is acting in such a manner that its own limitations are being perpetuated. This tendency, however, must be removed if a greater mind is to be constructed, because every action of the mind must aim to change itself into a larger action. To cause every aim or purpose to become universal in its action, the mind must transcend shape, form, space and distance in its consciousness of everything that it may undertake to do.

The power of mind to create a more brilliant mind increases as the mind places itself more and more in the consciousness of the absolute light of universal intelligence.

To cause the mind to become more brilliant, all the tendencies of mind should fix their attention upon the highest mental conception of mental brilliancy. Every expression of the mind should be animated with a refining tendency. Every force of the mind should rise towards the absoluteness of mental light.

From every word remove the sting. Speak kindly. To speak kindly and gently to everybody is the mark of a great soul. And it is your privilege to be a great soul. From the tone of your voice remove the whine. Speak with joy. Never complain. The more you complain, the smaller you become, and the fewer will be your friends and opportunities. Speak tenderly, speak sweetly, speak with love.

HOW CHARACTER DETERMINES CONSTRUCTIVE ACTION

Though the leadership of greater minds be necessary to the welfare of the race, it is also necessary for that leadership to be used, not for keeping the multitude in a state of simple-mindedness and dependence, but for promoting the intelligence of each individual until external guidance is needed no more. The true purpose of the strong is to promote greater strength in the weak, and not to keep the weak in that state where they are at the mercy of the strong.

A great many people go wrong because they do not know any better. To them, a better understanding of life is the path to emancipation. They will be made free when they know the truth, but the majority of those who go wrong do know better. Then why do they go wrong. The cause is lack of character. When you fail to do what you want to do, your character is weak. The same is true when you preach one thing and practice another. When you fail to be as perfect, as good or as ideal as you wish to be, or fail to accomplish what you think that you can accomplish, your character is at fault. It is the character that directs the action of the mind. It is the lack of character, or a weak character that produces misdirections; and when you fail to accomplish what you feel you can accomplish, something is being misdirected.

What you feel that you can do, that you have the power to do. Therefore, when you fail to do it, some of the powers of your being are being misdirected.

To be influenced to do what you would not do if you were normal, means that your character is weak, and to be affected by surroundings, events, circumstances and conditions against your will, indicates the same deficiency. A strong character is never influenced against his will. He is never disturbed by anything, never becomes upset, offended or depressed. No one can insult him because he is above small states of mind, and is stronger than those things that may tend to produce small states of mind.

If you are in the hands of worry, your character needs development. The same is true if you have a tendency to submit to fate, give in to adversity, give up in the midst of difficulties, or surrender to failure or wrong. It may be stated, without any exceptions or modifications whatever, that the more temper, the less character. Anger is always a misdirection of energy, but it is the function of character to properly direct all energies. Therefore, there can be no anger when the character is thoroughly developed.

A strong character will keep all the faculties and forces of life moving in the right direction, no matter what obstacles we may meet in the way. We shall turn neither to the right nor to the left, but will continue to move directly towards the goal we have in view, and will reach that goal without fail.

Thousands of people resolve every year to press on to higher attainments and greater achievements. They begin very well, but ere long they are turned off the track. They are misled or switched off by counter attractions. They have not the character to keep right on until they have accomplished what they originally set out to do. True, it is sometimes wisdom to change one's plans, but it is only lack of character to change one's plans without reason, simply because there is a change of circumstance. To change with every circumstance is to drift with the stream of circumstance, and he who drifts can only live the life of a log. He will be a victim of every external change that he may meet. He will control little or nothing, and he will accomplish little or nothing.

That person who complies with the mental laws but who violates the moral laws, wastes fully one-half of the energies of his mind, and sometimes more. His attainment and achievement will, therefore, be less than one-half of what they might be if he had moral character as well as mental character.

The same is true, however, of that person who complies with the moral laws, but who violates the mental laws; fully one-half of his energy is wasted and misdirected. This explains why the so-called good characters are not any more brilliant than the rest, for though they may be morally good, they are not always mentally good; that is, they do not use their minds according to the laws of mind, and therefore cannot rise above the level of the ordinary.

The true character tries to turn all the energies of the system into the best and most constructive channels, and it is the mark of a real character when all the various parts of the being of man are working together harmoniously for the building of greatness in mind and soul. When the character is weak, there is more or less conflict among the mental actions. Certain actions have a tendency to work for one thing, while other actions are tending to produce the very opposite. The same is true of the desires. A character that lacks development will desire one thing today and something else tomorrow. Plans will change constantly, and little or nothing will be accomplished. In the strong character, however, all actions work in harmony and all actions are constructive. And this is natural because it is the one supreme function of character to make all actions in the human system constructive – to make every force in the human life a building force.

Be good and kind to everybody and the world will be kind to you. There may be occasional exceptions to this rule, but when they come pass them by and they will not come again.

Ideals need the best of care. Weeds can grow without attention, but not so with the roses.

THE ART OF BUILDING CHARACTER

Character is developed by training all the forces and elements of life to act constructively in those spheres for which they were created, and to express themselves in those actions only that promote the original purpose of the being of man.

To develop character it is necessary to know what life is for, to know what actions promote the purpose of that life, and to know what actions retard that purpose. When the secret of right action is discovered, and every part of man is steadily trained in the expression of right action, character may be developed. But whatever is done, character must be applied in its fullest capacity. It is only through this full use, right use and constant use that anything may be perpetuated or developed.

Character develops through a constant effort to cause every action in the human system to be a right action; that is, a constructive action, or an action that promotes the purpose of that part of the system in which the action takes place. This is natural because since character is the power of right action, every effort to extend the scope of right action will increase the power of character. To have character is to have the power to promote what you know to be the purpose of life, and to be able to do the right when you know the right. To have character is to know the right, and to be so well established in the doing of the right that nothing in the world can turn you into the wrong. The first essential is therefore to know the right; to be able to select the right; to have that understanding that can instinctively choose the proper course of action, and that knows how each force and element of life is to be directed so that the original purpose of human life will be fulfilled.

The second essential is to create a subconscious desire for the right – a desire so deep and so strong that nothing can tempt the mind to enter into the wrong. When this desire is developed, one feels a natural preference for the right; to prefer the right under all circumstances becomes second nature, while every desire for the wrong will disappear completely. When every atom in one's being begins to desire the right, the entire system will establish itself in the right attitude, and right action will become the normal action in every force, function and faculty. In addition, this same desire will produce mental tendencies that contain the power of right action, which always means constructive action.

It is a well known fact that all the forces and energies of the system and all the movements of mind follow mental tendencies; therefore, when the mental tendencies are right actions, everything that takes place in the system will produce right action; and everything will be properly directed.

The desire for the right may be developed by constantly thinking about the right with deep feeling. Every thought that has depth, therefore, will impress itself upon the subconscious, and when that thought is inspired with a strong desire for the right, the conscious impression will convey the right to the subconscious. Every impression that enters the subconscious will cause the subconscious to bring forth a harvest of that which the impression conveyed; therefore, when the right is constantly held in mind with deep feeling, the right thought will soon become the strongest in the mind; and our desires are the results of our strongest thoughts.

You always desire that which is in your strongest thought. You can therefore change those desires completely by thinking with deep feeling about that which you want to desire. The two fundamental essentials, therefore, to the development of character are to know the right and to desire the right, but the term "right" as employed here must not be confounded with that conception of right which includes only a few of the moral laws.

To be right, according to the viewpoint of completeness, is to be in harmony with all the principles of life, and all the laws of the present sphere of human existence. To know the right, it is necessary not simply to memorize rules that other minds have formulated, but to inwardly discern what life is for, and what mode of thought and action is conducive to the realization of that which is in life. To desire the right, according to this view of the right, the mind must actually feel the very soul of right action, and must be in such perfect touch with the universal movement of right action, that all lesser and imperfect desires are completely swallowed up in the one desire.

It is the truth, that when we come into perfect touch with the greater, we cease to desire the lesser, and the closer we get to the one real desire, the less we care for our mistaken desires.

First ask yourself what you would have all the energies, powers, functions and faculties in your system do. Answer that question in the best manner possible, and upon that answer, base your picture of right action. Whenever a new line of action is undertaken, the mind should continue in that original line of action until the object in view has been reached. To do this in all things, even in trivial matters, will not only cause every action to produce the intended results, but real character will steadily be made stronger thereby.

The habit of giving up when the present task is half finished and then trying something else is one of the chief causes of failure. The development of a strong character, however, will remove this habit completely. To constantly think of the highest and the greatest results that could possibly follow the promotion of any undertaking or line of action will aid remarkably in causing the mind to keep on. To expect much from what we are doing now is to create a strong desire to press on towards the goal in view. To press on towards the goal in view is to reach the goal, and to reach the goal is to get what we expected.

An essential part of great importance in the building of character is the proper conception of the ideal. No mind can rise higher than its ideals, but every mind can realize its ideals no matter how high they may be. Our ideals therefore cannot be too high. The ideal should not only be a little better than the present real, but should be perfection itself. Have nothing but absolute perfection in all things as the standard and the goal, and never think of your goal as anything less. Do not simply aim to improve yourself in just one more degree. Aim to reach absolute perfection in all your attainments and all your achievements, and make that desire so strong that every atom in your being thrills with its power.

To form all one's ideals in accordance with one's mental conception of absolute perfection, will cause the mind to live above the world of the ordinary, and this is extremely important in the building of character. A great character cannot be developed so long as the mind continues to dwell on the ordinary, the trivial or the superficial. Neither can true quality and true worth find expression so long as thought continues on the common plane; and the life that does not continue to grow into higher quality and greater worth has not begun to live.

High mental color will be given to every characteristic, and the nature of man will cease to be simply human. It will actually be more.

Examine the tendencies of your mind and character, and fix clearly in consciousness which ones you wish to remove and which ones you wish to retain. Those that you wish to retain should be made strong by daily directing the subconscious to give those tendencies more life, more power and more stability.

Build up those qualities that constitute real character, and every bad trait that you have inherited from your ancestors will disappear.

To build up those qualities, picture in your mind the highest conceptions of those qualities that you can possibly form; then impress those conceptions and ideas upon the subconscious. Such impressions should be formed daily, and especially before going to sleep, as the building process in the subconscious is more perfect during sleep.

By impressing the idea of spotless virtue upon the subconscious every day for a few months, your moral tendencies will become so strong that nothing can tempt you to do what you know to be wrong. Not that physical desire will disappear; we do not want any natural desire to disappear, but your control of those desires will be so complete that you can follow them or refuse to follow them just as you choose. And your desire to remain absolutely free from all wrong will become so strong that nothing can induce you to do what your finer nature does not wish to have done.

There are millions of people who are morally weak in spite of the fact that they do not wish to be, but if these people would employ this simple method, their weakness would soon disappear, because by impressing the idea of spotless virtue upon the subconscious, the subconscious will produce and express in the personality the power of virtue; and if this process is continued for some time, the power of virtue in the person will become so strong that it can overcome and annihilate instantly every temptation that may appear.

Hold yourself constantly in a positive, masterful attitude, and fill that attitude with kindness. The result will be that remarkable something that people call personal magnetism.

There is enough power in any man to enable him to realize all his desires and reach the highest good he has in view. It is only necessary that all of his power be constructively applied.

THE CREATIVE FORCES IN MAN

If you would turn your mind upon some desire that was directly opposite to the desire that feeds your habit, and if you would give over your whole attention to that opposite desire, you would soon draw all the energy away from that desire which perpetuates the habit. The habit in question therefore would soon die of starvation. In the same way, people who are inclined to be materialistic could overcome that tendency entirely by concentrating attention constantly and thoroughly upon the idealistic side of life.

In learning to apply the law of transmutation, our first purpose should be to employ all surplus energy either in promoting our work or in developing faculties and talents. This process alone would practically double the working capacity of any mind, and would steadily increase ability and talent; and also to turn energy to good account that cannot be used in its own channel now.

To illustrate, suppose you have a desire for a certain physical or mental action, and you know that it would not be possible to carry out that desire at the time. Instead of permitting the energy that is active in that desire to go to waste, you would turn that energy into some other channel where it could be used to advantage now. Our second purpose should be to direct all surplus energy into the brain and the mind in case we had more energy in our body than we could use, or that was required for physical functioning, and thereby become stronger and more efficient in all mental activities. Our third purpose should be to transmute all reproductive energy into talent and genius when there was no need of that energy in its own particular sphere. And in this connection, it is well to mention the fact that a man who is morally clean, other things being equal, has in every instance, greater agility, greater capacity and greater endurance by far than the man who is not. While the latter is wasting his creative energies in useless pleasures, as well as in disease producing habits, the former is turning all of his creative energy into ability and genius, and the result is evident.

In carrying out these three purposes we can prevent all waste of mental and personal power. We can control our desires completely; we can eliminate impurity, and we can turn life and power into channels that will invariably result in greater mental power and brilliancy, if not marked ability and rare genius.

To experiment, turn your whole attention upon your mind for a few minutes, and desire gently to draw all your surplus energy into the field of mental action. Then permit yourself to think along those lines where the mind is inclined to be most active. In a few moments you will discover the coming of new ideas; and in many instances, you will for several hours receive ideas that are brighter and more valuable than what you have received for some time. Repeat the process later, and again and again for many days in succession, and it will be strange indeed, if you do not finally secure a group of ideas that will be worth a great deal in your special line of thought or work. Whenever you feel a great deal of energy in your system, and try to direct it into the mind, you will have the same result. Ideas will come quickly and rapidly, and among them all you will surely find a few that have exceptional merit.

In learning the art of transmutation, the first essential is to train your mind to think that all surplus energy is being turned into the channel you have decided upon; that is, if you are a businessman, you naturally will want all your surplus energy to accumulate in your business faculties. To secure this result, think constantly of your surplus energy as flowing into those faculties. This mode of thinking will soon give your energies the habit of doing what you desire to have done. It is a well-known law, that if we continue to think deeply and persistently along a certain line, Nature will gradually take up that thought and carry it out. Another law of importance in this connection is that if we concentrate attention upon a certain faculty or upon a certain part of the system, we create a tendency among our energies to flow towards that faculty or part. We understand therefore the value of constantly bearing in mind the idea that we wish to realize.

What we constantly impress upon the mind through our thoughts and desires finally becomes a subconscious habit, and when any line of action becomes a subconscious habit, it acts automatically; that is, it works of itself.

Before taking up this practice, however, it is necessary to determine positively what you actually desire your surplus energy to do. You must know what you want. Then continue to want what you want with all the power of desire that you can arouse. Most minds fail in this respect. They do not know with a certainty what they wish to accomplish or perfect. Their energies therefore are drawn into one channel today and another tomorrow, and nothing is finished. If you are an inventor, train your mind to think that all your surplus energy is constantly flowing into your faculties of invention. If you are a writer, train your mind to think that all your surplus energy is flowing into your literary talents; or whatever it is that you may be doing or want to do, direct your energy accordingly. You will soon find that you will increase in power, ability and capacity along the lines of your choice, and if you continue this process all through life, your ability will continue to increase, no matter how long you may live.

The second essential is to desire deeply and persistently that all your surplus energy shall flow into those functions or faculties that you have selected for greater work. Wherever your desire is directed, there the force of your system will also tend to go, and herein we find another reason why persistent desire has such extreme value. The use of desire in this connection, however, must always be deep and calm, and never excited or overwrought.

The third essential is to place your mind in what may be termed the psychological field, and while acting in that field, to concentrate upon that part or faculty where you want your surplus energy to accumulate. This essential or process constitutes the real art of transmutation, though it is by no means the easiest to acquire.

To master this method a great deal of practice will be required, but whenever you can place your mind in the psychological field and concentrate subjectively upon any part of your system where you want surplus energy to accumulate, all your surplus energy positively will accumulate in that part within a few moments time. Through the same process, you can annihilate any desire instantaneously, and change all the energy of that desire into some other force. You can also, in the same way, reach your latent or dormant energies, and draw all of those energies into any channel where a high order of activity is desired; in fact, through this method, you can practically take full possession of all the power, active or latent, in your system, and use it in any way that you may wish. That you should, after you learn to apply this method successfully, become highly efficient in your work, is therefore evident, though this is not all. Extraordinary capacity, mental brilliancy and genius can positively be developed through the constant use of this method, provided, however, that nothing is done, either in thought, life or conduct, to interfere with the underlying law of the process. To place your mind in the psychological field, try to turn your conscious actions into what may be termed the finer depths of the personality; that is, try to become conscious of your deeper life; try to feel the undercurrents of mind and thought and consciousness, and try to act in perfect mental contact with those deep, underlying forces of personality and mentality that lie at the foundation of your conscious activity. An illustration in this connection will be found valuable. When you listen to music that seems to touch your soul, so that you can feel the vibrations of its harmony thrill every atom of your being, you are in the psychological field. You are alive in another and a finer mental world, a mental world that permeates your entire personal existence. You are also in the psychological field when you are stirred by some emotion to the very depth of your innermost life. A deepening of thought, feeling, life and desire will take the mind, more or less, into the psychological field; and whenever the mind begins to act in that field, you should concentrate your attention upon that faculty or part of your system where you wish extra energy to accumulate.

Make your concentration alive, so to speak, with interest, and make every action of that concentration as deep as possible, and all your surplus energy will positively flow towards the point of concentration.

THE BUILDING POWER OF CONSTRUCTIVE SPEECH

Every word that is spoken exercises a power in personal life, and that power will work either for or against the person, depending upon the nature of the word. You can talk yourself into trouble and poverty or you can talk yourself into harmony and prosperity. In brief, you can talk yourself into almost any condition, desirable or undesirable.

That person who retains poise and self-control in the midst of trouble, will pass through it all without being seriously affected; and when it is over, is much wiser and stronger for the experience.

When you feel that better days are coming, and express that feeling in your speech, you turn all the power of your being towards the ideal of better days, and those powers will begin to create the better in your life.

Whether the inner life force of a word will be constructive or destructive depends upon several factors, the most important of which are the tone, the motive and the idea. The tone of every word should be harmonious, wholesome, pleasing, and should convey a deep and serene expression.

The words that wound others do far more injury to the person who gives them expression. Words of constructive power are always deeply felt. They are never loud or confusing, but always quiet and serene, filled with the very spirit of conviction.

To talk for the mere sake of talking is to throw precious energy away, and no human chatterbox will ever acquire greatness.

The motive back of every word should be constructive, and the life expressed in every word should convey the larger, the better and the superior. Such words have building power, and are additions to life of extreme value. Every word should express, as far as possible, the absolute truth, and should never convey ideas that are simply indicated by appearances.

The man who constantly thinks he is easily disturbed, disturbs himself. When we are in harmony with everything including ourselves and refuse to be otherwise, nothing will ever disturb us.

There is but one strength in the universe – the strength of the Supreme – and that strength can never fail. You may have as much of that strength as you desire. All that is necessary for you to do is to live in perfect touch with the Supreme, and never think, do or say anything that will interfere with that sublime oneness. The strength of the Supreme is just as able to fill your system with life and power now as it was at any time in the past. Therefore, there is no real reason whatever why your powers should diminish. Be true to the truth and your power will perpetually increase.

The belief that there are no opportunities for you is caused by the fact that you have hidden yourself in a cave of inferiority. Go out into the life of worth, ability and competence, and you will find more opportunities than you can use. The world is ever in search of competent minds, and modern knowledge has made it possible for man to develop his ability. No one therefore has any legitimate reason for speaking of hard luck or hard times unless he prefers to live in want.

No day would be hard if we met all things with the conviction that we are equal to every occasion. Live properly, think properly, work properly and talk properly, and trouble and ill-luck will not trouble you seriously anymore.

When wrong things come, set them right and look upon the experience as an opportunity for you to develop greater mastership.

Remember, you are mentally living with everything that you talk about, and there is nothing that affects us more than that which we take into our mental life.

The greatest essential is to make all speech constructive. Search for the real truth that is at the foundation of all life, and then give expression to such words as convey the full significance to that truth. The results, to say the least, will be extraordinary.

In daily conversation, the law of constructive speech should be most conscientiously applied. What we say to others will determine to a considerable degree what they are to think, and what tendencies their mental actions are to follow; and since man is the product of his thought, conversation becomes a most important factor in man.

We steadily grow into the likeness of that which we think of the most, and what we are to think about depends largely upon the mode, the nature and the subject matter of our conversation.

All conversation should be so formed that it may tend to move the mind towards the higher domains of thought, and should make everybody more keenly conscious of the greater possibilities that exist within them. Conversation has exceptional value in the training of young minds, and in many instances may completely change the destinies of these minds. To properly train a child, his attention should be directed as much as possible upon those qualities that have worth and that are desired in his development; and the way he is spoken to will largely determine where he is to give the greater part of his attention. To scold a child is to remind him of his faults. Every time he is reminded of his faults he gives more attention, more thought, and more strength to those faults. His good qualities are thereby made weaker while his bad qualities are made worse.

Our conversation must be in perfect accord with our ambitions, our desires, and our ideals, and all our expressions must aim to promote the real purpose we have in view.

Our conversation should deal with the strong points of character and the greater possibilities of mind. We should so frame our conversation that we tend to make everybody feel there is something in them. Our conversation should have an optimistic tendency and an ascending tone. It should deal with those things in life that are worthwhile, and it should always give the ideal the greatest prominence.

IMAGINATION AND THE MASTER MIND

Hang up pictures in your mind that will inspire you to do your best; hang up pictures in your mind that will cause you to think constantly of that which you desire to accomplish, and this you may do by imagining yourself being that greater something that you want to be and doing that greater something that you want to do.

An excellent practice is to use your spare moments in creating such pictures in your imagination and placing them in the most conspicuous position of your mind, so that all your faculties and powers can see them at all times. We are always imagining something. It is practically impossible to be awake without imagining something. Then why not imagine something at all times that will inspire the powers within us to do greater and greater things?

To aid the imagination in picturing the greater, the higher and better, we should "hitch our wagon to a star." The star may be something quite out of reach as far as present circumstances indicate, but if we hitch our wagon to something in such a lofty position, our mind will begin to take wings. It will no longer be like a worm crawling in the dust. We shall begin to rise and continue to rise.

First, make up your mind as to what you really want in every respect. Determine what surroundings or environment you want. Decide upon the kind of friends you want and what kind of work you would prefer. Make all those ideals so good and so perfect that you will have no occasion to change them. Then fix those ideals so clearly in mind that you can see them at all times, and proceed to desire their realization with all the power of mind and soul. Make that your first step.

Your second step should be to imagine yourself living in those surroundings that you have selected as your ideal; then make it a point to live in that imagination every moment of every day. Instead of imagining a number of useless things during spare moments, as people usually do; imagine yourself living in those surroundings and those ideals. Imagine yourself in the presence of friends that are exactly what you wish your ideal friends to be, and permit your fancy to run as far as it may wish along all of those idealistic lines. If you have not found your work, proceed to imagine yourself doing what you wish to do. If you have already found your work, imagine yourself doing that work as well as you would wish, and imagine the coming of results as large as your greatest desires could expect. Devote every moment of your spare time to the placing of those ideals before your attention, and you will give your power and forces something strong and definite to work for.

Your third step should be to proceed to apply the power of desire, the power of will, the power of scientific thought, and in brief, all your powers, in trying to realize those beautiful ideals that you continue to imagine as your own. First make your prediction. Then go to work and make it come true. What you imagine concerning your greater future is your prediction, and you can cause that prediction to come true if you apply all the power in your possession in working for its realization every day.

The constructive use of imagination therefore will enable you to place a definite model or pattern before the forces of your system, so that those forces may have something better and greater to work for. In brief, instead of permitting most of your energies to go to waste and the remainder to follow any pattern or idea that may be suggested by your environment, or your own helter-skelter thinking, you will cause all your energy to work for the greatest and the best that you may desire.

This is the first use of imagination, and it easily places this remarkable faculty among the greatest in the human mind. Another use of the imagination is found in its power to give the mind something definite to think about at all times, so that the mind may be trained to always think of that which you really want to think; that is, through this use of the imagination, you can select your own thought and think your own thought at all times; and he who can do this is gradually becoming a master mind.

The mind that does not master itself forms its thoughts and desires after the likeness of the impressions received through the senses, and is therefore controlled by those conditions from which such impressions come; because as we think, so we act and live. The average mind usually desires what the world desires without any definite thought as to his own highest welfare or greatest need, the reason being that a strong tendency to do likewise is always produced in the mind when the desires are formed in the likeness of such impressions as are suggested by external conditions. It is therefore evident that the person who permits himself to be affected by suggestions will invariably form artificial desires; and to follow such desires is to be misled.

The master mind desires only that which is conducive to real life and in the selection of its desires is never influenced in the least by the desires of the world. Desire is one of the greatest powers in human life.

The master mind is never misplaced because he does not live to do what others are doing, but what he himself wants to do now. He wants to do only that which is conducive to real life, a life worthwhile, a life that steadily works up to the very highest goal in view.

Every object that is seen will produce an impression upon the mind according to the degree of susceptibility. This impression will contain the nature of the object of which it is a representation. The nature of this object will be reproduced in the mind, and what has entered the mind will be expressed more or less throughout the entire system. Therefore, the mind that is susceptible to suggestions will reproduce in his own mind and system conditions that are similar in nature to almost everything that he may see, hear or feel. He will consequently be a reflection of the world in which he lives. He will think, speak and act as that world may suggest; he will float with the stream of that world wherever that stream may flow; he will not be an original character, but an automaton.

Every person that permits himself to be affected by suggestion is more or less an automaton, and is more or less in the hands of fate.

The principal reason why the average person does not realize his ideals is because he has not learned to think what he wants to think. He is too much affected by the suggestions that are about him. He imitates the world too much, following desires that are not his own. He is therefore misled and misplaced. Whenever you permit yourself to think what persons, things, conditions or circumstances may suggest, you are not following what you yourself want to think. You are not following your own desires but borrowed desires. You will therefore drift into strange thinking, and thinking that is entirely different from what you originally planned. To obey the call of every suggestion and permit your mind to be carried away by this, that or the other will develop the tendency to drift until your mind will wander.

Concentration will almost be absent and you will become wholly incapable of actually thinking what you want to think. One line of constructive thinking will scarcely be begun when another line will be suggested, and you will leave the unfinished task to begin something else, which in turn will be left incomplete. Nothing, therefore, will be accomplished.

THE HIGHER FORCES IN MAN

Every mental process, or every mental action, that takes place in our wide-awake consciousness will, if it has depth of feeling or intensity, enter the unconscious field, and after it has developed itself according to the line of its original nature, will return to the conscious side of the mind. Here we find the secret of character building, and also the secret of building faculties and talents. Everything that is done in the conscious field to improve the mind, character, conduct or thought will, if it has sincerity and depth of feeling, enter the unconscious field; and later will come back with fully developed qualities, which when in expression, constitutes character. Many a man, however, after trying for some time to improve himself and seeing no results, becomes discouraged. He forgets that some time always intervenes between the period of sowing and the period of reaping. What he does in the conscious field to improve himself, constitutes the sowing, when those actions enter the conscious field to be developed; and when they come back, it may be weeks or months later, the reaping time has arrived. Many a time, after an individual has given up self-improvement, he discovers, after a considerable period, that good qualities are beginning to come to the surface in his nature, thereby proving conclusively that what he did months ago along that line was not in vain. The results of past efforts are beginning to appear. We have all had similar experiences, and if we would carefully analyze such experiences, we would find that not a single conscious process that is sufficiently deep or intense to become an unconscious process will fail to come back finally with its natural results.

Many a time ideas come into our minds that we wanted weeks ago, and could not get them at that time; but we did place in action certain deep, strong desires for those ideas at that particular time, and though our minds were not prepared to develop those ideas at once, they finally were developed and came to the surface.

The fact that this process never fails indicates the value of giving the mind something to work out for future need. If we have something that we want to do months ahead, we should give the mind definite instruction now and make those instructions so deep that they will become unconscious processes. Those unconscious processes will, according to directions, work out the ideas and plans that we want for that future work, and in the course of time, will bring results to the surface.

Try to feel what you want done either in the conscious or the unconscious mental fields, and you will place in action forces that correspond to what you want done. Those forces will enter the unconscious mental world and produce processes through which the desired results will be created.

Whenever you want to redirect any force that is highly refined, you must feel the way you want that force to act. To illustrate, we will suppose you have certain emotions in your mental world that are not agreeable. To give the energies of those emotions a new and more desirable force of action, change your emotions by giving your whole attention in trying to feel such emotions as you may desire. And here let us remember that every emotion that comes up in the system is teeming with energy; but as most emotions continue to act without any definite control, we realize how much energy is wasted through uncurbed emotions. We know from experience, that whenever we give way to our feelings, we become weak. The reason is that every uncontrolled feeling wastes energy.

Here is a good practice. Whenever you feel the way you do not wish to feel, begin to think deeply and in the most interesting manner possible, of those things that you wish to accomplish. If you can throw your whole soul, so to speak, into those new directions, you will soon find your undesired feelings disappearing completely. Every individual should train himself to feel the way he wants to feel, and this is possible if he will always direct his attention to something desirable whenever undesired feelings come up. Through this practice he will soon get such full control over his feelings that he can always feel the way he wants to feel, no matter what the circumstances may be.

In building character we find the results to be accumulative; that is, we make an effort to improve our life or conduct, and thereby produce an unconscious process, which will later on, give us more strength of character to be and live the way we wish to be and live. This in turn will enable us to produce more and stronger unconscious processes along the line of character building, which will finally return with a greater number of good qualities. The result of this action will be to give us more power to build for a still greater character, and so this process may be continued indefinitely.

The same is true with regard to building the mind. The more you build the mind, the greater becomes your mental power to build a still greater mind; but in each case, it is the unconscious process that must be produced in order that the greater character or greater mind may be developed from within. In this connection, it is well to remember that the principal reason why so many people fail to improve along any line is because their desires or efforts for improvement are not sufficiently deep and strong to become unconscious processes. To illustrate, it is like placing seed on stony ground. If the seed is not placed in good, deep soil it will not grow. You may desire self-improvement for days, but if those desires are weak or superficial, they will not enter the unconscious field; and any action, however good it may be, if it fails to enter the unconscious field, will also fail to produce results along the line of self-improvement.

What may be called the higher forces in man act invariably through our most sublime states of consciousness, and as it is these higher forces that enable man to become or accomplish more than the average, it is highly important that we attain the power to enter sublime consciousness at frequent intervals. No man or woman of any worth was ever known who did not have experience in these sublime states; in fact, it is impossible to rise above the ordinary in life or achievement without drawing, more or less, upon the higher realms of consciousness. People are sometimes criticized for not being on the earth all the time, but it is necessary to get above the earth occasionally in order to find something worthwhile to live for and work for while upon earth.

If we would rise in the scale in the fullest and best sense of the term, we must pay close attention to those higher forces and make it a practice to enter frequently into close touch with higher states of consciousness; in fact, we simply must do it, because if we do not, we will continue to move along a very ordinary level.

Among the many important forces coming directly through emotion or feeling, one of the most valuable is that of enthusiasm. In the average mind, enthusiasm runs wild, but we have found that when this force is properly directed it becomes a great constructive power. When you are enthusiastic about something, it is always about something new or something better – something that holds possibilities that you did not realize before. Your enthusiasm, if properly directed, will naturally cause your mind to move towards those possibilities, and enthusiasm is readily directed when you concentrate attention exclusively upon that something new that inspires enthusiasm. By turning your attention upon the thing that produces enthusiasm, the mind will move forward toward those greater possibilities that are discerned. This forward movement of the mind will tend to renew and enlarge the mind so that it will gain a still greater conception of those possibilities. This will increase your enthusiasm, which will in turn impel your mind to move forward still further in the same direction.

Thus a still larger conception of those possibilities will be secured, which in turn will increase your enthusiasm and the power of your mind to take a third step in advance. We thus realize that if enthusiasm is directed upon the possibilities that originally inspired that enthusiasm, we will not only continue to be enthused, but we will in that very manner, cause the mind to move forward steadily and develop steadily, so that in time it will gain sufficient power to actually work out those possibilities upon which attention has been directed. In this connection, we must also remember that we can grow and advance only as we pass into the new. It is new life, new thought, new states of consciousness that are demanded if we are to take any steps at all in advance, and as enthusiasm tends directly to inspire the mind to move towards the new, we see how important it is to continue, not only to live in the spirit of enthusiasm, but to direct that spirit upon the goal in view. It is invariably the enthusiastic mind that moves forward, that does things, and that secures results.

Two other forces of great value, belonging to this group, are appreciation and gratitude. Whenever you appreciate a certain thing you become conscious of its real quality, and whenever you become conscious of the quality of anything, you begin to develop that quality in yourself. When we appreciate the worth of a person, we tend to impress the idea of that worth in our own minds, and thereby cause the same effect to be produced, in a measure, in ourselves. The same is true if we appreciate our own worth, in a sensible and constructive manner.

When we appreciate the beautiful in anything, we awaken our minds to a higher and better understanding of the beautiful. Our minds thus become, in a measure, more beautiful. The same is true with regard to any quality. Whatever we appreciate, we tend to develop in ourselves, and here we find a remarkable aid to the power of concentration, because we always concentrate attention perfectly, naturally and thoroughly upon those things that we fully appreciate. Thus we understand why it is that we tend to develop in ourselves the things that we admire in others.

Whenever you feel grateful for anything, you always feel nearer to the real quality of that particular thing. A person who is ungrateful, however, always feels that there is a wall between himself and the good things in life. Usually there is such a wall, though he has produced it himself through his ingratitude.

We all may meet disappointment at some time and not get exactly what we wanted, but we shall find that the more grateful we are, the less numerous will those disappointments become.

The most important side of this law, however, is found in the fact that the more grateful you are for everything good that comes into your life, the more closely you place your mind in contact with that power in life that can produce good.

Another among the finer forces is that of aspiration. No person should fail to aspire constantly and aspire to the very highest that he can possibly awaken in his life. Aspiration always tends to elevate the mind and tends to lift the mind into larger and greater fields of action. And when the mind finds itself in this larger field of action, it will naturally gain power to do greater things. We all realize that so long as we live down in the lower story, we cannot accomplish very much; it is when we lift our minds to the higher stories of the human structure that we begin to gain possession of ideas and powers through which greater things may be achieved.

The same is true of ambition. Ambition not only tends to draw the mind up into higher and larger fields, but also tends to build up those faculties through which we are to work. If you are tremendously ambitious to do a certain thing, the force of that ambition will tend to increase the power and ability of that faculty through which your ambition may be realized.

The force of an ideal is another among the finer forces that should receive constant and thorough attention. When you have an ideal and live for it every second of your existence, you place yourself in the hands of a drawing power that is immense, and that power will tend to draw out into action every force, power and faculty that you may possess, especially those forces and qualities that will have to be developed in order that you may realize that ideal.

Have an ideal, and the highest that you can picture. Then worship it every hour with your whole soul. Never come down, and do not neglect it for a moment. We all know very well that it is the people who actually worship their high ideals with mind and heart and soul that finally realize those ideals. It is such people who reach the high places and the reason why is easily explained. Give your attention, or rather, your whole life to some lofty ideal, and you will tend to draw into action all the finer and higher forces of your system – those forces that can create greater ability, greater talent, greater genius – those forces that can increase your capacity, bring into action all your finer elements and give you superior power and superior worth in every sense of the term – those forces which, when aroused, cannot positively fail to do the work you wish to have done.

A fact well known in this connection is that when the mind is turned persistently upon a certain ideal, every power that is in you begins to flow in that direction, and this is the very thing you want. When we can get all that is in us to work for our ideals and to work towards our ideals, then we shall positively reach whatever goal we have in view.

The power of love, if genuine, constant and strong, tends to improve everything in human life; and as this power is one of the higher forces in human nature, we readily understand the reason why. We can therefore without further comment, draw our own conclusions as to how we will use this power in the future.

The last of these finer forces that we shall mention, and possibly the strongest, is that of faith; but we must remember if we wish to use this force, that faith does not constitute a belief or any system of beliefs; it is a mental action – an action that goes into the very spirit of those things which we may think of or apply at the time we exercise faith. When you have faith in yourself you place in action a force that goes into the very depth of your being and tends to arouse all the greater powers and finer elements that you may possess. The same is true when you have faith in a certain faculty or in a certain line of action. The power of faith goes into the spirit of things and makes alive, so to speak, the all that is in you. The power of faith also produces perfect concentration. Whenever you have faith along a certain line, you concentrate perfectly along that line, and you cause all the power that is in your mind or system to work for the one thing you are trying to do. It has been discovered that the amount of energy latent in the human system is nothing less than enormous, and as faith tends to arouse all this energy, we realize how important and how powerful is faith.

When a man has tremendous faith in himself, he becomes a live wire, so to speak. It is such a man that becomes a real and vital power wherever he may live or go.

THE GREATEST POWER IN MAN

The principal reason why the average person remains weak and incompetent is found in the fact that he makes no effort to fathom and understand the depths of his real being. He may try to use what is in action on the surface, but he is almost entirely unconscious of the fact that enormous powers are in existence in the greater depths of his life. These powers are dormant simply because they have not been called into action, and they will continue to lie dormant until man develops his greatest power – the power to discern what really exists within him.

The fundamental cause of failure is found in the belief that what exists on the surface, is all there is of man, and the reason why greatness is a rare exception instead of a universal rule can be traced to the same cause. When the mind discovers that its powers are inexhaustible and that its faculties and talents can be developed to any degree imaginable, the fear of failure will entirely disappear. In its stead will come the conviction that man may attain anything or achieve anything. Whatever circumstances may be today, such a mind will know that all can be changed, that the limitations of the person can be made to pass away, and that the greater desires of the heart can be realized.

The idea that there is more of man than what appears on the surface should be so constantly and so deeply impressed upon the mind that it becomes a positive conviction, and no thoughts should be placed in action unless it is based upon this conviction.

When the average individual fails, he either blames circumstances or comes to the conclusion that he was not equal to the occasion. He therefore easily gives up and tries to be content with the lesser. But if he knew that there was more in him than what he had applied in his undertaking he would not give up.

It is therefore evident that when man gives attention to his greater power – the power to discern the more that is in him – he will never give up until he does succeed.

It is the truth that man is a marvelous being – nothing less than marvelous; and the greatest power in man is the power to discern the marvelousness that really does exist within him.

In practical life this mode of thinking will have the same effect upon the personal mind as that which is secured in a wire that is not charged when it touches a wire that is charged.

The great within is a live wire; when the mind touches the great within, it becomes charged more and more with those same immense powers; and the mind will constantly be in touch with the great within when it lives, thinks and works in the firm conviction that "there is more of me," – so much more that it cannot be measured.

We can receive from this deeper life only that which we constantly recognize and constantly realize, because consciousness is the door between the outer life and the great within, and we open the door to those things only of which we become conscious.

It is the law that we steadily develop and bring forth whatever we think of the most. It is therefore profitable to think constantly of our deeper nature and to try to fathom the limitlessness and the inexhaustibleness of these great and marvelous depths.

The average person lives on the surface. He thinks that the surface is all there is of him, and consequently does not place himself in touch with the live wire of his interior and inexhaustible nature.

This being true, we can readily understand why mortals are weak – they are weak simply because they have chosen weakness; but when they begin to choose power and greatness, they will positively become what they have chosen to become.

It is wrong, both to the individual and to the race, for anyone to remain in the lesser when it is possible to attain the greater. It is right that we all should ascend to the higher, the greater and the better now. And we all can.

VIII

JULIA SETON

The following quotes are from
The Science of Success, 1914

First Success Method

KNOW THYSELF

You can ask a thousand people what they call success and they will give you a thousand different answers. One calls money success and the ways and methods which will unite him with money, the power to manipulate these laws and to select and retain all the material which produces a continued expression of opulence, he does not seek to select or unite with anything else in the self because this is the lesson his soul has come to include.

There are many who call human love success, and they keep their human senses drugged with the narcotic of this race belief: they count themselves successful and go on each day rejoicing in their idol, and in just the degree that they demonstrate human love they feel they have made a success of their lives. When they fail in this and have to walk the pathway of life alone, uncompanioned, save by the crowd, they send forth a cry of sorrow and of failure, and do not understand that to be *alone* and not *lonely* is a part of the law of The One. There are others who hold success to be such material and methods as will link them in a great law of service to the race, they count the opportunity to give of their time and supply to others as the greatest success possible for them, and in the degree that they can select place and opportunity to serve the world they feel they are successful, but if they have to stand idle while every pulse is throbbing to serve, they send out the cry of failure and feel like a cast off atom and they join the mighty army of complaint that they are wasting their time, they never realize one of the highest laws is "he also serves who only stands and waits."

The new thought answer to "What is success" is: Success is the power in the individual to get the thing he *wants*, when he *wants* it, in the way he *wants* it, to keep it as long as he *wants* it and when he has included it, let go of it, and pass on to the fulfillment of a new desire.

There are those who have the power to get the thing they want and after they have quite outgrown the desire and included all that it can bring them, they are obliged to go on day after day, clinging to the dead body of their old desire. This is not success – this is failure; it takes its part indirectly in the fashioning of success, for on every step of their pathway they are learning in this way, the higher mastery and control that is necessary for them to know, and every ounce of power generated on this plane of failure, takes its place in the constructive work of the next step.

The power to get what we want when we want it, to keep it as long as we want it and then pass it up constructively, and go on to another want, is not won by a moment's contact with people, conditions or things, but it comes as the result of slow self mastery and comradeship with all forms of human experience.

Success is not a mysterious, metaphysical thing that waits around and then rushes unannounced into a life, but it is a sane, sensible entity, born from the consciousness of high power.

Success is the product of success methods and recognition of universal laws and it comes and abides with an individual in just that hour when he compels it.

There is no such thing as good or bad luck. The individual creates these conditions within his own consciousness and develops them into form by his thoughts and actions.

There are thousands of well defined success methods and the one who possesses the greatest number of these methods and uses them will be the greatest success.

The first success method includes all success but only a few people are clever enough to manifest this success method without further interpretation.

This first success method is: "Know Thyself." The one who knows himself and all that the self means, is straight in the middle of the divine channel of life, and he can steer his bark from end to end of the channel without fear of shipwreck, but among the great failure multitude there is only one in a thousand who has any idea of this law.

New Thought divides humanity into four planes of expression, namely, Body, Mind Soul and Spirit. We function through the body in *instinct*, through the mind in *reason*, through the soul in *emotion*, and the Spirit in *intuition*.

Men as we know them have one or two and sometimes all of these planes in expression and they have success or failure in just the degree that they know themselves and contact consciousness from their own plane of power.

A plane of consciousness is only a state of being in which man lives, and through which he has his own individual law of transference; and a complete understanding of these planes of consciousness and their laws, makes man master of himself and of life in all its forms. It has taken generations of thinking to at last evolve this truth that every life is named, numbered, chorded and placed in its own natural law of attraction, and when it works in unison with this law it has success, when it works in opposition it has failure.

When one has found himself and his natural contact, he is straight in the middle of the Divine channel of success and rowing with the full force of the tide in his favor; but where he does not know himself, he is rowing against the tide or drifting idly and at every moment he is dashed against the rocks of error in his channel.

The reason so many are seeking success, fame, money, love and recognition and not finding it, is because they have never learned the first necessary lesson of *knowing themselves*. First, they do not know what they want to do, and secondly, they do not know how to do what they want to do. They go on in aimless drifting and come at last to be some of the driftwood of life which is washed up onto the shore as the stream of success and failure flows on.

There is work and pay for all, success for all, in just the hour we know ourselves and connect with it. When one wants to be a farmer he goes among farmers; musician, among musicians; commercial, he hunts the marts of trade, and so on; and if he has in himself a fully fledged consciousness of his own indwelling power, nothing can keep him from dragging out from the Universal Supply Company the things which belong to his own life.

The first true law for success is; know to what part of the mighty system of the universe you belong, and then strike boldly out in that current of life. If you find that you respond to all that, physically, mentally, emotionally and intuitionally, you are vibrant with life, then choose the things which you like best.

The creative life can do more than one thing at a time and do them all well. Just keep inside your own power of concentration; the creative life does not think in time, it thinks in eternities; it does not think in states, it thinks in continents; it does not think in dollars, it thinks in millions, and as long as it holds its mental mastery all things fall before its power.

If you are only developed in one direction and in one plane of consciousness, then plunge your desire in that direction; get the work that fills your whole heart and stick to it, and put into operation every day all the fundamentals of New Thought, and if you do this, you will not be a failure, for you can think yourself straight into the very center of supply, and whatever you command to become your own will come and manifest for you.

With the knowledge of what you really can do, of just where you belong in the divine plan, and a consciousness of your latent energy and ability, you are straight in the middle of the road of success and it will never turn you one single step out of the way of peace, power and plenty.

Second Success Method

HAVE A PLAN

Often after one has found himself, and adjusted himself harmoniously in his own plane of expression, he finds that he is still not manifesting sufficiently the degree of success that he desires, and strive as he will, he cannot discover where he is going off the center of the law.

Sometimes it takes a deep perception to find that he is breaking the next essential and usually breaking it because he does not know that it is the next important thing in the Science of Success.

This next all important essential is Order.

"Have a plan," this is the second fundamental of success, for without a plan the human side of life must be always out of order and man himself adrift like a rudderless boat.

The whole failure world has this law of the lack of order somewhere in operation. There are thousands of planless, aimless, purposeless people everywhere. You can ask them "What do you want?" and they tell you that they have a profound idea of what they want to do and believe in their power to accomplish; but when you say "Well how, do you propose to do this?" they answer, "That's just it, I don't know," and often one finds them, after they have aimlessly drifted from pillar to post, and asks then "How did this happen?" "Why didn't you do differently?" they answer again in the same hopeless strain, "I didn't know."

The failure world is heaped high with those who "didn't know." They glut the marts of trades and professions, while there are positions calling insistently and constantly to the one who does know, knows that he knows, and knows how to express what he knows.

Have a plan, is the slogan of all success, from the man who breaks rocks to the master builder. The *plan* is the fulcrum which lifts the formless into form; until one has a plan of life, his world is void.

There are places on the path where the human mind cannot include all the law of the past, present and future, but there is never a place where the mind worth calling a mind, cannot include control and command the *now*.

The individual who hopes for success must become that success in his own mind, at once. He must build his plan as perfectly as a draughtsman draws the pictured house, or the sculptor sets his sketch. Nothing can ever pass into form that has not first been projected in consciousness. Everything must live first in the brain of the master builder. It does not matter what the desire is, it must eventually come out into manifestation.

No matter what we want to do, we must work it all out in our mind just exactly as we want it to be. We must not allow our minds to accept one single idea that links us with less than the perfect. We must know what we want, how we want it and what we are going to do to get it, and then, every day be more and more insistent in our demand.

The one who hopes to go on from good, to better and best, can only do so in the degree in which he brings the perfected vision of thought and action into unity.

Have a plan – then day and night live in the full realization of this plan – think, speak, be the thing itself. Do not accept anything less than all you desire, think it out to the smallest detail, for aimless drifting and formless drifting can take no part in the life of the one who would win.

Success by any other law than that of conscious, spiritual direction and control, is built upon the law of *change*. If you drift accidentally into success you can accidentally drift out again, but the success gained through the law of self knowledge, through the perfected spiritual arrangements and placing of our own human desires, is success forever, because it is the at-one-ment of human design with Universal intelligence.

When we, through higher understanding project the plan of our own human life and then resolutely command this plan to manifest, we will find that there is converted action between the universal and personal laws of life and we can speak this plan into the very silences of the Universal Mind and myriad forms of success will come out and gather round us.

Holding the plan up before our own inner vision, projecting it into the very face of the Infinite All, following it with unclouded eyes unwaveringly as the sailor tracks the polar star, success of any or all kinds begins for us and can never end, for we have *become* the very law that we are seeking.

Third Success Method

DON'T HURRY

When one has found his place in the great system of Universal Consciousness and has faithfully fulfilled all the personal side of the laws of adjustment; when his plan has become so crystallized that it hangs like a shining star of promise in his field of conscious thinking; when, sleeping or waking, he is one with the divine order of his desire, then he is really ready to receive fulfillment.

Why doesn't he receive it? There are many who have found themselves, built their plan with all the skill of a divine architect, yet the success which they seek eludes them. After days, nights, months, years perhaps, they sink down in despair saying, "There is no use trying."

This is the story of the multitude: "What is the next thing to do?" There is only one answer. Don't hurry – take your time – live each day for all there is in it. There is not a step on the path that does not bring its own compensation.

Life is a season; man is a new born plant and not all of life is born in us all at once. We ripen out of one law of consciousness and its embodiment, into others. There are many desires which take time to develop; they cannot come in a few days, hours or months.

If the thing you plan is a sublime and lasting thing to stand the test of time, it must draw inspiration from many moons of intensification.

We must remember that our today and our tomorrow of possession is linked with our yesterdays. We have often set many causes into operation in the past, which operates as a privilege or a lack of privilege in this new day.

Many hearts throw down their hope at the very moment when they are just ready to receive life's gifts; they send them away by their changed consciousness; they do not know that substance is always changing, as is our position towards it, and that if we want to succeed we must keep the same hope eternally renewed under every and all conditions. Time is an element in all human desires; time does not limit, it always fulfills, and waiting is one of the greatest human initiations.

After one has fully projected the plan, he has nothing to do but to water it continually with the rains, dews and showers of his expectations, and wait that hour when he has passed up the proofs of his own steadfastness. Some things by their own natural law will come slowly.

The life that can know itself and link up consciously with the Universal system of transference, by getting into its own natural groove, then steadily, unwaveringly, project its plan, and, flinging its whole conviction into it, wait patiently upon the law of the thing it desires, living in the consciousness of the eternal now, this life is one with the great Universal law of success; and as it sweeps on in rhythmic circles, it will come face to face with its desire, worked out in sane, sensible form.

Forth Success Method

CLEAN UP YOUR MOODS

We meet persons every day who have found themselves, who have a plan, who have patience and wait, and yet they are not a success.

They find one engagement, one position, one home, one friend after another, but they are never happy, never satisfied, and change and confusion is over them.

What is the matter? Why are they not successful when they are filling so many of the success laws?

This is the great question. *Why?*

Surely the reason is not very apparent, and one has to direct careful and deliberate attention to their life before the question can be answered for them.

After enough thought and attention has been given, the reason pops up like a "jack in the box" clamoring for recognition, and we are amazed that we did not know it sooner.

The answer is found in the unhappy disposition of the individual. Moods have wrecked tens of thousands.

"Clean up your moods!" This is the slogan of the successful person.

With a hateful disposition, no one can ever become a permanent success.

Self-culture is not a myth. There are negative, destructive states of mind that will destroy the finest genius if they are allowed to manifest and take part in the individuality.

There are persons with dispositions so vicious that they are like biting dogs. No one is safe for a moment from the outbursts of their spiteful tongues and temper.

Hasty temper has cost more than one person a good position; lost others a really valuable friend, and shut the door of grand opportunities.

No one wants as a friend, companion, wife, husband, employee or employer, one who is likely to fly into a rage and lose his head at the slightest provocation.

Every condition worthwhile calls for poised, calm, self-controlled states of mind. In these there is power and opportunity; in haste and rage there is nothing but lack of opportunity and waste of energy.

The dear ones in the home, who love us, may protect us in our destructive states of consciousness, and we make them the victims of our moods and tenses; but there will come a time and place when the world will teach us that if we sulk or act spitefully we will do it *alone*.

The whole world of successful business waits for the big, genial, loving person, who will be a mascot for it; but it has no place for the crabbed, uncontrolled, moody, sulking individual, who thinks the whole world was made to serve and adjust to him.

We have no more right to pour our discordant states of mind into the lives of those around us, and rob them of their sunshine and brightness, than we have the right to enter their houses and steal the silverware.

Unhappy black moods, discouragement, hasty temper, sulks and grouches are mental habits, and they have no more right to be allowed to persist than any other indelicate, uncultivated habit.

It is just as uncouth and ungentlemanly, to wear a sulk as it is to wear a soiled collar. Neither will be tolerated where the standards are true and high.

Gentleness, patience, consideration for others, self-forgetfulness and true selfness, are all the trophies of well-directed thought culture. They build up a personality that has one hundred percent of attracting force. We can be small, mean, narrow, bigoted and fault-finding, with our hand against every man, and his hand against us, but as the years go on, we lose our value in every respect; our room is preferred to our company.

We can set ourselves to clean up these endless little weaknesses of disposition, and put in their place through persistent self-culture, the states of mind and heart which bring us forth as a personality valuable in every walk of life.

We can be "big," true and kind, patient, forbearing, full of wisdom and understanding, and the world will come and gather round us, no matter where our feet may wander, bringing us the fruits of our life's greatness. Success then is ours, to remain with us. Everyone seeks to receive something from and give something to the one who stands ever ready to give and receive.

Our personality and character becomes, then, our guarantee of ability; and the gentle attention, the sympathetic understanding, endears us to our friends and home, while our geniality, patience, forbearance and tranquility make us indispensable in the big discordant world of work and conquest.

Fifth Success Method

MIND YOUR OWN BUSINESS

When one has found himself, made his plans, taken the attitude of active patience, cleaned up his moods, what is needed to precipitate into form his heart's desire? Many things; but chief among them all is the need of concentration; the power to know what he wants, to know the way he wants it, to be the divine thinker of his own thoughts; and, having done this, mind his own business. This does not mean that he will be blind to your business or mine, but that he will train his mind to be inclusive of all, but positive to outside desires.

To be positive, however, in the thought of outside things, and negative to our own desires, is a failure law: any external thing that we endow with the power over us, will use this power simply because we have made it possible by our own thoughts.

The Concentrated mind owns itself. It is success, and it thinks itself straight into the middle of the law of power.

The diverse, flitting, rambling mind is a failure from the start, because the power of life lies in being able to unify all action, either mental or physical.

The ten thousand changes and conditions of life through which we are forced to pass in the search for what we call our success, demands that we arrange every step of the path of life with a precision and definiteness that is unimpeachable.

No one else will or can mind our business but ourselves; the one who thinks differently is face to face that moment with failure.

We can so arrange our business that we mind it through a multitude of people who assist us, but these people are only a part of the plan of our business. They may assume complete control for that time and place, but if we drop them out of our consciousness, or worry about them, or break the law in any way, they will sometime become a rebellious factor and undermine our success.

The one who chooses what he desires must stand by this desire and vitalize it into perfect success through his own thought force.

Mind your own business after you know what it is. No matter what anyone does or does not, it cannot affect us unless we think it can and divert our power of creation and attraction by this thinking.

The law of divine attraction makes everyone *One* with his own, and *our* own is just what we create for ourselves; and deep nor high can take our own away.

In our own genius the germ of freedom, power and success lies, and day after day, with our eye single to our own business and double to the business of those around us, there will spring up for us such an eternal law of the action of finer forces that whatever our hand touches turns at once into that thing which we desire.

Our own business then, no matter what it is, objective or subjective, becomes a wonderful magnificent reality, which grows more and more brilliant as each day goes on and we intensify and re-intensify this great success law.

Sixth Success Method

THE USE OF POWER

When one reads the vast majority of books, with instruction of how to acquire success, he soon finds that all their instructions are directed toward the mass-man and devoted to calling the attention of the unfortunate and unsuccessful to his faults; all efforts point to the reconstruction of the life of those who are down and out.

It seldom occurs to the ordinary mind that all things work together for the good or bad of everybody, and when the last word has been said to the employer, the employed, and the unemployed, there yet remain vast books to be written for the use of the employer, the master, the leader, the controller of things and of people.

The employer, leader, or teacher and every life acting in a law of power and control has success and failure methods, and in the degree they operate them they take part in the upbuilding or destruction of their own and other's success. "The one who teaches learns," and as soon as anyone is in a position of power where his advice is given and acted upon, he is linked eternally with those who act upon it – this is Karma, or the law of cause and effect, and through this he learns to give finer and finer advice.

There is a great cosmic law of "live and let live," and those who are the fittest in the struggle for existence have the strongest will to work either rightness or iniquity. Our place on the path determines our power and the leader, employer or master who has the top round of the ladder of privilege and then deliberately kicks the one below him in the face, has the opportunity to do it, but not the *right* under the higher law of justice and he will do it at his own risk.

A little learning, and a little power is a dangerous thing, and power misused can bring the longest round of despair. There are men in every walk of life, strong, positive, creative, able to cope with almost any condition, who never give a decent word or thought to those who are inferior to them, they are building their own failure law to meet them further on. They live in a world of inferiors, they never accept an equal or dream of a superior, and they poise themselves in an exalted spot and deal out their ultimatum to the rest of the world.

Employers, and all who deal with the many, owe a great deal to the truth of harmonious association; the one who is right with the lives that serve him will prosper; there are places when a big creative life cannot stand for suggestions from one who is not struggling, as he is, to pull off big things, and then he does not need to allow it. Take for instance, an inventor sees his vision, and no one can expect to see it just as he does, and he has a right to be, to a marked degree, intolerant of others and their opinion, but to be so that no one can approach him and to be almost impossible to live with, so that all his assistants fear and despise him, this is not genius, it is pure uncontrolled moods and tenses, which, left to themselves, will destroy the very thing he desires. When one is really great in genius and understanding, he knows that the biggest life is the one which includes the most, and who most perfectly expresses the things he includes, and "he who conquers himself is greater than he who taketh a city."

Those who have the power to do, to say, to be, have also a great responsibility and as they act toward the very least of earth's children, they set the laws for themselves, *in the long run*. It has been written, "Ye shall not set your children's teeth on edge," and true leadership can only come to one who feels in all, and through all, the great law of justice and love.

"Do unto others as ye would that they should do unto you" is not too old to use in the New Civilization. Live for all you are worth yourself, but let others have a chance to live too. This is true success; team work is hard to do perfectly, but if we use our genius, our power, our mastery to help others, and rise in deeper patience and helpfulness to the majesty of our place on the path, then power becomes a wonderful possession, our word never comes back to us void, and we can know that we are the highest expression of our own type of consciousness; that we can command, everything will love to obey, because we are one with all, in truth, in justice, and in power.

Seventh Success Method

FAITH

Fear, more than any other thing, operates against success. No one can reach the summit of himself as long as he tries to climb with this ball and chain weighing him down.

Fear stands as a gloomy sentinel and will not let the Spirit pass onto possession of its best. The strands of failure are made from the fibers of fear; wherever fear is active, failure is its neighbor.

Looking at this very active agent we are obliged to ask the question, "where did fear originate, of what are we afraid, and why does fear dog the footsteps of the whole failure world?"

Try as we will to deny it, the fact remains that no matter how unfolded a human life is, there is always something of which it is afraid. Sometimes it is manifested as physical fear, sometimes as psychological fear, sometimes as spiritual fear, but fear of something and weakness of character in that particular direction is a part of the scheme of the race unfoldment. And where fear is positive in nature, controlling and limiting the life's natural forces, there is nothing on earth that will turn aside the negative results of this law.

Men fear new conditions, because they are outside of their immediate experiences. There are some who would as soon face a loaded cannon as break in a new position, or meet a new responsibility, but after they are acquainted with it they are brave as a lion. All things are easy and common-place as soon as they are *old*. There are crowds of failures simply because we are afraid of each other. Good actors and actresses have failed because they could not forget the crowd outside the footlights; fear brings self-consciousness, and this is death to all true greatness. Singers fail again and again because self-conscious fear stifles their breath and grips them so that they cannot express their best.

There is no cure for fear but *faith*. One has to first know the truth – that all life is the same life and everyone on the path of life is seeking the same things and going in the same direction. There is only one man on the path and he is ourself, yesterday, today or tomorrow.

There is no way of reducing life to a certainty. The years are always more or less full of things, people and conditions which are new. It is necessary for true progress, and to be afraid to meet each new day is soul cowardice, from which we must rescue ourselves. Life demands that we induce at a moment's notice an intelligence which will cope with any and all things around us and do it masterfully. The one who has *faith* in himself will never doubt other things; he will build his resolve on his ideal and fling himself resolutely after it.

The substance of things hoped for are not easily transmuted into things *gained* and the only thing which transmutes them is *faith*.

Faith makes the business man strong enough to venture and win. *Faith* teaches him to wait and trust until changing fortune again turns the wheel. *Faith* makes the friend, the lover, the mourner, all go forward with a hope that never fails. Fear has shut the door of success in the face of millions, but faith ever stands ready to open it and let the free spirit pass to new levels of peace, power and plenty. Success built upon faith is ever renewing. It remains because it is reborn over and over again through itself.

Eighth Success Method

SELFNESS

When one has arrived at the eighth fundamental, he is beginning to have an intelligent idea of just what life requires of him, and his success or failure gathers around him according to the magnet he has made of himself.

One cannot go very far in self-analysis before he finds that all things gather round, leave and return to the self, and this self becomes an absorbing study.

There is no such thing in the world as unselfishness, if there were we would cease to exist, for the self is the center of the magnet called "man"; it is man himself and always will be. There are two distinct expressions of self – one of these makes for the eternal and abiding success and is drawn from the varieties of living; the other often brings an apparent success, but it is built on the laws of change which manifest eventually in failure. The success method is called by these selfishness, but the new world calls one "selfness" or universality, and the other, separateness or personality. Upon these two great laws hang the past, present and future of every living soul.

Personality and universality are both states of consciousness and no one is to be blamed or praised because of them, but he must be taught of them, so that he will recognize the results of his own laws. The younger one is in the contact of the experiences of life, the more personal and separate he will be; he will only know himself, his own desires and his own aims and these will dominate his mind and actions. The everlasting *ego* stands out in pride and arrogance, and says to the whole world: "I – I want! I am! I must have," and I, me and mine is the trinity of his consciousness. On the path of life, in the association with men, we easily recognize this great army of egotists by their slogan, "what's in it for me?" This is their first and last word and unless there is something "in it" for them, they don't move.

Great wonderful things may be waiting everywhere, calling for a strong hand and a true heart to push them into form for the universal good, but their ears are deaf and their strength unattainable unless they can rise on these things of their own desires.

The personal egotist, separate, self-seeking often secures his own for a while, because he feeds upon everything in his environment. He uses everything as legitimate material to pave his way. He will rise to his immediate desire even if he steps upon the heart of his best friend, and he often drags to slaughter the fondest love which has laid itself at his feet.

They may have and hold till the want grows cold whatever is their desire, and may squeeze out of it all that is in it for them, but they are one with the law of their own relationship, and this is *change*.

The failures come to the personal life because in its own conceited selfhood it links itself with the method that brings failure. One must eventually lose his opportunities when everyone knows that he operates every action of his life by what he will get out of it.

Employees will leave a firm some day where only the employer's interests are served; the hour may be long delayed because of the lack of true selfness of the employees but the handwriting is on the wall and he must meet his own method. An employee who shows that his whole interest is personal and who works only for what there is in it for him is a failure. There are thousands of such failures because in their search for opportunities and work they were not really hunting these, but were really hunting a nice soft snap, where they could draw a good salary and get all out of it they can and give nothing in return; they want to get three hours pay for one hour of work; their employers soon discover it and above their exalted ego write the word "shirk."

The personal, separate life loses its value as a friend and in time finds itself forgotten and counted out, for tolerance ceases to be a virtue when it forces friendship into personal service. These people fail just as surely in love. True it is that "love suffereth long and is kind, does not take offense, seeks to give of itself," but love must love, and after a while it will turn away just as naturally as the sunflower turns to the sun, and claim its own where it finds it.

The personal success that comes to us through universal association with interest and helpfulness to others is a verity that time will only make more truly our own.

We cannot push our personal desires through the very center of another's hopes and find lasting success. We cannot fling down the aspiration and dreams of another and climb by them into eternal fame and glory. We cannot step over a broken human heart to continuous happiness; the law of life is not mocked, but we can link our life, our dreams, our aspirations, our love with the deep centralized desires of those around us and mount as by eagles wings to the very mountain tops of our hearts desires. We are only atoms in the whole, and in the long run, all love is plussed by love, all helpfulness by helpfulness, all service by service.

All small lives talk, live and act separateness, egoism and personalities, and they will by natural law register these things around them in failure until they learn through failure the weakness of their law.

All great lives talk, live and act principles of unity, love, understanding and service – this makes them one with the truth of life in the highest and around them must come an ever increasing success power.

Ninth Success Method

YESTERDAY, TODAY AND TOMORROW

There are few things about which the world is so genuinely stupid as the true attitude to *yesterday*, *today* and *tomorrow*.

The obsession of this trinity of time, stands as a sentinel and will not let the race mind pass into a peaceful mental or spiritual state.

Remorse about yesterday, uncertainty about today and dread of tomorrow drives the human consciousness on into a wild burst of psychical despair from which only the strong word of truth will ever rescue it. There are thousands of failure lives caught in the destructive obsession of yesterday; they have tried and failed; their past is full of regret, remorse and rebellion against conditions over which they apparently have no control; fortunes lost, friends gone, opportunities passed by, old age with them, they sink down in weakened courage and go round and round in the thought drag-net of their dead yesterday; they think of all they have not succeeded in accomplishing, think of deeds done which had better have been left undone. All these take the light from the eye, the spring from the step, the courage from their hearts, and there is no possibility of their accrediting themselves in a new way for they are one with the deepest degree of failure, and they never know that they are building it for themselves.

There is no such thing as a mistake; no such thing as lost opportunities; there is no such thing as the past – there is just life, and more and more life. Everything is the Eternal *now*, and every hour behind us on the path *was* that this hour might be, and our experiences of yesterday were simply the methods which life took to drive us on into higher things.

Everyone always does exactly the best he knows how to do, he often thinks that he did not do the best, but the fact remains that his actions are always based on his own consciousness, and somewhere in his own mind certain laws obtained which made it impossible for him to do differently just at that time. Perhaps he might have done differently had he known five minutes before what he knew five minutes after the doing, but this wisdom came as the result of doing. "Experience is a dear teacher, but fools won't learn any other way."

Since we know that life is for experience, expression and inclusion, we stop our failure method – we do not look back – we keep out of the past. It has no message that we can understand, save what it speaks to us in the today. What we built into yesterday must come out in our today, and if we are continually recreating our old hours with our thoughts of today we will never get free. If we want to go on to the new success awaiting us we must unwrap ourselves from the grave clothes of our yesterday.

There is no use grieving over anything; no use recalling a painful memory, let it go! Life is always a going on; man's face was set to go forward, walking backward he stumbles. And there are always big new things ahead if we keep after them.

One continuing and persistent obsession is the one of old age. "If I were young" has stood in the way of multitudes.

Old age is waning enthusiasm – as long as one keeps enthusiasm and interest and unity he will find his place waiting for him.

True it will not be among those of youth, nor in the occupations of youth, but age has its demands which youth can no more fill than age can fill youth's position.

There are thousands of places, positions and conditions of life which call for the poise and judgment of mature minds, and the person with age and wisdom can fill these places.

Youth has dash and glow and power to rush ahead and pioneer, but age has grit, endurance, steadfastness and power to hold on through hours of suspense and supreme tests, and these two avenues of life must forever be filled. The one who is obsessed with the thought of old age is shutting his own door of opportunity and no one says no to him but himself.

We have quit letting the croaker, the pessimist and the fatalist think and speak for the world. At fifty a man or woman is just beginning real life; they have finished their processes and are ready to begin a real existence; they have in them the wisdom born of many experiences, and their life can become a veritable cedar of Lebanon sheltering many tribes.

If they seek the things in life, the people or the opportunities where age is a valuable factor, they will be one with a success higher than they have ever conceived existed for them. With experience, poise, power, endurance and a young heart, and a clear mind that understands life and its needs, age is a royal pathway of power and wisdom and the young everywhere will come and gather around and bring the fruit of their lives greatness.

The *obsession of today* is another great stumbling block. There are thousands who expect to take out of today all their hopes and dreams, and weep because the day passes and nothing comes to them, they do not know that they are the cause of their own delay. Today is the product of our yesterday, and it is given us so that we may each day plus our own consciousness.

We can never take out of today anything that we did not create for ourselves in our yesterday.

What we build into today passes with us into our tomorrow, and when we face days and days of emptiness, it is a certain fact that in all our yesterdays, we did not accomplish the law of our desires. If one wants to meet a day full of joy, love, peace and opportunity, he must live these things every passing hour, holding fast to them in faith, then as time passes by, his days plus each other and in some unexpected day he will meet all his own power and a perfect day of joy, love and opportunity will come to him, which will continue according to the power which he has generated. No one is to blame but ourselves if our today narrows down to dull, dreary monotony, and our life to petty confines; we reap what we sow, and we can never reap the harvest of anything unless we have sown the seed somewhere; nothing and nothing make nothing, and the way to get something into expression for ourselves is to set about creating it for ourselves in each hour of living; we can always live unfalteringly in the ultimate until it comes.

If we begin to fill our today with true understanding everything will change for us.

Standing fast we can call and it must come, not by living months and years of waiting, but *now*, for in full realization a thousand years are but as one day!

The *obsession of tomorrow* is always recognized just as easily as one detects the traces of yesterday and today. The obsession limes out all over those who are caught in its negative drag-net.

"Going to do it" – this is their slogan. "Going to have it" - "Some day." The future, like a mighty ruler, stands before them and worshipping it they are blind, deaf and dumb to their present opportunities.

There are wondrous avenues of accomplishment opening on every hand, but something in their weak consciousness says, "wait" – "not now" – "some other time." "Going to do it" is the finished law of procrastination. Procrastination is the seed, and "going to do it" the true tree that springs from the obsession of tomorrow. There is nothing in this world that ever springs spontaneously perfect. Creation, emanation and evolution is cosmic law, and it is human law too. And no matter what we want, have, do or be, we must begin it before we can finish it and possess the fruition. The individual who caries a hope, a dream, a desire hidden in his heart, and drags through days, months and years without the courage of putting it to the test, must be a failure because he is standing ever before his own unfulfilled selfhood.

The world is full of those who are "going to do it" and so it is full of failures.

"Do it now," is the watchword of success. It is common sense to give ourselves a legitimate amount of time to get ready for anything. The bigger our endeavor, the more time and thought it demands, and it is well said, "fools rush in where angels fear to tread," but it is also true that without this quality in the human soul which causes the fool to rush in, there are many fools who would forever remain at the fool's level of unfoldment. The urge that sends the fool on is the urge that deifies and glorifies our human endeavor and the fool follows it in uncontrolled, undirected enthusiasm, while the wise man guides it, cherishes it as his most precious possession, training himself to allow it to urge him on and through almost impossible accomplishments.

"Going to do it" never gets anyone anywhere, and the one who rises powerfully to the top of his own mountain of success, is the one who first surveys the path to this mountain-pass and then taking the bit of the bridle of his own life in his teeth, runs away with himself.

It is then that the world seeing him rush on in what appears to be madness, stops and says, "what is this?" And with attention comes interest, and through interest comes praise or ridicule, and through these comes cooperation and his success is assured. Finding ourselves, knowing what we want to do, giving ourselves a legitimate time for perfecting our ability to do, then *doing* it – this is the *law* of *success*.

Do it now! We may have only one-tenth of one percent perfection when we start anything, but practice makes perfect, and out of the very crudest material will come a gem, polished by use into a resplendent brightness. It is better to do and fail and profit by the wisdom born of this failure, than to sit down in unexpressed genius and atrophy from disuse.

Tenth Success Method

PSYCHOLOGICAL SINS

The world is full of psychological sins. Every hour someone is transgressing the higher laws of truth, trampling down that which is fine and right and putting in its place the imperfect, the crude; defeating his own purpose through the blindness of his own consciousness. The old world has said, "life is just the difference between tweedledum and tweedledee, but the tweedledees have it" and this means that those who consciously or otherwise contact and express at all times the true law of a condition, time, place or person, have gained a power unknown and unpossessed by the blundering multitude who never see into the real center of things.

To be able to always say, do and be the right thing at the right time, demands a high degree of consciousness, but in the measure that we pass up the proofs of such a law there hangs our own personal privileges and opportunities for progress.

The names of psychological sins are legion, and each sinner has his own particular form of sinning, and it often demands microscopic spiritual examination to find the spot through which the law is operated.

Chief among all psychological breaks, a prime factor in the production of failure, is the lack of sense that will tell you when to hold your tongue. Talk has beggared thousands. No matter how carefully it is used it is bound to come that some day one will talk too much to the wrong man; it is not so much the sin of not minding your own business, as it is the love of talking.

There are always many things that the other fellow need not know; it is a violation of all true being to talk about these things. To hold our tongues about our own affairs and the affairs of others especially, this is power. We may tell our secrets to the idle listener if we choose, we only hurt ourselves thereby, but what we think about someone else, and pour out with our own senseless talk is double sinning and seldom one cares to hear it and we become a bore to be avoided. Again, there are those who say "you can believe that I always say what I think and if I think anything, I am going to say it." Wrong again! No real psychologist ever says just what he thinks unless his finer senses tip him off that that is just the moment for him to say that very thing. What one says often cuts no figure with the real truth. Our "think" and "say" are good for us to act by, but they might be entirely incorrect in analysis and the direction of others. It takes years of experiences and fine discrimination before the things which we say will not come back to us void, and we only get ourselves disliked and delay our own law of larger usefulness by meddling. Another sin is to play the traitor in small hidden ways to friendship, business or love; little suggestive insinuations behind the backs of others, a trifling betrayal of weak spots in their character or work or business, which they, unconsciously put in our hands, or which we arrived at through the intimacy of friendship, and a friendship which made it appear possible for them to live for a moment perhaps, off their guard.

Every human life is transmuting something either in the self or environment. The guise of friendship allows a closer intimacy than is accorded to others, and through this we enter into shrines and temples of lives which are kept closed and sealed to the big useless crowd outside. It is a sin of the deepest dye not to have a shrine of absolute truth in our own life, and then to sneak like a thief in the night into the holy sacredness of another's shrine and turn from this to the outside world, tear down this shrine and demolish this temple with insidious hints and half-veiled suggestions, until we have let loose a floodtide of suspicion around it. This is *theft* on the subjective side of life, and as nature avenges herself on the material thief, just so the Higher Avenger of truth takes strict account.

Amid all the great psychological sins, there are thousands of minor ones; lack of attention – lack of earnestness; lack of reverence for truly holy things; taking one's self too seriously; failing to give a legitimate interest to other people's problems; untidiness; vulgarity; unnecessary mannerisms which we would be better without; quick offense to a well-deserved correction or suggestion; white lies; procrastination; continuous evasions; pretensions – all of these eventually crystallize into some big failure law of character and consciousness.

Success is the product of psychological righteousness or rightness. Honor, integrity, truth, faithfulness, steadfastness – all these link us with a cosmic current of power which will manifest for us anything we declare.

Eleventh Success Method

BUSINESS, BUT NOT TRUTH

Nothing but truth will hold truth, and failure comes as the inevitable reaction of being continually just off the center of absolute truth.

Perhaps in no association are there quite so many false positions intensified as in what the world calls love. The world will say it truly loves and then lie with the next breath. A man writes: "I am so glad, dear, you are having a good time while you are away" which is pure sarcasm as he is sick with jealous pain because "dear" is away alone.

A woman says: "I love him with all my heart, but I pretend I don't; it wouldn't do to let him know it, he would be so domineering." Yet they call this love, when, in truth, love only loves, it never domineers, and true love is always glad, it is never jealous or unhappy; there cannot be any permanent success for such association, and it is this which has led the world to say – marriage and love are a failure; such marriages and such loves are failures because they are one with failure methods. But true marriages and true love are life's holiest success, because they are built upon the law of true understanding and not pretension.

The highest and greatest permanent successes are built around the lives of those who stand steadfast for truth, the whole truth and nothing but the truth.

Whoever wants business success, love or ambition to blossom into fruition, must have the absolute principle of truth in his heart. It is said that civilization today does not permit truth to be either spoken or lived – this is the *master lie*, hatched in the consciousness of the prince of liars, and sent forth by those who are living the life of business but not truth. It fits their development to say this and if possible hold the mass mind to their own levels.

There are in all this seething mass of misdirected energy seeds of mighty truth, and a new civilization is rising which speaks the truth and whose business, love, home and social relationships are assuming new and beautiful expressions.

We know today that the straight road of truth, through the jungle of the old civilization, is a hard climb, and truth is beset on every hand with opportunity to change horses with liars, but the quickest way to our perfect success, no matter what it is that we desire, is to live each hour in unfaltering steadfastness to the truths of life.

It is true that truth takes the long road and that sometimes the hour seems long delayed, but it is also true that when our ideals are accomplished by this law, they are verities and the true commercial world is waiting to pay us a big price for our verity. The world of friendship is waiting to worship at our feet, for truth has reached the heart of truth.

Twelfth Success Method

PERSONALITY AND INDIVIDUALITY

There is a great place for higher instruction in the subject of personality and individuality, and one of the greatest blunders of age comes in directing the race mind into a line of thinking which separates these two distinct expressions of the self; they are both important, and only as we understand them can we harmonize them for power, and when we do harmonize them, the world witnesses a gigantic success law which makes all other laws look puny and insignificant, then it seems as if all laws were finished in this perfect magnet called *man*.

Man is the visible and audible expression of spirit, the energy which comes from this expression is the unseen energy of life. It is spirit itself.

The external body of man, that which we see and touch, is simply thought energy materialized; we have been taught to call this "personality." Personality is really only that energy which we have thought into expression and it bears witness to our own estimate of ourselves. Our body or personality becomes the expression of just what we have created in the infinite energy and localized on the objective plane for our use.

The personality is the objective man, the individuality is the subjective man, and the work of life is to transmute the two into one, and make the outer man respond to the inner man.

One *sees* the personality, he only *feels* the individuality; it is the subtle something which radiates from us. One may possess a very displeasing personality and yet radiate a very pleasing individuality. There are personalities which are really repellent, but often after we know them we find a wonderful individuality hidden within them, and are charmed with it and so learn to forget the displeasing exterior.

Individuality is the positive pole of being and thinking, and our personality is the negative pole. The one who has a displeasing personality and a pleasing individuality tells every passer-by that he has lent himself to negative inharmonious lines of thinking, if not here then in some other state of consciousness, and that he has lived in the external mind and has been caught in the diverse currents, and the laws of common consciousness, and that in this life he has not yet learned to join the two forces within his own being. Often we have heard this expression, "He is a grand individual and his personality is in keeping with his character." This means that the same quality runs through and through, that the warp is the same as the pattern.

Individuality is an expression of conscious growth and our personality may be made the perfect objective expression of this growth.

The purely personal life is not a whole life at all; it is only a part, just as the body is only a part of the divine man. Individuality is often latent in every life and after the development of the personality is over, the individuality begins to speak forth; it is nothing but the finer thought life that has been growing throughout all time.

Every moment of our life individuality is adding to itself and personality is adding to itself and when the two become one, the same material is used for both and there is no longer need for transmutation. But as long as there is separation between them, one may know that there is some work yet to do in life. The whole scheme of existence makes for absorption of the lesser into the greater, the subliming of all matter into the manifestation of spirit.

The law of each life demands that the personality and individuality become joined so that the individuality may express externally as well as internally, that is, to become the visible as well as the invisible power. The personal must become refined and etherealized through the stimulation of the higher impulses.

We all know just how many beautiful thoughts we have which often fail to materialize because we do not believe them to be true. These thoughts are all creative ones and are generated in the individuality, which is often telling us what splendid radiant creatures we are, or may become, and how often we submit these imaginings to our personal mind and are told that they are too fantastical to clothe with form; we accept the verdict of our common consciousness and build our personality with the idea of something less than perfection, when the very soul within us is screaming out the message that we may become divine if we so desire.

Every positive creative thought is added to the individuality and each day developing a higher function of the body.

Every thought we carry is creative and must by natural law express somewhere; it must be localized in the physical body or it must be represented as energy which we radiate through the body. The more crude the thought generated, the more dense must the body and the radiations become.

Individuality will forever remain the twin of personality until mankind merges them together; they were born together and they will remain together until the higher absorbs and controls the lesser.

The visible world and the visible body are both under the same law. The external grows from a fuller rushing out of the inner life; the personalities grow and refine through the new truths learned; the closer it allows itself to follow the invisible but insistent individuality, the more beautiful and harmonious it becomes.

In the struggle for existence and the accomplishment of our success law, both personality and individuality have their power, and those who forget, find it out later on to their sorrow. Our personality is our introduction to the world, it is the real press agent to the multitude, it speaks a silent message and depends wholly upon us to make it tell a wonderfully attractive message. No matter how beautiful one may be in mind and character he is just that much more attractive if he has all this joined and expressed in his personality. No matter how unattractive anyone may be there is always one personal charm which can be made the center around which individuality can attract and manifest. The one who neglects to find his strong personal point of power and intensify it, does so at his own risk. Sometimes this point of beauty or attraction is only nice hair, it might be luminous eyes, perhaps a gentle smile or a tranquil expression, possibly good teeth, a supple figure, a splendid walk, broad shoulders, a cheery laugh – each one of these makes a fulcrum of power for the one who will use them and not go moping around because she or he does not have them all.

Business, more than anything else, calls for power personalities; personalities which have strong marked characteristics on which faith can be established. This will lead the seeking world on into at-one-ment with the individuality. I have often heard businessmen say, "Oh, I can't send him; he hasn't personality enough, and can't use what he has." All public opportunities and privileges call for personalities to fit them.

The very acme of success depends on our having one hundred percent of our personality expressed all the time, and one of the sure failure paths of life is to allow our personality to become so demagnetized that it has in it no hint of the true self. The world may say, "She is just as handsome as she can be, but, poor thing, she cannot be very handsome," and this may be true, but if we make ourselves just as handsome, strong, sweet, kind, neat and wholesome as we can, then we have fulfilled the true law of our own being and can laugh the whole world in the face. As we become more and more perfect in the transmutation and reformation of our personality, this fineness sinks in and stays in our consciousness and joins our individuality, and our individuality each day grows more wonderful, and this perfecting individuality plays all its strong impulses out through our face and form, and we again return them still finer through action and understanding, until our psychic circle of power is complete, then we become a magnet of attraction and in every walk of life there radiates from us a great love, power, success and energy, and our very presence becomes a benediction. We are not then seeking success, we are success and the whole world pays tribute to our individualized personality.

Thirteenth Success Method

ENTHUSIASM

There is nothing in all the world but life! Even Death itself is only life acting inversely.

One of the greatest success methods is to be full of a radiant energy. We are judged every moment by the law of whether we are "the quick or the dead." There are multitudes of dead ones everywhere, and these make the vast army in failure. You may go among the poverty-stricken, the unemployed or the loafing world, and you will find that the quickness of spirit is lacking in them; they are dead to opportunities; dead to enthusiasm; dead to faith; dead in vital understanding and dead to everything that will hold them fast to the great pulsing life current, everywhere waiting their own conscious contact.

These failure people are depressed below the level of the universal life, like the Dead Sea, or the parched sands of the desert, while within their own being are lying dormant the possibilities of life more abundant and the success that comes from this life.

One true eternal success law is enthusiasm; no one can ever expect to fan anything into a raging flame of completion unless he does so from the red hot coals of his own ambition, enthusiasm and aspiration.

Power, possession, attraction, name, fame, honor and success are all the product of a whirlwind consciousness.

It is our own life stream which rushes us on past valleys, hills and mountains to deliver our possessions to ourselves, and the one who does not generate within himself the divine energy of enthusiasm is one with the death of his own desires.

It takes a stout heart to always keep enthused in the face of prolonged disappointment and continued opposition, but it must be done if we aim to conquer.

The money magnet who lets his enthusiasm carry him into an interest of his very lowest employee, to see that labor is comfortable, will never hunt for laborers, nor meet strikes nor revolutions.

The friend who meets his friend with interest, joy and aliveness, will count his friends by the score. And the lover who gives being for being in perfect part, smile for a smile, truth for truth, heart for a faithful heart, will never die alone.

With the fire of a great enthusiasm within us we keep our own lamps trimmed and burning, and we become then a torch bearer and a lamp to the feet of the slumbering multitude. We are success then because we have set the law of our own life and believing in the law we come into the protection of the law.

Fourteenth Success Method

CONCENTRATION

Centuries ago it was written, "Whatsoever thy hand findeth to do, do it with thy might." And that subtle law of doing everything we do with our might is the very heart of the law of success. Upon concentration more than upon any other thing hangs our hope for ultimate self-perfection.

Concentration is the first step toward conscious direction and control, and without it we cannot hope to go far into the fulfillment of our own desires. The one who hopes to find something to do, who has an urging aspiration and then fails to do this thing with his might, is not fit to possess the thing for which he is longing.

There are thousands of failures simply because they did not have the genius to see an opportunity, but there are more failures because when opportunity was everywhere they lacked the thought force necessary to push it into form. This is not just the same as the law of "mind your own business."

There are many subtle breaks in this chain of doing and every break means failure. Living in one world and working there with our hands, while all our thoughts and wits are wandering in another, divides our forces. No one can serve two masters.

Success demands that our mind shall be in all things we do, and all things in our mind, until we have established a long line of things which we can do automatically.

The concentrated mind does not think in concepts, it thinks in ultimates, it does not think in pennies and dollars, it thinks in millions, it does not think in cities and states, it thinks in continents; nor does it think in minutes, hours, or days but in eternities.

"Do with your might what your hands find to do" and concentrate on that work until you are absolute master, no matter how much you dislike your work. If you had outgrown the thing you are doing, you would not have to do it, just as one lays down an old coat that is outgrown. The moment we are big enough to get rid of a thing, we are forced to leave that thing. We could not stay, for the larger law of our life displaces it, we cannot stay with it because the cosmic law will push it off.

Man's fitness is measured by his understanding and by his perfection in the place on his path; and so today if we are working in a place which we do not enjoy it is the measure of the state of consciousness we have intensified so highly that it cannot keep out of form.

When we know that no one gives to us but ourselves, and no one takes away from us but ourselves, and that we lose or gain through our own individual law of attraction, and that this attraction is based wholly upon our power of concentration and ability to pass up the proofs of our fitness, then we have a new idea of success and failure. We begin to put the blame where it belongs – upon ourselves – and to really know that the perfect or imperfect expression of life is in our own hands.

The tools of conquest are in our hands! Our concentrated mind, our thought force carefully directed and intensified, at our own pleasure, make us the master of our fate and no matter what our place in life may be, we can show our greatness.

Concentration first, then an unfaltering determination to do! Then, with eyes wide open to life's gigantic opportunities, the Gates of Success swing wide, never to close again.

Fifteenth Success Method

APPRECIATION

It is a part of the higher development of everyone to learn, not only to do his own work as thoroughly as is possible, but to create the conditions and atmosphere by which all others with whom we contact can do their work equally as well.

It is the work of us all, not only to unfold our own character and life, but at the same time to carry around with us that silent creative atmosphere which helps others to bring out and develop all that is best and desirable within themselves.

Go where we will, we find many people who must depend on other lives for the stimulus of their finer and higher growth; they have to be drawn out; they are in their shell; their sweetness and charm never find expression unless they are evoked by sincere encouragement and warm affection. The world is full of half starved lives; they go on day after day finding no legitimate expression for that mysterious something within them which cries out to be fed and expressed.

There are many others who are hungry for the affection which they often have, but never receive or possess, because those who hold it for them never give it voice.

Again, there are many who have possibilities within them of a very high order, but those possibilities remain undeveloped because nothing in their lives, and no one around them, brings out these latent powers.

There are some who can only express in the warm atmosphere of appreciation: "The hearts of men contract from cold suspicion; shine on them with warm love, and they expand. It is *Love*, not justice, that from a low condition, leads mankind up to heights supremely grand."

Many individuals throw out an atmosphere of chill instead of appreciation; they are totally unaware of the influence they throw out. There are many, many lives that go around antagonizing everyone they meet; driving friends and friendships from them; defeating their hearts' dearest purpose, and never understanding why, when it is plain to those who look on, that all their difficulties come from a lack of thought about the delicate and intricate adjustments of human life.

There are thousands of homes which are without sunshine and good cheer, not because they are really without love, but because they have missed the one line of transference of these things and that is, appreciation and the expression of appreciation.

There are thousands of offices, stores, workshops, factories, schools, and places where humankind beat out their lives, that are wholly without inspiration, not because they are lacking in earnestness, but simply because they have never formed the habit of recognition and have none of the cooperative appreciation which gives out to others and at the same time brings out the best for itself.

Companion with this lack of appreciation is the spirit of sullenness, crankiness, and complaint; a continual looking at the dark side of things, and a sourness which makes not only one's own atmosphere acid, but reaches out into the lives of all those around us.

Of course we may be a crank if we want to be; that is our own affair; but we have no right to crowd our smallness into the lives of others, and neither have they any right to allow us to do it.

We should all be taught to recognize such disagreeable natures and atmospheres at a glance, take them as a signal of undevelopment, and protect our own lives from them. Some time in our life we all meet one of these walking frosts and we never forget the chill they always give us, until we learn our true position toward them.

Whenever we feel all of the meanness of our undeveloped nature welling up within us, it is a good plan to just keep it to ourselves, and cultivate the appearance and atmosphere of recognition. After a while we will displace the chill by the sunshine we have willed into expression. If we conquer it a little, day by day, we will soon cease to have it. A smiling face, a happy life, a soul full of appreciation which shines and radiates from us; this is the proof which the soul offers to the world that it has learned how to create its own kingdom.

We should train our eyes to see the good, the true, and the beautiful in everything, and then recognize it by every avenue of expression. It is not always enough to a life that we think it is good or great; we should tell the life what we think.

When a life needs encouragement, give it. Don't see its limitations, even though they almost overshadow its power; help it to grow into what it believes it can be. Encouragement is only another name for appreciation. It is no harder to see the good qualities in others than it is to see the faults, and it is a whole lot more comfortable for everyone. Life is a continual process of selection, and since we cannot choose but select something, learn to make it from the beautiful and best qualities, and then hold them up before the eyes of the possessor and see it with all the high lights of love and appreciation turned upon it. If we make the most of all the good and great things we find in our lives we will have very little time left to grieve about what we do not have.

When we go into a store and find all the clerks who wait upon us cross, distraught and uncivil, don't report them to the proprietor; that will never cure them.

Just treat them yourself by appreciation; give them sunshine; pour out all the warmth of yourself upon them and watch the effect. It won't be five minutes until the effect begins to show; just the tones of your voice can start a new vibration. Do not be afraid to express your appreciation of them or for anything they do for you; there is no life on earth that can stand against real, sincere recognition.

When someone answers us in a hateful manner, don't answer them back in the same tone; stop a moment, give them a thought of warm love and a kind word and see the storm clear away. There is no force on earth higher than the constructive energy of appreciation, warmed by great love. There is a latent spark in every being which flares up in answer to the stimulation of appreciation; and the knowledge and use of this power widens our lives and our field of usefulness. The whole business world everywhere is clamoring for live, vital workmen, who can attract and hold the outside world. It pays big salaries to those who can prove themselves "mascots" in whatever work they represent, but there is positively no place whatever for the "dead ones"; they already glut the market.

Appreciation; the power of sincere recognition of our own abilities and capabilities; and side by side with it, the same approval of other lives; these are all factors in the foundation of a life success which cannot be fully understood until it is tried.

In order to get real appreciation, we must get real love into our hearts and then teach ourselves how to connect with our words. We may manufacture a grin and an artificial approval, but at the same time we must be getting the real thing into our inner being or there will come a time when our words will be only as sounding brass or tinkling cymbals. There is a great truth in the power of thought transference, and it is just as easy to create a mental atmosphere of appreciation as it is to speak it; and for some lives this is sufficient to encourage them, but be wise and *know* when the spoken word is necessary to complete their character.

Live appreciation; radiate it; let it shine through you, but by all means learn to make your lips declare the truth your heart has known. "Encourage people; tell them of their good qualities of mind and heart and person too; it will revive them; make them think they are understood; perhaps awaken hope and will and power to do"; and when this is finished be sure that we recognize and appreciate all that others do for us.

To aid others in developing to their uttermost and to "dare to be what they will to be," is the great testimony of our capacity of controlling, directing, and completing our own life.

There is no power so impressive, so strong for success, so powerful in life building, and so certain in its everlasting benefit to mankind in general, as this one great human attribute, appreciation, or the power of universal recognition.

Then each life is great in itself and increasing in its greatness with others.

Sixteenth Success Method

HATEFUL COMPARISONS

Comparison, both true and false, takes part in our success and failure. Comparison is everywhere on our pathway.

"By the mistakes of others wise men correct their own," and unless we are proud and self-arrogant we must find splendid opportunities of measuring our own ability with the ability or lack of ability of others.

Strong, positive ideals are necessary in the building of a perfected selfhood, and positive ideals are bound to keep one in a condition of comparative thinking, for only as we see the ultimate self clearly can we hew to the line along the path of our true development.

There are always those who can do the very thing we are doing and do it in a different way and better, perhaps, than we are doing it, and no matter how fine we are, we would be just that much finer if we added to our own method the methods of those who are our masters.

A master consciousness and a master expression is always to be emulated, and the one who does not know this and who stands fast bound to his own peculiar method, refusing to entertain even the idea of a change in his method is a cad, and a snob, who will meet his own defeat through his own egoism. He may be all right, but so are a world of others and it will do him good to take notice.

All art, literature, music, drama, commerce, politics, and industry have their living pictures of perfection and there follows, as incentives, ideals and examples to help bring out in us all that is capable of stimulation.

Healthy, normal and careful comparison of our own ability and our own expressions with the highest type of these things we can find in others, will keep us on the keen edge of finer effort and spur us on to accomplish still greater expression in action, and as long as we keep to this we are under a success law which cannot be broken.

Around this true law of healthy comparison there swings the negative destructive law of hateful comparisons. Hateful comparisons have ruined fine executive lives. Filled with a desire divine to be perfect in the thing it is doing, possessing a supersensitive nature, seeing the magnificent expression of others in the same work and company their own feeble effort with the fuller perfect one, they have sunk down in despair and given up all effort, when all that was needed was a little longer practice and steadfast application; keeping what they had, and without hateful comparison, using the expression of those who were their masters as examples to inspire them, instead of becoming discouraged and giving up all effort.

Whatever you have around you in things, people and conditions are just what you have the power to create, and they will remain until you change them by making new conditions, so don't belittle them or compare them – love them and call them good and try to displace them by finer attraction.

Comparisons for growth and example – this is only embodied stimulation to higher effort and purpose and is the ladder by which we climb past our dead selves to higher things.

Comparison for depreciation and rejection of our finer selfhood – this is failure – and the one who does it reaps what he sows.

The true self knows, and knowing, dares the way, turning aside, perhaps, to get a shorter path, but holding fast to the great mortal birthright which allows it to say, "I am that I am."

Seventeenth Success Method

HAPPINESS

There are those who are always sad, unhappy. Their gloom reacts on everything around them and carrying this load of despair they become a dread to their friends, their loved ones, business opportunities pass them by because no one wants a walking tale of woe which, by every look, tells to every passerby the negative failure method of their lives.

If we look deeply into every life that touches our own, we will find that each one is on the same journey; each hunting for the same object. It is plain that everybody is filled with only one great purpose, which stands paramount to all others, and that is, the desire to be happy, to find happiness, not the fleeting content which anyone can feel for an hour, a day, but that all sufficient, certain and abiding contentment which makes for peace, power and plenty at every point in our human existence.

We know that happiness is the law of life, and man's natural condition; that unhappiness is a disease and the sign of a life astray from the Infinite union.

Life is full of curious contradictions and conditions, all set in motion by our own and other people's ignorance, and it is the position we assume toward these conflicting forces which determine whether we shall be happy or otherwise. It is no one's fault but our own if we are unhappy; it is no one's fault but our own if we are poor or full of lack.

There are always two ways of looking at these things that we want, and which we think are necessary for our happiness. One is to determine whether from our viewpoint we consider them attainable; and if we are convinced that they are, then secure them; but if we are convinced that they are not, at least, without great striving and resistance on our part, then lay them down and let them alone for that time, get over wanting them until life brings them into our current. We must never forget that substance is always changing, and so is position, and the unattainable of today may become the attainable tomorrow, just from the fact that the law of supply and demand are equal.

We can never hope to possess anything until we feel and know that it is directly in our line of transference, and it is our own folly if we sit down and become unhappy over it, while we recognize its separation from our lives. As soon as our wills recognize that it is not our own, we put it beyond our reach for that time; we will never get it until time, and our own wills, bring it into our atmosphere.

We are only responsible for one thing in this world life, and that is ourselves; everyone else is responsible for themselves and do not need to worry about us. If we would only learn this, and refuse to put our hands on another's life, and not allow their domination in our lives, we would go a long way in this search for happiness.

It is not our own lives that make us unhappy; it is our fear of what others will think of us. We will never become happy nor know true happiness until we learn that it really does not matter what anyone thinks of us. There is only one true criterion of our actions, and that is ourselves. The only one we are responsible for is ourselves; it is impossible for us to tell what any one needs in his development save ourselves; no one can tell us what to do; in the last analysis we must stand alone, and if we learn this, we put ourselves and our affairs far beyond the reach of promiscuous direction into the great path of truth, where and whatever *is*, is right for us as well as for others.

The life that has found its own center and who knows that it is its own unaided law that stands amid eternal ways in the midst of changing and chaotic conditions, that walks on serene with mind alive to the divine teachings, has the Success law, and the true position toward the differentiations of life and the changes of substance.

Does it want wealth; it knows the opulence of supply and asks for it. Does it want wealth, love, possession, anything – it knows that there is abundance everywhere, and in the calm purpose of life, it has only to ask and it is given. This is realization, this is happiness; a realization which only is vouchsafed to those who have made a conscious union with the Infinite.

The life that sublimes itself into the plane above the human thought-plane of error, comes into the "perfect peace that passeth all understanding," for it has touched the Absolute; that life looks at all the conflicting expressions of this earth life with *all* seeing eyes, and knows that no matter what the expression may be, far above the heartaches, the self-made loss, the self-made pain or remuneration, the hand of the eternal Good is guiding this life, finds peace and happiness, and this brings power and power brings Success. It knows that every idol of our human hearts must somehow, somewhere be laid down unless we know how to take it with us as we pass onward to our own fulfillment.

We cannot lose anything which is our own.

Failure, loss, pain and grief are but words to the life that has awakened to this knowledge; it keeps its soul filled with the greatness of growth; looks at attainment from a grand pinnacle of feeling where pain, trouble, heartache, loss and unhappiness are unknown, but the happiness of an eternal realization is its soul. And happiness is a magnet attracting to itself all the free wonderful things in the world.

Eighteenth Success Method

POISE

Poise is that quality of the human mind which makes for perfect balance in all of life's relations. It is activity under control. It enables one to pass from end to end of the pole of human feeling and function normally at every point of contact.

Poise is to the human soul and body what the compass is to the mariner; it is the cloud by day and the pillar of fire by night to the soul adrift on the psychical ocean; it is one expression of the highest energy. When every other hope has failed, the soul that has poise is not altogether desolate.

Sensation is the direct cause of action; we are continually receiving sensations through mind, soul and body, and acting accordingly. The individual who can receive every sensation of his daily life, and regulate himself to vibrate with it, no matter how high or how low it may plunge him, has a poised life and is master of himself.

What constitutes a poised and an unpoised life? Simply this: The understanding and use of willpower, the application of natural laws to every phase of life, and the correct position toward everything on all planes.

Everyone is possessed of just so much willpower which by training and study he may increase to an unusual amount. Given a certain amount of this quality, it is easy to see that the one who understands and uses his willpower increases his growth on all planes far in advance of the individual who does not know or refuses to know his true worth. It is also easy to see that the greater the development, the greater the controlling power becomes and the more certain of results one may become because he has learned the inherent power of his own being.

A willpower that is halting, full of fear, and uncertain of its own creations, cannot hope for success in the activities of life. The changing substances of life with which we are obliged to cope make it impossible to intelligently direct our plane unless we have taught ourselves that fine balance which cannot be altered by external conditions.

We are all acquainted with the unpoised man – the self-conscious, negative creature; the one who "doesn't know" and who says "I can't." The whole world is full of a great skulking apologetic crowd, who cannot even come into our presence without carrying with them the atmosphere of begging to be excused for being born. This is the expression of the unpoised man, and it is he who has caused all the trouble between labor and capital in the world, and will continue to cause it until the "I" in all these individuals is lifted up and placed where it should be by themselves.

Be sure that we are the highest expression of life on this plane and have absolute dominion over our lives; we must never waver in our mental mastery; after we have secured our own freedom, set about getting it externally; we can have what we want and what we want is the very best thing for us to have; it is our consciousness trying to get into expression; do not let anyone else think for us, we have to become our own masters before we can have any force with anyone else; advice is all right but it does not amount to anything only as it helps us to reach our own conclusions.

Absolute perfect union with our own selves and common sense relations to all external life; belief in our own power of accomplishment and our own Divine right to be "what we will to be," faith, hope, love toward all others and that great worldwide charity that "thinketh no evil," – this is *poise*, and as we learn it on the human, physical plane of expression, we pass into the unseen psychic world of laws and become one with that great invisible world-poise which never faileth.

Nineteenth Success Method

THE RULES OF THE GAME

This throwing and lacking the craft to load the dice is the failure side of effort, and the winner in the game is he who plays with a complete and perfect understanding.

Every game has rules; there is not the simplest thing in the world which is not governed by its own law, and to learn how to operate this law is the game men play everywhere.

The thing we call "life" is man's master-game, and the one who understands all the rules of life is the winner in just the degree that he plays fair; he may cheat and lie and shift his hand and win for a time, but the universal master of the game checkmates him when, in some unguarded moment, he lays down his hand.

There are great eternal rules in the game of life which must be regarded, and we violate these rules at our peril. Before we can begin to study the rules we have to learn that one-half of life is wholly dependent upon man.

When we link ourselves with the universal and create our own in consciousness, men must pass it to us by divine law; it is the great universal rule of the game of supply.

If men can give, then men can take away, and the one who works with this belief in his heart, is playing false to the true rule and he must fail, for he builds this law for himself; the one who rises through the power and influence of another has only passive possession, and he must somewhere surrender everything that is not his own, and pass it into the higher law of active possession. No one can take our own away and our own is just what we create for ourselves, and we create it by recognizing it in the universal, and then looking to men to bring it to us or connect us with it.

The one who forgets that his source of supply is universal and not personal, but who links his life with the personal, will have to fight his way through the changes of men and things until he becomes the example of his own game of life.

To think the thoughts which will give ourselves the environment, people, everything just as we would have them – this is the great command, and "there is not a thing in all the world but that thinking makes it so." What folly it is to spend our hours thinking of everything in the world that we do not want, when with another thought move we can change the whole game for ourselves and for others.

Every day men speak themselves out of their hearts' desires. If we listen to the words of the failure multitude we will soon learn that by their words they are justified and condemned. They say, "What's the use?" "I know I can't," "There is nothing in it for me." "There is no use trying, I have tried and failed, I know I can't get it." "He wouldn't help me, business is awful," "I expect that I will lose," "I shall not try any more," "I am too old," "I hate life." Yet the rule of the game says: "Ask, seek, knock," but standing just before the doors they have closed by their own ignorance they turn away and in despair say: "I've played out, the game was never fair."

When we take our wants into our hearts and step out into the multitude of men, and having asked the universal, ask men also with the poise born of this higher authority, they will hear and heed and become then and there a direct line of transference between us and our own. Then, listening to those around who are asking us, we fulfill the rules of service, and as we go on seeking wider and deeper fulfillment of our desires, we can knock at the door of the hearts of men and they will arise and bid us enter.

The universal rule says, "I have set before thee an open door no man can shut." The only part of the game man makes perfect is to open the doors of life around him. As he goes on playing his part in unison with the universal rule, he comes ere long into perfect mastery, his hand no longer lacks the craft to load the dice and his throw is swift and sure because he is one with the *law*.

Love – born of an understanding deep as life itself, reaching out for the distraught faltering human heart, loves on through doubt and darkness until the impossible becomes the possible through the inspiration of love's own spark.

A life that pledges itself to a certain action, a certain development, gets that thing and all the other things which go with it, of which he was unconscious when he signed away his freedom. The law takes every man at his word.

Let us look at the question of compensation from an everyday practical standpoint. Do we want to become artists, actresses, physicians? The first thing we do is to consecrate ourselves to that work; the next thing is to begin along the line we have chosen. If an actress, we bear the poverty, the disappointments, the hours of toil and hardship, the chagrin and despair, until in some unexpected moment the compensation draws near: the time of our service ends in a larger service which we have brought for ourselves by our consecration.

If we want to become artists, it is the same story, the hours of useless labor (when viewed from a world's position), the wasted daubs, the mistakes, the hours of waiting for public approval, and at last the goal. The same thing holds good in every field of labor, but the soul which has fully felt the consecrating power, never lays down the struggle. It follows the beautiful vision of its inner senses.

We must learn, too, that we can make no demand on the world in any way with any hope of realization, if we are not prepared to supply equal value to the world with the gift of ourselves.

No matter what we want, we will find that we can get it if we are willing to pay the price, not always in our way, but in the way that will bring us towards the thing for which we have asked. Left to our own way we would now and then go in a directly opposite path from our desires, for we cannot see the end from the beginning, but once we have made the consecration, if we find the path rough and winding, we cannot choose but go on.

We get what we ask for. If we mourn over our supply it is because we do not understand the causes which we have set in motion and are expecting perfect returns from imperfectly formulated plans.

Those lives which seem so destitute of compensation are not really so; they have only made a mistake in interpreting it. In order to understand compensation, we must understand cause and effect, and know that we only reap what we sow. The life which sows for service reaps service; for knowledge gets knowledge; love gets love; there is no escaping the harvest, but we do not always recognize the compensation for it does not come to us invariably in the guise we expect.

Compensation is always near us, but often we do not recognize it as our own; it may meet us in a new garb at any turn in the lane of life, but while our eyes are blinded with hot tears of loss we cannot see it.

The life that sows service, pleasure, joy, peace, money, power and every hope of its soul, will gather the compensation of its sowing in some way or another, day by day, because it is the unchanging law of the Infinite substance. The human mind has limited itself; it has distorted the soul vision and forgotten the eternal promise "seek and ye shall find."

To plant for the highest compensation is a matter of growth. Look deeply into your own lives and find out just what you want, then ask yourselves if you are ready to pay the price for it? If you are ready, then consecrate yourselves to it and all that the consecration brings, and when you are looking for returns or recompense, be sure that you recognize your own when it comes. Do not limit yourselves; take with you into this consecration everything that you want, and then do not complain of what you are called upon to pay for your gifts.

IX

MARY A. DODSON

ELLA E. DODSON

The following quotes are from
Positive Thoughts Attract Success, 1920

The life each one is fitted to live depends on his mental development. The life each one does live is largely a matter of choice, and the choice is too often on a much lower plane than that to which the natural capabilities point.

One man makes a mere living; another man gains great wealth. The only difference between them is the difference between their desire and will.

Desire is mental; will is spiritual: and both control the physical. As man's mental nature is educated, as his will is developed, so will he acquire the power to change his circumstances, and create whatever environment he desires.

All the elements that make up man's outer conditions exist in the ethereal realm which pervades all space.

Positive thought attracts these elements, and forms them into that which has been strongly stamped on the mind. Whatever image is intensely impressed is thus created in the ethereal world. The manifestation in physical form is as sure to follow as that the clay of the pottery takes the shape of the mold into which it is poured. When the mind has learned to concentrate intelligently, the mental pictures will be so clearly defined that outward visualization is only a question of time. A little definite knowledge combined with the correct mental attitude gives the ability to perform every day wonders almost miraculous.

The spiritual atmosphere surrounding us is full of inexhaustible treasures in such liberal supply that there is more than enough for all. Every one could be living in opulence and plenty.

The well trained mind is magnetic, and can draw to itself any desired substance, in any desired form – whether in life or financial conditions. An affirmative attitude is necessary to gain possession. Positive thoughts attract whatever is wished for and willed. In exact ratio to the knowledge of the marvelous power of the mind and the creative energy of the will, the ability to attract to one's self from the universal supply will be developed.

The mind must be trained to plan, and to concentrate with a clear vision; the will must be strengthened to act with intensity. Concentration includes attention, and our perception of values is that which arouses the will to action. We think what we perceive, and we act what we think. Let us then think strongly only of that which we would like to have expressed in our lives. The most vivid mental picture is the one that will be out-pictured even though it may be something undesirable or something that we fear. But we have the power to choose and direct our thoughts. We should exercise this power and bring our minds to dwell only on that which is desirable.

Thoughts are things. By thinking wisely we can surround ourselves with whatever "things" we wish, and so create our own life atmosphere.

Positive thoughts attract results equal to their strength. Whenever the image is definite and well-defined in thought, and the will energized, intense in purpose, the thinker is divinely led to the use of means to accomplish even the seemingly impossible.

One can be whatever one wills to be; one can do whatever one wills to do; one can have whatever one wills to have – but willing means infinitely more than merely wishing.

You are Beauty. You are Will. You are Faith.

You are Spirit.

Your potentiality is infinite.

You are Love. You should rule only by love. You are in Divine Love's care.

You are the child of Intelligence. Through intellect, you should make your life a life of reason, and through reason, should the emotions be governed, and you, reach perfection.

The garment of a man's character is cut from the pattern of his thoughts.

Whoever watches for the light of life will never see its shadow.

Change and progress are the watchwords of evolution.

Even an umbrella has to be raised to be of use. Therefore, no matter how bad a man appears to be, raise him in your estimation and he will show the best there is in him.

It requires great strength to carry great abundance.

That which will never bend must stand a chance of breaking.

Every person is at every moment unconsciously sending out dynamic rays, invisible impulses, powerful agencies for good or evil. Through these rays, so strongly and unmistakably felt, radiates not only the man with his mode of life, his manners, and his social habits, but also the very constitution of the man – the foundation upon which he rests. Few realize how truly one is enveloped by one's own power, this subtle, magnetic atmosphere.

This unknown quantity in human nature cannot be measured; neither can it be bounded by any lines. It cannot be computed mathematically, but it is there, and not to be ignored. This mysterious force can no more be separated from the man than can the fragrance be taken from the rose, or the grace from the flying bird. It is analogous to the strength of a tree, or the sound of some sweet symphony.

Untiring, unswerving, unfailing, this electric-like energy reaches out from each person, and is what constitutes his personal influence.

An education in the School of Thought is the best preparation for the School of Career.

AFFIRMATIVE

I will drink freely of the waters of truth.

I will eat plentifully of the bread of omnipresent wisdom.

I will bathe in the sunlight of love and honor which everywhere surrounds me.

I will absorb power from the omnipotent forces with which the whole universe is filled.

I will think spiritual thoughts and free myself from the depths of ignorance, by raising myself above it.

Your path is harmony and your duty, adjustment to harmony.

The perfection of personality is the perfection of resplendent intelligence and light.

THINGS I MUST DO TODAY

I must be strong and energetic.

Whatever I do today must be vital.

I must reflect universal kindness.

I must concentrate my energy, and direct it into the right channels.

I must keep my mental windows open to the sky.

I must receive nothing but good from all the world, that I may give back nothing but good to all the world.

As Dawn proudly marches in, Night flees abashed at her approach.

Each day is a new day – for a new conflict with the world and a new conquest of the world.

Life, to be complete life, must be chock-full of poetry and inspiration.

Even though everything around you is upside down, don't let that upset you.

Sometimes it takes bitter doses of misfortune to cure bad cases of unkindness.

Our best weapons are happy work and cheerfulness. No enemy is strong enough to hold out long against them. Do what you can do best, and do it cheerfully. Don't be a slacker!

"A good way to help the world is to become a good listener," said Silence. "Voluble people must have their talk out."

"But," said Speech, "they do not know what they are saying. They talk without thinking."

"That is very true," said Silence, "but when they have tired themselves out they will stop talking. Not until their wagging tongues are still, will they take time to *think*."

Unless your heart sings the word, it would be better left unuttered.

There are many good but weak persons with aimless vacillating methods, who have as bad influence on the community as those whose characters are positively wicked.

In every conclusion the thinker has a share as important as the subject which he is considering.

Making a new plan altogether is sometimes more feasible than changing an old one.

Of course, trouble is likely to come at any time – but to anticipate it constantly is to have it before it *has* come.

Life is not stationary and true life is free.

Instead of always preparing to enjoy life, why not be happy now?

The sweetest voice is that of kindness.

What follows the vision? Power and realization.

Shepherds, we? Yes, each with his herd of sheep to tend – emotions, passions, and desires to lead into right channels. We are often very careless shepherds, sadly neglecting our duty, and then our sheep scatter in every direction.

When they are no longer under our control, we become the playthings of the scared sheep and they control us – poor shepherds at the mercy of our half-crazed flocks!

Patience is the twin sister of genius.

When you see the person, you see the principle.

Worry is the most useless occupation in the whole world. There is simply nothing to worry about if we only knew it.

Worry is the belief in the non-triumph of justice, in the impotence of goodness, in the lack of power, even in the lack of omnipotence itself.

You may have tried – you may have failed – but that does not convince me that you need give up the attempt. If we would develop the good, we must keep our eyes and minds fastened on good.

It is not our power that is limited, but the consciousness of our power is limited.

To learn how to assimilate more and more of the universal life-force is the highest purpose of man. The man who succeeds is the man who opens his pores to the clear, bracing atmosphere of the universal life which surrounds him.

You can be disturbed by externals only when there is some weak spot in your mentality.

See harmony everywhere – think harmony at all times, and those with whom you come in contact will feel your harmonious vibrations, and manifest accordingly.

The *substance* of gold is not equal to the *shadow* of love.

Losing interest is the first step toward losing success.

First, he lost his temper – then, he lost his bearings – then, he lost his cause.

Do you wish higher ideals? *Think* them into your personality.

Do you wish a larger world? *Think* more friends into your circle.

Do you wish to be more successful? *Think* more power into your vocation.

Do you wish to have more ability? *Think* more intensity into your scheme of values.

Do you wish to be happier? *Think* more joy into your consciousness.

Do you wish each year of your life to be sweeter? *Think* more beautiful thoughts each day.

The boundless skies are in your eyes; in them I see Infinity!

Effective thought requires discrimination and concentration. The efficient thinker conserves thought-energy and does not waste it on what is unimportant.

Could we but understand the past, we would already have the future.

Our disputes and competitions often hang on definitions.

Let us not be envious, but remember that whoever has success deserves it.

Run from the wrong thought as from the plague!

Truth is a jewel so fair, and love is a gem so rare, that in contrast with either of them, stars, planets and suns are dim.

The tiny point proves the infinity of space; the shortest moment, the eternity of time.

Definite purpose is the advance agent of success.

The budding human mind ever unfolds into a divine flower, just as naturally as the chrysalis changes into a butterfly.

If your estimate of yourself is small, your accomplishment will be correspondingly small.

Begin it now. If you wait until tomorrow somebody else may have done it.

Unless a man can convince himself of his worth, there is no need for him to try to convince others.

Every man is bigger than his circumstances.

Your true wealth is your richness of thought.

That which is fair and lovely attracts what is fair and lovely to itself.

The whole question of life is a question of truth.

Love is a tree, fragrant and sweet – lasting and strong. It bears flowers and fruit at the same time. The flowers are most beauteous, and the fruit, exceedingly pleasant.

Whoever carries a load of hating thoughts is in danger of being crushed by his burden.

What you can do is the straightest road to what you think is impossible.

Our feeling of warmth is a physical reaction on the day; our being pleasant is a mental reaction on the times; our doing good is a spiritual reaction on eternity.

Alcohol preserves natural history specimens; temperance preserves joy.

If we cannot be great, why not be trustworthy?

This is the critical hour; this moment, the decisive moment.

The spirit needs nourishment. Doing good is spiritual food.

The sunshine of sympathy lights up the darkest caverns of despair and gloom.

Nothing shines like Sincerity.

Why not keep on at the work while waiting for the result?

We may defy convention when we have something better to take its place.

Until one has learned to respect one's self, one cannot reasonably demand the respect of others.

What is the excuse for wrong? After all, the only ultimate result of any of our strivings is the illumination they impart to us. Our most difficult tasks are our best teachers. They make us think and plan and study. They call out our most earnest endeavors and our mental muscles become stronger from the hard struggle with them. No matter what the outcome may be, the enlightenment we gain from any experience is the only real reward. What excuse can there possibly be for wrong?

It is always in our power to create new habits to displace old ones.

Men will try to be what you think they are.

Beware! When you fight another's battle you are apt to get one of your own.

The road of inquiry is a much more direct route to the realm of knowledge than is the road of exposition.

The lessons taught by failure are well worth the cost of tuition.

Lack of concentration is one of the principal human frailties. It keeps many from reaching heights which they might otherwise attain. There can be little success unless one concentrates on his task with energy, and energy is sure to be forthcoming if all the thoughts are gathered together and focused on one subject.

Not all wealth can be represented by the dollar mark.

The ignorance of time is lost in the knowledge of eternity.

Learning to notice little things teaches a man big things.

Learning to take needed rest is the most profitable of all work.

Do not work grumblingly – leave that for slaves.

The world of the egotist is very small. Its average weight is about one hundred and fifty pounds.

Abridgment is sometimes enlargement.

Faithful practice each day will accomplish wonders in mental discipline. But the work must be kept up daily – each day and every day, holidays and workdays, rainy days and sunny days, days when you feel well because it makes you feel better.

The largest houses are made by laying one brick upon another. "A little done this hour and a little the next hour, day by day, and year by year, brings much to pass." The careful gleanings of the miser of moments who hoards up odd minutes, and half-hours, and holidays, will some day have accumulated a solid and substantial block of intellectuality.

Every moment is bright – the sun is shining always. We may not see it, but the spirit knows that this is true.

"I envy no one so much as the man who is rich," said the poor man.

"Only the poor man is happy," said the millionaire.

Nothing is oftentimes better than something.

The analysis of life is a most interesting experiment. It is instructive, too.

You belong to the Boundless. You are eternal.

There are many voices in the universe but only one song.

Love has already won the everlasting victory.

Sometimes agility gets ahead of ability.

You have talked a great deal but what have you told me?

If you don't blow your own horn it may never be blown.

Living is a lifelong job.

In the winter of adversity, prepare for the summer of prosperity.

The ignorant man cannot comprehend why some of his fellows desire knowledge. No more can the snail understand why the bird delights in flying.

Little deeds often fill great needs.

We cannot give to others what we do not possess ourselves. Therefore, be happy, if you wish to give out happiness to the world.

Instead of finding fault with another's earnest work, I will try to draw from it the priceless message it reveals.

A duck, even with peacock's feathers stuck in its tail, is still a duck.

Counting too much on the other fellow – counts yourself out.

Reason compels attention and dispels opposition.

The ugliest truth has more beauty than the most beautiful lie.

A knowledge that all is one is the basis of true understanding.

The world is the marble; your mind is the sculptor; your thought is the chisel.

Do not depreciate yourself constantly; because, the depreciated man might come to rule.

The endurance of life is an essential part of the life of endurance.

Whether our lives shall be rich with promise or filled with despondency depends on our mental condition. If we dissipate our energy we impair our strength and retard our progress. But by concentration we secure unity of purpose, and assure the accomplishment of otherwise undreamed of achievements.

It is good to produce new pictures, new statues, new ideas, new books – but the one who produces something greater than all these is the man who produces new hearts.

The person who is too easygoing makes it hard for himself and for everybody else – while he who struggles hard for what is right makes easy work for all who follow.

The universal precedes the particular as the plan precedes the building.

No, I will not say it is inevitable until I have done all in my power to prevent it.

I am a holy temple, and send out love and good to all the world.

The King of Life has ordered all good to be distributed among his subjects. Now is the day of distribution.

Come and receive your share.

What can't be endured can often be cured.

Start the ball. Its own momentum will keep it rolling.

What you accomplish is often determined by what you attempt.

Dread is the champion of misfortune.

We build our own mental worlds. We must blame no one but ourselves if we fail to draw the proper plan on which to build.

Everything animate and inanimate is governed by the one great power – the power of love.

Strictly speaking, thought and the thinker are not two different logical entities. Each is embodied in the other, and it is impossible to find any thinker existing apart from the thought, and equally impossible to find a thought in which the thinker is not incorporated.

AFFIRMATION

I *will* to be whatever I intelligently desire to be.

I *will* to be a magnet and attract those things which I desire.

I *will* to begin now with what knowledge I have, and to add continually to my knowledge.

I *will* to go on from strength to strength, from character to character, until I have developed a powerful personality.

I *will* to make of myself what it is my divine right to become.

Rebellion is one of the first steps to progress.

If you are concerned with eternal matters, if your mind dwells only on eternal thoughts, if your soul feeds only on eternal food, I now pronounce you living in eternity.

Intelligence is the best foundation for your house of reason.

Satisfaction is Stagnation.

Life is highest when we have ascended to the top of life's greatest hills.

Your surest need is your surest guide.

The most permanent characteristic of humanity is its tendency to change.

The world is apt to judge that what you are doing is what you want to be doing.

Nothing but practice can outwit theory.

The things we love photograph themselves on our faces.

Who tries to deceive another, doubly deceives himself.

It is natural to the spiritual man to prefer wisdom above earthly riches.

Whoever fights with a spiritual sword, wins joy and gladness, as his reward.

Is it best because it is universal? Or, is it universal because it is best?

Rivers of good suggestions make lands fertile in good actions.

A *dreary* failure became a *cheery* success.

For the luster we gather from the world, we are expected to shed back luster on the world.

Fear to lose a good and the good is already lost.

Man is individualized intelligence, and it is his duty to reflect Universal Intelligence at all times and in all places.

The admission of ignorance is sometimes a declaration of knowledge.

Our struggles with discouragement are half over, when we have begun to learn the truth. When we have ever so little a hold on truth, we must remember that truth has a much bigger hold on us. Hear her: "Be still, and hope always, for that which thou seekest, has been seeking thee since time began."

The world will shove him forward, who refuses to go backward.

The man who is lucky is the man who is above luck.

If you understand yourself, you will understand everybody else.

My Resolution: I will think but gracious thoughts; I will sing but songs of praise; I will love with all my heart; and will trust the livelong days.

What grows in life was born of thought.

The most beautiful eye is the eye which sees only the beautiful.

A good disposition is needful seven days in the week.

What you did wrong yesterday – banish it from your mind. It no longer exists – it is but a memory.

Neither dwell too much on what you will do tomorrow, for that is hidden by the veil of the future.

But on that which you do today, think well and ponder – for today you live: yesterday, you were; tomorrow, you will be; today, you are.

Good for this moment only: to make this a high moment in life.

You can't expect to reap a harvest of love, if the seeds you sow are those of hate.

Intelligence, force, and substance – one great trinity.

An extensive fund of information is not requisite for the man who talks only about himself.

When dyed with fear, darkness becomes many shades darker.

Scientific knowledge is knowledge for its own sake. Unscientific knowledge merely feeds intellectual curiosity.

We don't apprehend one another's spiritual nature.

I greet Your Majesty! I see in you dynamic force enough to move the world.

The end of all moral action is to find our eternal relation.

The man who is not afraid to be inconsistent, who gives full expression to his ever broadening ideas, is the man who will be the big man of his day.

If we rely only on haphazard plans, we should not be surprised at getting haphazard results.

To realize life-force everywhere – is to be forceful in every way.

Wonderful poise means exalted vitality.

It is not for the world to discover you – it is for you to discover yourself.

To the art of life must be added the craft of life.

Squelch troubles with scant ceremony and they are lost.

The action of the will is effective, because will exists in the spiritual realm – in the realm of causes.

The eyes often carry more information than the tongue.

Desire is the great motive power of ambition.

Examine your thought and ask this question: "Is it important, or is it trivial?"

Let go fear – let go anger – let go desire – then watch yourself as you grow, higher and higher.

The scientific thinker is the one who considers values.

If one aspires always, one will have little to regret.

If one desires good always, one will not wish to forget.

The mind should assert its power, and only the desirable thoughts should be allowed to enter. The subconscious mind never sleeps, and will untiringly persist until it has worked out the pictures impressed upon it by the conscious mind.

It is not the repression of the wrong emotions at which we aim, but their eradication.

Leave the path of fear and lamentation, and cross over to that of hope and cheer and happiness.

Take care to remove the cause – before the effect has a chance to remove you.

Being brave enough to fail is being strong enough to succeed.

A lashing tongue cuts its possessor first; a boiling temper scalds its owner worst.

Humility that makes me believe myself a good-for-nothing, a cipher, a nobody – is not humility – no, indeed, it is servility – the most depraved.

Since eternity is so long, why such rash haste?

Peace, Power, and Plenty, follow concentration.

Constructive people believe in the rights of others, the same as in their own.

All is impersonal with Truth. Everyone who goes to the Source of All Power will be blessed. Each is led step by step as he is ready for it.

Some men are force – some are power – and some are cosmic tenderness.

To become magnetic, one must learn concentration of energy and self-control.

You desire to be something – choose it, become it.

Look at yourself truthfully. People all about you are studying the limitations to which your egotism is blinding you.

Self-neglect is base idolatry.

Let no man think that he is alone in his greatness; neither let any man believe that he is alone in his meanness – we are all so very much alike.

Every man you meet is greater than he appears to be.

A little weakness inside is a great menace outside.

HOW TO UNDERSTAND HUMAN NATURE

Love is the key to understanding human nature. Without it, one can be deceived by friend or foe.

Love should be the first ray of the human lamp.

Good, honest intentions with love, count far more than wonderful accomplishments without it.

Don't forget that spiritual expression is the perfection of love's reflection.

Love is a lamp which shines into all men's hearts, and reveals all the good which is hidden away there.

Love is the great leveler and equalizes the greatest and the lowest.

Love is the key to the human heart, and love is the key to the understanding of human nature.

What the world needs is courage, honesty, and kindness. Smile!

X

RALPH WALDO TRINE

The following quotes are from
Character-Building Thought Power, 1899

A thought – good or evil – an act, in time a habit – so runs life's law: what you live in your thought-world, that, sooner or later, you will find objectified in your life.

Unconsciously we are forming habits every moment of our lives. Some are habits of a desirable nature; some are those of a most undesirable nature. Some, though not so bad in themselves, are exceedingly bad in their cumulative effects, and cause us at times much loss, much pain and anguish, while their opposites would, on the contrary, bring us much peace and joy, as well as a continually increasing power.

Have we it within our power to determine at all times what types of habits shall take form in our lives? In other words, is habit-forming, character-building, a matter of mere chance, or have we it within our own control? We have, entirely and absolutely. "I will be what I will to be," can be said and should be said by every human soul.

After this has been bravely and determinedly said, and not only said, but fully inwardly realized, something yet remains. Something remains to be said regarding the great law underlying habit-forming, character-building; for there is a simple, natural and thoroughly scientific method that all should know. A method whereby old, undesirable, earth-binding habits can be broken, and new, desirable, lifting habits can be acquired – a method whereby life in part or in its totality can be changed, provided one is sufficiently in earnest to know, and, knowing it, to apply the law.

Thought is the force underlying all. And what do we mean by this? Simply this: Your every act – every conscious act – is preceded by a thought. Your dominating thoughts determine your dominating actions. The acts repeated crystallize themselves into the habit. The aggregate of your habits is your character. Whatever, then, you would have your acts, you must look well to the character of the thought you entertain. Whatever act you would not do – habit you would not acquire – you must look well to it that you do not entertain the type of thought that will give birth to this act, this habit.

It is a simple psychological law that any type of thought, if entertained for a sufficient length of time, will, by and by, reach the motor tracks of the brain, and finally burst forth into action.

The thing to clearly understand is this: That the thought is always parent to the act. Now, we have it entirely in our own hands to determine exactly what thoughts we entertain. In the realm of our own minds we have absolute control, or we should have, and if at any time we have not, then there is a method by which we can gain control, and in the realm of the mind become thorough masters. In order to get to the very foundation of the matter, let us look to this for a moment. For if thought is always parent to our acts, habits, character, life, then it is first necessary that we know fully how to control our thoughts.

Here let us refer to that law of the mind which is the same as is the law in connection with the reflex nerve system of the body, the law which says that whenever one does a certain thing in a certain way it is easier to do the same thing in the same way the next time, and still easier the next, and the next, and the next, until in time it comes to pass that no effort is required, or no effort worth speaking of; but on the contrary, to do the opposite would require the effort. The mind carries with it the power that perpetuates its own type of thought, the same as the body carries with it through the reflex nerve system the power which perpetuates and makes continually easier its own particular acts.

Thus a simple effort to control one's thoughts, a simple setting about it, even if at first failure is the result, and even if for a time failure seems to be about the only result, will in time, sooner or later, bring him to the point of easy, full, and complete control.

Each one, then, can grow the power of determining, controlling his thought, the power of determining what types of thought he shall and what types he shall not entertain. For let us never part in mind with this fact, that every earnest *effort* along any line makes the end aimed at just a little easier for each succeeding effort, even if, as has been said, apparent failure is the result of the earlier efforts. This is a case where even failure is success, for the failure is not in the effort, and every earnest effort adds an increment of power that will eventually accomplish the end aimed at. We can, then, gain the full and complete power of determining what character, what type of thoughts we entertain.

Shall we now give attention to some two or three concrete cases? Here is a man, the cashier of a large mercantile establishment, or cashier of a bank. In his morning paper he reads of a man who has become suddenly rich, has made a fortune of half a million or a million dollars in a few hours through speculation on the stock market. Perhaps he has seen an account of another man who has done practically the same thing lately. He is not quite wise enough, however, to comprehend the fact that when he reads of one or two cases of this kind he could find, were he to look into the matter carefully, one or two hundred cases of men who have lost all they had in the same way. He thinks, however, that he will be one of the fortunate ones. He does not fully realize that there are not short cuts to wealth honestly made. He takes a part of his savings, and as is true in practically all cases of this kind, he loses all that he has put in. Thinking now that he sees why he lost, and that had he more money he would be able to get back what he has lost, and perhaps make a handsome sum in addition, and make it quickly, the thought comes to him to use some of the funds he has charge of. In nine cases out of ten, the results that inevitably follow are known sufficiently well to make it unnecessary to follow him farther.

Where is the man's safety in the light of what we have been considering? Simply this: the moment the thought of using for his own purpose funds belonging to others enters his mind, if he is wise he will *instantly* put the thought from his mind. If he is a fool he will entertain it. In the degree in which he entertains it, it will grow upon him; it will become the absorbing thought in his mind; it will finally become master of his willpower, and through rapidly succeeding steps, dishonor, shame, degradation, penitentiary, remorse will be his. It is easy for him to put the thought from his mind when it first enters; but as he entertains it, it grows into such proportions that it becomes more and more difficult for him to put it from his mind; and by and by it becomes practically *impossible* for him to do it. The light of the match, which but a little effort of the breath would have extinguished at first, has imparted a flame that is raging through the entire building, and now it is almost, if not quite impossible to conquer it.

Shall we notice another concrete case? A trite case, perhaps, but one in which we can see how habit is formed, and also how the same habit can be unformed. Here is a young man, he may be the son of poor parents, or he may be the son of rich parents; one in the ordinary ranks of life, or one of high social standing, whatever that means. He is good-hearted, one of good impulses, generally speaking – a good fellow. He is out with some companions, companions of the same general type. They are out for a pleasant evening, out for a good time. They are apt at times to be thoughtless, even careless. The suggestion is made by one of the company, not that they get drunk, no, not at all; but merely that they go and have something to drink together. The young man whom we first mentioned, wanting to be genial, scarcely listens to the suggestion that comes to his inner consciousness – that it will be better for him not to fall in with the others in this. He does not stop long enough to realize the fact that the greatest strength and nobility of character lies always in taking a firm stand on the side of the right, and allow himself to be influenced by nothing that will weaken this stand. He goes, therefore, with his companions to the drinking place.

With the same or with other companions this is repeated now and then; and each time it is repeated his power of saying "No" is gradually decreasing. In this way he has grown a little liking for intoxicants, and takes them perhaps now and then by himself. He does not dream, or in the slightest degree realize, what way he is tending, until there comes a day when he wakens to the consciousness of the fact that he hasn't the power nor even the impulse to resist the taste which has gradually grown into a minor form of craving for intoxicants. Thinking, however, that he will be able to stop when he is really in danger of getting into the drink habit, he goes thoughtlessly and carelessly on. We will pass over the various intervening steps and come to the time when we find him a confirmed drunkard. It is simply the same old story told a thousand or even a million times over.

He finally awakens to his true condition; and through the shame, the anguish, the degradation, and the want that comes upon him he longs for a return of the days when he was a free man. But hope has almost gone from his life. It would have been easier for him never to have begun, and easier for him to have stopped before he reached his present condition, but even in his present condition, be it the lowest and the most helpless and hopeless that can be imagined, he has the power to get out of it and be a free man once again. Let us see. The desire for drink comes upon him again. If he entertains the thought, the desire, he is lost again. His only hope, his only means of escape is this: the moment, aye, *the very instant* the thought comes to him, if he will put it out of his mind he will thereby put out the little flame of the match. If he entertains the thought the little flame will communicate itself until almost before he is aware of it a consuming fire is raging, and then effort is almost useless. The thought must be banished from the mind the instant it enters; dalliance with it means failure and defeat, or a fight that will be indescribably fiercer than it would be if the thought is ejected at the beginning.

And here we must say a word regarding a certain great law that we may call the "law of indirectness." A thought can be put out of the mind easier and more successfully, not by dwelling upon it, not by attempting to put it out *directly*, but by throwing the mind on to some other object, by putting some other object of thought into the mind. This may be, for example, the ideal of full and perfect self-mastery, or it may be something of a nature entirely distinct from the thought which presents itself, something to which the mind goes easily and naturally. This will in time become the absorbing thought in the mind, and the danger is past. This same course of action repeated, will gradually grow the power of putting more readily out of mind the thought of drink as it presents itself, and will gradually grow the power of putting into the mind those objects of thought one most desires. The result will be that as time passes the thought of drink will present itself less and less, and when it does present itself it can be put out without difficulty, and eventually the time will come when the thought will enter the mind no more at all.

Still another case. You may be more or less of an irritable nature – naturally, perhaps, provoked easily to anger. Someone says something or does something that you dislike, and your first impulse is to show resentment and possibly give way to anger. In the degree that you allow this resentment to display itself, that you allow yourself to give way to anger, in that degree will it become easier to do the same thing when any cause, even a very slight cause, presents itself. It will, moreover, become continually harder for you to refrain from it, until resentment, anger, and possibly even hatred and revenge become characteristics of your nature, robbing it of its sunniness, its charm, and its brightness for all with whom you come in contact. If, however, the instant the impulse to resentment and anger arises, you check it *then and there*, and throw the mind on to some other object of thought, the power will gradually grow itself of doing this same thing more readily, more easily, as succeeding like causes present themselves, until by and by the time will come when there will be scarcely anything that can irritate you, and nothing that can impel you to anger; until by and by a matchless brightness and charm of nature and disposition will become habitually yours, a brightness and charm you would scarcely think possible today. And so we might take up case after case, characteristic after characteristic, habit after habit. The habit of faultfinding and its opposite are grown in identically the same way; the characteristic of jealousy and its opposite; the characteristic of fear and its opposite. In this same way we grow either love or hatred; in this way we come to take a gloomy, pessimistic view of life, which objectifies itself in a nature, a disposition of this type, or we grow that sunny, hopeful, cheerful, buoyant nature that brings with it so much joy and beauty and power for ourselves, as well as so much hope and inspiration and joy for all the world.

There is nothing more true in connection with human life than that we grow into the likeness of those things we contemplate. Literally and scientifically and necessarily true is it that, "as a man thinketh in his heart, so *is* he." The "is" part is his character. His character is the sum total of his habits. His habits have been formed by his conscious acts; but every conscious act is, as we have found, preceded by a thought. And so we have it – thought on the one hand, character, life, destiny on the other. And simple it becomes when we bear in mind that it is simply the thought of the present moment, and the next moment when it is upon us, and then the next, and so on through all time.

One can in this way attain to whatever ideals he would attain to. Two steps are necessary: first, as the days pass, to form one's ideals; and second, to follow them continually whatever may arise, wherever they may lead him. Always remember that the great and strong character is the one who is ever ready to sacrifice the present pleasure for the future good. He who will thus follow his highest ideals as they present themselves to him day after day, year after year, will find that as Dante, following his beloved from world to world, finally found her at the gates of Paradise, so he will find himself eventually at the same gates.

Life is not, we may say, for mere passing pleasure, but for the highest unfoldment that one can attain to, the noblest character that one can grow, and for the greatest service that one can render to all mankind. In this, however, we will find the highest pleasure, for in this the only real pleasure lies. He who would find it by any short cuts, or by entering upon any other paths, will inevitably find that his last state is always worse than his first; and if he proceed upon paths other than these he will find that he will never find real and lasting pleasure at all. The question is not, what are the conditions in our lives, but, how do we meet the conditions that we find there? And whatever the conditions are, it is unwise and profitless to look upon them, even if they are conditions that we would have otherwise, in the attitude of complaint, for complaint will bring depression, and depression will weaken and possibly even kill the spirit that would engender the power that would enable us to bring into our lives an entirely new set of conditions.

In order to be concrete, even at the risk of being personal, I will say that in my own experience there have come at various times into my life circumstances and conditions that I gladly would have run from at the time – conditions that caused at the time humiliation and shame and anguish of spirit. But invariably, as sufficient time has passed, I have been able to look back and see clearly the part which every experience of the type just mentioned had to play in my life. I have seen the lessons it was essential for me to learn; and the result is that now I would not drop a single one of these experiences from my life, humiliating and hard to bear as they were at the time; no, not for the world. And here is also a lesson I have learned: whatever conditions are in my life today that are not the easiest and most agreeable, and whatever conditions of this type all coming time may bring, I will take them just as they come, without complaint, without depression, and meet them in the wisest possible way.

Each one is so apt to think that his own conditions, his own trials or troubles or sorrows, or his own struggles, as the case may be, are greater than those of the great mass of mankind, or possibly greater than those of any one else in the world. He forgets that each one has his own peculiar trials or troubles or sorrows to bear, or struggles in habits to overcome, and that his is but the common lot of all the human race. We are apt to make the mistake in this – in that we see and feel keenly our own trials, or adverse conditions, or characteristics to be overcome, while those of others we do not see so clearly, and hence we are apt to think that they are not at all equal to our own. Each has his own problems to work out. Each must work out his own problems. Each must grow the insight that will enable him to see what the causes are that have brought the unfavorable conditions into his life; each must grow the strength that will enable him to face these conditions, and to set into operation forces that will bring about a different set of conditions. We may be of aid to one another by way of suggestion, by way of bringing to one another a knowledge of certain higher laws and forces – laws and forces that will make it easier to do that which we would do. The doing, however, must be done by each one for himself.

And so the way to get out of any conditions we have gotten into, either knowingly or inadvertently, either intentionally or unintentionally, is to take time to look the conditions squarely in the face, and to find the law whereby they have come about. And when we have discovered the law, the thing to do is not to rebel against it, not to resist it, but to go with it by working in harmony with it. If we work in harmony with it, it will work for our highest good, and will take us wheresoever we desire. If we oppose it, if we resist it, if we fail to work in harmony with it, it will eventually break us to pieces. The law is immutable in its workings. Go with it, and it brings all things our way; resist it, and it brings suffering, pain, loss and desolation.

But a few days ago I was talking with a lady; a most estimable lady living on a little New England farm of some five or six acres. Her husband died a few years ago, a goodhearted, industrious man, but one who spent practically all of his earnings in drink. When he died the little farm was unpaid for, and the wife found herself without any visible means of support, with a family of several to care for. Instead of being discouraged with what many would have called her hard lot, instead of rebelling against the circumstances in which she found herself, she faced the matter bravely, firmly believing that there were ways by which she could manage, though she could not see them clearly at the time. She took up her burden where she found it, and went bravely forward. For several years she has been taking care of summer boarders who come to that part of the country, getting up regularly, she told me, at from half-past three to four o'clock in the morning, and working until ten o'clock each night. In the wintertime, when this means of revenue is cut off, she has gone out to do nursing in the country round about. In this way the little farm is now almost paid for; her children have been kept in school, and they are now able to aid her to a greater or less extent. Through it all she has entertained no fears nor forebodings; she has shown no rebellion of any kind. She has not kicked against the circumstances which brought about the conditions in which she found herself, but she has put herself into harmony with the law that would bring her into another set of conditions. And through it all, she told me, she had been continually grateful that she has been able to work, and that whatever her own circumstances have been, she has never yet failed to find someone whose circumstances were still a little worse than hers, and for whom it was not possible for her to render some little service.

Most heartily she appreciates the fact, and most grateful is she for it, that the little home is now almost paid for, and soon no more of her earnings will have to go out in that channel. The dear little home, she said, would be all the more precious to her by virtue of the fact that it was finally hers through her own efforts.

The strength and nobility of character that have come to her during these years, the sweetness of disposition, the sympathy and care for others, her faith in the final triumph of all that is honest and true and pure and good, are qualities that thousands and hundreds of thousands of women, yes, of both men and women, who are apparently in better circumstances in life can justly envy. And should the little farm home be taken away tomorrow, she has gained something that a farm of a thousand acres could not buy. By going about her work in the way she has gone about it the burden of it all has been lightened, and her work has been made truly enjoyable.

Let us take a moment to see how these same conditions would have been met by a person of less wisdom, one not so farsighted as this dear, good woman has been. For a time possibly her spirit would have been crushed. Fears and forebodings of all kinds would probably have taken hold of her, and she would have felt that nothing that she could do would be of any avail. Or, she might have rebelled against the agencies, against the law which brought about the conditions in which she found herself, and she might have become embittered against the world, and gradually also against the various people with whom she came in contact. Or again, she might have thought that her efforts would be unable to meet the circumstances, and that it was the duty of someone to lift her out of her difficulties. In this way no progress at all would have been made towards the accomplishment of the desired results, and continually she would have felt more keenly the circumstances in which she found herself, because there was nothing else to occupy her mind. In this way the little farm would not have become hers, she would not have been able to do anything for others, and her nature would have become embittered against everything and everybody.

True it is, then, not: What are the conditions in one's life? But: How does he meet the conditions that he finds there? This will determine all.

Thought is at the bottom of all progress or retrogression, of all success or failure, of all that is desirable or undesirable in human life. The type of thought we entertain both creates and draws conditions that crystallize about it, conditions exactly the same in nature as is the thought that gives them form. Thoughts are forces, and each creates of its kind, whether we realize it or not. The great law of the drawing power of the mind, which says that like creates like, and that like attracts like, is continually working in every human life, for it is one of the great immutable laws of the universe. For one to take time to see clearly the things he would attain to, and then to hold that ideal steadily and continually before his mind, never allowing faith – his positive thought-forces – to give way to or to be neutralized by doubts and fears, and then to set about doing each day what his hands find to do, never complaining, but spending the time that he would otherwise spend in complaint in focusing his thought-forces upon the ideal that his mind has built, will sooner or later bring about the full materialization of that for which he sets out.

There are those who, when they begin to grasp the fact that there is what we may term a "science of thought," who, when they begin to realize that through the instrumentality of our interior, spiritual thought-forces we have the power of gradually molding the everyday conditions of life as we would have them, in their early enthusiasm are not able to see results as quickly as they expect, and are apt to think, therefore, that after all there is not very much in that which has but newly come to their knowledge. They must remember, however, that in endeavoring to overcome an old or to grow a new habit, everything cannot be done *all at once*.

In the degree that we attempt to use the thought-forces do we continually become able to use them more effectively. Progress is slow at first, more rapid as we proceed. Power grows by using, or, in other words, using brings a continually increasing power. This is governed by law the same as are all things in our lives, and all things in the universe about us. Every act and advancement made by the musician is in full accordance with law.

No one commencing the study of music can, for example, sit down to the piano and play the piece of a master at the first effort. He must not conclude, however, nor does he conclude, that the piece of the master *cannot be* played by him, or, for that matter, by anyone. He begins to practice the piece. The law of the mind that we have already noticed comes to his aid, whereby his mind follows the music more readily, more rapidly, and more surely each succeeding time, and there also comes into operation and to his aid the law underlying the action of the reflex nerve system of the body, which we have also noticed, whereby his fingers coordinate their movements with the movements of his mind, more readily, more rapidly, and more accurately each succeeding time; until by and by the time comes when that which he stumbles through at first, that in which there is no harmony, nothing but discord, finally reveals itself as the music of the master, the music that thrills and moves masses of men and women. So it is in the use of the thought-forces. It is the reiteration, the constant reiteration of the thought that grows the power of continually stronger thought-focusing, and that finally brings manifestation.

All life is from within out. This is something that cannot be reiterated too often. The springs of life are all from within. This being true, it would be well for us to give more time to the inner life than we are accustomed to give to it, especially in this Western world.

There is nothing that will bring us such abundant returns as to take a little time in the quiet each day of our lives. We need this to get the kinks out of our minds and hence out of our lives. We need this to form better the higher ideals of life. We need this in order to see clearly in mind the things upon which we would concentrate and focus the thought-forces. We need this in order to make continually anew and to keep our conscious connection with the Infinite.

We need this in order that the rush and hurry of our everyday life does not keep us away from the conscious realization of the fact that the spirit of Infinite life and power that is back of all, working in and through all, the life of all, is the life of our life, and the source of our power; and that outside of this we have no life and we have no power.

For we then realize that of ourselves we can do nothing, but that it is only as we realize that it is the Divine life and power working within us, and it is only as we open ourselves that it may work through us, that we are or can do anything. It is thus that the simple life, which is essentially the life of the greatest enjoyment and the greatest attainment, is entered upon.

We give so much time to the activities of the outer life that we do not take sufficient time in the quiet to form in the inner, spiritual thought-life the ideals and the conditions that we would have actualized and manifested in the outer life. The result is that we take life in a kind of haphazard way, taking it as it comes, thinking not very much about it until perhaps, pushed by some bitter experiences, instead of molding it, through the agency of the inner forces, exactly as we would have it.

In this Western world, men and women, in the rush and activity of our accustomed life, are running hither and thither, with no center, no foundation upon which to stand, nothing to which they can anchor their lives, because they do not take sufficient time to come into the realization of what the center, of what the reality of their lives is.

If we in the Occident would take more time from the rush and activity of life for contemplation, for meditation, for idealization, for becoming acquainted with our real selves, and then go about our work manifesting the powers of our real selves, we would be far better off, because we would be living a more natural, a more normal life.

To find one's center, to become centered in the Infinite, is the first great essential of every satisfactory life; and then to go out, thinking, speaking, working, loving, living, from this center.

The life of everyone is in his own hands and he can make it in character, in attainment, in power, in divine self-realization, and hence in influence, exactly what he wills to make it. All things that he most fondly dreams of are his, or may become so if he is truly in earnest; and as he rises more and more to his ideal, and grows in the strength and influence of his character, he becomes an example and an inspiration to all with whom he comes in contact; so that through him the weak and faltering are encouraged and strengthened; so that those of low ideals and of a low type of life instinctively and inevitably have their ideals raised, and the ideals of no one can be raised without its showing forth in his outer life. As he advances in his grasp upon and understanding of the power and potency of the thought-forces, he finds that many times through the process of mental suggestion he can be of tremendous aid to one who is weak and struggling, by sending to him now and then, and by continually holding him in the highest thought, in the thought of the highest strength, wisdom, and love.

The one who takes sufficient time in the quiet mentally to form his ideals, sufficient time to make and to keep continually his conscious connection with the Infinite, with the Divine life and forces, is the one who is best adapted to the strenuous life. He it is who can go out and deal with sagacity and power with whatever issues may arise in the affairs of everyday life. He it is who is building not for the years, but for the centuries; not for time, but for the eternities.

He is building for the centuries because only that which is the highest, the truest, the noblest, and the best will abide the test of the centuries. He is building for eternity because when the transition we call death takes place, life, character, self-mastery, divine self-realization – the only things that the soul when stripped of everything else takes with it – he has in abundance.

In life, or when the time of transition to another form of life comes, he is never afraid, never fearful, because he knows and realizes that behind him, within him, beyond him, is the Infinite wisdom and love; and in this he is eternally centered, and from it he can never be separated.

The following Ralph Waldo Trine quotes are from
The Higher Powers of Mind and Spirit, 1917

We are all dwellers in two kingdoms, the inner kingdom, the kingdom of the mind and spirit, and the outer kingdom, that of the body and the physical universe about us. In the former, the kingdom of the unseen, lie the silent, subtle forces that are continually determining, and with exact precision, the conditions of the latter.

To strike the right balance in life is one of the supreme essentials of all successful living. We must work, for we must have bread. We require other things than bread. They are not only valuable, comfortable, but necessary. It is a dumb, stolid being, however, who does not realize that life consists of more than these. They spell mere existence, not abundance, fullness of life.

We can become so absorbed in making a living that we have no time *for living*. To be capable and efficient in one's work is a splendid thing; but efficiency *can be made* a great mechanical device that robs life of far more than it returns it.

Our prevailing thoughts and emotions determine, and with absolute accuracy, the prevailing conditions of our outward, material life, and likewise the prevailing conditions of our bodily life. Would we have any conditions different in the latter we must then make the necessary changes in the former. The silent, subtle forces of mind and spirit, ceaselessly at work, are continually molding these outward and these bodily conditions.

He makes a fundamental error who thinks that these are mere sentimental things in life, vague and intangible. They are, as great numbers are now realizing, the great and elemental things in life, the only things that in the end really count. The normal man or woman can never find real and abiding satisfaction in the mere possessions, the mere accessories of life. There is an eternal something within that forbids it. That is the reason why, of late years, so many of our big men of affairs, so many in various public walks in life, likewise many women of splendid equipment and with large possessions, have been and are turning so eagerly to the very things we are considering. To be a mere huckster, many of our big men are finding, cannot bring satisfaction, even though his operations run into millions in the year.

And happy is the young man or the young woman who, while the bulk of life still lies ahead, realizes that it is the things of the mind and the spirit – the fundamental things in life – that really count; that here lie the forces that are to be understood and to be used in molding the everyday conditions and affairs of life; that the springs of life are all from within, that as is the inner so always and inevitably will be the outer.

To present certain facts that may be conducive to the realization of this more abundant life is the author's purpose and plan.

THE SILENT, SUBTLE BUILDING FORCES OF MIND AND SPIRIT

There are moments in the lives of all of us when we catch glimpses of a life – our life – that is infinitely beyond the life we are now living. We realize that we are living below our possibilities. We long for the realization of the life that we feel should be.

Instinctively we perceive that there are within us powers and forces that we are making but inadequate use of, and others that we are scarcely using at all.

Practical metaphysics, a more simplified and concrete psychology, well-known laws of mental and spiritual science, confirm us in this conclusion.

Our own William James, he who so splendidly related psychology, philosophy, and even religion, to life in a supreme degree, honored his calling and did a tremendous service for all mankind, when he so clearly developed the fact that we have within us powers and forces that we are making all too little use of – that we have within us great reservoirs of power that we have as yet scarcely tapped.

The men and women who are awake to these inner helps – these directing, molding, and sustaining powers and forces that belong to the realm of mind and spirit – are never to be found among those who ask: Is life worth the living? For them life has been multiplied two, ten, a hundred fold.

It is not ordinarily because we are not interested in these things, for instinctively we feel them of value; and furthermore our observations and experiences confirm us in this thought. The pressing cares of the everyday life – in the great bulk of cases, the bread and butter problem of life, which is after all the problem of ninety-nine out of every hundred – all seem to conspire to keep us from giving the time and attention to them that we feel we should give them. But we lose thereby tremendous helps to the daily living.

Through the body and its avenues of sense, we are intimately related to the physical universe about us. Through the soul and spirit we are related to the Infinite Power that is the animating, the sustaining force – the Life Force – of all objective material forms. It is through the medium of the mind that we are able consciously to relate the two. Through it we are able to realize the laws that underlie the workings of the spirit, and to open ourselves that they may become the dominating forces of our lives.

There is a divine current that will bear us with peace and safety on its bosom if we are wise and diligent enough to find it and go with it. Battling against the current is always hard and uncertain. Going with the current lightens the labors of the journey. Instead of being continually uncertain and even exhausted in the mere efforts of getting through, we have time for the enjoyments along the way, as well as the ability to call a word of cheer or to lend a hand to the neighbor, also on the way.

The natural, normal life is by a law divine under the guidance of the spirit. It is only when we fail to seek and to follow this guidance, or when we deliberately take ourselves from under its influence, that uncertainties arise, legitimate longings go unfulfilled, and that violated laws bring their penalties.

It is ours to find these laws. That is what mind, intelligence, is for. Knowing them we can then obey them and reap the beneficent results that are always a part of their fulfillment; knowingly or unknowingly, intentionally or unintentionally, we can fail to observe them, we can violate them, and suffer the results, or even be broken by them.

Life is not so complex if we do not so continually persist in making it so. Supreme Intelligence, creative Power works only through law. Science and religion are but different approaches to our understanding of the law. When both are real, they supplement one another and their findings are identical.

There are now definite and well-defined laws in relation to thought as a force, and the methods as to how it determines our material and bodily conditions. There are now certain well-defined laws pertaining to the subconscious mind, its ceaseless building activities, how it always takes its direction from the active, thinking mind, and how through this channel we may connect ourselves with reservoirs of power, so to speak, in an intelligent and effective manner.

There are now well-understood laws underlying mental suggestion, whereby it can be made a tremendous source of power in our own lives, and can likewise be made an effective agency in arousing the motive powers of another for his or her habit-forming and character-building. There are likewise well-established facts not only as to the value, but the absolute need of periods of meditation and quiet, alone with the Source of our being, stilling the outer bodily senses, and fulfilling the conditions whereby the Voice of the Spirit can speak to us and through us, and the power of the Spirit can manifest in and through us.

SOUL, MIND, BODY
THE SUBCONSCIOUS MIND THAT INTERRELATES THEM

Speculation and belief are giving way to a greater knowledge of law. The supernatural recedes into the background as we delve deeper into the supernormal. The unusual loses its miraculous element as we gain knowledge of the law whereby the thing is done. We are realizing that no miracle has ever been performed in the world's history that was not through the understanding and the use of Law.

Ignorance enchains and enslaves. Truth – which is but another way of saying a clear and definite knowledge of Law, the elemental laws of soul, of mind, and body, and of the universe about us – brings freedom.

The life force of the soul is Spirit. If spirit, then *essentially one* with Infinite Divine Spirit, for spirit, Being, is one.

The higher insights and powers of the soul, always potential within, become of value only as they are realized and used. Evolution implies always involution. The substance of all we shall ever attain or be, is within us now, waiting for realization and thereby expression. The soul carries its own keys to all wisdom and to all valuable and usable power.

Spirit being the real man, it follows that the great, central fact of all experience, of all human life, is the coming into a conscious vital realization of our source, of our real being, in other words, of our essential oneness with the spirit of Infinite Life and Power – the source of all life and all power. We need not look for outside help when we have within us waiting to be realized, and thereby actualized, this Divine birthright.

Browning was prophet as well as poet when in *Paracelsus* he said: "Truth is within ourselves; it takes no rise from outward things, whatever you may believe. There is an inmost center in us all, where truth abides in fullness; and around wall upon wall, the gross flesh hems it in, this perfect, clear perception – which is truth. A baffling and perverting carnal mesh binds it, and makes all error: and, to know rather consists in opening out a way whence the imprisoned splendor may escape, than in effecting entry for a light supposed to be without."

It was Dr. Hiram Corson who said: "It is what man draws up from his sub-self which is of prime importance in his true education, not what is put into him. It is the occasional uprising of our sub-selves that causes us, at times, to feel that we are greater than we know."

The precept for life in general and for every one is: *Exhibit only thy spiritual, thy life, in the external, and by means of the external in thy actions, and observe the requirements of thy inner being and its nature.* Here is not only an undying basis for all real education, but also the basis of all true religion, as well as the basis of all ideal philosophy. Yes, there could be no evolution, unless the essence of all to be evolved, unfolded, were already involved in the human soul. To follow the higher leading of the soul, which is so constituted that it is the inlet, and as a consequence the outlet of Divine Spirit, Creative Energy, the real source of all wisdom and power; to project its leadings into every phase of material activity and endeavor, constitutes the ideal life.

Failure to realize and to keep in constant communion with our Source is what causes fears, forebodings, worry, inharmony, conflict, conflict that downs us many times in mind, in spirit, in body – failure to follow that Light that lighteth every man that cometh into the world, failure to hear and to heed that Voice of the soul, that speaks continually clearer as we accustom ourselves to listen to and to heed it, failure to follow those intuitions with which the soul, every soul, is endowed, and that lead us aright and that become clearer in their leadings as we follow them. It is this guidance and this sustaining power that all great souls fall back on in times of great crises.

"That the Divine Life and Energy *actually lives in us*," was the philosopher Fichte's reply to the proposition – "the profoundest knowledge that man can attain." And speaking of the man to whom this becomes a real, vital, conscious realization, he said: "His whole existence flows forth, softly and gently, from his Inward Being, and issues out into Reality without difficulty or hindrance."

There are certain faculties that we have that are not a part of the active thinking mind; they seem to be no part of what we might term our *conscious intelligence*. They transcend any possible activities of our regular mental processes, and they are in some ways independent of them. Through some avenue, suggestions, intuitions of truth, intuitions of occurrences of which through the thinking mind we could know nothing, are at times borne in upon us; they flash into our consciousness, as we say, quite independent of any mental action on our part, and sometimes when we are thinking of something quite foreign to that which comes to, that which "impresses" us.

There are two realms of mind, the conscious and the subconscious. Another way of expressing it would be to say that mind functions through two avenues – the avenue of the conscious and the avenue of the subconscious. The conscious is the thinking mind; the subconscious is the doing mind.

The conscious is the sense mind; it comes in contact with and is acted upon through the avenue of the five senses.

The conscious suggests and gives directions; the subconscious receives and carries into operation the suggestions that are received.

The thoughts, ideas, and even beliefs and emotions of the conscious mind are the seeds that are taken in by the subconscious and that in this great *realm of causation* will germinate and produce of their own kind.

A noted thinker and writer has said: "Whatever the mind is set upon, or whatever it keeps most in view, that it is bringing to it, and the continual thought or imagining must at last take form and shape in the world of seen and tangible things."

The subconscious can do and does do whatever it is *actually* directed to do by the conscious, thinking mind. "We must be careful on what we allow our minds to dwell," said Sir John Lubbock, "the soul is dyed by its thoughts."

Thought is a force, subtle and powerful, and it tends inevitably to produce of its kind.

Praise to those who do not allow any one or any number of occurrences in life to sour their nature, rob them of their faith, or cripple their energies for the enjoyment of the fullest in life while here. It's those people *who never allow themselves in spirit to be downed*, no matter what their individual problems, surroundings, or conditions may be, but who chronically bob up serenely who, after all, *are the masters of life*, and who are likewise the strength-givers and the helpers of others.

THOUGHT AS A FORCE IN DAILY LIVING

Thought transference, which is now unquestionably an established fact, notwithstanding much chicanery that is still to be found in connection with it, is undoubtedly to be explained through the fact that *thoughts are forces*. A positive mind through practice, at first with very simple beginnings, gives form to a thought that another mind open and receptive to it – and sufficiently attuned to the other mind – is able to receive.

Wireless telegraphy, as a science, has been known but a comparatively short time. The laws underlying it have been in the universe perhaps, or undoubtedly, always. It is only lately that the mind of man has been able to apprehend them, and has been able to construct instruments in accordance with these laws. We are now able, through a knowledge of the laws of vibration and by using the right sending and receiving instruments, to send actual messages many hundreds of miles directly through the ether and without the more clumsy accessories of poles and wires. This much of it we know – *there is perhaps even more yet to be known.*

When a thought is born in the brain, it goes out just as a sound wave goes out, and transmits itself through the ether, making its impressions upon other minds that are in a sufficiently sensitive state to receive it; this in addition to the effects that various types of thoughts have upon the various bodily functions of the one with whom they take origin.

Of one thing we can rest assured; nothing in the universe, nothing in connection with human life is outside of the Realm of Law. The elemental law of Cause and Effect is absolute in its workings. One of the great laws pertaining to human life is: As is the inner, so always and inevitably is the outer – Cause, Effect. Our thoughts and emotions are the silent, subtle forces that are constantly externalizing themselves in kindred forms in our outward material world. Like creates like, like attracts like. As is our prevailing thought, so is our prevailing type or condition of life.

The type of thought we entertain has its effect upon our energies and to a great extent upon our bodily conditions and states. Strong, clear-cut, positive, hopeful thought has a stimulating and life-giving effect upon one's outlook, energies, and activities; and upon all bodily functions and powers. A falling state of the mind induces a chronically gloomy outlook and produces inevitably a falling condition of the body. The mind grows, moreover, into the likeness of the thoughts one most habitually entertains and lives with. Every thought reproduces of its kind.

Says an authoritative writer in dealing more particularly with the effects of certain types of thoughts and emotions upon bodily conditions: "Out of our own experience we know that anger, fear, worry, hate, revenge, avarice, grief, in fact all negative and low emotions, produce weakness and disturbance not only in the mind but in the body as well."

The one who does not allow himself to be influenced or controlled by fears or forebodings is the one who ordinarily does not yield to discouragements. He it is who is using the positive, success-bringing types of thought that are continually working for him for the accomplishment of his ends. The things that he sees in the ideal, his strong, positive, and therefore creative type of thought, is continually helping to actualize in the realm of the real.

Successful men and women are almost invariably those possessing to a supreme degree the element of faith. Faith, absolute, unconquerable faith, is one of the essential concomitants, therefore one of the great secrets of success. We must realize, and especially valuable is it for young men and women to realize, that one carries his success or his failure with him, that it does not depend upon outside conditions. There are some that no circumstances or combinations of circumstances can thwart or keep down. Let circumstance seem to thwart or circumvent them in one direction, and almost instantly they are going forward along another direction. Circumstance is kept busy keeping up with them.

When she meets such, after a few trials, she apparently decides to give up and turn her attention to those of the less positive, the less forceful, therefore the less determined, types of mind and of life. Circumstance has received some hard knocks from men and women of this type. She has grown naturally timid and will always back down whenever she recognizes a mind, and therefore a life, of sufficient force.

To make the best of whatever present conditions are, to form and clearly to see one's ideal, though it may seem far distant and almost impossible, to believe in it, and to believe in one's ability to actualize it – this is the first essential. Not, then, to sit and idly fold the hands, expecting it to actualize itself, but to take hold of the first thing that offers itself to do – that lies sufficiently along the way – to do this faithfully, believing, knowing, that it is but the step that will lead to the next best thing, and this to the next; this is the second and the completing stage of all accomplishment.

We speak of fate many times as if it were something foreign to or outside of ourselves, forgetting that fate awaits always our own conditions. A man decides his own fate through the types of thoughts he entertains and gives a dominating influence in his life. He sits at the helm of his thought world and, guiding, decides his own fate, or, through negative, vacillating, and therefore weakening thought, he drifts and fate decides him. Fate is not something that takes form and dominates us irrespective of any say on our own part. Through a knowledge and an intelligent and determined use of the silent but ever-working power of thought we either condition circumstances, or, lacking this knowledge or failing to apply it, we accept the role of a conditioned circumstance.

The thoughts that we entertain not only determine the conditions of our own immediate lives, but they influence, perhaps in a much more subtle manner than most of us realize, our relations with and our influence upon those with whom we associate or even come into contact. All are influenced, even though unconsciously, by them.

Thoughts of goodwill, sympathy, magnanimity, good cheer – in brief, all thoughts emanating from a *spirit of love* – are felt in their positive, warming, and stimulating influence by others; they inspire in turn the same types of thoughts and feelings in them, and they come back to us laden with their ennobling, stimulating, pleasure-bringing influences.

Thoughts of envy, or malice, or hatred, or ill will are likewise felt by others. They are influenced adversely by them. They inspire either the same types of thoughts and emotions in them; or they produce in them a certain type of antagonistic feeling that has the tendency to neutralize and, if continued for a sufficient length of time, deaden sympathy and thereby all friendly relations.

We have heard much of "personal magnetism." Careful analysis will, I think, reveal the fact that the one who has to any marked degree the element of personal magnetism is one of the large-hearted, magnanimous, cheer-bringing, unself-centered types, whose positive thought forces are being continually felt by others, and are continually inspiring and calling forth from others these same splendid attributes. I have yet to find anyone, man or woman, of the opposite habits and, therefore, trend of mind and heart who has had or who has even to the slightest perceptible degree the quality that we ordinarily think of when we use the term "personal magnetism."

If one would have friends he or she must be a friend, must radiate habitually friendly, helpful thoughts, goodwill, love. The one who doesn't cultivate the hopeful, cheerful, uncomplaining, goodwill attitude toward life and toward others becomes a drag, making life harder for others as well as for one's self.

Ordinarily we find in people the qualities we are mostly looking for, or the qualities that our own prevailing characteristics call forth. The larger the nature, the less critical and cynical it is, the more it is given to looking for the best and the highest in others, and the less, therefore, is it given to gossip.

The chief characteristic of the gossip is that he or she prefers to live in the low-lying miasmic strata of life, reveling in the negatives of life and taking joy in finding and peddling about the findings that he or she naturally makes there. The larger natures see the good and sympathize with the weaknesses and the frailties of others. They realize also that it is so consummately inconsistent – many times even humorously inconsistent – for one also with weaknesses, frailties, and faults, though perhaps of a little different character, to sit in judgment of another. Gossip concerning the error or shortcomings of another is judging another. The one who is himself perfect is the one who has the right to judge another.

Life becomes rich and expansive through sympathy, goodwill, and good cheer; not through cynicism or criticism.

THE DIVINE RULE IN THE MIND AND HEART:
THE UNESSENTIALS WE DROP – THE SPIRIT ABIDES

With Divine self-realization the Spirit assumes control and mastery, and you are saved from the follies of error, and from the consequences of error.

The lower propensities and desires will lose their hold and will in time fall away. You will be at first surprised, and then dumfounded, at what you formerly took for pleasure. True pleasure and satisfaction go hand in hand – nor are there any bad after results.

It was Edward Carpenter who said: "In order to enjoy life one must be a master of life – for to be a slave to its inconsistencies can only mean torment; and in order to enjoy the senses one must be master of them. To dominate the actual world you must, like Archimedes, base your fulcrum somewhere beyond."

You can trust any man whose heart is right. He will be straight, clean, reliable. His word will be as good as his bond.

Personally you can't trust a man who is brought into any line of action, or into any institution through fear. The sore is there, liable to break out in corruption at any time.

The ordinary mind is slow to distinguish between tradition and truth – especially where the two have been so fully and so adroitly mixed.

Fear can never be a basis of either religion or ethics. The one who is moved by fear makes his chief concern the avoidance of detection on the one hand, or the escape of punishment on the other. Men of large caliber have an unusual sagacity in sifting the unessential from the essential as also the false from the true.

SOME METHODS OF ATTAINMENT

It is the material that is the transient, the temporary; and the mental and spiritual that is the real and the eternal. We must not become slaves to habit. The material alone can never bring happiness – much less satisfaction. These lie deeper.

Abundance of life is determined not alone by one's material possessions, but primarily by one's riches of mind and spirit.

Why be so eager to gain possession of the hundred thousand or the half-million acres, of so many millions of dollars? Soon, and it may be before you realize it, all must be left. It is as if a man made it his ambition to accumulate a thousand or a hundred thousand automobiles. All soon will become junk. But so it is with all material things beyond what we can actually and profitably use for our good and the good of others – and that we actually do so use.

A man can eat just so many meals during the year or during life. If he tries to eat more he suffers thereby. He can wear only so many suits of clothing; if he tries to wear more, he merely wears himself out taking off and putting on.

All the time spent in accumulating these things beyond the reasonable amount, is so much taken from the life – from the things of the mind and the spirit. It is in the development and the pursuit of these that all true satisfaction lies. Elemental law has so decreed.

We have made wonderful progress; or rather have developed wonderful skill in connection with things. We need now to go back and catch up the thread and develop like skill in making the life.

When the mental beauties of life, when the spiritual verities are sacrificed by self-surrender to and domination by the material, one of the heavy penalties that inexorable law imposes is the drying up, so to speak, of the finer human perceptions – the very faculties of enjoyment.

He whose sole employment or even whose primary employment becomes the building of bigger and still bigger barns to take care of his accumulated grain, becomes incapable of realizing that life and the things that pertain to it are of infinitely more value than barns, or houses, or acres, or stocks, or bonds, or railroad ties. These all have their place, all are of value; but they can never be made the life.

Yes, life and its manifold possibilities of unfoldment and avenues of enjoyment – life, and the things that pertain to it – is an infinitely greater thing than the mere accessories of life.

One of the great secrets of all successful living is unquestionably the striking of the right balance in life. The material has its place – and a very important place. Fools indeed were we to ignore or to attempt to ignore this fact. We cannot, however, except to our detriment, put the cart before the horse. Things may contribute to happiness, but things cannot bring happiness – and sad indeed, and crippled and dwarfed and stunted becomes the life of everyone who is not capable of realizing this fact.

All life is from an inner center outward. As within, so without. As we think we become. Which means simply this: our prevailing thoughts and emotions are never static, but dynamic. Thoughts are forces – like creates like, and like attracts like. It is therefore for us to choose whether we shall be interested primarily in the great spiritual forces and powers of life, or whether we shall be interested solely in the material things of life.

But there is a wonderful law which we must not lose sight of. It is to the effect that when we become sufficiently alive to the inner powers and forces, to the inner springs of life, the material things of life will not only follow in a natural and healthy sequence, but they will also assume their right proportions. They will take their right places.

Infinitely better is it to know that one has this inner source of guidance and wisdom which as he opens himself to it becomes continually more distinct, more clear and more unerring in its guidance, than to be continually seeking advice from outside sources, and being confused in regard to the advice given.

Not that problems will not come. They will come. There never has been and there never will be a life free from them. Life isn't conceivable on any other terms. But the wonderful source of consolation and strength, the source that gives freedom from worry and freedom from fear is the realization of the fact that the guiding force and the molding power is within us. It becomes active and controlling in the degree that we realize and in the degree that we are able to open ourselves so that the Divine intelligence and power can speak to and can work through us.

Judicious physical exercise induces greater bodily strength and vigor. An active and alert mental life, in other words mental activity, induces greater intellectual power. And under the same general law the same is true in regard to the development and use of spiritual power.

It, however, although the most important of all because it has to do more fundamentally with life itself, we are most apt to neglect. The losses, moreover, resulting from this neglect are almost beyond calculation.

To establish one's center aright is to make all of life's activities and events and results flow from this center in orderly sequence.

We are so occupied with the matters of the sense-life that all unconsciously we become dominated, ruled by the things of the senses. Now in the real life there is recognition of the fact that the springs of life are all from within, and that the inner always leads and rules the outer. Under the elemental law of Cause and Effect this is always done – whether we are conscious of it or not. But the difference lies here: The master of life consciously and definitely allies himself in mind and spirit with the great central Force and rules his world from within. The creature of circumstances, through lack of desire or through weakness of will, fails to do this, and, lacking guiding and directing force, drifts and becomes thereby the creature of circumstance.

We can bring our minds into rapport, into such harmony and connection with the infinite Divine mind that it speaks in us, directs us, and therefore acts through us as our own selves. Through this connection we become illumined by Divine wisdom and we become energized by Divine power. It is ours, then, to act under the guidance of this higher wisdom and in all forms of expression to act and to work augmented by this higher power. The finite spirit, with all its limitations, becomes at its very center in rapport with Infinite spirit, its Source. The finite thereby becomes the channel through which the Infinite can and does work.

There is perhaps no more valuable way of realizing this end, than to adopt the practice of taking a period each day for being alone in the quiet, a half hour, even a quarter hour; stilling the bodily senses and making oneself receptive to the higher leadings of the spirit – receptive to the impulses of the soul.

Things in this universe and in human life do not happen. All is law and sequence. The elemental law of cause and effect is universal and unvarying. In the realm of spirit law is as definite as in the realm of mechanics – in the realm of all material forces.

If we would have the leading of the spirit, if we would perceive the higher intuitions and be led intuitively, bringing the affairs of the daily life thereby into the Divine sequence, we must observe the conditions whereby these leadings can come to us, and in time become habitual.

The law of the spirit is quiet – to be followed by action – but quiet, the more readily to come into a state of harmony with the Infinite Intelligence that works through us, and that leads us as our own intelligence when through desire and through will, we are able to bring our subconscious minds into such attunement that it can act through us, and we are able to catch its messages and follow its direction. But to listen and to observe the conditions whereby we can listen is essential.

I shall always remember with great pleasure and profit a call a few days ago from Dr. Edward Emerson of Concord, Emerson's eldest son. Happily I asked him in regard to his father's methods of work – if he had any regular methods. He replied in substance: "It was my father's custom to go daily to the woods – *to listen*. He would remain there an hour or more in order to get whatever there might be for him that day. He would then come home and write into a little book – his 'day-book' – what he had gotten. Later on when it came time to write a book, he would transcribe from this, in their proper sequence and with their proper connections, these entrances of the preceding weeks or months. The completed book became virtually a ledger formed or posted from his day-books."

The prophet is he who so orders his life that he can adequately listen to the voice, the revelations of the over soul, and who truthfully transcribes what he hears or senses. He is not a follower of custom or tradition.

His aim and his mission is rather to free men from ignorance, superstition, credulity, from half truths, by leading them into a continually larger understanding of truth, of law – and therefore of righteousness.

When a man finds his center, when he becomes centered in the Infinite, then redemption takes place. He is redeemed from the bondage of the senses.

It is a new life that he has entered into. He lives in a new world, because his outlook is entirely new.

XI

THOMAS R. GAINES

The following quotes are from
Friendly Thoughts, 1924

TODAY

Gladness will be my aim today. I will be happy, I will, I will. I will rise above every handicap or obstacle that might hinder or retard my quest for happiness. I will see only the good in life and in others. I will smile deep down in my heart. I will be considerate of others and help all those with whom I come in contact. I will have unfailing patience today. Nothing can take from me my sense of joy and gladness. Yes, today I will be really and truly happy, poised, contented and optimistic.

ACHIEVEMENT

I know that I spin the web of my own life. If I think success and joy, it will be attracted and be woven into every phase of my daily existence. I pray that no sickly, grumbling, faultfinding thoughts will dominate me today or at any future time. Positiveness, courage, self-confidence and determination are the forces I will dwell on, and I know they will inspire me to do my highest, finest and best.

THOROUGHNESS

Life is but imperfectly lived if thoroughness is lacking. If I skim through my daily tasks, I am narrowing my vision and sowing a destructive harvest to reap in the future. If my reading and thinking are of the shallow kind, I express shallowness and mediocrity in my conversation and contact with others. May I ever have the impulse to complete what I start if it is worthy of completion. May my life's slogan be, "I will do all things well."

ENLIGHTENMENT

Give me faith to know that all power is within, that by my thoughts and acts I build or destroy myself. Without the recognition that good is indwelling within me, I realize that I cannot find true happiness or make constructive progress.

PROSPERITY

Concretely visualizing prosperity for a little time each day will ultimately create it for me.

An ample supply for all my needs and comforts is my aim. In all nature there is an amazing abundance and it is my birthright to demand and expect a generous share. With hand and brain I will labor until I win. Then I can best serve those who are needy or discouraged.

EXPECTANCY

The Happiness Spirit will dwell with me today. I will endeavor to express normality, saneness and wholeness in thought and action. I will walk with the feeling of youthfulness in my step. My eyes will be keen and observant to focus on the pleasant sights of life. I believe in the promise "Seek and you shall find." So with contrite, expectant heart I will confidently seek.

THANKFULNESS

I desire today to have an unlimited view of life.

I will be grateful for even the simplest thing, the trust of a child, the glint of sunlight, the beauty of a simple flower, or a friendly smile. My prayer is that I may ever have an understanding heart so that I can magnify the little beauties and glories of life and see them as they should be seen – rich treasures.

OPPORTUNITY

The Supreme force behind life is so generous and fruitful that it has provided an abundance for everyone. Opportunity calls every day. Let me recognize that fact so that I will lose no time repining over lost opportunities. May I be prepared to seize the next chance for success when I sense the presence of opportunity.

POISE

Let my steps be placed in the right direction. Today I will travel on with life's good companions, Peace, Calmness and Tranquility. Serenely facing every handicap and problem, I will rise above them all. Not once will I swerve from my purpose. Today I will smile with supreme self-control. The poison of anger and envy will be far removed from me and the sweetness of peace will fill my every minute.

GOOD

Simple desires, mental serenity, wholesome modesty, constructive achievement, quest for good, these are the steps which I must daily tread to find true happiness, success and joy of living. Facing these supreme heights with outstretched hands and a hope-filled heart, I go forward until I arrive at the top, a victor. There I will redouble my efforts to continue to live the life worthwhile.

SMILES

Pleasant thoughts, sunshine of soul, buoyancy of spirit, gladness of heart, these will be my guiding forces through life. Today I will live with the spirit of optimism percolating through my being. I will be happy and glad. I will shut out all the poison of negation and doubt. My atmosphere and personality will be endowed with the radiance of smiles and good cheer. This will be my happiest day.

I CAN

I realize there is really no limit to advancement if I use the forces of life in the scientific and proper manner. First, the creation of a goal of attainment, then, visualizing daily the completion of that ambition. Bending my steps day by day in the direction of my aim, combined with constructive work will ultimately achieve and bring to fulfillment my desires. May I ever be guided by the highest and noblest purpose in all I think and do.

LOVE

To appreciate love, life's undying force, I must give back love in return; otherwise I violate the immutable law of love. With my life radiating love, I realize I am indeed blessed, and my prayer ever will be "Teach me how to give so that I shall receive more abundantly."

FRIENDSHIP

Friendship, like love, is unpurchaseable by gold. I know that I can win friendship only by loyal service and generous giving. Unless I personify genuine friendship in my intercourse with others, I cannot hope or expect to have many real friends. May I prove the depth and quality of my own friendship toward my friends so that they will extend to me what I earnestly crave: the warmth of true, soul-deep, golden friendship.

WISDOM AND KINDNESS

My desire is all-round development, and this is possible only through the expression of harmony, kindness and wisdom.

ASPIRATION

I realize my two greatest enemies are Indolence and Fear. Ambition, confidence, and determination are the master keys that unlock the treasure doors of life. Let me live so that fear and indolence will not find a place in my mental and physical life. My thoughts must be so positive, so filled with aspiration, that my consciousness cannot entertain a negative suggestion or fear condition.

SYMPATHY

Let me in a humble way try to express by loving and giving that I have the sympathetic spirit alive in my heart. But ever must I express sympathy wisely so that selfishness will not be engendered in those to whom I proffer it.

LIFE AND WORK

To know that I am a free agent, unhampered, unbound, my own master, pulsating with life, means so much. That I can express and direct the energy of my body and mind to the constructive performance of labor that I enjoy, is indeed a positive blessing. Life requires but little more to make it ideal.

COURAGE

Fear and doubt are tireless enemies and I must live so that they cannot find an entrance into my life. With undaunted courage, squared shoulders and unflinching eye I shall advance and fight life's battles. If I am knocked down I will arise again after the fury of failure has spent itself.

DESIRE

I will absorb the noblest and finest things in life. I will break away from bad habits and undesirable thoughts. The flame of desire is burning brightly in my heart; desire to do good and to be good day by day. My sincere wish is to draw sweetness, patience, and mental sunshine into my life; to be simple in my desires, wholesome, charitable and filled with sympathy for all humanity and ever to see the sunlight bursting through life's darkest clouds.

JOY

Let me walk in the sunshiny streets of life. Let me see the radiance of cheer and happy skies as I wend my way. From the depths of my soul I cry for more light, increased hope and greater faith, so that I may irrefutably know that all things are possible to those that look for good. I consecrate my life on the altar of joy, not only joy sufficient to bless and fill my own life, but an abundance of joy to extend to those needy souls who so grievously lack it.

SOWING

I pray for strength to practice mental gardening day by day. Let me root out of my life the weeds of selfishness, anger, criticism, unfairness, envy and jealousy! Then I will plant instead the seeds of love, friendship, poise, joy, cheer, hope and faith. These goodly seeds will germinate and later will richly bless and endow my life. May my harvest be these finer, higher, nobler and sweeter things; a harvest good to reap.

CRITICISM

I pray that the evil of criticizing others will be far removed from me. Let me learn the vital importance of these two great words, magnify and minimize, to learn to magnify the fine qualities in others and minimize their faults and follies, to magnify even the littlest blessing in life.

HAPPINESS

The warming, vitalizing influence of true happiness is a condition I greatly desire.

If I keep in a cheerful, joyous mood I shall be more successful in life. Magnet-like, happiness attracts joy, cheer and love. May my soul ever be filled with the gladness and sweetness of unadulterated happiness.

REACTION

Thought is metaphysical, but the vibration of thought is physical; actual living waves that travel through space. I pray for vision to ever remember that fact. I will carefully guard my lips so that no stinging, negative word will issue from them. And I will harmonize my life so that my thoughts will be pleasant and beautiful. Then even my littlest act will be directed by noblest inspiration and I will later reap a harvest of good.

THE PAST

Memory is a precious possession, but a good extinguisher too is essential in life. May I think only of the pleasant and profitable things of the past. I shall strive to consider the past a closed book as far as mistakes, failure, errors and omissions are concerned. I will start each morning from where I stand looking to the future with hope and confidence, determined to enrich every hour with constructive thought and achievement.

PERSONALITY

I will strive for sincerity, enthusiasm, ambition, poise and wholesomeness. I will mold into my atmosphere also the good qualities of charm, tact, friendliness, kindness and other fine traits.

The following Thomas R. Gaines quotes are from
The Achieving Life, 1926

PURPOSEFUL LIVING

Do the very best you can wherever you are, and as you do your best, make your best count for something; make it really productive, useful and worthwhile.

Thrust all confusion out of your life. Work to have poise, order and equilibrium firmly established, so that you may think without confusion and live your life in an orderly and efficient way.

Ours is a universe of law and order and we should try to emulate the majestic principle of our world, banishing confusion and encouraging order and harmony. Begin the morning well; try to awaken with a happy heart and a song on your lips. Smilingly look out of the window to greet the sun with a positive thought and carry that smiling, sunshine atmosphere with you all through the hours of the day.

Good cheer is one of the radiant essentials of life; it attracts happy souls to you because like attracts like. Wonderful indeed is the life that constantly manifests good cheer and happiness.

"Sing, and the hills will answer. Sigh, it is lost in the air." The song of gladness is wafted back to you and its vibration will ever bless you and also those around you, but sighing loses itself in the ether and is not productive.

Do not weight your joy with lead. Get genuine, wholehearted happiness pulsating within you. Be glad at every opportunity. Doubt and jealousy are factors destructive of joy. Live the happiness way; it is the preferred manner of living because it is constructive and a promoter of smiles and contentment.

Do not be like the thrush that keeps vigil over an empty nest. Rather be like the robin that sings in the rain. Utilize time, understand its significance; then you will comprehend that time is not given you to waste. It is too precious to be frittered away in complaining about the past, in self-pity, in talking about lost opportunities.

It is never too late to achieve in life, so be up, alert and doing. The past is dead, it is a closed book. Blot out all its errors and omissions and live your best today; do your supreme work now. "Make good"; that silences your critics and stamps you as a successful man.

Live an achieving life; show that by constructive thought, by hard work, by vision, by merit and superiority, you have won. "Make good" – that answers all.

Never say you are a victim of fate; that means self-pity, and self-pity is a destructive trait. Rather say with Henley: "I am the master of my fate, I am the captain of my soul." That triumphant attitude will lift you above self-pity, fear and remorse.

Life will always be a series of trials and problems. Each unfolding day will reveal its own burdens. Realizing that fact will enable you to meet your obstacles in the right frame of mind; you will know that there are toilsome heights to be climbed in life, that clouds will sometimes discomfort you, that handicaps will confront you, but there are also babbling brooks, fertile meadows, green places and cool, shady spots. Learn the laws of life; then will you understand life, and this understanding will at all times be a beacon and a guide to triumphant living.

Faith is an achieving factor. The spirit of faith will help you to drive darkness and fear out of your life and inculcate within you a sense of freedom and mastery.

Yes, faith will enable you to climb undreamed-of heights in life. It will give you the power to ring darkness and gloom out of your life and ring in lightness, brightness and happiness.

Divorce yourself from envy; cast it out of your life. Be glad for the prosperity of others; think kindly about them and you attract kind expressions from others into your own life. Be glad that your neighbor is prosperous.

Study life more deeply. Successful living is indeed the greatest of all sciences and its achievement requires constant perception and reflection. Develop the spirit of thoroughness as a precept in your daily life; do not be a skimmer or a skimper.

Develop the power of observation. Look around you with seeing eyes and an understanding mind so that you may promote the quality of appreciation and comprehension.

If you look with comprehending eyes you will find even the most commonplace thing has the potentiality of higher expression. Suitable unfoldment will bring to fruition that higher something that can be developed, thus enabling you to glimpse the deeper and greater meaning of life.

THE MOLDING OF PERSONALITY

Personality is something most difficult to define. You can see it and feel it, yet you cannot tangibly locate it. It is a subtle force for good or ill, depending on the kind of personality you have developed. Roughly speaking, there are three grades of personality: the magnetic or positive, the aspiring, and the negative types.

The positive type is exemplified in the successful man who has won happiness and success by vision, hard work and fair dealing. He has learned how to keep poised under the most unusual conditions; he has a cheerful, optimistic outlook in life. He has developed the qualities of personal magnetism and personal power; he is a good listener, a fluent talker and an omnivorous reader. He believes in friendship, love and inspiration. He is a student of life and is a good mixer and a keen judge of men. He aspires to daily growth and aims to advance by sincerity, ability and by giving genuine service.

He ever endeavors to climb life's supreme heights through the medium of hard work and a fertile imagination. The man of positive personality is a good leader because he is master of at least one thing. Others recognize his ability and believe in him. He believes in encouraging others and never unduly criticizes or condemns. He is wide-awake, level-headed, with a keen sense of humor and enjoyment of life, practical, thorough in his work and courteous to all those with whom he comes in contact.

The aspiring personality is the man who yearns to express himself in the positive range; he is ambitious for success and independence.

He works hard and visualizes advancement and the winning of opulence. He has pertinacity of purpose, and in spite of the slurs of his well-meaning, though mistaken friends, he keeps up his program of advancement. Naturally he encounters obstacles and disappointments, but the glow of ambition is firing his blood; he smilingly sticks to his set purpose until he finally arrives. He is a student of right thinking and aims to live a positive life.

The negative personality is the man in the rut of indigence, indifference, cynicism, ignorance, envy, limitation or discouragement. The negative personality should follow the example of the aspiring personality and dare to desire to reach a higher plane of living. He should arouse himself to the fact that all things are possible. He should become wholesomely discouraged with his hampering conditions and determine to improve them.

Some of us must be the crew to serve in the vessel of life. We cannot all be captains, but the fact that you are reading this book proves that you are reaching out for a higher life. Strongly assert, "I want to climb higher; I want more success, more abundance, more of the good things of life." Desire is necessary for growth. Demand alone brings supply. Resolve for the next year that you will spend fifteen minutes each day in the molding of a positive personality. Daily check up on your mode of living. Life is like a big garden and your mind is part of it; weeds and fair blossoms grow in the garden of your mind. See that you dominate; pull out the weeds that seek to choke the higher growths in your garden of the mind. Carefully keep on the alert to improve your mental garden and soon a vast improvement will take place. Know that symmetrical all-around improvement must be developed. If you really want to be known as a positive, radiant personality, you can reach that desirable stage, but only if you are truly and sincerely in earnest. It is worth trying. Step out of your rut of mediocrity. Remove yourself from the clutch of negativeness and learn how to live a supreme, triumphant life.

The aspiring man is not content to remain an automaton, nor is he willing to live a cheap, narrow life. He is reaching out for bigger and richer things. The urge for the greater life is goading him on to accomplishment. Anyone can live a cipher life, a little life, but it requires ambition, desire, confidence, pluck and determination to strike out toward emancipation and the adoption of a plan of living and thinking that will cultivate and develop an achieving personality.

A SERENE MIND AND EMOTIONAL CONTROL

You are creatures of habit, walking bundles of it. Your daily habits are assets or liabilities. Your thoughts and habits of the past have made you as you are today. Impartially check up on your habits. Are they positive or negative? Are they helping you to rise in life, or are they impeding your progress? Your past is gone forever, but the future lies ahead and the measure of a man's intelligence is how he utilizes his past experiences. If you keep on in the old blundering way, rare intelligence is certainly not demonstrated. If your personality is not all you wish it to be, improve your habits, and accordingly your personality will improve.

Believe in the principle of the "Golden Rule" if you wish to be rated as a great personality; treat others as you would wish to be treated by others. Fair dealing at all times leaves its indelible imprint on your personality; you cannot disguise crookedness or dishonesty for any length of time.

You cannot be insincere in private and feign sincerity in public; you must be consistently sincere, otherwise you will be found out and disgraced. Steadfastly adhere to the principles of high character, sincerity and square dealing, then you are well advanced on the road that leads to the attainment of a great personality.

The crowd lacks achieving personality; that is why the crowd is in a rut. The average man wants success and happiness, but he balks at the price he is asked to pay. Life above all is fair and impartial; no work, no reward, is the rule. Realize that personality must be won, it has to be fashioned; it is not an inheritance; it must be artificially created and it pays rich dividends for the energy you expend in its acquisition.

Your voice has much to do with your personality, cultivate a rich, full, attractive voice. When you express a well controlled, pleasant, agreeable quality in your voice, you have a decided advantage over the individual who has not improved his voice. Your success is often won by the tone of your voice.

Express energy, dash and power in your work, in your walk and in your daily life. Emerson says: "The earth belongs to the energetic and the wise." Weakness begets weakness; strength favors courage and self-confidence. People judge you by the kind of emotions and traits you express, so cultivate the qualities of daring, strength, force, spirit and enthusiasm. Your life will be lived in an ascending way when you are dominated by such positive tendencies.

The radiant, optimistic spirit should constantly be manifested. Be a reflector of joy, and gloom will not be attracted to you. All negative, harsh, gruff emotions tend to wither the attractive side of personality. All positive, happy, confident, enthusiastic emotions foster the development of a magnetic, winning personality. To reach the higher type of personality, be constantly on your guard against the expression of any of the lower, baser, unattractive emotions. Envy is a destructive emotion and you are going backward if you are so unwise as to express such an unfortunate tendency. Jealousy is an indication of inferiority and littleness. Divorce yourself from all jealous emotions; unhappiness lies ahead of you if you cling to these destructive animalistic traits. Cast off all thoughts of a narrowing, stultifying nature. Rise above these baser expressions of life. Cast aside life's dross and brass. Hold to the gold, the good, the fine, the inspirational and the best. Then it will be the ascending upward road on which your steps will be daily bent.

Tact is necessary to the winning of a pleasing personality. Consider the feelings of others. Recognize your responsibility to others. Realize that others have rights and privileges. Get the spirit of harmony into constant expression.

Learn the art of diplomacy and burnish off your rough edges; do not be too assertive or unwholesomely aggressive. Use moderation in all things; your greatest assets, if used beyond the point of moderation, becomes a menace.

Be thorough and consistent, develop the quality of application. Learn to stick to one thing until you are through with it; lack of concentration, inability to focus on one subject for a period of time, is opposed to the building of a great personality. Hold on to the job on hand until you push it through to a conclusion. Finishing the thing you start, adds to your self-confidence and personal power.

Ambiguity in conversation is destructive to a high personality. Speak clearly, effectively and to the point. Let your conversation count for something.

Just thrill with the sheer joy of living and with the thought of being free to think for yourself and being able to live a life of growth and freedom. All expression of fear and worry is unfavorable soil for the propagation of a dynamic personality. Aim to express poise, tranquility and the sense of mastery. Know how to dominate conditions and not be a creature of circumstances. Timidity is the stumbling block to success; develop self-assurance and self-confidence and carry about with you the consciousness of self-control and great inner power.

As you win the right kind of personality, you will discover that you attract the right kind of friends. Like brings like. Your improved personality will help to increase your efficiency. Your financial status will likewise improve.

There is practically no limitation to the principle of high personality as an influence for power and success. Gather knowledge from every source, and use it, and thereby it becomes wisdom. Accomplish! Let the spirit of building, doing and achieving reign within.

Your state of mind develops your success; believe in yourself and others will believe in you and will follow you. Hold to a definite goal; aim to accomplish some concrete thing. Vacillation weakens; determination strengthens. Push on with all your powers and forces of mind and body. It is marvelous to be successful, to have plenty of money in the bank, to enjoy the privileges of a car, and fine home and every comfort for yourself and your family. All these blessings are within your reach.

A compelling personality is the great magnet that will attract these good things to you. Let your thought be "Only the best is good enough for me," "I want the best and I am prepared to pay its price in service, thought, application, energy and time." There is no need to be poor. Gold is everywhere. Improve your personality and you increase your ability to get rich. When your personality improves, you are favorably noticed and opportunities in plenty come knocking at your door.

An ordinary man, devoid of the earmarks of a magnetic personality, is not noticed. The great personality is always observed, in a crowd or outside of it; that undefinable something attracts and compels others to notice and favorably comment.

Study life, study yourself. Do not be like a helpless piece of driftwood in the current of the river. Life is not given to you to live in a slave-like way. Discover your real self, your higher self and let it express itself.

VISUALIZATION

Have a definite purpose in life. Do not aimlessly drift. Find out what you want, then mentally photograph and impress that thing upon your brain and mind. Make it an idea through your sense of sight. Speak it aloud and use your auditory sense, then determinedly concentrate on it. Thus you begin constructively your process of visualization.

In checking up the history of successful people we find that the law of visualization has often played a most important part in their achievements. Unless you visualize in a concrete way and allow your mind to center on this mental picture a few moments each day, success through mental imagery may be long deferred.

Time may reveal that you have created an imperfect picture. In that case do not hesitate to blot it out at once from your consciousness and mentally photograph a superior picture. Visualize each day; let directed purpose play an important part in your life. Have a definite incentive toward which you may daily bend your steps. Visualization, hard work and the wise use of time are the foundation stones of a successful, achieving life.

ENERGY

Energy is a vital principle and should be considered in connection with time. You have time and you have energy; therefore spend your energy constructively in the time you have allotted to you. Make your energy productive. You can use energy on trifling matters that will bring but a slight return, or the same amount of energy may be given to more profitable things which will bring you a most munificent reward. Particularly if you are advanced in years should you aim to get greater returns for energy expended.

Plan to do bigger things; let experience be your guide, develop your fund of knowledge, improve your work, then you can reasonably demand a higher price for your services.

Young people must travel the same path of experience over which you have passed. As a rule youth is unwilling to profit by the experience of others. It must purchase wisdom in the same manner that you have, by the way of personal experience. Those who are advanced in years and are enriched by experience are entitled to a larger return for the use of their services. Their ability, acumen, intellect, knowledge, have been dearly bought.

OPTIMISM

The optimistic man is welcomed everywhere. The grouch, the joy-killer, the gloom-bearer, is a source of depression to others. Let your eyes sparkle with the fire of optimism. See the bright side of things; do not look for gloom and despair. Ride on the sunbeams of life. Look for happy skies. Be filled with the spirit of mental sunshine so that your very presence will radiate the joy of living.

The optimistic man is a life-builder; he is a reflector of inner joy, hope, faith and charity. Become a radiant optimist. Optimism pays precious dividends. Do not allow your mind for one instant to harbor thoughts of pessimism and despair. The pessimist is a cloudy person. He reminds one of a gray day. The optimist carries with him the vibrancy of sunshine, good cheer and uplift. Let optimism be a steppingstone to lead you to the higher life of mastership and achievement.

VISION

Vision is a brightening principle of the achieving life. Vision discloses joy to heart and soul. Vision enables one to lift the shades that most of us keep eternally pulled down. Vision imparts the desire to look beyond the mere confines of ordinary life and sense its full beauty and real meaning. Express vision so that your life may be filled with a deeper sense of understanding.

With vision there is no repining, no weeping, no complaining. From vision comes that wisdom that enables one to see the light shining behind every cloud.

Without vision we are in the clutch of limitation. We are narrowed, earthbound, self-centered, we are victims of prejudice and selfishness.

Let the power of vision stream through your consciousness. Let it be your beacon and searchlight through life; then all the rough and thorny paths will be lighted. There will be no darkness or hampering of your progress – with vision as your faithful guide and friend.

ATTITUDE

Attitude is an intimate quality and its harmony or disharmony depends on the condition of your mind. If you have a healthy state of mind you will hold a healthy attitude toward life. If you have a morbid state of mind your attitude toward life will be unhealthy.

In the same environment a healthy state of mind will find honey and an unhealthy state of mind will find bitterness. It is all a mind condition. Try to adjust your attitude so that common sense, reason and sound judgment will be displayed at all times. Learn how to give and take; do not stand like a rock, claiming that you alone know what is right and best. Polish off your rough edges, look at things from the other fellow's standpoint. The mighty tree bends and sways with the stress of the storm; it adjusts itself to changing conditions. So, too, must you.

Learn the law of attitude and adjustment so that you may live sweetly and serenely, without unnecessary friction. Then the nagging cares and disappointments of life will not bring you unhappiness. As life's problems daily arise you will know how to deal with them successfully.

The law of attitude is one that should be carefully studied. A healthy attitude blesses your life and sweetens the lives of those around you. Encourage yourself to develop healthfulness of mind; it brings in its wake precious returns.

LOVE

Love is the one thing in life that never fails. Love is the one force that always lives. Keep your spirit young with the vibration of the fountain of love. Keep love close to you and you will never be lonely. Love is the foundation of everything that is good, fine and noble in life. Love is the most precious possession you can have; with it you are rich beyond measure. When you harmonize your daily life with the sweetness of love you are blessed indeed. Love is a vital necessity of existence, and to understand love and to appreciate its divine worth you must give it. To be a recipient only means that you cannot comprehend the real power and glory of love; give abundantly and you will receive abundantly.

Love is the only force that will bring into the world peace and brotherhood of man. Nations will cease warring only through the expression of love; love alone can bring into the hearts of men everywhere the sense of friendship and brotherhood. Speed the day when an ocean of love will be welling up in the hearts of all the people of the earth; then can we say goodbye to hate and war and destruction forever. Love alone will accomplish these miracles.

GRATITUDE

Express gratitude for all the blessings you enjoy. Even the smallest blessing in your life should be a source of heart-deep gratefulness and thankfulness. What is gratitude? It is the memory and forgetfulness of the heart. Never forget the kind turn that has been done you by some friend. Always keep alive and green the remembrance of that kindly deed.

HAPPINESS

A life that is not expressing the tonic effect of happiness is gray and empty. Happiness is merely the law of adjustment and attitude. The unhappy man needs the medicine of optimism and good cheer.

Instead of looking for the poison in life he should look for its honey. The part that environment plays in regard to happiness is exceedingly small. To keep one's attention focused upon some undesirable part of his environment keeps him continually unhappy. Fight discord and confusion. Do not allow others to bring unhappiness and care into your life. Smiles and serenity of mind are steppingstones to happiness. Learn how to bend and unbend; adjust yourself to the changing conditions of life.

Happiness is not a thing that is easily won; it requires a thorough knowledge of the laws of living, so set to work and win for all time this very necessary element of supreme living, the spirit of contentment and happiness.

Refuse to worry. Live abundantly today. Look for joy and smiles and happiness today. Let every contact with others be vital with gladness and good cheer; thus you insure constant happiness for yourself and you spread mental sunshine around you wherever you go.

TIME

Spend some of your time in growing in a positive way. Utilize some minutes each day in the practice of mental gardening, rooting out the mental weeds and thistles. Whatever else you do with your time, spend it wisely.

Time is a great revealer. If you discard constantly the whims and negative traits which make people dislike and avoid you, in a short time a marvelous transformation will happen in your life. You will become more positive, more self-reliant, and your personality will take on a more pleasing and friendly aspect.

Time should never be wasted in useless gossip. Never fritter away a moment in vain regretting or talking about the past; your time must be spent in a more useful way if you want to grow in power and leadership.

Look upon time as something sacred; guard it jealously; make every minute count. Be able to look back at the close of each day and know that you have created something worthwhile during the hours that have passed.

PERSONAL POWER

Personal power is molded by the quality of poise, observation, perception, and dependence upon one's self. When you have that mighty possession as a constant force in your life, you are not easily led astray and your personality becomes most magnetic and attractive. Personal power is not won overnight. You cannot jump into it. It is a thing won by slow plodding and natural growth.

SERVICE

Cheating is never profitable; down through the ages men have deceived themselves by thinking they could get something for nothing, but it never succeeds. You must give to receive. Serve with a full recognition of your responsibility to others. Let your service be profitable not only to yourself, but to your employer as well.

If you are not putting the spirit of love into your service it cannot be fully successful. Inculcate more love, more joy, more wisdom, more energy, more vision in your daily work, and within a very short period a greater reward will be yours.

UNDERSTANDING

When you realize your closeness and oneness with the Divine Source of all good, life takes on a new thrill, a new depth, never experienced before. The spirit of understanding enables you to look at life with seeing eyes; it points the way to the attainment of the finest, noblest and best in life.

THE WINNING OF SUCCESS

There is no success without happiness; it would be far better to live in a humble cottage by the side of the road with happiness than to live in the finest mansion where unhappiness abides.

The first outstanding principle of success is that of starting out in the right direction. Find out what you want to do; by doing the work that you love to do you will win success much more easily; then create a mental picture of that which you wish to win and hold that picture persistently in your conscious and subconscious mind.

Sir Thomas Lipton, the famous sportsman, once told me that he achieved his marvelous success because of three vital principles. He said: "My first principle of success in life is that of a visualized goal. When I worked for fifty-two cents a week as an errand boy in the city of Glasgow, I determined that some day I was going to have my own store; and that that store would be the nucleus for a chain of grocery stores throughout Great Britain. I held to that thought. I was determined to have a store, and, as focused thought is the seed of all action, presently the visualized store became a reality."

Then Sir Thomas Lipton added: "I worked hard. Hard work was the second principle of my success. I used my mind constructively; I visioned my goal and then I labored incessantly, working many days twelve, fourteen and sixteen hours. But, hard work never injured me and I am a young man today, although beyond three score and ten."

Then he said: "My third principle was Love. I inherited from my mother the desire to entwine my life with the spirit of love. I loved my mother sincerely and devotedly. She told me, as a child, that success could only be won and retained by the power of fair dealing and love. I have put love to work for me in all of my stores; I give my employees a square deal.

We have love as a partner in all of my enterprises, and I owe my great success to these principles."

"Having a goal and a constructive vision, working hard day by day, then having the spirit of love, sterling character and fair play permeate through every phase of my business life, these are the three forces that have enabled me to lift myself from the struggling rut of mediocrity to the position that I occupy today."

Live a constructive, productive life. Do not waste your time; make every moment count. Time is life's greatest asset. When you live usefully you create, thereby harmonizing with the creative laws of life.

There are three master keys that will enable anyone to win success in life. The first one is Ambition – "I must." Wholesome ambition will urge a man on to do his best. Unwholesome ambition sometimes will cause a man to sacrifice his future for some temporary gain. Let your ambition be of the worthy kind; let it be founded on the rock of high character, with the idea that you are going to advance by merit, by intelligence, by the creation of a goal, by service, by doing unto others as you would have them do unto you. Let the fire of true ambition burn within you. Listen to the voice of ambition. "You must," it says, follow its purposeful call, and Confidence, the second step to advancement, is disclosed.

Confidence is the second master key. Listen also to its urging, silvery voice as it whispers, "You can, you can." "You must," Ambition says. "You can," Confidence echoes back. But when ambition urges you and when confidence inspires you to go on, you will have foes to contend with. Indolence will strive to take away your ambition, to impede your desire to achieve in life, and in its subtle, siren way will urge you to think of pleasure instead of hard work; it tempts you by promising easy paths – but you must not listen to the tempting voice of indolence. Let ambition be your guide, let confidence be your constant aid, and you will drive away the enemies that tend to keep you in a rut.

Fear is a giant enemy of success. When you limit yourself, when you are afraid to advance, you must use the forces of ambition and confidence to rout fear, as you have driven away indolence; then, when you are released from the clutches of indolence and fear, you generate a driving power within, that of determination, the third master key and achieving quality of success-building.

Do not think that life is always going to be a constant time of joys, romance and adventure. Problems must come; life is more successfully lived when crosses and burdens present themselves. We grow by overcoming. We become strong by doing. Patience is necessary in life; impatience quite frequently drives from us the best. When obstacles confront you, do not become impatient and retreat; just study your obstacle and you will find a way to master it. Do not become so obsessed with your handicap that it will cause you to stop trying and give up. Keep going on, recognizing that life tests you by obstacles.

When tested and tried, the aspiring life rises to meet conditions and to do its best. Necessity is the most powerful force in the universe; it promotes thought, and forces one to do his utmost. Any weakling may abandon and lie down in the battle of life, but the one who sticks, the man who refuses to stay down, is the man who will achieve and win, in the long run, in the battle of life.

When you keep on, when you turn your eyes towards the light, when you dare to do, when you struggle to your feet after the fury of the storm has spent itself, then you fit yourself for success in the future.

Do not give up. No matter if life has bludgeoned you a dozen times. If you have been knocked down repeatedly, keep up your faith; keep the spirit of hope alive, and as long as hope is registering within, you can "make good" in life. You cannot fail to triumph ultimately if you keep hope and faith alive and active within.

Dare to dream, dare to aspire in life, but do not let your dreams and aspirations make you unbusinesslike. Dream and aspire wholesomely and know that the best in life is rightly yours. It is no sin to desire success. How can you give to others if you lack?

Go forward day by day with the thought of winning success. Desire success not only for yourself, but also for the benefit and happiness of your family and of your friends.

Have a soul-deep wish to aid others who are struggling in the rut of poverty and ignorance and who have not yet found the way out. Give to others the best you have, and that which you give so generously will bless the giver as well as the receiver.

Visualization is a marvelous force for success. Dr. Orison Swett Marden tells a story about John Wanamaker, how he visualized for success, and how his mental picture, plus square dealing and superior hard work, won him well deserved prosperity.

There is danger in visualizing if it takes away the desire to work. Good service and visualization must go hand in hand. If you sit down and expect success to fly to you merely by thinking about it, time will reveal that you have acted most injudiciously. Instead of success, unhappiness and failure will probably come your way. Know how you are leading in life; see that you are headed toward success. Otherwise every step you take is away from your goal instead of toward it. Carry around with you the success atmosphere. Check up on yourself occasionally; question yourself as to whether you have embodied in your life the necessary elements to win the birthright that is rightly yours – real, unadulterated success.

That is the indomitable spirit in which you must start out in your quest of attainment. There is no failure with such a program outlined; through such a plan success cannot be long deferred.

Let your courage be of the duty order. Do your duty. It is an obligation to be brave and courageous in life. Courage will lead you to the higher levels in life.

Self-confidence will help you to win success. Many a man with a mediocre education is occupying a high position because of the spirit of self-confidence. The world has a high place for the self-confident man. Some highly educated men are occupying almost menial positions because they lack the driving force of self-confidence. "Timidity is the stumbling block to success," says a Japanese proverb. When you are self-effacing, when you speak in a strained way, when you carry around a shrinking atmosphere, you depress others. The world judges you by the way you look, speak and act; it has no time to dig down and investigate your real ability and powers. Be a living advertisement of success.

By keeping everlastingly at it, by having pertinacity and stick-to-it-iveness, by having patience and perseverance, by keeping the optimistic spirit alive, you cannot be denied. That which is rightly yours must become a part of your life.

No life is properly lived; no success is real success, unless the spirit of the Golden Rule is observed. Do unto others as you would have them do unto you. That is life's golden law, and that aspiration will be a giant magnet to attract success.

So many of our businessmen fail because they lack this great knowledge of the law of success, since success is found by following and harmonizing daily with its own specific laws. Sometimes it is more difficult to hold success than it is to achieve it. Learn the laws of winning and retaining success. Link in with these laws; then when you attain success you will also have the assurance that it will abide with you.

The spirit of optimism is one that greatly affects success. The businessman who is going around looking for trouble or failure usually finds it. I read a story recently of a man who inherited a thriving business from his father. Not being well versed in the ethics of business management he developed a supercritical attitude toward his employees. He came to business each morning with the destructive idea of finding fault, he scanned the furniture to find traces of dust, he looked for cobwebs. He hourly searched for something to criticize; he made his stenographer nervous by his erratic actions, he scattered his papers around his desk. He discouraged his manager and found fault with his saleswomen. He rarely smiled. Little did he realize that he was daily sowing the seeds of failure.

Within three years, because of his unwholesome attitude and irrational, unbusinesslike methods, his store was in the hands of a receiver. He was a bankrupt because he violated the ethics of success and achievement. He lived in a state of confusion instead of one of harmony.

Do not speak about poverty. Do not live in a poor neighborhood; it is better to have one room in a neighborhood of respectability and affluence than to have six rooms in an environment of want and need. Vibrations affect you, and if you constantly mingle with those who are poor, these vibrations are of a destructive nature and will hold you down.

Never belittle yourself in life. Always think well of yourself. How do you expect the world to believe in you, to reward you, to respect you, unless you think well of yourself? Get your blood fired with the spirit of enthusiasm; keep fresh your desire to win success by superior methods alone. Success won by personal endeavor, high ideals and hard work, is lasting success – do not try to win success cheaply. Do not be discouraged if you are a failure at forty; many of our most successful businessmen were almost penniless at forty-five. Your success must take time. What comes to you easily will go from you easily.

A kind deed, prompted by the spirit of helpfulness and unselfishness, is always productive of good. Scatter seeds of uplift and helpfulness along the highways and byways of life wherever you go. Someday they will return, bringing you a full measure of joy, inspiration and success.

Some of us are held in bondage by our thoughts of limitation. We do not recognize that around us is a superabundance for all our worthy wants. The Great Giver of Life did not put us here to express need and poverty. By arousing the achieving spirit within, by constructive thinking, by carefully planned hard work, by expressing the spirit of the square deal in everything we do, by ability and enthusiasm, we can all go forward; finding rich reward and recompense for the outlay of thought and labor, and failure will forever become a thing of the past.

UNDERSTANDING

There is nothing solid in the universe; all is vibration, all is energy, all is movement. Stagnation is not tolerated in life. A process of disintegration takes place whenever death is present. Service is the opposing force to stagnation; service means movement, life, action.

To harmonize with the laws of life, give and you will bountifully receive. There must be an outflow as well as an inflow. Giving the best that you have to others insures a space for intake and better than the best you have given will return.

This is a world of law, and to live serenely and properly one must find the laws and harmonize his life with them; otherwise, constant violation is sure to occur and the ensuing friction will breed confusion and chaos, and unhappiness will result.

Have a thirst for wisdom. Search until you uncover the great fount of understanding. Your quest for wisdom may have to be kept up for a long period, but do not become faint-hearted; keep up your patience until you discover the greatest force in life – understanding, the true comprehension of life, its meaning and its laws.

A story has been told about a young man who wanted to cultivate wisdom. He came to a wise man and said: "Sir, teach me how to find wisdom." The wise man did not make a reply; instead he turned and walked away. A few days later the young man came to him again and said: "Sir, I want to know the way to wisdom." Once more the wise man walked away. Several days later the young man returned and propounded the same question; then the wise man said: "Come with me." Taking the young man by the arm he led him down to the edge of the river; wading into the center he grasped the young man by the neck and forced his head under the water. He struggled vainly to release himself, but after ten or fifteen seconds the wise man allowed him to lift his head out of the water.

"While I held your head under the water," he asked, "what did you most desire?" "Air, sir, air." "Did you think about riches, love, honor or success?" "No, sir; I just wanted air, nothing else." "Well," said the wise man, "desire wisdom and understanding just as much as you wanted air, and ultimately wisdom and understanding will become part of your life."

Self-effort is the great ladder on which to climb toward soul-development. The desire to lead a better life, the inclination to help yourself, the wish to grow daily so that you may climb to higher levels, are rungs on this ladder of life.

Growth of the soul is indeed retarded when one lacks culture, refinement, dignity, and education. Vision is necessary to enable one to see clearly the rare value and great necessity of soul-culture.

There should be a desire and a hunger for soul-expression in every life, to understand not only life in its fullness and beauty, but also the method of living in a higher way so that one's very presence will be a benediction to those with whom one comes in contact.

Meditation practiced daily will help toward your goal of soul-development. Sit down quietly. Lock your fingers to keep them from straying and diverting your attention from your desire. Close your eyes for at least five minutes and get your thoughts filled with the desire to live a nobler, better life. Have a sincere wish permeating your consciousness to so live that your life may add to the happiness of others. This meditation will quicken your higher self; an awakening will take place and you will be reminded of the truth of these words: "Seek and you shall find." Your hungry soul is seeking complete expression and this message of promise will bring peace to your mind.

The second step is the realization that you have awakened your higher self, and you recognize that all things are possible. Through the medium of this newly aroused soul-development you begin a new life: a life of joy, of abundance, of happiness.

Then the third step – the cleaning. No soul development is obtainable until you undergo a spiritual cleansing. Cleanse your heart. All lower emotions are destructive to spiritual unfoldment.

The fourth step of soul development is that of strengthening. Hold your head high. Keep up your courage. Have a hopeful heart. You thus will progress more favorably toward your goal. Then comes the vibrant spark of faith.

You will receive into your life the prize of unaccountable worth, the richness of surpassing peace and tranquility of mind – a reward that is more precious than all the gold in the world.

The more completely you keep your mind filled with radiant thoughts, the more deeply and permanently this great channel of beautiful thoughts will deepen and develop within your soul. Do not limit yourself. Do not drive away the best in life by narrowness of mind and prejudice.

All power is given unto you. Why not live as a king? Why trail along in the dust? Why live in an inferior, struggling way? The possibilities of human life are stupendous and amazing. Through soul-power one can lift himself above all the nagging cares of life; one can elevate himself to undreamed-of heights.

The physical body must be kept in good condition by harmonizing with the physical laws. The mind must be kept attuned to serenity and cheerfulness by radiant thinking. But above all the soul needs its own special work; it, too, must be tutored and fashioned by sincerely desired soul unfoldment. Life, to be successfully lived, must be radiantly expressed on all three sides so that it may be rounded and harmonized from every standpoint.

With soul-development as a goal, new strength will be given to you daily. The will to do will become your guiding star; you will have the power of dominion, a force that will aid you to overcome all the handicaps of life. Glorious indeed is the reward of the rounded life.

Your life's mission cannot be fully accomplished without soul expression. It is no great ordeal, no complicated thing to connect with your higher self. Formulate the desire, then go forward, with faith constantly expressed, and the attunement will be realized.

THE POWER OF THOUGHT

Life is yours to do with as you please. You are your own builder; in the workshop of life you forge and fashion your mode of living just as you desire.

Life is a building process. We are adding something to it all the time, and what we add becomes a liability or an asset, just as we determine to have it. We can only build rightly when we possess the power of understanding and harmonize our life with its great majestic laws.

Think good within, and you externalize good without. Recognize that by the power of right thinking alone can you live an ascending life, a life devoted to the expression of the higher principles of existence.

Thought is the seed of all action. It precedes all visible things. It is the forerunner of all the realities of life.

Positive thinking is an asset of incalculable value. When you have constructive thought as a constant associate in your life it enables you to develop a wholesome, superior personality. Try to comprehend that life is just loaned to you for a time, so make every effort to live a serene and useful life.

How are you using your life? Are you living it as a master or as a slave? Forceful, dynamic thinking will lift you above the enslaving conditions of life, and will advance you towards the higher levels of successful living.

Try to cultivate such radiant, uplifting thoughts that your very presence will reflect the sublimity and beauty of optimistic, constructive thoughts within; then your association with others will be harmonious, uplifting; your presence will reflect peace, poise, harmony and power, and you will bless and elevate all those with whom you come in contact.

How necessary it is that we should guard our thoughts, because one cannot do his best unless his personality is of the positive, winning type, and right thinking alone will bring him that desirable condition.

The mind has been compared to a garden, and to properly cultivate a garden it is necessary to fertilize it and to keep the weeds and the thistles from growing there and injuring the fair blossoms.

Fertilize your mind by reading choice literature of the past, gems from the learned minds that lived centuries ago. Read the vibrant thoughts of today.

Life is a school, living is a science, and, to live properly, plan to be a student of life every day. There is so much to learn, so much to comprehend, that even a day cannot be wasted. Be a discerning, persistent student of life, and then the laws of life will be gradually unfolded as you gain in knowledge and understanding.

In many lives there are clouds and darkness because of destructive thinking. These depressing conditions would dissipate like a snowflake in the summer's sun if happy thinking were daily made a definite practice.

Limitation is the dreariest thing in life. How you are held back when your thoughts are morbid, self-depreciating, pessimistic and negative! How can you do your best unless the spirit of aspiration, the urge of optimism, the fire of enthusiasm are registering within?

When you have the quality of right thinking firmly established, you recognize that all things are possible; you cannot be held down; you realize you have the will to do, and with force and unwavering enthusiasm you continue to forge ahead until you attain the supreme heights in life.

Think superior thoughts. Do not belittle yourself. You have as good a right to enjoy life, to win success, to be gloriously well, as any other individual on earth. Every time you think a low, morbid thought you send out these vibrations, and the reaction spells failure and unhappiness. Positive thinking will help you to achieve success.

Stand triumphantly, walk triumphantly; assume the victorious attitude at all times. Carry yourself in a superior way so that you may favorably impress all those whom you meet.

There are fetters to be broken; there are bonds to be burst asunder in almost every life because of wrong thinking in the past. But determine with the assurance and inspiration of radiant thinking that you will achieve in life; that you will do good work for humanity, and make the world a better place because you have lived. With such a determination go boldly out into life and you will find your problems will be greatly minimized, and, because of your understanding, they will be speedily solved.

You are not a slave save when gyved by the fetters of enslaving thought; change the current of your thoughts and you may begin to live a life of mastership and leadership. Thoughts of tranquility will bring you poise and peace, and a harmonious life is to be much desired and admired.

Do not allow your mind to express hate thoughts, or thoughts of envy, jealousy, or any of the lower and baser emotions of life. Divorce yourself from all these distractive expressions. Let your thinking be uplifting, purposeful, progressive. Let fear be far removed from you. Remember these two points in thinking:

What you fear you attract – what you hope for you create.

In quietness there is strength.

Drop everything that would tend to embitter or harass your life; cleanse your heart and let your soul express and guide your thinking during this time of renewing silence.

There is marvelous power in contemplation and meditation, and when silently thinking visualize that you are attuned with the Divine Giver of life, and that you confidently wait for the blessings of joy and abundance, so that you may better be able to help others, as well as to improve your own life, and home and business conditions.

Do not be afraid to think new thoughts. Try to originate; often a simple idea brings great wealth. If you find that you lack the faculty of origination, plan to improve some existing principle.

At the close of each day be able to review your work and know that your hours have been productive.

We hear people moving the furniture and rattling the dishes; we hear the sound of their voices and their chatter, but when the day is done what have they accomplished? Very little, almost nothing to show from a constructive standpoint; and life should be a busy building workshop day by day.

There is much to be done in life and time is your greatest asset. The manner in which you use your energy and your time today paves the way for accomplishment or for failure in the future.

Instead of going around seeking to find fault, looking for something to condemn, endeavoring to find some flaw in others, why not go about with a tolerant smile, wishing to minimize the follies and frailties of others, magnifying even their smallest good quality, and minimizing their greatest failure? We get back in life about what we deserve. If we unduly criticize others, if we gossip about others, if we lie about others, the law of reaction in its own good time will bring back to us the quality we have given out.

A life that would give its best must let its lower and baser thoughts die. You can only rebuild, in a positive way, by vibrant, constructive thinking; get that motive established every moment in your life – the hours of life are too wonderful to be wasted in destructive thinking; hold to the determination to grow and develop through the power of uplifting thought.

Remember that you consciously or unconsciously impress others by your thoughts; so consider it a sacred obligation on your part that only the vibration of right thinking will stream from you; then you can smile with satisfaction, knowing that you are brightening up your own corner, thereby proving yourself a sterling influence for good.

THE SUBCONSCIOUS MIND

To impress the subconscious mind one must think with conviction, intensity and clearness. The subconscious mind will store away positive or negative thoughts with equal impression. The subconscious mind harmonizes and obeys the desire of the conscious mind and also thinks for itself.

ACHIEVEMENT

Affirmation – I will choose wisely.

Put wisdom at the steering wheel of your vessel of life. Choose your friends wisely. Avoid parasitic friendships; the clinging ivy will in time sap the vitality and destroy the life of the forest's mightiest oak. Choose your reading matter wisely. Why feed your mind with trash when there is a wealth of good literature easily obtainable? Choose your food wisely. Your body is built by the food you eat; even your thoughts are influenced by the kind and quality of food you consume day by day. Wisdom is the great propelling force for normality, saneness and constructiveness; let it be your constant guide and friend.

Wisdom is the utilization of knowledge. Knowledge in itself matters very little; it is merely academic unless rightly used; then only does it become helpful.

Affirmation – I will act convincingly.

Do not do things in a slipshod, haphazard manner; put conviction and energy behind all your actions. With wisdom and positiveness persistently manifest in your life, there are no heights that are impossible for you to climb. The world follows the positive man, the man of backbone and quiet determination. Do not vacillate from one thing to another; be positive, forceful, and convincing. Concentrate on some one thing; then unswervingly push it through to success.

There is an old proverb: "The world belongs to the energetic and the wise." Mold your life so that you follow out the precepts of this aphorism, then success will not be long delayed. The positive, energetic and enthusiastic man is always a doer and a builder. He usually wins major success.

Affirmation – I will think serenely.

Serenity of mind is a necessary adjunct to the life of achievement. When you are supercritical, fault finding, nagging, you drive away friends, love and happiness. Sweet thoughts, wholesome thoughts, serene thoughts, draw their kind into your life. When you live negatively, when you are supersensitive, when you magnify the failings of others, and minimize their good qualities, when you are snobbish, or lacking in the quality of gratitude, then your life is all awry. Your future harvest will be sad and destructive; you are sowing seeds of poison and hate, instead of good seeds that would later bless and sweeten your life.

Stop your nagging and fault finding ways; change your thoughts; smile. Get the spirit of cheeriness and friendliness around you; then life will smile back at you and it will become a joy to live. Your atmosphere will no longer be depressing and negative, but will radiate mental sunshine, joy, cheer, service, inspiration.

Affirmation – I will hope sanely.

Let the spirit of understanding be your guide all through life. You cannot hope to have a better or more successful future than you have today unless you strive to improve your daily work. Do not dwell on the past. You have been paid for the past; close the book of the past and be busy with your work of today, obliterating everything that would tend to retard your present progress. Blot out and extinguish all memory of long-forgotten errors of omission and commission.

Today is the steppingstone of tomorrow. If you determine to do better work today, to be happier today, to inspire others today, and will carry out this worthy program every day, then you can hope, and hope with assurance, that the future is rich with promise, because the seeds you are planting are good seeds, and the future gives only what the present sows.

Affirmation – I will serve joyously.

Unless you get joy from your work there is something radically wrong in your work or in yourself. If you despise your present work, then seek to secure work more to your liking. Improve, delve, investigate, do everything in your power to know more about your work each day so that you may continuously improve your service; by aiming to improve your present work, higher work will be attracted to you in time and promotion is always assured. If you cannot feel a deep joy in your present vocation, then change your work; one can do his best only when he serves with a spirit of joyousness.

Joyless work is grinding and destructive. You are not fair to your employer or to yourself if you continue to draw a wage for work that you despise. If the urge of wholesome ambition is rising within you, then seek to find the niche you can best occupy. Look for the place that will bring you happiness; thus may you fulfill the law because you are putting joy into your service. Serve to the utmost; serve usefully and constructively; do your best and make your best supremely worthwhile. Then you will know you are heading in the direction of success and abundance.

Affirmation – I will seek purposefully.

The life that drifts aimlessly is imperfectly lived. Have sincere purpose behind everything you do. Create a goal, not an easy one, and bend your steps day by day in the direction of that which you desire to bring to fruition. With purpose there is a definite incentive for living. Let your purpose be of the highest type so that it may bring you a rich reward when it is finally achieved. Do not be satisfied with a trifle; you can bargain with life for a penny or for a lordly competence.

Affirmation – I will live upliftingly.

Dedicate your life to the advancement of others. Scatter seeds of kindness day by day in the shape of smiles and kind words. So many lives are gray and morbid because they lack that inspiring spirit of uplift. The key to receiving is to give; when you withhold you are always filled, and there is no chance to take in. When you give there is always space within to receive, whereby you may constantly draw in from an inexhaustible supply. Let good cheer, faith, enthusiasm be woven into every phase of your daily life; then your very presence, wherever you go, will reflect that inner strength and power, the soul quality of a life dedicated to uplift, purpose and progress.

When uplift is your daily motto and watchword you become a reflector of the things that lead to the higher levels of living. Sometimes it is difficult to establish that spirit of true optimism and sincere uplift, but make the effort, and time will reveal it was gloriously worthwhile.

Affirmation – I will grow daily.

When properly lived, life is a scientific school of growth and attainment. Be a student of life every day. There is so much to learn, so much to understand in this marvelous world of ours. The glory of studying life is this: when you uncover one law it automatically leads to the discovery of some other majestic law. Life then becomes one constant round of higher development.

We grow by doing; therefore the desire to grow daily means that you will expand daily. You will not have a single moment of loneliness or discouragement. The wonder and grandeur of human life will be revealed to you, and though life may seem complex to others, you, being familiar with its laws and manifold windings, may solve, with very little difficulty, life's problems as they present themselves day by day.

A life that is devoted to the principles of daily growth is keeping on the offensive. There is no retrogression in such a life. Onward, ever onward, no going back! Just a forward life of growth and expansion! Such a program can only mean joyous living, a life that spells progressiveness and constructiveness.

Affirmation – I will judge charitably.

Live a tolerant life; do not be hasty to form opinions. Do not judge by first appearances. Judge not, that ye not be judged, for who can set himself up as an authority to judge others?

THE WILL TO DO

When you formulate a good resolution do not procrastinate; do not settle back and wait for something to turn up.

What dynamic power is charged into these words, "I will rise!"

You are unhappy; let the magic driving force of these three words be the impetus to raise you beyond the conditions or environment of unhappiness.

If you are a failure, hold to that thought, "I will rise," and at once you will be carried towards the hill that leads to true success.

Express the "I will rise" spirit, and the sordid things of life will pass you by.

Get the "I will rise" spirit pulsating and percolating through your being; let it be the challenging stimulus to overcome every impediment to your progress in the battle of life.

Fear and strife will vanish with that forceful thought. "I will rise" will reveal happy skies and impart the sense of liberty to your mind.

Need, want and limitation that blight so many lives may be instantly overcome by the "I will rise" resolution. Its magic potency will draw fine lives, beauty and wisdom into your life.

So many of us are living in the murky valleys of life when we might be dwelling on the mountain tops.

The "I will rise" message cries to you, "It can be done, and let it be done." "I can't" is a childish expression. "I can" and "I will" backed up by deeds is always a building force.

"I will rise" will carry you past bitterness, scowls and frowns and the hindering things of life. With that force operating within you, you may sweep aside life's dregs and froth, and, entwined with smiles, your spirit may go forth to do and to conquer.

You can always be a free man when you manifest the victorious spirit evolved by the vibrant "I will rise" attitude.

The "I will rise" spirit will give you that faith and hope that will lift you above to the supreme heights. It will clothe you with joy and sparkling cheer. Its message will vibrate and thrill through your consciousness with the assurance that all is well. Constantly use the affirmation, "I will rise"; let it be a spur, an urge, a goad, to go forward to victory, to attainment, to achievement.

THE POWER OF CHEERFULNESS

Dedicate your life to the spreading of goodness, hope, inspiration and beauty. Relegate to the attic of the past thoughts of gloom, hate, fear, worry and weakness. Have your life interwoven with the creed of love, kindness, helpfulness, optimism and good cheer; you are a benefactor to mankind as well as to yourself when you carry around with you these expressions of joy and uplift.

Cheerfulness is welcomed everywhere. It is a promoter of health and magnetism. Be happy now, today, not postponing it for some time in the dim future.

Seek good within. The spirit of mental healthiness will help you to discover the inner kingdom of joy. Keep your eyes lifted toward the star of good cheer. Do not stand in your own sunshine; then no shadows can beset you.

The sour-visaged pessimist is always going backward. The optimist has no time for grumbling; he is too busy reaping the harvest of happiness and success. Affirm: "Cheer is part of me; I harbor no hate; I think kindly of everyone."

Then practice what you affirm and you will become a better man and a more worthy citizen.

Stop worrying over your so-called troubles; constant thinking about your troubles magnifies them.

Talk happiness and success every day! You attract these essentials when you make them part of your daily conversation. Think of yourself as enjoying these blessings, for thought brings its kind. The world is sad enough without your contributing your tale of woe. Forget your clouds and burdens for a while; look for happy skies. Cast aside your blue goggles of pessimism and depression and see the silver lining to your clouds.

Let your song of cheerfulness ring soul-deep, an undercurrent of happiness sweeping you forcefully on to the state of blessed contentment.

When cheerfulness is made a permanent partner of your life, you reflect and radiate mental sunshine; thus you bless and brighten every life with which you come in contact. A pessimist and faultfinder pauperizes every life he touches, because of his disintegrating, negative personality.

Cheerfulness is a pearl of great price; express it, and you enrich your surroundings. You bless other lives; you contribute something to the betterment of mankind.

Be filled with the spirit of good cheer. You do not realize you have so much to be thankful for until you sit down and begin to check up your blessings. You may have a bitter trial confronting you, darkness may seemingly encompass you, but behind it all there is freedom, liberty and light. Just hold on, drop bitterness, morbidity and worry; soon the passing weeks will reveal that the experience you have undergone has made you a better man. Even a casual look around you will reveal thousands of people worse off than you are.

Cheerfulness is an essential of a magnetic personality. One cannot visualize a grumbling, fear-stricken, faultfinding individual as possessing a radiant disposition; a whining man is avoided, he is marked as a depressing influence and those who know his character shun him.

Form the habit of rejoicing at every opportunity for the gift of life; give thanks for your "littlest" asset as well as your greatest.

Cheerfulness ennobles your character and helps to attract superior friends to you; you cannot stay down if imbued with the spirit of cheerfulness. You rise undaunted after some testing failure or disappointment if you have wisely held on to your sense of optimistic good cheer.

Sometimes it takes great effort to remain serene and cheerful in the face of discomfiting and trying circumstances, but it is by self-discipline and the experience of overcoming that we grow. You grow in power, personality and character by struggling toward attainment. It is not what you win in life that counts most; it is how you have won the victory. If you fought the good fight in the face of seemingly overwhelming odds, if you kept alive your pluck and grit when disaster loomed imminent, if you fanned your dying flicker of faith and hope into a bright flame when faith and hope seemed well nigh extinguished, then all the glory is yours.

Be constant in well doing, not spasmodic; day by day, year in and year out; live the happy way, the cheerful way. It is the straight and narrow path that leads the traveler to the heights of a life supremely and triumphantly lived.

THE CULTURE OF PERSONAL POWER AND PERSONAL MAGNETISM

There is little hope for a man who leads an aimless, shifting life; when you drift you are weakened; you are strengthened by personal effort and by overcoming.

Do not rest idly on the current of life and placidly allow it to carry you where it will; there is no dynamic force, no lighting vision, no dominant urge in a life that just drifts.

The power of purpose will enable you to lift yourself above the blight of a meaningless life. Try to find yourself. Endeavor to see yourself as others see you; thus will you be enabled to discover why others avoid you and to find the reason for your lack of success.

To live rightly, one should endeavor to make his life a forward one; then he will register a series of gains day by day. Being continuously on the merely defensive in life means that you are marking time or going backward. A steady growth of energy and positive power should be your ambition, to go forward slowly and sanely. Do not expect that a life of power will be won in a day. You must have patience. Power develops through use; you grow by doing.

Study your subconscious mind; let it help you achieve your desires.

Your greatest enemy to development will be that of shallow thinking. Develop the spirit of thoroughness in everything you do; eliminate the surface things that are so universally of moment to the average individual. Let your desire for mastership be a soul-deep urge. Constant check-ups are necessary, so that you may keep on the right road to your goal. The man who expresses personal power is a conserver of energy.

The man who expresses power is able to control his emotions under all circumstances. He is not a victim of the jumping habit when the telephone bell rings or a messenger boy appears on the scene. He registers emotion in the brain and not in the heart. He has developed the rare qualities of poise, harmony and relaxation; his very presence is a living advertisement of self-confidence and power.

Wholesome indifference is a path to power; not to be callous, hard-hearted or hardened, but to have a masterly control of the emotions at all times and under most trying conditions.

Curb your ire, control your emotions, keep cool.

To be magnetic, one must be poised to a marked degree. He must not show his inner feelings. "Still water runs deep."

A life of mastership can be attained only by deep, beautiful inner feelings, by a dominant intellect and will. Gossip is destructive of personal magnetism. To reveal a secret or to indulge in gossip or cheap talk will bring in time a harmful reaction. Only ordinary people, only those who are shallow and flighty, will divulge the secrets of a friend or gossip about others; the man who aspires to lead a life of mastership will be far removed from the desire to be a gossip or a scandal-monger.

Creative energy flows to the one who expresses personal power. He looks to improve things and conditions.

The man of power is a doer and a builder. He realizes that power is obtained only by pushing things through to conclusion, so he hangs on in spite of all handicaps and impediments. He advances with power and energy towards looming obstacles and triumphantly battles them down. The man of power realizes that he should have dominion; he dominates, but he does not domineer. He is approachable, he is friendly, he expresses the spirit of compassion and sympathy in his association with others, but, behind it all, there is a sense of superiority, of dignity, of a deep self-reliance. He advances because of superior merit and masterly service.

Concentration is a steppingstone to a life of power and achievement. Meditation and contemplation are daily practiced by the man who desires to lead a superior life.

This principle of meditation is a true source of power building; daily practiced it will keep up the inflow that is necessary to build and maintain a life of power and triumphant leadership.

The man of power and magnetism constantly gives. He realizes that only by giving can he receive; there is little possibility of winning a life of magnetism and power unless it is actuated by the spirit of wholesome giving. That must be made a living and earnest ideal. The superman understands that a smiling face is a password to the higher levels of life.

Wear a smile as you wend your way through life, knowing that it will bring a rich reward.

The man of power will not stoop to criticize others adversely. He will frankly state his opinions if requested; but he realizes that harsh criticism is not a builder, so he wisely refrains from it. He lives such a superior life that it is a shining example to others to emulate and follow.

With it all, the man of power is wholesome, natural, and his life is one of radiant simplicity. He is not living up in the clouds; his feet are planted firmly on the ground, though his eyes may be fixed on the highest star.

He is not a bluffer or a pretender. He is not conceited. He never tries to advance over the failure of someone else; personal effort, personal endeavor, plus genuine merit, are the tools that he uses to win a competence from life. He is generous, forging, and good-hearted, yet is far-seeing and makes few mistakes.

A constant study of the laws of life should be a daily practice for one who aspires to power and leadership. It is indeed a most interesting study; almost daily a new unfoldment, revelation or discovery will take place. The intelligence becomes sharpened and the mysteries of life will be revealed when the faculties of perception and observation are persistently employed.

The life of power is not affiliated with monotony or any tiresome drudgery. It can choose the work that it wants to do. The man of power can be what he wants to be; he can dictate to circumstances and conditions and rise above them because of faith in himself. With indomitable faith in his own ability, the man of power can lead a life that challenges all handicaps and conditions, and by his knowledge of living he can victoriously surmount even the highest obstacle.

By directing your powers into right channels you prevent friction and save time. Do not take roundabout methods to accomplish your ends. Efficiently organize your methods of conducting your home and business affairs. Let your energy flow in the right direction; wisely directed your power becomes doubly valuable and productive.

To live successfully one must demonstrate the right spirit, and the right spirit is that of helpfulness. Never do a mean action. Be fired with the spirit of noble thoughts. Strive to bring pleasure and profit to all those with whom you do business; that is a propelling step to the achievement of power and of magnetism.

In your quest for superior development, aim for constant improvement of your personality. This is best accomplished by eradicating all narrow traits and personal idiosyncrasies which make people dislike you; thus will you be enabled to have a broader comprehension of life and keep alive a sense of your responsibility toward others. If you desire power, depend on your own ability, live your own life. Do not interfere with the happiness of others. Do not attempt to advise others unless you are earnestly requested to do so.

The man of power recognizes that time is his greatest asset and that he has not a moment to spare in criticism or trying to live someone else's life; he is constantly kept busy improving his own life, physically, mentally and spiritually.

Above all, every expression of hate must be cast out of the life of power. No positive power can permanently reside in the same chamber as hate. The man of power recognizes that hate is weakening and blighting. To overcome hate he will ever cultivate the spirit of love, the mightiest force in life.

Independence is an attribute of the achieving life. If someone thinks you cannot exist without him, he is not a true friend. You must show that you have personality and ability sufficient to get along anywhere, at any time, by your own personal efforts; this will tend to give you a mighty force of self-confidence, freedom and personal independence.

The reading of good books will help you to achieve power and personality. Make notes as you read. Try to apply the principles that appeal to you in your plan of living; this will make for a system of continuous growth.

Personal power is a priceless possession. The man of power can dictate to life and life will yield him that which he rightfully demands.

XII

GEORGE WINSLOW PLUMMER

The following quotes are from
Consciously Creating Circumstances, 1935

THE SOURCE OF POWER

It is evident that the great, successful or happy people of this world have access to some power that obscure, unhappy failures know little or nothing about – "a power which erring men call chance."

Perhaps you think it's just good luck that brings success, and let it go at that. But you miss something very important if you think that.

This is written for those willing to consider the possibility that something other than just luck or heredity bestows happiness on one and failure on another. This book describes a method of attack on the problems of life that thousands of happy people of merely average abilities have successfully employed. Yes, *countless* thousands, even though many of them did not realize what they were using.

If you seek help and are not afflicted with a closed mind, you can use the same power that has served these people. I *can* and *will* tell you about it.

As we look about us in the world our senses inform us that it is full of objects of all sorts: houses, trees, people. We give the general name of "things," or *forms*, to these objects.

Closer inspection informs us that each object has its individual characteristics, such as odor, density, firmness, weight, color, and we find that these objects are made of the same substances in varying physical or chemical combinations. So we say that the objects composing our environment are made of *matter*, and the state in which matter usually appears is *visible*.

Now as we look more intently, we observe that there are other conditions in our world that are *invisible*. We see the *fall* of an apple to the ground from a tree; the *cause* of the fall remains invisible. Forces of many kinds are evidently in play. We do not see the forces or energies themselves, but they are the *causes* of all that we do see. What we see are the results – called *phenomena*, or *actions* and *states of being*.

Plants, animals and human bodies change in size, but we do not *see* the energy that makes them increase. We observe people moving about, but we do not see what makes them move about. We think, but we do not see our thoughts. We listen to the radio, send telegrams, speak over the telephone, or push a button for lights in our rooms but we do not see the energy on the way.

So observation teaches us, correctly, that we live not only in a visible world of matter, but also in an invisible world of forces and energies that produce the visible things in our environment.

We recognize these visible forms and we sense the invisible forces behind them through a power we call *mind*.

Everything in this world about us that *man* has produced began as a thought in the mind of some man. Your home existed in the builder's mind before it took form. Your car took form first in the maker's mind. Everything that we do, individually or collectively, begins first in the *thought of the thing*. No matter how suddenly we do a thing at times, we *think of it first*. Sometimes we act quickly on the thought; sometimes we have to wait until we can develop conditions favorable to its accomplishment.

Also, as we look about us, we observe many forms of matter that were *not* produced by the hand of man, for they express characteristics that no human being has ever produced. Man cannot create a tree, for instance, or an ocean, or a robin. Yet they too must have begun in *a* mind. *In what mind and with what thought did they begin?*

Before answering the last question, let us look around us some more. We observe that the plant of yesterday is a bit higher today. The little child of last year is larger and abler. We note certain changes in ourselves with the advance of time. We cannot *see* what causes this increase in size, ability, etc., but the fact stares us in the face. Look again, this time at another class of things. That building, begun a few weeks ago, is steadily increasing in size. A railroad has increased its mileage. A bridge is ready for the last span. We *can* see that what makes *them* increase is the hand of man.

So we have before us two different pictures of increase. One springs from the efforts of man, on the visible plane. The other is directed from some invisible plane, and is *not* due to man's efforts. These changes in our environment we call *growth*. We note that this growth is effected by man in some cases, and by some other power or agency in other cases. But originating in some *mind, somewhere,* in every case.

Now let us try to discover whether there are *really* two kinds of growth, one caused by man and one caused by something else. There *seem* to be two, but is it truly so?

No sensible person believes that man just happened. He too is a phenomenon, *a fact*, with an invisible cause. We have agreed that this cause can only be man or something other than man. But man did not cause himself: something else brought him into being. Therefore this something else causes not only mountains and oceans, which are beyond man's control, but also causes everything that man *appears* to cause, *because it caused man himself to come into existence.*

Thus we see that there is but *one basic cause* of all things that are or ever were. We therefore call it the *great first cause*.

Some call it *spirit*. Whatever term we use, we remember that it operates through *mind*, and, since it causes all things, *universal mind*.

All power comes from one source today, just as it did before the beginning of "things."

This great, invisible cause acts through what we term *universal mind* – the Intelligence directing all the forces that produced man and through which man, on a much smaller scale, produces the various changes in his environment.

DUAL ACTION

We agreed at the beginning of this discussion to start with some things so evident that we could easily agree on them.

From there we arrived at an analysis of what was behind those things that we agreed on. We decided that everything in Nature or Man's World arises from one basic cause, which is invisible, universal, mental, creative, and *not material*, and we called the expression of this great first cause the *universal mind*.

What does that mean to us *personally* and *practically*? If, for instance, we should discover that *each* of us can use that fact consciously to our own advantage, wouldn't that be a great discovery? Let us see.

How can we get at least a partial idea of what mind is? I suggest a comparison that has been helpful to many people in gaining a better understanding of this very important point.

On any electric circuit we find different kinds of appliances functioning. Vacuum cleaners, lamps, bells, motors, are all drawing their power to operate from the dynamo in the powerhouse. A lamp draws much less *power* than a big motor uses, but they all operate on the same electrical voltage. Break the circuit to the dynamo; the lamp goes out, the motor slows down to rest, the vacuum cleaner stops whirring, proving that the one source supplies them all.

Mind is something like that. Mind itself is the *source* of power, comparable to the dynamo. Individually we are tied in to that one infinite source, just as the lamps and motors are tied in to the dynamo. And we individually vary a lot in the amount of power we develop from the same voltage, just as the big motor develops much more power than the little motor does. But we are all tied in to that dynamo of limitless power called the Universal Mind.

The development and bettering of your own life depends on your learning how to draw *more power* from that great source, for the beautiful fact is that human machines can *increase* their own power, whereas mechanical contrivances cannot.

So we see that when man thinks, he is drawing power from the infinite "voltage" of the Universal Mind.

But in the human being, the Universal Mind takes on two different aspects. One aspect includes the direction of activities pertaining to man's normal material environment exterior to himself. Therefore we call it the *objective* mind. Sometimes we speak of it as the *"conscious* mind." It is simply that part of our thoughts that we direct upon outward things, necessary to our mortal, mundane or material welfare.

The other portion of the Universal Mind within each of us takes charge of the direction and utilization of forces that operate independently of our conscious or objective phase of mind.

This phase of the Universal Mind within us we term the "*subjective,*" sometimes called "*subconscious.*"

The two – subjective and objective – are physically one, but ordinarily are occupied in different ways, the subjective with the various activities of sustaining life and promoting growth, and the objective with receiving the reports of the senses and with reasoning, etc.

The stream of force can go either way, or even both ways at the same time. You might conceive of their connection as being like a revolving door at the entrance to a building; through the same door you can go from the building into the street, or vice versa, and different persons can go in opposite directions at the same time through the same door.

This distinction between objective and subjective mind is extremely important.

Ordinarily these two phases of mind operate independently (though they are connected). They do not conflict with each other. Yet, from time to time, we find ourselves forced to control the activity of the subjective mind by the action of the objective mind. For instance: We get a stomach ache. That means that the subjective processes of digestion have gone awry. So the objective mind has to step in, select a medicine, and thereby help the subjective mind to do its work properly.

In the foregoing paragraph is contained a very great fact. The objective mind, under certain circumstances, *can* and *does* control the subjective. Likewise the subjective can influence the objective, for the connection works both ways.

You get pleasant or unpleasant results from your actions depending very largely on how fully you realize and act with the infinite power of the Universal Mind, of which you are a vehicle for expression.

ALL IS ONE

Now we begin to catch a glimmer of what it is that enables some people to succeed far beyond their *apparent* abilities. Remember that we do *not* see their *real* abilities. Perhaps some of those whom we may have envied or called lucky have got hold of this great truth that is beginning to unfold to us in our study of the *invisible causes of visible effects*.

We see that all of these invisible causes focus down to the action of the Universal Mind, of which our individual minds are an expression. We see too that these individual minds of ours operate in two ways, subjectively and objectively. And that this subjective mind in each of us *can be controlled* by our objective mind, and that the activity of the subjective mind is directed solely toward carrying out orders, *absolutely automatically*, without any will of its own.

This point will be found to rest on the absolute unity of all things in the Universal Mind, regardless of their apparent physical separateness. This idea is so essential to further understanding of our theme that we shall devote some time now to getting clearly fixed in our consciousness how this can be, and *is*.

I do not propose to lead you through a maze of metaphysics on this search. So we shall take an illustration or two that will fully explain this idea of unity, and the absolute necessity of realizing it.

You are familiar with a cog wheel. Have you ever realized what a wonderful symbol of cosmic truth it is? Probably not, for we do not ordinarily look for symbols in such commonplace articles. The cog wheel has its hub, spokes, rim and teeth. Now, let the hub represent the Universal Mind. Let each spoke represent a human being, a race, a nation. Call the rim the cycle of life. Let the teeth on the rim represent the individual incidents and experiences of life.

First to engage our attention is the fact that all the spokes have their common origin in the hub – the Universal Mind. The next thing is that *in* that common center or origin each of the spokes contacts and *is a part* of the central hub. Likewise, in the Universal Mind all men, races and nations are *one* and a *part of each other*.

But as each spoke goes out toward the rim (toward the cycle of life) it becomes *seemingly* separated and the place where each touches the rim is far apart from its neighbor. I say "seemingly separated," for in *reality* each spoke joins each other spoke in the hub, and each is part of the whole wheel.

Human spokes in the wheel of life too often entertain the false idea that they are separate, that individuality means to be different from each other; right here is where human error begins. The coherent, united nation is all-powerful. Groups of men who work in unity become all-powerful. The individual man who thinks himself a law unto himself *fails*. He has lost his strength in losing his realization of the essential value of unity. Let him recall with Emerson that "everything in Nature contains all the powers of Nature. Everything is made of one hidden stuff."

Now, as a cog wheel revolves, each spoke in turn has to bear its own share of weight and strain. And as each tooth is engaged, representing an incident of experience in the cycle of life, so each human spoke has to bear the full force of that experience, and each human spoke *also receives the transmitted force of the experiences that every other human spoke bears*.

Perhaps one human spoke, thinking itself alone, separated from its brethren, deserted, neglected, picked on, feels that it is bearing an undue share of the burden. Really it is not, for it is simply performing its own share, in its own time, obeying the law, "Bear ye one another's burdens." So much for that illustration. Think it over before going on, and realize the *actual unity* of all *seemingly* separated things.

Now take a sheet of paper. Punch five holes in it and insert your five fingers through them. To a person opposite you, the five fingers represent five separate things. Each finger seems to have the power of individual motion and *seems* to be completely separate and apart from its neighbor. But to *you*, back of the paper, behind the scenes, *beyond the veil* as it were, appears the inescapable fact that all the fingers *are united*; that they spring from one common unity; that they derive their power from the same source.

Now do you get the point involved? When we get discouraged, when the world seems haywire, when we feel that our backs are to the wall with no help visible, it lowers our ability, our power, our stamina, force and energy, because we are thinking wrong. We think we have been cut off from our source. We think ourselves deserted, left alone, badly used, unappreciated, undervalued, unrecognized.

Our very first task in remodeling the things in our lives that do not suit us, is to get fixed fast in our memories this *fact* of our Unity with all things in the Universal Mind, for that fact gives us access to far greater powers than any we could ever before imagine as accessible *to* ourselves *by* ourselves.

Do not go on until you realize and *accept* that fact. We are coming to the specific details of how to *use* that fact for yourself. But they will do you no good whatsoever unless you *see* the truth of what has been stated up to now.

Go into a huge power station. Observe a great dynamo, capable of generating tremendous power. Its armature may be revolving at an amazing speed. The dynamo is ready for business at a second's notice – the mere pressing of a button or the throwing of a switch. But that huge dynamo is useless until *a demand is made upon it for power*. The moment demand is made by throwing the right switch, the current goes forth over the wires. But the demand *must be made*. Not a unit of power goes forth until that demand makes it possible.

But if you do not know that the dynamo exists, or do not believe it after having been told so, there is no use in telling you *how* to use it, is there?

Now let us bring this picture right home to ourselves. We have the source of power *within ourselves*, ready for business. But no power will come from it to help us do the things we wish to do until we recognize its existence, and make a call on its power and direct it to the desired purpose. There is a specific way in which we can make that demand, a way in which we can set that power to work for us. It is the greatest power in the world, far greater than any dynamo invented by man, for it is the *power* that enabled man to invent the dynamo.

THE GREAT LINK

If you have followed the discussion carefully so far, you have thoroughly in mind these ideas:

(a) All is One in the Universal Mind.

(b) You personally are an individualized channel for expression of that one Mind.

(c) In your human existence you use that Mind both objectively and subjectively.

(d) Your subjective mind can be controlled by your objective mind, and it carries out orders automatically.

(e) Ordinarily these orders relate to the usual body-regulating functions of the subjective, but it will also act on orders about other types of activity.

Let us now set ourselves definitely to see that there are, in fact, other kinds of orders which the subjective will accept from the objective and *carry out*.

Ordinarily *your* subjective mind is only dealing with *your own* objective mind. But it can deal with somebody else's objective mind *without knowing the difference*.

Your subjective mind is therefore entirely impersonal. That is only another way of saying that your subjective mind is *universal* in its reactions – it does *not* discriminate as to persons, or reasons why, or pros and cons.

How different in this respect is your objective mind! It is very keenly aware of the difference between persons. It sifts reasons. It argues pros and cons. It definitely *does* discriminate. Hence your objective mind is *not* universal in its use by you – it is decidedly *specific*, and rightly so for being of use on the plane of the specific, or, in other words, the world in which you live.

Now we are ready to take the big step forward.

We have already found that the basic source of all power on all planes – physical, mental or emotional – is the Universal Mind.

Now we have just discovered that only one aspect of your mind's activity – the subjective – is *likewise universal* in its reactions.

Hence we see that your individualized *subjective mind is your immediate personal link with the universal mind*. It is your *great link* with all else that is.

And since all things are possible to the Universal Mind, the power of an individual expression of that Universal Mind – such as *your own subjective mind* – is limited only by the arbitrary conditions of time, space, force and the other natural laws under which you as a human being are limited. But it has no further limitations.

In other words, your subjective mind could not cause you to rise up from the chair where you are sitting and float about the room. It could not cause you to expand instantaneously to a height of twenty feet. It could not enable you to scratch your right elbow with your right hand. All those things are physically impossible, made so in our arbitrary world of time and space.

But your subjective mind, having access to the vast power of the *Universal* Subjective Mind, can accomplish *anything* which is not prohibited by the laws of time and space.

It can attract to you the kind of life mate that you want. It can make you a capable citizen of your community, with proper compensation to you for your services. It can, in short, make you successful and happy.

How it does so comes next.

But don't go on to that until you are sure you understand the trend of our thought so far. Do you see – truly – that you are an expression of Universal Mind? Do you realize that this is made manifest in you through your subjective mind? Do you see why this subjective mind can accomplish anything for you that is not contrary to the laws of our world? And, finally, do you recall that your subjective mind is under the control of your objective mind, ready to obey it down to the last detail?

If you have come so far without lagging behind you are now ready to take the most important step of all.

FORMING THE PICTURE

Again let us review briefly what we have done so far. We have found that:

(a) As Shelly says, "Nothing in this world is single, all things by a law divine, in each other's being mingle." In other words, All is One in what we term Universal Mind. Seeming separateness is an illusion of the senses.

(b) Each of us is an individual expression of that Universal Mind. It functions in us both outwardly, through our objective mind, and inwardly, through our subjective mind. These are really but two aspects of the One Mind, but they function differently because of our nature.

(c) Your objective mind, circumscribed in its abilities by your experience, your judgment and your mentality in its outward dealings with *this* world, has but limited power. But your subjective mind, directed inwardly to *all the worlds* on inner planes, drawing life from the very source of *everything that is*, has access to *unlimited power*.

(d) Despite the incredible difference in their respective potential powers, your objective mind can control your subjective mind, give it orders and plan its activities. So it sets at work for you (by consciously cooperating with your objective mind) infinitely greater forces than your comparatively feeble conscious mentality can command alone.

Our next step: to discover *how* the objective can control the subjective – how, in other words, can we *consciously create circumstances*?

Through our five senses we distinguish objects in our visible world according to what we "form." If we look at a picture or a landscape, we see the form it presents by means of our eyes and brain. If we close our eyes, we can still preserve that picture by a *"mental vision" of what we have seen*. But the picture we see with our eyes and later reproduce in our minds is the picture of something that *already* exists. It is the result of some *previous* creative activity.

Now approaches the big point to which we have been working since we first began this study. *In consciously creating circumstances we reverse the process of physical sight*. Instead of seeing mentally a picture of what we know already exists physically, we use this giant power within us by impressing our individual subjective mind *with the picture of what we want to see come about physically*.

That is how simple it is. Simple, I said, not easy – but entirely *possible*.

When we view a picture or landscape, we see it *first* with our physical eyes, then in our minds. Now throw the gears into reverse. In your work of consciously creating circumstances you are to see the picture of what you want *first in your mind*, and later with your physical eye after it comes into externalization.

You originate pictures and then, by means of a definite technique, you make them come true before your very eyes, in due time.

Put another way, creating circumstances requires you first to impress on your subjective mind what you want to perceive later with your objective mind.

This is a revolutionary thought to some people. "How can you reverse a natural process," they say, "and expect to get results?" Well, you do it with other natural processes.

You can make your automobile go backward – even though it usually goes forward. You can make the electric motor run the steam engine, although it usually works vice versa.

You can turn your dark night of trouble, of discord, disappointments and delays into the glorious day of accomplishment, joy and happiness by *reversing the usual process*. Do not wait to accept whatever may come before your eyes! Determine for yourself what *shall* come before your eyes! You *can* and *will do it*, if you will follow directions.

But, first and foremost, *know what you want*. Many people fail in life because they do not realize what they want. Have a clear, well-defined understanding with yourself before you start consciously to create circumstances.

Do not make up your mind hastily. In dealing with an infinite force you cannot afford to be hasty; if you insist on being so, you will have only yourself to blame when your efforts fail as they surely will. *You cannot hurry the infinite*!

Now let us say that you have a particular desire. We will assume that it is a desire that you can, with the warm approval of your conscience, take to the Universal Mind for fulfillment. How do you get results?

To some extent we all enjoy a faculty of "imagination," which Einstein has said is more important than knowledge. Imagination differs in degree and in kind in the individual according to temperament, vocation and evolutional status, but wherever there is human consciousness there also is *some* degree of imagination. So, when you have a distinct desire you automatically form a mental picture of it; incomplete as it may be, it requires the use of your imaging faculty.

Having satisfied yourself that your predominating desire is worthy; that it involves no harm or detriment to another, and that it will work out to the advantage of others besides yourself, *fix that desire*. Use your imagination to the utmost to develop a perfect, well-defined picture of it, not as you hope it may be, but *as if it were already a fact*. See yourself in that picture actually occupied in doing exactly what you would do if it were already externalized. Hold this mental picture as long as you can. Concentrate on making the image complete. *Do not strain or try to will it into being*. Just keep the image in mind, thinking of it objectively as often as your activities permit.

Now what are you really doing? Clearly, you are using your objective mind to decide what you want and to build up a perfect picture of that desire brought about in your life. Lots of people go that far.

But here is where 999 out of 1000 go wrong. They make the objective mind, greatly limited in its knowledge and power, try to do the rest of the job which properly belongs to the subjective mind, with its direct access to the *unlimited* power and knowledge of the Universal Mind.

Once you have formed your picture objectively, give the poor tired conscious mentality a rest. Leave the remainder of the job to the Universal. Not as a request or a hope that it will see you through, but in perfect faith, born of *knowledge*; that your image has already been built and is bound to come to pass.

Why should you have that faith? Why will your images, if persisted in and adhered to constantly, come true in the circumstances of your daily life? What, so to speak, are the mechanics of the process?

Let's go back a little.

We agreed that the objective can control the subjective, which means that an image formed by the objective can be impressed on the subjective *as an order to be carried out*.

Your unconscious (subjective) mind receives an order from your conscious (objective) mind; for instance, to get you money, or whatnot: your subjective mind immediately accepts the order and goes to work.

What tools does the subjective mind have to work with? My answer is: *all* the tools, known and unknown, in the universe, because it is *your personal link* with the Universal Subjective Mind which knows all, sees all, and can accomplish all things. And it *will* do whatever you command, because it is impersonal and has no will of its own, any more than a great reservoir can refuse to let the water run out of a single spigot that is turned on.

Therefore you can entirely, with reason, have the faith that your demand will be met, that your images will come to pass in your own life, that the circumstances you consciously create mentally will come about physically just as surely as you are reading these words.

These images we generally term "thought-forms" because they *are* real forms in the world of thought. You decide *objectively* what they shall be. You work *subjectively* to bring them about. Do not confuse the two. Let each aspect of mind do the work it can do best.

The ways and means of doing so come next.

IMPRESSING YOUR DESIRE

We will assume that a desire has taken shape in your mind, due to the absence of something in your life or environment that must be supplied to complete your happiness or welfare.

The desire has been picturized by your imagination as a definite thought-form. All this has taken place in your objective mind.

Your next step is to impress this thought-form upon your subjective mind, for there *the real work begins.* Talk to your subjective mind as though it were directly to an individual. Some people find it helpful to direct their speech toward the solar plexus, for the reason that the solar plexus, or center of your subjective mind, is the individual's link with Universal Mind. To us the most important thing in the outside Universe is the sun, giver of life, center of our system. That is why the solar plexus is very aptly named.

When you speak to your subjective mind you may do so mentally, if you prefer, or if audible speech would be disconcerting to others. But if possible, do so audibly to assist in crystallizing your thought-form.

When you speak to your subjective mind, close your eyes – not for any weird or occult reason, but simply that your mind may not be diverted by the sight of things in your environment that provoke distraction of thought.

In the darkness of closed eyes, try to feel that which you cannot see, namely the subtle body of the Universal Mind flowing through your organism.

If you do not bring yourself at first to this definite *feeling*, at least bring yourself to the state of mind in which you accept it as unseen, unfelt, but incontrovertibly *true*.

Then, with your eyes closed, bring the picture of your thought-form to mind, and describing it clearly, speak to your subjective mind, which you conceive of as in the solar plexus. Say something like this to your subjective mind:

"It is my *desire* and my *will* that you do thus and so, using me as a focal center of attraction. It is a worthy request. I ask it unselfishly. I desire to be in perfect harmony with all constructive activity. I *know* you have the power to bring about what I order through your connection with the all-powerful Universal Mind. *You are doing it now*, and I thank you for hearing me."

What is worth having is worthy of thanks.

Your subjective mind, being a function of the Universal Subjective Mind, then impresses the image with which you have charged it upon the potency of the whole body of the Universal Mind with you as a focal center. By the Law of Attraction the elements necessary to the externalization of your thought-form in your life are built up. To put it simply, the thought-form comes true, because this archetypal mental form must build a corresponding set of circumstances in the world of matter.

All the *power* of that Universal Mind is brought to focus at any point at which it may be contacted, and the results at one point will be equally present at any other point.

When talking to your subjective mind, remember one thing above all. *Do not attempt to tell it its own business, which is the means of carrying out your order*. It knows far more than you can possibly know. It manipulates forces that you cannot even dream of. Let it do its work in its own way. Make your order as simple, clear and uninvolved as possible. The clearer and simpler your charge, the quicker will you attain results. Just give the plain outlines of what you want to realize. *Do not limit the subjective as to time*. Do not stipulate how or through what channels your money, your friendship, your job or whatnot is to come. Hold fast only to the image itself, and the details will be filled in later.

The principal matter to keep in mind at this stage is the necessity of sublime faith. We are not teaching "faith-cures" or anything of the sort.

What you are learning is based absolutely upon *knowledge and fact*. But faith plays an important part in all human experience. If you asked a friend to do something for you and then began to question whether he would be *able* to do so, if you began to *hope* that he might, or *fear* that in some way he would not, how much do you think that friend would do for you if he knew just how you felt? Well, the Universal knows far more about how you feel than any human being could possibly know, because you are a part of the Universal, and you therefore communicate every state of mind within you to the Universal Mind, even though you do so unconsciously. Therefore you must not doubt its ability, no matter how great a demand you make on it.

In our present discussion we are not dealing with the cumbersome faculties of human individuals but with the all-potent medium of the Universal Mind itself, upon which all the thoughts of all the individuals through all the ages have been impressed.

The technique we have given is simple. The results will depend entirely upon the mental attitude and spiritual trust you can develop. *Do not worry about results*. Let them take care of themselves. They will manifest according to your ability to contact the Universal Mind in an attitude of understanding and true faith.

The great majority of people, through ignorance or lack of faith, use a child's tin hammer to drive home their desires when they could use a ten-ton pile driver. They put a toy electric motor behind their ambitions when they could harness up a giant turbine. In other words, they use only their confused, helter-skelter, feeble *objective* minds when they could tap the infinite resources of the *Universal Subjective Mind*.

THE LAW OF ATTRACTION

Here let us pause to survey more closely the means by which your thought-form, correctly evolved and stamped on the Universal Mind, will become manifest in the facts of your life.

We have already discussed the point, but it will be well here to study further, and *understand*, the great Law of Attraction on which depends the success of your thought-forms.

It is a law in physics that "unlikes attract, and likes repel," meaning of course "polarities," the term used to express opposites.

We are used to this expression in dealing with electricity and magnetism, but by careful observation we shall find that this law operates throughout Nature's entire domain. Now note carefully how we make the law operative in accordance with our *legitimate* and *reasonable* desires as expressed in thought-forms.

Universal Substance manifests the two polarities of Matter and Spirit, and as a corollary to that fact, formations in the invisible mental and spiritual worlds seek manifestation in the visible material world. In this search for material expression Nature's forces generate and develop tremendous activity and this activity is the cause of all action and reaction, urging and restraining, positive and negative, in cosmos. It produces the phenomenon we ordinarily call "life."

The principle holds true in regard to your thought-form. First you formulate and develop it on the inner, invisible plane. Then the invisible thought-form, which is the positive polarity, seeks the negative polarity or material expression of itself. All that is visible in the mundane world about us is the expression of the activity of invisible archetypes in the inner worlds.

If you have ever watched frost crystals form on a window pane during cold weather, you will have noticed how the lines of crystallization radiate in very definite directions, always in geometrically correct proportions of balance and symmetry – a fine illustration of Nature's maintenance of equilibrium.

Your thought-form operates in exactly the same manner. In the case of the frost crystal, we *see* the lines of crystallization becoming visible and these lines are called the "lines of force," i.e. the direction taken by the operative force in crystallizing the moisture. Your thought-form does the same thing. You cannot see it visibly in just the same way as you see the frost crystals, but you *can* see it by observing carefully the various incidents in your daily life, which will become apparent to you as indicating just how conditions are shaping themselves toward the ultimate realization of your desire.

Little by little, you will note apparently insuperable obstacles being eliminated, providing you with *greater scope and opportunity*, with the way being made clearer for you to *progress* toward your goal.

The frost crystal does not spring into visible manifestation instantaneously; neither will the realization of your thought-form. The frost crystal is a manifestation wherein the constructive material is of the most attenuated character. Your thought-form is complex, involving a vast array of constructive materials, and possibly also involving other individuals, and much time is necessarily required for the operative activities to bring all the elements together in visible realization.

But the realization will surely come, if you are patient and persistent and, above all, conscientious. Lines of force will radiate out from your growing thought-form just as the tiny roots radiate out from the fast-growing plant or shrub. These roots radiate in ever-widening areas in search of nourishment, and that nourishment consists of material substances which they can assimilate.

The length of time necessary for the thought-form to "come true" will depend on its nature; whether it is simple or complex, whether it involves just you or others, whether the obstacles to be overcome are few or many.

The two factors of thought-forms and the Law of Attraction are the prime working tools of the mental scientist, and on them depend the amazing phenomena of metaphysics, psychology and mental science.

There is an interesting and true analogy between the workings of a thought-form and the growth of a plant which will help you to understand this extremely important point of *why* thought-forms "come true."

A tiny seed is planted in the ground. You plant it, let us say. Probably, if you are wise in such matters, you first clear away stones, weeds and rubbish from your garden. You select the seed carefully, studying the different grades or brands offered to get just the flower you want.

After planting the seed, you see that it has the right conditions for growth, including moisture and *freedom from disturbance*. In the dark earth the creative processes of nature – which you cannot see – are bringing the seed along, and soon comes the day when it pokes its bright green shoot above ground.

Sunlight, moisture, air and, again, *freedom from disturbance*, eventually bring the plant to full growth, and the beautiful flower spreads its fragrance for you *and others* to enjoy.

Obviously the seed is the thought-form. You select it carefully – either the seed or thought-form – to make sure it is the *one* you want. You prepare the ground for your thought-form by clearing away the stones of envy, the weeds of sloth and discontent, and the rubbish of belief in limitation.

You stamp the thought-form in the Universal (plant the seed in the earth) carefully and earnestly. Then, just as you do not disturb the seed after planting, you do not disturb the thought-form by doubting its power, or by fussing with its details.

And just as the invisible powers of nature cause the seed to sprout, so do the equally invisible powers of the Universal cause your thought-form to "sprout." You cooperate with nature by providing moisture and possibly fertilizer for the invisible seed; likewise you cooperate with the Universal by providing *meditation* and a calm, sure *expectancy* that the thought-form *will* sprout.

And inevitably one day the first tiny shoot of the thought-form will become visible, that is, the first specific result of it will appear in your life. Glad day! From then on, if you continue to aid it with the life-giving waters of *meditation* and hearten it with *sunny* expectation of its eventual completion, it will continue to grow, and sooner or later it will stand forth in your life an accomplished fact. And, like the flower, it will gladden *others* as well as yourself.

Really, are thought-forms and their working out any more miraculous than the sprouting of a seed? They are both based on the Law of Attraction. We are used to the one, unused to the other, that is all. But think how great was the amazement of the first man who planted a seed of wheat, and later found it growing into a plant that would nourish him! In those days it required *real faith* to take the trouble to plant, when no results were immediately apparent. And today it requires the same faith to plant a thought-form, at least until you *know from experience* that they *do* sprout.

But this faith is just the one thing you *must* have, and we have seen the logical basis for it in this explanation of the Law of Attraction.

It is difficult to believe that we have received something, when our senses tell us to the contrary. Yet this is *absolutely necessary* for the individual who seeks success through the use of thought-forms.

It certainly seems like "putting the cart before the horse." Nevertheless it is quite sound, and to the extent that we can bring our consciousness to an understanding and acceptance of this truth will our results be successful or unsuccessful.

We may resort to another illustration to clarify the point. When we take a photograph of a landscape, the momentary flash of light has imprinted the picture of the subject on the sensitive plate *permanently*. As long as that plate lasts, many positives or prints may be made from it. That is what the plate or film was made for. The landscape may change with the seasons or by the hand of man, but the print of it on the negative will be preserved as long as the owner of the camera desires to keep it.

What you have asked for *has* come into being at once, and you may logically believe that you *have* received it, although the realization of your reception of it will be delayed until it has been brought into physical manifestation, when the time is ripe.

When *you personally* begin to study the use of thought-forms and begin to make them part of your mental equipment, shaping circumstances by them consciously, you will have taken a tremendous step forward – perhaps the most significant single step forward that you ever will take.

You will then have begun to take the first steps in the kindergarten of conscious creation. You will naturally stumble and fall, probably cry a bit, but then you will try again and sooner or later accomplish the first steps. I promise you, my friend, that few things on earth equal the joy you will get from learning that first lesson. When you know that this marvelous new power is *yours* – you will sing for joy. You will then *know* that all things on Earth are yours to command. That you yourself can solve your own problems, be they what they may. That you have within yourself the seeds of your own success.

This may sound exaggerated if you have not learned that first lesson. Yet I *know, personally,* scores of men and women of *only average mental equipment* who have learned this lesson. Once gained it can never be lost, no matter how slowly or with what difficulty the further lessons are mastered.

And the very fact that you are reading these words and thinking about these mysteries, for they *are* mysteries, demonstrates that you personally are marching in the vanguard of evolution because very few people know about the power of thought-forms.

Nature wastes nothing. If you had not earned the right to know about thought-forms, you would not hear of them! If your past had not brought you to the point where you could accept this great power and use it, you would not be told about it. The very fact that you know about this throbbing dynamo waiting for you to throw the switch is proof that you are entitled to use its power.

Whether you use it is, of course, entirely up to you.

I do not ask you whether you want this power, or urge you to take it. In fact, I warn you that use of this power for evil ends will hurt you badly.

Do not hesitate to use thought-forms because of a fear that your *method* will be wrong. That will not hurt you. You simply will not get results, in that case, and no harm is done. But *be sure* that your thought-forms do not intend any harm to another person, because that will inevitably react on you quite unpleasantly, as we shall discover later on.

And if you would ask just how to begin to use this vast power – what kind of a thought-form to fashion first – I would suggest this:

Immediately set to work to clean out of your heart any bitter, destructive, unkind, uncharitable feelings. You cannot build a new house with rubbish from the old one cluttering up the lot.

When you are satisfied that you have honestly done that, begin to build up an image of yourself as a conscious agent of Universal Mind, receiving inspiration from the source of all things to aid you and others in making life more worth living. Some find it helpful in forming a picture of this kind to imagine themselves receiving floods of light and power from the Sun, and this is a good method, for the Sun blesses us with much besides daylight and warmth.

But I shall not go into particulars about the details of this basic thought-form of yours. If I did, it would be mine, not yours. Meditate on the idea. Let it mature in your own mind. When you are satisfied with it, adopt it definitely and see it already *done*. Add to it from time to time if additional details occur to you. Concentrate on it whenever you can.

The important point is your realization of yourself as an instrument of Universal Mind. A feeble instrument now, perhaps, but one that can build itself into a bigger, finer person by surveying your possibilities, and then consciously developing them as you will be instructed.

Work first on your basic thought-form. Never mind that specific want in your life that needs to be filled. That will be taken care of more quickly if you first make sure of your *general* alignment with nature's constructive forces.

In passing, let us clear up one point. We began this study by saying that successful people have access to something that failures do not know about. Now we are talking about thought-forms. Does that mean that *all* successful people use thought-forms? By no means; or rather, they do not all use them *consciously*. But even if they are used unconsciously, they have *some* power.

Electrical engineers know that a current of electricity flowing through one wire will *induce* a current in a wire laid alongside it, even though the second wire is not connected with it or to any battery. The effect is *slight*, and as nothing compared with the current in the first wire, but it exists.

In a similar way, a strong image of a desire in one's objective mind will have *some* effect on one's subjective mind, even though it is not *consciously* impressed on it as a thought-form. The results will be minor compared with the results of *consciously* stamping the thought-form. It is this unconscious activity, small though it is, that has enabled many people to achieve success, because they knew what they wanted, and they wanted it vigorously.

Now let us review again, briefly, to be sure that we understand each other so far.

Each of us functions mentally in a dual fashion. Objectively we work through our brain, with its powers of observation, comparison, reasoning and imagination – relating to things on our limited mundane plane. Subjectively, we work through our solar plexus, with its access to the unlimited power of the Universal Subjective Mind.

Your brain can direct the activities of your solar plexus – or, to put it another way, your objective can direct your subjective mind. For convenience we speak of these as two minds, though in reality they are but different expressions of the one mind.

By deciding objectively what *shall* come into your life, and impressing the picture of that desire forcefully on your subjective, you can bring about those conditions as you wish, before your very eyes, in due time.

These images which we impress on the subjective we call thought-forms. The process of using them we call "consciously creating circumstances."

The successful people of this world are chiefly distinguished from the laggards by reason of their use of thought-forms – consciously or otherwise.

This takes us in outline through our previous discussions. Now let us go on to further details of your basic thought-form. You are probably anxious for me to give you specific suggestions about how to get a job, or a better job; money, a wife or husband. But please listen to me: do *not* form any *specific* thought-form for a while. Stick to the basic, general thought-form. It won't be easy to be patient. But it *will* be worthwhile.

Let me give you seven reminders:

(1)   Make your thought-form constructive.

(2)   Include benefit to others as well as yourself.

(3)   Make it practical.

(4)   Concentrate it on what you want to *be* or *do* – *not* on what you want to *have*.

(5)   Visualize the thought-form as worked out *now*.

(6)   Make the thought-form relate to *yourself* as the agent of Good.

(7)   Act constantly in full faith that your thought-form *is* working out.

Your life can be just as wonderful as *you* decide to make it. Now keep that brain of yours quiet, with its habitual objections and doubts and hesitations.

I repeat, *your life can be just as wonderful as you decide to make it* – provided only that you use the truths which the real *you* does not need to be convinced of – *for it already knows them* – but which the shell you call your body needs to be stirred into using *actively*.

The great laws of the Universe have brought you to the point, after eons of eons, where, as a self-conscious, individualized entity, you have had the *key* to Nature's great storehouse *put right into your palm*.

All right. Now you have just created your *basic permanent thought-form*. So far you have only created it consciously – with your objective mind. *Hold fast to it*. Perhaps you will want to write it down.

But that is only part of the process. Now let's complete it. You are now to speak mentally to your subjective mind – concentrating on your solar plexus as your link to Universal Mind.

Never mind whether you are doing it *just* right. You are making a start. You will do this many, many times more!

Say to your real self mentally: "This is what I desire to be. All power is yours to create those circumstances. You *have* created them in the world of thought. I joyfully await their manifestation in the objective world, for lo! my own shall come to me."

Do that right now. Do not go on for even one paragraph until you have done so.

It is the infinite power of the Universal Subjective Mind that builds the mansion for you, and when it is ready, throws it open to your possession. You decide what shall be created for you. Then you *hold fast* to that image: you *keep out* contrary or diluting ideas.

Your beginnings may be small, but they will be obvious to you in many ways that will encourage you if you heed the little things. Be not greedy for the big things immediately. The *big things will come in due time* and that time of waiting will be a test of your faith and your "endurance unto the end."

One swallow does not make a summer, nor can one or two minutes spent on a constructive thought-form undo the destructive influence of the countless weakening thoughts you may have *ignorantly* and *unconsciously* sent into Universal Mind for years.

Yet a beginning must be made somewhere and at some time. If you have participated actively in our little exercises, you have made an excellent beginning.

YOUR BASIC ATTITUDE

Again I am going to ask you to be patient and not skip over to the details of technique. You have one more important idea to solidify before getting down to the fine points.

That idea that I want to impress on you is this: *Act* daily in full faith that your basic thought-form *is* working out. Perhaps that does not sound so terribly important, but let me assure you that it is.

It would be easy here to give you a long list of Don'ts in the use of thought-forms. But instead, for the time being, we shall concentrate on one *big do*. And we may find that, by inference, it will provide all the Don'ts.

Now read this carefully: The degree of success which you enjoy in using thought-power will correspond exactly with the degree to which your *habitual*, daily attitude toward Life is *constructive*. Why? Because your habitual, daily attitude toward Life reflects your *real underlying* thought-form. If it is constructive your results will be so. And *vice versa*.

Now suppose a man has a head full of black thoughts. And suppose that by chance he let one little white thought into it. Obviously, his head would still be full of *black* thoughts.

Going still further, if over a period of years a man has poured a stream of black thoughts into the Universal, and then suddenly introduces one little white thought – the Universal remains, *to him*, a sea of black. These black thoughts need not be what we usually call evil ones. They can be just careless ones, or doubtful, or hesitant, or unhappy and distrustful.

Such a man need not expect *one* constructive thought-form at once to undo the harm of millions of destructive thought-forms he has consciously or otherwise impressed on the Universal. Such a man will require perhaps *years* of effort to nullify his previous ignorant actions. This seems like hard lines, in a way – yet we may be sure, on the other hand, that once this has been accomplished, the evil has been put behind *forever*.

Now let us consider the man of good heart, jolly cheerful and optimistic by nature. His *basic* thought-form of life *is* constructive and *has been* for years.

To the optimistic man things come easily, but for the pessimistic man life is a burden. You have noticed that yourself, I am sure, speaking by and large.

And here is the scientific, convincing reason for that fact which you have observed: the optimistic, good-expecting man creates good conditions for himself by his daily, inherent thought-forms – unconscious, to be sure, but nevertheless *somewhat* effective. And the pessimistic individual creates his own bad conditions, by a like process.

The mental scientist who is alive to his task will, curiously enough, exhibit to the world a perfect bevy of the homely virtues. He will be anything but spectacular in his actions, and perhaps seem even stupid to some bright minds because he is not continually scheming to advance his interests.

But how incredibly *superior* is such a mental scientist? The one great lesson he has learned leads him to leave ways and means to the Universal Ways and Means Committee, once he has decided the direction and manner in which that power shall manifest in *his* life.

This does not mean that he sits back and does nothing! Far from it! He will be decidedly active in discharging his duties, and doing well the thing at hand.

The worker in thought-forms leaves to others all worry as to whether he will get his just reward. He *knows* that he will. He radiates good cheer and confidence – not because some "pep-up-artist" has told him to, but because he *cannot* be any other way.

He knows that *life* has a *real meaning*, and he is eager to enter its experiences on the credit side of his ledger. He seeks every opportunity to enlarge the useful sphere of those experiences, both with ideas and with people.

He knows that Love and Beauty walk hand in hand down the byways of life, as twin agents of the Universal Mind, and he finds them equally in the song of a lark or the glad cry of a child, in a lump of soft clay or a dancing sunbeam, in the caress of a loved one or the smile of a friend.

Such a person, who has come to *at-one-ment* with Universal Mind, and who understands its infinite bounty, truly inhabits a world of the wondrous, "far surpassing wealth unspoken."

Does anyone doubt that such a world is indeed possible? It awaits only the will to find it, to open the door – in short, to use the key which already has been placed *in your hands*.

It requires mainly the formation of your basic thought-form, and then living your life in full confidence that this thought-form *is* working out in your life.

Do not worry if you find it difficult at first to frame your desires completely and simply. Your *real* meaning will be clear to the Universal Mind without lengthy and detailed instructions. But be sure you do have a definite idea yourself. If you find it hard to phrase, it may be that you have not yet as definite a desire as you think you have.

Some students, with all sincerity and the best intentions in the world, begin to concentrate on wealth. Now wealth in itself need not be despised, but wealth sought merely as an end generally destroys the individual who gets it. You have seen that yourself. Wealth does not always accomplish the purpose originally desired.

Many times in the passing years have I heard people say: "Wait till I have made enough money and then I want to devote my entire time to humanitarian work." And I have watched and waited and I have never seen *one* of them acquire what he considered enough to enable him to relax and devote himself to the really useful side of life. Yet many of them have made what the world calls "wealth."

When you concentrate to impress your thought-form upon the Universal, do *not* ask for money or wealth first. *There may be a better way.* Follow the rules given and picturize yourself doing the exact work you desire to do, *regardless of money*. The fact that you become able to do the thing you desire to do is evidence that the means for you to do so will be forthcoming. The best plan for all thought-forms is to see yourself in them doing the actual work you want to do.

Then do not "cramp" the Universal by trying to impress it with the idea of just what the desire will cost or when the means shall come or through what channels. What do you care how the supply comes so long as you are doing your work? This is the big thing – the *only* thing for you to concentrate on.

If and when you find it difficult to follow the precepts of the great laws of nature which are bound to produce harmony, it is because somehow you are thinking wrong. Stop where you are, and wait until your inner guidance tells you that you are back on the clear road to straight and correct thinking, for as your thoughts are, so will the results be, and if you are jangled in your thoughts you will be jangled and confused in your actions and affairs.

Jot this rule down in your memory and, paradoxical as it may seem, *believe* it. If you are as poor as the proverbial church-mouse, never think poverty. If you are as rich as Croesus, never think of yourself as wealthy. But *always think of yourself as opulent*. Many a financially poor man is so rich in courage and stamina that he is bound to rise out of his poverty. Many a rich man is so poor in spirit that his money is the only thing that gets him by, and he frequently loses that.

Talking and thinking poverty, whether of means or of spirit, creates or perpetuates poverty. Talking or thinking of wealth crystallizes the mind to such an extent that one forgets that riches sometimes take wings, or else develops a spirit of aloofness and arrogance. Talk and think *opulence*, or having an abundance of the good things of life, including the opportunity to serve others.

Remember always that you are a part of and a channel for all the Power in the Universe. That Power will manifest through you in just the degree that *you* permit.

EMPLOYMENT

These days a job or the absence of it seems to be uppermost in the minds of many. How can you get a job – or a better one – by using a thought-form?

Not so long ago a man I know was out of a job. He knew about thought-forms, but – having had an easy life up to then – had not bothered to use them. After several months of idleness, with his funds disappearing rapidly, he suddenly woke up to the fact that he was merely doing what everyone else was doing who was out of work – walking from place to place wherever he hoped there might be a job, and advertising in the newspapers. And he was rapidly getting nowhere.

He decided that he would "come to life" and use the power of thought-forms. But *how*, was the question?

There was a certain office where he felt sure he could be useful. He had once worked there, could do certain things for that organization, and believed that he might, without loss to anyone, well be employed there.

So he set up a picture of himself at work there, right in the office and at a certain desk he knew was not then being used. He clearly outlined the kind of papers he would be working on. He visualized himself receiving a pay envelope. He built up many details of the picture, and then impressed it hard and often on the Universal Mind.

He got the job.

Was that a successful thought-form? Apparently so, for he got what he was after. But he failed in one important point, and soon afterwards lost the job! What was the thing he did wrong and which therefore brought him only temporary and mild success with that thought-form? Do you see it?

His mistake was in specifying the *particular* office he was to be employed at. He believed they needed him, and the power of his thought created a temporary condition that agreed with his idea. But basically he was wrong – they did *not* need him, and his thought-form could not permanently overcome that fact.

What should he have done? Just what he did, except that he should not have specified the office. He should first have meditated fully on the manner in which his talents could well be used by *somebody* – not a specific person. He should have pictured himself in *an* office doing the kind of work he wanted, as part of a chain of effort that was giving his community a real service of some kind – and receiving a pay envelope.

What is really the essence of employment? Is it not *service*? That is a much-abused word these days but it is an honorable one, nevertheless. If you desire – honestly and completely – to be *useful*, and impress that idea on the Universal Mind, the way will be found. The answer may be entirely different from what you expect, but, when it comes, accept it whole-heartedly and put all of yourself into whatever it suggests.

The story about the man which I have just related – a true one, by the way – has a happy ending. After being discharged from the job he secured, he had wit enough to realize his error. He went right to work on another thought-form of a more general nature, without specifications as to how or where it would work out. His emphasis was put on himself as really serving. A close friend of his soon came to him and hired him for a totally unexpected kind of work, which he was glad to undertake, and that job he has held, with his pay increased twice since.

I cannot tell you the exact nature of the thought-form you should set up to get yourself a job. I can and have told you what to do in a general way.

Now let me add a few Don'ts.

Do not see yourself replacing anyone in a job. That would probably be bad for the other person, and so could not do you good.

Do not specify minutely the kind of work you want to do. *There may be a better kind of work for you.*

Do not say that you are going to get a job *by such a time.* Your best work may not be ready for you, and no matter what your present needs may be, your best work will be better for you in the long run if you have the courage to wait for it!

Do not see yourself getting money by clever deals with other people. Those clever deals may not be good for the others, so they will not be good for you.

These are a few of the principal errors to be avoided. There are others that you will find for yourself unless you stay close to the general rules laid down. And above all, remember that after you have made up your thought-form correctly, and consistently stamped it on the Universal Mind, you must act in full confidence that it *has* become a fact in the world of thought, and *will* come true before your very eyes.

HOW TO CONCENTRATE

In the technique of forming mental pictures we must emphasize the importance of *concentration,* a principle about which many people talk and write – but which few know how to put into actual practice. It is easy to form a mental picture. Everyone has done so and continues to do so to a greater or lesser extent. Daydreams are such pictures. Even the most "unimaginative" person forms pictures in his mind of the desires or longings closest to his heart.

Ideas *must* express themselves, and in order to become full fledged ideas they *must* picturize themselves in one's consciousness. If you propose to build a house, you may be hazy about details but you have *some idea* of about how you expect it to look and you try to convey your general mental picture to your architect, leaving the detailed drawings and specifications to him, if you are wise.

In forming thought-forms you are commending your ideas to the Great Architect of the Universe.

The more you retain your pictured idea in your mind, seldom letting it out of your consciousness, even though you may be engaged on other matters, the stronger that picture becomes. It grows by its own nature, for growth is a cosmic law that applies to things on the mental plane as well as on the physical.

We keep our mental picture or thought-form in continuous, healthy growth by the process and faculty of *concentration*. An eastern philosopher, Patanjali, defines concentration as "the hindering of the modifications of the thinking principle." In plainer words, it means the prevention of thoughts that interfere with any important matter on which we have set our minds. It means devoting one's unhindered mental energies to the particular matter that stands out in importance above all other things in our life at any one time.

Concentration means being of "one mind" for the period in which you are holding your thought-form for impression upon the Universal Mind. There must be no confusion. You cannot develop your thought-form and impress it upon the Universal and at the same time allow side thoughts to flit across your mental vision. Development of concentration is natural to some, difficult for others: but any normal person *can* develop it by simple perseverance.

If, at the start, your mind wanders, bring it back to focus again and again until your picture remains clear and unobscured. Again, if your mind persists in wandering, in spite of all your efforts, it shows that what you *think* you desire does not take the precedence it should and that it is not, for the moment, the all-absorbing interest in your life. To be successful, it *must* be the all-absorbing interest, to the exclusion of all else at that time. This does not mean that you must think of nothing else at any time. Go about your ordinary affairs, but with the knowledge that the thought-form upon which you are working is very close beneath your surface consciousness and can be brought up to focus at any moment. Have an underlying consciousness of your supreme desire, and as many times as possible each day bring it to focus and impress it again and again upon the Universal Mind.

In concentrating upon your thought-form, hold it steady, clear and fixed. But there is another way in which you can help. *Meditate* upon it. Meditation is somewhat like concentration but not the same. In concentration the thought or picture is held fixed. In meditation the general idea is held, but one allows the mind to revolve the idea in every direction, developing its possibilities, and then adding such developments to the fixed idea. Meditate *first* to build up a fine thought-form. Then contemplate calmly and expectantly its working out.

Now notice carefully that it is *not* by concentration or meditation that you consciously create circumstances. It is *only* by impressing your thought-forms on the subjective and visualizing them worked out that you bring them about. Concentration and meditation are needed to help you do this stamping. Your *will* holds the thought constant to its purpose – but the thought alone *creates*. Probably you have seen a steel die or copper plate from which stationery is engraved. The surface of the metal is hallowed out in the form of the monogram to be printed. As a die alone it is practically worthless. Yet when the ink is put into it, and transferred under pressure to the paper, the finished product is useful.

Conceive of your thought-form as the die. When the proper materials come to hand, the die or thought-form impresses your life with events as determined by its own form. The common expression, "The die is cast" takes on a greater significance in this connection.

The sort of concentrative ability you need must be the vigorous, active kind that will operate anywhere and under any conditions without an external stimulus. In seeking this, first relax. Close the eyes. Take a comfortable posture. In other words, *remove* external distractions. Allow your mind to calm down. Then –

Develop the picture of your desire. Fill in as many details as you can without specifying how they shall come about. Gradually, like a photographic film developing, the picture will take on more and more meaning, until it suddenly jumps into completion. Then *fix it*. Hold on to it for a few minutes. Then banish it and forget it. Relax.

Later on, recall the picture to your mind. Repeat this process often. There is no such thing as too much concentration, unless you do so much of it at any one time that you become over-tired.

Remember that the Universal Mind is constructive. Yet because Universal Mind is impersonal, it has no choice but to follow the plan laid down in the charge, mission or burden that is given it by you. Therefore it will work for you, and on returning your plan or thought-form completed and in objective manifestation, it will involve you just as you wanted to be involved. If, therefore, your thought-form has in it any element of personal grievance or harm for another, it will come back to you and you will still be involved, which is just what you do *not* want.

Sometimes the question is asked: "Can I function more than one thought-form at a time?" The answer is that only one thought-form can be impressed upon the Universal Mind at one "stamping."

But having with deep concentration impressed the Universal Mind with a fundamental thought-form, there is nothing to prevent you from making other impresses upon the Universal Mind for other purposes. The real test is whether you can focus your objective mind on more than one purpose without weakening the varied purposes you have in mind. Sometimes a person may have several desires which, when properly put into definite shape, indicate that one single, well-expressed thought-form will furnish the basic essentials to cover all those desires.

If it is desired to develop two thought-forms and to impress them upon the Universal Mind, the individual must make sure that his mind is entirely clear of the one while he devotes it to the other.

It is better to set one well-defined thought-form into activity and wait until it is firmly started on the way to externalization, and then later impress the second thought-form as a distinct entity by itself.

Take the first steps slowly. Ponder your objectives carefully. Then work hard on one basic thought-form before you clutter up your mental workshop with a lot of half-built, weak structures.

FEAR AND FAITH

Some people feel that they understand the law perfectly as soon as their attention has been directed to it. They begin to practice it and as soon as they begin, they also begin to nullify it by their doubts. It seems so simple at first that they begin to question: "How is it possible to secure what I need merely by closing my eyes and speaking to myself?" That is one question that arises. "I wonder if it is true; if it will work out for me just as I have been taught?" is another. And so on.

When an individual begins to wonder, or question a thought-form's power in any way, he has only one thing to do, and that is to begin all over again, for he has sent out thoughts that have weakened or destroyed his brain children almost the moment they were born.

These mental states of wonderment, hope, questioning and similar conditions all evidence an inner fundamental doubt, and doubt is fatal to success in any phase of activity. Doubt is a mild form of expressing something stronger and more dangerous – *fear of failure*. "Our doubts," as Shakespeare has it, "are traitors, and make us lose the good we oft might win, by fearing to attempt."

Fear must be conquered before you can reasonably expect to attain real success in *anything*, and the conquest of fear may be one of the very best things you can ask first from the Universal Mind. All doubts *must* be eliminated, and you can start to accomplish this by forming a mental picture of yourself doing courageously and positively just the thing you are most fearful of. It will be a self-discipline that will stand you in good stead for the rest of your lifetime.

Many failures in this world, where the individual is apparently gifted with every working tool that destiny can furnish him, arise from this deep, inner *fearfulness*, fear of criticism, fear of ridicule, fear of competition, fear of superior power, education, place, financial status. All these produce an inferiority complex that breaks down many a useful man or woman.

When you impress your thought-form upon the Universal Mind, you must remember that because the Universal Mind is universal it operates through *all* human individual minds. Therefore, your thought-form is going to make a definite impression upon others.

More than this, the fact that your thought-form is going to be impressed upon other individual minds, and that they are going to react to it according to their capacities for reception, shows us that we do not live unto ourselves alone, but impress ourselves most potently upon others for good or ill. It behooves us to make sure that it *is* for good and *not* for ill. This impression is made upon others through their subjective minds, and will manifest according to the measure by which their subjective minds can react upon their objective mentalism. It shows the underlying unity that is the basic principle of the real concept of human brotherhood.

So it is emphasized all through the subject of mental science that you must make your thought-forms constructive. Note well – not that such are the *only* kind that will ever work. But that constructive thought-forms are the only kind that will *surely work* to our ultimate advantage every time. And that is the only kind you are interested in.

Only a supreme confidence in one's relationship to the Universal Mind will beget results.

All requests made upon the Universal should be formulated from the standpoint of becoming an instrument through which the Universal can work in greater freedom of expression to reach the greatest number for good.

Do not get the idea that you are using something new and untried. The law of supply through impressing the Universal Mind with your particular needs has been known for ages, but the vast majority of mankind has lost sight of it in their haste to secure their ends through what they consider visible, tangible means, relying in false pride upon what they call "their own ability." Well, our ability, so-called, is simply the measure by which we utilize the vast power within us, whether we do so consciously or unconsciously.

THE SPIRIT OF YOUR THOUGHT

Be very, very sure when you use a thought-form for another that it is to his or her advantage. What you *think* would be good for another might not be good at all. Hesitate always before taking action on the mental plane for another (as well as for yourself), for in working a thought-form for another you are involving yourself in the results of it, and you may not like them if things do not work out as you think they should, through your imperfect use of the idea.

One safe way to help another – and in my opinion the very best way – is to *help him to help himself*, for then he puts his own efforts into the work and the results will mean more. This applies to thought-forms in particular. You may even go so far as to talk to the person who needs help, *about* thought-forms, so that he can use them for himself, if he is open-minded enough to concede the possibility of their value.

Wherever the Universal Mind is, there also we find love – love for its own creatures like the love of a parent for his children – only on a grander scale, and never failing. And love in a human being "is ever the beginning of knowledge, as fire is of light."

Love and Life are inseparable. Sometime we may discover that they are one and the same Principle, in creative and ethical polarities. Life being everywhere, creation is therefore still going on everywhere. Your thoughts, reaching out into this ocean of creative activity, can direct its energies to your purposes, and if those purposes are in alignment with the nature and intent of the First Creative Purpose, and if they betoken Progress for All, your desires will be more speedily realized.

To become or to make one's self a chosen vessel implies a direct personal responsibility, one that we have not generally observed to be stressed by most self-help philosophies of the day, which are devoted mainly to the subject of "How to get what *you* want."

The correlative responsibility is *to use what you get*. It seems to be a law of Nature that only use brings out or keeps up what we have. If we do not use our brains, they do not develop. If we do not use our muscles, they atrophy.

Truly, anything that is right, constructive and worthy, *is* within the reach of any intelligent human being, if that being will only set himself in alignment with the forces whose assistance he seeks. When you have formulated your thought-form, by impressing it upon the Universal Mind, you create a *mental prototype*. It is actually accomplished. That is why you *have* received, even before you see it in manifestation. This prototype grows, by the law of growth, according to the intensity and frequency with which you "pray without ceasing," i.e. fix it deeper and deeper into the Universal matrix. As it grows, it attracts to itself just the material its complete expression calls for until finally it comes into externalization.

By going about it in the right way, ready always to conform his individual will with that of the Universal Will, so to speak, one can effect such a rapprochement with the Universal as to be able to enter into its creative activities and direct those activities to an individual measure of realization. This is what Judge Troward, a great mental scientist, meant when he described this process as one wherein the "Cosmic Intelligence becomes individualized and the individual intelligence becomes universalized. The two become one." So I urge you to use thought-forms in this spirit – *if you use them at all*. Yes, they will work even if you use them for some entirely worthy *personal* motive. But they will work with much greater power if you seek to conform them to Universal Motives, so far as you feel you understand them.

Whatever your purpose, let it serve also the purpose of the power that has brought you to the point where you are permitted to use thought-forms. In other words, *provide for the equity* – Universal Mind is going to do a lot for you: what are you going to do to serve the purposes of Universal Mind?

XIII

E. V. INGRAHAM

The following quotes are from
Wells of Abundance, 1938

FIRST PLANE OF SUPPLY – THE LAW OF ABSORPTION

At the root of most human difficulty lies the eternal problem of supply in some of its phases. In fact, supply must include that which supports every phase of man's nature and every difficulty involves some lack of proper support. The ancients called imperfection a matter of "under-nourishment." To thoroughly understand the question of supply would, therefore, enable us to understand the whole problem of successful living.

There is a logic to be followed in the matter of supply.

If we approach supply in the order of its most vital importance, the following sequences will not be difficult. At the beginning, it should be noticed that the more necessary any element is to the sustaining of life, the more there is of it, the easier it is to contact and the more impossible it is for anyone to separate you from it or charge you anything for it. Take the following elements and consider how relatively important they are in sustaining life; how they are increasingly available as they increase in importance:

Shelter, Clothing, Food, Water, Air, Consciousness, Hope, Aspiration – and finally, that *mysterious something* which is the very essence of life itself.

That which increased hope and the realization of more abundant life would be the most essential element of supply.

The fact is that most of the supply that we work for only feeds 2% of our nature. That which feeds the other 98% is *free* for the effort involved in receiving. If this 98% of our nature were habitually fed, the matter of taking care of the other 2% would be simple and easy. Let us, therefore, try to consider supply in its broadest and fullest sense. Let us also be diligent in applying ourselves to every phase of supply in order that we may be most fully provided with all things needful. If we can feed some of the inner hungers first, we may find it a more simple matter to feed the remaining outer hungers.

Life is seven-fold and supply functions on *Seven Planes*. In other words, there are seven degrees or ways in which supply moves. Or, we might say, there are seven ways in which we may approach the matter of supply.

The simplest form of Supply is Absorption. In this field, an organism merely absorbs from its immediate surroundings all of the elements necessary to its maintenance and growth. This method of obtaining supply belongs primarily to the vegetable kingdom. From seed to fruit, a plant absorbs moisture, the elements of the earth, air, and sun.

When human beings descend to this plane, they "vegetate" or retrograde. Man belongs on a plane much higher than the vegetable. He must learn to live upon his own plane if he is to flourish as a human being. Humans who try to live on this plane think the world owes them a living. They become leeches and parasites, expecting supply to be furnished by those who are more industrious. They are the beggars who have lost their station in life by expecting support without giving an equivalent in return. The law, "give and it shall be given unto you" works with precision. Where there is no voluntary giving for what is received, something is taken from you.

The voluntary offering plan in the religious field has pauperized millions of people. It has not been made clear that voluntary giving is a plan for individual development. It is a way of preserving the sense of balance between man and his surroundings. Not understanding this phase of the plan, too many people have imagined that spiritual service is free and that they need only receive. Spiritual and often physical and material bankruptcy has been the result.

Let everyone who receives instruction or help from any spiritual avenue take due note of this law and he will doubtless find the reason for his lack of progress. If you can afford to go to picture shows, for your own sake and well-being, you can afford to sacrifice the show if necessary to give to the one who serves you spiritually.

The foregoing is not suggested with the idea of increasing the income of spiritual workers, but to help the student attain to a basis of more certain spiritual as well as material progress. "With what measure you mete, it shall be measured to you again." Nothing is of value to you except on the basis of the value placed by yourself. It cannot truly be yours until you have given value in return for value received.

Give to those who serve you in any way and in every way that you can devise. Then see if the blessings you have been seeking are not released to you.

You are part of the entire Universe.

Every Law of Supply applies to you in some way. The *Law of Absorption*, or receiving, does enter into the process of your supply. However, you are primarily a spiritual being and you receive upon a spiritual plane, first, at least. Learn to receive the very essence of all things that surround you. Absorb the very presence of life, love, wisdom, power, and substance, just as you might absorb the light of the sun or the warmth of the air.

Wherever you go, absorb everything that is pleasing to your soul – beauty, music, the odor of flowers. Learn to drink in everything around you that you can enjoy and appreciate.

All the Universe is your storehouse from which to receive. The world is your field of radiation or expression.

MEDITATION

That force which sustains the Universe, sustains me. I am sustained, supported, and supplied by a self-operative process that sustains and supports the entire Universal system.

My supply is at hand. It fills me, surrounds me and is poured out upon me from everywhere. Supply flows to me wherever I am and in whatever I do.

I receive my invisible and visible supply constantly and I am increasingly rich within and without.

SECOND PLANE OF SUPPLY – THE LAW OF FORCE

All future progress in the matter of supply will be strengthened if you are grounded in the first steps. Faithfulness in first things is the secret of progress in any direction. Outer supply is often delayed because fundamental requirements have not been met. When the inner nature is fully supplied, the matter of outer supply will be easily taken care of.

Each degree of supply is only the increased momentum, or expansion, arising from a simple starting point. All that we think say or do regarding anything began with a simple idea. It is futile to hope for full knowledge or power in any direction except through a logical procedure from start to finish in the process.

Supply begins with the simple idea of *receiving* as outlined in our previous lesson. Receiving awakens increased desire and capacity and we accordingly begin to make greater demands. Man is more than a sponge; therefore, the mere act of receiving does not meet the requirements of his more complex nature.

Moving on the scale of supply, we find the next *Law* to be a matter of *force*. This Second Plane of Supply, materially considered, belongs to the carnivorous animals. These animals get their supply by forcefully taking it from others. In most cases, they prey upon the lesser beasts themselves. When this Law of Supply is employed by the human being, he descends to the animal plane and becomes the thief, the robber, the grafter, the racketeer, the extortionist and the usurer. By force, cunning, deception, or advantage, he preys upon those who have. He is not intelligent enough to use his skill and talents to produce for himself. He devotes all his energy to getting what others have produced. Such men are vultures and beasts of prey in human guise.

Descending to a plane beneath the human status exacts its terrific toll, for the law of compensation is exact. Such humans lose their peace of mind, their sense of security, their liberty and often life itself. They lose their own self-respect and the respect of those about them. One can maintain his standing in the world as a man only if he *lives* as a man. Man is co-creator with his Source and to find the fullness of life, he must become a producer and not live by what others produce.

Man, being a replica of the Universe, has something of every plane within him. The application of the various laws must be according to his high estate. He is a spiritual being and the application of the *Law of Force* is on a spiritual and not a physical plane. It may be a new idea to you that *force* is a Law of Supply on the spiritual plane. Nevertheless, it is so.

Force here has no semblance to the forceful measures characteristic of the material or animal world.

Human beings too easily surrender to the apparent. A little positive assertion is often all that is necessary to turn the tide of events. Sometimes a more enduring persistence is necessary. But the tide must be turned if we are to rise into the realm of creative men where we belong.

A little wrestling with facts will inevitably break the struggle with appearances. And the chances are that if we do not exert the necessary *force* in wrestling with facts, we will have plenty of opportunity to struggle with the apparent.

Ordinarily, breathing is a process of simply absorbing or inhaling the air. But if you ever had the "wind knocked out of you," that simple process of absorbing the air was not sufficient to meet the situation. You had, in this instance, to fight for the air. Some *force* had to be exerted. Perhaps, at times, you have had to fight for your reason in much the same way. At times, you have faced a difficult rule, or complex saying. The ordinary process by which the mind absorbs – easily comprehends – does not seem to suffice. A definite assertion of the mind, a forceful effort to drive the mind until it penetrates through to the meaning seems necessary.

The foregoing may serve to somewhat illustrate that manner of *force* as applied to man's supply. When you get the "financial wind knocked out of you," so to speak, it may be necessary to forcefully drive the mind in the direction of your Source.

At such times a "wrestling" with the spiritual fact seems essential. If no positive effort is put forth in this direction, you are likely to curl up in the cruel clutches of poverty and defeat.

Exercising *force* in the matter of supply is not exercising the will or driving the flesh to get outer results.

Faith is a much greater *force* than the Will. Will is only efficient when used to awaken or conform to faith. Faith is a real wealth for it is a *force* that produces.

Faith sees into realms where the eye of the mind and the eyes of the flesh cannot see.

Living in faith, one comes to the point of Knowing. "Knowledge is power," we have so often been reminded. Here again, we have another transcendent force. It keeps one calm in calamity and victorious in seeming defeat. The outcome is seen and *known*, therefore, the incidents intervening are of little consequence. "*Knowing*" acts like magnetic force in a bar of steel. Its power of attraction is irresistible. It pulls into being that to which it is attached. If you are knowingly convinced of poverty, there is no human power that can prevent poverty from springing into manifestation all around you.

Learn to reach out into the Universe. Absorb all that it naturally radiates toward you. Once the sense of its abundance awakens in you, a great hunger for more will also awaken. Then you will wrestle with the wealth that is there for you until it is visibly manifest in your mind, body, and affairs. The wealth of the Universe *is* yours. Take it! The timid seldom arrive at great fulfillment.

MEDITATION

I refuse to be drawn into the entangling illusion of appearances.

If Source, it must be the Life, the Substance, and sustaining Power of my whole being. My Supply, then, is immediately at hand and instantly available to me.

Awake or asleep, my whole being constantly and intently pursues the truth until I possess it in the secret depths of my own soul.

The spirit and Substance of Abundance fills me and surrounds me. It feeds my flesh, revives my mind, restores my soul. It fires me with renewed power and creative ability and I am aroused in the might and power of the inner man.

THIRD PLANE OF SUPPLY – THE LAW OF WORK

The Third Plane of Supply is where it is earned by Work. This is where man, who considers himself a mere human being, should logically expect his supply. But to work only for what you can get is but little better than the thief. You have not yet caught up with the law of compensation but it is still at work in you. Until you reach the place where there is a free giving for what you are receiving, you are never on a secure footing. Your salary is or should be a just balance for the service you give. To advance, you must get ahead of the law and begin to give more than you receive. Sooner or later, you will see the law of balance at work. Your increased supply will inevitably come. Profit and service in righteous balance is what makes this Plane pleasingly effective. "He profits most who serves best" is not a mere axiom but it is a living truth. Voluntary giving of the best you are capable of giving takes the place of exacted toll. Then the returns begin to voluntarily increase.

Following this procedure, it finally dawns on you that a sort of mysterious change has taken place. At first, you were always trying to get something. Now the very thing you were trying to get is seeking you. This new thing also has a way of compounding itself. Not only do you receive more return for your work, but new opportunities for work with still greater returns present themselves. This is one of the most joyous experiences in the path of life. There comes the sense that you are not only making real progress but that you are in harmony with the law of life.

When one realizes the entire motive of work is the development and expression of skill – a means of growth and advancement – then the individual has reached the turning point in the matter of supply. Work, then, loses its strenuousness and becomes a fascinating pursuit. He also discovers that the same degree of joy and eagerness with which he goes forward in this motive is returned in the good that comes back to him. The law gives back in exact ratio and kind that which you express in giving. Once this process is clearly experienced, one becomes as fascinated with his work as in the most intriguing game.

"Wealth gotten by vanity shall diminish; but he that gathereth by labor shall increase." One may find courage in the possibilities of securing work if they will contemplate a statement of Gladys M. Relyea in Collier's for April 30, 1938, that "according to occupational experts, there are 25,000 ways to make a living in the United States." This information should be interesting enough to start everyone looking for opportunities for service instead of explaining how and why there is nothing to do.

Once abundance is attained, there is a greater need in inward ability than before because both yourself and your money must be sustained.

Unless strong character is builded in our accumulation of outer wealth, we only get into greater unrest than before.

Physical work is only a means of outward expression. It builds muscle but not character. It is the *working* of the mind back of the muscle that builds skill. The *attitude* in work makes character. Motives govern the whole nature of the outer man. Ability is fed from inner sources of supply and only when we are inwardly fed, can we expect the outer nature to be well.

Mental and spiritual *work* are the first tasks of the individual who would express the greatest achieving power in the world. A proper conditioning of the soul is fundamentally important in all undertakings. Outer work can be no more effective than the motives which prompt the performance of tasks, just as the performance of an engine is no better than the fuel used in it. The kind of *inner work* that builds up the highest and most vital motives should be the first consideration. We so often make the mistake of tackling the outer aspect of a problem before we have mastered its inner aspect. In supply, we should first *work* to master the sense of lack by *building* an inner sense of wealth. This is done by prayer, meditation, and the intelligent use of affirmation.

It is all right to pray for both money and bread. But it is more important to pray that the spirit of abundance fill your heart and mind.

This sense of the Universal and inward flow of supply must sooner or later loosen every element of outward supply and move visible abundance to you. "Straws show which way the wind blows" and driftwood follows the current of the stream. So does your outer supply flow on the current of inward supply.

Affirmation, another phase of spiritual work, is a definite laying hold of an attitude of accepting and appropriating supply that has been uncovered and set into operation by *prayer* and *meditation*. Affirmation does not take the place of *prayer* and *meditation* but it supplements and coordinates them with the outer world. Give yourself daily to your *spiritual work* in the matter of supply. Keep the mind first interested in the spiritual sense of supply. Only let the mind turn to include outer supply when the inner realization is strong throughout your entire nature.

FOURTH PLANE OF SUPPLY – THE LAW OF ATTRACTION

By this time in our study and practice, we begin to realize that supply is not so much a matter of material form as of spiritual forces. Furthermore, as we avail ourselves of the ever-accessible spiritual forces, it is much easier to gain the material forms. This experience may be continued indefinitely and the more this order of supply is followed, the more readily the outer supply comes. The ultimate, of course is the discovery of the secret of instant fulfillment. This is the fascinating goal ahead of the faithful.

When one really breaks through into the realization of the power of this procedure, a great sense of freedom comes. It is like passing from a stuffy room into the freedom of the great out-of-doors. Every weight of lack and oppression of poverty falls off and you clearly sense the presence of Divine Wealth. Abundance fills and vitalizes the very air you breathe. Instead of forebodings of lack, you are filled with the promise of abundance. When the might and power of the inner man is supplied, the whole aspect of life changes.

In this stage of progress in developing inner supply, you find that the things you formerly pursued are now seeking you. A sort of inner magnetic force seems to attract jobs, opportunities, money. This *Law of Attraction* is the Fourth Plane of Supply. At this point, to strengthen your knowledge of the process involved, we suggest that you buy a small horseshoe magnet, such as boys play with. Spend some time each day watching needles, pins, and metal objects jump to it until it dawns upon you that a radiant, inner force always has power to attract its own kind from the world of form.

Now consider your own being in place of the magnet and your own deep feelings in place of the magnetic force. Here you have the key by which all manner of things are attracted to you. A feeling and conviction of poverty attracts poverty conditions in the world of form. A feeling and *conviction* of abundance attracts outer abundance.

Go on from here now and realize that all of your procedure up to and including this point is only for the purpose of building up the forces of your inner nature until they are so strong that outer evidences of supply begin to move toward you. Do not spend your time merely hoping and expecting everything to come to you. Be equally willing and ready to go to them. But above all, be continually active in building and maintaining the realization that the abundance of the Universe *is* yours, that it flows to you from every source, and that the *Law of Attraction* opens wide every channel of supply.

In taking up this method of spiritual work, one does not cease to work outwardly. In fact, one does more outward work and that work is the more effective. It is also joyous work. But the motive is completely reversed. You work always to increase your realization of spiritual power and abundance, *knowing* that all the Universe is working with you, guiding your mind, feeding and supplementing your ability and sustaining your flesh.

What you thus build into your character attracts to you from the world that which exactly conforms to your newly awakened realization.

When we begin to see that the foregoing is an accurate explanation of why certain things come to us, we will also understand what we have previously considered rank injustice. We have so often asked why certain people, apparently good, faithful and sincere workers, are always getting the "tough breaks." You see, it is not what we seem to do or be in the outer that counts most.

What goes on inside of man's consciousness is what determines the status of his outer life. "To him that hath shall be given" and it is given in kind and degree according to what you have. What you have is what you are most conscious of in your mind and feeling nature. That is what determines your *power of attraction*.

The purpose of life must take into first consideration the perfecting of man himself; not the accumulation of money and possessions. Only as the man himself grows in wisdom and power can he expect his outer world to grow. The outer must and always will be a product of the inner. One can, therefore, see that the important thing in supply is to build up the consciousness and realization of abundance. Money does not build the consciousness of abundance and security.

Your world changes as inevitably and under the same law as the expression on your face changes. It is not the smile that makes a joyous heart, but a joyous heart that produces the smile. This same law applies to the condition of your body generally, to your clothes, your home, your business, and your finances as well.

What you radiate determines what your manifest world will be.

Remember, it is a matter of building up your spirit, of increasing the *forces of abundance* within yourself. Potential wealth exists as your storehouse of inner powers and capacities. The realization of eternal facts and the consciousness that all of the wealth of the Universe is yours comprise your limitless supply.

FIFTH PLANE OF SUPPLY – SUPPLY AS AN INHERITANCE

It is a self-evident fact that the more frequently you associate with anything, the more you feel a part of it and the more its operations vitally affect you.

Spiritual practice is no exception to the rule. The faithful application of spiritual law brings a consciousness that you are not a product of, nor a part of, a material world. Everything seems to move out and become a part of the larger system.

The world did not produce itself and it did not produce the things that live upon it. The things that appear upon the earth are but further expressions of the same system that produced it in the first place. Should the Universal system break down, then every part of the system would break down. It can then be seen that even a single blade of grass is supported by the Universal system.

The Law of Nature causes a plant to grow, provides all of its requirements and sustains the plant as it is growing.

At a certain point in your growth, you awakened to the fact that you were a conscious being.

The Universe owes you a living, is glad to give it to you and furthermore, it is your natural heritage. Please note this statement again: *"the Universe owes you a living"* – not the world!

Truly, the Universe *owes* you a living. Not only that, but it is willing and eager to give it to you.

Man cannot live by bread alone. Quite truly he cannot, for bread does not feed his mind, spirit, or life.

You should dwell much upon the fact that you are more dependent upon invisible forces than forms for your support. Think often how much more your nature depends upon air than water, and so on. What keeps your mind going, what feeds your hopes and ideals? What keeps your life going on and on? It is best for your own progress that you trace these answers through for yourself. Some day, if you will be faithful to this practice, the whole matter of supply will clear up.

Then go on with the idea that air is something you inherit in the very process of living.

From here on to the highest forces of the Universe, you inherit all things. They are yours by Divine right.

Yours now, not something you come into possession of at a later date. It is all *yours,* an *inheritance now*!

Now is the only time you can accept supply.

Claiming, accepting, receiving and building this Universal supply into your character is a most vital and satisfying procedure. By it, you get back into harmony with basic facts and the sense of wealth and security become living realities to you. Here outer supply seems *eagerly* seeking you. The magnet here works stronger than ever. You realize as a practical reality the statement made earlier in these lessons that "outer supply rides on the current of your inner supply."

This practice leads to an actual inrush of your supply. Abundance begins to crowd in upon your mind and feeling. You know the negative experience of this stage of realization when trouble or lack crowd in. This stage of your progress is just the reverse aspect of the same law.

"My supply, as my inheritance, has arrived. It is mine! It is my birthright." *Knowing your own* is a sort of coming of age spiritually.

The *absolute knowing* that a thing is yours is an irresistible force. "That which I *know* is *mine* must come to me by the very law of my being."

If you knew your Divine supply as firmly, as feelingly, as spontaneously, you would have enough to procure anything in the outer that you needed.

Keep it up until the radiant sense of *"mine"* comes over you. Here you will enter into a new and wonderful world where you belong.

You will still work. But your work will not be labor for reward. It will be the joyous expression of such inward wealth that you must work to express the great joy and abundance of life. You work in order that others may be enriched by your efforts.

MEDITATION

Being a product of the creative Law of the Universe, I inherit all of the Life, Intelligence, and Substance of Infinite Space.

Give me now, the fullness of supply that is rightfully mine!

SIXTH PLANE OF SUPPLY – SUPPLY AND THE CREATIVE PROCESS

How fascinating this whole matter of supply becomes as its various phases unfold. Like everything else, it unfolds only to those who study it. We discover only what we search for. This explains why so many of us have not found and manifested abundance. We really have not searched for it. The discovery of supply is not only interesting because the supply itself is desirable, but the progressive unfoldment of the idea is fascinating in itself. It is like finding the solution to a puzzle or discovering the secret of some very complex situation. Once this point of fascination has been reached, the rest of our progress will be easier.

The Sixth Plane of Supply brings a new and more fascinating discovery. As we search out the mystery of supply, we find something vastly more important is involved in the process. It is something that sets aside all the struggle and uncertainty in our pursuit of the needful things in life.

Wherever there is an inheritance, there must be a source from which it originated. Furthermore, there must have been a willingness and an activity that the inheritance pass from the source to the inheritor. A gift implies a giver and the act of giving.

There is an impelling force and actual movement which urges the gift or inheritance upon you. This, after all, is the real principle of nature. Seemingly vegetation absorbs its supply from the sun, air, and earth. But in reality, its supply is forced upon it. It is the activity of its inheritance that supplies it with life, action, and form and is that which causes growth. Its supply is, therefore, an *active* process already providing needful elements before it starts to grow and continuing during its entire process of development.

How *heartening* even to consider that every moment of your life your good is seeking you out; that all things needful for your progress are moving toward you. But to awaken to the realization of this fact is to arise to the state of absolute certainty in the entire matter of supply.

Perhaps, you can better understand the terrific urge for your supply to express in you if you think for a moment how all living forces move toward expression. Notice all the eagerness which impels you to *tell* everything you know, or to *express* what you feel, or *produce* what you idealize. The desire for full expression seizes your whole nature whenever creative ideals fill you. The singer longs to sing, the dancer to dance, the artist to paint.

Remember that "outer supply moves on the tide of the inner." Do not be drawn away from the realization of this self-acting, eager force that moves to supply you with every good and perfect gift. Too much concern about results will insulate you from its full and free expression through you. To live in absolute assurance that the results are inevitable is to keep the circuit through you flowing at full force. Here is another vital fact that appears in considering supply at this point. Since it moves eternally, all that you have not used is cumulative. It is stored up for you, just as water has piled up behind a dam. That is the cause of the pressure you feel. You think the pressure is the weight or oppression of lack, but it is not. It is the pressure of your Universal bank account, the unused resource of your nature that is crowding itself upon you.

Life moves on and unless we keep up with it, we feel its pressure. Some day, you must express the abundance of Spirit. It is the order of life. All that you have lacked is stored up back of your nature. It is a priceless Universal bank account waiting for you to adjust yourself to its tendency, that it may flood you with blessings until you shall be unable to contain them all.

The great secret in swift results in supply is in the knowledge that Omnipotence *moves upon you* to bless and to prosper you. Study this law; watch for its action wherever you go, consider it until at last you grasp it.

MEDITATION

My supply of all good is at hand.

I inherit the Wealth of the Universe and it eagerly and actively seeks me out, pouring its great Wealth upon me.

I am richly and abundantly supplied within and without from the eager storehouse of the Universe, a supply that is more eager to manifest Wealth through me than I am eager to receive it.

SEVENTH PLANE OF SUPPLY – SUPPLY IN THE ABSOLUTE

It may be a bit difficult for those unaccustomed to considering abstract things to grasp supply in its absolute sense. This is a realization that one is more likely to grow into than to grasp off-hand. But to those who can grasp it, it is the direct approach to supply. It all centers around the fact that cause and effect are one, that they are always synonymous and therefore, simultaneous.

The mind schooled to appearances does not readily grasp this. Such a mind trying to apply this logic creates a conflict in one's nature; and confusion and vague uncertainty results.

One who does not readily grasp the idea of this plane had better approach it by the easy stages of the preceding lessons. But those who can at least sense its truth will find swift progress in following this highest fact; it can hardly be called law for it is not a movement by which results are realized but self-evident and self-expressed facts.

The process by which we arrive at this state might be likened to a very wealthy man falling asleep and dreaming he was very poor. In the dream, he may have all the experiences and feelings of poverty but it would only be a dream. Finally, he awakens and his wealth is there. The only attainment involved is to "wake up." A man once explained his escape from danger in the same way. He dreamed a lion sprang upon him. He was so frightened, he awoke and, of course, he awakened to safety because there was no lion there in the first place.

All sense of lack and disease has always been classed as "illusion" by those who have attained illumination – those who have awakened.

This is a proclamation of fact, regardless of appearances to the contrary. In like manner, we must school ourselves to facts until we awaken and see the truth thereof. When we see and *know* the truth, we are free of the illusion.

The individual attains to the Seventh Plane of Supply – *Supply in the Absolute* – only when he has expanded his consciousness to comprehend the Universality of all things visible and invisible and has entirely lost the sense of separateness.

A sponge immersed in water becomes completely saturated in it.

So man, returning to his Source, abiding in it, reaches the point of complete saturation.

To help awaken yourself to this state, try to *feel* yourself in the midst of Infinite abundance much as you might feel yourself in the warmth of the sun while taking a sun bath. After a while, you feel the warmth all through you. At the point of complete *oneness*, you say "I am warm."

MEDITATION

All that I can use is always at my command for it is in me and I am in it.

Do not let money or the lack of money dull your vision of reality. Do not allow appearances to lull you back into the earth sleep. Awake!

The following E. V. Ingraham quotes are from
The Silence, 1922

In this changing world it is necessary for man, if he would stabilize his life, to have some dependable foundation upon which to build his life's structure and from which to evolve his ideals.

The silence is not in any sense the discovery of a new process of mind, but is a practice known very well to every genius, every inventor, every philosopher, and in fact every individual who has in any degree outstripped his fellow men and brought back to the world some new idea or invention from beyond the range of habitual thought and experience.

"Be still, and know" is a clear command to let the mind rest from its own activities and record knowledge that the infinite waits to reveal.

To gain new knowledge, man must be willing to leave his former ideas behind. No mind is capable of receiving instruction from any source when it is preoccupied with other ideas.

PURPOSE

Shakespeare said, "All the graces of mind and heart slip through the grasp of an infirm purpose."

Much of the difficulty experienced in connection with the silence is due to the fact that many people have no clearly defined purpose in view. These people try to get still, to stop the turbulent activity of their mind, to put ideas out of consciousness, or to go through various other processes that are wholly negative. Others merely give their time to holding specific thoughts, affirmations, and the like. Each of these methods has its rightful place, but there is a purpose above and beyond them all, and in attaining this higher purpose, these negative phases of the silence take care of themselves.

He should also go into this presence in an expectant attitude, knowing that he is to receive, and therefore should be in a receptive mood. It is foolish for one to go to a spring for a bucket of water, without a bucket in which to receive the waters thereof.

If a student is to become a mathematician he must devote himself to mathematics. The businessman must devote himself to his business. Irrelevant thinking, irregular practices, conditions foreign or opposed to our undertakings must delay our progress and defeat our purpose to the very degree to which they occupy our attention. Complete devotion to a single purpose is the secret of true and quick success.

To be true to the fact that there is but one Presence and one Power is to be possessed of the key to a correct solution of all life's problems. To the degree in which we recognize other powers, we fall short of even the possibility of a correct answer.

THE SILENCE NOT NEGATIVE

The silence is not negative or an inert state of the mind. Many persons, not realizing this, have allowed their minds to become inert, and through this false conception of the silence they have lessened their executive ability to no small degree. These persons, when attempting to practice the silence, often fall asleep. Can you not see how utterly ridiculous this is, to say the least? One would hardly say that this is respectful of the presence of Divinity.

Can you picture anything but the most perfect attention, the most absolutely awake and alert mind, the most profound interest? Of course not; and yet when we enter the silence we are approaching this same presence.

After reading this chapter one should be thoroughly alive and awake with a divine enthusiasm. Approaching the silence in this attitude of mind one would be alert with vital attention, lest something of the divine nature escape one's notice.

RELAXATION

It is said, "You cannot pour into a vessel already full." This is true of the individual whose mind and body are already preoccupied with some tense or strenuous state of mind or feeling.

The true function of both mind and body is service to Spirit.

Relaxation is not lapsing into a state of inertia, nor is it sinking into physical negation. True relaxation, as we refer to it in this connection, is a complete surrender to the presence and power of Spirit.

Truly there could be no burden to mind or body in such an attitude, and relaxation would come naturally.

This is part of the receiving process by which we appropriate the gifts of Spirit and incorporate them into our being. Nothing ever becomes ours until we accept it, because acceptance is the first requisite to ownership. Any amount of wealth may be yours potentially, but until you lay hold of it you do not possess it for any practical purposes.

Physical relaxation is not inertia. It is a state of absolute physical freedom. It is that state in which the body cells are free from the consciousness of strife and strenuous effort, and are perfectly responsive to Spirit.

TENDENCY TO SLEEP

Many persons, in their attempts to practice the silence, have great difficulty in overcoming the tendency to go to sleep. This tendency arises from two general causes. The first is that the individual needs a greater realization of physical vitality. Sleep is a process of revitalization of the body, and in sleep the same thing happens to the individual that happens to the storage battery when it is being recharged. The energies projected during the day reverse their direction and are reabsorbed by the body.

The second reason for this tendency to sleep is lack of genuine interest. Have you not at some time been deeply interested in reading a book of fiction? During the reading of that book did you get sleepy, or was your difficulty in going to sleep, once you felt it your duty to lay the book down? Undoubtedly your mind was thoroughly interested in and awake to the action of the story.

ATTENTION

Difficulty sometimes arises in the control of the mind, because one does not realize the basis from which all mental action evolves. For instance, one strives through various methods to control the course of thought and feeling, whereas the basis of all mental control is in the point of mental focus, which we might call attention – the eye of the mind, or the vision of the mind.

Where the vision is centered the thoughts forgather, and the character of the thought is determined by the object upon which the attention rests.

The necessity for one-pointedness is easily discerned by anyone who knows the laws of mind. To make the discovery of underlying Truth the supreme objective is to lay the foundation for the greatest possible attainment.

Gradually, from that center of attention, the revelation of the actual facts of that presence will begin to draw upon his waiting consciousness.

The matter of centering the attention upon an invisible force is not a difficult thing. Just sit quietly for a moment and give your attention to the air. You cannot see it, hear it, smell it, taste it, or feel it though you may have heard and felt its action. Likewise you can contemplate the fact that there is an electrical ether, finer than the air, existing in you, through you, and around you, just as the air is. Transcending the electrical ether is the spiritual ether, the very essence of everything that has being, and it is from this spiritual ether that every lesser force or thing emanates. Contemplation of the fact of its presence is just as easy as contemplation of the fact of the presence of the air. When you realize that Spirit is a presence, a reality as the air and electricity are realities, yet infinitely finer than these, infinitely more important, it is but a slight task for the mind to comprehend its existence.

MEDITATION

Attention is only the beginning of one's mental evolution in relation to this most important fact in life. The spiritual ether is not only omnipresent, "over all, and through all, and in all," but it contains all life, all substance, all power, all love, and in fact all that has being, for it is infinite. The mind therefore should be allowed to expand in its concepts of this one Presence and one Power. The mind should go on to speculate, as it were, on the character of the spiritual ether, on what it contains, how it moves and what it conveys to the mind of man as it moves in and through his being. This mental speculation, this allowing the mind to expand in its estimate of the nature of the one Presence and one Power, is what we might call meditation.

Meditation is a process of association with the divine Presence, a method of forming an acquaintance with it.

Does not your mind grow and expand through your association with nature? Much more ought the mind to grow in comprehension through its association with the presence of the All.

CONCENTRATION

Concentration is singleness of mind or purpose.

True concentration is that sort of interest in which all the forces of your being are intent upon a given objective, or unified in a given purpose.

Concentration, like relaxation, is attained not through strenuous effort, but through quiet means, reasonable processes, by which the mind's interest is awakened and complete attention is attained.

Above all, make the approach to the silence pleasant, interesting, joyous.

INSPIRATION

Have you not at times noticed yourself taking on or absorbing something of your environment, particularly when you have been thrown into close and prolonged touch with that environment? You simply absorb the impressions coming to you from the environment, and these impressions give you a new understanding of your surroundings, which in turn affects your nature to some extent. In like manner he who associates much in thought with his divine environment receives impressions from it, and his nature is altered accordingly.

Listen! This is the approach to the secret place of the Most High. What could more fascinate your mind? What could more absorbingly hold your interest to the exclusion of everything else?

LENGTH OF SILENCE PERIOD

The question is often asked, at this point in the lessons, "How long should one remain in the silence?" It is just as impractical to attempt to answer this question as it would be to tell a person how long he should take for eating his meals.

It should be remembered that man develops in his nature that which he exercises. In practicing the silence, therefore, one should exercise only the attitudes of mind which tend to bring out the most desirable experiences. For instance, many persons put forth so much effort in holding their attention on what they consider the silence that "effort" is the dominant factor in the practice. The effort habit is therefore developed until it becomes the dominant experience, and the entire being rebels at the thought of the silence, because it seems to mean nothing but hard work.

"Let us reason together" does not apply only to a relationship between persons. It applies likewise to the various departments of your own being.

Interested attention can be cultivated by a reasonable appeal to the mind, rather than by a resort to forceful or dominant measures. Just as you respond to reasonable methods more readily than to forceful measures, so does your mind follow and respond to processes that are agreeable to it. Talk things out with yourself. Even talk aloud, if need be, to get your mind's attention.

What could be more interesting than to delve into the realm that contains everything that a being could wish or desire? Such is the realm of the divine presence. By reminding yourself of this fact, you will find the mind eagerly giving its complete attention to this wonderful communion. When you have reached this conception of the silence, you will find that the length of the silence period will increase. Genuine interest has little regard for the passing of hours.

Knowledge and realization gained in the silence become motive power that governs the outer life of man and quickens him with the magic power of attainment.

The most important thing to consider in connection with the silence is the conscious revelation which comes from Spirit.

PLACE AND POSITION

These questions are often asked: "Where should one go for the practice of the silence," and "In what position should the body be placed." As to the place, it might be well in the beginning for one to find a place as free as possible from disturbing influences.

The quiet place should be looked upon only as a retreat for special communion. In leaving the quiet place, endeavor to feel that the one presence, of which you become aware in the silence, is a tower of strength to you in every way.

As to one's physical posture: The only suggestion we would make is that one should be physically comfortable, free from strain, so that the body itself is not a disturbing factor or a distracting influence.

THE LIGHT

In the days that follow, ask yourself many times whether you are truly interested in receiving this light. If you are interested, keep your attention turned toward it; that you may not lose a single ray of its radiance. Keep physically relaxed so that every ray of this light may penetrate the innermost and the outermost parts of your being.

WHAT THE SILENCE REALLY IS

Many people fail to gain a realization of what the silence really is, because they have some false ideas regarding the silence and are practicing these ideas instead of seeking a clearer understanding of it.

The silence is not an end in itself; it is merely a means to an end.

Once you have entered into the light, continue to walk in the light, for the light becomes your life.

Man's life is as limited as his ideas. If his ideas have been developed through material associations alone, his life is held in confinement to the measure of material standards. In other words, knowledge is to man what light is to the plant. Only the measure of light which the plant succeeds in incorporating into itself becomes its life.

As we have said, the silence is very simple; in fact, it is one of the simplest functions of the mind. Every time we stop to listen, every time we open our minds to receive a new idea, a new impression, or a new inspiration, we practice consciously or unconsciously, all the processes of the silence. Whether we receive the intended idea, impression, or inspiration is another thing, for these impressions pertain to the realm that we have designated as "beyond the silence."

The processes are identical, but the objects are to gain knowledge of different kinds from different sources. In the first instance the knowledge gained is of the external world, and in the second instance the knowledge gained is of the inner, spiritual facts back of the external world.

The process of the silence might be simply illustrated by the case of a child saying to its mother, "Mother, tell me a story." There necessarily follows a period of stillness between the asking for a story and the time when the telling of the story actually begins. This period may be long or short, according to conditions in the mind or conduct of both the child and the mother. However, sooner or later the revelation of the story begins, and while the child continues to be silent it is at the same time receiving the revelation, which comes only after it has become still. The revelation continues only so long as the child remains still. The child's stillness is the silence, and the unfoldment of the story is what we refer to as "beyond the silence."

Receptivity to impressions depends largely on the importance that we place upon the thing or condition that we wish to know about. The less important it seems to us, the less likely we are to be still, with interested attention. On the other hand, the more important it seems to us, the stiller we automatically become and the more intent is our interest. In proof of this statement, observe what takes place when we sit in an audience before a lecture.

If the speaker is a person of note, one in whom we have great interest and from whom we expect great things, we instantly become still when he arises to speak, and one could literally hear a pin drop. This stillness is in direct proportion to the interest of the audience in the speaker. If the speaker lives up to our expectation we continue to keep still; but the moment he fails to interest us, we begin to plan ways of possible escape. A speaker who was considered of no importance would have great difficulty in quieting an audience so as to be heard at all.

You may gain further help in this direction by saying to every disquieting thought, "Peace, be still."

AFFIRMATION

The question naturally arises at this point: What part does affirmation play in the practice of the silence? You may best understand the place and function of an affirmation if you will consider it in the same relation to the divine principle as you would consider a mathematical rule in its relation to the principle of mathematics.

Affirmations may be presented to our consciousness in any one of three ways: firstly, by someone's formulating an idea and stating it to us either verbally or in written form; secondly, by our formulating in our own intellectual mind an idea that expresses a certain truth or condition which we wish to realize; thirdly, by a spontaneous expression of some truth about man's being, which the very soul realizes is the fulfillment of divine purpose. This is the most potent form of affirmation and carries the greatest degree of creative power. You can say "I am happy," affirming a desired condition, and such a statement will be helpful; but when you say "I am happy," expressing an inward joy, it carries the power of your conviction.

Affirmations that are taken from outside sources may or may not have in them a great deal of quickening energy for the one that uses them. The effect of an affirmation is determined largely by the individual's understanding of the truth and meaning back of the words.

One can affirm that 2 and 2 equals 5, yet the statement is not an affirmation of mathematical truth. An affirmation of spiritual Truth must conform to the principles of Truth, regardless of apparent facts. If you saw "2 plus 2 equals 5" on the blackboard, you would immediately say, "2 plus 2 equals 4." The power of your statement, the authority with which you speak, and the results which follow are all determined by the fact that your declaration expresses the underlying truth, regardless of all appearances.

The incorrect problem on the blackboard and your declaration of the mathematical truth about it brings up another important point in the use of affirmation. Do you make the correct declaration to compel something to be so, or is it because it is already so? The fact is that you make the declaration because it is true, and this truth causes a rearrangement of the figures on the board. Always remember that the power of an affirmation is in the spiritual fact described, and this, when understood and applied, compels a corresponding change in outward appearances.

In the first place, affirmation is to be used merely for the purpose of educating the conscious self to a knowledge of that which is true in a universal sense. Faith is your vital contact with anything in life. If you understand your affirmation, if it is true to principle, and if you thoroughly believe it, then make it in the fullest assurance that it will inevitably bring forth perfect results, for it has back of it all the authority and power of the universe.

Through use of the intellectually formed affirmation the conscious mind becomes sufficiently purified to enable it to record the pure impulses of the soul. The affirmations are spontaneously formed from within and are spoken in the realization of Truth rather than for the purpose of developing a realization of Truth. It is like the change which takes place with a child in studying the piano. First he practices that he may become a musician. Finally, when he arrives at a certain point of musical development, his playing is an expression of his developed musical sense. However, the preliminary practice helped him to attain to this point.

The point in connection with affirmation that we wish to make very clear is this: In the use of affirmations, feel that they are but a means by which you are carried into a realization of the truth which they describe. Try to feel that as you are making these statements you are being carried closer and closer into the very heart of the one Presence and one Power, and that your words derive their power from the infinite action of the one Presence and Power.

To practice an affirmation in the silence is to accept it as a vehicle through which the activity of Spirit is manifesting in your being.

No matter how great yesterday's experience may have been, we should look forward each day in anticipation of still greater revelations. Sometimes, however, because of our own mental lethargy or for some other reason we do not pass quickly over the transitional period; consequently we experience a depression.

Such periods are not only evidence that our former ideas have run their course, but are prophetic of a new cycle of experience, the dawn of a new creation in us, the herald of the next step in our spiritual growth. Instead of being times of despondency or discouragement, they should be times of keenest anticipation, of a new hope arising from the fact that we have arrived at the point of spiritual revelation.

GOING WITHIN

At this point it would be well for us to consider the idea of "going within," and its application to the silence.

This going within literally means going to the spiritual fact that lies back of the outer manifestation. Let us go back to our reference to mathematics in a previous paragraph. To consider the mathematical fact back of the figures on the blackboard is equivalent to going within. The figures themselves are the without, the appearance; whether they are right or wrong, the inner fact, or the within, is the truth. In addition to this, however, a knowledge of the fact must exist in the consciousness of the individual.

Again, to be conscious of the inner facts of Spirit involves a faculty of the mind not understandingly used in man's daily affairs; this faculty is the discerning power of the intuitional nature. Intuition has its seat in the more sensitive portion of man's sympathetic nervous system, known as the solar plexus; man's spiritual revelations come through this inner sense, which seems to have its means of contact with man's consciousness in the very innermost parts of his being.

The silence might be likened to the experience that was the writer's when he first saw the Grand Canyon. The train arrived early in the morning, and before the tourists went into the hotel for breakfast it was quite natural for them to run over to the rim of the canyon for a first glimpse of it. It was so immense and beautiful that the mind could not take it in. After breakfast another visit to the rim, and still there was the utter inability of the mind to grasp the grandeur of the scene. In fact, the canyon was so immense that one's attempt to comprehend it seemed to paralyze the mind. After each visit to the rim it seemed necessary to retire into the quiet of the surrounding woods in order that the mind might adjust itself to the grandeur and beauty and immensity of this marvelous spectacle. It was awe inspiring.

The simplest and perhaps most effective means of making the silence, and the process of entering into it, perfectly clear is the illustration of the echo. No doubt you have at some time stood in a canyon or other place where you could hear the echo of your own voice. After you said "hello" and paused for a moment, there came back to you from the depths of the canyon the echo of that same hello. Your call echoed and re-echoed, softer, fainter, and farther away, until it eventually died away entirely. Many people are interested only in the echo and they keep the canyon vibrant with the noise of their own voices. One who might be interested beyond this point has but to continue to listen, and finally a great sense of stillness and perfect calm seems to settle down around him. In that moment he touches a phase of life that is never known to those who busy themselves only with the processes of their own minds or voices.

As man waits until the reaction of his own thought processes ceases, he finds himself face to face with the Infinite.

BEYOND THE SILENCE

One of the most important things to remember in connection with the silence is the fact that it is only a means to an end. In order that the fullest benefits may be derived from the practice of the silence, one must constantly go beyond the point of mere mental stillness and allow the elements of the spiritual realm to come forth into consciousness. For beyond the silence is the answer to every question, the fulfillment of every desire, and the solution to every problem that can arise in the experiences of life.

All the progress of the race in any direction has come from a knowing or an unknowing practice of the principles involved in the silence.

THE GUIDES

In exploring a strange country it is always wise for the traveler to have guides who lead the way. Aimless wandering among strange surroundings seldom yields satisfying results. The guides into the realm beyond the silence are faith, interest, and a steadfast vision toward the highest. These factors of the mind lend stability to its action and keep the individual from wandering into bypaths. They insure the possibility of realizing the objective beyond the silence, by leading the traveler into the one Presence and one Power of the universe, where all things are revealed.

We follow where attention and interest lead, and there comes to us a revelation of the nature of the object upon which our attention and interest are centered. If they are centered upon the bypaths, or the mere results which we think that we desire, we may receive but the by-products of life; but not the satisfaction that comes with genuine spiritual attainment, wherein is life itself. If they lead into the very heart of Being, there comes to us the Truth that makes free, the knowledge that makes alive.

ACQUAINTANCE

Acquaintance comes through association, and association involves a mutual exchange of thought and feeling. We become acquainted with others as they express themselves to us in terms of thought and feeling.

Be *still*, and know.

No doubt everyone has had some experience with the type of mind that belongs to the person who might be termed the "talkative questioner." This person is very eager to ask you some question – or usually questions. No sooner is the first question out of his mouth than he begins talking, sometimes about the question in his mind, and sometimes on unrelated subjects.

Should you be given an opportunity to attempt an answer, instead of listening to your answer this person is formulating still another question, and so on indefinitely. Finally, after a session of considerable duration he exhausts either himself, his time, or his breath and bids you goodbye, entirely forgetting about the question that he originally asked. Every metaphysician has met minds of this type. You can become very well acquainted with a person of this sort, but he himself receives little from the acquaintance except the reaction of his own thoughts.

In our search for divine revelation, do we not often proceed somewhat after this fashion? Do we not too often keep up an incessant clamor of some sort, either prayers, affirmations, or rituals, until it is quite impossible for the Spirit of truth to make itself known to us?

One may gain a knowledge of the difference in the force of various ideas by studying the difference between the casual thought and the thought that comes from one's deepest conviction. It is therefore easy to comprehend how thoughts coming from the very foundation of one's being, from the very source of life itself, convey a transcendent power. It should be kept in mind that ideas convey power in accordance with the source from which they arise and the realm in which they function. It is especially important that this be remembered in connection with the use of affirmation.

AFFIRMATION

The mere repetition of an affirmation carries only the power that is characteristic of the mental plane. A parrot might be taught to repeat the most intricate mathematical rule, but would it be possible for the parrot to speak with the authority and power of a mathematician who fully comprehended the meaning of the rule?

This is the exact difference between "vain repetitions" and speaking from an inner conviction of Truth. Ideas expressed in the realization or understanding that they are statements of absolute Truth, and that within the idea itself is a moving force which is spiritual, increase to a very great extent the power and authority of the affirmation. The most potent thought, however, is the one that comes forth as a conscious revelation from the Spirit within man and its potency is retained just so long as the thought is allowed to function consciously as an expression of Divine Mind, unadulterated by the efforts, emphasis, or other characteristics of the purely personal mind.

THE ANSWER

It is impossible to foretell just what your response from beyond the silence will be, or in what form it will come. It may come from within your own nature, or it may come through the word of a friend or through the printed pages of some book. We do know, however, that it will be whatever is most needed in your spiritual development and that it will come by any channel through which your consciousness can be reached.

Your work is to prepare your entire consciousness so that you may be most receptive to the inspiration of Spirit.

You can more easily understand some of the things that will come to you in response to the practice of the silence, if you will recall your experience with the echo to which we have previously referred. If you were sufficiently interested to listen after the echo had entirely died away, you would first have become aware of a great calm or sense of stillness that would have seemed literally to settle down and to permeate the entire atmosphere of your surroundings. Two planes of discovery may be opened to you out of or from beyond this stillness. First, you may record through your senses the sights and sounds that come through the keenness of mind that is possible only in moments of intense stillness.

Again, you may record impulses of nature that are not discernable to the seeing eye or the hearing ear. But beyond this is a still greater and more significant fact, for the silence itself is your direct revelation of the very first characteristic of the divine nature.

Silence ceases to be mere stillness, and becomes the unfolding presence of Divinity itself.

You may be conscious of this as a quickening energy, filling your entire being.

It is the divine Presence manifest as the vitalizing life of Spirit, and the whole being should be relaxed and open to receive it as such.

Revelation is likely to come to you through whatever avenue of your mind is most open or receptive to Divine Mind. Some people receive their revelations in symbols, or in mental pictures, or in symbolical dreams. To these is given the additional task of interpreting the symbol and discovering the hidden meaning. But many who receive these symbols are content merely to contemplate the mental picture or to recite the mere "story" part of a dream without regard to the meaning. If any practical value is to be gained from these visions or dreams, their meaning must be understood. "What is the meaning of these things?" is the question for such a person to ask of himself and of the infinite mind from which all true knowledge comes. The interpretation follows easily if one recognizes that the symbols come from Spirit and if one then seeks in Spirit to find their meaning. Through seeking thus to understand the direct meaning of all such experiences, one becomes more and more conscious of the inspiration of Spirit, and sooner or later one's revelations will assume more direct form and the symbols become fewer and fewer.

But very often someone will say that even though he has practiced the silence faithfully, seeking an answer to some question, the answer is not forthcoming. The truth is that the answer was present all the time. The very fact that the one all-knowing mind interpenetrates your mind and being, just as light interpenetrates glass, involves the further fact that the answer to your question is in that mind and that the answer is therefore in you, through you, and around you. Often we hinder the progress of the answer in its coming forth into our consciousness by denying it. We say, "The answer did not come," thereby closing the door of our consciousness so that the answer, awaiting us, cannot come in.

The silence is not the opening of the mind to anything that may choose to come along; neither is it a search into the subconscious mind to discover things of the past, or the purported powers contained therein.

SELF-CONTROL

As a natural result of practicing the silence, there is a marked increase in the mental and physical forces of the individual. It is therefore of greatest importance that every seeker after Truth begin consciously to direct all his forces into channels that seem at the time to be most desirable and tend toward the furtherance of his highest ideals. In other words, self-control becomes a necessary part of the practice of the student. Here, however, a distinct difference must be recognized between suppression and direction of one's forces. One may, by mere force of will, dominate any mental or physical force, and seem to control it; but the ultimate result of this method is detrimental.

BEYOND THE ANSWER

We can but illustrate in a general way the infinite blessings that come from beyond the silence, from beyond the present range of our sense perception, and hence from beyond the comprehension of our present understanding.

Out of the points that have been presented take those that seem to be of help in your specific case; apply them in earnestness, looking to the infinite mind within you for your own revelations as to just what the silence is and what the great secrets of life are.

That this voice of Truth may continue to speak to you long after the lessons are forgotten is the real object of the lessons themselves.

The Spirit of truth you have always with you, and it is your eternal and sure guide into the way of all Truth; it will speak to you if you listen for its words.

THE PRACTICE OF THE SILENCE

The first thing that you should do in your attempts to practice the silence is to be comfortably seated, so that your mind will be as free as possible from any thought of the body.

With all the interest that you can arouse, become very still, listening with your whole being to catch whatever degree of the divine presence that may be revealed to you.

A time just after arising in the morning and a time just before retiring at night are good periods for your meditation. These periods, however, are no better than any others that may seem better adapted to your requirements.

Never be discouraged if your experiences do not come as you have anticipated, or if you do not seem to make the progress that you would like to make. Only by practice does one become a musician, and it is by practice that you develop the new consciousness of spiritual things.

You have finished reading volume one of

A Course In Materialization.

For information about volumes two through five go to:

www.thefreedomreligionpress.com

or

www.seeseer.com

AFTERWORD

Most of the modern living teachers of the manifestation teachings have left out hundreds of important safeguards. The importance of morality, ethics, integrity, unselfishness, compassion, character building, and genuine concern for others are examples of some of those safeguards. There are no modern living teachers of the manifestation teachings being recommended here. Most of the teachers in *A Course In Materialization* spent decades perfecting their understanding and practice of the Materialization Teachings. The fact that there are hundreds of safeguards in *A Course In Materialization* is an example of the expertise of the Teachers. The Teachings found in *A Course In Materialization* are not in need of improvement. The Infinite Consciousness has not changed in all eternity, and the best methods of approaching it have not changed.

Near Sedona, Arizona a popular author and modern living teacher of some of the manifestation teachings led a course that included a "sweat lodge" experience. Three people died. This is being mentioned here because it is an example of what can happen to students of modern teachers who do not include the hundreds of important safeguards.

One of the errors many modern teachers make is creating a spiritual soup from many different traditions. For example sweat lodges have nothing to do with the manifestation teachings. Many modern teachers mix various practices from various traditions with the manifestation teachings. This is an error because the Materialization Teachings are not in need of help from other practices or traditions. This is also an error because it is very rare that one person is a master of even one teaching and extremely rare that one person is a master of more than one tradition.

Another red flag is when a modern teacher charges a huge sum of money for a course, workshop, lecture or seminar. If the teacher is truly a master of how to draw abundance, they do not need to charge huge sums of money. If their primary source of income is teaching the manifestation teachings in workshops, seminars, lectures, etc. that is more like a Ponzi scheme or a chain letter. There is a saying "Those who can do. Those who cannot do teach." That saying is true in some fields and not true in other fields. In the realm of the modern living manifestation teachers that saying is almost always true.

As long as a teacher has not brought the impostor self to its final end, the potential for harming the students is present. When the impostor self is brought to its final end, only the Infinite Consciousness remains. The best book on the subject of what the impostor self is and how to bring it to its final end is *The Most Direct Means to Eternal Bliss* by Michael Langford. There is a link on the seeseer.com website to where you can purchase that book.

It is recommended that you never become part of any public experiments relating to the manifestation teachings. There are many reasons for this. The fewer people involved in your wishes the better because there is a violation of other people's free will when you try to change them. Also, limited humans may think they know what would be truly helpful, but usually they do not. The Infinite Consciousness from its infinite perspective knows what is truly helpful.

For example, suppose a public experiment is organized to pray for peace in Sri Lanka. Then suppose that thousands of Tamil Tigers and suspected sympathizers are killed. Then, because one side has been almost completely annihilated, what might appear to be a "peace" ensues. However, those participating in the experiment did not expect that the "peace" would have come at such a high price, the killing of so many people.

Before the impostor self has ended in you it is best to use the teachings only to improve your life and not to interfere with the lives of other people. When the impostor self has ended in you and all that remains is the Infinite Consciousness, then you will know what true help is without any unforeseen negative consequences.

Many of the teachers from which the teachings in *A Course In Materialization* are drawn included statements about healing the body in their teachings. Those statements were not included in *A Course In Materialization* because modern medicine is much better now than it was at the time those teachers were writing. The place to start when one has an illness is with modern medicine. If after obtaining many opinions from modern medical doctors, they all agree they can do nothing for your particular illness, that would be the time to consider alternatives. Unfortunately, many people die from illnesses that modern medicine could have easily treated if it were only given a chance. That which is not curable today may be curable tomorrow or a week from now or a year from now because modern medicine is making new discoveries every day.

The best teacher is the Infinite Consciousness within you. The teachers in *A Course In Materialization* give some tips on how to contact and learn from the Infinite Consciousness within you. Set aside some time every day to shut your eyes and ask the Infinite Consciousness within you: "Oh Infinite Consciousness, source of all that is good, please reveal yourself to me and please teach me. Show me the way to the happiest, most loving, most kind life that is possible." Then let go of all your thoughts and wait for the answer. Let go of yesterday's answer and discover the Infinite today.

LaVergne, TN USA
05 May 2010
181601LV00003B/1/P